Reasoning Otherwise

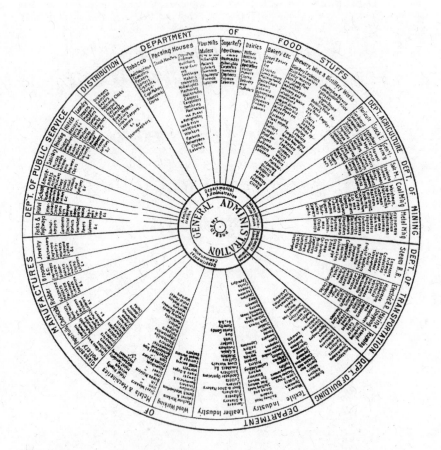

The imagined "Russian Soviet System," as featured on the front page of Winnipeg's *Western Labor News*, 25 April 1919, weeks before the city's General Strike. Such charts had a long pedigree on the left. In 1905, Thomas J. Hagerty, a left-wing former priest, published a version of a similar "wheel" that demonstrated how a revolutionary industrial union could evolve a new form of industrial democracy – a workers' co-operative republic. As rational reconstructions of the social world, such models – which went through many twentieth-century variations, some of them embracing the producers of the entire world – suggested that workers could reason about the evolving structure of the world in order to transform it.

Reasoning Otherwise

Leftists and the People's Enlightenment in Canada, 1890–1920

Ian McKay

Between the Lines
Toronto

Reasoning Otherwise: Leftists and the People's Enlightenment in Canada, 1890–1920

First published in 2008 by
Between the Lines
720 Bathurst Street, Suite #404
Toronto, Ontario
M5S 2R4

1-800-718-7201

www.btlbooks.com

McKay, Ian, 1953-
        Reasoning otherwise : leftists and the people's enlightenment in Canada, 1890–1920 / Ian McKay.
Includes bibliographical references and index.
ISBN 978–1–897071–49–6

1. Socialism – Canada – History.   2. Canada – Politics and government.   3. Right and left (Political science).   I. Title.
HX103.M34 2008   335.00971   C2008-906079-2

Cover design by Jennifer Tiberio

Front cover photo: People of all ages gather for a concert in the community hall of Sointula, the Finnish socialist utopian colony, Malcolm Island, B.C., 1903. Rare Books and Special Collections, University of British Columbia.

Back cover portraits: author's collection except where noted. Top row, left to right: Colin McKay, c.1904; trapper boy Dannie Robertson as depicted in R.A.H. Morrow, *Story of the Springhill Disaster* (1891); Margaret Haile, *Social Democratic Red Book* (1900); Charlie O'Brien, courtesy Glenbow Museum, Calgary; Gaylord Wilshire. Bottom row: R. Ernest Bray, photo by Lewis Benjamin Foote, courtesy of Archives of Manitoba; John Spargo, courtesy Special Collections, Bailey-Howe Library; J.S. Woodsworth; James Simpson, from *Citizen and Country*, Toronto (1902); and Marshall Gauvin, courtesy Archives and Special Collections, University of Manitoba.

Page design and preparation by Steve Izma

Printed in Canada

Between the Lines gratefully acknowledges assistance for its publishing activities from the Canada Council for the Arts, the Ontario Arts Council, the Government of Ontario through the Ontario Book Publishers Tax Credit program and through the Ontario Book Initiative, and the Government of Canada through the Book Publishing Industry Development Program.

Canada Council   Conseil des Arts
for the Arts   du Canada

Canada

ONTARIO ARTS COUNCIL
CONSEIL DES ARTS DE L'ONTARIO

Creating a new culture does not only mean one's own individual "original" discoveries. It also, and most particularly, means the diffusion in a critical form of truths already discovered, their "socialisation" as it were, and even making them the basis of vital action, an element of co-ordination and intellectual and moral order. For a mass of people to be led to think coherently and in the same coherent fashion about the real present world, is a "philosophical" event far more important and "original" than the discovery by some philosophical "genius" of a truth which remains the property of small groups of intellectuals.

– Antonio Gramsci

Contents

Acknowledgements

I owe a great debt of thanks to six stalwart scholars who worked through earlier overweight drafts of this book: Richard Allen, Robin Bates, Peter Campbell, Sean Mills, James Naylor, and David Thompson. I must also thank Ian Angus, Gary Burrill, and Linda Kealey for responding helpfully to specific chapters, and Michel Beaulieu, Margaret Bedore, Mikhail Bjorge, Nancy Butler, Andrew Cooke, Karen Dubinsky, Ingrid Ericson, Stefan Epp, Peter Graham, Don Macgillivray, Chris McCreary, Ian Milligan, John Riddell, Travis Tomchuk, and Gerald Tulchinsky for suggestions and leads, and Bryan Palmer and *Labour/Le Travail* for suggesting the article that got me thinking about this project almost ten years ago.

Paul Eprile as an editor at BTL and Jamie Swift as its Kingston sparkplug offered guidance and inspiration. I should also like to thank David Brownstein, Amanda Crocker, Sue Galvin, Dave McKay, Robin McKay, Matt McRae, Carmen Neilson, Kate Shaughnessy, Tena Vanderheyden, and John Varty for research assistance. Archivists and librarians across Canada have been most helpful, but I particularly single out the Special Collections department at the University of British Columbia for service above and beyond the call of duty.

Without Robert Clarke, my editor, this book would not have attained its present shape, and without Robert Vanderheyden, my partner, its author would not have cheerfully faced the many 4 a.m. mornings that its research and writing have demanded. This book could also not have been written without the many books and articles of scholars who, since the 1960s, have generated a library of books on the Canadian left. Many discussions in this book build directly on their works, and I hope I have acknowledged all my borrowings in the abundant notes, which serve here in place of an extensive bibliography. I would be delighted to enter into a correspondence with any readers interested in exploring more sources than I have been able to list in this book.

In this case the normal caveat about the author wearing all his or her mistakes applies in spades: not only are the inevitable errors of fact and interpretation strictly my own, but I take a certain pride in them. I hope they will function as *useful* errors, inciting an emergent cohort of scholars and activists to correct and transcend them in new work.

I dedicate this book to Ruby, in the hope that someday she will read and enjoy it.

A Note on Usage

As much as possible, I have tried to use quotations from the texts of this period in their original form. Rather than inserting "[sic]" wherever they diverge from contemporary usage, I insert a slightly altered reading in square brackets. An unavoidable bugbear for any Canadian historian writing on this period is the vexed "labor/labour" conundrum. Today's Canadian usage calls for "labour," but *fin de siècle* Canadians – for example, those in the Socialist Labor Party or Trades and Labor Congress – tended to use "labor." Then, sometime about the time of the Great War of 1914–18, Canadians started preferring the "our" spelling of such words – for example, the All-Canadian Congress of Labour. The result is that we have a vast thicket of independent *labor* and independent *labour* parties, and even different ways of spelling "labour" within one and the same organization. Here I generally adopt contemporary practice and refer to the organizations by the name they themselves adopted, but use "labour" myself when I am talking about them. Although I have adopted gender-neutral forms when speaking about humanity and the persons making it up, Canadians of this period often used "he" as a generic pronoun, and "mankind" and even "man" as a designations of humanity. I report their words as I find them.

Introduction:
Reconnaissance and Resistance

When I embarked on writing this book, initially intending to cover a much longer time period in a much shorter volume, I thought it would be a rather easy job. I would just generalize on the basis of all the histories that we have – about organizations, the left and religion, the left and women, the left and radical immigrants, the impact of the Great War, the coming of the postwar labour revolt. Then came a chilling discovery. Many of these histories do not exist.

Canada is unusual in this respect. Many other similar countries – Britain, the United States, France, Italy, for example – can boast of at least a half-dozen books about their turn of the century leftists. Not so Canada. I would have loved to have had at my side *The Canadian Social Democrats and the Challenge of War*, or *La gauche québécoise, 1890–1920*. There are no such titles. Some reasonably well-developed patches do exist – on Winnipeg 1919, the social gospel, the traditions of the Socialist Party of Canada, and the women's movement, notably – interspersed with tracts of empty space. In Canada, on topics that elsewhere have generated vast debates and even libraries, we are often lucky to have one or two unpublished theses.

In taking up this challenge – in setting out to describe and analyze the history of the Canadian left from 1890 to 1920, the three-decade period in which a distinctive and multifaceted socialist movement established itself as a permanent presence in the country – I engage in what I call a mission of reconnaissance. It is an approach that eschews what has been called "scorecard history," in which the historian assigns stars and demerit points based on his or her present-day politics.[1] In one sense, reconnaissance means "a preliminary examination or survey, as of the territory and resources of a country." It carries a second military meaning, "the act of obtaining information of military value, especially regarding the position, strength, and movement of enemy forces." Both definitions suit my purpose. A left historian is engaged in obtaining information of use in the lengthy war of position that, as Antonio Gramsci observed, Western leftists since the early 20th century have necessarily had to fight. In addition to recognizing and learning all we can about the ruling regime's strengths and weaknesses, we also need to pass on what has been learned by past left cohorts about how to survive and thrive in such a setting.

A reconnaissance is several steps down the ladder of comprehensiveness from a polished and final synthesis. As the name implies, reconnaissance entails accepting that, on issues big and small, the latest word is not going to be the last word. The point of reconnaissance, both in real life and in metaphor, is to awaken us to little-explored realities, in an age when – philosophically and politically – the quest for rock-solid foundations seems more and more quixotic. One of the implications of reconnaissance is that any exploration of past formations of thought and activism must be governed by the understanding that, in time, our own frameworks of understanding will almost certainly seem "dated," as is the fate of all the thoughts and things that humans construct.

At the same time a reconnaissance entails something other than the pursuit of knowledge for its own sake, for the amusement and edification of the reader. As the name suggests, reconnaissance does not confuse objectivity with neutrality[2] – it does not pretend either that intellectual work is mere diversion or entertainment, or that the knowledge it produces is politically inconsequential. Reconnaissance is a political act of research. It is not a strategy that says, in effect, "it does not matter if one side or the other dominates a question or the pace and direction of change." It says, instead, "To win this terrain, this multi-generational and protracted struggle for equality and justice, a re-emergent left needs to see its past more clearly, its present more strategically, and its future more ambitiously." Indeed, it needs to *live* its history, to grasp rigorously the extent to which what might seem straightforward and obvious about our present day is not exactly what it seems – not, as Gramsci might say, "identical with itself" – because on closer inspection we find traces and structures of the past, and trends and developments pointing to the future. A left that understands its own past, that "acknowledges its own determination," has a far better chance of strategic interventions in the present.[3] Escaping from the unilinear, onwards and upwards master narratives that it has conventionally applied to itself, socialist historiography can say something more original and more useful to a movement that deserves not sectarianism or sentimentality, but a principled and critical realism.

A useful reconnaissance of Canadian socialism entails no ancestor worship of past socialists, and no sense of certainty that ultimately the "right side" is going to win. It may actually involve sightings of once-promising paths that turned out to be dead ends. Neither trial by jury nor exculpation by biography, reconnaissance explores those paths because doing so can suggest important parallels with contemporary strategic alternatives.

In this sense, "reconnaissance" and "polemic" are antonyms. Polemics can by their very sharpness lead to new forms of knowledge and a crystallization of theoretical and political alternatives. No left would last long without them. Yet they can also lead to self-satisfied mystifications, to the stale repetitions of positions whose plausibility and logic are not rigorously interrogated. Polemical history can, even in its most professedly "revolutionary" guise, thus play an essentially reactionary and regressive role if it is not supported by a grounded realism. Reconnaissance recommends a post-polemical approach to the history of the left. It emerges during a time of reflection upon a century of political violence and polemical turmoil, and with an awareness of the left's near-death experience in the 20th century's neo-liberal closing quarter. Rather than celebrating the leftists about whom we talk as our pioneers, or rebelling against them as our symbolic parents, we acknowledge the profound chasm separating their world from ours. We do not seek to rescue the figures of past leftists as icons of the true faith, or to silence the ne'er-do-wells whose heresies, betrayals, and apostasies can be preserved as bad examples of what happens when you diverge from the true path. Instead, we acknowledge that the true path is often, for us as for them, difficult to discern – which is not the same as thinking that all paths are the same, or that it does not matter which one we choose.

The writing of a post-polemical reconnaissance does not mean either that we think the positions associated with past lefts have been decisively transcended, or that they are all of equal worth. What is living and what is dead for us within each of the lefts of the past is something to be argued about in the present. Yet, paradoxically, unless such arguments are simply going to confirm what we already think we know about our politics – which raises the question, why then bother to go to all the time and trouble of historical research, if we already know what it is going to tell us? – they have to be both *present-minded* (there are urgent reasons why we need to undertake this research) and *anti-presentist* (accurate and politically useful answers can only emerge if we reconstruct past lefts as much as possible in their own terms).[4] We have to explore these histories with an awareness that one point of doing so is to explain the present; yet we can only effectively use them to do that if we acknowledge that they come from different historical contexts. There is in reconnaissance itself a drive to *reason otherwise* in left historiography – to replace the consolations of morality tales and onwards and upwards master narratives with a more intellectually challenging and politically useful methodology.

For me, reconnaissance notably differs from the scholarly approach that strains for completeness, authoritativeness, and (rhetorically if not actually) certainty. A scholar taking up this other approach would try to "hold the field" against competitors, generate a "commanding synthesis," and if possible persuade acolytes and competitors to see the field in exactly the same way. Reconnaissance accepts the contingency, difficulty, and political riskiness of any and all attempts to generalize beyond the particular – and the inescapable necessity of doing so. The point of a reconnaissance is to provoke a network of focused investigations. If a work of synthesis is (at least in imagination) meant to brood over its landscape for the generations, a reconnaissance knows itself to be but one step in a co-operative struggle to understand a contested terrain, just one step in the struggle to reclaim left history from the "enormous condescension of posterity."[5]

Some Questions of Definition . . .

Until recent times most leftists in Canada would have agreed to define themselves as socialists and spoken of socialism as a set of principles whose inner presence is attested to by outward signs: mastery of certain texts, participation in defining struggles and movements, identification with particular leaders. In conventional historiography, seeing socialists and socialism this way often ushers us into a polemical world of irresolvable debates about who is *really* a socialist.

Following Raymond Williams and Margaret Cole, we might agree on a very general definition of socialism as an outlook holding that any society founded on large-scale private ownership entails injustice; that a more equitable and worthwhile form of society can be established; and that attaining that society will require a social revolution, hopefully peaceful, perhaps not. Especially if we were interested in maintaining a critical connection with the Marxist tradition, we might also add a fourth point from Karl Marx and Friedrich Engels: socialism is not just an *ideal* but something *actually emerging*, a "set of objective possibilities," in the actual social and economic world around us.[6]

A leftist in Canada is generally someone who thinks that capitalism is unjust and an equitable alternative is feasible, that social revolution (peaceful or otherwise) is needed to attain that alternative, and that capitalist social relations, about which we can acquire reliable if always improvable knowledge, are making that revolution a real-world possibility. It is my working principle that anybody whose words and deeds can be plausibly connected with these four key insights – into capitalism's injustice, the possibility of more equitable democratic alternatives, the need for social revolution, and the development of the preconditions of this social transformation in the actual world around us – counts as a leftist.

Canada is by geographical area the second-largest and one of the most thinly populated countries on the planet. It is an archipelago of different regional and national identities more than a homogeneous and culturally unified nation-state. What brought the country together in the mid-19th century was the practical project of founding a liberal order – premised on restrictive readings of the ideals of liberty, equality, and property – under the aegis of the British Empire.[7] In Canada this goal meant resistance to U.S.-style radical republicanism, to previously established Tory notions of hierarchy and community, and to "democracy," particularly as it had emerged in revolutionary

Europe. Although the formula of the state and the tone of its politics were drawn from Britain, the homeland of many thousands of settlers from the 1760s on, before them the country was settled by settlers from France, and before them the Aboriginal peoples – with the result that within this "British Dominion" were large spaces dominated by the non-British. Massive waves of emigration from continental Europe after the 1890s added a further complexity. Such patterns made Canada hard to govern in the past, and make it difficult to describe accurately in the present – because any brave generalization about the whole can always be refuted with a divergent finding from one, often many, of its parts.

Once a group, usually closely tied to a class, achieves power, it works to make its historical choices – for instance, constructing a *liberal order* – appear to be natural phenomena to which no sensible person can object. This is in part, but not only, a question of developing a convincing political language. Gramsci calls this process "hegemony," which is not quite the same as "ideology." The theory of hegemony refers not just to ideas, but also to the material forms that generate them and the social agents they attract. Challenging one of its aspects often means calling into question a vast network of assumptions, institutions, and values. In Canada since the 1840s, liberal hegemony has worked at the deepest levels, organizing the very ways in which the "individual," "state," and "economy," for example, are framed, analyzed, and changed. To be a leftist in Canada has historically meant not only contesting the injustices of capitalism but also coming to terms with the cultural complexity of the country, with its capitalist political economy and mainstream political assumptions.

Reconnaissance includes an emphasis on the underlying patterns of politics – an interest in political formations. A *left formation* is an analytical term used to describe a specific constellation of parties, people, issues, and texts. Each formation is united by its own distinctive interpretation of an overriding political objective – that of *reasoning and living otherwise*. Each formation is, in its heyday, "the section that pushes forward all others" on the left. It might have a party (in the conventional sense) at its core; it might have several parties; or it might have no one dominant party. Left formations may share many words and even concepts with each other – those participating in them are, after all, engaged in pushing forward left ideals of equality, democracy, and freedom championed since the 1790s. Yet each formation gives these ideals a different articulation. Hence a word – "freedom," "evolution," "revolution," "science," even "socialism" – that means one thing in one formation may mean something quite different in another.

Research into left formations focuses less upon the specific events of a time frame and more upon the underlying principles, the "axiomatics," that distinguish one left formation from another. While reconnaissance focuses particularly on the statements left behind by the people of a given political formation, this research is even more interested in the general rules and assumptions, the grammar and syntax, underlying those statements. As historian Robert Stuart suggests, rather than asking "Who really spoke?" and "How well and how authentically," this approach asks, "How did this language of socialism function? Where, how, and for whom did it work?" Rather than focusing exclusively on the individual speech-acts and great men (and much more rarely women) of the conventional historical accounts, it focuses on the constitutive language characteristic of a given leftism. Rather than viewing ideologies as passive reflections of an external world, reconnaissance interprets them as active elements of the social and political order. It counsels acute sensitivity to their nuances, silences, contradictions, and cohesion. It urges that they be understood "in time and place" – that is, placed within the "social whole which conditioned their development and was conditioned by that development."[8] Rather than just asking, as various left-wing versions of "Great Man History" tend to do, "Did these people get Marx right?" reconnaissance asks, "How did these people put texts, events, things, and memories to work, so that they themselves felt that their politics was consistent and coherent?"

Each left formation organizes a conceptual system, which – at the limit – comes to be defended as an integrated science. Such a system provides categories through which the world can be logically understood, and through which actions in the present can be connected with possible future outcomes. Such a system thus allows leftists to discriminate between the real and the unreal, the true and the false, the we and the them. It entails a new *practice* of leftism, political and cultural, that both reflects this new understanding and – as categories and descriptive terms are repeated over and over again – constructs and reconstructs it, day after day. The formal organizations – parties, unions, co-operatives, study groups, publishing houses – take shape as so many instantiations of theory; as they themselves develop, and people within them invest themselves heavily in the framework, these institutions in turn alter what it is possible to think within them. Ideas, practices, and institutions combined create a formation, whose basic outlines are dictated by what that formation seeks to accomplish and how those within it try to achieve those goals. In Canada most formations imported their leftism from other places, but over time they generated their own homegrown understandings, intellectuals, and memories.

We learn that we are in the presence of such a formation when large numbers of leftists – often a cohort drawn from the same generation – start naming new problems and using new words to announce a radical break with existing reality and pre-existing theory. To make the case that a given formation exists, we must at a minimum be able to show that, notwithstanding the splits and divisions to which the left is particularly prone, large numbers of people embraced the formation's conceptual system. Even when leftists were arguing with each other, they were at least sharing enough of a common language of leftism that their positions were mutually intelligible. Even when they were not connected by shared institutions, we can, judiciously, bring them together within the analysis of a formation if it can be shown that they were connected through a shared language of politics.

Every formation in Canada has wrestled with the fundamental question of how to make the socialist vision "real." How does one bring into the mainstream a movement requiring a radical disengagement from, indeed, a scathing and damning critique of, the surrounding socio-political order? How do you convert the events of everyday life into a cumulative struggle for a world that is truly *otherwise*?

It might be possible to imagine an infinite number of leftisms organized around an infinite number of themes, from anti-materialism to Zoroastrianism. Yet in a critical realist reconnaissance such leftisms can only be described as formations if they can be shown to have attracted and influenced thousands of people, generated hundreds of publications, and created long-lasting institutional networks. The people working within them developed sustained critical movements, usually lasting for more than two decades. Some were more coherent, and hence more easily discerned, than others. Yet the key to their existence is a widely shared language of analysis and resistance, one isomorphic with given patterns of political organization. Each of these experiments merits our respectful and detailed attention, because – separated as we are from them by the traumatic experiences of the late 20th-century left and the rise of neoliberalism – we can no longer tell the story of the left as an onwards and upwards narrative. Such master narratives are no longer plausible.

Yet, living as we do in a time in which postmodernism itself stands revealed as a flawed framework, incapable of addressing our own principal issue of human survival, we can also not summarily dismiss any of these past experiments, writing them off as so many dark moments before the dawn of our own age. We need, in other words, to step back and, by seeing these experiments afresh, measure them for both their meaning (what this leftism meant for those caught up in it) and their significance (the unintended consequences and implications of this leftism as they have become evident to subsequent generations).[9]

I can summarize this developing approach in the form of a five-point program.

1. A given socio-economic situation generates problems and contradictions – objective possibilities for change – that provide a niche for leftists, for people who want to change their societies in egalitarian and democratic ways. But to become "real" in any meaningful sense, these possibilities must be *known* –

that is, taken up within a system of concepts and integrated into a form of *reasoning or living otherwise*. The very process of articulating this alternative future stimulates people to take up positions for or against the leftist vision that activists and thinkers have made, as best they can, a real possibility.

2. Structure-shifting "matrix-events" spark sudden and drastic moments of rebellion. It suddenly seems imperative to many people to *refuse* the social world around them – that is, not just reactively *reject* their circumstances in unreflective ways (such as taking drugs, vandalizing public buildings, or attacking real or perceived enemies) but articulate reasons why they have chosen such a path of resistance. It may end there – especially if there is no organized political formation to channel this refusal into more lasting shape. But if there is such a formation, *refusal* leads to *supersedure*: the sense not only that the immediate oppression should be resisted, but also that the entire structure making it possible should be contested. This moment of supersedure – the epiphany of understanding that the suffering and oppression being experienced emerges from underlying contradictions in the social and economic structure, that it can be logically explained and actively contested – can in turn lead to *systematization* – the energetic pursuit of models and narratives that will make sense of this moment and further the cause of resistance.

3. The applied sociology, historical analysis, and cultural networks developed by such systematizing socialists, although they achieve many individual articulations and give rise to many different constructions, can – if only in retrospect – be seen to share a common language, common interests, and a widely diffused sense of long-range historical patterns. Intellectuals and institutions develop conceptual tools to master the world around them – constructs that work both in theory and in more day by day activism. These conceptual systems – analogous to the paradigms or research programs described by philosophers of science[10] – represent a significant investment in the time, energy, and sometimes even lives of those who become leftists. Consequently, these radicals defend them militantly as the precondition and prefiguration of the freedom for which they are fighting. Often, as a cohort drawn from a generation that has been shaped by the same matrix-events, they defend the conceptual systems against earlier and later leftists, whose political languages they find inadequate to the many challenges posed by the big events of their time.

4. Leftism reaches a certain fixity in formal institutions, manifestos, position papers, debates, and other manifestations. For the historian this organizational detail can be both useful and misleading. It is useful because the organizations were often important in their own right as historical actors; it can also open a window into underlying patterns of left thought. But it can also be misleading, in part because it can tempt us to equate the particular party with

the whole formation. A formation does not require unanimity, nor does it imply unequivocal domination of a left inescapably shared with other, emerging or declining, formations. Many leftists who share a common language of leftism and cohabit an institution may come to differ radically about how best to interpret their program and further the organization's agenda. The left, which takes ideas and their implications very seriously, is almost predestined to be characterized by fierce debates and organizational divisions.

Yet, if from the participants' point of view, each and every one of these debates or divisions might be construed as the initiation of a new paradigm, in fact and in retrospect such is not the case: historical perspective allows us to determine which ones truly indicated an epistemological and political break – that is, a new systematization – and which ones were merely aspects of the normal functioning of left political discourse. The methodological implication is that anything substantial that comes out of a left formation must be scrutinized not only for its self-evident meaning to participants, but also for its historical significance. Words do significant work in the world – and for that very reason just how they are put together within a past left formation can tell us a great deal, sometimes inadvertently, about that formation's underlying logic and dynamics.

Looking back, we might be tempted, for instance, to measure the impact of a particular "left" in straightforward quantitative terms – seats won, union positions acquired, strikes led, members signed up. Indeed, all such measures can be helpful indications of how a party (and beyond that, a formation) is faring. But none of them can be taken as the benchmark. A formation might be a jumble of weak institutions – short-lived organizations, intermittent campaigns, ineffectual and minority parties – yet still be judged important in forcing the pace of social and political change in many spheres apart from official politics.[11]

5. An inclusive narrative of a given moment of leftism in Canada can be written in terms of the major figures, parties, currents, texts, and debates. The logic of transition to the "next moment" lies in the (implicit and explicit) contradictions inherent in any socialist network; and especially in the gap between the post-liberal socialist ideal and the contingencies of survival in a liberal order. Each formation can be identified not only in terms of its typical texts but also by the core contradictions and the "questions" characteristic of the formation.

A full history of socialism in Canada would thus trace both the continuities and the discontinuities between one moment and the next. Rather than arguing for a unilinear pattern of development, which would encourage us to think of the "third formation" as necessarily an improvement over the "first," our history would tend more towards setting up each "left" in its own terms, as a relatively autonomous (if never isolated) experiment specific to a time and place. Reconnaissance would pay special attention to innovations and to silences, to the moments in which the formation has seemingly "sealed" a contradictory reality within its own terms, and to those in which the "seal" is broken and previously stable definitions and constructions are in flux.

Reconnaissance would also pay equal attention to the spatial complexities of any articulation of socialism, for it cannot take for granted that "socialists in Canada" were "Canadian socialists," with horizons determined principally by the boundaries of the Dominion. The left in Canada has always been intensely involved with movements outside the country, and the extent to which any given formation saw itself as Canadian and wrote its manifestos and programs with Canada in mind is a complex question that can only be answered by empirical research. There is often a considerable time lag between the introduction of a new left program and its indigenization in Canada; and a further gap between that first rooting and the development of a strong challenge to the reigning political and cultural order.

... *and Some Implications*

Understanding Canadian left history in this way allows for a different perspective on the success or failure of succeeding leftisms. Although all major socialisms in Canadian history have ultimately been contained by liberal order, they have also worked to transform the country. When we evaluate any particular leftism or socialism in Canada, we might ask: During the years of a particular left project as it arose in the interstices of liberal order, how much change did it bring about? What were its (foreseen and unforeseen) consequences? Anyone who wants to reinvent the left in the 21st century has everything to gain from a critical understanding of the prior efforts of past leftists – without any implication that we necessarily can or should share all of the same political goals.

If we want to *live otherwise* in the future, we will have to not only live our present differently, but also find new ways of exploring and re-experiencing our past. We have to imagine generations of radicals past and generations yet to come as our co-investigators and co-activists – not people standing before us, awaiting our God-like judgment. We have to transcend our immediate temporal limitations to re-create the ways of thinking and seeing with which many previous radical democrats identified. Doing that we will be able to understand their leftisms more clearly. We have to have an acute and respectful awareness of the political and social order that we want to change – and an equally precise sense of the many attempts made before us to do so.

Throughout this book, then, I seek to explore the underlying grammar of a particular left formation, attending closely to its organizing concepts and characteristic rhetorical tropes and the questions that most profoundly agitated its adherents. For the most part, reconnaissance downplays the drive to bring past leftists before the bar of history – in part because it arises from an ethic and a politics suspicious of the power relations involved in such imaginary show trials, and in part because it imagines not a unitary, but a sharply differentiated, reading public. Hence, I am generally less interested in reaching negative verdicts – even in cases in which the leftist is articulating a position that today could be described as, say, classist, intolerantly anti-religious, sexist, homophobic, or racist. (In truth, there are few reactionary positions in today's world that cannot claim some Canadian left articulation.) Although now and again my own Gramscian politics will inescapably influence how I represent a past position, I try to invest most of my time and energy in describing the position as accurately as I can and saying as much as I can about its fit within the overall framework. Neither do I seek to airbrush such flaws from the account in order to save reputations. Sectarianism and sentimentalism, and point-scoring histories, have become tiresome and, much worse, politically counterproductive.

Each period makes its own leftism. Each one of these is a particular dialect of a more general language. What may seem a frivolous and insubstantial leftism to most of us today may well prefigure the most crucial issues tomorrow. That there are many paths to the left means that, at any given time, it may be misleading to imagine that one of them is truer or more serious than the others. To say that some of these paths are more important than others in a specific period is not a sly way of saying that they are more worthwhile; rather, it is a critical realist attempt to provide an accurate assessment of an actually existing situation.

My not so hidden agenda, then, is to persuade the reader that the vanished world of left politics in turn of the century Canada is a fascinating and exciting field of study. In my eyes this book will find its place by generating new conversations and debates, not for the purpose of filling journals and monographs with evidence of erudition but as a means of reimagining the past of the left, and anticipating its future. This is indeed an urgent task as we debate not just the characteristics of this particular formation of the left but the future hopes and prospects of those that are yet to come.

A strange new play called Modernity: here in Winnipeg, 21 June 1919, as before in such cities as Halifax, Saint John, Toronto, and London, a streetcar becomes part of a bonfire of corporate vanities. Provincial Archives of Manitoba.

1

Socialism: The Revolutionary Science of Social Evolution

S pringhill, Nova Scotia, 21 February 1891. When the explosion came, 13-year-old John Conway was sitting on the edge of the front box of a train of coal cars, driving his horse on the 2,000-foot level far below the surface of the mine. The fire killed his horse, which fell upon him, and there he lay, crying, "Mother! Mother!" The rescue parties had given up hope of finding more survivors, but when his feeble cries reached their ears, they turned the horse's body over, found John only slightly affected by the poisonous mine gas, and led him to safety.

Little Dannie Robertson was driving a rake of empty boxes when he was struck by a blast of flame so forceful that it instantly killed his horse "Jenny" and knocked him backward into one of the boxes. He was momentarily stunned, and when he came to he found his clothes afire and the mine roof falling around him. Throwing off his burning coat and vest, he began to crawl his way out of the pit. After going a short distance he overheard the cries of 12-year-old Willie Terris. Robertson's hands were so badly burned he could not bear to pick Terris up, but he told him to climb up on his back. Then, so burdened, he made his way to safety.

When he caught a glimpse of the flames, 14-year-old Adolphus Landry threw his hands over his face and crouched behind his horse. The animal fell onto him. In pinning the boy to the ground, the horse also probably saved his life – although Adolphus spent the following hours in such intense suffering that he prayed for death to swiftly come.

Other boys were not so lucky. Out of a total death toll of 125 that day in Springhill, 16 boys under the age of 17 would die. The body of Lemuel Morrison's 13-year-old boy was cut in two and damaged beyond recognition. Morrison had gone looking for him, and had walked by the mangled body several times. His wife took a second look and, spotting the lad's shirt, came upon the telltale traces of her needlework from the night before. All she could say was, "This is my poor boy! This is my poor boy!"[1]

In the late 19th and early 20th centuries such events were repeated with brutal regularity in mining towns, lumber camps, and manufacturing centres from Nova Scotia to British Columbia. Death stalked the coal mines. In an average two years more people died in late 19th-century Nova Scotia mines than died in all the battles of the Northwest Rebellion of 1885. Coal disasters had occurred in Nova Scotia for decades, some worse than that of 1891. It would seem but common sense that such institutionalized child abuse would rouse outrage throughout a liberal society that prided itself upon the civilization and humanity of its institutions, with its schools high among them. It might also seem that the coal communities above all – witnessing the cruelty and carelessness with which a social and political order regarded their offspring – would have been swiftly radicalized by such events.[2]

Yet, before the late 19th century, the experience of coal mining – its supposed isolation, class polarization, and fatality rates – did not often lead to many outbreaks of political radicalism. In Springhill in 1891 the biggest crowds of mourners came out for the ceremonies commemorating manager Henry Swift. There was much praise for the company for its "generosity" in donating land for burial plots, and little apparent dissent with the exculpatory Coroner's Inquest, which cleared the management of all responsibility. (Interestingly, however, the regulations on gaseous mines were then tightened up.) Perhaps grievously bereaved parents were more likely to move inwards, to religion or despair or drink, than proceed to a radical rejection of the system that had allowed their children to work in the mine – and, of course, many families had depended on the money that their children made, took pride in the young workers' advance up the mining hierarchy, and may have well have felt guilty when they died. Before the late 1890s, blood on the coal did not often lead, as today's socialists might presume, to a radical refusal of the killing pits of capitalism.

Yet once an alternative ideological framework was abroad in the land – a new way of thinking, talking, and organizing about class – it became possible to see the wounds of industrial capitalism in a new way. Such enormities were transformed, in part at least, from natural to social catastrophes. They were delivered from the province of providence and rearticulated into the counter-hegemonic frameworks of a new radicalism. When a similar coal-mine disaster took place in New Waterford, Nova Scotia, in 1917, the conventional pieties about submitting to the inscrutable Will of God or accepting the turn of Fortune's Wheel were displaced by a new discourse, palpably influenced by the new 20th-century left, which led not just to an indictment of the coal company for "causing grievous bodily harm" but also to charges of manslaughter against two company officials and the deputy mines inspector.[3] It was a sign, in large measure, of the deep-seated cultural change involved in the diffusion of radical socialist ways of interpreting the world. There were now "normal" aspects of modernity that, redescribed in a new framework, seemed utterly monstrous.

During strikes these moments of refusal and supersedure were common occurrences. Although Canadian historians can track strikes back into the 18th century, down to the late 19th century they remained primarily local affairs. In the *fin de siècle*, they started to take on worldwide dimensions. In the Maritimes, for example, when the large coal companies threatened to roam the world – from Turkey to China – to find strikebreakers, resorting to recruitment as far away as Constantinople, the notions of a "world economy" and a "world working class" no longer seemed abstract. The relatively new word "capitalism" itself gradually – from 1905 to 1910, approximately – became something that many on the Canadian left started using to denote the *systematicity* of economic and social patterns. They started to see a connection between the body of Lemuel Morrison's boy and the balance sheets of the Cumberland Railway and Coal Company.

For leftists of the early 20th century this moment of supersedure came with shattering, novel, and difficult implications. If they had truly internalized the truths of liberal political economy – and very few Canadian schoolchildren would not have done so, given the intensity with which these givens were promoted in the educational system – such a moment of supersedure would cast into doubt the very core of the system: the reality-status of the category of "the individual." What did "the individual," so pivotal to liberal theory, mean in the *fin de siècle*, when the most powerful people in society – the industrialists, politicians, and financiers – were not really "individualistic" in any real way? If for most people what really mattered was how they functioned within a structure they had not themselves created? Surely, many contemporaries reasoned, the very boundaries of the "individual" at the heart of liberal theory had been irretrievably eroded. And with them went many of the cultural resources of capitalism – from the "rags to riches" narratives that crowded the newspaper columns to stories that blamed the death of mining children on the feckless disobedience of the individual children themselves.

In November 1898, at an Amherst, N.S., meeting of the coal miners' union, the Provincial Workmen's Association – which had recently expanded beyond its coalfield base to organize some of the town's boot and shoe workers – a young man of 22 presented a long, detailed address on "The Social Problem." It was none other than Adolphus Landry, one of the lads injured in the 1891 explosion. He began by drawing a glowing picture of Thanksgiving (which in those days took place in late November). He saluted the peacefulness and good harvests of the surrounding countryside, and the marvels of industrial progress. Then, citing copious U.S. statistics, he turned to the "terrible mockery" of poverty, unemployment, and industrial violence. Look, Landry cried, at the consequences of the system! Look at "all the stunted undeveloped inarticulate brains, all the bent and aching backs, all the tired and weary limbs, all the rheumatism racked frames, all the wrecked hopes and aching hearts of youthful manhood." Think of "all the anxious hours and painful heart beats of hungry mothers, all the bitter cries and untold suffering of children, children robbed of their childhood, that have been, and shall be." We can imagine his voice rising: "Cry halt! Stop in the name of your God given sense, stop in the name of justice and truth, refrain from such hypocritical mockery." Think of the Rockefellers, the Goulds, the Astors – the money they made in a day would feed a working-class family for a year! And consider the trusts, for as the "Capitalists" became "more powerful," slowly but surely the workers were "being enslaved." Think of Charles Tupper, the local Tory and former prime minister (not to mention a well-rewarded investor in the local coal industry). Did Tupper even understand the system he stood for? Tupper spoke of business crises as "cyclones" – natural disasters. It was, Landry said, a very telling metaphor, because it suggested a man still trapped in the Dark Ages, who spoke of economic patterns as superstitiously as earlier humans had spoken of thunder storms. What a relic! An echo of a time when a "hundred thousand bonfires" had lit up the skies, and human beings had been done to death "in the name of God and Christianity," before a more enlightened age of religious tolerance and freedom.

But now, Landry urged, we should all draw the necessary lesson. Realize that just as "superstition, narrowness, bigotry, prejudice, ignorance of God's laws and man's true relation to man" had once created such horrific suffering, "today we are suffering from effects that are the results of our ignorance of political economy." Dare to know! Confront the teachings of Karl Marx, Ferdinand Lassalle, and the others who had elevated socialism into a movement of millions, inspired by "the science of reconstructing society on an entirely new basis," that is, "the substitution of the principle of co-operation for that of competition, in every branch of industry."

"I am young and inexperienced," Landry confessed. Yet he claimed some expertise in the workings of the system. "The Springhill explosion nearly eight years ago found me among its victims and the marks it left upon my hands are no deeper than the marks it left upon my heart." Remember, then, along with the great message of the socialists' scientific enlightenment, that "Boys of 13 years old were killed there." Think of the people who had sent them down there. "I tell you," he cried, "there is injustice in this society of ours."[4]

Landry's voice conveys the impression of someone who has at last found the words to refuse the injuries of class that were so manifest in 1891, someone who could describe such evils within a framework in which even his own injuries could take on a different meaning. The crashing liberal assumptions in Landry's speech were like a distant echo of the sounds of crashing timber from that moment in February 1891.

A Monstrous Modernity

For one writer in the Montreal *Herald* on 15 December 1896 – anonymous, but the fingerprints of radical writer and merchant seaman Colin McKay (1876–1939) are all over the piece – the moment of supersedure came in a profile of "Two Men." One of them is the head of a prosperous business. He is surrounded by all the luxuries money can buy. The other is a poor sailor wintering in the city, much (it is safe to hypothesize) like the writer himself. The sailor is alone, "with the awful solitude of a vast, strange city." His face is weather-beaten. All around him are wealth, beauty, and happiness, but "in these he had no part." A woman in shimmering clothes walks past. She gazes upon him contemptuously and moves to the other side of the walk. A policeman hustles him along. Reflecting on his position in life, the lonely sailor thinks to himself: "It was money, and money alone, [that] was the cause of his utter desolation. It was this that forbade the true man to give him a hand; it was this that made the true woman gather up her skirts and hurry past."[5]

In a modern city like Montreal, appearances were deceiving. The silk-clad woman and the weather-beaten sailor, experiencing vastly different worlds, were in fact part of one process – for "he and his ilk had risked life and limb" to bring home her silk "from far, far lands." As a Marxist of a later generation might put it, they were profoundly alienated from each other and from the socio-economic world of which they were both a part – even while being connected by the unseen web of the social relations of production.

Such mutual estrangement and disconnection seemed remarkable to many in the 1890s. Many had, like McKay, emigrated from small towns that, however they might have romanticized them, provided an experience of the "social" that was profoundly different from that of the bustling metropolis. The big cities unsettled and also inspired them when juxtaposed to more knowable communities. Whom could you trust? What did the signs of urban life mean? Sometimes leftists have been almost palpably impatient with the combined and uneven development of the Canadian social and political archipelago; they generalize on the basis of the big, class-divided cities without really imagining the different rhythms and strata of the countryside or the vivid, sometimes radicalizing "shock of the new" experienced by generation after generation of internal immigrants, arriving in cities that were shockingly indifferent to the ties that bind people to one another and to a land.[6] Even the smallest details of urban modernity – the crowds, shop windows, smells, dangers and pleasures, the vortex of unceasing and driven change – could be articulated, "defamiliarized" within *fin de siècle* social thought, and described as unsettling signs of human disconnection, from fellow human beings and from the natural world.

Stephen Leacock (1869–1944), who incongruously combined the roles of a prominent liberal political economist and Canada's best-loved humorist, beautifully captured this raw edge of modernity. The transition from his *Sunshine Sketches of a Little Town* (1912), with its fond nostalgia for the "knowable community," to *Arcadian Adventures with the Idle Rich* (1914) reveals a movement from the human scale of small-town life, with all its pettiness and peculiarity, to the monstrous maelstrom of the metropolis. The coldly plutocratic Plutoria (Montreal) depicted in *Arcadian Adventures* is eviscerated with a satirical venom worthy of Karl Marx himself. Everywhere in the city categories are fetishized, as city-dwellers see each other only as instruments of personal profit. The satire extends even to the children of Plutoria, babies who are perambulated as so many personifications of monopoly capital: "Here you may see a little toddling princess in a rabbit suit who owns fifty distilleries in her own right.... Near by is a child of four, in a khaki suit, who represents the merger of two trunk-line railways.... A million dollars of preferred stock laughs merrily in recognition of a majority control going past." Leacock, a lapsed "utopian socialist," had not quite lost his sense of the inhumanity of the city around him. The spirit of ethical outrage so carefully removed from his writings on the political economy returns to haunt the humour and give *Arcadian Adventures* its midnight laughter.[7] Later he speaks even more directly of the monstrous disease that had malformed the plutocrats – they suffer from an "elephantiasis of individualism." Everything – religion, the "life of the mind," the rituals of a supposedly democratic politics – has been reduced to a money sign. Nobody is what they seem to be. They are all apparitions, projections from a process we can barely glimpse.

Today perhaps the knowing "nightmare hilarity" of *Arcadian Adventures* stands up more effectively than does the small-town earnestness of so many standard critiques of the big, bad city – but we should not miss the contradictory unity binding these positions together, their shared sense of shock. Was this urban alienation, both McKay and Leacock would implicitly ask, really the unavoidable outcome of social-evolutionary forces of such power and depth that only a fool could resist them? Although an apologist for liberal laissez-faire and the competitive system, Leacock shared with the radical McKay an awareness that "only by a confusion of thought" could processes of the struggle for existence in nature be used "to explain away the death of children of the slums. The whole theory of survival is only a statement of what is, not of what ought to be."[8]

Arcadian Adventures achieves its extraordinary rhetorical impact by exploring this unresolved contradiction. Its writer, and its readers, seemingly did not know whether to laugh at, or simply succumb to, the logic of a modernity wherein all that had once been solid – community, place, custom, identity – appeared to be "melting into air," as so eloquently predicted decades earlier in *The Communist Manifesto*.[9]

Still, not all human solidarities had melted into air. As labour historians have long demonstrated, working-class families constructed vibrant worlds of meaning and memory around the mine shafts, foundries, and steel mills of modern capitalism. In Springhill are preserved the coal-dust-covered old subscription books, recording the nickel-and-dime donations collected from comrades to cover the medical costs and funeral expenses of members of the knowable community. Yet, often, when we listen to many voices from the early 20th century, voices like those of Adolphus Landry, we are hearing from the grievously injured and the shockingly bereaved – people who have suddenly awakened to a new, almost post-human, reality: a monstrous modernity.

Often, too, if we listen carefully, we hear these voices in unexpected places. The urban skilled workers – the "labour aristocracy," many both then and today have called them – often nurtured a sense of standing apart from and well above other workers. In Halifax, for example, urban artisans had since the 18th century evolved associations, networks, and traditions that insulated them from the rural riff-raff and the common urban labourers. Nobody would sensibly include slow-growing Halifax on any short list of the "shock cities" of capitalist modernity, or place it among the Dominion's emergent "red bases." Nonetheless, in the minutes of many "conservative" craft unions we find the shocked acknowledgement of a new order of things, intimations of a modernity both terrible in its scope and intimate in its details.[10] Writing early in the 20th century, the recording secretary of the carpenters' union left a note in the minutes concerning the funeral of a member of the local. In the past, just as they had often come together for craft celebrations, masters and journeymen alike would attend such funeral services in honour of men they had known for years. But now, the secretary noted, things were radically different. Although the deceased had been a member well known in the craft and had worked for the same firm for 40 years, "not one member of that firm were men enough to spend a half hour of their valuable time at that grave side of our departed brother. . . . 'God help us all,' when we have such a class of employer to deal with. Just think and remember, a faithful employee for 40 years, more than a life time." Half an hour might seem like a small price to pay, to acknowledge a community. Yet in this fast-changing world, it might seem too steep a price, for an employer rushing to wring a profit from yet another rooming-house contract in the city's working-class North End.[11]

Whatever the human qualities of the deceased carpenter, the networks and traditions of craft that vested much of his life with meaning now shockingly seemed *passé*. For there was another, more powerful logic at work in this secretary's world. Within this logic, the deceased carpenter, notwithstanding his own conception of himself as above and beyond the common herd of labour, was just another bearer of "labour-power," bringing a commodity for sale, his ability to work, to an impersonal labour market.

The rage-filled, often seemingly irrational, riots of the urban crowds provided a parallel to the quiet grief of the recording secretary. Throughout turn of the century Canada, in city after city, with peculiar similarities, crowds would rise up, seemingly out of nowhere, as though performing in some strange new play called *Modernity*. From Halifax to Saint John to London to Winnipeg, the play entailed many of the same props and happenings: the overturned streetcar, possibly set alight; sabotaged gear boxes; crowds that suddenly appeared and just as quickly dissipated. Many down-to-earth labour issues often lay behind such moments – wages, hours of work, union recognition. Yet the involvement of non-strikers and their unusually forceful performances of protest suggested something else: that the streetcars themselves had become the deeply resented, potent signs of privilege and alienation in the modern city. They were grotesque corporate monsters, the embodiment of the acquisitiveness and compulsion of the age. It was as if, victimized by trusts and monopolies in so much of their daily existence, and fed up with rising fares and shoddy service, citizens seized the opportunity of enjoying a fleeting moment of freedom in a bonfire of these corporate vanities. The words and acts of bitterness were rarely at first directed at "the system." They flew more often towards the foreman, the mine boss, the owners of the local streetcar company, even the streetcars themselves.

It is to this age that we owe the stereotypical cartoon image of the bloated plutocrat – or "plute," to give him the nickname attached to him by the left press of the day, including the Canadian socialist movement's most widely circulated paper, *Cotton's Weekly*. Published from 1908 out of Cowansville, Quebec (before moving to Toronto in 1914), *Cotton's* in turn borrowed the term from the sensationally popular U.S. left publication *Appeal to Reason*.[12] The plute was of monstrous dimensions. His bulging vest-coat was a trophy case full of meaningless watches and medals. His jowls were distended from dissipation. He was, in his starchiness and artificiality, the antithesis of the honest workingman. His monstrosity arose not only from his corpulence but also from the squalid details that explained it. Each cartoon plutocrat was a visual aid in teaching how the rich preyed upon the working class. Each told, not just of the pathologically greedy exploiter, but also, implicitly or otherwise, of the deprived and maimed worker – whose gaunt cheeks and sunken eyes bore visual witness to the source of the plute's parasitical obesity. The body politic as a whole, socialist activist and journalist Will R. Shier of Toronto explained, was "falling under the dominion of an industrial autocracy that has its knee upon the stomach of the nation and its fingers in the pocket of every man, woman and child throughout the world." What other phrase better for this plutocracy than "a monstrous growth within the body politic"?[13]

Marx, no stranger himself to gothic imagery, would speak in *Capital* of vampire-like capitalists sucking surplus value from the working class.[14]

William Lyon Mackenzie King opens his unjustly neglected treatise *Industry and Humanity* of 1917 with images drawn from Mary Shelley's *Frankenstein*. Later his gothic imagery comes horribly closer to reality with his account of Ottawa-area women, former workers in the match factories, one suffering from "phosphorous necrosis" whose slowly decaying jaws have condemned her to the slow agony of chronic toxemia, and another who in abject misery even pulls out her own jaw.[15] Even in the shadow of stately Parliament Hill stalked a monstrous modernity.

Much of the literature on the slums and sweatshops is only superficially about the sufferings of the downtrodden; at another level, it is about the newly visible realities of social connection. Rev. J.S. Woodsworth (1874–1942) brought his readers a vintage experience of the "shock of the new" in *My Neighbor* (1911), when he told the story of a bargain-hunting woman returning gleefully with her prize – an inexpensive garment made by a poor girl suffering from tuberculosis.[16] Many commentators were registering the connections, and contradictions, woven by modernity. Beneath the deceptive surface of events they were seeing disturbing links and terrible problems. The much-noted horrors and sufferings of the day included infant mortality statistics from Montreal more reminiscent of Calcutta than North America, the horrific nightmares of isolation and oppression in the labour camps awaiting many freedom-seeking immigrants from Europe and Asia, and the blind brutality of the transcontinental railway construction sites, which consumed thousands of expendable lives in an ultra-modern conquest of space by time.

The Best of Times ...

This emphasis on modernity's hardships captures half the truth. The other half lies in the equally persuasive evidence of the astonishing and brilliant success, after decades of sluggish growth and political uncertainty, of the Canadian liberal project.

By some measures Canada from the late 1890s to the Great War was the fastest-growing place on the planet. As Gregory P. Marchildon remarks, no country in the Western world enjoyed a faster rate of economic growth than did Canada from 1870 to 1913. Real growth in Gross Domestic Product (GDP) in Canada was 4.1 per cent per annum from 1870 to 1913 (as compared to 3.9 per cent for the United States); the real GDP per labour-hour was 2.3 per cent in Canada (versus 1.9 per cent in the United States, Germany, and Japan). From 1896 to 1913, Gross National Product (GNP) per capita in Canada clocked in at an annual average real growth rate of a phenomenal 6.6 per cent (as compared to 4.4 in the United States). Foreign, primarily British, capital flooded in – a "deluge of foreign investment" in Marchildon's phrase; Canada may have absorbed as much as a third of British lending in a surge that started in 1902 and lasted until the war. Canadian securities were easily marketed in London, where Canada was seen as tightly connected with "The City."[17] Ken Norrie and Doug Owram reach similar conclusions in their survey of Canadian economic history. In the decade that opened in 1900, they observe, the Canadian economy grew at nearly double the U.S. rate. Looking back at the pattern from the 1870s to the early 20th century, they note that data on real per capita GNP "suggest that Americans were increasing their standard of living faster than were Canadians in the 1870s, but that the opposite situation held for the other three decades, with the greatest difference coming between 1900 and 1910."[18]

Canadian economic structures were also changing. Under the National Policy instituted in 1879, a home market for manufactured goods had been encouraged through tariff protection, and with the building of railways the Prairie West was opened up for immigration. Capitalist development in early 20th-century Canada meant the development of a modern coal and steel industry, the modernization of ports and grain-handling facilities, a process of bank mergers that saw scores of community banks swallowed up by their much larger competitors until only a few big banks were left, and the establishment of modern stock exchanges. From the 1890s to the 1920s the Canadian economy was transformed by the development of capital goods and by new primary resources and heavy industries – a veritable second Industrial Revolution, as historian Craig Heron suggests.[19] Perhaps even more than in the United States, the early 20th century in Canada was a time when a relatively sleepy colonial backwater was quickly if unevenly transformed into a far more industrial, and increasingly corporate, capitalist society.

Rather like Ridley Scott's *Blade Runner* (1982), the dystopian vision of Los Angeles in 2019, which succeeded brilliantly because it just slightly exaggerated observable tendencies in the world of the 1980s, Leacock's *Arcadian Adventures* was, disturbingly, just a slight exaggeration of actually-experienced Montreal. In real life, one capitalist, Herbert Holt, wove himself a phenomenal web of corporate interests, from Montreal Light, Heat, and Power (gas and electricity), the Royal Bank of Canada, Dominion Textile, the Steel Company of Canada, and Imperial Life Assurance: it might be difficult, some have speculated, for an adult to go through a Montreal day without encountering some proximate or distant manifestation of the good Mr. Holt. Leacock's fictional cutthroat capitalists had little to learn from the likes of Max Aitken (Lord Beaverbrook), who would eventually parlay the fortune he made in Montreal into a commanding position in British business and politics. Mergers in coal and steel made that industry the epitome of a new age of capital. Across urban Canada, this was "monopoly's moment," an age of great expectations and windfall profits.[20] Meanwhile, in the city below the hill in Montreal, the infant mortality rate was almost double that of New York or

Toronto. Between 1897 and 1911 about one in three babies died before reaching the age of 12. Many of them were the victims of gastroenteritis, attributed to unhealthy food. In sweatshops, women worked brutally long hours in ill-ventilated quarters. Many of the garments they made were sold to the large department stores. Between 1901 and 1921 the number of working children between 10 and 15 years of age increased "both absolutely and as a proportion of the age group." From cotton mills to coal mines, employers realized that tiny hands could make for tidy profits.[21]

It would be hard to find a major or minor socialist who did not position this matrix-event of the coming of a new capitalism – described in words like "the problem of trusts," or "monopolies," or "the labour problem" – at or close to the centre of his or her analysis. Sometimes lucidly, sometimes with voices shaking with rage, sometimes with a radiant and transformative hope, sometimes with bitter despair – people on the left could be heard to say, "The world into which we were born has been changed forever." They looked to the factories belching smoke over neighbourhoods of squalid houses and poisoned rivers. They witnessed railways that sliced through whole mountain ranges, built at the cost of thousands of working-class lives. They knew of the vast new underground cities where the coal miners worked and died in their hundreds. Their newspapers were full of news of extraordinary new sciences. They looked to this world transformed and they wondered not just about what the future might hold, but whether they would live to see it. Even if Canada had yet to generate a fully fledged Rockefeller or J.P. Morgan, the question of a new form of capitalism was central. Canadians raised questions about the "rings" that were dominating certain vital urban trades, the monopolistic power that certain entrepreneurs enjoyed in supplying urban Canadians with vital necessities, and the diminution of "trust" that was implied by the anonymity of capitalism's new seemingly irresponsible and reckless "trusts." Much larger corporations, new forms of managerial expertise, a scientific revolution in agriculture, forestry, and manufacturing – all seemed to call out for unprecedented ways of grasping the world.

Treated like so many interchangeable and anonymous units of labour-power, workers responded readily – more than it is now fashionable to remember – to analyses of society that told them, in language either abstract ("the labour theory of value," as variously interpreted) or down-to-earth ("while you're working yourself to death, the fat cats are getting rich off your labour"), that they had to do *something*. The strike movements in Canada from 1901 to 1914 were on a different scale than those of the 19th century (at least to judge from those places where comparative statistics are available). The Maritimes, for example, saw 411 strikes from 1901 to 1914, accounting for 1,936,146 striker-days. Halifax from 1901 to 1914 saw more strikes (54) in this period than in the entire half-century before 1900 (42).[22] Farmers were also mobilizing. Treated like expendable foot soldiers in Canada's struggle to assert its sovereignty in the West, often disappointed that dreams of yeoman-like independence had turned to dust, many primary producers struggled to improve their material conditions through co-operatives and to undo their political powerlessness through collective struggle. The year 1911 would mark the first of many Western On-to-Ottawa treks, this one by agrarian producers angered by, among other things, the Liberals' seemingly wilful abandonment of the free-trade principles that had brought them to office. The atmosphere crackled with tension as the Empire, having already fought a deeply controversial war against the Boers in South Africa, mobilized itself against enemies in Europe. Women, whose labour was indispensable on the Prairie homesteads and in urban factories alike, were transformed in the minds of many liberals from being the helpless victims of sweatshops to rights-de-manding fellow citizens. Still, many liberals would, down to the years of war, resist socialist pressure to extend full political rights to them. All of the contradictions – of gender, class, race, and sex – that we now associate with modernity were emerging in a Canada still governed by a mid-Victorian polit-ical framework, whose pivotal document – the British North America Act – made no mention of democracy, citizenship, or society.

The liberal order appeared in one of its purest manifestations on the Prairies. There the First Nations societies that liberal Ottawa bureaucrats of the 1880s had regarded suspiciously as examples of "communism" were forcibly marginalized.[23] Ethnic cleansing left a land fit for property lines and fence posts. Saskatchewan's wondrous rectangular shape in defiance of all nat-ural contours was itself proof of the power of the liberal imaginary. The province was duly divided into a massive quilt of townships and quarter-sec-tions. Each homestead was contained within a larger geometrical unit, yet each was also "independent," acting as a free unit within a free market. As Gerald Friesen shows, there was a chasm between this image of the Prairies and many of its socio-economic realities. The rationale of building this new Western Canada lay in the benefits that it would supply to the powerful in the old Canada of the East. The farmers of myth were the self-sufficient captains of their "little houses on the prairie." In reality they were interchangeable ele-ments in a vast state-building enterprise.

Through a five-pronged National Policy – the dismantling of First Nations communities, the North-West Mounted Police, the Canadian Pacific Railway, tariff protection, mass European immigration – the state effected a vast socio-economic revolution on the Prairies. Reservations, pass laws, residential schools, and the violent suppression of rebellions in 1870 and again in 1885 removed the First Nations and Métis as real or imagined obstacles to the new order. The North-West Mounted Police force was, Friesen points out, "an es-sential part of the National Policy because it ensured that peace would prevail in an area that could have been extremely violent," and at a cost far lower than the price of fighting Indian wars on the U.S. model. The force, in a departure from British common law traditions, acted directly as an agent of the central government, supervising not only criminal but also important aspects of civil law and administration. The Canadian Pacific Railway, later taken to be the very epitome of Canadian nation-building, was a multinational consortium (with one-sixth of its stock held in Canada, and the majority ownership shifting from investors in the United States to those in Britain). As Friesen notes, drawing a suggestive parallel with similar railway projects in Africa, the CPR combined commercial calculation with evolutionary uplift: its arrival was meant to substitute civilization for barbarism, a project the state so mightily endorsed that it vested millions of acres and dollars in the scheme and gave the corporation distinctly aliberal monopoly powers. Through tariff protection, raised significantly in 1879, the Canadian state committed itself to a strategy of import substitution, a home market, and a secure environment for the consolidating business class.

Mass immigration and the creation of a vast agrarian population represented the culmination and justification of these policies. Advertising "free land," in as many as a million pieces of propaganda per year, the Canadian state provided 56 million acres for homesteads; about 60 million acres on the Prairies were available through purchase. The proceeds from land sales helped achieve the state's other objectives – "railways, schools, swamp drainage, military service, and the extinguishing of Indian title and the Hudson's Bay Company charter." Although the initial results were unimpressive – only 1.5 million immigrants entered Canada from 1867 to 1899, a figure dwarfed by results achieved in the United States and Australia – after 1900 the numbers rose steeply. By 1928, Friesen observes, "Canadian wheat sales constituted nearly half the world export market."[24]

In short, a proud liberal could boast of the Prairies as an example of what an energetic state, seized with the spirit of improvement, could accomplish – and there was a world listening. By 1914 almost half of all Prairie residents had been born in another country; as late as 1931 the proportion was still one in three. The population soared from 419,512 in 1901 to 1,956,082 in 1921 – 64 per cent of it rural – a rate of growth far exceeding that of the country as a whole. Many were called to the turn of the century Prairies from a Europe cluttered with the social detritus of feudalism and from the land-hungry Maritimes and rural Ontario. As elsewhere, the promise of a propertied independence often proved deceptive. By one early estimate, borne out by subsequent research, perhaps four in ten homestead applications were never fulfilled, and the failure rates in Saskatchewan and Alberta may have exceeded 40 per cent. Many of those who arrived with some capital and secured good land prospered. Many others spent decades struggling on marginal farms, only to end in failure. Surveys revealed that the countryside was socially and economically stratified; in one district the bottom third of the farmers owned but 18 per cent of the farm wealth.[25]

The contradictions of corporate liberalism were most manifest in the new immigration policy, crafted by Clifford Sifton, minister of the interior. Agents, some operating on the edge of legality, scoured the world. Labour contractors shipped out thousands of workers; the North Atlantic Trading Company offered monetary encouragement to shipping agents who might be induced to send agricultural settlers to Canada. As many as 10,000 Chinese were brought to Canada to build the railways, work in the mines, and provide urban services; Italy, Scandinavia, and the Balkans provided thousands of railway and timber workers. Many of these workers were unskilled labourers, often imported under dubious circumstances, and exploited without mercy.

With a shrewdly calculating eye, Sifton specified the sorts of nationalities he preferred and that would conform to the needs of a liberal (and now Liberal) regime.[26] Whole peoples and cultures were weighed in terms of how much they would help to build up the new economic order. Today we might idealize this stance as "multiculturalism." Then the leftists called it "buying labour-power." Immigrants were propelled into relationships that were both ancient and new. Italians, for instance, often settled in "Little Italies," vestiges of which remain today. There, they could retain strong connections to their homeland (and in many cases to their home regions and villages). They might even return to Italy, having sojourned in Canada for a spell. Yet each of these "pre-modern" moments plunged them into an international labour market operating according to its own logic, often dominated by hiring agencies, and existing in a "shadow world" outside official reality. In theory, to take another example, each railway labourer on the Canadian Pacific Railway was a human individual entitled to dignity and respect. Each was working on a project of national significance. Yet in actual practice all were so many units of labour-power, commodities for sale on a world market. Some mining companies were supplied with Italian workers by the shadowy Cordasco agency of Montreal, and with Armenian and Syrian workers from agencies as far away as Constantinople. Emigrants were required to sign contracts concerning their future employment and wages. The middlemen in these operations often extracted a huge percentage of the workers' salaries. Employers also used immigrants as strikebreakers, who would often arrive in mining towns and find themselves caught in the middle of massive labour disturbances.[27] If they died in industrial accidents, as so many did, they might not even be buried under their own names. No one had bothered to write them down.[28]

Through countless books, advertisements, and recruiting drives, the Prairies were constructed as the promised land of individual freedom. The liberal ideology of the Department of the Interior hailed indomitable individuals who came to the new land and "stuck to their task until they had achieved success." The one man who "surmounted all obstacles" inspired other men "determined to do likewise."[29] Many encountered a different reality. The Maritime region's pre-eminent socialist activist and intellectual, Roscoe Fillmore (1887–1968), journeyed from the Maritimes to the West in 1906 to work on the harvest and was struck by the wretchedness of the Hungarian immigrants, lured by state promotions that promised them prosperity. "There had only been one thread of truth in the whole story – free land," Fillmore said. "The free land was here but the people who flocked in watered it with their blood, sweat and tears."[30]

At its heart the liberal experiment on the Prairies led to an almost palpable dialectical tension.[31] On the one hand the Prairie provinces were the individualistic laboratory of an Ottawa-ordered liberalism. On the other they were the plutocrats' playground, with some of the period's most flagrant experiments in corporate monopoly. On the one hand the region drew hundreds of thousands prompted by the dream of a propertied independence. On the other, when that dream was violated these people were open to listen to the various voices of the new democracy. Early, powerfully, magnificently – almost as soon as the century began – the three Prairie provinces experienced the great stirring of the liberal order's democratic nemesis. Even in British Columbia, which was never placed in the same structural relationship with the federal government, a certain logic appeared in a progression from the almost pure liberalism of the province's mid-19th-century colonizers, as vividly elucidated by historian Tina Loo and others, to the dialectical overcoming of that tendency in one of the continent's most vibrant and culturally creative socialist movements of the early 20th century.[32] For a time, but only for a time, the West was where the Canadian liberal order's contradictions were most fully in evidence – and not coincidentally, where radical democracy most powerfully developed.

When the *Trades Journal*, published by Nova Scotia's Provincial Workmen's Association, complained in the 1880s that "labour is treated as a commodity, like corn or cotton, the human agent, his human needs, human nature, the human feelings, being kept almost completely out of view," it was gesturing towards a post-liberal ideal of democracy and solidarity.[33] Marx would have immediately known what this writer meant. After the general abolition of slavery in the Western hemisphere in the second half of the 19th century, working people were not literally commodities for sale. They enjoyed human rights as individuals above and beyond the marketplace. But, said the left-wing democratic critics of liberal order, such rights were actually closely circumscribed – so much so that they routinely spoke of "wage slaves" and "wage slavery." Labour-power, they argued, is a commodity unlike any other, in two respects. It is inseparable from living human beings; and (under the right conditions) it can generate other commodities with a value greater than itself. If you look around you, Marx would say, it becomes clear that labour is free only in a restricted sense. No one in Canada is literally forced at gunpoint to go down the mine or work behind the cash desk. They do not need to be so forced. The *free labour market* works to create the happy outcome that they spend countless hours in activities that answer not to their own subjective needs, but to the requirements of capital. Sceptics, at least those without private incomes, may readily put this theory to the test by declining to be part, indirectly or directly, of the capitalist labour market. When this testing of the theory was carried out in massive reality, as in a major depression in 1912–14, many people had their own moments of supersedure, epiphanous insights into the cold logic of modern "freedom." For all its cruel irrationality, mass unemployment was a fine tutor to many left activists.[34]

Still, for many people these were years of golden opportunity. For prosperous farmers, "liberal utopianism" could seem like a plausible portrait of reality. Nobody was pinned down and forced to elect pro-business liberal parties. The Klondike Gold Rush of 1897–98 provided fresh energy for the myth of the self-made man, an ideal massively diffused throughout the continent. Here was the epoch of Canadian history that the neo-liberals of today would cherish above all: no welfare state; no public medical insurance; by and large, no secure and powerful trade union movement; almost no environmental legislation; no employment equity; no publicly funded universities; no minimum wage; only a few legal restrictions on working hours or child labour; no income tax. It was a time, in many places, of feverish, amazing growth – outrivalling the most exalted dreams of avarice. In the big cities populations grew rapidly from 1891 to 1921 – Toronto shot up from 181,215 to 521,893; Winnipeg from 25,639 to 179,087; Vancouver from 13,709 to 163,220; and Montreal from 219,616 to 618,566. Fortunes were made and lost in real estate and wheat, fox farms and patent medicines.

Plutocratic mansions were erected from Victoria to Halifax, providing lasting, eloquent monuments to this past age of excess and extremism. Craigdarroch Castle in Victoria, completed in 1890, commemorates the business prowess and entrepreneurial vigour of Robert Dunsmuir, the wealthiest man in turn of the century British Columbia. In Toronto from 1911 to 1914 Sir Henry Mill Pellatt spent about $3.5 million and employed more than 300 workers to build Casa Loma, whose flamboyant architecture combines 16th-century Scotland with 20th Century Fox.[35] Such urban castles arrogantly combined a version of European high culture and a conspicuous display of buying power – and perhaps, more subtly, suggested that even the very wealthy wanted to erect some stout quasi-feudal fortifications against an age in which so much that had once been solid had melted into air.

From Darwin to Spencer to Socialism

The first formation can be defined as a school of socialists who saw their movement as a practical science of social transformation founded upon the insights of evolutionary theory. It was not inherently simplistic, positivistic, or vulgar – to cite some epithets commonly used in the literature. "Vulgar Marxism" and "Socialism of the Second International" work best as slogans, not as tools of understanding this cohort. The term "first formationists" suggests both the time and the complexity of these socialists: their underlying axioms, patterns of activism, and strengths and weaknesses. If they often look and sound strange in and to 21st-century eyes and ears, the members of the first formation fit perfectly into the cultural terrain of the mid- to late 19th century.

If a certain middle-class anti-modernism captivated the likes of Dunsmuir and Pellatt, almost without exception the leftists of the early 20th century were those who, finding modern capitalism both unendurable and re-placeable, vested their hopes in a science of social evolution. They believed that they could explain and change society with the same success in which scientists had explained and helped "master" nature. They were "naturalists," believing that social patterns could be analyzed in a scientific language drawn largely from three great thinkers of the 19th century: Karl Marx (1818–83), Charles Darwin (1809–82), and Herbert Spencer (1820–1903).

Therein, too, lies one of the major hurdles confronting any reconnaissance of this cohort. If they are thought of as "social Darwinists," or as straightforward apostles of Herbert Spencer, notorious for his ultra-reactionary classical liberal views on the poor and the state in the 1880s, one polemical response will be to associate them with all the horrors of 20th-century totalitarianism. Any turn to evolutionary theory can be represented as an anticipation of racism, or Nazism, or a betrayal of socialism. A dominant image of Spencer has seen him painted as the starkly reactionary scourge of the halt and lame – which is by no means a completely inaccurate interpretation, especially of the cantankerous texts he turned out in the 1870s and 1880s. In this Spencer, failure is a sign of weakness and degeneracy. Death, ultimately, is the just reward of those who cannot compete. Pervading all nature is a stern discipline, which is a little cruel that it may be very kind. Herein lies the kernel of truth behind so many first-year sociology textbook descriptions of him as a supposed racist, anti-feminist, and "social Darwinist." (The most flagrant abuse of Spencer is the one that attempts to link him to eugenics.)[36] Yet modern scholarship has revealed a far more complex Spencer, a theorist of *radical organicism* – that is, of the concept of society as a whole as an organism – and disputes the argument that such a philosophy led ineluctably to totalitarianism, scientism, or intolerance. It was by emphasizing Spencer's thorough-going organicism, and opposing the reactionary conclusions that

Spencer himself derived from it, that the left was able to make use of his evolutionary theory – and did so for about four decades, especially in the Americas.

Contrary to many more hostile polemics aimed against them, on this reading these first formation socialists were often ardent, critical, and realistic explorers of capitalist modernity. Some Canadian socialists looked back with fondness on the fishing and farming villages of their youth, and some looked ahead to egalitarian countryside communities: but they and most of their comrades agreed that modernity was here to stay. Capitalism had allowed humankind for the first time to escape from the "dead hand" of history and to reshape its own future. Many were especially inspired by Walt Whitman, John Ruskin, and William Morris – men who combined a romantic critique of the deadening aesthetics and life-denying atmosphere of capitalist life with a democratic vision of living otherwise.[37] Yet these mentors were not construed as intellectuals seeking to return to the past, but rather as thinkers who might sharpen protests against the barrenness of a capitalist civilization and articulate the steps by which that particular society could be transcended. The socialist who bought into the perspective of the *Western Clarion* or *Cotton's Weekly*, the two most famous left publications of pre-war Canada, was expected to engage with the massive experiment in social engineering that capitalism had unleashed, not to search for escapes from it in the pursuit of older or better ways.

Again and again, with hammering insistence, leftists said that beneath the visible social world – family, friends, local communities, national institutions – were the much more powerful and formative hidden forces of the economic base, of class power, of capitalist accumulation, and sheer brutal greed. As Zygmunt Bauman reminds us, the point of these often ruthless exposés of the familiar "solids" was not to liquefy everything, but to clear the site for "*new and improved solids*; to replace the inherited set of deficient and defective solids with another set, which was much improved and preferably perfect, and for that reason no longer alterable."[38] In other words, this socialism was not value-free but value-saturated. The socialist of this period could swing, in the space of a sentence, from the most hard-boiled, deadpan evisceration of some encrusted, "medieval" holdover to the most sentimental, glowing evocation of the human solidarities that would replace it.

In publications such as the *Western Clarion* and *Cotton's Weekly* readers characteristically moved, with dizzying speed, from up-close descriptions of experiences and events to the very "distanced" language of abstractions and grand theories. This cohort of socialists loved to dissect the hypocrisies, shallowness, and misrepresentations of the capitalists and their liberal apologists. Beneath the liberals' pious pronouncements about individualism, their pathetic self-help books, and their pompous self-serving speeches could be found the barely concealed facts of exploitation and repression. In both publications, and across a wide range of other productions, we hear a raucous, liberating, disquieting laughter. Capitalism is depicted as a cunning confidence game. The people deceived by it are often mocked as wet behind the ears innocents and dumb as a doorpost know-nothings.

The first formation socialists proclaimed from the rooftops: everywhere and everything can be understood in terms of a great massive force – evolution. This big new word – revealingly, it had no synonym – would be at once the scientific *explanation* of change, the *process* of change, and the *political practices* predicated on the awareness of this change. Around the term revolved a vast galaxy of organic metaphors, all of which – whether drawn from St. Paul or Marx, the medical dictionary or the tract on sanitary reform, the latest armchair anthropological discussion of life among the "savages" or a balance sheet from U.S. Steel – testified to the same overpoweringly significant new reality of social interconnection. Society is an evolving organism – a functioning system of interdependent parts that resembles (for some, it literally *is*) a living creature, with organs and tissues, membranes and cells. And this organism itself is deeply imbedded in the whole universe, the cosmos, evolving according to laws and patterns discoverable by science.[39] The point of socialism is to understand society's patterns of evolution, to accelerate those that are beneficial and fight those that are not. Socialists stood over the process of social evolution like anxious midwives – one of the most popular of the many embryological and obstetrical metaphors that flourished in the first formation.

Evolution was massive, impersonal, all-embracing, and progressive. A turn of the century socialist did not view "evolution" as a narrow political prescription – such as the avoidance of violence and a focus on parliament – but as a much more all-embracing scientific paradigm, whose political implications were open to debate. All serious socialist thinkers and activists, in Canada and internationally, believed that they had to master the theory that explained it. Evolutionary theory by 1900 had come to be considered as an organic part of the socialist intellectual tradition, a body of literature "about which one should at least be able to speak intelligently."[40] Biological theories were conscripted directly into politics – indeed, many famous international socialists started their journeys on the left with Darwin, well before they studied Marx. Their numbers included Karl Kautsky (1854–1938), often considered the leading Marxist theorist of his time. Then, too, especially in North America, Spencer was seen as a thinker who could put both of these master thinkers together. Socialists could combine Darwin's theory of descent with modification, Marx's analyses of the capitalist system, and Spencer's seemingly powerful theory of social and cosmic evolution.

As historian Stephen Kern remarks, across a very wide swath mid-19th-century thinkers were drawn to "determinism" – the first cited reference in the *Oxford English Dictionary* dates from 1846 – and were confident about the existence of an "undeviating law in the material and moral world." All phenomena could be explained in terms of matter in motion, "governed by law-like mechanical forces in addition to electromagnetic, thermodynamic, and gravitational forces." In the 21st century many of us are acutely aware of what Kern calls the "specificity-uncertainty dialectic" – that is, "the more causes we understand, the more we realize how many causes there are to discover and how little we actually know about the causes we think we know." As scientific specificity – implying precision and validity – expands, so too does uncertainty – implying "multiplicity, complexity, and probability."[41] Yet for that very reason we should hesitate before glibly dismissing or oversimplifying the character and impact of earlier forms of social-scientific thought.

In the years following its publication, the full philosophical and social implications of Darwin's *Origin of Species* (1859) were not immediately obvious, even to Darwin himself. (Notoriously, only one sentence in the entire book refers to humanity.) Darwin, whose theory of evolution was generally paralleled by a host of other researchers – the very word "evolution" was popularized by Spencer, not Darwin – did not settle in his own mind what it was he had discovered. It was by no means as simple as Darwinism = Natural Selection. In many ways Darwin himself was often not much of a Darwinist, if that meant a down the line commitment to natural selection, the theory of which, simply put, is that "since more organisms are born than can survive and reproduce, a struggle for existence ensues, and success in that struggle is a function of the features that the successful organisms possess."[42] In successive editions of *The Origin of Species* Darwin would make room for other mechanisms, and by the end of the 19th century, in the absence of much progress around the question of identifying just *how* evolution happened, Darwin's theory was widely considered to be in trouble (and so it would remain until the rise of a neo-Darwinian synthesis in the second quarter of the 20th century, one that combined Darwin's theory with Gregor Mendel's rediscovered work on genetics).

Similarly, the social and political implications of Darwinism remained highly debatable. Those who used natural selection to justify capitalism, the so-called "social Darwinists," received considerable attention, but equally as visible in the *fin de siècle* were "reform Darwinists" and "socialist Darwinists," who used what they took to be Darwinism to emphasize the connections that bound members of society together. The moment of evolution was not so much a quick, sharp break as a gradually unfolding tectonic shift in human perception, whose social and cultural implications are still intensively debated. It was less a well defined scientific discovery and more a developing, all-inclusive, highly complex change in scientific and historical perspective.

Thus, in our reconnaissance, we cannot realistically upbraid the socialists of this generation for not being good Darwinians, or for making different readings of evolutionary theory than are prevalent in the 21st century. After all, as the Genomics Revolution suggests, many of the social implications of Darwinism are still being worked out in our own day.

At the time all the readers of Darwin's influential work, and especially his working-class and socialist readers, confronted the flexibility of the doctrine of evolution and the ambiguity of many of his explanations.[43] Darwin's approach to evolution did not necessarily see history as a story of progress. Vast eons of evolutionary time might culminate in a dead end. Evolution has no intrinsic purpose: we cannot even be sure if, millennia from now, anyone will remember a species called "humanity." For many, this was a hard pill to swallow.

One of Spencer's contributions was to give ordinary people a sense that they could navigate Darwinism without despair. Spencer's key theme – the inevitable organic adaptation, through processes of functional and structural differentiation and integration, of society to its environment – seemed to provide an explanatory framework for a vast range of phenomena. Spencer's "law of differentiation" enraptured many leftists. It hypothesized that, like the cosmos itself, society passes from the homogeneous to the heterogeneous, from the simple to the complex, from the local and atomistic to the global and interconnected. All of these developments made many people think of how human beings evolved from simple cells to an intricately interwoven system of organs. Evolutionary theory provided a way of connecting the sights and sounds of modernity with a sense of its underlying logic in discoverable and contestable patterns of development.

There is just no escaping that without Spencer and the theory of social evolution – subsequently filtered through Marx and a host of other writers – the first formation would have been very different. Almost all of those who committed their radical ideas to paper had something to say about these concepts. They would reach for the four great truths of social-evolutionary theory – that both organic and social bodies grow naturally in mass, become increasingly complex, attain an ever greater mutual interdependence of parts, and live beyond the lifetime of any one individual unit.[44] They might fight with or against these ideas, argue about their deterministic implications, or wrestle with their bearing on religion and morality; but they could not ignore them. Whenever we hear the socialists of the day using words like "cells," "organic," "development," "structure," and "function," we can be reasonably confident that they have been reading Spencer or, perhaps as likely, the works of one of his numerous acolytes.[45] Indeed, it was about as easy to evade Spencer if you were a turn of the century socialist as it is today to evade Michel Foucault if you are a student of social theory.

Even those who might otherwise have avoided the Spencerian net often ended up echoing the great guru. Many Protestants turning to the left in this period, for example, were reluctant to fully endorse Spencer because of his widely known agnosticism. Rev. J.S. Woodsworth was impolite enough to call Spencer's *Synthetic Philosophy* "Conglomerate Rubbish."[46] Yet even such thinkers would turn to evolutionary thinkers in theology, like Rev. Henry Drummond, whose explicit mission in life was to work out for theology the same ideas that Spencer had established in "sociology" – a term that Spencer himself naturalized in the English-speaking world.[47]

Social Statics (1849), Spencer's first book, was ardently admired by North American leftists. It reveals the certainty of a young man whose truths are self-evident and unalterable. In a beautiful passage Spencer imagined the sadness of a true scientist viewing the clumsy mechanisms and antics of political schemers: "After patient study, this chaos of phenomena into the midst of which he was born has begun to generalize itself to him; and where there seemed nothing but confusion, he can now discern the dim outlines of a gigantic plan. No accidents, no chance; but everywhere order and completeness. One by one exceptions vanish, and all becomes systematic." Underlying the evident transformations in human society was a natural law, argued Spencer, that was setting them in motion. These modifications must end – in "completeness," the entirely harmonious adaptation of all living beings to the social state.[48]

From his initial 1860 essay on "The Social Organism" to his multi-volume *Synthetic Philosophy*, Spencer consistently argued not only that society was *like* an organism, but also that in many respects it actually *was* an organism – with human beings, society, and the universe as a whole governed by the same evolutionary laws. The "life of a society is independent of, and far more prolonged than, the lives of any of its component units; who are severally born, grow, work, reproduce, and die, while the body-politic composed of them survives generation after generation, increasing in mass, in completeness of structure, and in functional activity."[49] As one interpreter audaciously put it, "Society is the fourth power of the cell," composed of "individual animals ... living in organic relations."[50] The enthusiasts of "Spenceria" happily and quickly moved from a discussion of the circulatory systems of fish to the transportation system of a modern society.

Spencer also contributed important work on religion, feminism, and pacifism. *First Principles* (1864), the first volume of *Synthetic Philosophy*, was one of the most treasured books of the freethinkers; feminists frequently consulted the highly egalitarian passages of *Social Statics*; and anti-militarists drew repeatedly on Spencer to show that war was a counter-evolutionary reversion to the vanishing age of warlike "militant societies." Working-class and left intellectuals found in Spencer answers to big questions that they could not find in their churches or in the available texts of Marx or Darwin.

Although it may be difficult today to imagine exhausted coal miners, bruised lumberjacks, and bone-weary working-class mothers curling up with Spencer's *Synthetic Philosophy* (or the almost innumerable works inspired by it) after a hard day's work, a surprising number did. In turn of the century Canada, you could pack a large lecture hall for abstract debates about Marx's economic ideas and the latest struggle between "religion" and "science." So many merchant seamen seem have come down with "Spencerism" that it could have been listed as one of the occupational hazards of a seafaring life. Certainly the labour organizer Peter Wright, who later toured Canada as the working man's anti-Bolshevik, numbered Spencer, Darwin, and biologist T.H. Huxley among the pantheon of authors he had studied at sea. "The fo'csle," he remembered, "was a fine spot for books." The left-wing libraries that once dotted the country reserved space for heavy theoretical books alongside the popular novels. Local socialists invested their own meagre funds and many hours in reprinting and in some cases translating social-evolutionary classics. The past really is a foreign country, and even labour historians sometimes have had difficulty in accepting that there was once a time in which hundreds of workers would gather for debates about how best to understand wages, prices, and profits, or that many of them would pour their hard-earned dollars into the newest publications from the remarkable Charles H. Kerr publishing house, the Chicago-based firm that from the 1890s on provided an entire generation of anglophone leftists with a remarkably diverse diet of international left theoretical literature.[51]

When he died in 1903 – and although his star had been fading in Britain since the early 1880s – Spencer was celebrated from coast to coast in Canada. For his eulogist in the Montreal *Star*, Spencer's *The Data of Ethics* was a book that would "delight and enchant the reader." Spencer had "unified our knowledge of everything into a system."[52] Victorian and Edwardian Canadians could identify with the austere majesty of Spencer's quest for truth. Many admiring accounts might begin with the miserable sales figures for *Social Statics* – it took 14 years to sell just 750 copies – and end with the triumph of Spencer's scientific method of studying human life, which had won support among "young students of philosophy" and "the working-men, who gave up their evenings to the study of technical or social sciences," and even among fellow scientists. He was admired by John Stuart Mill and a galaxy of other Victorian notables. Darwin, who disliked him but held a grudging respect, referred to him as "our great philosopher." Alfred Russel Wallace, the co-discoverer of natural selection, went so far as to name his son Herbert Spencer Wallace. (Even Karl Marx sent him, for unclear reasons, a complimentary copy of *Capital*.) Spencer, an overwhelming and indefatigable writer, seemingly covered every topic under the sun, "and under every head," enthused the eulogist in the ardently liberal *Manitoba Free Press*. "He surprises you with the multiplicity of effects which he clearly proved to be the necessary requisite of these facts on conditions considered as antecedents." Beatrice Webb, a towering figure on the British left, on reading *Social Statics* and *First Principles* at the age of 18, cried out: "Who could wish for a grander faith than this." Even Sam Gompers of the American Federation of Labor (AFL) was a fervent admirer.[53]

Spencer also had a massive and long-lasting impact on the North American left. Spencerian language permeated the U.S.-based Socialist Labor Party (SLP), which was the first organized socialist party organization in the Canadian cities of Halifax and London. The concept of the society as a social organism was one that would structure much of the outlook and the politics of the Canadian left for six decades of the 20th century, at least down to the end of the Co-operative Commonwealth Federation in 1961 (that party's very name, as we shall see, was Spencerian). As for the Socialist Party of Canada (SPC), soon to emerge in 1905 as an important focus of political and cultural energy, by 1914 its recommended reading list, as Peter Campbell observes, contained as many books by Spencer as by Marx.[54] Very few notable radicals in this period expressed a disinterest in evolutionary philosophy. Most everybody else on the turn of the century left, religious and secular, revolutionary and reformist, feminist and non-feminist, was working within a powerful and pervasive framework that combined Marx and Spencer. They would fit additional authorities into this framework, and after about 1910 there was a gradual dropping off in citations to Spencer.

Yet Spencer was superceded in large part by two equally "cosmic" evolutionary thinkers, Joseph Dietzgen (1828–1888) and Ernst Haeckel (1834–1919). Both of them were apostles of monism, a philosophical position sometimes associated with the 17th-century Dutch-Jewish thinker Baruch Spinoza. As researcher Nolan Heie describes it, this position proposed that "the theistic world view – one based on dualistic distinctions such as those between matter and spirit, organic and inorganic, living and dead, God and Universe – be replaced with one that would overcome these antinomies by regarding all phenomena as manifestations of a single, underlying substance."[55] Haeckel's *The Riddle of the Universe*, first published in German in 1899, had sold 310,000 copies by 1914, 250,000 of them in English translation; differing with Dietzgen in his politics, he shared with him the conviction that dualistic concepts of God and humanity were no longer tenable "in light of educated modern humanity's awareness of the immense span of geological time, the infinite duration and extent of the universe as a whole, and the suffering that humans and other organisms inflict on one another." He set in their place a holistic concept of a beneficent cosmos, guided by evolution, an "unguided process that results in overall improvement."[56] When Haeckel died in 1919, *Red Flag*, the organ of the Socialist Party of Canada, interrupting its rather busy schedule in following the revolution seemingly sweeping the world, gave up most of its entire front page to an obituary. Acknowledging the German scientist's anti-socialist politics and his support of the recent war, *Red Flag* still proclaimed Haeckel's world-historic significance to the cause of proletarian enlightenment: "His tremendous labors in his special fields of zoology and embryology will command the attention of mankind, long as the written word remains a factor in human affairs."[57]

In some treatments, the "Darwinian Revolution" was a short, sharp, mid-19th-century crisis, swiftly contained by pre-existing structures of thought, or conversely rapidly overturning them. In Gramscian language, the "moment of evolution" was not so much a sudden "war of manoeuvre," pitting scientists against clerics – although there were many such pitched battles, in Canada and elsewhere, from intensive debates over geology in the 1880s to a vitriolic debate over school textbooks in Nova Scotia in the 1930s – as it was a "war of position," in which debates unfolded over decades. Rather than confronting a fixed and firm body of certainties, contemporaries faced the daunting, deeply modern dilemma of wrestling with probabilities and uncertainties.

Darwin himself was at times an inconsistent "Darwinist," combining his most original discovery of natural selection with a variety of other explanations for evolutionary patterns, from "sexual selection" to the inheritance of acquired characteristics (a theory associated with the French scientist Jean Baptiste Lamarck). He was acutely aware that he had not identified the mechanisms of evolutionary change and was not always clear in his own mind about the implications of his discovery for the classical liberal principles he also upheld.[58] By the end of the 19th century many critics thought that Darwinism's day had passed, especially given new work in heredity that was thought to call into question his basic findings. Only in the second quarter of the 20th century, with the advent of the "neo-Darwinian" synthesis combining the genetics inspired by Gregor Mendel's mid-19th-century experiments and natural selection, did the Darwinian paradigm rise to unrivalled dominance in natural science, though the debates are, even today, far from over.

Gems of Socialism

In the first formation, another word rivalled "evolution" as a master concept: "socialism." It was a radiant word. In 1903 poet Bliss Carman remarked that "socialism" was a term that was both safe and perplexing, with a meaning "so vague and undetermined" that even conservatives could "take it upon their lips without trepidation." Socialism, he reported, was prolific: "The divers kinds of Socialism are as mushrooms in the morning; they spring up fresh every day, until it seems that every man may be his own prophet in matters pertaining to the commonwealth." They were all so many "formulae for the solution of a difficult problem in the science of life."[59] *Gems of Socialism* (1916), a pamphlet from Lindsay, Ont., socialists, compiled scores of aphorisms, axioms, prophecies – and definitions: "Socialism means plenty for all. . . . Socialism is not a dream, and it is not based on any sentiment. It is but an economic expression of the ages. . . . Socialism is common sense, it is the best of everything for everybody, here, now and forever. . . . Socialism is administration of things in the interests of people. Capitalism is administration of people in the interests of property laws and in the interest of property owners."[60]

New political parties, visiting speakers, editorialists in both the mainstream and alternative press, party manifestos – all of them seemed to be "talking socialism."[61] On behalf of "socialism" new songs were sung, poems were published, people marched behind red flags in parades through the hostile streets, and letters and editorials in the newspapers punched and counterpunched their imagined opponents. People organized study groups and enlisted children in special socialist schools. To an extent that we would find unbelievable today, daily newspapers ran thousands of articles on socialism, many of them theoretically sophisticated; and an editor who raised issues of socialism could, it seems, expect to be deluged with letters smugly telling him that he had not grasped the idea and offering to enlighten him. Yet each of these writers would in turn have "a conception of Socialism at variance with every other writer's conception."[62] As one New Brunswick stalwart of the struggle wrote in the Saint John *Globe*: "Now, what it this socialism? What is this movement that has shown so unprecedented [a] growth? I have been asked this question hundreds of times during the last six months in St. John."[63]

O.D. Skelton (1878–1941), later to become a major architect of the Dominion's foreign policy, brought out the first major Canadian book on socialism in 1911 – and it was perhaps a sign of the peculiarities of the country's left history that this book was published in the United States and, as one part of its more all-embracing critique, was pleased to note the unlikelihood of the political tendency ever being a serious force in Canada. In Skelton's liberal mind, "socialism" denoted an evolving set of concepts: a "living movement, changing insensibly with every change in the mental horizon or material conditions of the time." This made the movement impossible to "label with the cheerful finality with which the scientist treats a paleolithic fossil." Still, even given its changing character, "socialism" did have discernible features that could be agreed upon by most people using the word. It combined four elements: an indictment of any and all industrial systems based on private property and competition; an analysis of capitalism; a substitute for capitalism; and a campaign against capitalism. "In each of these aspects – indictment, analysis, panacea, campaign," Skelton wrote, "socialism is intelligible only as the antithesis of the competitive system. It has followed private property like its shadow."[64]

Socialists, then, were those who *indicted* capitalism as an obstacle to social evolution; they *analyzed* it according to concepts derived from a variety of sources. They sought to substitute for capitalism a "co-operative commonwealth," a social and political system designed to function efficiently and harmoniously as an organically unified body. They campaigned to make this future a reality, principally through newspapers, reading circles, and small groups and parties, many of them organized to educate the industrial working class, which was seen as the primary force of "progressive" (that is, evolutionarily advantageous) social changes. Like all ideologies, this socialism drew in both people who made it a huge part of their lives, and others who merely dabbled in it.

Vigorous and sometimes violent debates occurred over the *how* of socialism, but there was broad and deep agreement about the *why*. The socialism at the core of the first formation was the application to social and political life of the laws of social evolution. Virtually all socialists saw themselves as the guardians of scientific evolutionary theory and the partisans of a democratic future built according to its laws. Socialism, explained one authoritative voice of the movement, "is the name given a scientific force in human events which may be retarded, but cannot be stopped by individuals. Disagreements may arise between Socialists on matters of tactics, method and whatnot; but as to fundamentals there can be no wide divergence of opinion." Socialism, said another, was both the inevitable product of "inexorable social forces," as "inevitable as death," and the science by which those forces could be understood and mastered.[65]

"Socialism I regard rather as a theory of life than a set of special economic doctrines," added G.G. Pursey of Toronto. "When we have obtained a unified view of life, the facts of history and experience cluster around that view which serves as a nucleus."[66] Today we might imagine that "intellectuals" and "activists" inhabit different worlds and talk different languages, but in this earlier time such identities were far more porous. For, if socialism was *the science of social evolution*, a socialist was one who, having mastered something of that science, that "theory of life," sought to put its precepts into action.

This "unified view of life" included a reverence for the Enlightenment, whose achievements in the 17th and 18th centuries on behalf of science, reason, and rationality were kept fresh in the left's historical memory. In Skelton's terms, socialists *indicted* existing society for its irrational interference with the progress of human understanding. They cast themselves in the role of latter-day Galileos and Newtons, leading their societies to states of rational progress after a long "Dark Age" of tradition, superstition, tyranny – and capitalism.

For, although it had once been progressive in having stimulated science and undermined religious and monarchical authority, capitalism had now become an obstacle to human advancement. The leftists' analysis of human society required the creation of a counter-system of concepts based on a scientific analysis, and more particularly a mastery of the social-scientific approach upheld by a galaxy of great thinkers. Spencer, Darwin, Marx, and U.S. anthropologist Lewis Henry Morgan (1818–81), among others, were all seen as figures in the new *people's enlightenment*, which would wrest from the decaying capitalist and liberal order the principles of science and reason that it could no longer embody.

To *substitute* socialism for capitalism and liberal order required the creation of a mass democracy, which was the only way in which the majority of people could be enlightened as to their true interests. Although very few, if any, Canadian socialists of this period were insurrectionary, that is, engaged in the actual planning and implementation of a violent overthrow of the state,[67] neither were many of them strictly parliamentary, that is, inclined to imagine that electing the right party to parliament would realize the program of the people's enlightenment. Instead, they believed that, whether through industrial or political action, deep-seated forces of social evolution would allow a scientifically educated working class to bring about a vast and rational transformation in social and political life. In that sense, evolution was not the antithesis but the precondition of revolution.

Finally, to *campaign* for socialism meant bringing together everything that would make the *possibility* of a more enlightened and equitable society a thing, not of some distant world, but of this one. On this reading, "socialism" was indeed an intricate and interpretable doctrine, but it was also a deeply coherent and cogent one. It supplied not only the dream of a better egalitarian world but a scientific language through which that world could in time be made a reality.

Karl Marx and the Triune Formula

The "Marx" gradually constructed within this evolutionary problematic was a social scientist – along with Friedrich Engels and Spencer, the most important in the history of the world – who had worked out the human implications of the theory of evolution.[68]

For first formation socialists, Marx contributed three great theories to the understanding of the past, present, and future of humanity: a scientific view of history that explained the necessary stages through which humanity had passed; a framework of economic reasoning that unlocked the secrets of capitalist profit-making; and a science of society that explained the existence of irreconcilable classes based upon relationship to the means of production, distribution, and exchange. All three breakthroughs were fully compatible with the theories of social evolution identified by other writers. Building upon the distillation of Florence Custance, a towering Canadian figure in the second formation but also a force in the first, we can refer to these core Marxist ideas – historical materialism, economic determinism and the theory of surplus value, and the class struggle – as the "triune formula."[69]

Socialists saw Marx's approach to history – historical materialism – as a view showing that – to quote Engels's *Anti-Dühring*, which in abridged form became a foundational text for socialists in this period – "the economic structure of society always furnishes the real basis, starting from which we can alone work out the ultimate explanation of the whole superstructure of juridical and political institutions as well as of the religious, philosophical, and other ideas of a given historical period."[70] Most North American leftists would have encountered Engels via a more accessible 1892 translation and abridgement of his 1878 polemic, *Socialism: Utopian and Scientific*. In that work he used "historical materialism" to "designate that view of the course of history, which seeks the ultimate cause and the great moving power of all historic events in the economic development of society, in the changes in the modes of production and exchange, in the consequent division of society into distinct classes, and in the struggles of these classes against one another."[71] Marx and Engels inherited older patterns of Enlightenment thought about "modes of subsistence" forming parts of a single sequence. First formationists tended to be sceptical of any notion of a society "skipping" stages – moving directly, say, from feudalism to socialism – a tendency reflecting the continuing impact of the concept of social evolution as drawn from Darwin and Spencer.

Spencer's viewpoint – that humans advanced in history "through a predetermined sequence of stages," in a purposeful process bound to culminate in a new kind of society – chimed with many mid-Victorian scientific arguments. Auguste Comte, Georg Wilhelm Friedrich Hegel, Darwin, Mill, and many others could be listed as supporters of the view that, in Kern's words, "philosophies, nations, social systems, or living forms become what they are as a result of progressive transformations in time, that any present form contains vestiges of all that has gone before."[72] Of particular significance for the history of socialism were those models derived from embryology, which emphasized "progressive development through increasing complexity." Such developmental schemes also fit well with Spencer's overall philosophy of evolution – a word, after all, derived from the Latin *evolutio*, meaning "the unrolling of a pre-determined plan."[73]

Both Darwin and Marx would have delivered more qualified answers. Although both could be and were cited to provide such a determinist and "sequentialist" interpretation, it was actually a reading open to contestation. It overlooked, in Darwin, his emphasis on the "non-directional logic" at work in nature – the millions of years of evolutionary change that might culminate in a dead end, for instance. It forgot many contrary indications in Marx, emphasizing multiple paths to modernity and the significance of path-changing events in the lives of societies.[74]

The research program into patterns of human history launched by Marx in the middle of the 19th century proved remarkably fertile, even without leading to a version of human history about which all Marxists now agree. It was more a revolutionary method than an orthodox doctrine. Sometimes Marx emphasized the forces of production, the factories and technologies; more often he emphasized the social relations of production, all the institutions, laws, human relationships, and bodies of knowledge necessary for the forces of production to function or even to exist. In both cases, for the first formation, the stress was placed on explaining history in terms of how societies were organized to meet their material preconditions. It was by looking at how people made their living and in what contexts that one could learn most about what they were thinking and how they were likely to be governed.

Marx's second great discovery, economic determinism, gave socialists a way of saying that their political project was not just a critique of capitalism, a campaign against it, or a vision of its replacement – but, more powerfully, an actually existing tendency, an observable force in the world. Socialism was "an economic 'is' rather than a moral 'ought,'" argued Paul Lafargue (1842–1911), Marx's son-in-law, a heavyweight theorist in France's Parti ouvrier and a widely esteemed figure on the North American left. Lafargue saw socialists as "simply spokesmen" who were "translating the language of economic facts into human language." It was in the economy, and "there alone," that one could locate "the irresistible force of our revolutionary theory." In an even more determinist metaphor, Lafargue described socialists as "mere thermometers" indicating the boiling point of the masses "under the pressure of the economic phenomena which victimise them."[75]

By taking up the labour theory of value earlier worked out by Adam Smith and later developed by David Ricardo, Marx unlocked the secret of capitalist profit-making. He proved conclusively that the value of commodities was determined by the amount of socially necessary labour-time involved in their production. As members of the Social Democratic Party of Canada (SDPC) learned from the definitions printed on their party cards at the time of the First World War, these definitions were crystal clear. "Value and Surplus," ran the headline. "Value: Is the social labor embodied in a commodity, the amount of which is measured by the average social time required to produce the commodity under average conditions and with average ability on the part of the laborer." Then: "Surplus Value: Is a value created by the laborer over and above what he receives in wages. That part the capitalist takes which he does not pay for." Many academic Marxists today, and virtually all self-taught

Marxists then, would regard it as self-evident that a socialist formation must place at its heart Marx's analysis of value.[76]

Among the first formation socialists of 1890–1920 Marx's economics provided an important warrant of scientific authority for ways of conceptualizing "the social" through which workers could be represented as not just fighting for their own interests, but also engaging with the core economic processes reshaping all of society. British North Americans and Canadians had experienced fairly large coal-mining strikes since the 1840s. Now, within the political language game of the first formation, such events were seen as the risings of "wage slaves" against a capitalist class that robbed and exploited all other workers. They were not local labour wars, but manifestations of the general struggle of the working class to reclaim the full value of the commodity it produced. True socialists inscribed on their banners: "Every one to receive the full value of his or her labor."[77]

Sometimes these early Marxists, diverging considerably from the position of Marx himself, promised that under socialism all workers would receive "the undiminished proceeds (or full product)" of their labour. Whatever the slogan's orthodoxy, there can be no doubting its deep roots and wide popularity. It chimed with older notions of the "producer ideology," which held that the *really* productive members of society were the manual workers, small manufacturers, and farmers – the men who worked with their hands – and not the lawyers, tavern-keepers, and property speculators who lived off their hard work.[78] The labour theory of value was a more sophisticated way of saying what was obviously true – that at bottom, without the workers and their often dangerous and ill-paid labour, there could be no professors, priests, politicians – or profits. When you put value theory in down-to-earth terms, it made (and still makes) abundant sense. If capitalists really paid the workers as much or more than their products were worth, they would readily go out of business. Even when you cast your ballot, said the first formationists, you were in essence voting for – or against – the proposition that "commodities sell or exchange on the average, for what it costs in necessary social labor time to produce them." Only socialism would take "man out of the category of commodities," advised the *Western Clarion*.[79] For many in the first formation, and especially among the *Clarion*ites, socialism essentially *was* a politics founded on the labour theory of value.

Yet just as clear as the theory seemed in such down-to-earth applications, its implications were intensely debated. This was especially so after the release of the first major critiques of Marx's economics, which fastened on the discrepancy between volumes 1 and 3 of *Capital*. As Skelton pointed out, with a certain undisguised satisfaction, the first volume held out the possibility of a conformity of prices to values, at least ultimately; the third volume that they were normally at variance.[80] First formationists could easily brush aside a critique from a liberal like Skelton, but not one coming from Ernest Untermann – the very man whose Charles H. Kerr text had introduced scores of Canadians to the "socialist mode of economic reasoning." When Untermann seemed to qualify his belief in the labour theory of value as a touchstone of revolutionary politics, partisans of the Socialist Party of Canada were quick to denounce this erstwhile pioneer of Marxian economics in North America as "confused," engaged in "vulgarizing the theory of Karl Marx," and a person whose "conception of both price and value is a hazy one." That Untermann, previously considered an expert and someone who had spent years studying and expounding Marxian economics, could be so mistaken, gave pause. As Peter Campbell has shown, early Marxists strongly resisted any tampering with the labour theory of value, as they understood it, because doing so would remove a vital element of their entire project.[81] Their fierce opposition to what they might dismiss as the new "jazz economics" was not misplaced, for the neoclassical economists' reduction of value to price, and their derivation of prices from an equilibrium between abstract "supply" and "effective demand," often meant that the propertied and the wealthy were represented as the "fountainhead of wealth." In this new economics, in historian Robert Stuart's words, "Labour (read 'workers') became a 'cost of production', rather than the source of value identified by the classical economists from Mandeville to Marx."[82]

Early Marxist thought in Canada and elsewhere had a marked tendency to stress industrial production at the expense of every other aspect of the capitalist economy. The Marxists did pay some attention to exchange relations and the financial system, but their discussions tended to return, again and again, to the relations of production. They were *Capital*, volume 1, Marxists, perhaps for the very good reason that volumes 2 and 3 were not accessible to most of them.

Contrary to present-day assumptions about what by definition must constitute the left, first formationists were by no means universally, or even generally, in favour of the extension of the existing state. Many first formation socialists, on the contrary, saw the state as intrinsically the enemy of all producers. "When slavery came into being in the dawn of history, there also came into being as a direct result of it, the germ of law and government – the modern state in embryo," Roscoe Fillmore explained in 1915. Even in a day in which most workers enjoyed the right to vote, the state was their enemy: "All the forces of the existing state and of society were and are to this day enlisted in the effort to confuse the slaves and therefore preclude the possibility of . . . revolt." It followed that those who argued for the public ownership of the post office or railways were profoundly mistaken. The notion of "winning socialism" through the "peanut politics" of forming a government was, on this reading, a shallow delusion. It stemmed from conscious efforts to confuse and distract the proletariat from its chief historical goal – the abolition of wage labour.[83] Since the a priori conviction of many early socialists was that all competition led remorselessly to monopoly, they were inclined to think that the state itself, as the executive committee of the ruling class, was in the pocket of the monopolists.

The Marxists' hope that the trusts would serve as the catalysts of the revolution suggested the extent to which they internalized organic notions of the political and social order. Trusts were like very large organisms, digesting the smaller fry in their midst; when their evolutionary time had lapsed, they would be easily taken over by the enlightened people. Many first formation socialists – including Gaylord Wilshire, for a time a luminary of the Canadian Socialist League (CSL) – tended to focus resolutely on the trusts as harbingers of a new social order. As Wilshire and others argued, when large monopoly corporations negotiated with and provided social welfare for workers, they were showing signs of evolutionary insight (without necessarily staving off the day of their inevitable extinction). The corporations were fleeting phenomena within a much longer-term evolutionary pattern. When they showed signs of having understood their organic connection to society, for example, by indicating that they knew workers collectively had rights and needs, they were furthering the work of evolution; but this had no real bearing on their long-term chances of surviving, which were nil. Conceivably the lessons they learned in providing social services might be of use to the new post-capitalist humanity that was inevitably, as a matter of natural and social law, going to replace them. As many socialists would say, and keep on saying down to the 1940s, after the revolution they would find that much of the work of rationalizing and planning a new order had already been carried out because corporations had centralized and consolidated the economy. The formation of the corporation, its provision of welfare services for workers, and the growing "consolidation" and "centralization" of capital all anticipated the ultimate and inevitable withering away of capitalism itself.

As Stuart observes, the "revelation of the monstrous anatomy of capitalism, when wielded with force, has repeatedly ruptured the libertarian and egalitarian camouflage which otherwise conceals the system's predatory nature from its proletarian victims," thereby puncturing "the liberal illusion of equal exchange between the propertied and the propertyless." But, he notes, the same analytical rigour did not generally accompany Marxist analyses of the working class.[84] First formationists remained very much influenced by the Spencerian concept of the social organism, according to which the working class was a living entity as much destined to achieve its mature life-mission as a young child was destined to become an adult.

Could Marxian economics sustain the weight that the first formation asked it to bear? It was striking how sketchily the labour theory of value, for instance, was actually presented – often serving more as the distant anchor of a rhetorical argument than a thesis to be tested against current economic data.[85] Many took the political upshot of the theory to be that labourers should receive the full product of their toil. Yet, said one commentator – reading the fine print with that intensity that gave socialists a name for being rather ponderous souls – the position of the Socialist Party of Canada actually was that "labour produces all wealth and to the producers it should belong" – not quite the same thing. This writer, C.W. Springford, was trying to defend orthodoxy from an obvious objection: if the labourers received all they produced, "what was going to keep up the afflicted, the old and the orphan?" If one answered, "general taxation," this too conflicted with one reading of orthodox Marxism. "If there is any one who objects to taxation it is a Socialist," wrote Springford in 1910. "Taxation suggests a ruling power which has a whip to enforce payment – the very thing we are trying to overthrow, viz., our masters. I believe the explanation of our platform is, that under a co-operative system all would be in the producing class and as such would have a right to share in the wealth owned by the commonwealth; those who are unable to produce through sickness, etc., would be provided for."[86]

Such debates even reached into the daily press (at least if the Maritime papers, which may have been surprisingly fascinated with socialism, are any indication). "Can any honest, reasonable person," asked L.M. Brown in a letter to the Halifax *Herald*, "dispute that capital is the result of productive labor?"[87] Nova Scotia's P.F. Lawson, who was later to emerge as a major theorist and activist in postwar industrial unionism in Western Canada, also entered the lists on behalf of the labour theory of value in a letter to the *Herald*. He pondered the gold fountain pen that he was using to write his letter to the editor: it incorporated the labour of some miner; those who tended the machines that stamped the pen; those who made those machines; the cooks who prepared their sustenance: "all round the production is clustered a tremendous subdivision of labour." In the simple pen one found the historical outcome of dangerous ocean voyages, work in tropical forests, the labour of those who had perfected the mechanisms that polished metal – the list was almost too long to imagine. "It is safe to say that ten thousand times ten thousand human beings played a part in the production of my highly-prized pen."[88]

Partisans of conventional liberal laissez-faire economics faced a host of critics – economists steeped in the historical method, marginalists who wanted to transcend the value debate altogether, and Marxists who wanted to translate economic theory into language suitable for the revolutionary transformation of society. "That labor is the source of exchange value is known to everybody except the dodgasted idiots who perform the labor," said the *Western Clarion* in its vintage hard-boiled language. Those workers who did not understand that they were literally being robbed by capitalism were the "damphool workers" – these damn-fool workers – who hugged "chains of wage-slavery" and denounced "those who wish to enlighten them to freedom." Or, as the Lindsay Socialists explained, with their customary pithiness, "Every dollar made in profits adds to the world's poverty and misery."[89]

Workers who could not see such an obvious truth were being taken in by a "clumsy hoax," and – at least in *Western Clarion* discourse – were "victims without brains." Others more colourfully transposed the labour theory of value into monstrous images. Capitalists were transformed into carrion-eating animals. One description freely mixed Christian and naturalistic metaphors in describing the workers "crucified" upon "the cross of exploitation and their flesh consumed upon the altar of profit because the stink of it smells good to the capitalists." If Frankenstein's monster haunted the imagination of Mackenzie King in *Industry and Humanity*, socialists for their part often warned workers of vampires abroad, capitalists who formed a "vampire class which sucks their blood."[90]

Explaining the world according to "socialist economics" was, in some Marxist representations of the socialist movement, the top priority of every real leftist. On the subject of "exploitation," the *Western Clarion* remarked, "This word should be writ large and pasted in every Socialist's hat. Every time he is in doubt as to what stand he should take on any question he should look in his hat." If the issue being discussed had nothing to do with the exploitation of labour at the point of production, "chances are ten to one it has nothing to do with the Socialist." For the worker the beginning of wisdom was to know that he was being exploited. Once he had grasped that, he had found the clue to the maze. If he followed that clue, he would soon find out by whom he was exploited, how he was exploited, why he was exploited, and how to stop it.[91] For Fillmore, writing in 1915, it was obvious that the movement had lost its way when its advocates no longer knew their economics:

> True, there is an alleged party collecting dues and sending out 'organizers,' many of whom are absolutely guiltless of any knowledge of Socialism and are put on the platform merely because they have big reputations and can "lead" the slaves. How many of them elucidate clearly the Marxian law of value and thus show the worker just where the robbery takes place? How many have digested "Value, Price and Profit" or "Socialism, Utopia to Science"? How many of them could take the platform against a good capitalist economist and hold their own? A very small percentage, if we are to judge by the slush that is their stock in trade. If it's sentiment that we want the workers to learn, then these fellows have the goods, but sound economics – never.[92]

Young spc members keen to win their spurs in the movement were well advised to master the economics of Marx. Whether they received good or bad reviews in the *Western Clarion* was largely determined by their grasp of the labour theory of value. Comrade Porritt of Toronto wowed the *Clarion*'s reviewer with his début as a speaker, with an address on "The Different Modes of Exchange." It showed, his critic remarked in his "two thumbs up" review, that Porritt was "not going to be, but is, one of the best-posted comrades we have around Toronto."[93] Comrade Pearson was no less stellar in his conscientious approach to the science of socialism. Having heard in a lecture an argument that he did not quite understand, he went home and studied it. After two sleepless nights, he had thus been able to "qualify himself for argument. It is this attitude, together with a mathematical mind, that has made Pearson the star economist of the speakers' class, and that is no little thing."[94] Another man, poor Comrade Young of Nanaimo, B.C., provided a sorry illustration of exactly the opposite habits. Before he opened his mouth one more time, he needed to read up in socialist economics, J.Y. wrote in the *Clarion* in 1908. "Comrade Young is very enthusiastic, very rash in his ut-terances and not too well informed in economics." And so he ran up against "the rock of accepted Socialist principles as defined by better informed or more dogmatic comrades" of the "Old Guard." They had given him a "drastic application" of the " 'big stick' of economic truth."[95]

And beware if you incautiously put forward a position that inadvertently went against the letter, if not the spirit, of Marx. The controversy aroused by Frederick J. Urry, a Port Arthur, Ont., architect who became closely identified with the "gradualist" position within the SPC, was fought out in part over Urry's understanding of socialist economics. Urry had advanced what may have seemed (to non-Marxian outsiders) the relatively benign argument that the Socialist Party stood for "a fair day's pay for a fair day's work." Nonsense, cried the *Clarion*: this was "exactly what the Socialist Party stands, not for, but against." Urry's proposal meant that socialists would be bound forever by the market price for labour-power, the current rate of wages, and "that is just what we DON'T want."[96]

In any given capitalist society, then, one either owned the means of production, distribution, and exchange or was forced (indirectly or directly) into dependence on those who did; and on this basis "classes" – the third great Marxist theme – were fundamental, inherently in conflict, and ulti-mately represented different historical trajectories. If working people man-aged to shorten the working day, for example, capitalists would lose out on some of the surplus value that could be squeezed from labour. Capitalists would inevitably try to use every means at their disposal – the state, religion, ideologies like liberalism, even distracting campaigns for temperance – to dis-organize the working class and preserve their hold on power.

There was nothing indefinite or ambiguous about class. Indeed, a class itself could be considered a kind of social organism – that is, we recall, a body growing in mass, becoming increasingly complex, with ever-more interdependent parts, and outliving any one of its individual units. For these Marxists, and for most of those who would follow them for the next six decades, the innermost secret of monstrous modernity, and the key to its supersession, lay in the working class. As Marx had told the First International in 1871, "The economical subjection of the man of labour to the monopoliser of the means of labour ... lies at the bottom of servitude in all its forms." Hence the emancipation of the "man of labour" from this servitude was "the great end to which every political movement ought to be subordinate as a means."[97]

Yet although "class" was utterly central for first formationists, not many of them confidently developed accounts of how one was to build "consciousness of class" among the workers. The leftists were often content with a priori assumptions about working-class attitudes and interests that were not matched by careful empirical investigation. They dealt, much of the time, with a "philosophical" or an "abstract" proletariat – not the actually living workers. Much of the Marxist commentary was influenced by a kind of "miserablism" and "catastrophism" – that is, an emphasis on the wretchedness of working-class life and the imminent collapse of the economic system. That the workers were steadily becoming more and more pauperized was an article of faith that oversimplified and even contradicted substantial statistical evidence on living standards, and misread Marx. It also stimulated some of the most dismissive things that first formation socialists had to say about working-class struggles. Colossal defeats and enormous suffering, of the sort undergone by Canadian coal miners and other workers in the labour revolt of 1907–13, could be interpreted as *good things* – since, as they became more wretched and miserable, the "damphool workers" would become more sharply opposed to the system. Having had sense knocked into their wooden heads, they would realize that the mere "commodity struggles" of their unions were useless when compared to the socialists' "political struggle" to wrest control of the state. Even if the state dragged the working class into war, this might lead to beneficial results – such as exposing the class dictatorship of the capitalists and leading to new and sharper levels of upheaval. Once workers were educated in economics, sociology, and biology, they would desire to achieve the end of capitalism. That they would have the ability to do so was, according to Stuart, "a *non sequitur* of massive proportions."[98]

At their most controversial, early Canadian socialists sometimes derided as stupid or self-interested those workers who held a "false consciousness" of their class interests. Did one need an explicit and accurate understanding of class to merit being considered "conscious"? What of workers who were well aware that they were in a subordinate position, but deferred to the boss? And how did militant class warriors arise? As Stuart argues, three answers to these questions can be associated with Marx – "first, that class consciousness arose spontaneously from social location, that class warriors sprang fully-armed from the fertile soil of class society," second, that "class warriors graduated after long suffering in the brutal boot-camps of the class war," and, third, "that class consciousness infiltrated its designated class through the agency of autonomous scientific investigation of society," with the Marxists themselves as its most proficient disseminators.[99] This third option was (and remains) attractive among many orthodox Marxists, partly because it vests in them the power to decide who "makes the grade," and partly because it shields them from any reflexive consideration of how well their language of socialism is functioning as an instrument of emancipation. One can always blame the "damphool workers," with their "false consciousness," for the mixed results or failures of any political initiative.

One could also blame *particular* elements of the working class, those which obstructed its road to unity. The "labour aristocracy" was routinely denounced and as rarely analyzed, partly because doing so would have compromised any "absolutist understanding" of the capitalist mode of production. Will Shier, a supposed "moderate" within the SPC, argued that the "proletariat of today" was increasingly led by an "aristocracy of labour," consisting of "brain workers and skilled mechanics," and some of them were now seeking "a field for the play of their superlative abilities in the professions." These jobs in turn were becoming overcrowded, and generating dissatisfaction with the social order. Meanwhile, others, recognizing that they could only better themselves by rising with the working class as a whole, had joined the revolutionary movement.[100]

Shier and others were noticing something that their more fiercely orthodox two-class comrades did not, or would not, see. It may have been an article of faith for many in the first formation that society was simplifying itself into two great classes. To point out the contrary was to incur the charge of theoretical laxity and even apostasy. Yet the worse danger to socialism as a science of social evolution was to ignore actually existing realities. The emergent reality under modernity was an ever-growing tertiary sector, exemplified by a vast new army of white-collar workers – as was suggested by the emergence of unions and associations among them.[101] A glaringly obvious reality in our own time, these massed "middle-class" white-collar employees were already a force at the turn of the 20th century. But first formationists tended to shield themselves from any acknowledgement of the extent and cultural resonance of social mobility and the internal stratification of the working class. The "two-class" model would have extraordinary staying power.

The irony was that many socialists were themselves white-collar participants in the professions and in the service sector. Few of the first formation's prominent thinkers, such as its many articulate newspaper editors, were themselves producing surplus value at the point of production. Many of those who, like eventual Communist Party leader Tim Buck, were found in industrial employment were characteristically in supervisory positions – in Buck's case, as a foreman. The *Western Clarion*, the spc's newspaper published in Vancouver, offers rich examples of this class ambiguity. The same paper that so often, and so confidently, predicted the imminent disappearance of small business was not above accepting advertisements from small businessmen. Victoria socialists in 1906 were lured by *Western Clarion* advertisements for Smith & Champion's furniture, E. Shaper's fall suits, food from the Colonial Bakery, and bicycles, guns, and ammunition from Harris & Moore. Nor did the *Clarion* spurn an advertisement from A.F. Cobb, Merchant Tailor of Okotoks, Alta., and evidently a strong spcer: for every made to measure suit (selling at from $15 to $30) that he sold because of his *Clarion* ad, Cobb promised to donate $2 to the paper. Real estate investors were solicited in another *Clarion* ad to invest in "big lots" in the Vancouver Heights extension, costing upwards of $1,000 each.[102]

The "performances" of socialism in theatres and parks often drew crowds that did not look at all like proletarian revolutionaries. As Joseph Adams said of a socialist event in Vancouver in his 1913 travel account *Ten Thousand Miles Through Canada*, "It was quite evident from a glance at the audience that it was not comprised of those who espouse Socialism as a possible solution of problems of which they are the immediate victims. Many of them were in evening dress, and the occupants of boxes at the sides of the building, which included ladies, looked as if economic laws had not dealt unkindly with them, Socialism or no Socialism."[103]

Socialism was a science to be learned and an art to be performed, as much as it was a definite political program. Yet if socialism was a science, it mattered little in one model of class-consciousness if the "scientists" were themselves workers. It mattered that workers be taught about their history and interests. The working class *had* to become educated. In *The 1913 Vancouver Island Miners Strike*, issued by the B.C. Miners' Liberation League, spc organizer Jack Kavanagh offered a blow by blow account of the Vancouver Island coal wars from September 1912 to December 1913. Kavanagh then offered this implicit critique of top-down education: "The emancipation of the wage-slaves will not fall, like manna, from heaven. Nor yet will they be led into freedom, as into the promised land, by inspired leaders of mankind."[104] This work was highly unusual – it may well have been a historic first in Canada – in focusing socialist attention so closely and consistently on a specific aspect of Canadian working-class history. In general, Canadian socialist discourse followed the international pattern of framing analysis in a telescopic or cosmic way. C. Osborne Ward's writings on class struggles in the ancient world and other works about the history of ancient civilizations were given a limelight denied to mere occurrences in the neighbourhood – even the tumultuous revolts in the Lakehead towns of Fort William and Port Arthur, which were perhaps the most deadly of all the era's many battles for the workers, or the 22-month-long battle of the Nova Scotia coal miners to win recognition of the Socialist-led District 26 of the United Mine Workers (UMW), which received only a few detailed and not especially analytical stories in the socialist press.[105]

In this regard respect and leadership went to the person (with very few exceptions in this age, a man) who had excelled in socialist science. After 1907 some provincial units of the Socialist Party of Canada – for instance, that of Ontario – demanded entrance examinations in socialist economics. Socialist orators were rated in the socialist press according to how well (or often, how badly) they had understood the clear-cut scientific principles outlined in the first nine chapters of Marx, *Capital*, volume 1. "No Compromise, No Political Trading" was emblazoned on the literature of both the SPC and later its rival, the SDPC. *What* was not to be compromised? Briefly: the socialist form of *reasoning otherwise*: historical materialism, the labour theory of value, and class analysis, which only a socialist party could uphold. Whatever distinctively extreme styles some Canadian leftists may have brought to its rendition in the Dominion, this triune formula was found throughout the international left from the 1880s to the late 1910s. From the first formation perspective, for a leftist to compromise on any of these doctrines was akin to a doctor prescribing quack medicines instead of making a serious scientific diagnosis.

First formation promotions of Marx and Engels sometimes suggested the influence of contemporary languages of advertising and exhibitions. "Mr. Wage Slave, you have the brains, develop them, and you can do that by reading Karl Marx and Engels," one pamphlet barked out. "Pin your faith to them, read their works, study them, criticise them, find faults or errors if you can (I know you can't) . . ." Marx and Engels would help the Wage Slave to avoid deception by "an adventurer from the capitalist or the fast-dying middle class." He or she would also come to understand that "you have all the forces of evolution on your side. Socialism must follow capitalism as sure as light follows darkness. Its speedy coming depends on the devotion and the energy of those who have already seen the light."[106]

Socialists had three irrefutable reasons for their confidence, a Saint John leftist proclaimed in 1910 – the understanding of surplus value, the class struggle, and, first and foremost, the theory of evolution. Evolution simply was the "materialistic conception of history," and it taught that "the systems under which men have lived are continually changing, that man is ever rising higher and higher. The law of surplus value and the class struggle prove that the next step will be from capitalism, the system under which we live at present, to socialism." Fillmore, who in 1905 studied Ruskin, Wallace, Mill, and the inevitable Spencer, would have approved. According to "materialistic monism," he later argued, any notion of a separation between economic, political, cultural, and intellectual spheres was an illusion. James Simpson, a prominent Toronto socialist, told members of the Toronto School Board that, according to an overriding "social demand," students should be educated to become "units," so that "social evolution is not impeded."[107]

Just like doctors, socialists equipped with their scientific knowledge could "diagnose the malady of our social ills, expound the course the disease will run and foretell the final outcome of the fitful capitalist fevers from which society suffers," an article in the *Western Clarion* explained. "The body politic suffers ills in the same manner as the individual." Scientific knowledge could help turn aside "those forces which make a fevered and corrupt state of society." For one sympathizer from Springhill, N.S., in 1906, the socialist was the scientist who, by treating a diseased constitution by enabling its "original law" to recover, sought to find ways to "assist Nature." The true socialist had no wish to "recast the natural functions of the body, and no desire to remodel the disorders to which it is subject." The objective was to eradicate the disorders and cure the body. *Cotton's Weekly* agreed: "Man has risen only by searching out nature's laws and obeying them." For UMW activist Dave Rees, "chronic diseases," whether in the human family or in industry, did not call out for "darning and patching," but "drastic remedies." If the "family doctor," that is, Parliament, did not "prescribe intelligently and effectively," then the patient, "Mr. Labor – head and brain" – would "raise itself in its majesty and might do away with its doctor, and apply the remedies and the cure itself."[108]

For such people, scientific theory was simply the most important single weapon in the leftist's arsenal. Those who truly possessed it were qualified to speak on behalf of socialism. Those who did not possess it were quacks, fakirs, poseurs, sentimentalists, and amateurs. For many activists the exposition of Marx's scientific discovery of how surplus value was extracted from labour at the point of production – for this formation, the only rigorous definition of the word "exploitation" – was *the* core socialist position, to be defended in every circumstance. Such people agreed with Marx's argument to the First International that the end of exploitation in *this* sense was the fundamental key to emancipating society from the worst aspects of a monstrous modernity. Once production for profit became production for use, virtually all social evils would disappear. Production for profit accounted for "all of the abnormalities, paradoxes and pestiferous phenomena that beset and afflict human society today," argued William Davenport in his pungent 1912 pamphlet *Why Not Enjoy What You Produce?* Once the "enslavement of labour" was brought to an end, "the vices, crimes, corruption and degradation incidental to slavery must inevitably disappear."[109]

The labour theory of value provided scientific depth to the fundamental tenet that society was divided into two conflicting classes, between which there could be no lasting compromise. The scientific status of the system of concepts developed by the early socialists hinged, in both their eyes and in those of their opponents, on the actual existence of a working and an employing class; in labour and capital; or, in language less frequently used, the proletariat and the bourgeoisie.

For first formation socialists, everything depended on the working class – which, paradoxically, in a sense could be counted on for nothing. It was, on the one hand, the class that held human history in its hands. On the other, it seemed hopelessly confused, duped, even stupid. In many respects, at least down to 1910, many first formationists seemed to be in love not with actual workers, but with the "philosophical proletariat," the "fit protagonist" that would fulfil a "transcendental historical destiny."[110] Moments confirming a socialist analysis of the stark divisions and inhumanity of the system – with the coal miners often providing the best examples – were described in the socialist press, but even here the strategy was often not one of providing exact descriptions of "This is what it is like to be a worker," but "Here is yet one more detail confirming our theory." Socialists often talked as though they were addressing, or speaking on behalf of, a great unified class of workers: yet, as historian Geoff Eley remarks, "The 'unity' of the working class was an idealized projection, an abstraction from the disorderly and unevenly developing histories of industrialization in the 19th century."[111]

An Army of Cosmic Redressers

To become a socialist in this period meant joining a vast international army of intellectuals and activists pushing similar agendas in a shared social-evolutionary discourse. To be a socialist in Canada generally meant an actual or imagined relationship with English-speaking socialists in Britain and the United States. The word "Marxist" itself was still relatively new. Marx himself wasn't sure he was one, and many texts now taken to be canonical were either not available in English or conceptually inaccessible to leftists unfamiliar with their philosophical and economic undergirding. Even the redoubtable British socialist William Morris confessed that he was "blankly ignorant of economics" and had not mastered Marx's *Capital* when he joined the Social Democratic Federation (SDF) in 1883.[112] A host of other leftists mistakenly asserted that Marx was an advocate of the "iron law of wages" – with its central point that workers' attempts to increase wages through organization would result in a general price increase for commodities, thus nullifying any benefits. Such reasoning led some early socialists to deride the economic struggles of trade unions.[113]

Marxist ideas were almost always integrated into a framework drawn from evolutionary theory, which seemingly held insights into everything from plant cells to political institutions. Aside from Marx himself, some of the most important members of this army of redressers – and I am deliberately confining myself to authorities who I know were influential among Canadians – included Laurence Gronlund (1846–99), a Danish emigré to the United States; the German Friedrich Engels (1820–95), best known as Marx's collaborator; Grant Allen (1848–96), Spencer's Canadian disciple; socialist feminists Charlotte Perkins Gilman (1860–1935) of the United States and Olive Schreiner (1855–1920) of England; Peter Kropotkin (1842–1921) of Russia; and the U.S. novelist Jack London (1876–1916), perhaps the most wildly popular and controversial figure of the first formation.[114]

Of all the major socialist Spencerians to influence Canadians, the status of pioneer must probably go to Gronlund, a founding father of North Atlantic socialism. His book *The Co-operative Commonwealth: An Exposition of Socialism* (1884) sold over 100,000 copies in the United States and Britain within a decade of its publication. Cleverly drawing upon the arguments of T.H. Huxley ("Darwin's Bulldog"), Gronlund equated the law of differentiation, thought to govern all organic change, with "mutual aid." He also argued that just as the brain was the organizing headquarters of the human organism, so too could the state be considered the indispensable governing agent of the social organism. For Gronlund, an enlightened social order could not only understand the evolutionary processes shaping it, but also govern those processes so that they worked for the general benefit.[115]

Gronlund took Spencer literally. Spencer's use of the term "organism," Gronlund insisted, was not just a matter of the British philosopher developing an analogy. For Gronlund the state was indeed a "living organism, differing from other organisms in no essential respect." The state, "including, with the people, the land and all that the land produces – literally is an organism, personal and territorial."[116] The "co-operative commonwealth," a term that would resound in the history of the Canadian left until the 1960s – one of the most significant moments in Canadian left history would be the emergence of the Co-operative Commonwealth Federation in 1932–33 – was the name that Gronlund used for Spencer's "Social State," that harmonious integration of heterogeneous units within an organic social whole towards which the processes of social evolution were tending. The duty of the co-operative commonwealth, in historian Mark Pittinger's words, "was not to protect the 'natural right' of individual capitalists to exploit workers for profit, but to protect the welfare of all its constituent parts." Here was a *constructive vision* of socialism that could appeal to a wide variety of leftists.[117]

The first formation was also, in a very real sense, "Engelsian" as much as it was "Marxist." Engels's status as co-author with Marx of *The Communist Manifesto* (1848) would tightly link the two names (although Marx did most of the writing), especially after Marxism became the official doctrine of the Second International. Engels's graveside eulogy to Marx praised his comrade as a man who had extended Darwin's theory to the study of human society.[118] Marx and Engels were neither perfectly in unison on everything, nor implicitly working on entirely different projects. Engels was undoubtedly a far more interested and capable explorer of natural science, and also more inclined than was Marx to a cosmic theory of evolution. That scientific turn became particularly pronounced from 1870 on, when Engels undertook such works as the *Anti-Dühring* (1878), *Dialectics of Nature* (1883, but unpublished until the 1920s), and *The Origin of the Family, Private Property and the State* (1884). Canadian socialists read an abridged version of *Anti-Dühring* in large numbers. "More than any other single publication," historian David Stack remarks, this version, in a pamphlet called *Socialism: Utopian and Scientific*, worked "to encourage socialists to look to Darwinism for the foundation of their politics."[119]

Like Spencer, Engels enjoyed reflecting on the position of humanity within the *cosmos* – the really big picture. Also like Spencer, Engels was immensely impressed by the interconnectedness of this cosmos, the way in which "everything acts upon everything else and vice versa." Humanity is inextricably part of nature – "we by no means rule over nature like a conqueror over a foreign people, like someone standing outside nature – but that we, with flesh, blood and brain, belong to nature, and exist in its midst, and that all our mastery of it consists in the fact that we have the advantage over all other creatures of being able to learn its laws and apply them correctly."[120]

His *Socialism: Utopian and Scientific* became the Bible of the first formation because it seemingly provided a succinct statement of the "materialist conception of history." In "every society that has appeared in history," Engels explains, "the manner in which wealth is distributed and society divided into classes or orders is dependent upon what is produced, how it is produced, and how the products are exchanged" – a process that in the end becomes "the Darwinian struggle of the individual for existence transferred from nature to society with intensified violence."[121]

The contradiction built into the capitalist mode of production was bound to come to an end, "like the movement of the planets, by collision with the centre." Once brought under the control of the producers, the "productive forces themselves" – active social forces that worked "exactly like natural forces" – could be transformed, much as electricity could be harnessed in the telegraph. In transforming "the great majority of the population into proletarians," the capitalist mode of production was creating a power that, "under penalty of its own destruction," was forced to complete the rebellion of the mode of production against the mode of exchange, by seizing political power and turning the means of production into state property. The proletariat, having accomplished this mission, would then abolish itself, because when "it becomes the real representative of the whole of society, it renders itself unnecessary." The state dies out, anarchy in the economy is replaced by systematic organization, and the "struggle for individual existence disappears."[122] First formationists could derive considerable justification from this canonical work for their belief in capitalism's inevitable downfall, which would be the consequence of the unfolding of forces inherent in its emergence centuries before, and beyond the influence of any individual or class. This was, in a sense, a cosmic interpretation not only because it gestured through strong and direct references to Darwinism to the unity of the natural and social sciences, but also because it could be read as an analysis of how the structures and functions of a capitalist order, or the "forces" driving it, generated patterns over which one could exert little control.

Like Engels, Charlotte Perkins Gilman believed firmly in the Lamarckian theme of the inheritance of acquired characteristics. Often referenced in Canadian writings and sometimes a visiting lecturer in Canada, Gilman produced the magazine *Socialist Woman*, a substantial treatise called *Women and Economics: A Study of the Economic Relation Between Men and Women as a Factor in Social Evolution* (1898), and a series of utopian novels – *Moving the Mountain* (1911), *Herland* (1915), and *With Her in Ourland* (1916) – that were socialist-feminist answers to Edward Bellamy's highly influential utopian novel *Looking Backward: 2000–1887* (1888). A rapt Spencerian since young adulthood (but resistant to the call of Marx), Gilman believed passionately, as Pittinger puts it, "in the promise of science" and that "ideas could modify both human heredity and social environment." *Women and Economics* presented a classically cosmic account of the "woman question," analyzed in light of Darwinian "sexual selection" – staking Gilman's claim to be the major voice of Spencerian socialist feminism in North America.[123]

Evolution had made "man" the "human creature," whereas "Woman has been checked, starved, aborted in human growth; and the swelling forces of race-development have been driven back in each generation to work in her through sex-functions alone." Imprisoned in the domestic sphere, women were reduced to a stationary status akin to that of the gypsy moth, whose female, with aborted wings, was consigned to a subordinate role: "She waits humbly for the winged male, lays her myriad eggs, and dies." So it was with human beings. Men could travel far and fast, into "industry, commerce, science, manufacture, government, art, religion," while women were condemned, like the female gypsy moth, to make sexuality and love the focus of their entire world. They were forced to become prisoners of sensuality and ornament, to "all that is luxurious and enervating," and as "over-sexed" creatures they made "unintelligent and ceaseless demands" that worked to hinder and pervert "the economic development of the world." The confinement of women to the domestic sphere meant that they had been perversely forced into a permanent homogeneity, which constituted "a definite limit to social progress."[124]

Moving the Mountain spoke to an equally pervasive demand to imagine a future that would be radically otherwise. In Gilman's imagined world of the distant 1940s women had reasserted the powers that rightfully belonged to them as the decisive figures in sexual selection; they were no longer, for instance, subjugated by motherhood. Gilman adapted a recent sociological argument that women constituted the essential "race type," the "trunk" of the species. In her future world, along the lines suggested in *Women and Economics*, women would decide which men would win the competition among men to reproduce.[125]

From Gilman's point of view, monogamy had been "proven right by social evolution" as the "best way to carry on the human race," and the "depth and purity and permanence of the marriage relation rest on the necessity for the prolonged care of children by both parents, – a law of racial development which we can never escape."[126] Once it was recognized that the birthrate was for women alone to settle, they could play an actively selective (or "eugenic") role in the reproduction of the species, breeding out anti-social traits of aggressiveness, perversion, and excessive sexual energy that had been carried over from the distant past.

With some ingenuity, Gilman thus transformed the unpromising materials of Darwin's theory of sexual selection into an outlook and a strategy that socialist feminists could find both optimistic and empowering. Leftists could now argue for socialist feminism not by resisting Darwinian arguments that women were unique, but rather by upholding them. Women were not "outsiders of evolution," but (potentially) its decisive actors.[127]

Novelist and evolutionary theorist Grant Allen also qualifies as something of a Spencerian feminist. Born near Kingston, Ont., Allen acquired much of his fascination with Spencer from his father, a clergyman who filled his young son's ears with the master's philosophy. Young Grant Allen brought some of this fervour with him to Merton College, Oxford, where he devoured *First Principles* and the *Principles of Biology*, and became a full convert in Jamaica, where he went to teach at a college. He even wrote an ode to Spencer, and in 1874 established a correspondence with him that led to one of the eccentric philosopher's few close friendships. Later, in London, England, Allen busily turned out commentaries, novels, and articles, pursuing, rather like Spencer himself, the renaissance ideal of the perfect generalist – ranging over such subjects as colour-perception, botany, and physics as well as current affairs, politics, and religion. He believed himself to be a scientist, even though, again like Spencer, he never darkened the doorway of a laboratory or conducted a stringent field investigation.

Allen rivalled Marx in his acute perception of the liquefying impact of capitalist modernity – "Chaos appears to be swallowing up everything. 'The natural relations of classes' disappear. Faiths melt; churches dissolve; morals fade; bonds fail; a universal magma of emancipated opinion seems to take the place of old-established dogma" – and in his positive representation of such a time of transformation: "There will be a new heaven and a new earth for the men and women of the new epoch." In such a period of accelerated modernity, he wrote, "We can have no certainty. Save only the certainty that no element will outlive the revolution unchanged – not faiths, not classes, nor domestic relations, nor any other component factor of our complex civilization."[128]

In addition to making arguments for the complementary relationship of Darwin and Spencer,[129] Allen firmly believed that private property and the existing system were deeply immoral. Although he is often classed with the gradualist British Fabians, he seems closer in spirit to William Morris, with whom he shared a deep disgust at the "iniquities of the capitalist system, the miserable inadequacies of a culture based on 'getting and spending' . . . and the selfishness of restricting access to private land."[130] Just as significantly, and most notoriously in his own day, he was a sexual radical who (like Engels) disdained the institution of marriage, which he believed enslaved women and encouraged immorality. He pursued this theme in his widely read novels *The Woman Who Did* (1895), a scandalous anti-marriage romance, and *The British Barbarians* (1895), about a time-travelling anthropologist who returns from the distant future to gather anthropological data from Victorian Britain.

Finally, Allen would be widely esteemed on the left in the North Atlantic anglophone world as the scourge of religious faith – the courageous writer who showed that, far from being a divine revelation, Christianity was a product of nature and history. The various gods were just the ghosts of father figures (an idea Allen inherited from Spencer's *The Principles of Sociology*). *The Evolution of the Idea of God: An Inquiry into the Origins of Religions* (1897) sold 55,000 copies from its time of publication to 1903. Its theorization of religion surfaced in countless rationalist polemics throughout the international socialist world – including in one significant pamphlet published by the Socialist Party of Canada after the Great War and in another, originating in Britain, that was actually endorsed as the Party's official line on religion in 1915.[131]

Olive Schreiner was an equally powerful figure within socialist feminism. Born in South Africa to missionary parents, and later active as a socialist in England, Schreiner brought out *Woman and Labour* (1911), a Spencerian epic that made a significant impression on the discussion of the woman question in Canada. She argued that technological progress had opened up vast new fields for men, undermined the economic value of large families, and swept away the traditional functions of women without replacing them. This, in a nutshell, was "our modern 'Woman's Labour Problem.'" "Women's work" was shrinking, leaving women to lead lives of pointless and soul-destroying parasitism. In resisting this pattern, socialist feminists were not merely acting in the interests of women, but were resisting "*for the race.*" For while many causes might lead to the "enervation and degeneration of a class or race, the parasitism of its child-bearing women *must.*"

Schreiner, like Gilman, believed that women were "the final standard of the race. . . . As her brain weakens, weakens the man's she bears; as her muscle softens, softens his; as she decays, decays the people." Drawing on contemporary biological theory, Schreiner argued that parasitic women bred parasitic children – primarily through the inheritance of acquired characteristics. Modern women who delegated to others the tasks of mothering and relied upon their male relations for economic survival were little different from the prostitute, "who affects no form of productive labour, and who, in place of life, is recognized as producing disease and death, but who exists parasitically through her sexual attribute." In an analysis that anticipated later forms of feminist pacifism, Schreiner also argued that women were *naturally* predisposed to oppose war, because unlike men they had endured "months of pressure and physical endurance" to bring new life into the world. It was of the essence of men that they were intrinsically inclined to set a low stock on the value of life, and that of women that they set a much higher one. Schreiner thus drew upon evolutionary theory to present some of the earliest arguments for the importance of an autonomous socialist movement of and for women.[132]

Another prominent voice among those who wrestled with the challenge of evolutionary theory was that of Peter Kropotkin – sometimes referred to as Prince Kropotkin (in recognition of his former status within the Russian nobility).[133] The "Anarchist Prince" was lionized in much of the turn of the century anglophone socialist world, including Canada, where he played an important role in the immigration of the persecuted Doukhobors to the Canadian West. The sheer romanticism of a Russian prince who had adopted the cause of the oppressed no doubt added to his allure. His works were widely and intensively read in Canada (which he visited in 1897). A. Percy Chew in *The Voice*, Winnipeg's outstanding labour paper, hailed Kropotkin's work as a foundational contribution revealing how "we, the bond-slaves of capital, cannot do better than take a leaf out of the book of nature." Toronto radical Phillips Thompson was so taken with Kropotkin that he paid him a visit in England, where the Russian, having escaped from czarist imprisonment under hair-raising circumstances, lived for much of his life.[134]

Kropotkin was originally a scientist, and like many European socialists he was a Darwinian *before* becoming a socialist. His extensive geographical researches in Eastern Siberia and Manchuria persuaded him that the evolutionary patterns of that thinly settled region did not correspond to the theory of a ruthless competition of each member of a species, and of each species with others, in the struggle for survival.[135] Instead, in line with a rich tradition of left celebrations of pre-capitalist societies, associated especially with Morris, Kropotkin extolled the pre-capitalist village communities, which for centuries had thrived by adhering to certain fundamental principles of socialism, notably "the common ownership of the chief instrument of production, the land, and the apportionment of the same according to the labour capacities of the different families."

In his interpretation of social history, all of the scientific and technical wonders of the age were the results of the labours of untold millions of human beings who had gone before. Far from being insightful "captains of industry" who had single-handedly succeeded in transforming a benighted world, capitalists were merely the beneficiaries of the achievements of past generations of workers. Millions of people had laboured for thousands of years "to clear the forests, to drain the marshes, and to open up highways by land and water." Every yard of European soil had thus been watered "by the sweat of several races of men," and "every mile of railway, every yard of tunnel, has received its share of human blood." The upshot of all this pain and suffering was a society in which the benefits of centuries of evolutionary development were unjustly monopolized by a few.[136]

Kropotkin, a proponent of "anarchist communism," took care to emphasize that anarchists were integral parts of a wider left. For him, anarchism was not so much a completely free-standing body of radical theory as a branch of a wider system of socialist thought – the "no-government system of socialism."[137] Kropotkin himself saw no contradiction in calling himself an anarchist, a socialist, and a communist – all at one and the same time. Although he generally accepted the labour theory of value, Kropotkin argued that the true evil of the present system resided not in the expropriation of surplus value by the capitalist, but in the very possibility of a surplus value, for this meant "that men, women and children are compelled by hunger to sell their labour for a small part of what this labour produces, and still more so, of what their labour is capable of producing." This evil would last "as long as the instruments of production belong to the few," and with it went a culture of "hypocrisy and sophistry" that had become "the second nature of the civilized man."[138] The entire social and political order was founded upon a lie. Its inhabitants could not flourish unless they returned to the truth.

In the meantime, Kropotkin said, Darwin's formula of the "Struggle for Existence" provided an excuse for every "infamy" of civilized society and for "the relations of the whites towards the so-called lower races, or of the 'strong' towards the 'weak.'"[139] As he pointed out in his book *Mutual Aid* (1902), only in its narrowest sense – and Kropotkin argued that Darwin himself understood this – could the "struggle for existence" be confined to "a struggle between separate individuals for the sheer means of existence." Moreover, he noted, Darwin had urged that the term be taken in a "large and metaphorical sense," which would include "dependence of one being on another, and including (which is more important) not only the life of the individual, but success in leaving progeny."[140]

Kropotkin did not dispute that "an immense amount of warfare and extermination [was] going on amidst various species," but he did maintain that there was as much, perhaps more, mutual aid and mutual defence belonging to animals of the same species. Hence "sociability is as much a law of nature as mutual struggle." As Kropotkin noted, Spencer had already had the "grand idea" that "association" was found in the animal world at all degrees of evolution.[141]

For Kropotkin the philosophy of evolution and socialist anarchism were tightly interwoven. Again, typical of many socialists of the day, Kropotkin refused any suggestion that the human sphere was separate from the natural world. Nature taught, and humanity should learn, that mutual aid was the key to flourishing in both spheres. Socialist anarchism had developed out of Spencer's doctrine of the "survival of the fittest," which in this reading could be applied to the anarchists themselves: "'the fittest' will prove to be those who combine intellectual knowledge with the knowledge necessary for the production of wealth, and not those who are now the richest because they, or their ancestors, have been momentarily the strongest." Sociable species were simply destined to prosper, whereas "the unsociable species, on the contrary, are doomed to decay."[142]

Even the comfortable members of the middle class, inherently inclined to protect their own privileges, might be drawn into the movement after realizing the injustice underlying their supposed rights, Kropotkin argued. Socialists had to make sure that their new ideals penetrated "into the very class ... whose economical and political privileges had to be assailed."[143] Even more than unleashing the workers, socialism essentially meant the unlocking of the "immense power" of knowledge – a genuine people's enlightenment. Knowledge had to become the possession of all. Revolution itself was distinctively defined within this conception of socialism as the science of social evolution – as a moment in which long-standing evolutionary processes were rapidly accelerated.

Anarchism was not a *style* or a *faction*, but a "*principle or theory of life* and conduct in which society is conceived without government." It aimed at the creation of a new kind of society, which was to be "an interwoven network, composed of an infinite variety of groups and federations of all sizes and degrees" carrying out a wide diversity of shared tasks and striving "for the satisfaction of an ever-increasing number of scientific, artistic, literary and sociable needs." This network itself was to be seen, in words that might have been written by Spencer himself describing the "social state," as a harmonious equilibrium of organisms.[144] Entire pages of Kropotkin's "synthetic philosophy"of anarchism resemble discussions of "synthetic philosophy" in Spencer.

Compared to Kropotkin, novelist Jack London had a very different way of combining Darwinism with socialism. London, North America's most widely read socialist writer, enjoyed a mass readership in Canadian lumber camps and coal towns. Any socialist fond of reading, and many non-socialists fond of adventure stories, were likely to be found consuming London's bestselling books, and *Call of the Wild* (1903), London's tale of the Yukon, was especially beloved. In it, the dog Buck, pampered offspring of a St. Bernard and Collie, lolls about in California, until he is stolen, sold, and shipped to the Klondike. Here he "reverts to type," descending the evolutionary scale from dog to wolf. In a 1903 review in *Wilshire's Magazine*, Toronto writer and activist Margaret Haile twice referred to Spencer's dictum of the "survival of the fittest," a slogan that she thought applied not just to Buck but to the author, who, "like a strong runner stripped for the race, has discarded every superfluous ounce of weight." The *International Socialist Review* noted, "You do not need to search for social philosophy in it unless you want to. But if you do, it is one of the most accurate studies of 'reversion to type' that has ever been published."[145]

The Sea-Wolf (1904), amazingly popular throughout North America, revealed something of the same evolutionary dynamic. Wolf Larsen emerges as the "fittest" to "survive" in the brutal world of North Pacific sealing, thanks to his astounding natural strength and abiding interest in evolutionary philosophy.[146] London's highly autobiographical *Martin Eden* (1909), which chronicles a working-class man's desperate attempt through education to achieve social standing and romance, includes a moment when the hero, after hearing Spencer's name invoked at park meetings, signs out Spencer's *First Principles* from his library.[147] It is truly his "Eureka!" moment.

In London's world rugged rebels fight for justice, often with their two strong fists. His heroes, and London himself, appealed to many a socialist's apocalyptic fantasies. The *War of the Classes* (1905), a collection of speeches and articles, transposed Spencer's passages on the weak and inefficient into a direct analysis of the "surplus labor army," comprising "the men who cannot hold jobs, – the plumber apprentice who could not become a journeyman and the plumber journeyman too clumsy and dull to retain employment. . . . In short, the failures of every trade and profession, and failures, many of them, in divers trades and professions." Poverty was the reward of mediocrity, the "inferno where ignorance festers and vice corrodes, and where the physical, mental, and moral parts of nature are aborted and denied." Hence, London argued, the tramp was "self-eliminating," his kind incapable of reproducing: "And, while it is not nice that these men should die, it is ordained that they must die, and we should not quarrel with them if they cumber our highways and kitchen stoops with their perambulating carcasses." He was virtually repeating Spencer's *Social Statics*.[148] Nature, in Spencer in 1851 and London in 1905, was individually cruel in order to be organically kind.

London's most overtly political (and deeply disturbing) work was *The Iron Heel* (1908). Like Bellamy's *Looking Backward*, it involved the imaginary reconstruction of human history from a distant time – in this case, the year "419, B.O.M.," or "since the Brotherhood of Man," some seven centuries in the future and a time when socialism had finally triumphed. Through the eyes of Ernest Everhard, a working-class hero, and Avis, his middle-class beloved, London painted a portrait of a monstrous modernity in which the rich had become grossly hypocritical and the poor and unemployed had been transformed into "people of the abyss."[149] Ernest, a swashbuckling heroic "sociologist," defies crowd after bourgeois crowd with his command of theory and the rhetorical bodychecks he effortlessly delivers. An ideal-typical autodidact, he has taught himself French and German and translates scientific and philosophical works "for a struggling socialist publishing house in Chicago" (Charles H. Kerr and Co., many readers of the time would have inferred). His own economic and philosophic works were helping to pay his tuition at Berkeley, where he is (predictably) taking special courses in biology and working on a new book called *Philosophy and Revolution*. Avis is attracted by his boylike charm, delicate and sensitive spirit, and (we surmise) his "bulging muscles and prize-fighter's throat." Her father, having encountered Ernest as a soapbox socialist in the park, seems drawn by his "splendidly disciplined mind." Many a young male socialist would have patterned himself on Ernest, who time and again can be seen "mastering men in discussion, the war-note in his voice." Ernest "never gave quarter to an enemy," Avis marvels admiringly.[150]

Ernest Everhard's socialism was something to be performed – almost an experiment to be carried out in various social circumstances. London mapped social divisions onto biological categories, with muscular proletarians relentlessly confronting their befuddled, effeminate, soft-handed, paunchy, and absent-minded opponents. To a large extent he treats class identity as much as a biological as a socio-economic phenomenon. Ernest is a professional writer, collector of royalties, university student, and later a Congressman – all roles that, in the conventional Marxist sociology of the day, would have placed him firmly in the middle class, outside the two great contending classes. How, then, did he get to become the "voice of the working class"? By virtue of his ancestry, his background as a craft worker, and apparently because of his *style* – that of the fighting man, who punches it out with his theoretical opponents with the gusto of a barroom brawler. He also just happens to have a great command of evolutionary philosophy. As Ernest explains to a sceptical crowd, his synthetic philosophy, based so squarely upon the inductive method, "fuses all particular sciences into one great science." Many of the social facts of the day could be explained by the class struggle, a "law of social development" that was fully as scientific as Newton's theory of gravitation, and which was in essence Spencer's law of the survival of the fittest transposed into the social world. The revolutionary science of evolution clarifies all the questions that are put to it. Trusts and the new corporate capitalism? They were the irresistible and inevitable consequence of a system "in the midst of a transition stage now in economic evolution." Still, London could be interpreted as revealing the futility of trying suddenly to create an instantaneous revolutionary order: in the novel it will take seven centuries of slow evolutionary progress before the socialist order is securely in place.[151]

The Iron Heel is a self-undermining text in that the scientific infallibility, "everhard" masculinity, and proletarian purity advertised in the first four-fifths of the book are radically questioned in its closing pages. It proclaims a "hard science" of social evolution that is incapable, even after seven centuries, of explaining why its predictions, strategies, and tactics so conclusively failed. Instead of a people's enlightenment, the socialist revolution, although it successfully creates a number of co-operative commonwealths and recruits the mass of workers to its standard, culminates in the bloodthirsty rule of the Oligarchs. The cosmic message that, seven centuries from now, all of this difficulty will be behind us, rings a bit hollow, given the bloodstained mayhem that takes up so many pages, and the worrying inability of the wise man of the future to explain how it could have been that the laws of social evolution were overturned for such an extensive period of time. If its apostles had led social evolution into a centuries-long cul-de-sac, how much faith could they credibly command?

Jack London was a bundle of contradictions – a "womanizer" whose most vivid and admiring descriptions of bodies are almost always about muscular men, an ardent proletarian who would become a millionaire from his novels and erect a vast mansion with his royalties, an ailing alcoholic who worshipped the "everhard" austere revolutionary. *The Iron Heel* would receive praise, Stack notes, from "as unlikely a trio as Trotsky, Eugene V. Debs and Aneurin Bevan."[152] Bill Haywood and Mary Marcy, on the left of the U.S. Socialist Party, also thought well of it. Writing in October 1937 to Joan London, Leon Trotsky reflected on the "deep impression" the book had made upon him: "The book surprised me with the audacity and independence of its historical foresight." The novel sold over 50,000 copies in hardback, and, as Alex Kershaw points out, was "devoured by many in the iww [Industrial Workers of the World] who were inspired by Jack's uncompromising stance."[153] It undoubtedly stirred many workers: one report from Nova Scotia's Pictou County remembered young local activists who, inspired by London, organized a secretive club that took the name of the "Iron Comrades."[154]

London, for good or ill, introduced thousands of working-class people to the concept of socialism as the revolutionary science of social evolution. Wilfred Gribble, the unofficial poet laureate of Canada's first formation, originator of *Rhymes of Revolt* (1911) and a prisoner of conscience in the early years of the Great War, thought so highly of London that he wrote a poem in his honour:

> No need above his dust to place
> A graven stone;
> No need his epitaph to trace –
> He wrote his own!
> He wrote it with a flaming pen
> Upon the throbbing hearts of men.[155]

Why Must a Socialist Be a Scientist?

This diverse and imposing array of *fin de siècle* thinkers important to the left were not tied together by any one party or movement. They were diverse in nationality, *métier*, and talent – from Engels, whose disciplined intelligence radiates from his every page, to London, who was critiqued in his day for churning out mere potboilers just to pay the bills. Each had Canadian followers.[156]

For all its diversity, this group reveals arresting shared affinities. In addition to contributing, in their own way, to a global social-evolutionary framework – and priding themselves on their in-depth mastery of evolutionary theory – they all considered it a primary duty to defend science and the legacy of the enlightenment in general. They were Darwinians, though only in the loose turn of the century sense of believing that Darwin's concept of descent with modification, acted upon by a variety of selective mechanisms, was an indispensable guide for scientific and political theory alike. They did not necessarily emphasize, or even accept, natural selection.

Even those who wrote "utopian" fictions – Gilman, Allen, and (in a certain respect) the primarily dystopian London – were not idly spinning fantasies: they were engaged in literary forms of experiment. By using the device of time travel, they were able to expose and critique the limitations of the present day. Even those who wrote "scientific" treatises – Engels, Allen, Kropotkin – were interested in using evolutionary theory as a way of predicting the future. Even those who devoted energy to day to day politics – Gronlund, Engels, and (in his youth) Kropotkin – saw what they were doing in this "practical" realm as a fulfilment of the ideals they held in the "evolutionary" and "scientific" realm. If some of them were often otherworldly "utopians," dreaming in often unsettling detail of the futures that awaited an enlightened humankind, others were the "practical theorists," who nonetheless made it their business to interject into their contemporary world radiant images of a future of which they could have no direct experience. In an entirely non-pejorative sense, Engels – whose time-travelling imagination extended to the death of the planet and the species, and the re-creation in distant galaxies of new minds – was literally the most "other-worldly" of them all.[157]

Perhaps the most distinctive trademark of this generation of leftists was their enthusiastic recourse to the most cosmic and telescopic forms of evolutionary theorizing. All of them believed it fully possible to grasp universal patterns, and that, once grasped, these understandings could work to change present-day conditions. A 21st-century leftist who opens Schreiner's book on *Women and Labour* or, to cite a 1920 Canadian example, William Irvine's *The Farmers in Politics* might innocently expect to encounter theoretically framed empirical investigations of actual women and farmers, respectively, but instead is jarred by finding lengthy reflections on the infinitely small parasitical creatures of the micro-world or, conversely, the "whirling orbs of fire" and the evolution of the higher intelligence as so masterfully mapped by Spencer.[158] Those who viewed social evolution through a theoretical "telescope" that gave them access to the patterns of the universe often saw no need to bring out a "microscope" to understand events on their doorstep. When huge coal strikes erupted, east and west, and when Lakehead workers at the land's centre were engulfed in violent class conflicts, such events did not dominate the socialist press, which were seemingly preoccupied with issues of more universal significance. This taste for the cosmic was an indication of the underlying evolutionary approach that flourished from 1890 to 1920 (after which, entering into a period of stiff competition with an alternative Bolshevik framework, it gradually declined).

Of central importance was the self-taught proletarian intellectual – the autodidact. As Jonathan Rée remarks, the autodidacts' athletic enthusiasm for self-improvement through intellectual exercise provided them with their own personal model of social progress: they had a sense that they themselves were shifting, by their own efforts, from a crabbed, superstitious, and fearful parochialism to a bold and oceanic inclusiveness of vision, in which the infinite universe could be grasped as a whole. They would also all have agreed that the laws of social evolution allowed researchers to demarcate one type of society from another, and position these in an evolutionary hierarchy, from "savages" to the "civilized."[159]

Perhaps the most striking of the first formation's naturalistic images was that of the parasite. As Stack argues, parasitology, a hitherto neglected strand within socialist theory and one that drew eclectically from Darwin, Lamarck, Spencer, and Francis Galton, the father of eugenics, provides a vital key to how leftists took up evolutionary ideas.[160] Both Darwin and Spencer in their scientific writings had pondered the presence of parasites in the natural world. Parasites were puzzling because they defied Spencer's law of differenti-ation – that is, "Rather than moving from the homogeneous to the het-erogeneous, parasites became less, not more, complex over time." The parasitological *motif* gave first formationists a convincing comeback to the hard-nosed sceptics, those who were more inclined to hard-core "natural se-lection" and who, in the 20th century, were drawing upon the new findings from genetics. Just as parasites in the natural world could be explained as or-ganisms that had acquired their characteristics in response to given host en-vironments, so too could one explain social parasites – the plutocrats or "plutes" – by looking at the underlying structure of the "social environment" that allowed them to prey upon the "social organism." When we encounter parasitism directly in Schreiner and Gilman, and indirectly in London's fic-tion, we are really meeting up with the outcrop of an extensive and at times sophisticated development of one politically useful "organic concept" developed within evolutionary theory.

Socialists could build on older "producer ideology" arguments – which maintained that those who worked directly in production had a moral and economic right to benefit from their labour – to distinguish the preying and idle parasite from the virtuous and industrious worker. A bevy of prominent socialist intellectuals and practical politicians studied parasitology seriously, as did a number of intellectuals seeking to bridge the gap between science and religion.[161] One of the contradictions of "radical organicism" was that it seemingly disabled the possibility of critique and alternative because, as Pit-tinger nicely puts it, how could "one criticize the physiology of a living crea-ture?"[162] To that, parasitology offered an alternative: not the "living creature" itself, but the parasites preying upon it, could be singled out as "counter-evolutionary."

Engels, Allen, and Kropotkin were all militant non-believers in God – in Kropotkin's case, to the point of attributing countless deviations from the law of mutual aid, in all manner of societies, to the malign influence of priests. None of them invoked God as an explanation, and some (Allen in particular) spent considerable time and energy trying to advance the cause of free thought. Others – London is a good example – identified the church as a central enemy of human progress; its "religious" functions were to be sub-sumed by the socialist movement itself. All of these writers opposed, with varying degrees of sophistication, dualistic positions that separated mind and body, matter and soul. All of them would have sharply disagreed with the sug-gestion that socialism could be invented holus-bolus without the adoption of an "organic conception of incremental change." The task of socialism became not one of instituting "a new society," because realistically no such thing could be imposed upon "the social organism." Rather, as Stack puts it, "The task of socialism was simply to put society back on its path of natural evolutionary progression."[163] Socialists were "progressives" – they were those who, having studied universal patterns of growth and development, could seed beneficial changes and nurture the emergent plants as they *progressed* towards maturity. The name has outlived the heyday of the paradigm.

For these thinkers, the lessons of social evolutionism extended to personal life – and, at the very least, socialism should be centrally concerned with everyday moral issues. The ever-contradictory London, sexist and self-seeking, wrote as though he believed sincere progressives should seek to simplify their lives and avoid luxury and pretension. Kropotkin, who was similarly if less offensively blind to the position of women, nonetheless believed that socialism would transform and simplify daily life, and did imagine the benefits that women might derive from the new technologies of the better day. Engels, Allen, Schreiner, and Gilman all put gender issues at the heart of the revolution in personal life that they hoped would be ushered in by the advent of socialism. That the personal is the political was, in theory at least, a given.

Above all these important figures demonstrate that the emergence of socialism and of evolutionary thought cannot be regarded as separate and distinct phenomena. The interpretive implications are significant. If we go back over the past and scan for "Marxists," often with the implicit idea that they were (or should have been) well versed, free-standing, and self-sufficient, we can either engage in lengthy and self-deluding exercises in trying to shoehorn such figures into our present-day definitions, or we can acknowledge that most of the period's Marxists, with an unavoidably partial grasp of Marx, were drawing extensively upon evolutionary theories associated with Darwin, Spencer, and (especially in central Europe) Haeckel. Leftists could look to evolutionary theory as confirmation of their own acute sense of the flux of history and the historical character of all categories and analytical frameworks – here most closely converging with Marx's own formulations after his reading of *Origin of Species*. They could see in natural selection an analogue of the class struggle (a move that could be associated with Engels and London), in "mutual aid" an inspirational reminder of the "naturalness" of socialism (Kropotkin), or in "parasitology" the natural equivalent of the appropriation of surplus value by capital or the oppression of women by men (Schreiner). They could see in natural science more generally the cultural legacy of the Enlightenment that they were sworn to uphold, which once released from the fetters imposed upon it by capitalism would flourish all the more remarkably. They would find in evolutionary theory a materialist rejoinder to religion (Allen); and they could find in evolution support for a revolution in personal politics, through arguments linking "woman's" subordination with limitations on her powers over sexual selection (Gilman) or by noting how capitalist modernity was creating sexual degenerates incapable of reproduction (Allen and Gilman). In the North Atlantic world of socialist movements and ideas, a socialist uninterested in or opposed to a politics that linked the street corner and the stars, the "cell" and "socialism," was an oddball indeed.

The Axiomatics of the First Canadian "Marxists"

Turn of the century socialists were not being ill-informed and naive when they combined natural selection with a host of other factors – mutual aid, the inheritance of acquired characteristics, sexual selection, rapid environmental changes – in their explanations of nature and society. Many of them were intelligently responding to the state of play within biological thought itself, within which Darwinism was not clearly defined. Darwin himself had introduced many of these elements into his theory, and there was as yet no "scientific consensus" about the mechanisms of evolution. Contrary to their image of credulous scientism, many first formationists read the available evolutionary theory sceptically and with an eye to its contradictions and paradoxes.[164]

A striking sign of this sophistication came in 1919, when an article by Chapman Cohen (1868–1954), one of the most formidable British autodidacts of his day, was reprinted in *The Indicator*, a publication of the Socialist Party of Canada.[165] Cohen asked his readers to understand that the adaptation of a particular species to its environment, hinging on the acquisition of particular qualities that spell survival, might pave the way to "what we call progress," or it might mean "the reverse." Nature levelled neither "up" nor "down." In nature there was "neither better nor worse, neither high nor low, there are only differences, and if that had been borne in mind, a great many theistic apologies would never have seen the light, nor would non-theists have so often weakened their case by using a watered-down form of the theistic argument."

Construing evolution as a progressive force was a way of smuggling theology into science, Cohen provocatively maintained. "There are certain lowly forms that were in existence long before the appearance of man, and which will most probably be the last form of life to disappear from a worn-out globe." From the scientific point of view, theological talk of a universal plan was so much meaningless chatter. "Science knows nothing of a plan, or an end, or even of progress in nature. All these are conceptions that we humans create for our own convenience." To treat human measures as though they were those of nature itself was "sheer anthropomorphism. It is the ghost of God imported into science."[166]

Others highlighted the "teleological temptations" involved in evolutionary theorizing, a problem current among 21st-century philosophers of biology. Many first formation writers were acutely aware of the complexities of evolutionary theory and alert to counter-evidence suggesting regress.[167] They clearly knew how well Spencer's "survival of the fittest" could work within right-wing liberal discourses of private property and anti-unionism. As the *Western Clarion* put it: "A most striking illustration of the working out of 'the law of the survival of the fittest' may be seen in the case of the capitalists and the workers. The former get fat on no work. The latter starve on no work. As idlers and loafers the capitalists are the more fit to survive."[168]

Yet they did not on that account reject, but rather sought to adapt, evolutionism. In the imagination of early Canadian socialism, the people's enlightenment meant not a doctrinaire and unintelligent insistence upon certain texts, but an openness to science as a new way of thinking and acting in the world. In Arthur M. Lewis's *Evolution: Social and Organic* (1908), a runaway bestseller among leftists in Britain and North America – it deeply impressed scores of Canadian activists, including such notables as Roscoe Fillmore and Tim Buck – even the conventional Marxist contradictions between the forces and relations of production were replaced by a new driving force of history: that between bourgeois narrowness and *working-class enlightenment.* Having unwittingly released science from its fetters, the bourgeoisie were now struggling to suppress it, "or at least prevent its reaching the proletarian brain." No such strategy could work. The bourgeoisie was "bound, more securely than Prometheus to the rock, to a mode of production which makes the education of the proletariat a relentless necessity."[169]

In this audacious rewriting of the base and superstructure model, the enlightenment of working people was inevitable. As Lewis would explain in his *Vital Problems in Social Evolution* (1917), the working class had inherited the best of the 19th century, which had been distinguished more than anything else by the "amazing development of positive science. The only thing that at all compares with it is the growth of machine industry." In the scientific enlightenment socialists could find their truth and their salvation. "The hope of Socialism," he proclaimed, "does not lie with the Socialist lecturer or editor who proclaims its superior justice. It will triumph because back of the lecturer and the newspaper stands the inexorable economic evolutionary process which grinds capitalism to powder and moves majestically forward to the dawning of a new day."[170] This working-class enlightenment touched virtually every problem a person might confront. If one truly desired the coming of a new way of life, the scientific education of these worker-intellectuals, without whom the whole system would founder, was of pivotal significance – more so than their mere organization on economic issues.

Social-evolutionary theory only ostensibly evicted values from "scientific" analysis, and even when its practitioners tried to evict "hope" from their hard-boiled first formation vocabularies, as an undefinable vision of living otherwise, it kept coming back in. A good example is Jim Connell, author of a long series of articles on "Socialism and the Survival of the Fittest" reprinted in the *Western Clarion* in 1913.[171] Connell stressed that the term "fittest" should not be taken in a "teleological" sense – the "fittest" merely were able to survive and reproduce in a given environment. Yet Connell and the *Clarion* would only follow Darwin so far, and they actually worked with a much more teleological doctrine derived from both Engels and Spencer. Connell's "Nature" is no blind watchmaker, to reference Richard Dawkins's imaginative metaphor for a logical but non-teleological evolutionary pattern, of a type often championed by 21st-century theorists,[172] but an enthusiastic, if sometimes somewhat inefficient, Master Planner. In Connell's words: "Nature always accomplishes her purposes in the end. We know that her aim is Communism, for some of the higher species have already reached it, and all are tending towards it. It will come." Echoing Jack London, Connell suggested that socialists, in their prediction of the new society, could be as certain of it as ocean watchers were about the coming tides. "We know what is coming. Today Capitalist individualism seems firmly rooted and strongly knit, but the laws of nature are fighting on our side. It may hold its ground for many years yet, but the time is coming when the waves of the evolutionary tide will break and roar far, very far above it."

Although Connell conceded that "low down in the organic scale," nature "makes many failures in order to achieve one success," he associated mutual aid with the higher end of that scale and implied its inevitable triumph. He presented, in essence, a radicalized version of Kropotkin (who had emphasized mutual aid, but only as a "factor in evolution") and a more determinist, even fatalistic, stance than anything found in Spencer. Connell's musings occupied column after column in a *Western Clarion* that in many issues gave more space to such theory than to analyses of the country's slide into recession and the rise of a working-class revolt.

Analysis, Substitution, and Campaign

Did social-evolutionary theory entail particular political and ethical positions? In principle, no. Science, contemporaries believed, concerned itself strictly with the logical, dispassionate analysis of the facts. "A fact is a fact," the *Western Clarion* proclaimed, much as London's Ernest Everhard might have said. Even if you were to show that, as individuals, socialists were all horse thieves, bad men, or even bankers, the socialist position, based upon scientific factual analysis, "would remain sound and its interpretation of material development be absolutely correct," the paper stated in 1906.[173] Socialism was not just a politics inspired by the scientific Enlightenment – it *was* the Enlightenment in its 20th-century democratic incarnation, "the logical and indestructible outcome of all the scientific and intellectual activity of the nineteenth century," in the words of the Italian socialist Enrico Ferri, one of the *Western Clarion*'s favourite European theorists.[174]

Yet in Canada first formation leftists happily merged the concepts of evolutionary science with the language of right and wrong. J.S. Woodsworth, before and after his conversion from liberalism to socialism c.1917, was prone to demonize whole realms of the animal kingdom. One of the many eccentric pleasures afforded by his book *Strangers Within Our Gates* (1909), which focused on recent immigrants to Western Canada, is a paranoid riff on Mormonism, whose menace to all that is noble and fine in Canada is brought to life by the vision of a monstrous octopus, its tentacles stretching all the way from Nevada to Canada.[175] After his conversion to socialism, Woodsworth preferred spiders: a graph depicting a Dominion-wide spider web, spun by financial interests, proved to audiences that finance capital had become the unworthy, because spider-like, beneficiary of social evolution. Woodsworth's web conveyed not only a sense of the new interconnections of modernity, but of how workers could, like insects, be trapped and sucked dry by bloodthirsty capitalists.[176] Metaphorical octopuses and spiders were demonized as appropriators of surplus value. As one SPC polemicist wrote in 1909, "The feudal system gave birth to industrial capital; that giant octopus whose insatiable maw crushed the individuality out of humanity, made them the creature of things, and forced their obedience to its demands."[177]

The very general equation of the natural with the valid also had an ethical overtone, and made an inadvertent bow to scholastic philosophy. Socialists turned the tables on their liberal opponents by demonstrating that not socialism but capitalism was "against nature." For Connell, capitalistic individualism, without a prototype in nature – not even Kropotkin had gone *that* far – was unnatural.[178] Opponents of socialism were often shown to be physically as well as morally repulsive, their very bodies a theatrical display of parasitical excess. Only "white-livered humbugs" would have been repelled by the "straight dope" of comrade Wilfred Gribble, in the opinion of W.E. Anderson, the Dewberry, Alta., correspondent of the *Western Clarion*. Another Western socialist poked savage fun at a Liberal Party audience, which he depicted in a series of grotesque images: a "fat lady" perspiring like a frog, a "young lady in a low necked dress" sporting "five rings with precious stones," and a "bald-headed old satyr . . . with a nose like a huge wart" who sat there "wiping the spots of grease coming out of his bald cranium." Ralph Smith, first elected as a labour man but who then betrayed the Enlightenment and became a Liberal politician, was described as "the oleaginous Smith," a foretaste of the "vermin" who fed on fat pensions or other benefits in other labour movements.[179]

For the first formation, socialism was not in essence either a wispy ideal or a pragmatic program. Rather, socialism *itself* was a science, which had to be learned, taught, and developed. In 1887, before he became a fully fledged socialist, Phillips Thompson was already complaining about "political economists, capitalistic editors, full-fed optimists, and sleek pulpiteers," who were keen to discredit socialism but entirely ignorant of its "scientific sense." People were complaining about the slipperiness of the word "social-ism" before the movement was even launched in Canada. James Simpson of Toronto would complain in 1908 that there was no word in the English lan-guage that had been "more misrepresented, which is more maligned than that word 'Socialist.'"[180] Part of the problem of definition lay in the many paths – religious, secular, scientific, ethical – that had led people to name themselves "socialists." Yet in this diversity socialism remained profoundly connected to – indeed, in many minds it was the application of – social-evolu-tionary theory.

H. Martin, the national secretary of the Social Democratic Party of Canada, spelled out in 1913 what it meant to him (in his capacity as a party functionary) to be a socialist. He started out with the science of sociology that every adherent should have mastered. "Sociology," he wrote, "is a scientific in-quiry into the actual conditions of society. It is a new conception of society, including its development, in strict contradiction to the theological theory of society." Then what was socialism? It was

> the new science of sociology ... the philosophy of social development that treats
> of the great economic laws, according to the working of which each of these
> stages of society must naturally be a development from its predecessor. Social-
> ism is therefore not a scheme, not a plan to reform the evils of our society, but
> an analysis of social misery which explains the causes (primarily) of poverty,
> crime, prostitution and the many kindred evils of capitalism.

This socialism should not, said the SDPC secretary with some asperity, be confused with "wishy-washy sentimental humanitarianism," and it had "nothing to do with any fantastic idea of prophecy." No. Socialism was the sci-ence of social evolution, which could affirm "with mathematical certainty, that the current of human evolution is in a general direction of a continuously and progressively increasing preponderance of the interests and importance of the community over the interests and importance of the individual."[181]

As far as organizing a substitute for capitalism, socialists looked to promising signs within their own society. Socialism was not a dream – it was really happening. "In some of its phases Socialism is already here," Thompson reported in 1887, responding to those who easily dismissed the entire notion as utopian. He noted as harbingers of socialism "every advance from the primitive system of isolation and self-dependence," and every improvement that brought the productive forces closer together, simplified exchange and distribution, facilitated the division of labour, and accentuated the dependence of the individual upon the community. All were advances to-wards socialism "in its co-operative phase." After all, as the often-cited Rev.

F.M. Sprague of the Canadian Socialist League remarked, "Socialism being the product of social evolution, the only danger lies in obstructing it."[182]

As a scientific campaign to replace capitalism, socialism meant developing, both collectively and individually, a new "theory of life." Once, said G.G. Pursey, in a nice distillation of the moments of supersedure and systematization, "we have obtained a unified view of life, the facts of history and experience cluster around that view which serves as a nucleus." The predominant interpretation that many socialists placed upon this unified view of life was that the working class had a special mission to change the world. The "Socialist Faith" for *Cotton's Weekly* in 1909 called for "Justice to all mankind; the same chance for every creature born. No tyranny, no oppression. The watchword – labor; and laziness a crime." In 1907 the *Western Clarion*, breaking for once with its trademark sarcasm, showcased an ecstatic vision of socialism written by Ferri. "Socialism is the deepest, the most majestic movement, intellectual and moral, ever known in the annals of the human race," proclaimed Ferri. "And that is the secret of its irresistible march onward, with the welfare of humanity as its goal."[183]

Conceding in 1915 that he did not know what the future held for the socialist movement, Fillmore felt obliged to enunciate what he held to be its basic truth.

> When all's said and done, the one function of the Socialist movement is to educate the workers. . . . Our function is to educate. Educate and then *educate* the workers. The revolution will come as the result of the growing inability of capitalism to provide us with the means of life coupled with the intelligence that we and those who come after us display in revolt. Without working class education, class rule can continue in some form or other indefinitely. It's up to us.[184]

All of this analyzing, substituting, and campaigning presupposed a well-functioning democratic public sphere. The people's enlightenment required a radical democracy. It meant the defence of the right to free speech and a critique of its enemies – superstitious priests, craven academics, and bullying patriots.[185] It also meant contesting the limits of liberal order. Most socialists understood very clearly that they were working within and upon a political landscape already thoroughly colonized by liberalism. An increasing number of socialists proclaimed themselves Marxists, seeing in Marx a figure whose theories combined Darwinism with the class struggle. Others were reluctant to do so, all the while using many Marxist concepts of class and value in their theoretical and practical work.

From Polemic to Reconnaissance

Today this is a left most often remembered in epithets – Vulgar Marxism, "Socialism of the Second International," Positivism, Scientism, social Darwinism. Around it has congealed a vast vocabulary of dismissal and patronage. This is a left remembered for its fevered quarrels, futile polemics, and failed politics. It is often scanned for premonitions of coming disasters and disparaged for its primitiveness.[186] Historian Richard Hofstadter pictured a time and place – a country store, I have always imagined – in which the "cracker-barrel agnostic" entertained a crowd of credulous bumpkins with his "comprehensive world-view, uniting under the generalization everything in nature from protozoa to politics."[187] The period is often painted as a time and place when badly educated yokels fell for crackpot schemes of social regeneration – Vulgar Marxisms for Vulgar People. Some Canadian historians describe "impossibilism," a doctrine they attribute to the SPC and by dubious extension the entire movement, in terms that suggest a kind of fevered madness.[188] Others remember insults to women and racial minorities. When a serious politics of the left commenced in the 1920s and 1930s, historians of various political persuasions suggest, it was small wonder that so few cared to look back upon the blighted soil of 1890–1920. Land of barren sectarianism and arid scholasticism, that earlier period does not signify, even as a time and place of humble beginnings.

This reconnaissance has found something different. I see this time and place not as a toxic waste dump but as a freshly planted field. I see it as the time of the first formation of the Canadian left – that first time when people who wanted to live otherwise came together to construct an enduring socialist counter-narrative to liberal order. I see it as a time of scientific enlightenment – of curiosity, discovery, and debate. Here I find not ignorant yokels mangling Marxism but fiercely independent working-class men and women – autodidacts – doing original and important things in Canada with an unavoidably abbreviated "Marx" whom they often read with discernment and adapted with intelligence. I generally do not find social Darwinism but socialist Darwinism – not a heedless embrace of natural selection and biological determinism, but a more judicious attempt to weave themes from evolutionary theory and revolutionary politics together.

As for "impossibilism," I see it as a stylistic aspect of *part* of the movement, but not as a valid characterization of the whole. Although there were some figures, especially in British Columbia and Toronto, who gloried in extreme forms of socialist discourse designed to put off all but a few adepts, what is often meant by "impossibilism" is an insistence on socialism as the revolutionary science of social transformation. If only a minority of first formation socialists went in for the arrogant in-your-face rhetoric of some members of the SPC's Dominion Executive Committee, a vast majority would have identified with the ideal of a socialist science, enlightening the people on the irrationality, cruelty, and replaceability of capitalism. What distinguished the first formation socialists from their ancestors and descendants, and also from their liberal and labour competitors on the left, were the specific moments of refusal, supersedure, and systematization that progressively distanced them from the liberal capitalist mainstream. As the historian E.P. Thompson might have said, a "river of fire" separated them from those who could or would not see the intrinsic evils of capitalism and the liberal order with which it was intertwined.[189]

I do not see simpletons seduced by the political equivalent of snake-oil salesmen, but autodidacts struggling for coherence in a fast-moving, threatening world. And I see 14-year-old Adolphus Landry, stumbling in the smoke of an unsafe child-killing coal mine, one small unit of labour power squeezed to produce the revenues of the provincial government, a mansion for the colliery manager, and handsome returns for the Montreal investors – and the same Landry, eight years later, reaching for the teachings of Marx and Co., grasping for a "science of reconstructing society on an entirely new basis," and understanding his own scars as products, not of providence or blind luck, but of an evolving social system. I see a formation that, like a constellation, set many ideas and forces in motion, not all of them easily reconciled – but centred on a dynamic nucleus, that of socialism as the scientific key to reasoning and thinking otherwise.

Most socialists were for, but some were against, the organization of trade unions as primary and efficacious weapons for the defence of the working class. Many socialists were for, and a few were against, and some were highly conflicted about, religious belief in general and Christianity in particular. Most socialists were for, but a few were against, equality for women. On these and many other fundamental issues, socialists did not speak with one voice. Yet within the dominant conceptual framework of the first formation from 1890 to 1920, they could not be for or against the concept of social evolution. Socialism by this definition *was* the revolutionary science of social evolution. It was only through the application of this science that a people's enlightenment would become a reality. Socialism was the applied science of a great movement of enlightenment – nothing more, nothing less. "Socialism is a star," proclaimed *Cotton's Weekly*. "It shines in the present night and speaks of a coming day."[190]

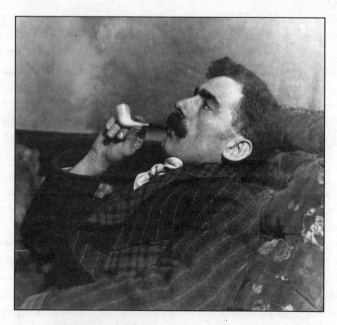

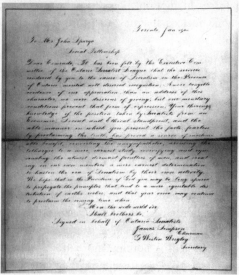

John Spargo, a major transatlantic figure in pre-1914 socialism, whose speech at a foundational CSL conference in Toronto would be remembered decades later; and a testimonial from James Simpson and G. Weston Wrigley Jr., thanking him on behalf of the Toronto socialists. Special Collections, Bailey-Howe Library, University of Vermont, Burlington.

2

The Emergence of the First Formation in Canada, 1890–1902

*T*oronto, 28 November 1901. As great turning points in history go, it was an understated moment. Certainly, few of the 70-odd people gathered at Victoria Hall that Thanksgiving weekend – back then Canadians followed the U.S. timing for the holiday – would have felt overpowered by any sense of historical significance. The meeting did not receive much press coverage. It was sponsored by the Canadian Socialist League and advertised as being dedicated to the formation of the *Ontario* Socialist league – which would mislead many of those who later thought about it at all to disregard it as a merely provincial happening. Those who were there that day would remember it in markedly different ways.

Yet this humble provincial gathering in Toronto marks the first time in Canada that homegrown radical and socialist organizations got together to merge simple local clubs and units into a more complex interprovincial body. The people in attendance that day had been active in Ontario and Quebec locals of the League, which had itself had been born only three years earlier, in the summer of 1898, in the Point St. Charles neighbourhood of Montreal. CSL Local No. 1 in Point St. Charles drew from a working-class community in which many worked at the Grand Trunk Railway shops nearby. It included within its ranks many veterans of old reform and recreational clubs, and had recycled its name from that of a short-lived league from earlier in the decade. Soon after, in that same summer, a larger Local No. 2 was established in Toronto and quickly became the core of the organization, which then spread to small and medium-sized communities across Ontario and parts of the West. In March 1900, after briefly sharing "top billing" as the twinned headquarters of the movement, the Montreal group ceded place to Toronto.[1] Interest grew in creating a larger, more truly Dominion-wide Canadian Socialist League.

The gathering in November 1901 was thus the first concrete step to the organization of a Canada-wide left-wing movement. The 20th century opened with many dispersed groups and movements questioning the political and social order, drawing upon an increasingly coherent and articulate international socialist alternative. Previously local socialist parties and groups and spinoffs of U.S. socialist parties had existed, but no one homegrown cross-Canada movement for the left. With its founding in 1901 the Ontario Socialist League would function as the nucleus of a larger body. From it would emerge activists who would then take leading roles in other regions of the country, especially British Columbia, where the socialist movement was growing fast. A half-year earlier G. Weston Wrigley Sr. (1847–1907), a veteran socialist, had noted that the Canadian socialist movement itself was like a child learning how to walk. It had been born, it had evolved through the crawling stage, and now "in the swift evolution of events it will soon be beyond the walking and into the running stage."[2] The relatively modest meeting of November provides a distinct vantage point into how the first formation ideas of this early stage were put to work in turn of the century Canada.

Attending the 1901 meeting were three activists whose practice and approach provide a sharp insight into the surprisingly complicated and dynamic world of first formation Canadian leftism. One was a Toronto-based journalist with a long track record on the left. He brought to the 1901 convention his own experiences with democracy on both sides of the border, and in 1902 he would become the League's Ontario organizer. The second was a Montreal-based merchant seaman and labour journalist instrumental in launching the movement in Point St. Charles. The third was a British émigré to the United States who was invited to present the first socialist convention's keynote address. All three men were ardent proponents of a science of social evolution that they had learned at the knees of Herbert Spencer. Together they and the CSL would work to consolidate not just a new movement but a new language of the left that would prove enormously influential down to 1920.

If we can imagine an instrument capable of measuring the "leftist earthquake" in the larger turn of the century world, it would, at least outside Canada, pick up distinct signs of a vast transnational political disturbance. Our imaginary seismograph would detect the construction on socialist principles of Germany's largest single political party – the Social Democratic Party, the SPD (the acronym arising from its name in German, *Sozialdemokratische Partei Deutschlands*). Our political Richter scale would definitely pick up massive stirrings in Italy, Belgium, Finland, Australia, New Zealand, and even the United States, where by 1912 the Socialist Party was capable of winning almost a million votes in the presidential contest, and inspired almost 300 publications – weeklies, monthlies, and even daily newspapers.[3] It would register the rise of mass anarchist movements in Italy and Spain. It would undoubtedly note the prominence of the Socialist International, whose first stirrings were felt as early as October 1881, and which held its founding congress in Paris in July 1889, at which delegates from 20 countries pledged allegiance to the principles of the International Workingmen's Association, founded in Marx's day 25 years earlier (and hence the popular designation, "the Second International"). Throughout the years 1889 to 1914, leftists in various countries saw the conferences of the International as truly major international events – the conference held at Stuttgart in August 1907, for instance, drew 884 delegates from 25 countries. If the first Marxist government in the world was that of the remote French mining town of Commentry in 1881,[4] three decades later the Marxists of the Second International, having withstood repression and ridicule, were serious contenders in the political life of a half-dozen European countries. Large socialist parties, with dozens of elected members, were making serious bids for power. The ever-growing millions of socialist voters worldwide were commonly celebrated in North America, where even in the United States the Socialist Party was a force to contend with.

Yet in Canada our imaginary seismograph would scarcely have budged.[5] In essence, Canadian socialists had no institutional relationship with the Second International. True, members of its European parties could sometimes use their party cards as passports into Canadian organizations; and true, many Canadian leftists wanted to join the International – but the SPC staunchly refused to do so on revolutionary grounds, and the SDPC, whose break with the SPC was fought out partly on this issue and did affiliate, never managed to send a delegate. Not only were these parties essentially non-starters in international left politics, but at home they were negligible electorally – you could count the socialist legislators in Canada on your fingers, and still have enough left over to play "Chopsticks." True, in British Columbia, James Hurst Hawthornthwaite and Parker Williams were able to parlay well-located voting blocs and weak Liberal results into becoming Canada's first socialist leaders of an official opposition (in 1910 and 1912 respectively). Nonetheless, according to 1913 estimates emanating from the Socialist Party of America, Canada (with a socialist vote *generously* pegged at 15,857 out of a population of 7,300,000) ranked dead last of the 13 countries assessed in terms of the strength of its socialist movement.[6] Some of the country's large international labour organizations – especially Districts 18 and 26 of the United Mine Workers of America, the International Ladies' Garment Workers' Union, and the Industrial Workers of the World – were, especially in 1907–14, hotbeds of socialism. Even so, across Canada as a whole the size of the pre-1914 organized left, broadly speaking, and on the most generous estimate, cannot be pushed beyond 50,000. This was a numerically weak left, by any measure.

Later on, even in Canada, the imaginary seismograph would finally register a massive earthquake – dramatized by the Winnipeg General Strike

(1919) and a pan-Canadian labour and socialist revolt (1917–25), and the emergence of powerful and lasting organizations, including the Communist Party (fd. 1921) and the Co-operative Commonwealth Federation (fd. 1932–33). Down to the mid-1920s, 33 provincial and two federal members could be classified as socialists; by the mid-1930s, both communists and socialists had developed significant bases, enough to elect civic politicians and provincial and federal members.[7] In the 1930s a disproportionately large contingent of volunteers went off to fight for republican Spain. By the 1940s the "Canadian left" could boast an international and domestic strength. Dozens of left politicians – labourites, socialists, and even communists – had been elected, and in 1944 the first socialist government in North America was elected in Saskatchewan. The laggard had seemingly become, to a modest extent, a North American leader.

The puzzle, then, is how a Canadian political landscape seemingly lacking many socialists in 1914 came to be one teeming with them such a short time afterwards. Perhaps our Richter scale itself might be part of the problem. An exclusive focus on parties and organizations, votes, and elections can blind us to more deep-seated – or, as Gramsci would say, "organic" – elements of the situation. As historian Peter Campbell notes in his classic account of this period, the focus of early Canadian socialism was on "making socialists," that is, educating and training a cohort of activists who understood social science and could defend it against all comers.[8] Much of this effort took the form of winning converts in churches, unions, and reading circles, often among immigrant groups only loosely attached to formal Canadian politics. Many of the left's energies were invested not in electioneering – which itself was often interpreted not as a bid for parliamentary power but as a way of broadcasting the truth of the socialist enlightenment – but on education. What might have seemed a barren field when seen from the lofty heights of the International Socialist Bureau in Brussels, the Second International's headquarters, was actually teeming with ideas. What might seem like nothing from an institutional perspective – no governments, big parties, or even major thinkers – takes on a different aspect when we start to think of it in terms of *an emergent historical bloc*, a "party" in a much broader sense, within which economic class relations could be metabolized into political ideals, a vivid sense of shared history, and even an internationalist myth-symbol complex, complete with rival heroes, anthems, holidays, and hallowed texts.[9] A socialist historical bloc was emerging organically out of the complicated Canadian terrain – a process that would be only partly complete by 1920 – and, especially on the local level, was gradually exerting pressure on established elites – within the old parties, the business class, and even the craft unions. Although centred on the working class, this historical bloc was not confined to it: women, ethnic minorities, and religious radicals could all find their own voices, sometimes discordant with the rest of the left, but more often, through a unifying goal of the people's enlightenment, harmonized within it.

Even those labelled "impossibilists" were able to create a nucleus of opposition around which a much broader radical left could cohere after 1916. The unintentional paradox of revolutionary purism – that is, its *significance* rather than its *meaning* – was to help make a grounded revolutionary politics a postwar reality. Like so much of the formation in which they sometimes functioned as often awkward and divisive elements, the early socialist organizations had much more to offer – a entire substrate of the socialist enlightenment thought and activism – than was evident on the surface of their formal politics.

Democrats in a Liberal Order

The emergence of liberal order through which the Dominion of Canada acquired its key political institutions entailed an intricate mid-19th-century historic compromise between Tories and Reformers, a compromise that curbed the enthusiasms of both in the interests of a more stable and profitable political environment. Whether the emergent Dominion was "democratic" is a vexed question. Certainly "acceptance of public opinion and deliberative democracy" had come to seem conventional with respect to some issues. Yet the country remained a colony. Its constitution was never democratically approved, and in many liberal quarters the very word "democracy" designated a virus more than a virtue. Thus, when Canadian leftists hoisted the flag of "Democracy" into the mastheads of their publications of the 1890s, they were being deliberately provocative. In the context of a hierarchical and conservative liberal order – the "Liberal-Conservatives" ruled Canada for much of the latter 19th century, before being replaced by the quite conservative Liberals in 1896 – the word "democracy" was associated with American mob rule, and, after the revolutionary events of the Paris Commune of 1871, it also carried the overtones of an even more thorough-going social upheaval. When working-class men and women started talking about democracy, they were demanding a "capacity to judge" that Canadian liberal order was not predisposed to recognize.[10] Assessed even by the minimal standards usefully enumerated by Geoff Eley – "free, universal, secret, adult, and equal suffrage; the classic civil freedoms of speech, conscience, assembly, association, and the press; and freedom from arrest without trial" – the Canadian political system was only partially democratic, since it routinely denied the suffrage to women (as late as 1940) and to racialized minorities (as late as the 1960s).[11] It included many institutions, most notably the appointed Senate, whose very reason for existence was to curb the supposed excesses that might arise from a free and unfettered recognition of the people's "capacity to judge."

Canada was a slowly industrializing colonial backwater through much of the fourth quarter of the 19th century. Engels was hardly alone in finding it a somewhat unprepossessing and dilapidated place. The feudal French Canadians were "going to ruin" and the English Canadians were "also slow," with "much dilapidation" even in Toronto, in contrast to the "genuinely capitalist" United States.[12] Yet the "backwater" was, on closer inspection, more like a diverse archipelago of very different societies, some very "slow" and others as "fast" as any to be found in a global capitalist world-system.[13] Canadian liberal order was shaped in the middle years of the 19th century by a succession of intellectuals who sought to re-create in Canada the social and economic bases of a liberal order designed according to British or U.S. specifications. The socialist refusal, supersedure, and systematic critique of liberal order was no less North Atlantic in its genesis. In a real sense, the left in Canada was born transnational.

As in the United States and Great Britain, many thoughtful Canadian democrats of the 1880s – often in the labour movement or churches – were drawn to the comprehensive critique of capitalist social relations put forward by economist Henry George, outlined in his famous book *Progress and Poverty* (1880), one of the most widely circulated books on economics in world history. George's ideas were boiled down, and in many places partially adopted, under the heading of the "Single Tax." From Halifax to Victoria, and with particular vigour in Toronto and Winnipeg, "single taxers" could be found pressuring old political parties and new social reform movements to change tax regimes so that speculators would pay tax on the "unearned increment" they had received from speculating in land that, thanks to no particular skill on their part, had increased in value. Such was the single taxers' persistence in their crusade against "unearned wealth," historian Gene Homel observes, that they called to mind the joke "about the funeral at which the minister failed to appear. The undertaker requested an eloquent-looking fellow to speak, and the latter, confessing he didn't know the deceased, added that he thought it was his duty to use the occasion to defend the single tax."[14]

Goldwin Smith (1823–1910), the one-time Regius professor of history at Oxford who became, after resettling in Toronto, an anxious ideologue of Canadian liberalism (and inspiration and mentor to Mackenzie King) worried that single taxism menaced liberal order. Instead, it turned into a limited, single-issue campaign focused on tinkering with land taxes.[15] Still, Smith had a point. George was critical of the heavy costs, to both labour and capital, of private land ownership. To follow him rigorously was to reject, along the lines set out by that young Chartist sympathizer and radical firebrand Herbert Spencer, private ownership of land as an unreasonable infringement on the rights of citizens. Both labour and capital were unfairly burdened by the owners of land, who claimed exclusive rights over a natural phenomenon that – no less than air or water – was essential to all. What might now seem to have been a quibble over how urban lands should be taxed actually stemmed from a much more comprehensive critique of the emerging capitalist economy as a threat to individualism. As journalist S.T. Wood argued in 1898, George, working on the basis of economist David Ricardo's premises, became the most penetrating defender of a core liberal doctrine: freedom of contract. "He argued," said Wood, "with logic as irresistible as that of the Ricardo school, that there could be no such thing as freedom of contract unless all men were granted equal right of access to the planet on which they were sailing through space." Many would find in George, as Wood did, a "chain of reasoning" in which there was no "false link."[16] In Toronto an Anti-Poverty Society (1887) took up George's ideas and connected them to a broader campaign against social inequality.[17]

Those who refused poverty and suffering as inevitable parts of the social order often articulated them within a Georgeite political economy. They found in George's work a systematic way of understanding what they felt to be true – that both wealth and poverty were increasing exponentially all around them. Georgeism allowed them to articulate this problem within a system of concepts centred on the questions of landownership and speculation. In retrospect we can see that when capital became truly multinational, less firmly connected to any particular location, and more clearly distanced from the working class, this way of thinking was unlikely to retain its power. As historian Martin Robin suggests, "Single tax ideas and organizations prevailed among labour reformers at a time when the factory system and industrialism were not highly developed, and when land was still available to the urban artisans."[18] The single tax spoke eloquently to those who saw the central class struggle as pitting rentiers and speculators on the one hand against the "industrial classes" – including both manufacturers and workers – on the other. As David Stack points out, George had an additional theoretical significance: he accomplished a "subtle shift in the left critique" of capitalism – in essence shifting the basis of that critique away from timeless values rooted in an unchanging natural order towards a more secular and materialist argument building on the notion of human evolution.[19]

A diversity of 19th-century resistance movements in Canada had raised profound questions about capitalism. The 1870s rocked with massive and often violent strikes, in Londonderry, N.S., Saint John, N.B., the Cape Breton coalfields,[20] and Quebec, and the 1880s resounded with the far-reaching activism of militant local unions, the Knights of Labor, and the Provincial Workmen's Association. But Georgeite economics may well have provided the first intellectual bridge between such moments of refusal and the moments of supersedure in which they could be simultaneously honoured, critiqued, and (tentatively) transcended. One of the most exciting indications of this quiet revolution in working-class confidence came in the hearings of the Royal Commission on the Relations of Capital and Labour, convened in 1886 by the Liberal-Conservative government as a response to mounting pressure from labour movements (and, indirectly, a way of showcasing the achievements of the National Policy of tariff protection). Here, working-class Georgeites presented, to a noticeably hostile Commission, their alternative readings of the capitalist economy.[21]

George – whose own views were not really pro-labour – lectured in Toronto, Ottawa, and Montreal in 1881, and his admirers were widely distributed – from Toronto and Montreal to Listowel, Ont., and Amherst, N.S., for instance. From 1883 into the 1890s, the Trades and Labor Congress (TLC) passed Georgeite resolutions opposing land monopolization and favouring the imposition of a single tax; and the economist himself was greeted with a mass demonstration in fast-industrializing Hamilton, where he unveiled the single tax as a panacea for a monopoly-plagued society.[22] The single tax would gradually fade from radical view – though its partisans could still be found in some numbers down to the 1920s – but the biography of many a socialist included an apprenticeship in Georgeite economics.

The other intellectual godfather of the movement was Edward Bellamy, the renowned U.S. novelist and social reformer whose *Looking Backward* (1888) was a sensation of the North Atlantic world, selling some 200,000 copies during its first year in print in the United States, and perhaps 100,000 copies by early 1890 in England. The book was part of the great wave of utopian fiction in the *fin de siècle*, although readers today, in the good company of William Morris, might well find *Looking Backward* a "deadly dull" production.[23] The plot line follows the story of a Bostonian protagonist, the aristocratic and insomniac Julian West, who succumbs to the ministrations of a mesmerist and inadvertently falls asleep for over 100 years until awakened by one Dr. Leete. West then becomes tediously intertwined with the doctor's daughter. The tale is enlivened mainly by the quaintness of certain technological details of this imagined future, such as the orchestras that ply their violins 24 hours a day; every Bostonian, simply by pressing a button, can be connected to the chamber in which the music is produced.

Yet, dull though the story itself may have been, at the time many men and women experienced Bellamy's book as a revelation. As Matthew Beaumont suggests in his study of utopian fiction, they encountered in it a haunting vision of their own time, including an image of 19th-century Boston, a world of "rampant commercialism that amounts to a state of siege," with the mills and shops all engaged in a ruthless and interminable war with each other. The city was "symbolic of the crisis of civilization itself," both destroyer and deliverer – reducing individuals to "monadic fractions of the 'festering mass,'" but at the same time creating a new collective conscience.[24]

Here too was a temporal reconnaissance of the city of the future, described in exquisite, if at times numbing, detail: a system of production encompassing vast industrial armies (made up of conscripts between the ages of 21 and 44) that carry out the necessary labour of production and distribution; a "Nation" that has become a giant trust, and that scientifically manages the entire social order; and a society of ease and abundance, without useless labour, with all the good things of life available via free and easy credit. As the good doctor tells Julian West, "the solidarity of the race and the brotherhood of man, which to you were but fine phrases, are, to our thinking and feeling, ties as real and as vital as physical fraternity." *Society had evolved.*[25]

As Morris pointed out in his critique of Bellamy, the whole book was saturated with a sense of contentment with modern civilization, "if only the injustice, misery, and waste of class society could be got rid of" – as though these could be simply snipped off, leaving Western civilization much as it already was.[26] Stephen Leacock, a repentant ex-Bellamyite himself, would describe this "Socialism" (incidentally a word that *Looking Backward* never uses) as "a bubble floating in the air. In the light of its opalescent colours we may see many visions of what we might be if we were better than we are, we may learn much that is useful as to what we can be even as we are."[27] To a 21st-century reader this "bubble" is reminiscent of the distant paradises summoned forth by the tourism industry, especially resorts offering unlimited refreshment, free entertainment, and other manifestations of centrally planned bliss, all available, at least to those who can pay the admission price, on easy credit. It is a vision that was particularly appealing to middle-class people who, although genuinely troubled by the wretchedness of the city, did not find capitalism spiritually impoverishing. They wanted, in the deepest sense, not its abolition but its perfection – a state capitalism in which the nation did collectively all the things that the trusts were doing, only more efficiently and fairly. To some 20th-century critics Bellamy's middle-class utopia seemed like an anticipation of the worst excesses of authoritarian socialism, with its omniscient expert-run state and its hierarchical industrial armies.[28] Even in the book's own day Laurence Gronlund was denouncing Bellamy's pro-militarism as "unsocialistic." The thriving progressive intellectual circle around the Unitarian Church in Halifax, although once rather enthralled by Bellamy, heard a similar critique of *Looking Backward* and his later work *Equality* in 1898. The discussion included an interesting attack on the "drabness" of Bellamy's utopian vision.[29]

Yet, as was the case with George, Bellamy's halfway analysis set many critical minds going in Canada. Bellamyites in Canada, as in the United States, flocked for a time to "Nationalist Clubs" – not as "nationalists" in a contemporary sense, but because they identified with the utopian "Nation" that Dr. Leete had so convincingly described. W.A. Pritchard (1889–1981), perhaps the greatest of the first formation's Marxist intellectuals – his theoretical reflections in the *Western Clarion* and *Red Flag* can be compared without puffery to those running in the *International Socialist Review* – would even write a foreword to the Canadian edition of *Looking Backward* in 1934. Pritchard hailed a book that "probably had a wider sale and exerted greater influence than any other book published in America." Bellamy, wrote Pritchard, perhaps with half an eye on Leacock's critique, had been made the "butt of that ridicule which Tory minds in all ages launch against prophet, dreamer, and the man with a new idea."[30]

"The Parable of the Water Tank," drawn from Bellamy's *Equality* (1897), was one of the most successful popularizations of this "new idea." Indeed, the story was circulated throughout the Dominion in tens of thousands of copies under the auspices of the fledgling Canadian Socialist League.[31] In this "Parable," Bellamy describes a simple capitalist economy with one principal industry, the collection and storage of water. The workers are paid a penny for every bucket of water they bring to the market; but they have to pay two pennies to buy back water for their own use. The workers obviously cannot afford to buy back the water they carry to the tank, and consequently it overflows. The workers are then laid off, and the community remains in an economic crisis until the water tank is at last emptied by its improvident and foolish owners. Depressions occur because people are not paid enough to buy the goods they produce. The upshot is a crazy world with an endemic waste of scarce resources, a growing gap between the wealthy and the poor, and a mounting sense of political crisis and injustice. Although Bellamy's "Parable," with its focus on distribution and consumption, is a far cry from the orthodox Marxist analysis of surplus value, in a more general sense it nonetheless gave radicals a practical picture of a profoundly irrational and crisis-prone capitalist system enmeshed in contradictions.

Contemporaries read Bellamy as someone who had held up to his own society a mirror capturing its most negative and controversial features. John A. Cooper would argue in *The Canadian Magazine* in August 1897 that Bellamy had usefully warned the "middle-class Canadians who are the backbone of our country" that a society divided between monopolies and workers was headed for trouble.[32] Right down to the 1940s, many socialists would include Bellamy along with Spencer in the narratives they so often constructed on the theme, "Why I Became A Socialist."

Other influences of the time arose from the country's own stormy past. By the 1880s, despite the islands of industrial modernity that the National Policy had helped to create, Canada was lagging far behind both the United States and Britain. The left of the Liberal Party, for whom William Gladstone was a veritable saint, often also expressed heartfelt admiration for the freedom and democracy of the Americans. They articulated a "popular liberalism" that posed the "masses" against the "classes," the free traders against the protectionists, the down-to-earth Grits against the pampered Tories. Although such working-class and democratic liberals had to look past compellingly adverse evidence, such as the impressive webs of patronage and privilege that the Liberals were themselves evolving on the provincial level, they rose to the ideological challenge. Many a Marxian socialist of 1901–14 began political life as a Laurier Liberal, and many a Laurier Liberal, not excepting future prime minister Mackenzie King, would listen raptly (if only for a short period) to the siren sounds of the socialists.[33] It was only after the Liberals came to power federally in 1896, and undermined much of what remained of their populist critique of protectionism and the National Policy, that we see the rise, to their left, of somewhat influential socialist movements that could capitalize on the acute disillusionment of many rank and file Gladstonians.

An additional line of demarcation between mainstream liberals and radicals could be found in the imperial connection itself. Revulsion against the vestiges of British aristocratic privilege rose like a massive wave from 1900 to 1917. *The Palladium of Labor*, a publication associated with the Knights of Labor, anticipated this radical sentiment in the 1880s: "No more military tomfoolery, vice-regal trips at public expense, usher-of-the-Black-Rod nonsense, court costumes or fur and feathers generally. The business of the country is to be done in a common-sense, democratic fashion."[34] Many aspects of Canadian life, from quasi-official churches to property qualifications for elected and non-elected offices, were blatantly elitist and old-fashioned – in a country increasingly tied economically and culturally to the ostensibly democratic and ultra-modern United States.

Across Canada in the 1880s workers initiated dozens of experiments in autonomous political organization, among them the Workingmen's Political Club of Cape Breton, People's Political Party of Kingston, Hamilton Labor Political Association, London Workingmen's Association, and Workingmen's Party on Vancouver Island.[35] Of particular long-term significance was the democratic revolution in British Columbia. In November 1886, two Vancouver Knights of Labor assemblies issued a joint manifesto for the approaching municipal elections, and a "Working Man's Party" in the B.C. provincial election of that year put forward candidates in Victoria and Nanaimo.[36] In Nova Scotia the coal miners' Provincial Workmen's Association, the largest union in Nova Scotia, put forward candidates in 1887 to challenge the reigning Liberals (with the unexpected outcome of elevating their leader, Robert Drummond, to the unelected Legislative Council of the province).[37] Many working-class people were now arguing for their own "capacity to judge." If many of these workers still found their place in a Liberal party that they persisted in idealizing, others were turning to "mixed" liberal-labour alternatives, and still others were poised to make a more radical socialist break with the existing system.

The Radical Journalist

At the CSL's November 1901 convention, the man who best exemplified this long complicated history of local and international activism was the dapper 58-year-old Thomas Phillips Thompson (1843–1933). Born in Newcastle-on-Tyne, Thompson had a journalistic career in Toronto that stretched back to 1867, when he began work as a police court reporter. He served from 1874 to 1876 as editor of *The National*, a weekly newspaper designed to promote the views of the Canada First Movement. Then he spent three years working in Boston as literary editor of the *Evening Traveler*. As Pierre Berton, his grandson, noted, Thompson's turning point came when he was sent as special correspondent to Ireland by the Toronto *Globe* to cover struggles over the land question. His dispatches were reprinted in an extra edition, and he was "tendered a public banquet and lionized in the press." It was as a result of this Irish experience, Berton suggests, that this self-taught man became a radical.[38] A visceral rejection of British hierarchy and colonialism would not be an unusual moment of epiphany for Canadian leftists, although in the 1880s there was not much of a coherent "left" within which Thompson could articulate and develop this moment of refusal.

In 1883 E.E. Sheppard acquired the Toronto *News* and recruited Thompson from the *Globe* to become his assistant editor and chief editorial writer. As historian Russell Hann reveals, Sheppard was committing himself to making the daily newspaper into a force for "Democracy," by which he meant "the extension of the elective principle into all areas of public life."[39] Sheppard put his formula of "simple democracy and common sense" to the electoral test as an independent labour candidate in West Toronto in 1887, losing by a close vote of 3,891 to 3,334. In this early left, "democracy" was emphatically *not* to be confused with "socialism, nihilism, or annexationism" – the first kept alive by the memories of the heroic Paris Commune in 1871, the second by more contemporary struggles for democracy in Russia, and the third by the quite popular agitation to have Canada join the United States.

In part the noble exponent of the people's democratic emancipation, the *News* was also devoted to stirring the pot of scandal and sensation – a not uncommon admixture of the day. The two could be combined in provocative attacks on the "upper tenth," with their odious airs of superiority; on the English who paraded through Canada with bogus titles; and on the foppish idlers at Kingston's Royal Military College, whose "scarlet-coated and epauletted loaferism" was made possible only by exploitation of the "hardworking people of Canada." It was a suggestive vocabulary of outrage, drawing upon the venerable notion, as much associated with John Locke as with Karl Marx, that labour was the source of all true value. As Hann astutely suggests, the *News* was primarily concerned "with the fostering of a new kind of opposition to the basic political, social, and cultural assumptions of late 19th century Canadian society."[40]

Thompson was in the democratic forefront of this somewhat hazily defined oppositional politics. By discreetly combining two ventures – the *News* and a weekly column in the *Palladium of Labor* – Thompson functioned inside and outside the conventions of mainstream journalism. Like many other self-taught leftists of the day, Thompson found in the newspaper world a way of combining social radicalism with economic survival. He was able, in his labour journalism, to denounce as platitudinous and banal the very self-help "vernacular liberalism" (exemplified by such popular writers as Samuel Smiles and Horatio Alger) that a newspaper like the Toronto *News* upheld in its columns. Thompson also brought his critical sensibility to the Knights of Labor. He was a driving force in the Victor Hugo Assembly, organized for "brainworkers" and named after the French writer who epitomized a democratic resistance against the exactions of the rich. When the Royal Commission on the Relations of Capital and Labour of the mid-1880s came to town, Thompson was prominent among the Torontonians who made the case for George's single tax.[41]

Thompson was in a good position to make such Georgeite arguments, because the economist had become his friend and mentor in the mid-1880s. In 1887, with George's assistance, Thompson brought out *The Politics of Labor*, an eloquent defence of a working-class democracy. It enacted a long refusal of liberal political economy rather more than it suggested a coherent alternative to it. So disgusted was Thompson with the party machines running much of the United States that he urged true democrats to spoil their ballots by writing "Labor Reformer" on them. That way, they would demonstrate the pointlessness of casting a vote for one or the other of the corrupt current parties.[42] Both parties were distant from the most urgent questions, raised by George, relating to the obsolete privileges associated with land. With "labour organization on a greater scale, and the growing determination to use the ballot as a remedy for social abuses," the political power of the masses was ready to sweep away dysfunctional distinctions.

Thompson's emphatic book, pitched to an American more than a Canadian audience, was one long call for "power to the people." Labour, "in working out its own emancipation, will regenerate the world." Hesitant about committing himself fully to a socialist vision, indeed honestly in doubt about what the expression meant, and seized by the horrific repression associated with the Paris Commune, Thompson in 1887 was much closer to the ideas of George than he was to Marx, quoted but once (and that briefly) in his book. Thompson was a man who knew what he refused, but was less certain about what he could affirm. He explicitly drew attention to the absence of a theoretical vocabulary that could fully capture the idea of how the few had monopolized the earth's resources and forced the many to compete with each other for the means of livelihood. "There is no word in the language which will answer," he exclaimed. "Exploitation" he rejected as too general. "Capitalism" he knew, but only as an epithet. Like Duncan's murder in *Macbeth*, the "social crime" that condemned so many to poverty was, he remarked, "a deed without a name."[43]

Thompson would continue to be the ardent democrat, the enemy of class distinctions, the champion of the "simple citizen." He may well have had himself in mind when he later described the single taxers as preachers of "Unitarianism." They broke ground for heretics departing from the orthodox religion of liberal political economy, without giving them more than a half-solution to their most burning questions.

Yet in *The Politics of Labor* Thompson was plainly steering towards Spencerian evolution as a way of systematizing his moment of supersedure, and in a way that went far beyond his witty deconstruction of Spencer's ultra-individualistic political economy. When Thompson wrote, "Evolution is not a blind, inexorable force," and that it was working through the increasing aggregation of social units, he was echoing Spencer's evolutionary law. Often in this text he quoted Spencer directly. He brought Spencer forward specifically at exactly those decisive moments in the text when he sought to go beyond the refusal of the injustices of the present day to reach for a systematic understanding of their origins and remedies.[44]

Thompson, like leftists worldwide, was inspired by Spencer's vision of inevitable social evolution and his firm defence of the possibility of a people's enlightenment uncontrolled by the existing religious and political hierarchies. Left Spencerians endorsed this evolutionary philosophy. They critiqued Spencer's perverse unwillingness to see that society's evolution led directly to socialism. If society was a complicated organism, it surely required a brain – and that could be nothing other than the educated working class in a reformed democratic state. For left Spencerians, this merely meant that the Master Sociologist himself was being overtaken by the processes of social evolution that he, more than anybody else, had illuminated.

If *The Politics of Labor* suggests a "Labour Reformer" refusing the blatant irrationalities of capitalism, but not knowing quite where to go after that, a subsequent manuscript of 1888 reveals Thompson's further struggle with this dilemma. It seemed to Thompson that "All roads lead to Rome" – that is, that all the discussions of his time led back to the challenge of labour reform and the quest to right the imbalance of classes in society. "Temperance, religious, educational reformers all find their attempts to doctor the symptoms futile so long as the root remains untouched."[45] But how to grasp them? Thompson refers to the teachings of Spencer in *Sociology*, especially those regarding the "Internuncial System" – the railways, telegraphs, and the rest of the system through which society was both co-ordinated and subordinated to common purposes. In developing this analogy between nature and society, Spencer was in effect undermining his own fierce individualism, almost tending (said Thompson perceptively) to an anarchist position against all "governmentalism." Yet governments themselves were "but the products of Evolution – not imposed on the people but emanating from them. Governments in countries such as England, U.S., & France, based on extended suffrage, fairly represent the average intelligence, honesty & justice of the people." As he wrote these words in the late 1880s, Thompson had clearly come to believe that George and the land reformers, whom he had defended so stoutly before the Royal Commission a few years before, really offered no profound solution to the problems besetting modern industrial society. Even if rent was abolished, the "mass of people would still be enslaved by capital."[46] Thompson was nearing a turning point into an alternative system of concepts.

After announcing his conversion to the socialism of Bellamy in December 1890, Thompson went on to become chairman of the Municipal Committee of the Bellamyite Toronto Nationalist Club, which became active in 1891.[47] Perhaps Thompson's greatest contributions to the Canadian left were his writings in Toronto's *Labor Advocate*, a weekly he founded. The *Advocate* cannot be counted an outright success. It lasted less than a year and reached only a few people, and just a handful of institutions – the Toronto Builders' Laborers' Union No. 2, the Bricklayers' Union No. 2, the Cigar Makers' International Union, and the Knights of Labor hand laundry – offered tangible support in the way of advertisements. Yet his *Labor Advocate* writings secure his position as one of the great founding figures of the Canadian socialist movement.[48]

In the 13 March 1891 *Labor Advocate*, Thompson, once the defender of orthodox liberal political economy, now argued in the language of a new theory. "Capitalism," he said, "is the power by which labor is robbed of the greater portion of its earnings." *The Politics of Labor* and his earlier journalism had revealed an assumption that capital and labour might fairly and democratically arbitrate their differences. Now the *Labor Advocate* was arguing for the essential and irreconcilable conflict between the interests of capitalists and wage-workers. The wealth of the capitalists was pumped from the labour of the workers.[49]

Much of the logic of the new position appeared in discussions of trusts and monopolies. What Georgeites lamented – the growing consolidation and centralization of capital – the Bellamyites hailed as the first sign of a better-organized society. Dr. Leete's world had depended, after all, on one giant trust called "The Nation." Why shed tears for the little businesses swallowed up in the process through which this advanced social organism had evolved, in much the way Spencer had predicted? Why, Thompson asked, devote time and energy to trust-busting, when the trusts, as they became more and more all-powerful, would raise prices, lower wages, and extort vast profits from the public – all of which would have an educative effect on the public and hasten the day when the people would decide to exterminate capitalism altogether? This eminently Bellamyite argument would prove to have great staying power right down to the 1940s.[50]

So, like many radicals of his generation, Thompson graduated from George to Bellamy and Spencer. Was he a Marxist in the 1890s? Only in a few left circles did this very new concept of being a Marxist forcibly set one apart from those who reasoned their socialism on biological and evolutionary grounds.[51] Given that Darwinism and Marxism tended to be inextricably linked in the *fin de siècle*, a host of the socialist movement's most powerful leaders were arguing forcefully for a socialist Darwinism. The evidence suggests that in the 1890s Thompson was only partway towards adopting the triune formula – historical materialism, economic determinism and the labour theory of value, and class struggle. For instance, he accepted without any qualms Bellamy's water tank parable, which he termed "perhaps the clearest and most convincing exposition in popular language of the economic absurdity and wastefulness of the profit-mongering system ever published" – whereas someone immersed in Marx's *Capital*, only just becoming generally available in North America, would most likely have worked to distinguish Marx's scientific analysis of production from Bellamy's focus on distribution. His analysis of the "predatory classes of Britain, the United States, Germany and other great countries" and their relentless pursuit of foreign markets has a more Marxist ring: "Wars of conquest are the logical and necessary consequence of the profit-mongering system. When labor is organized on the basis of mutual service, instead of individual profit, the great incentive to war will be done away with."[52]

In some sentimental narratives, Thompson is the Grand Old Man of Canadian Socialism. His photograph suggests a white-haired genial philosopher. His reputation as the humorist "Jimuel Briggs," his salty style, and his moral earnestness all seemingly stamp him as a 19th-century utopian. Compared to the supposed ranters of British Columbia, he is the "nice" Ontario socialist – a radical one might bring home to meet Mom and Dad.[53] "It is hard to understand now why so much calumny was heaped on the head of this earnest and selfless man. So many of his causes seem mild enough to us today," Berton remarked, mentioning the Toronto *Star*'s obituary of this "always soft-spoken and sincere man," who was "on the side of lost causes."[54] He was simply one more beautiful dreamer, we are invited to think, unappreciated by the world around him.

Thompson's own contemporaries sensed something more rigorous and more revolutionary within the man. His growing reputation for intellectual acuity and moral stature was reflected in a 1895 Toronto *World* reflection on

Thompson's transformation from humorist to socialist. There had come a time in his life, the *World* remarked, when Thompson, earlier noted for his fine humour, had not known "whether to laugh or cry over human affairs." Some said that Thompson believed that the "human being belongs to the state," and others described him as "a cross between Malthus and Bellamy." It would be up to a future historian to assign him his "proper location in the historical firmament."[55]

This long-awaited future historian might well want to ponder complications in the received wisdom about Thompson. He became, in many respects, as unflinching a revolutionary intransigent as any of the more flamboyant B.C. "impossibilists." In a critique of Bellamy, for example, he spent no time enjoying the futuristic fantasy of Boston in the year 2000, and focused rather on Bellamy as the structural critic of capitalist economics. Like others in the spc, to which he ultimately gravitated, Thompson treated the question of public ownership with a stern realism. Public ownership was not socialism. It was not necessarily even close to socialism. It represented the extent to which liberal capitalist governments shirked the work that they should have undertaken in the public interest. Through franchises, contracts, and special privileges, governments handed the economy over to outsiders who bet against each other for the privilege of "despoiling the public." In December 1899 Thompson intervened, from an "anti-imperialist direction," to denounce jingoism, the Boer War, and any truck or trade with imperialism.[56]

By the early 20th century Thompson had learned many things about the left. He retained from George a strong sense in the necessary progress of social evolution. He kept from Bellamy an idea of the irrationality of the capitalist system. If some of the Bellamyites of the 1890s were probably middle-class folk temporarily drawn by the allure of utopia, the "moment of Bellamy" involved getting longer-haul radicals to think structurally and functionally about the social order. Well down into the 1940s, it was *this* Bellamy, the "water tower" Bellamy, who appealed most to Canadians. Drawing on the social-evolutionary insights of the religious writer Benjamin Kidd, who in turn was dependent, almost to the point of indelicacy, upon the works of Spencer, Thompson became intensely interested in reconciling the ideal of the "free development of individuality" with the achievement of socialism. The first and most famous of the Canadian Bellamyites, Thompson was perhaps less a "fading beam of the 19th century" than a glowing "beacon" of the first formation intransigence that was to become so significant in the 20th.[57] Within the csl and its successor organizations Thompson would be a consistent hard leftist. Although he was undoubtedly a kind and generous soul, he was also a convinced enemy of capitalism, a critic of the liberal order that perpetuated it, and ultimately a zealous advocate of the pure and hard "no compromise, no political trading" philosophy of the Socialist Party of Canada.

The Martyr from Montreal

If we imagine the 70 people or so milling about Victoria Hall, before the beginning of the meeting, we might speculate that around the grandfatherly white-haired Thompson a few old Toronto comrades would have paused to pay him homage. We might also imagine a much younger gentleman, with brown hair and the beginnings of a bristling little moustache, on the fringes of the crowd, a young man from the provinces who had been invited to the meeting as a representative of the Socialist League of Montreal.

Colin McKay (1876–1939) was 33 years younger than Thompson. In the 1890s he had been a wet-behind-the-ears Christian, attracted by the Liberal Party, moral reform, and the trade unionism of the American Federation of Labor. Born in Shelburne, on the South Shore of Nova Scotia, McKay had spent his childhood in and around his family's small shipyard. At 15 he had "followed the sea," which he would continue to combine with other jobs down to 1914. He had sailed on U.S. vessels on which the "scuppers ran red" with the blood of merchant seamen. He had seen sailors brought to "the verge of cannibalism." McKay spent many winters between voyages in Montreal, where he garnered a reputation as a leading anglophone labour journalist – the writer you went to if you were after a story about municipal corruption, sweatshop conditions, or the relationship of workers with the Church.

He combined small-town naiveté with a truly cosmopolitan experience of the seafaring world. He often wrote about Montreal as a troubling metropolis, one whose anonymity and indifference assaulted his low-church Anglican sense of right and wrong. For McKay, Montreal – with its anonymous streets, dank factories, secretive sweatshops – was the face of a new capitalism. These capitalists reminded McKay of murderous sea captains he had met, but they were even worse. If at least the actual seafaring captains were bound by a rough and ready code of honour, the land-based captains of industry were governed only by their own crude selfishness. A sea captain who ran his ship aground would be fired. A captain of industry whose acts helped run the economy aground suffered no such indignity. These capitalists could drive their workers harder and harder, and fight with each other mercilessly to dominate conglomerates, amalgamations, consortia. They often watered their stock, selling shares to investors at prices grossly in excess of their actual value. Such capitalists could draw on the increasingly combined strength of the banks. To McKay they seemed a shockingly new breed of humanity.[58]

Exposing their misdeeds became his passion. Sweatshops, which McKay investigated in Montreal at about the same time as Mackenzie King was undertaking similar research in Toronto, could be seen in isolation as examples of human cruelty and suffering. To understand why workers were putting in 12 to 14 hours a day in clammy, unregulated, ill-ventilated workshops and garrets, you had to grasp the urban and rural economies that made such wage labour possible. Appearances were deceptive because they distracted from underlying connections. To understand these connections meant struggling to change them – such as organizing unions for the workers and designing union labels to distinguish clothes made under reasonable conditions from those made in sweatshops. At the turn of the century the AFL was energizing many Canadian working people, especially those in skilled urban trades, with an impressive organizing drive. McKay, an ardent trade union man, was in the thick of it. He was a keen and capable union organizer. "In Montreal during the past three or four years the labor movement has made the most remarkable progress," McKay wrote. "The great interest that International trades union officials have recently manifested in matters here is a striking testimony to the development and possibilities of the movement in Montreal."[59] McKay worked directly for some of the unions. Garment Workers' Union No. 140 asked him to take on an inquiry into sweatshops in 1899. The Wholesale Cutters asked for his expertise on the union label.

In short, Colin McKay was a crusader. As the Montreal *Herald*'s law-shy editor remarked to Deputy Minister of Labour Mackenzie King, McKay was "not a man that we can make much use of on a paper like the Herald." He was so devoted to the cause of the labouring class "that on occasion he is something of a crank."[60] Like countless other leftists of that day and later, he became quite familiar with the sights and sounds of jail cells. Never one to turn down an opportunity for on the spot social commentary, he provided a blow by blow account of one visit to jail and then concluded, with the period's trademark sociological earnestness, that its harsh conditions (terrible food, surly guards, filthy bedding) fit within the overall irrationality of crime and punishment in capitalist society: "A doctor would not be content with merely plastering a running sore, while his patient's system was full of bad blood. The law – which occupies the position of social doctor – should treat social disease scientifically."[61] McKay had already started reading Herbert Spencer.

He was, even more than Phillips Thompson, the archetypal working-class autodidact, driving himself with a Jack London intensity to master as much sociology, philosophy, and political economy as he could. At this stage he was greatly influenced by Grant Allen, whose novels especially seemed to appeal to him. Whether in the Economic Association of Montreal, over which he sometimes presided, or in the informal socialist networks of Point St. Charles, which organized frequent picnics and brought in visiting speakers, McKay was anchored by his stalwart belief in evolutionary theory, both as a guide to abstract principles and as the key to advancing the cause of the workers. Ultimately his path through life would lead him to the philosophies of Hegel and Dietzgen; to Marx's labour theory of value; to the rival strategies of craft and industrial unionists for organizing the workers. Yet every step along that path was consistent with an underlying theory that held that all reform, all progress, and all "socialism" entailed the development of a rigorous science of social evolution.

In addition to his immersion in turn of the century social science, McKay was also deeply moved by the writings of the social gospel, that movement within Protestant Christianity to ground the teachings of Christ in the world of everyday life. He was a proponent of the religious left, a significant force in his native South Shore of Nova Scotia.[62] In his adopted city of Montreal, reform-minded clergymen frequented the Pleasant Sunday Afternoon Society of Point St. Charles, a more iconoclastic group than its name implied. The well-known U.S. reverend Herbert N. Casson, M.A., spoke in both 1896 and 1897, and was said to have won large numbers to the cause of Christian socialism. A Montreal *Herald* report, filed in all likelihood by McKay, remarked that Casson had conclusively demonstrated that "man was but a fraction of the great union of humanity; that there was the strictest interdependence between all men in all the ages." It was also probably McKay who filed a report from a meeting of the Philosophical Society, where Roswell Fisher had explained that socialism, a doctrine evolved from the most ancient religions, found a niche in the ethics of Christ, and had then received fresh Enlightenment energy from a pantheon of thinkers from Voltaire to Marx.[63] McKay himself took his religion seriously enough to dispute the infallibility of the Bible.[64]

McKay was particularly taken with the teachings of the charismatic Rev. William Thurston Brown of Rochester, N.Y., whose books *The Real Religion of Today*, *The Relation of Religion to Social Ethics*, and *After Capitalism, What?* had all been published by Charles H. Kerr. "No drop of water in the river can separate itself from the rest," Brown would proclaim to his congregation. "It cannot have a separate existence. It is a part of the stream. It is the stream that is the unit, not the drop." The implication of this image and of Brown's overall theology was that the "individual" at liberalism's conceptual core was a kind of fiction. "No individual in this vast stream of humanity can isolate himself from the rest and say that he stands alone, that he owes nothing to the mass," Brown argued. "Human life, find it where you will, but especially in the midst of civilization, is one vast tissue of relationship and interdependence. . . . The destiny of one depends upon the destiny of all."[65]

Derived from Spencer and a host of socially minded Protestant thinkers, McKay's leftism c.1901 was of a more recent vintage than Thompson's. The younger McKay was far more attached to orthodox Christian teaching and to philosophical idealism. For him, the distinctive character of socialism, as of Christianity, was that it defined and placed "duties before rights." You could not, McKay said, consciously paraphrasing Immanuel Kant, derive "ought" from "is." The laws of science could not, ultimately, yield the new ethics that the world was crying out for. Socialism could not be materialistic, nor could it ultimately be strictly scientific. It was based on "moral intuitions, rather than natural principles." These intuitions were, in essence, assumptions that were like the "fundamental axioms of Christianity, namely, the current conceptions of eternal justice, absolute, transcendental moral law, and the immortality of the soul." Socialism was, above all, more an ethical system than an economic system. The labour movement itself could be seen as an effort to rehabilitate Christian ethics in political and social systems – which was why it was pitted against institutional "churchianity," which had reduced the radical message of Christ to a meaningless rote and ritual.[66] All of these sentiments suggested a first formationist who was not yet in agreement with the Marxist sense that socialism was immanent in capitalist social relations, that it was growing in the interstices of the system itself.

A Christian socialist like McKay was repulsed by the Socialist Labor Party, which had come across the border into Canada from the United States in 1894.[67] The SLP did not share McKay's gentle vision of a socialism that meant living by the Golden Rule and carrying out Kant's categorical imperative. When McKay dropped by a Montreal meeting of the SLP in 1899 at St. Joseph's Hall on Ste-Catherine Street, he found a tiny, shouting group obsessed with military tactics. The SLP's splitting tactics had already sparked many anguished debates in the labour council, and, McKay observed acerbically, the council had not "waxed stronger for it." The SLP, in his interpretation, was hampered by its lack of local roots, but more significantly by its philosophy of materialism, which amounted to a "repudiation of the only tenable basis for a socialistic system of society," which was a new system of morality.[68] The next year McKay could be found writing poems in honour of Liberal prime minister Wilfrid Laurier.

Despite this lapse in judgment, McKay brought an impressive resumé of labour struggle to the CSL convention in Toronto, and one episode in particular may explain why he was invited as a special guest. McKay had confronted J.M. Fortier, a notorious Montreal employer, and gone to jail, once again, because of it. In some ways Fortier was a Montreal success story – as the proprietor of a cigar factory, he had managed to make money in a trade fast becoming tightly integrated into a global marketplace. Some of his employees looked to him as a father. His 275 workers in the late 1880s included 75 small boys and girls – a few of the many children who supplied much of the labour-power that made Canada's industrialization possible.[69]

Also among Fortier's workers in the 1880s were 14 union cigar-makers who were part of a craft tradition dating back to the 1860s. Some of these very workers had demanded a royal commission to look into labour conditions, which the federal Conservative government – anxious to win support from labour and to document the fast-growing economy it had created through the National Policy – set up as the first substantial federal royal commission in

Canadian history. So it was that in 1888 the Royal Commission on the Relations of Labour and Capital had the privilege of being addressed by Fortier. It emerged from his testimony that the factory owner maintained an unheated room in his basement, which he used for coal storage. He also used this dark room as a detention room for his child employees. If a child employee "lost time" – for some reason not producing at the prescribed rate – he or she would be locked in this "black hole," and left there, perhaps for many hours, until the factory closed. Other workers were beaten over the head if they were not sufficiently diligent in their labour. "Was it a general rule to beat apprentices?" one royal commissioner asked. "Not precisely," was Fortier's answer. "But whenever there was a chance, they made use of it."

"What do you mean by a 'chance'? Did that child do any act that deserved such punishment?" asked the Commission. Fortier's reply: "If a child did anything, that is, if he looked on one side or other, or spoke, he [the superintendent] would say I'm going to make you pay 10 cents fine, and if the same were repeated three or four times, he would seize a stick or a plank, and beat him with it."

Fortier had himself beaten children with an implement called a "mould cover." The child labourers were not, it is true, quite beaten senseless. Some reported that they felt the effects of being hit on the head through much of the rest of the day. Fortier would argue that his employees were actually grateful that they had been disciplined in this manner. Curiously, not one of them offered up this opinion when asked by the Commission, even with Fortier and other employers sitting in the audience.[70]

Canada as a liberal order safeguarded freedom of speech on questions such as tariff reform and the virtues of the Liberal-Conservatives over the Liberals. It did not provide much protection for a worker who was angry about low wages and capitalist child abuse. Within this liberal order, a man of substance like Fortier could even call upon the police department to arrest workers who were absent from work. Those who were sick with no doctor's certificate were merely fined. When Montreal's deputy chief of police was asked whether or not he approved of such goings-on in Fortier's factory, the policeman expressed the classical liberal view that such issues really came down to "internal" matters. Within the four walls of his factory, according to many turn of the century liberal minds, an employer could do pretty much what he wanted to do. Fortier was within his rights to discipline his workplace family, just as a Victorian patriarch was perfectly justified to inflict corporal punishment on his children.

In the late 1890s Fortier was in the news again. This time the cigar manufacturer had discharged a number of employees, then rehired some of them selectively, taking care to avoid bringing back those suspected of being trade union leaders. This was, of course, his perfect right, as an individual running a private business. He added insult to injury, from the trade unionists' point of view, by presenting each of his rehired, loyal workers with a Christmas turkey. It was a situation custom-made for a first formation firebrand. In stepped Colin McKay.

McKay wrote an impassioned critique of Fortier's approach to labour relations in a radical broadsheet publication that flaunted its challenge to liberalism by its very title: *Canada's Democracy* – once again employing that fighting word of the left. McKay did not mince words. Borrowing some choice phrases from his beloved Rev. Brown, McKay called Fortier a "moral dynamiter" and an "industrial copperhead." McKay condemned employers like Fortier, who refused to negotiate with his employees, defied democracy on the basis of his "divine rights," and refused to recognize the interests or rights "of those who invest their stock in trade, their labour, in their businesses." They were, he argued, "dangerous obstructionists," bosses who "create dissension, excite passion, and misrepresent the attitudes of the generality of employers." As McKay's parallel to "dynamiters" was intended to suggest, such crass businessmen were the equivalent of bomb-throwing anarchists who, throughout Russia and Southern Europe, were blowing up heads of state and, closer to home, were soon to be blamed for the assassination of a U.S. president. The parasitical, monstrous Fortier had grown fat on the bodies of his often underaged and underpaid workers. McKay even attacked the gesture of giving out Christmas turkeys. Were the turkeys really such generous gifts if Fortier was paying a lower wage than were other cigar manufacturers, and could thus afford to give every employee several dozen Christmas turkeys, not just one?

Perhaps understandably chagrined at being simultaneously cast as a cannibal and a terrorist, Fortier sued McKay for defamatory libel. Opening 15 September 1899, the trial in the Court of Queen's Bench provided a glimpse into the strange world of turn of the century liberal law. Defamatory libel, the judge explained, consisted of a statement published without justification or excuse, and "of such a nature to injure someone by exposing him to the hatred or ridicule of the public. Thus it was that the peace of the land was endangered by such publications, as men's passions were thereby aroused and crimes were committed." Now, a newspaper could moderately criticize the law of the land. Truthful criticisms might be in the public interest. This loophole did not protect labour journalists. They spoke merely for a "small body of citizens, forming a class." Even if workers had some rights to combine, "personal liberty should not be lost sight of." Of course any employee, as an individual, could refuse to work. Equally, any individual could freely decide to take his or her place. Attempts to change this perfect freedom in the labour market were (on this orthodox reading of classical liberal theory) infringements on the rights of the individual. They would constitute "a great abuse of personal liberty," pronounced the judge. Thus, only *if* the charges were true, and *if* they were made in the general *public* (and not the working-class) interest, could the defendant be found innocent.

It became, in part, a question of whether McKay, in calling Fortier a "moral dynamiter," a person who had grown rich on the flesh and blood of his workers, and an "industrial copperhead," had been writing the literal truth. Had Fortier in fact been seen with dynamite? Was he in fact a dynamiter – which the judge translated into French as "assassin"? If these and other allegations were not accurate, the jury had no choice but to return a verdict of guilty against McKay. And, even if Fortier had been captured – perhaps in one of the newfangled newspaper photographs just starting to become popular in the daily press – personally feasting upon the body and blood of his workmen, there would still be another barrier to McKay's acquittal. Not many people had actually bought *Canada's Democracy*. Indeed, the newspaper had been, in some cases, distributed free of charge. Was it then really operating on behalf of the general public? Or was it published in the interests of a small group of citizens?

Operating outside the liberal market, McKay had been *forcing* upon the public a paper that they would not willingly patronize. The crusading journalist could not pretend to speak for "the public," but only one small part of it, one "class." The jury retired. Some ten minutes later they returned. McKay was found guilty and sentenced to three months in jail. J.M. Fortier was exonerated. The liberal individuals of Montreal could sleep soundly at night, reassured that the manufacturer could return to the governance of his factory family. As for McKay, he could once more experience the delights of jailhouse cuisine.

McKay, of course, was not going to let things go at that. Imprisoned, despite ill health, he wrote from his "martyr's cell" in Montreal that the judge's verdict had, backhandedly, actually conceded the truth of much of the factual case he had been trying to make against Fortier. Interestingly, McKay also wanted to take the judge up on his Christian theology. The learned judge had remarked that "Canada was a Christian country." Well, said McKay, what about Matthew 18: 15–18? – an apt allusion during a time when the Bible was ready to hand and most adult readers would get the point. Almost everyone in the first formation – atheists, agnostics, and fervent believers one and all – seemingly had the Bible at their fingertips for metaphors, precepts, historical narratives, and war cries.

Matthew 18:15–18 advises the believer, "If thy brother shall trespass against thee, go and tell him his fault between thee and him alone; if he shall hear thee thou hast gained thy brother." If the sinning brother will not listen, the believer is enjoined to "take with thee one or two more, that in the mouth of two or three witnesses every word may be established." Failing that, the wrongdoer's errors should be announced unto the church, and if he still proved recalcitrant, "Let him be unto thee as a heathen man and a publican." By exposing Fortier as a union-busting tyrant, McKay, in his own books, had followed the advice of Scripture.

McKay then turned from the Bible to quote from the only slightly less authoritative words of Spencer: "The well-ordering of human affairs in remotest communities is beneficial to all men, the ill-ordering is injurious to all men." In this instance the philosopher and sociologist sounded remarkably like the rabble-rousing Rev. Brown of Rochester. Even if citizens were only slightly affected by good or evil influences, the cumulative effect of such influences should not be underestimated. While men performed as "social units," they could not transgress "the life principle of society without disastrous consequences somehow or other coming back upon them. . . . A nation is a living organism analogous to the human body."[71]

Here was first formation socialism, condensed in a dialectical image. The image contains Fortier triumphant, an *individual* who has vanquished his opponent in a court of law. But here were his workers, also – but much more ambiguously now – *individuals*. Did they have the right to combine and demand changes? The law was truly murky on this point. Neither they nor employers were bound to each other by any ancient communal bonds. Everyone in this world was *free* – but free in the specific sense explored by Marx's *Capital*, that is, free to participate in a *free labour market*. Even the factory children – "individuals" in training, so to speak – were evidence of this liberal style of freedom. Such discipline as they received – being beaten over the head or imprisoned in black holes – might well build their individual characters.

Fortier was acting in his factory as many men acted at home, exercising discipline over their children and wives. The miracle of this system was that Fortier, by buying his workers' capacity to labour, was able to pay their wages and still pocket a handsome profit for himself. He could make the labour he bought in the free marketplace generate a surplus, which he could reinvest in Christmas turkeys or in his factory, to help it grow and grow as he himself accumulated and accumulated yet more capital. Marx, an author whom McKay had yet to explore in any detail, but whose *Capital*, volume 1, he would soon virtually memorize, would unforgettably distil the essence of this process. Marx would also explain how, under capitalism, it was likely that Fortier would be bought out – not by the state or by the workers, but by a bigger, more aggressive, more efficient version of himself.

Then came the turn to Spencer. McKay, in explaining the wider context of Fortier's social role, turned to an argument of *radical organicism*: "individuals" under conditions of modernity are so interdependent, so much "members of one another," that a man like Fortier, by his conduct, was attacking not just his workers, but the entire body politic.

McKay was one of the founding spirits of the CSL in Montreal, and he most likely had a hand in writing its foundational *Program and Declaration* of 1899 – the first homegrown detailed program to come out of the socialist left in Canada. What is fascinating about the *Program* is its silence on the very "Christian socialism" that was supposed to be the CSL's essential characteristic. Even on the question of temperance, the largest mass movement in Canadian society and one that many Christian socialists put at the core of their activism, the *Program* simply declared for the nationalization of the industry and local control over liquor sales – not for prohibition.

Within the Point St. Charles milieu McKay was quite possibly coming up against former SLP members, more radical influences, who were subtly altering his outlook on life. In his mid-twenties, McKay was still working out the implications of theories and questions that Thompson, nearing his sixties in 1901, had pondered much longer. They had read different books and lived in different cities. Had they sat down for a long discussion they would probably have furiously disagreed with each other. Or maybe Thompson would have cut the young martyr some slack. As an old Bellamyite, he might have warmed up to McKay, as the cocky young man explained to him that in *Looking Backward* and *Equality* radicals were just developing Christian ethics as they might concretely apply to industry.[72] Most profoundly, they would have shared a common formative experience in wrestling with Spencer's rich, provocative, and seemingly inescapable sociology.

The Celebrity from New York City

Yet if we might imagine those 70 people in November 1901 acknowledging Thompson as the local "great man of the left" and perhaps nodding at McKay, as a young man from far away, the buzz in the room would probably have been about a third man, the star of the hour, the keynote speaker at this formative convention. That honour would fall to John Spargo (1876–1966), who was not even a Canadian, but a Cornish immigrant to the United States. Years later people would remember him vividly – and very differently.

Spargo's biography crystallizes many of the most significant highs and lows of international socialism at the turn of the century.[73] Born in the Mabe Burnt House, just outside Penryn in the parish of Stithians, Cornwall, England, Spargo worked at a wide range of jobs – in a shoemaker's establishment, pork butcher shop, foundry, tin mine, and stone quarry. He came by his early class-consciousness honestly. His family derived its meagre sustenance from poorly paid work in the treacherous Cornish tin mines. In the Methodist church of his childhood, according to his biographer, Marku Ruotsila, "Sons of workers like himself were strictly cordoned off from the rest of the congregation and bidden to worship among their own kind."[74] When he sought to explain these and other injustices, the teenaged Spargo initially lacked any "matrix of interpretation" apart from Methodism within which to place them; but in short order he discovered Christian socialism, and then, converted to Marxism by *England for All*, a book by H.M. Hyndman of the Social Democratic Federation (SDF), he threw himself into the literature of British socialism (especially Ruskin and Morris) and political and social theory (Mill, Huxley, and Spencer). As Ruotsila remarks, although all of these influences were significant, it was Spencer who most impressed Spargo: he became a "lifelong disciple" who "never wearied with the conflation of Marx and Spencer that he had made so early on." As for practical political guidance, it was Hyndman himself who became Spargo's "model, mentor and friend."[75] Arriving with his job-seeking father at the town of Barry Dock, within a year the 25-year-old Spargo had become the president of the local labour council and a member of the SDF's National Executive Council, where with rare exceptions he saw the political world through Hyndman's spectacles.

The Hyndman perspective provided the particular vision of Marxism of a man, famous for his bourgeois top hat and waist coat, who was a Tory by background, a believer in Empire, stock speculator, and absentee mine owner – yet who had known Marx and believed deeply in his analysis of a capitalist system driven by its contradictions into revolutionary crisis. One of Hyndman's favourite stage devices was to appear nattily dressed before working-class audiences and tauntingly remind them that his evident paunchy prosperity derived from the profits squeezed out of their working-class hides. He was something of a maverick and an adventurer – a not uncommon figure in the left of the day. E.P. Thompson remarks that Hyndman, while rarely giving the impression of wanting to conduct a sustained fight for any half-measure, would happily employ any issue as "a useful temporary peg on which to hang an agitation, to advertise the Federation and himself: not with the intention of using it for the education of the workers in Socialism, but in order to build up a loyal mass following who could be called upon when the next agitation arose." In this period, Hyndman was capable of expressing the utmost contempt for the donkey-like people who might be seduced by mere palliatives. Friedrich Engels described Hyndman as "a skilful and good business man, but a petty and hard-faced John Bull, possessing a vanity considerably in excess of his talents and natural gifts."[76] Yet Hyndman's emphasis on the cultural revolutionary side of socialism, his respect for the worth of arts and ethics, and his insistence that the working class had to develop the intellectual capacity to use its potentially awesome collective powers were innovative, and many found him a gifted and inspiring teacher. A vast number of the luminaries of British socialism learned their Marxism from him, and over young Spargo he exerted a formidable power, as the one *true* Marxist.

Spargo himself would reveal many conflicting political selves. His belief in the slow, gradual education of the working class – a process to ensure that they would eventually become worthy of political power – went hand in hand with a disgust at the inability of that class to realize their own interests. He also believed in direct action, hailing, for instance, the assassination of the Spanish prime minister in 1897. At home he joined a little band of SDFers who took up training, with broomsticks substituting for rifles, for the coming Red revolution. He believed in Christianity, yet was also an atheist, who even for a time celebrated science as a new religion that would eliminate all superstition. Unifying this bundle of contradictory stances was an underlying belief in social evolution. Socialism he defined in 1898 as the "conscious endeavour to substitute a system of co-operation for existence instead of the competition for existence that exists today." This project was to be pursued through "education to make people conscious of the inevitable material and spiritual progression towards the socialist order." He believed that "social revolution" would come about when "social evolution had reached the point where a transformation is not only possible but inevitable." A properly educated people – as distinct from the anarchists, whom he abhorred, or the *lumpenproletariat*, whom he disdained – would desist from any premature resort to violence, "either in resistance to, or in order to speed up, a process of socialization that was as inevitable as it was slow."[77]

The John Spargo who showed up in Toronto in November 1901 was enmeshed in an even harsher contradiction: that of trying to make a business out of socialism. Although he later tried to make people believe that he had selflessly left Britain in order to make way for the emerging labour luminary Keir Hardie, and that he planned to return to his home country in two or three years, in fact Spargo had arrived in the United States in February 1901 primarily because he saw a chance for a new life for himself. Recently married, Spargo urgently needed money, and his mother had written him to say that the newlyweds might live with her in New York, where John might manage his stepfather's store. Alas, when the Spargos arrived in New York, both his mother and stepfather were dead, the store had been left to someone else, and the young couple found themselves homeless and penniless. Spargo begged money from the socialist leaders he knew, stood in breadlines, and finally acquired his first North American job – sweeping snow from the New York streets for $7.50 a week. Only slowly did he make his way into the good graces of the city's socialist movement – winning a job as an organizer for the Socialist Labor Party, doing a stint as a contract lecturer with the religious Fellowship of the Socialist Spirit, and taking an unsalaried editorial position with *The Comrade*, the new cultural organ of the party. The Spargos were able to move into a humble apartment on the East Side, although it was "so small that their dining table had to stand in as Spargo's writing desk, workbench, and bed," all at the same time.[78]

In inviting Spargo to be the keynote speaker at its 1901 convention, perhaps the CSL saw in him a man who had rubbed shoulders with the greatest figures in the world socialist movement – people such as Wilhelm Liebknecht, August Bebel, Jean Jaures, Jules Guesde, and Enrico Ferri. More prosaically, the dirt-poor, desperate lecturer undoubtedly came fairly cheap. Socialism was a great dream and a shimmering ideal. It was also a business – for the organizers who brought Spargo in, who wanted to sell newspapers and pamphlets, and for poor Spargo himself, who was singing hard for his supper. Like vaudeville, like the new moving pictures, like the Toronto Exhibition, the science of socialism was in part a spectacle, a "demonstration" of the deeper quandaries of modernity.[79] For the many platform leftists who visited Canada through these years – Emma Goldman, Charlotte Perkins Gilman, Keir Hardie, William Haywood, Eugene V. Debs – socialism was something you *performed* as well as *believed*. The left lecture circuit rewarded those celebrities who arrived with star power and could keep an audience entertained for an evening, and it cruelly dismissed the plodders who had only their earnest convictions to fall back on.[80]

Spargo could only have been in Toronto as the outcome of a local choice by the CSL, which in 1901 had made the momentous decision that as of that year the body would adhere to "the principles of International Socialism." This move reflected the organization's belief that it should be not only a Canada-wide body, but one connected to currents of socialism the world over. One can well imagine that Spargo was invited as part of that internationalist mandate. Years later, in 1937, someone who had been in the audience that night remembered his "strong cockney accent" and his "extremely ill-fitting suit of clothes." Although over time Spargo would become more polished, and his speeches would have the flow and poise that Edwardian audiences found so captivating, in 1901 the fresh-off-the-boat Englishman gave the distinct impression of being on the "B" rather than the "A" list of socialist celebrities – which explains why the CSL was able to slot him in, not just in Toronto, but in Belleville and other venues not renowned as hotbeds of left-wing intellectual ferment. It was a sign of the CSL's provincial dependence upon transnational socialist circuits that it apparently needed someone like Spargo to add lustre to the important socialist convention – an element further demonstrated when Spargo made no attempt to acknowledge, and perhaps was not even aware, that he was speaking to an important gathering in a different country.

Decades later Colin McKay remembered a routinely sentimental socialist speech, so hackneyed that a reporter in the audience could anticipate his every platitude. (Asked about Spargo's subsequent renunciation of socialism, McKay remarked acidly that his "defection" was "partly immanent in his sentimentalism.")[81] No, quite the reverse, ran another memory: Spargo had expounded the "soundest Marxism," which was "well, even enthusiastically, received," but had then gone on to give a second speech, which "intimated in the plainest terms that the existing order could and would be overthrown only by force, which would have his personal support."[82]

The text of the speech, printed as a pamphlet, *Where We Stand: A Lecture by John Spargo*, indicates that, in a way, both memories were right. The text combines conventional platitudes with predictions of a coming violent storm. It *is* a kind of "boilerplate speech," of the sort that a beleaguered man fighting hotel fleas, exhaustion, and ill health might pull out of his back pocket, if he really needed to. As such, it is a superb introduction to the "common sense" of much of the first formation.

In his address Spargo endeavoured to tell the fledgling CSL about *the* Socialist position on matters "Economic, Ethical and Political." For Spargo, the matrix-event of recent world history was the emergence of a new predatory capitalism, dominated by a mere handful of men – Carnegie, J.P. Morgan, Rockefeller, and Co. – who were building, out of the unpaid labour of the proletariat, a despotism that put all past tyrannies to shame. Think of the widows and orphans who had lost their breadwinners in the tycoons' mines and factories, all because these fat cats would not pay to protect the workers' lives and limbs. Think of the motherless babies and the childless mothers, victimized by the "ghoulish greed" of predatory landlords. Capitalism was killing the working class. Those who did not die outright were reduced to a pitiless slavery, a "wage slavery" that was comparable – perhaps even worse – than that experienced by 19th-century slaves from Africa.[83] At least the slave sold at auction had been kept alive, as an investment, by his or her master; whereas the modern wage slave could be ground down relentlessly, in an ever-deepening pit of poverty, by an employer who cared only whether the worker did the job. When workers ran out of work, they were infinitely degraded: "We sell ourselves on the instalment plan – and heaven knows the price is small!" This was a "speaking of bitterness," a moment of refusal, that culminated in a heartfelt conclusion: "Our position, then, leads us to condemn as wrong and immoral the whole fabric of society."[84]

What, then, was to be done, in Spargo's mind? And with whom? Not liberals – they were the enemies to be exposed. For liberals began with "individuals" – not as living, human beings, but as *abstractions* – and through this sleight of hand they were able to overlook all manner of injustices and crimes. For socialists it was a fundamental political, economic, philosophical, and ethical error to begin with the individual. For, as a matter of scientific fact, society was "not merely a large number of individuals; evolution has made it an organism, and each unit of the whole being interdependent upon all the other units."[85] How could one unit do good, without changing the organism of which it was a part? And so from the moment of refusal – a description of wage slavery as a crime – we pass to a moment of supersedure, placing this crime in its context. And once we do that, we can see that at least it was possible and necessary to live otherwise.

History had demonstrated this tendency over and over again. The one fact most plainly written on "the blood-stained pages of world history," Spargo urged, was that "things have not always been what they are to-day; that the present form of society is the result of a long series of changes logically consequent upon each other, and all the signs of the time portend that we are on the eve, nay, in the very midst of, further great and far-reaching changes."[86] The system that forced workers to generate surplus value, which was then expropriated by idlers and corporations, had to be overturned. Look around you, at their mansions! And look at the workers in their hovels! What a "tragic paradox" that, while all wealth was produced by labour, only they who laboured were without wealth!

Nor were mansion-dwelling idlers the only "Others" in this performance of socialism. Also numbered among socialism's enemies were the "pseudo-philosophers," new-style economists, or religious prophets who turned to "one God or many Gods" for their understanding of right or wrong. Away with such muddle-heads! They were like quack doctors, incapable of seeing the diseases racking the social body. A real surgeon, treating a man suffering from cancer, did not prattle on about the shared interests of the cancer cells and the patient. "He doesn't try to find something that will help both at once." No, he tried to eliminate the cancer. Well, "Capitalism is the cancerous growth in the social organism that must be eliminated in the interests of the organism as a whole.[87]

That was by no means a new insight. As Spargo remarked, "We believe in evolution. Everybody believes in evolution nowadays." Yet an emphasis that may have struck many in the Toronto audience was Spargo's insistence that socialism was a *science*, which had discovered that natural processes of evolution were at work in society itself: "There is a law of social evolution which is but the counterpart of the law which pervades the organic world."[88] As Marx had promised in 1844, there was to be *just one science* – embracing the known and knowable universe – and *just one world-process of enlightenment*, expounding and exploring and extending its truths.[89] "Just as in the evolution of organic life it is necessary to find a determining factor – a force that determines the time and the character of each successive change – so [it is] in this process of social evolution," Spargo told his Toronto audience.

> Therefore we ask ourselves, "What force was it that determined the time and the manner of the great changes we have seen?" . . . The propelling force behind all history is not ideal, or moral, but economic, centered in man's power over the forces of external nature. What the determining force summed up in the old adage, "Self-preservation is the first law of nature," is to organic evolution, economic pressure is to social evolution.

For Spargo, Marx – or rather, Marx as glossed by Engels – had captured this unity of the natural and the social perfectly in his "theory of the economic determinism of historical development," which held that "in every historical epoch the prevailing mode of economic production and exchange, and the social organization necessarily following from it, form the basis upon which is built up and from which alone can be explained the political and intellectual history of that epoch." Life itself was "finally dependent upon the supply of its material requirements." Thus any "far-reaching change in the means of producing those material necessities must affect the whole of life."[90]

In addition to Marx, named twice in this lecture, the man who emerged as the Hero of the People's Enlightenment in Spargo's rendition of socialism was Herbert Spencer, who illuminated the great vistas, the massive landscape, of social evolution.[91] Spencer allowed for a new understanding of the past – as the history not of kings and queens, but of working people and their exploiters. It was Spencer who so convincingly traced human history from "rude tribal communism" through the "militant phase" in which prisoners taken in war could generate a surplus for their captors to the rise and fall of feudalism, followed inevitably by the rise of a system "in which the worker became a wage-earner, and, ultimately, the mere adjunct of a machine." From Savagedom to Slavedom to Serfdom to Wagedom: the "law of change" would make the next phase of human history that of freedom.[92] This vintage first formation socialist rhetoric compressed the millennia of human history into one compelling and cosmic formula.

Socialism was inherent in the very logic of evolution, as Spencer and Marx had analyzed it. Marx had provided the theory of the economic base, upon which social organization was established. Following this logic, socialism might flow inescapably from the transformations wrought by capitalist modernity. Yet, Spargo suggested, evolution could also be thrown into reverse. For example, the contemporary "wage slave" was, in terms of freedom, in a much *worse* position than the pre-capitalist "savage": "The savage without any idea of exchange, but with all his felt needs plentifully supplied, was a comparatively wealthy man."[93] "Savagery" as a point of origin for the great narrative of human history was itself rather contradictory. It might mean "that which has been overcome as civilization has inevitably advanced," or it might mean "that which is *sauvage*" – that is, closer to nature, freer, more abundant. Spargo, and here he was typical of the first formation in general, cannot even in one short speech quite decide whether humanity is ascending ever upwards or inevitably descending into the depths.

This was the keynote address of a foundational conference of the CSL, which most historians have painted as an organization of gentle, middle-class Christians, so mild in its politics and middle class in its social composition that it would not have said "Boo!" to a mouse.[94] Spargo, to the contrary, ruled out any resolution of the social question through conventional politics. The extension of public ownership, in and of itself, was beside the point. Why strengthen the existing legislative and governmental forces, which provided the exploiting class with its greatest strength? "If we beg we are scorned and derided; if we strike we are shot down by their troops or bludgeoned by their police!"[95] Reformers who sought to improve the state were like doctors prescribing worm powder for consumption. Why, if we were convinced of the fundamental wrong of capitalism, should we be content with "anything short of its removal?" What was needed was not just a "patching and stitching of the old" but – and here Spargo suggestively cited the romantic revolutionary William Morris – "a world new-builded." How? Education, of course. But let us not disregard the possibility that armed rebellion might be needed to overthrow such evils. "Force may prove to be as Marx has it, 'the midwife of Progress,' and out of the travail of bloody and ruinous rebellion may come Liberty and Comradeship." Or force, as Hyndman warned, might prove to be "the deadly abortionist, strangling the new society in the womb of the old."[96]

No wonder that memories of the speech did not agree on whether or not Spargo had recommended the violent overthrow of the state. On the one hand, his audience could sharply appreciate – especially so soon after the assassination of U.S. president William McKinley in September 1901 – the controversies lying in wait for those radicals who seemed "soft on terrorism." The CSL's Toronto leadership had been backpedalling furiously lest anyone associate them with the anarchists thought to have been implicated in the killing.[97] On the other hand, if one took Marx's analysis seriously, and was committed to the socialist position on democracy, it was difficult to avoid the conclusion that the entire capitalist system itself was based upon robbery and terror. The liberal promise that the citizen could speak truth to power had been repeatedly shown to be empty. Both the rise of the trusts and the vicious subjugation of the Boers in Africa suggested the violence at the heart of the ruling order. Piecemeal approaches to these political problems were bound to miss the key issue. For the many Marxian socialists who were gradually coming to predominate on the international left, to express sympathy with anarchism was problematic, but – such was the tenor of Spargo's exposition of socialist doctrine in 1901 – to condemn the anarchists out of hand was also difficult. At least they had done something to challenge the rule of capital in North America.

It was precisely on this question of the anarchists that Spargo ran into trouble in his second major address to the Canadian Socialist League, delivered on the very next day, 29 November 1901, to Toronto Local No. 2. The title of Spargo's address was "Socialism and the Anarchistic Peril." After expressing conventional (but in Toronto highly controversial) positions against the Boer War and British colonialism in India, Spargo then opened fire on the anarchists. Like his mentor Hyndman, he used "anarchist" as an all-purpose word designating chaotic, foolish, and dangerous people. "There were hundreds of Anarchists, the speaker declared, in high places whom it was impossible to imprison, and they were not only law makers, but law breakers," noted a report on the meeting. Anarchists, Spargo contended, "advocated the supremacy of the individual, while Socialists on the contrary advocated the general good of society as being of far greater importance than that of the individual. Socialists further endeavored to bring about a better system of society by means of the ballot, rather than by the bullet." This statement recalled the balance that Spargo had attempted to strike the night before: "Force is always justifiable as a last resource, but not otherwise. At present we possess constitutional means whereby we can do all that is needed, and we Socialists urge that these should be used."[98]

Many in Spargo's Toronto audience that day must have been expecting something more in line with the moderate Christian socialism so often unveiled in George Wrigley Sr.'s *Citizen and Country*, the country's second major socialist newspaper. They heard instead a man who distinguished socialism from anarchism by arguing that socialists were more radical and more anticapitalistic than the anarchists. Spargo's critique contained no outright rejection of anarchist direct action. Instead, Spargo thought of anarchism as unbridled individualism – liberalism carried to an extreme – and as such, the antithesis of socialism.

> Socialism, as the word implies, is founded upon the idea of social interest, and recognizes a moral responsibility based on that social interest. Wherever the desire or interests of any individual are opposed to the interests of society they must be subordinated to them. The paramountcy of society over the individual is the very essential quality of Socialism, while anarchism places the interest of the individual first, and does not recognize any social obligation, in the strict sense of the term.

Hence, between "Socialism and Anarchism there is unending war," as evidenced by the history of the International in Marx's time. This "war" was one of the "most cherished traditions" of the socialist movement.

Spargo was misleadingly simplistic about the intricate and complex socialist/anarchist relationship of the 19th century – as, at some level, he must have known. Many people of the time, including Kropotkin, thought that "anarchism" and "socialism" were merely two ways of thinking and acting on the underlying science of social evolution. Anarchism was simply a no-government form of socialism. But more apparent is Spargo's sense of a socialism that is *both* evolutionary *and* revolutionary.

Spargo critiqued anarchists because they were not *radical enough*. In 1937

Owen Sound–area veteran A.H. Ross recalled that Spargo in this address had "intimated in the plainest terms that the existing order could and would be overthrown only by force." That was also the impression conveyed by a report in the Toronto *World*. The *World* reporter thought that Spargo had "started in to defend the possible ultimate appeal to force in order to carry out the principles of Socialism. He also expressed the earnest wish for the day that would see the East Indians' successful rise against Great Britain. The Boer cause was also strongly defended by the speaker." According to the same report, in the "heated general discussion" that took place after the address, one member linked Count Leo Tolstoy's doctrine of non-resistance with Christ's words: "Resist not evil." Such words, retorted Spargo, were those of an anarchist. Spargo confusingly denounced the anarchists both for their pacifism and their direct action. Suggestively, in 1901, he himself was intent on proclaiming his allegiance to socialist revolution, even if it did involve, as a last resort, the use of force from below.[99]

In proclaiming himself a "Revolutionary Socialist," Spargo repeated what could be emblazoned upon the tombstone of the first formation as its great defining insight: there is no necessary antagonism between evolution and revolution, as any scientist will tell you. Social revolution simply means that social evolution has reached a stage at which transformation is not only possible, but inevitable. *Revolutions are but necessary stages in the general process of evolution.* That was a classic formulation of a stance that, try as one might, does not neatly fit within the pigeonholes of either "social democracy" or "revolutionary Marxism." As the applied revolutionary science of social evolution, socialism in this version was neither "idealist" nor "materialist," but "monist," holding that education into the workings of the world could itself work wonders in its transformation. As Marx famously observed in 1844, "Theory . . . becomes a material force as soon as it has gripped the masses."[100]

Socialism was a science of modernity. Socialists believed that society was an evolving organism. Those we might tentatively call the left Spencerians, men like Thompson in the 1890s (and William Irvine in the 1920s), often argued for a functional democracy – a form of government that reflected the social structures and integrated functions characteristic of a modern society. For others, whom we might call the stricter Marxian socialists, men like Spargo in 1901 (and Pritchard in the 1910s), the core belief in a science of social evolution led to what we have called the "triune formula." This social-evolutionary "triple formula" of historical materialism, value theory, and class struggle created the sense that many aspects of social existence could be mapped according to the scientific co-ordinates devised by Marx – which complemented those of Spencer.

Marx and Engels on the one side and Darwin and Spencer on the other had arrived at their theorizations of evolution separately, and they had evolved systems of thought that today might not seem to go together. But those ideas did seem compatible to most participants of the first formation. A narrative in which the "Marxists" neatly and plainly succeeded the "Spencerians," although it might be polemically attractive, is contradicted by too much evidence of hybridity to be persuasive. As Spargo's Marxist-Spencerian speech suggests, the reality was much untidier. The social evolutionism associated with Darwin and particularly with Spencer was not superseded by the three-part formula of the Marxists. Rather, contemporaries ran these different theoretical traditions together. Socialism was, so to speak, a specific instance of the more universal, cosmic phenomenon of evolution. Just as the cosmos was evolving ever more integrated and complex aggregations made up of once-distinct homogeneous units, so too were socialists aiming at constructing their politics based on one big theoretical system, integrating all scientific knowledge about the natural and social world.

First formation socialists generally believed in positive social-scientific knowledge, in a unified science of humankind that mirrored in its precision and determinism the natural sciences of physics and biology. Left Spencerians believed that democracy could prosper only if groups necessary for the economy were given decision-making power over their lives. The increasingly more numerous Marxian socialists held that the workers were the key to socialist revolution. Since this revolution was imminent, they spared no efforts in trying to educate the workers as to their true interests in furthering the people's enlightenment. Many people like Spargo were left Spencerians in one moment of their social analysis and Marxian socialists the next. They articulated the two systems of thought in combination, without a sense of any contradiction. At one end of the non-Marxian continuum were a few whose outlook was mainly that of "Spencerism," and at the other a rare few who were more oriented to defending "Marxism" as its own free-standing mode of historical inquiry and political activism. The overwhelming majority of socialists of this period, within and without the organized parties, stood somewhere between these two poles.

The Three Gentlemen of Spenceria

We might wonder what these three gentlemen of Spenceria – drawn from such different corners of the globe, under such different circumstances – had to say to each other. There is, to my knowledge, no record. There were ample grounds for disagreements on a host of issues, and their future paths would take them in different directions. Thompson was to persist for another two decades as a leading light of the Toronto left, throwing his energies into the emerging League, then the Socialist Party of Canada, and later the Social Democratic Party of Canada. In some ways McKay's path would be similar –

at least into the League and the SPC – but he would devote most of his life as a socialist to refining the movement's analysis. Spargo would go on to become a highly influential intellectual whose writings on themes such as class struggle, religion, and women became world famous (and sharply contested) statements of "the socialist position." At the time of the Great War he underwent a second epiphany and broke with his Socialist Party comrades. Under the thoughtful guidance of the Fascist Benito Mussolini, he played a significant role in crafting U.S. policy towards the fledgling Soviet state, which he viewed as the monstrous product of the anarchists whom he and Hyndman had been denouncing for decades.

So far as I know, these individual men were rarely if ever in touch with each other. Nor, apparently, can we even record in detail what they said and did in 1901, since the conference was sketchily reported and the CSL apparently left a very small archival footprint. Nonetheless the CSL conference of 1901 did initiate a complicated process of consolidation on the left – in essence, setting up a bare-bones Toronto-led framework, first for Ontario, then exported elsewhere, that would eventually lead to far larger organizations. Both Spargo and McKay would become honorary members of its executive. Thompson, who seemingly played a much larger role, became an organizer. As a possible birthdate of the organized movement in Canada, the November 1901 conference has much to recommend it. After the de facto formation of the CSL as a Dominion-wide presence in 1901, Canada would always have at least one widely based socialist organization that could claim deep roots in the country. After 1901, however wispy it may sometimes appear, there would always be a socialist network in the country, integrating as best it could the many influences from elsewhere, and struggling to adapt them to politics in a particular place.

Then again, this moment is probably more interesting for what it reveals about an emergent socialist paradigm than for its organizational significance. The vast range of positions inferable from the turn of the century texts of these CSLers, and sometimes even the conflicting positions held firmly by one and the same individual, reveal an arresting theoretical commonality. All three men defined themselves *against* what they considered a liberal (or "individualist") and capitalist order. Interestingly, all three would polemicize against Goldwin Smith, who, as Homel's fascinating research reveals, was seen to be something of a supportive senior statesmen by working-class activists in Toronto – the liberal "Sage of the Grange" who had a surprisingly soft spot for the labour movement.[101] The opinions of this Luminary of Liberalism, who brought to backwoods Toronto the inestimable status of an Oxford professorship, were too conspicuous a part of the ideological landscape to be overlooked by any self-respecting radical.

McKay, at this stage working primarily within a Christian framework of assumptions, railed at a callous and complacent polemic penned by Smith on the occasion of the suicide of an unemployed man, which the liberal guru presented as the unavoidable result of there being too many "hands" and not enough jobs: that Smith's orthodox liberalism allowed him to see the suicide as inevitable and avoid the obvious solutions of more working-class organization and shorter hours "must make the angels weep."[102] When Spargo penned his malicious if seemingly unctuous anti-Smith pamphlet in 1907, he ungently suggested that Smith was simply the fossil of a bygone liberal age who seemed to be losing his marbles.[103] Spargo made much of Smith's abuse of economic concepts that, for socialists, had meanings completely different than those attributed them by Smith. Both men used "labour" and "capital," but in radically conflicting ways. By labour, Smith meant "manual" or "physical" labour (and so, it would seem, did many Marxists). How could an educated man like Smith, Spargo demanded in his most smarmy voice, make such an elementary blunder? Spargo evinced "amazement indescribable" at Smith's "ignorance" of what labour actually means. "It is simply inconceivable that you should be ignorant of the fact that all the great political economists ... use the term 'labor' to connote all useful, productive energies regardless of whether they be mental or physical."[104] Socialism entailed, for many, the correct use of a scientific terminology.

The wittiest and most memorable attacks on Smith came from Thompson, who indirectly satirized the hypocrisies of Smithian laissez-faire liberalism in his brilliant satire, "The Political Economist and the Tramp," in which the learned apologist for survival of the fittest is given a taste of his own medicine. Thompson directly attacked Smith for his complacent conviction that if workers did not find their jobs pleasant, they could simply leave them. Once more turning the rhetorical tables on the good professor, Thompson imagined him sailing back from England and being kicked out of his comfortable quarters, forced to sleep on deck, condemned to a bread and water diet – and then, "on remonstrating with the captain, being told: 'Well, my dear sir, there's no need for you to stay on this ship for a moment longer than you wish. You are at perfect liberty to get out and walk!' "[105] So it was with wage slaves the world over.

For all their obvious differences, then, these three men shared a common-sense notion of what they were against: a cruel and irrational liberal order, founded in capitalist social relations. Indeed, their shared moment of refusal involved (over time) the textual representation of exactly the same ideologue, who epitomized for them the Other against whom they must fight. In coming together in Toronto, they at least offered an inkling of how the moment of supersedure was to be conceptualized – in new leagues, alliances, and meetings. They had more than the beginnings of a way of linking their insights into the pitfalls of liberalism into a much more elaborate, even cosmic, framework of

concepts derived from Spencer and mixed to varying and sometimes confusing degrees with Marx. This framework, they would have agreed, could be
called "sociology" or, more combatively, "socialism."

If the moment of supersedure meant the realization that there could be no
genuine liberty if a master class exploited and oppressed the wage slaves, and
if the moment of systematization meant that this insight must be placed
within a general social-scientific understanding of history and economics, it
was still not very clear in 1901 how this would translate into practical politics.
It was plainly insufficient simply to dabble in reform, when underlying all the
evils of the modern world lay the reality of capitalist oppression. As Spargo
explained, if you owned "all the means of a man's life," he became your slave,
and you his master, as surely "as if you owned him by right of purchase or
conquest."[106] A labour leadership that did not challenge this condition was
failing to grapple with reality.

Spargo put it provocatively when he said that, when he read of the shooting down of strikers, he refused to "join in the cry of Shame!" because "It is
we ourselves who should hide our faces, for it is our own power that is behind
the legislator, the judge and the policeman." Unless the working class was educated in social evolution and united as a revolutionary force, it was
hypocrisy to pretend to be shocked when the defenders of the system exploited children and shot strikers. "We" were letting them do it. Were the
cslers dismayed by this transparently revolutionary message? Perhaps the
young organization could handle these insights because Spargo had prefaced
his bitterly realistic words with that seemingly magic phrase: "To paraphrase
some words of Herbert Spencer . . ."[107]

One useful way of depicting the Spencerian turn is to see it as the creation,
within a pervasively hegemonic liberalism, of an alternative discursive space.
"Spenceria" was a *langue*, not merely a *parole* – it not only provided a memorable way of putting things, but also, more substantially, entered into what
could be seen and said. Yet it did not *determine* in any exact way the content
of the discursive forms it generated. When they invoked Spencer, and through
him the cosmic processes of evolution that seemingly justified their politics,
the radicals of 1901 were constructing a cogent, rigorous, and "scientific" language of politics, but this is not to say that "left Spencerism" was itself an ideology, one that strictly determined the positions a radical might take on a host
of issues. Rather, left Spencerism was a language of politics, and the fascination of the texts of 1901 is that of watching it slowly emerge to a position of
influence among the cohort.

To fully enter the first formation was to learn a new vocabulary of politics
and economics. Even ordinary words like "rich" and "poor" functioned in a
radically different way once they were integrated into a framework within
which the labour theory of value was so emphasized. "The poor owe no duty

to the rich, unless it be the duty which an honest man owes to the thief who has robbed him. The rich have no right to any of their possessions, for there is but one right, and that is the right of the laborer to the fruits of his labor, and the rich do not labor."[108] So much, in the words of the *Western Clarion*, for Christian philanthropy.

Socialisms do not fall from the sky. They emerge, dialectically, from the practical experiences and problems confronted by human beings. This socialism, the first such formation in Canada, offered a way of identifying, organizing around, and ultimately transforming the concrete, real-world problems it encountered by situating them within an all-embracing evolutionary theory, which found common patterns in nature and in society. Working-class autodidacts in Canada successfully "reconstructed" their own Spencer to suit their needs and circumstances. The key is *which* Spencer the socialists were reading and *how* they were reading him. Spencer's vision of one great process of evolution, at work on the street corner and in the stars, yet directed towards ultimate human goals, could ultimately be both comforting and uplifting. Spencer's great theme – the inevitable adaptation, through processes of functional and structural differentiation and integration, of that social organism called "society" to its environment – was so sweeping and universal, so cosmic, that it seemed to provide a logical and complete explanation for a vast range of phenomena.

For all three socialists, the force of the new way of seeing was such that they drew upon the "organic analogy" whenever they talked about any serious issue. Socialism meant standing back from the day to day world and subjecting it to a scientific and ethical critique moulded in the fires of evolutionary theory. "Socialism" here meant something bigger than a preoccupation with parliamentary contests, winning strikes, overthrowing the government, organizing a League, or rebuilding the state, although it also included those actions. It meant the mass education of working people in a great people's enlightenment and, through that, ultimately the foundation of an entirely new politics. Science would set working people free – from superstition, from national prejudice, from exploitation.

Spargo and McKay, and a host of others, were also clearly working within a Christian frame of reference, even if the lapsed Methodist Spargo was concerned about making a fine show of his agnosticism. But the conventional framework of Christian socialism – a gentle strategy for moral and social reform, a campaign of uplift focusing on temperance and respectability, a movement dominated by clergymen appalled by poverty and selectively integrating some of the findings of the new sociology into a middle of the road Christian theology – does not neatly enclose the politics of the CSL. We are tempted to overlook what was incendiary, iconoclastic, and "revolutionary" about this integration of radical Christianity with social-evolutionary theory.

When McKay spoke of industrial life in Montreal as "this industrial Egypt," for example, he visualized the socialists as a collective Moses, rising up against so many despicable Pharoahs. Similarly, in adopting St. Paul's most organic metaphors – for example, "We are all members of one another" – McKay was not just enlisting the saint as a very early forerunner of Spencer, but also driving home a political lesson: no person should dominate another. "We are all members of one another" is not, in truth, a mild thing to say, when denouncing the privileges and status of a turkey-dispensing patron. The Christ that appealed most powerfully to those who thought like these gentlemen of Spenceria was Christ-the-liberator, whose methods were neither ingratiating nor gradualist.

The CSL also had deep connections with a host of system-challenging social movements in Ontario, from temperance to campaigns for kindergartens, as the issues of *Citizen and Country* clearly indicate. Still, evolution as a social theory prompted a good number of its radical adherents to refuse as "palliatives" many of the reforms championed by progressives. The long-range "cosmic" perspective it encouraged allowed some first formationists to see in each "limited" demand the possibility of something far more ambitious. Even the "impossibilist" intellectuals of the SPC who emerged a few years later – whose avowed program eschewed gradualism, immediate demands, and feasible reforms – can be heard making the argument that, if you really wanted to shake reforms from the apple tree of capitalism, the harder and tougher the shake, the better. What seems paradoxical to us – that "reformists" in the CSL in turn listened to, applauded, and afterwards honoured the uncompromisingly revolutionary language they heard from Spargo in 1901 – is less so when it is interpreted within an evolutionary framework. Even the CSL's founding program itself contained the "ultimate" demand for the "entire abolition of the present form of society" – which sounds Spencerian, but not "reformist" in any easily recognizable sense. Only a few of the "evolutionary socialists" talked as though winning elections, extending public ownership, and rationalizing the state formed the pith and substance of the new socialist vision.

Very likely the moment of 1901 suggested a CSL that was of at least two minds. Some may have been rather startled by Spargo's revolutionary address. Among their numbers would be those who identified with its many mainstream ministers and with founder George Wrigley Sr., the veteran Toronto and St. Thomas journalist and promoter of the *Canada Farmers' Sun* (a paper affiliated with the farmers' Patrons of Industry) and then *Citizen and Country*. Others, who more closely identified with Wrigley's son, George Weston Wrigley Jr. (1875–1944), Phillips Thompson, and James Simpson, may have been keen to hear a much more aggressive and secular statement of the socialist case.[109] In January 1902 the Executive Committee of the Ontario Socialist League wrote to Spargo to tell him that "the services rendered by you to the cause of Socialism in the Province of Ontario merited well deserved recognition." The chairman and the secretary of the Ontario socialists praised Spargo for his "thorough knowledge of the position taken by Socialists from an Economic, Social and Ethical standpoint." It hailed him as a man who, "fearlessly proclaiming the truth," had helped to convert the unsympathetic, aroused "the lethargic to a more earnest study," and rejuvenated and revivified "the almost dormant faculties of men." Thanks to this great labour of enlivening enlightenment, the Ontario socialists were now far more united in their "more earnest determination to hasten the era of Socialism by their own activity." They closed on a religious note, hoping that "in the Province of God you may be long spared to propagate the principles that tend to a more equitable distribution of earth's riches, and that your voice may continue to proclaim the coming time when 'Men the wide world o'er/ Shall brothers be.' "[110] The CSLers enclosed an "appreciation plaque" to the man they had made an ex-officio member of all their committees. On the one hand the gesture honoured Spargo, but on the other the middle of the road sentiments of its closing lines, and the appeal to the "Province of God," seemingly reinscribed his message into a moderate Christian socialist framework at variance with the fiery visitor's actual words.

In 1901 the moments of refusal and supersedure were evident. Those of systematization and organization – pertaining not just to a theoretical system capable of tentatively situating these insights but also to a consistent real-world political organization wherein they could be deepened and developed – were not. There were models upon models of "other socialisms" that Canadians could follow (and Spargo was probably in Toronto because he was so closely identified with one of them, carrying the allure of the Great Motherland), but there was no unified certainty about how to translate evolutionary scientific understanding into political reality.

First formation socialists were gripped by both an extraordinary optimism and an equally marked sense of crisis. There was a tremendous certainty about the vast, hidden social forces that were remaking the world, and the imperative requirement that they be understood and harnessed. There was an equally acute anxiety that if this science did not take hold, the costs to working-class humanity would be horrific. It was a time of utopian fervour, when imagined futures – including the work of Bellamy and his countless imitators and successors – became astonishingly effective mobilizers in the present. It was a time when many activists and thinkers believed that socialism as a science could translate that utopian fervour into reality. "Oh, when will [the socialist world] come?" asked a British socialist election flyer in 1895. "God is ready, nature is ready." It answered: "When will you, the producers of wealth . . . stretch out your hands . . . and will this thing? Then – then – that very minute, it shall come."[111]

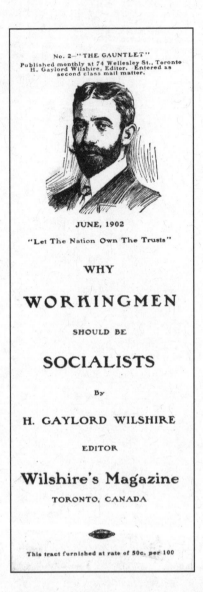

Two images of Gaylord Wilshire, the millionaire socialist: "Why Workingmen Should Be Socialists," brought out in 1902, the same year as his candidacy on behalf of the Ontario Socialist League; and an advertisement from his later career in the 1920s as a promoter of magnetic health devices. Author's collection. Lower right: James Simpson, in *Citizen and Country* (Toronto), 16 May 1902.

3

The Class Question

Montreal, 1 May 1906. The city was abuzz with the prospect of the socialists' first May Day parade. Would they really go through with it? Would the "foreigners" turn out in full force? Would they fly the red flag of revolution? What would the police do? Was the renowned Russian writer Maxim Gorky going to make an appearance? Would there be violence? According to the previous day's *La Patrie*, the socialists were basically all foreigners, mostly "Russian Jews." Although they must have been aware that the red flag was a provocation in so Catholic a city, Albert Saint-Martin threatened to place it at the head of their parade, which was going to begin and end at Empire Hall, after appearing on Ontario, Bleury, and Saint-Laurent streets.

The socialists did march, and not only was the red flag unfurled, but Saint-Martin as leader emphasized that it was "the flag which breaks the fetters of the oppressed and which will overthrow the tyrants." About 600 showed up, "the least enthusiastic of whom were assuredly not the women." The downtown streets echoed with socialist slogans: "Down with the clergy!" for the benefit of Catholic university students and "Travailleurs du monde, unisons-nous!" for the more enlightened.

The next year, suitably forewarned (as we learn from Claude Larivière's fascinating account, upon which I heavily rely), the city patriarchs readied themselves for a repeat performance.[1] Montreal city council, the Archbishop of Montreal, the nationalist *Société Saint-Jean-Baptiste*, the students of Laval, and the chief of police all exerted themselves to prevent a second scandalous parade. On 29 April 1907, the mayor ruled that there was to be no parade of socialists through the streets of Montreal. He graciously allowed that individual socialists who might wish to discuss questions of public interest could go to the Champs-de-Mars and hold a public meeting, but they were forbidden to assemble in groups on the street or make a display of banners and insignia. They would be allowed to express their opinions – the mayor was not going to get into the martyr-making business – but they must play by the rules. They must agree not to disturb the peace of the city.

Gathering *chez* Saint-Martin to assess the situation, the socialists disingenuously read the mayor's seemingly oppressive restrictions as a backhanded declaration favouring their democratic right to proceed to the Champs-de-Mars. On 1 May, the socialists gathered at the Saint-Joseph Hall, which they had rented for the occasion. Normally decorated with religious paraphernalia, the Hall was now bedecked with the signs and symbols of international socialism: "Liberté, Égalité, et Fraternité," proclaimed one. In the afternoon, while most of the male socialists were away at their waged jobs, the hall had echoed with the voices of women and children, preparing for the evening. At 6:30 the socialists began to move towards their headquarters, all of them carrying, in their buttonholes, a little red ribbon. "A half hour later," Larivière says, "the hall was full with 200 to 300 persons, socialists or would-be socialists, the greater number of them Jewish, Russian, Italian and Syrian."

Meanwhile, on Rue Ste-Catherine, a large crowd of the curious had assembled. The police were out in large numbers to see that there was no parade. Nor was there. At 7:30, 20 carriages pulled up, and the socialists decided, individually of course, that they would now proceed, in carriages or otherwise, to the Champ-de-Mars, there to discuss "questions of public interest." The first ones out of the hall carried "red flags, torches, transparencies and candles." The crowd was incensed. "In an instant, the flags were taken from the hands of those who carried them and ripped up, the torches and transparencies destroyed." Four brave socialists – two men and two women – managed, in the middle of the general commotion, to enter a vehicle and flourish their colours at its windows. "The car was surrounded immediately by a group of police officers who gave an order to the occupants to remove their colours." The crowd tumultuous, the police thrown back on their heels, red flags ripped up and flagpoles broken: it was a moment pregnant with riot.

A massive crowd gathered at the Champs-de-Mars – possibly as many as 10,000, made up of many of the curious and fewer of the converted – to listen to a band playing "the national melodies of every country imaginable." Gradually, allowed by Police Chief Campeau to emerge from their citadel two at a time, the socialists showed up. Saint-Martin arrived and mounted a makeshift platform. He was wearing a red sash. Was he allowed to do so? "If you wish, M. Charpentier, I will remove these socialist insignia," he said politely to the attending police officer. "No," came the reply. "It is not presently necessary for you to make your ribbon disappear."

"But I am ready to obey all your orders, my dear chief, and we socialists will do as you instruct us . . ." The beribboned Saint-Martin then made a brief speech, which he concluded by congratulating the police and the mayor for the protection they had offered the socialists.

An American luminary from Illinois presented a rousing pro-socialist address. He was shouted down by students from Laval and McGill. The socialists counterattacked by striking up the band, which played *La Marseillaise* – the great anthem of the French Revolution, and now closely identified with the anticlericalism of the Third Republic. It was a controversial melody in a Montreal in which Catholic ultramontanism was highly influential. The crowd was not assuaged when, after the visitor's speech was finished, the socialists struck up *The Internationale*, the increasingly popular hymn of the world socialist movement born of the Paris Commune – "C'est la lutte finale; groupons-nous, et demain, l'Internationale sera le genre humain," which in the loose translation popular in North America declared, "'Tis the final conflict/ Let each stand in his place/ The international working class/ Shall be the human race." This musical affront was swiftly rebutted with *O Canada*, an anthem that in French is replete with gallant Christian soldiers bringing the cross to the Natives. As Larivière's account demonstrates so well, the cacophony of political modernity had truly arrived in Montreal.[2]

Such civic uproars over the socialists' right to speak in public could be found across Canada, in cities big and small. In 1908 the Toronto socialists took up the struggle for free speech by organizing open-air rallies, virtually daring the police to arrest their leader. They even invaded the meetings of their Tory opposition and remained sitting during the customary three cheers for the King. After a police riot against leftists in "The Ward," the downtown immigrant neighbourhood, the spc likened the Toronto constables to the brutal Russian Cossacks.[3] In Brandon, Man., local activist Edmund Fulcher wanted to stage a big public meeting in honour of Charlie O'Brien (c.1871–1952),[4] the newly elected (and first) Socialist member of the Alberta legislature. He roused the mayor out of bed, addressed a special meeting of the town council, and finally won their reluctant approval, "for one night only," for a gathering at one of Brandon's prominent intersections. "They don't object to us speaking on street corners here so long as we get on a back street where nobody comes," grumbled Fulcher, who skewered the councillors' shallow sympathy with the cause. "We believe in socialism; it must come – in about two thousand years," he imagined them saying. Still, his band of socialists, "a small number, but real revolutionary," was able to stage a successful event.[5]

In Vancouver, spc Sunday propaganda meetings were held right through the year. Possibly audiences would hear the same message repeatedly, but that was all to the good: socialism was "a subject that will bear and need constant repetition before the mass of wage-workers become conscious of their position as slaves of capital, and the revolutionary spirit is stirred within them."[6] In 1909 Vancouver would erupt in what was perhaps the most famous free speech fight of them all, after police swooped down on a January meeting orchestrated by the Industrial Workers of the World as well as by Socialist and trade union leaders. They hit out again the next week, dispersing a peaceful crowd. The socialists fought back, with such slogans as "Shall British Freedom of Speech and Assemblage be Denied? I say *No!*" Temporarily blocked on the land, the combined forces of the left took to the sea, from whence speakers could safely and perhaps even legally address the land-based crowds. In a further imaginative countermove, the free speech agitators also raised the possibility of hiring balloons. The tactics proved successful – at least for now, and to an extent. A similar struggle followed in Victoria in 1911. Radicals had won significant if partial rights to free speech.[7]

The liberal public sphere, which had allowed certain select members of a stratified population the public right to the exercise of reason, had been won in the 1840s.[8] The democratic public sphere, which envisaged a universal right of all citizens to open debate, one extending even to the rationality, legitimacy, and longevity of liberal order itself, was only just emerging. To extend the concept of free speech to the inarticulate and the downtrodden, to make it possible to reason otherwise in the city squares, about topics that raised doubts about the very assumptions of the system – this was one of the great objectives that the newly organized left hoped to wrest from the guardians of liberal order. It was one essential component of the "class question."

The Three Phases of Left Debate

The rallies, songs, and free speech struggles dramatized the emergence of a new collective actor in parts of Canada: an organized socialist movement. All such moments arose out of complex, even byzantine debates about how the working class should be organized – the class question, in short. In the first formation it was axiomatic that class struggle was the essential key to social transformation. How else could wage slavery be abolished and social evolution safeguarded unless the wage slaves themselves were activated to do so? Why these rallies, songs, and struggles? Underlying the organizational dynamics of the left, in all their immense complexity, was a coherent debate centred on the question: How best can we rouse, channel, and develop the consciousness of the working class? It was a debate fixed within the context of a contradictory liberal order, which both validated the socialists' right to openly debate their politics and severely circumscribed the ways in which they could do so.

Unlike the hierarchical liberal parties, with their access to patronage appointments and contracts, the fledgling socialist bodies had relatively modest material advantages to bestow upon their members. In fact, joining a socialist organization was asking for trouble. Occupying a leadership position could mean losing one's job, and taking part in a left demonstration could mean injury, public scorn, deportation, and on rare occasions death. Yet in this period these risks were run by thousands of Canadians, by people who impressed even their enemies with their zeal for the new democratic public sphere. They also brought with them a tremendous capacity to split hairs, engage in battles of unbridled ferocity over issues whose urgency no longer seems apparent, and to run each other down with an almost malign enthusiasm. Dozens upon dozens of socialist bodies were established in this period. The elaboration of this new democratic public sphere was neither quiet nor tidy. Often the left seemed inchoate, yet in many contexts the combination of theoretical austerity and institutional prolixity was a strength. Alongside an inability to generate powerful Dominion-wide institutions was a success in matching the socialist message to particular circumstances. Most crucially, the educational programs launched by organs, organizers, and organizations did succeed in "making socialists," in forging activists and intellectuals who would defend their hard-earned insights through decades of adversity.

At least four Dominion-wide socialist organizations were in place for varying lengths of time in this period: the Socialist Labor Party (1894–1910s), Canadian Socialist League (fl.1898–1903), Socialist Party of Canada (fl.1905–1925), and Social Democratic Party of Canada (fl. 1911–1920) – plus, after the Trades and Labor Congress decided cautiously to support a political arm for organized labour in 1904, a daunting diversity of local labour political organizations and (fleetingly) a Canada-wide labour party. Yet none of these experiments can be categorized as "parties" in the way the word is usually used today – meaning well-disciplined organizations with thousands of members, regular conventions, broadly recognized leaders, well-defined programs, and stable bureaucratic structures. The Socialist Labor Party – the U.S. offshoot planted in Canadian soil in the mid-1890s – was (it seems) so closely tied to its U.S. parent that it was not exactly a free-standing party in the Dominion, although it did adopt its own Canadian constitution in 1901. The Canadian Socialist League gave each of its locals a marked degree of autonomy; it also had a relatively short life. The Socialist Party of Canada, the rebellious offspring of the CSL, emphatically *did* have a platform, some leaders who achieved a degree of recognition across Canada, a coast-to-coast network, and a relatively long life. Yet in the entire course of its existence it never managed to organize a national convention, it remained very much focused on propaganda, and its relatively unaccountable Vancouver executive was often visibly uninterested in integrating local rank and file members into the party. The Social Democratic Party of Canada, which grew to be bigger than the SPC, did hold Dominion conferences, and its very name inspired some historians to imagine it was a "Social Democratic" party along the lines of the German SPD or one of today's mass parties. Yet in fact it was, at least for much of this period, seemingly very much a loose federation of different linguistic or ethnic groupings, only episodically able to speak with one voice. It was also essentially confined to the decade of the 1910s.

Throughout the period 1890–1920, while many of the experiments in organizing "labour parties" were strictly ad hoc local affairs geared to electing a particular candidate thought to favour trade union demands, some of them stood out as conspicuous powerhouses. The Canadian Labor Party was formed in 1917 with the backing of the TLC, and was subsequently revived in a different form in the 1920s. An impressive number of postwar provincial parties appeared in British Columbia, Alberta, Manitoba, Ontario, Quebec, and Nova Scotia, among them Quebec's Parti ouvrier (which elected four MNAs from the 1890s to 1920), Manitoba's Dominion Labor Party and Independent Labor Party (which helped elect 11 labour MLAs in 1920), and the Independent Labor Party of Ontario, which rocketed from modest beginnings in 1917 to elect 11 MPPs in 1919. Yet there was in truth no pan-Canadian labour party, and even many of the seemingly impressive local parties were ambiguously positioned vis-à-vis the Liberals and often, because of intense factionalism, short-lived.[9]

Compared to the German SPD, none of the Canadian attempts at party formation amounted to much. Canada, then, had *no real equivalent* to the Labour Party in Britain or Australia, the Socialist Party in the United States or Italy, or the Social Democrats in Russia or Austria. No party can be said to have been the voice of the left in this period. In fact, it is entirely possible, as suggested by the ease with which Canadian leftists entered debates in the United States and Britain, that many of them may have regarded the Socialist Party of America and the Independent Labour Party as more "authentic" voices of socialism than anything to be found in their own country.[10]

In addition, various other organizations, often loosely described as "populist," appealed primarily to farmers, but often included socialists. Examples are the League of Equity, the Non-Partisan League, and the amorphous, massive Progressive Party of Canada, which became the second-largest political group in the House of Commons in 1921. Attempts to create farmer-labour political alliances went back at least to negotiations between the TLC and the farmers' movement called the Grange in the 1890s. Then the TLC Executive Committee thought farmers and labour might come to an alliance in the face of monopolies. In April 1893 a joint meeting of representatives of the Patrons of Industry, Dominion Grange, Knights of Labor District Assembly No. 125, Toronto Trades and Labor Council, and Social Problems Conference sought ways of uniting to fight the monopolies. The many farmers' parties in the Dominion were certainly not "red," but they had within them stalwarts of a different social and political order.

The organizational form and ideological content of first formation socialism were deeply related. Socialism might be accelerated or impeded by a party, but in this formation it could hardly be constructed by one. Only the working class, taking ownership of what was rightfully its own, could construct socialism. To "seize state power," either through parliamentary or extraparliamentary means, was not really in these parties' job descriptions. They were much more like associations or clubs than they were either "fighting weapons of the working class" aiming to achieve the dictatorship of the proletariat or "broad alliances of progressives" hoping to win parliamentary power.[11]

With regard to electoral success, all of the socialists elected to legislatures from the 1890s to 1914 were located in the West. Indeed, according to historian A. Ross McCormack, "Canadian socialism came of age in British Columbia."[12] The first major electoral breakthrough took place in that province with the election of two members of the Socialist Party of British Columbia (joined later by a third) in the provincial election of 1903. The Vancouver-published *Western Clarion* influenced socialists across the country. Some of the most remarkable labour struggles, radical analyses, and socialist thinkers were to be found in the West – in the coalfields and metal mining camps of British Columbia and Alberta, and in such cities as Vancouver, Calgary, and Winnipeg. Even so, the Canadian movement, in *both* the East and the West, was virtually too small to notice. "Conservative East" and "Radical West" work better as slogans than as tools of analysis.[13]

British Columbia, as Ross Johnson concedes in his study of the province, was – in general – not a hotbed of socialism at all: "In the multiple riding of the City of Vancouver the socialist candidates always shared the bottom of the poll with any labour or independent candidates who ran. . . . Only in the coal mining communities of Vancouver Island and the metal mining communities of the Kootenay area did the workers support the socialist cause to a significant degree."[14] Even by Johnson's estimates the Socialist Party of Canada numbered in its heyday twice as many members *outside* British Columbia as within it.[15] More people (8,600) voted for the Socialist candidate for the mayoralty of Toronto in 1906 than voted for any Socialist candidate in the provincial election in the following year in British Columbia. In fact, the Toronto mayoralty candidate received almost as many votes as the 20 Socialist candidates in British Columbia combined (9,503).[16] Even the unequivocally Socialist candidate in a 1905 provincial by-election in Montreal gained more votes than many of the B.C. candidates did in their provincial elections.[17] Springhill, N.S., in 1910, was possibly the *reddest* spot on the map of Canadian liberal order. The official Canadian parties were so tiny that debating which region was the "most socialist" involves a fetishism of very small differences.

In his *Socialism: A Critical Analysis* Skelton happily observed in 1911 that socialism – in a Canada where "widespread poverty is unknown; the gates of opportunity are wide open" and "the power of the Catholic Church in Quebec erects a solid barrier in [its] path" – was pretty much a dead letter.[18]

In the 1911 federal election, in a country with a population of 7,206,643, not one of the 10 Canadian socialist candidates succeeded in saving his $200 deposit. *Altogether* they failed to break the 10,000 vote barrier. Skelton clearly had a point. In 1913 the leading socialist party probably had only about 5,380 members. The second biggest party might have accounted for about 2,500.[19] The members and supporters of a variety of mainly short-lived local labour parties, and the members and supporters of more durable ethnic institutions, such as the Arbeiter Ring among Jewish immigrants, the Finnish Socialist Organization of Canada (FSOC), and the Ukrainian Social Democratic Federation, were also more numerous. Some labour unions harboured socialists in significant numbers.[20] More difficult to estimate would be the penumbra of socialism in the various cities – the pacifists, urban reformers, temperance advocates, and others loosely connected to the movement.

The Canadian socialists who did exist were, as we have seen, deeply influenced by figures in both Britain and the United States, and foreign influences also held strong in the closely related sphere of political organization. For many U.S. (and some Canadian) writers, Canadian patterns were simply U.S. patterns worked out in a slightly different space – and, after all, the SLP and, later, IWW were both headquartered in the United States. Moreover, the central linguistic minorities, the Finns, Jews, and Italians especially among the ethnic socialists, shared cultural and political networks that operated across the border. In one of the first important elections for socialists in Ontario in 1902, one candidate was an activist who had held office in the Socialist Labor Party in Massachusetts; another was a U.S.-born publisher and propagandist temporarily headquartered in Toronto. Eugene V. Debs, the leading figure and folk hero of the Socialist Party in the United States, was widely revered in Canada. His comments on the (to him) unsatisfactory ("mixed-pickles") eclecticism of the emergent program of one important left party in British Columbia were important in scuttling it.[21] Emma Goldman, Bill Haywood, Arthur M. Lewis, and Ernest Untermann were as familiar figures in the Canadian setting as they were in the United States. Canadian organizers were buying up shares in the Charles H. Kerr publishing co-operative and selling its books by the bushel. They were also avidly reading such wildly popular U.S. left magazines as *Appeal to Reason* and *Wilshire's Magazine* – the latter of which was published for four years in Toronto, with significant Canadian coverage.

While a U.S. citizen would find much that was wholly familiar in the Canadian left – so much so that the Canada/U.S. border might seem to have vanished altogether – so too might a British subject visiting the shores of an Empire shared with the Canadians. Every coalfield contained its British miners, many with cherished memories of struggles in the homeland. Every large city had its British skilled workers, many arriving – like Tim Buck in pre-war

Toronto – with their heads full of socialist ideas. Sidney and Beatrice Webb, Keir Hardie, and Ramsay MacDonald were just four luminaries from the British left who visited Canada. The complicated "rise and consolidation of the British Labour Party," grasped in nuanced detail, was part of the consciousness of many Canadian leftists, especially those recently emigrated from Britain, who repeatedly sought to create local and federal labour parties analogous to those in the mother country. A debate over forming an independent labour party, stalled for a long time within the TLC, suddenly became much more focused and concrete when the Labour Party in Britain emerged as a parliamentary challenge to liberalism. One reason why one of the great debates of this period – socialism or labourism? – was argued with such intensity in Canada was because many Canadians saw in Britain a model of a liberal order under stress that spoke directly to Canadian politics. The B.C. SPCers have sometimes been seen as part of a northward extension of Washington state, but it is equally plausible to see them as militants working in a North American extension of Lanarkshire and Lancashire.[22] As McCormack points out, "In 1903 it was estimated that 'nine out of ten' of the *Clarion*'s readers had recently arrived from the United Kingdom. Even when eastern European immigrants began to join the party in important numbers, British domination was never threatened."[23] The very name *Clarion* echoed that of the most famous British left newspaper.

Many historians of continental European socialist history would also find familiar names, debates, and publications in the early left. It was the Canadian left's good fortune that the capitalists' urgent need for cheap labour-power, access to the most sophisticated means of persuasion known to modernity, and the drive to save Canada for the Empire – all factors in the great push for immigrants characteristic of 1896–1914 – coincided with the brutal repression of Jews, Ukrainians, and Finns in the vast Russian and Austrian Empires. The 1905 Revolution in Russia sent a stream of refugees to Canada, many of them left-wing opponents of czarist autocracy. The upshot of all these circumstances was a pattern of immigration that sent to Canada many workers with a latent or active penchant for radical activism. Many arrived with a sophisticated understanding of socialist theory and history and a proud conviction that they should be influential within any socialist movement. After around about 1907 they became key players on the left in many Canadian cities and regions.

Canada was thus wide open to a world of influences; but as a liberal dominion more than a unified nation-state, an archipelago of strikingly different social formations, it *itself* was a complicated world, simultaneously agonizingly parochial and old-fashioned (as Engels had so disparagingly noticed) and transnational and ultra-modern (as newcomers to the bustling cities and workers in the steel mills and mines could readily attest). Canadian left politics were not simply an extension of those in the United States – the ties with Britain had massive cultural and political implications. Still, Canadian left politics were never simply those of Britain overseas – because many Canadians felt themselves to be Americans, engaged in building a liberal order more vigorous, more "North American," than that of the British motherland (and, in Quebec, the majority inhabited an altogether different francophone imagined community). Canadian left politics could also never simply be an assemblage of the various minorities flocking to the Dominion's shores, because however initially faithful the transcription to America of particular patterns of leftism, ultimately the class question dictated that such groups reach out beyond their boundaries, while the weakness in Canada of democracy as a binding force meant that they could not do so within a master framework of "Canadianism."

Canada became home to different *leftisms* that were discernible in a diversity of organizations. The Canadian patterns were stitched together within broad international debates over the contours and meaning of socialism; and the parties in themselves were not the principal vehicles of the people's enlightenment. As important as any parties were the language-defined socialist groups, unions and some co-operatives, left publications, multihued campaigns for social justice, and particularly dynamic organizers.

In the peculiar Canadian social archipelago, individual local organizers and eloquent local and international organs were often more important than pan-Canadian organizations. Organizations, organizers, and organs of the left all wrestled with a central strategic and tactical challenge. How should the working class be organized to fight the capitalist system? How should ultimate and immediate demands be related to each other? The almost mind-defying complexities of the Canadian left's organizational debates might be distilled to three competing positions, each of them traceable back to Marx himself, on how best to make the working class conscious of its evolutionary mission: (1) class-consciousness might arise almost naturally, as workers respond to the practical problems of their everyday lives – what we might call the "spontaneous" position; (2) class-consciousness might result only from an understanding of social evolution and capitalist economics – what we might call the "scientific" position; and (3) class-consciousness might emerge only as workers themselves learned the harsh lessons of struggle with their masters, and would depend on them drawing the *right* lessons from their defeats and victories – the "struggle" position.[24] Over time organs, organizers, and organizations emphasized one or another of these positions – and over time they came to be internalized as the unexamined assumptions, the "common sense," of powerful players on the left. The earliest years of Canadian socialist organizations can be grasped as so many debates about these rival constructions of the "class question" – debates that were the lifeblood of the movement's thinkers and activists, because upon them hinged the meaning of their political lives.

The institutional patterns of the small Canadian left from 1890 to 1915 were immensely complicated. Oceans of ink, for example, were poured out on the question of how many planks a party platform should have. Should it have a "single plank" – in essence, "Socialism Now! No more wage slavery, no more capital!" – an approach that encapsulated the "scientific" option? Or should it have many planks running the gamut from free school textbooks to the more or less comprehensive nationalization of the monopolies? Although they might seem a prime example of left-wing hairsplitting, such debates crystallized important differences over the question of how class-consciousness could be aroused, channelled, and developed. If leftists advocated many planks, and allowed some people to affiliate because they were (for instance) particularly motivated by free school textbooks or temperance, they seemed to be buying into a more "gradualist" perspective on class: essentially, people could become conscious of class because of their spontaneous positions on everyday issues. Conversely, if they had one plank, calling for the abolition of wage slavery, and accompanied it by an educational program through which the aspiring member would come to grasp the underlying scientific logic behind the demand, they were implicitly saying that without the guidance and leadership of a socialist party, a genuine class-consciousness could not develop. Behind the seemingly arcane debates over "many planks" or "one plank" lay significantly different answers to the class question.

For these leftists in general, socialism was about the creation of a scientific enlightenment and a new way of life, not a shift in the balance of power in a local legislature or the Dominion parliament. They saw such parliaments as sounding boards more than as decisive arenas for socialist struggle, and they often saw the party as an instrument of, and not the pinnacle of, a process of sociological education. Within this consensus about the primarily educational focus of the first formation, parties wrestled through these three distinct stages with the question of how best to organize the working class and stimulate its class-consciousness: in the first phase, in a debate pitting the SLP against the CSL; in the second phase, in a debate between the SPC and the labour parties; and in the third a struggle among the SPC, the SDPC, and the militant organizations of a radicalized labour movement.

Of Mixed Pickles and Militant Proletarians: The First Phase, 1894–1904

On the one side: the intransigents in the SLP. On the other: the Liberals and Christian reformers active in the CSL. In the centre: a new (and weak) synthesis, also within the CSL, emphasizing the integration of scientific analysis with working-class struggles. Much of the fascination of this foundational period can be found within the CSL, within which much of this transition to a new way of thinking about socialism took place.

Initially a crucial question confronting socialists – organizers, organs, and organizations alike – was the determination of their stance towards pre-existing liberal institutions, including much of the labour movement as well as the Liberal Party. Indeed, the Liberal Party through these years – and until about 1911 – was the major working-class party, making a strong appeal to left-wing sensibilities (though admittedly it did confront significant continuing pockets of working-class "Tory" Liberal Conservatism in such places as Toronto, Hamilton, Saint John, and Southwestern Ontario).

The Liberal Party was seemingly pure (on the federal level) because until it won power in 1896 under Wilfrid Laurier it had been out of power since the late 1870s. It was associated with anti-monopoly positions – free trade, unrestricted reciprocity – that were promoted on the bases of "The Masses against the Classes," the working-class consumers against the pampered monopolists. It was linked on the provincial level, at least in Ontario and Nova Scotia, with regimes that had brought in far-reaching compromises with labour (including enhanced mine safety, compulsory education, and arbitration laws). It was headed by the charismatic Laurier, easily romanticized as Canada's answer to the revered William Gladstone, who was associated with Christian purity and the dignity of the working class (even some *Canadian* working-class organizations bore the name of this British prime minister). It was not an easy task to construct a socialist left when Liberals could so often point to pro-labour laws, sympathetic platform speakers, and the radiant image of that gallant white-plumed knight, Sir Wilfrid Laurier. It was only when the possibility of a working-class liberalism receded that significant opportunities would arise for organizing a socialist left.[25]

New currents were stirring within turn of the century Canadian liberalism.[26] A Liberal who attended closely and sympathetically to critiques of classical liberal economics and the findings of the new post-individualistic "historical schools" of sociology and economics was no oddity in 1901. The Liberal Party seemed to listen to the concerns of trade unionists, and some of its intellectuals, Mackenzie King most visibly, were *au fait* with recent currents in economics and social science. They had already become masters of the art of *trasformismo* – the conversion of erstwhile opponents into faithful supporters through the noble arts of persuasion and patronage. And if one general *material* manifestation of liberal (and Liberal) hegemony was the country's extraordinary growth rates, this had its *personal* dimension in the ability of the Liberal machine to grant jobs and favours throughout the Dominion. The coming to power in 1896 of the Laurier Liberals meant that the Liberals in Ottawa, and long-standing Liberal provincial machines throughout Canada, had a ready supply of patronage positions that they could use to make "friends" from coast to coast (the word "friend" acquired an almost sinister ring in the political correspondence of the day). The small-town mayor who fought the Liberals might find himself without a "Laurier Post Office," and the rebellious small-town worker might find himself out of a job.

Some of the Liberals' "friends" were working-class leaders recruited for Laurier with a few ego-stroking gestures. Such adventurers were using the labour movement as a way of winning political prominence. Others might need more substantial inducements. Prominent labour leaders breathing fire on appropriate occasions about the rights of the working class were often so many Tory and Liberal politicians in the making. D.J. O'Donoghue, Charles March, A.W. Wright, Robert Drummond, and H.B. Whitton were just a few of the 19th-century politicians who did well out of establishing favour with labour, often by winning genuine concessions to labour demands. When Adolphus Landry, the coal driver of 1891 transformed into the socialist of 1898, spoke to unionists in Amherst, one of the prominent men in his audience that evening was Hance Logan – a Liberal politician who had seized the renowned Charles Tupper's seat from the Tories, in part because Logan had defended rifle-wielding coal miners in nearby Joggins against charges arising from their struggles. This pattern of liberal hegemony explains not only the limited traction of the radical left, but also many of the debates raging within it, especially given how easily labour militants could turn into liberal milquetoasts. In the language of the day, some so-called "workingmen's friends" were "foxy" and some were "proxy." Some were "virtuoso labour friends" capable of the most heartwarming but insincere declamations on the rights of labour, and some were more organically tied to the trade union movement and felt genuinely obliged to do their best for it "within the system."[27]

The "spontaneous" argument in this period favoured the Liberals. If the primary political task was to wrest secondary reforms from the system – free schoolbooks or a better deal for the farmers – why go to the trouble of creating political organizations outside the Liberal Party? But if you believed there was something *structurally* wrong with a decades-old liberal order, if you had reflected on the child-killing coal mines that Liberal politicians defended and whose workers generated the surplus value from whence the Liberal governments themselves extracted royalties for the public finances, if you believed that something much more than absence of mind was at play in a social and political order in which unhygienic slums coexisted with monstrous mansions – then the sight of a "labour fakir" or a "foxy friend" inspired righteous rage. Intransigence might then seem a *necessary* strategy in a political atmosphere in which, like phagocytes engulfing and ingesting foreign particles, liberals were preternaturally alert to any sign that a socialist militant might be persuaded to become more "reasonable." In the many debates between the "spontaneous" and "scientific" positions, pitting the Socialist Labor Party against the CSL, the depth and subtlety of liberal hegemony are all too clear.

The Socialist Labor Party

The Socialist Labor Party was, historian Paul Buhle notes, "the first major party of American socialism." Founded in the United States in 1877, it expanded rapidly before appearing on the Canadian horizon around 1894, evidently first in Halifax, a city that often followed trends in the northeastern United States because of its province's deep cultural and economic links with New England.[28]

The intellectual accomplishments of the party's members included Gronlund's classic *The Co-operative Commonwealth* and Ward's magisterial two-volume *The Ancient Lowly*, both of them extensively read in Canada. Jack London cut his teeth as a socialist rabblerouser in the SLP. After mounting a surprisingly strong bid to win control of Gompers's American Federation of Labor, itself the product of an organization founded by socialist cigar-makers, the SLP settled into a position of sustained scepticism, perhaps not always expressed with a requisite degree of tact, about the existing U.S. trade union movement. Its most famous leader was Daniel De Leon (1852–1914), a brilliant orator who was among the first of many North Americans to attempt to find in Darwin and Spencer the message of social revolution, though he also ranked as high among his declared influences Lewis Henry Morgan's *Ancient Society, or Researches in the Lines of Human Progress from Savagery through Barbarism to Civilization* (1877), a book that "first convinced him of capitalism's inevitable doom."[29] De Leon, who put his legal training to good work in dissecting the arguments of his many opponents, was so much a socialist of his time that, even in a speech delivered to strikers in 1898, he would sternly advise his audience that, while they might need bread, they even more urgently needed the message of the socialist enlightenment, the "knowledge of a few elemental principles of political economy and of sociology."[30] In his model of socialist politics, workers did not spontaneously possess an accurate consciousness of their situation – they needed to be scientifically educated by the SLP.

The SLP-dominated Socialist Trades and Labor Alliance (ST&LA) was organized with the ostensible purpose of organizing the unorganized. Its real goal, according to Buhle, was that of giving "outright socialist leadership to a labor movement growing out of the ruins of the AFL."[31] Such strategies of "dual unionism" were not for the faint of heart. They involved a fundamental challenge to existing labour unions and the principle of labour unity, with the SLP militants vigorously critiquing the AFL and mounting a campaign to replace it – at a time when the AFL was set to embark upon a major organizing drive, one extending into Canada and drawing upon the talents of many of the Dominion's fledgling leftists.[32] Although few at the SLP's 1896 convention criticized their party's increasingly revolutionary stance, by 1898 disgruntled members had broken ranks and taken up cudgels against De Leon, who branded them "The Kangaroos." Factionalism descended to actual violence between the two sides in July 1899, in a struggle for possession of the party headquarters.[33] From the SLP perspective, the "labour fakirs" of the AFL were not to be trusted as exponents of the true interests of workers, and the organization came to argue that only a party with the single plank of socialist revolution merited their support.

The SLP that arrived in Canada was thus a complex beast. The SLP's basic message of the imperative necessity of working-class education was viewed in some circles as being high-handed and elitist, and SLP language was notoriously vitriolic – "the language of class hatred," in the ears of its CSL opponents.[34] Many local socialists may well have been put off by the occasionally aloof and hostile tone of the party's propaganda and the attempts to re-enact in Canada the same dual unionist strategies vis-à-vis labour that had proved so controversial in the United States. One writer in the Montreal *Herald*, most likely Colin McKay, satirized the SLP local and Richard Kerrigan, its leading militant, as a group obsessed with military strategy and bound and determined to split the local labour movement. *Citizen and Country* took particular umbrage at such vintage SLP terms as "labor fakir," "frauds," "decoys of capitalism," and "bogus party." There were "two classes of socialists which unfortunately exist in America," in its estimation: one led by "Prof. DeLeon a foreigner" attached to the "materialistic and anti-trades union section of the socialist movement," and that led by Eugene V. Debs, "who is at once a Christian, a socialist, and a trades unionist."[35]

Still, many SLPers, such as Kerrigan, went on to play distinguished roles as militants, and in such places as London, Brantford, Hamilton, and Toronto SLP activists made remarkably creative and energetic contributions to left-wing debates and activism. In the 1898 Ontario municipal elections the section in London broke new political ground with a municipal ticket that received 126 votes. In 1899 SLP candidates in London drew 1,948 votes. Fred J. Darch won 656 votes for mayor and Henry B. Ashplant 923 votes as water commissioner. In Toronto, in 1899, SLP aldermanic candidates polled 706 votes; in 1900 the party's candidates gained 1,453 votes. The SLP candidate won 2,402 votes in 1900 in a mayoralty contest in London, and an aldermanic candidate endorsed by both the SLP and the labour movement was elected. In the same year, five SLP nominees together took in 1,834 votes, with the tally in Ward 5 running as high as 591. It was all the more impressive, as *Citizen and Country* remarked, considering that "these candidates merely placed themselves before the people as the representatives of socialistic principles without conducting a campaign."[36]

London's Ashplant, one of the SLP's most eloquent advocates, was some-times called the SLP's "National Secretary." Ashplant explained "The History and Policy of the SLP" in Winnipeg's *Voice* in a series that started in February 1896, and he expounded on "The Socialist Labor Party: Its Principles" in the pages of *Citizen and Country* on 25 March 1899. Conspicuously worried about the ever-important debate about religion and socialism, Ashplant was also keen to demonstrate that, as a member of long standing of the YMCA and a fervent Methodist, he was, as the "most prominent Socialist Labor man in Canada," in *Citizen and Country's* description, a straight-talking and honest leftist. He emphasized that the SLP was "broad enough for Jew, Gentile, Greek or Barbarian," and that the party knew "neither color, creed, nor sex, in our demand for equality." With a note of resignation, he cited the SLP's opening manifesto in the Ontario provincial election of 1898: "We are not oblivious of the fact that in our pioneer campaigns we must anticipate misunderstandings, prejudices, misrepresentations and unfair criticisms, and regret that under present conditions we must accept these as inevitable."[37] Ashplant was plainly a figure who did not answer readily to the later standard critiques of SLP "im-possibilism." A Marxist Christian who wrote passionately against the anti-Chinese racism that permeated the contemporary liberal order, Ashplant also contributed writings on "Heterodox Economics," which were advertised in such places as the *Social Democrat* of Chicago. His writings were read well beyond the SLP.[38]

The Vancouver SLP's history was stormy. Founded in 1898 by a militant hailing from Brantford, the local claimed 22 members by December.[39] By 23 November 1899, "escaped" members of the SLP had broken away and made up the bulk of the membership of the Vancouver Socialist Club: "a taste of DeLeonism had made them cautious" of joining any larger body, and "the sentiment was in favor of an independent organization at first."[40] The result-ing United Socialist Labor Party ran a candidate, Will MacClain, an SLP veteran, in the 9 June 1900 provincial election, the first time a socialist had entered such a race. MacClain's platform broke with the SLP in containing, for the first time in B.C. socialist politics, an overtly "anti-immigration platform" that declared its sympathies with the "white British workers of this fair province."[41] As in the United States, splits affecting SLP members were fought out with fists as well as words, which the Party's Canadian critics cited as evidence of its unsuitability for the fair Dominion.

The Canadian Socialist League

On the other side of the spectrum imagined by the critics of the SLP, espe-cially those recording their views in *Citizen and Country*, was the Canadian Socialist League. The narrative spun around the "twin birth" of the CSL – being established first in Montreal in 1898 and then soon after in Toronto – has about it the whiff of folklore, but the exact story is difficult to reconstruct from the available documents. The primacy of Montreal is suggested by its designation as "Local No. 1," its status as the "headquarters local," and the 1899 appearance of the branch's sophisticated and detailed *Program and Declaration of Policy*. One plausible explanation for the dual eruption in 1898 would be that the Point St. Charles militants included some railway shop workers from Toronto, who brought with them memories of an earlier local Socialist League in Ontario. They were in touch with George Weston Wrigley Sr. of Toronto, who saw in them an opportunity to spread the influence and sales of *Citizen and Country*, and as part of this campaign incorporated them into his own fast-evolving plans for a country-wide network. Yet the extant evidence also suggests that the Montrealers were not entirely on the same page with the Torontonians – they were notably less inclined to construct their "socialism" in religious terms.

The *Program and Declaration of Policy of the Canadian Socialist League* (1899) was one of the most important and revealing documents of first formation socialism. If one were a De Leonite, or even a Debsian, it could be critiqued as a variant of the "mixed pickles" approach to constructing socialism,[42] since it listed no fewer than 25 demands, organized handily in four sections. "Secondary and Immediate Demands" included biennial parliaments, universal adult suffrage for men and women, public electoral finances, and (very interestingly, given the heavy legacy of Bellamyite centralism) "the utmost extension and application of the principle of decentralization in all legislative and administrative functions." The "Industrial Demands" ranged from the conventional Liberal-Labour calls for the eight-hour day, safety legislation, and workers' compensation – none of which would have worried the apostles of Sam Gompers – to a more surprising demand that workers be allowed to go on strike without notice, wherever their employers enjoyed a similar privilege to lock them out – a frontal attack on the unbridled management rights of liberal industrial relations. Under "Economic," the Montreal CSLers combined fairly conventional demands for the nationalization of public transportation facilities, old age pensions, a cessation of the alienation of unoccupied public land, a progressive income tax that exempted the working class, and, more combatively, the revocation of the charter of the Canadian Pacific Railway. Finally, under "Public and Social," the Montreal militants wanted free, secular, compulsory and locally controlled public schools, public hospitals to be controlled by national or local boards, legislation against the adulteration of food and drugs, the nationalization of breweries and distilleries, with communities given the power of "local option" to regulate the drink trades, and, more surprisingly, the municipalization of *all* theatres, concert halls, and other buildings used for amusement, recreation, and instruction – perhaps an imaginative pre-emptive strike against the emergent culture of consumption.

The long platform and miscellaneous demands, pitched at such a wide diversity of interests – temperance, suffrage, labour, farmers, urban reformers – would arouse the ire of all those who wanted a proletarian politics *pur et dur*, uncontaminated by the fussy particularities and uncertain class allegiances of those who might sign on by virtue of such secondary issues. Yet the *Program and Declaration* frames this 24-point program with something much more radical. It first proclaims itself an organization primarily focused on the education of the people. "Organization is an impossibility before the educationalist has done his work," it baldly declares. Only well-educated and informed socialists could build a new society – hence the absolute priority to enlightening the people. What is the first priority of the socialist party? "Win the next election," a contemporary social democrat might say. "Build the revolutionary party, and mobilize for the dictatorship of the proletariat," a 1920s Communist would answer. But here the overriding first objectives of the organization are – *Build the Library! Distribute the Literature!*

It was too early in the movement's evolutionary development to envisage a party along the lines of those outside the country, the *Program* warned: if leftists tried to plunk down a disciplined revolutionary party in Canada, without due regard for the nation's peculiarities, the result might well be an "abortion." Hence the Montreal CSLers' caution on questions of organization. They wanted as much local control and initiative as possible. Even on so basic a question as to whether the CSL would charge membership fees, the Montreal cadre believed that such a matter should be left "to the capacity and inclination to pay of the members of each branch." And what of the structure of membership? Could one belong directly to the CSL as a whole, or was one obliged to affiliate with a branch? Although leery of the first option, the Montrealers were not going to insist dogmatically upon the second. As for decision-making, conventions, rules of procedure in branches, the whole nitty-gritty of organizational life – all were left undefined. (Small wonder, then, that by November 1901 the CSLers felt the need to clarify and, to a very limited point, centralize their group.)

After having made these educational declarations, the League then modestly declared that its primary aim would be "*the entire abolition of the present form of society*" and the "*establishment of a co-operative commonwealth*." This meant that the "means and instruments requisite for the production and distribution of the necessaries of life shall be the collective property of the entire community" – a statement offering any De Leonites within the fledgling Montreal local some of the words of "intransigent opposition and critique" that they may have been looking for.

No doubt a strenuous debate occurred in the fashioning of this document. Indeed, echoes of the discussion came in the Montreal CSL's almost apologetic preface to its immediate demands. It flatly declared that none of the 24 demands, or all of them combined, constituted "a radical and conclusive remedy for pressing social evils." Rather, they were "retained chiefly for their educational significance." Conceding that living standards had risen to an extent, the *Program and Declaration* drew the orthodox conclusion that never had the "ratio of exploitation" been so high, for the total share of the wealth going to the workers was growing smaller and smaller. For every dollar's worth of wealth generated by the unprecedented productivity of the workers, only about 25 or 30 cents were going to the workers. The rest was "appropriated by those who are directly or indirectly living on the proceeds of exploitation."

Rather than a dismally liberal "jar of mixed pickles," the document appears to be a very early draft of a program seeking the organic fusion of immediate, or modest, and ultimate, or overarching, demands – in effect, an attempt to combine the spontaneous and scientific approaches. The *Program*'s rationale for its educational work, for instance, was "to develop a sound, logical conception of the truths on which Socialist demands are based, to the end that, sooner or later, those demands may become a power which the opponents of Socialism will find it necessary to reckon with." Such an argument would underline, especially, the Montrealers' unmistakably Marxist presuppositions underlying the analysis of relative working-class immiseration – a theme suggesting that this group was well aware of the debates over revisionism then shaking European socialist movements.[43]

The *Program and Declaration* ends with a wonderful denunciation of the world then emerging around these leftists. "No amount of tinkering with the social evil will ever solve it," it proclaimed. Capitalism was the "upas-monster." For if the "upas" – *Antiaris toxicaria*, a Javanese tree with white bark and poisonous sap that only became more vigorous and pervasive in its root structure if its branches were lopped off – was the image of capitalism, the "upas-monster" could only be effectively combatted by ripping it out by its roots. Pruning away its noxious branches – an anti-child-labour act here, an eight-hour-day there – would only leave the monstrous thing free to grow, perhaps even stronger. The Montreal cslers had found an original way of combining a penchant for gothic imagery with the more homey metaphors of gardening.

The *Program* offered a rousing and moving call to the "Men and Women of Canada." "Play a great and noble part in the great and glorious transformation which lies before the despised wealth producers the world over," it urged them. "You who have borne the burden of poverty, misery, wretchedness, shame, degradation, ignorance and humiliation for so long, to the end that others might wallow in their ill-gotten gains like fattened pigs in their swill," must now gather up your strength and "carve out . . . the glorious heritage of the future free and glorious people. . . . Strike a Blow for the Cause of the World." (Note that this resounding vision of the world transformed was notably secular: one was striking a blow for "the world," not for God, Jesus, or the salvation of a fallen people.) "Girdle on your armour and shoulder your weapons" to win "a life free from want, domination and tyranny of every kind." Bring on the future, when "the good, the beautiful and the ennobling in one and all" will flower in a liberated human race. Here is a cosmic but not religious socialism uniting the most specific reforms with the destiny of all of humanity.[44]

The Montreal CSL preached revolution; the Toronto CSL initially preached Christian social reform. As the Montreal CSLers seemingly anticipated, the League could only grow if such internal differences were tolerated. If working-class autodidacts were the heart and soul of the Point St. Charles cadre who created Montreal Branch No. 1, Toronto Branch No. 2 was in large measure the preserve of Protestant clergymen and strongly linked to a diversity of Christian social reform groups. The style of the Toronto local was reflected in *Citizen and Country*, which typically read like a four-hour-long church sermon about social harmony. Perhaps it was not surprising that the middle-class Toronto group gained the lead over their fellow socialists of Montreal given that they would have had the money, publishing connections, and cultural confidence to do so. Still, in 1902 the program of the Toronto CSL locals – now two in number – contained radical democratic demands such as abolition of the Senate, the people's right to directly initiate legislation and vote on it by referendum, adult suffrage, proportional representation, and public ownership of all franchises. It included a Spencerian call for land nationalization and "Public ownership of all Monopolies and ultimately of all means of production, distribution and exchange."[45] This far more moderate program lacked the Montrealers' Marxist emphases and vigorous rage – yet, even so, it by no means spoke a mild language of "Christian Socialism."

The early history of the CSL confusingly shades off into dozens of other contemporaneous social reform movements, all enthusiastically backed in *Citizen and Country*, and many of them involving the Wrigleys, father and son. The Social Reform League solidified in 1898, with a large conference in Toronto's Richmond Hall, attended by a who's who of concerned Torontonians: J.J. Kelso, social worker; J.A. Martin, single taxer; and Rev. William S. Rowe, perhaps Toronto's pre-eminent socially concerned minister. On 20 October 1899 the Canadian Socialist League held a unity conference, and the Social Reform and Social Progress leagues were brought into its fold. When Wrigley Sr. himself looked back on the history of the CSL, he noted the many other preceding social reform organizations that had participated in what he revealingly called "the social evolution." He remembered Bellamy's *Looking Backward* and George's *Progress and Poverty*. He remembered the Nationalist Club of the Bellamyites and the Anti-Poverty Society of the Georgeites. He recalled, frustratingly very vaguely, the *old* Canadian Socialist League, the Henry George Club, the Social

Reform League, and overall a veritable thicket of new organizations in 1890s Toronto.[46] Branch No. 2's over 100 members in October 1899 could thus draw on a well-established Toronto tradition. *Citizen and Country* cited the panoply of stars that could be found within its walls, including one noteworthy Protestant minister after another. Here, for example, was *Dr.* H.G. Hargrave – one rather suspects he would have insisted on being called "Doctor" – the holder of not one but *two* degrees from the University of Toronto!

A telling portrait of Branch No. 2 was published in the *Globe* in September 1901. The reporter began with the image that the "general public" might have of socialist meetings, "held in attics or garrets in obscure buildings, in back streets," and "composed of unshaven and unshorn men garbed in threadbare coats and trousers shiny at the knees." The public might well worry that such sartorially challenged socialists were listening to "opinions that, if acted upon, would shake society to its foundations." One can imagine many a middle-class householder shaking his earnest head in disbelief over breakfast crumpets at the very idea! Yet Toronto need not fear. Its local socialists were of a better sort altogether. Rather than shaggy-haired Karl Marx types, they were well-turned-out ladies and gentlemen, who gathered at the Woman's Christian Temperance Union (WCTU) on Elm Street, "with its lace-curtained windows, its Brussels-carpeted floor and its luxurious lounges and armchairs." The 17 such socialists that the reporter counted, all of whom were "well dressed, and professed the most benevolent intentions to society in general," included no fewer than seven "attractive young ladies," as well as "nine young men with smooth, clean visages." (Perhaps the one unaccounted-for socialist was a shaggy-haired Marxian reprobate, but we shall probably never know.)[47]

The conventional image of a CSL essentially mild-mannered and middle-class in its politics has a certain validity, then, though to a large degree it emanated from the pages of *Citizen and Country*, which preceded the CSL. The paper had long sought out ministers as its market on the Christian left. Only some of its contributors were oriented to the CSL. Only to a point, then, did the organ function on behalf of the organization. It must have struck many of the secular revolutionaries in Montreal as a rather particular and bland version of their politics, transposed into a religious and unradical key.

For the Montreal revolutionaries, both the immediate and the ultimate demands of their program stemmed from the overriding teleological proposition that in order to evolve towards a free and glorious future humanity must replace the "upas-monster" of capitalism. Yet in many other popular statements the socialist position came to be identified more narrowly with particular immediate demands. What seemed clearly reasoned for the proponents of the scientific position on class-consciousness was "impossibilist" and dogmatic for many proponents of the spontaneous position. A distinct moment in this struggle over basic definition came in the B.C. provincial election of 9 June 1900 when Richard McBride, the Conservative candidate in Dewdney, pledged to carry out the CSL's local platform after it was put before him by activist James M. Cameron. The platform included such un-Conservative measures as proportional representation based on free adult suffrage, free school books, decent jobs for the unemployed, and public ownership of monopolies. McBride later denied signing the pledge; the resourceful Cameron then circulated copies.[48] From the standpoint of the scientific approach to the class question, even had McBride stood by his pledge, the struggle to create a class-conscious proletariat capable of building socialism would have remained unresolved.

From this scientific perspective, there was something maddeningly vague about *Citizen and Country*'s take on "socialism" – notwithstanding the umpteen definitions of the concept proffered by the publication. Socialism seemingly took in everything and everybody who wanted a more humane and sensible world – from a scheming politician like McBride and a curious and sympathetic student like Mackenzie King (who might well, if pushed, have described himself as a "socialist" in 1895) to the systematically anti-capitalist George Weston Wrigley Jr. and Phillips Thompson. Socialism, in this moment, was something not only immense and fascinating but also infinitely amorphous. Socialism was a matter of attending lectures, joining reading circles, and pondering ways and means of improving society. All those who saw themselves as "regenerators" were welcome; and if they provided good copy and sold subscriptions to *Citizen and Country*, they were more than welcome.

Socialism offered a kind of "popular science" of society – one accessible to people with high-school educations and a burning sense that something was profoundly wrong with the social order. If we marvel at the doors that opened to socialist ideas throughout small-town and rural Canada – doors that in later years would be firmly closed – we might consider how well socialism fit into patterns of rural sociability – of visiting, soirées, a neighbourly sharing of insights. By virtue of this ideological and social heterogeneity, the CSL was able to reach into many parts of Canada, some untapped by any prior and, indeed, most subsequent leftisms. In Ontario, besides being quickly established in centres such as Toronto, Hamilton, Ottawa, London, Port Arthur, and Kingston, the CSL penetrated small-town and rural areas not generally associated with socialist movements: its presence was reported in such places as Manitoulin Island (in Lake Huron); Forest (in Lambton County, near Sarnia); Leith (in Grey County, near Owen Sound); Bobcaygeon (northwest of Peterborough); Malton (then a village some 16 miles distant from the city, now the location of Pearson International airport); Gananoque; Preston; Paris. (Some of these might, admittedly, have been semi-fictional "paper locals," perhaps made up of *Citizen and Country* readers who clubbed together to get the paper more inexpensively and perhaps gathered once or twice a year over tea.) By 1902 the CSL had organized in about 65 Canadian centres. In British Columbia it assisted in a great awakening the likes of which the Canadian left has rarely seen since.

In some places circles were sufficiently solidified to run candidates for office and host regular educational events. In 1901 CSLers R.N. Price and C.M. Durward, running on a "People's Union" ticket, won as aldermen in St. Thomas and Brantford respectively. In the 29 May 1902 provincial election in Ontario, 29-year-old CSL candidate James Simpson garnered 375 votes to the winner's 3,136 in the East Toronto riding, and across the city the CSL racked up over 760 votes. (The SLP, which received 285 votes in Toronto, was bettered by the CSL in all four of the constituencies in which the two left groups ran against each other.)

Of the three non-Toronto seats contested by the CSL – South Wellington, Manitoulin, and West Elgin – perhaps it was West Elgin that held the biggest surprise. Here H. Gaylord Wilshire (1861–1927), already a celebrity in the North Atlantic socialist world, contested the seat on behalf of the CSL. As editor of *Wilshire's Magazine*, one of the first formation's flagship journals, Wilshire had made a reputation as the "millionaire socialist," whose flashiness would earn him the nickname of the "P.T. Barnum of American Socialism." An unabashed Spencerian, Wilshire was one of the major theorists of socialism as the science of social evolution in North America, and here he was in St. Thomas, bringing cosmic evolutionism to the farmers and city-dwellers of Elgin County.[49]

Wilshire was able to contest the seat because, as he explained to readers of *Wilshire's Magazine*, "the law in Canada, as in England, does not lay down any restrictions as to who shall be chosen to represent the electors of a district in Parliament, provided that he is a British subject." Since his grandfather had been born in England, Wilshire – who had already run as a socialist in Britain – could claim British citizenship.[50] West Elgin as Wilshire presented it was an unlikely place for a socialist breakthrough. "The people are well contented with their country, climatically, industrially and politically," he advised his readers. "The farmers are all doing well."

In the campaign both of his opponents professed their profound sympathies with socialism, though they worried that their constituents might not be quite ready to embrace it. Still, they reasoned, they did not want to get too far ahead of their less enlightened constituents. Wilshire himself tried to put the best face on the agrarian question, arguing that farmers and workers shared essentially the same interests. "The farmer is really but little, if any, better off than the workingman, inasmuch as he must always sell his product on a competitive market and whatever advantage he should have by virtue of the ownership of his land is usually lost, owing to the high prices he must pay to the various combinations controlling the railways, and to the manufacturers of agricultural implements, etc., and other goods he must buy." As an inventor of quack remedies and future speculator in California real estate (Los Angeles' renowned Wilshire Boulevard is named after him), Wilshire had a genuine soft spot for small businessmen, and he appealed even to merchants threatened by the growth of department stores.[51] The election result, though, suggested the continuing balkiness of the "awkward classes," those who lay outside the classic proletariat/bourgeoisie binary: Wilshire won 425 votes, 375 of them in St. Thomas, where he had been able to build on Price's earlier work. This was 7.4 per cent of the total cast in the constituency as a whole, while his percentage in St. Thomas was 15 per cent.[52]

In British Columbia, perhaps the most important single CSL local was No. 6 in Port Moody, where the central organizers were James M. Cameron, born in Cornwall, Ont., and O. Lee Charlton, born in New Brunswick. Here many activists from the Ruskin co-operative colony, established in 1896 at the confluence of the Stave and Fraser rivers about 40 kilometres east of Vancouver, rallied to the banners of the CSL after the utopian colony failed in 1899.[53] Cameron, who had gone west to work with the Ruskin co-operative, was one of them. He moved from Ruskin to Ladner, B.C., where he set up a branch of an organization called the Christian Commonwealth of Canada. Later, funded by $150 from the newly named Ontario Socialist League, and a small donation from the socialists of Northport, Washington, Cameron would set the West alight with an organizing drive that culminated in the establishment of Local No. 62 in Winnipeg. Other amazing organizers of the great awakening, B.C.-style, included a trade unionist from the Toronto Typographical Union, G. Weston Wrigley Jr., the firebrand and militant who would eventually rename *Citizen and Country* the *Canadian Socialist*. After many permutations and combinations, it became Vancouver's famous *Western Clarion*.[54]

The great socialist awakening in British Columbia coincided with bitter fishermen's strikes and, happily for Canadian socialism, took place at a time when the provincial party system was only beginning. The result was that its socialist activism could, as compared to Ontario, more easily make a permanent institutional mark. The building of the Vancouver Socialist Hall, on the "no-money" basis (labour and materials donated against the possibility of future returns) suggested the new spirit of solidarity in the province. Soon the lower province had many locals. On 23 February 1900, Kaslo was proudly listed in *Citizen and Country* as "the latest town to turn its face to the rising sun of Socialism." Such was the rate and reputation of British Columbia's great breakthrough that the CSL received at least one request from Oregon for affiliation with the organization. It turned down the Oregonians on the grounds that "the Canadian Socialist League is a purely Canadian Institution."[55]

The early years of the 20th century also witnessed a remarkable growth of print media and, with them, the crusading socialist editor. The country was crowded with small carriers of "socialistic opinions." British Columbia not only was home to the *Industrial World* of Rossland and the *Independent* of Vancouver but also had a number of other papers friendly to socialism: *Sandon Paystreak*, *Nanaimo Clarion*, *Ferguson Eagle* (later the *Lardeau Eagle*). Manitoba had *The Voice* of Winnipeg. Ontario had *The Toiler* (a labour paper in Toronto), the *Bobcaygeon Independent*, and London's *Industrial Banner*. Montreal had *Canada's Democracy*. *Butler's Journal* could be found in New Brunswick. One study notes the characteristic impression of the *Slocan Drill* on 6 May 1900 that the province of British Columbia had been swept by a wave of socialistic enthusiasm: "More practical socialistic ideas are expressed today in the multitudinous platforms before the provincial electors than ever saw the light before in the west."[56]

In the thick of it all was *Citizen and Country*, that second great Canadian experiment in publishing the socialist enlightenment. Its publisher, the Social Progress Co. Ltd., a joint stock company, sold shares at $10 apiece to organizations and trade unionists, who paid 10 cents per month. A shareholder who bought more than one share was bound – whether by honour or law is not clear – not to demand more than one vote at the shareholders' meeting, and not to propose a one shareholder/one vote arrangement in the future. It was clearly a well circulated and important paper, the first such in Canadian history, sent out to over 600 other publishers in the country. "A few reproduce matter from it every week, and some less regularly," the paper remarked. As a "wide-awake" publisher on the left, the paper offered both reduced "clubbing rate" prices and book rewards for subscribers. In 1899 it offered subscribers two books and the magazine for three months for just 25 cents. Trade unionists who bought *Citizen and Country* as part of a "club" of subscribers paid only 25 cents a year for a subscription. Selling the paper throughout small-town Ontario (and even into the United States) required a contingent of devoted workers – some of the more dogged of them winning extended accolades for their salesmanship in the newspaper itself – though it is not clear from the evidence how much these "salesmen for socialism" were paid for their marketing efforts.[57] Like *Coming Nation* and *Appeal to Reason* in the United States, *Citizen and Country* was using the new commercial networks and new modes of transportation and communication against the very capitalist modernity that had created them. If a new subscriber was secured by an old subscriber, one of the books went to the sender and the other book, along with the magazine, went to the subscriber. In both cases, socialist consumers were receiving "75 cents in value for 25 cents in cash." This is an "ENDLESS CHAIN," the newspaper enthused. "Every person on our list can be a worker, and not only keep his own subscription paid in advance but send us as many news subscriptions as he may be able to secure."[58]

From coast to coast *Citizen and Country* thus tried to motivate people interested in "socialism," very broadly defined, to join its clubs and sign up new subscribers, and the Christian themes featured in its pages allowed it, although a Toronto-based publication, to reach out to small-town and rural people. Canada now had a Dominion-wide "Voice of Socialism," one so aggressively bent on influencing public opinion that many stepped forward to denounce it, thereby producing a controversy that probably added to its allure.[59] In a pitch to the family (and possibly inspired by the likes of the sensationally popular *Family Herald and Weekly Star*, which reached about 115,000 subscribers in this period), the Social Progress Company pledged itself both to wholesome values and family life. It regularly carried columns supporting the aims of the Woman's Christian Temperance Union, to which George Wrigley Sr.'s partner was firmly attached. It offered as gifts a diversity of wholesome children's books "worthy [of] a place in every family."[60]

As a business, *Citizen and Country* was preoccupied with establishing a solid subscription base. In April 1899 it reported sending out 6,000 papers to "business and professional men, farmers, and workingmen." The Maple Leaf Assembly of the Knights of Labor sent *Citizen and Country* a list of 17 subscribers in the same year. Comrade Hayes, secretary of the Cooks' and Waiters' Union of Rossland, sent along a "club of three yearly subscribers nearly every week." In a note Hayes remarked: "I am still working to add more names to your list, for I consider it the best method of getting the public to understand socialism and its works."[61] Readers were offered access to a daunting list of books, no fewer than 131 in March 1899, for example. Some of them were predictably geared to its Christian readers. Others were of a more directly Marxist or socialistic bent: Bellamy's *Equality*, George's *Science of Political Economy*, and a variety of books by Richard Ely and Thorold Rogers, for example. Even Marx's *Capital* was available, as well as Hyndman's *Socialism and Slavery*, Gronlund's *Co-operative Commonwealth*, and Henry Ashplant's *Heterodox Economics vs. Orthodox Profits*.[62]

The booklists, and the Montreal *Program*, suggest that within the CSL a struggle was taking place between meliorists and militants – or, in other words, between those who believed that consciousness would spontaneously manifest itself and those who believed it must be developed by well-trained authorities in socialism as the applied science of social evolution. In essence the CSL steadily moved towards a much more clearly defined, anti-capitalist program – as amply illustrated by the Spargo address to the 1901 conference. The existence of a "George Weston Wrigley Jr. faction" within the CSL might well have estranged the more conventional Christian reformers. Phillips Thompson had moved from lecturing on "Socialism by Evolution" in 1898 to "Class Conscious Socialism" by 1902. Strikes, mounting impatience with the Liberals, disappointment at the failure of "united front" approaches to social reform – all of these conditions fed into "the CSL's shift to unvarnished social-ism," heralded in June 1902 with the transformation of *Citizen and Country* into the *Canadian Socialist*.[63] That renaming – occurring in the same month as a major streetcar strike in Toronto – was a brazen declaration of a new "left turn." Marking this shift, the Ontario Socialist League's Thanksgiving Day convention in 1903 moved to adopt a single-plank platform with one de-mand: socialism. The meeting, writes Homel, "affirmed the 'materialist in-terpretation of history,' and the 'programme of international revolutionary socialism." It committed its members to a De Leon-like "party pledge," which meant that they must not support, vote for, or appear on the same platform with another party. It changed the organization's name to the Ontario Social-ist Party. Its leading Ontario theoreticians – Thompson, Simpson, Wrigley Jr. – were now all fiercely critical of a politics based on "mere trade unionism" and palliatives. The CSL had moved from spontaneity to science in its stance on the class question.

This transformation in Ontario was undoubtedly influenced by British Columbia, where events had moved with tremendous speed. The 1900 provincial election, in which the United Socialist Labor Party ran for the first time, did not result in the election of any socialists – but the vote tallies were encouraging. "If we could have contested all four [Vancouver] seats our vote would have been easily twenty-five per cent of the total," Ernest Burns of Van-couver marvelled. "This is the first time that candidates have been run on a Socialist platform in British Columbia and if such showing can be made on the first attempt, success is surely near at hand."[64] In October 1900 the United Socialist Labor Party and Nanaimo Socialist Club held a joint convention in Vancouver; at a second convention in October 1901, the Socialist Party of British Columbia was formed (although it did not have the endorsement of the Nanaimo socialists, who wanted a more revolutionary party). Drawing on the mighty traditions of the coal miners, who were fuelled by their passionate resistance to the inordinately wealthy and despotic mine-owning Dunsmuir family, the Nanaimo Socialist Club had more than 80 members as early as 1900 (compared to CSL Local No. 2 in Toronto, with 100). In 1902 the Nanaimo radicals, now in the Revolutionary Socialist Party (RSP), in search of a hard-core revolutionary, brought in E.T. Kingsley from Oakland, California. Kingsley would have a substantial influence over the B.C. left for the next quarter-century.[65]

In 1902 the Nanaimo Revolutionaries introduced a new program. Compared to the Montreal *Program* of 1899, its founding document was a model of scientific succinctness. The Revolutionary Socialists demanded "the transformation as rapidly as possible of capitalist property in the means of wealth production (natural resources, factories, mills, railways, etc.) into the collective property of the working class." They called for the "thorough democratic organization and management of industry by the workers" and the establishment "as speedily as possible" of production for use and not for profit. A fourth demand required candidates for public office on the Revolutionary Socialist ticket to pledge unqualified support to the program's principles and program. If elected, they must use "every legitimate means within their power" to further such objectives. In a grand rhetorical flourish, the Nanaimo revolutionaries threw down the gauntlet to all those who thought they might be bought out. "The Revolutionary Socialist Party of Canada proclaims itself the political exponent of working class interests," they proclaimed. "It will deviate neither to the right nor the left of the fine line laid down in its platform. It will neither endorse or accept endorsement. It has no compromise to make."[66] It pays to remember, when we consider the "in-your-face" tone of this manifesto, that these Nanaimo socialists had been fully exposed to the arts and science of liberal *trasformismo* and the devices of "political speculators" in the house of labour.

The B.C. socialists received a tremendous fillip in 1902 with the election of James Hawthornthwaite (1865–1926). He had once been the "left-hand man" of Ralph Smith, the Nanaimo politician who had drawn close to the Liberals. Hawthornthwaite had worked as a nightwatchman for the Vancouver Coal Company and a clerk in its land department before he ran for office on the Labor Party platform. In 1902 he abandoned the Nanaimo Labor Party for the Socialist Party of British Columbia (SPBC), which in 1903 ran nine candidates and won 4,629 votes out of the 59,688 cast. It elected two members, Hawthornthwaite and Parker Williams, a Welsh coal miner who had worked in the mines of Vancouver Island. George Weston Wrigley Jr., whose father had once written warm-hearted celebrations of such halfway measures as public post offices and government-owned railways, now proclaimed that victory in British Columbia had come about because the SPBC's platform was the "shortest and most uncompromising statement of the principles of revolutionary socialism that has ever been drafted in any country."[67] Even more astonishing, with only two seats – three if one counted that of William Davidson, elected on a labour platform but inclined to support the Socialists on most measures – the B.C. socialists could, with only some exaggeration, claim that they held the balance of power. Researcher Ross Johnson cites the rapturous comment of one socialist: "The Socialists are the power in this province today and although we permit the Conservatives to hold office, we are thoroughly aware that they do so at our pleasure. Conscious of the fact that we hold a balance of power, we intend to take a hand in the management of affairs in this province."[68] This socialist's triumphalism was perhaps inadvertently foreshadowing the dialectical tension at the heart of the project – that of transmuting parliamentary activism into revolutionary transformation.

In 1905, responding to appeals from the Socialist Party of Ontario and the Socialist Party of Manitoba (fd. 1902), an initially hesitant Socialist Party of British Columbia changed its name to the Socialist Party of Canada and, absorbing the Ontario and Manitoba parties, launched its Dominion-wide career. The growth of the movement in British Columbia was astonishing – according to Vancouver stalwart Ernest Burns, some 56 per cent of the party's membership in 1903 had converted to socialism within the previous two years.[69] Socialism had also arrived in the Yukon Territory, where a utopian community at Harmona associated with the Co-operative Commonwealth had earlier been active; in 1904 the 21-member-strong Socialist Party of the Yukon Territory affiliated with the SPC; in 1905, it claimed no fewer than 90 members. In 1906 the SPC even spread into the then-independent Dominion of Newfoundland, with a ten-member local organized in St. John's.[70]

By that point the CSL was no more. Contemporaries claimed that its leading lights, having decamped for British Columbia, had left it in ruins; moreover, its Toronto militants were gravitating en masse themselves into the SPC. The SLP persisted for a while longer. It had a continuing presence in Montreal, as suggested by news stories in April 1907, where it was associated with members of the United Garment Workers of America and would figure in the May Day manifestations of 1908.[71] The debate over how best to organize the class and create a new political order would survive it.

"No Compromise, No Political Trading": The SPC Against the Labourites, 1904–11

In some accounts the SPC seems to emerge with an almost miraculous speed out of Nanaimo – the product of the very exceptional conditions of the far west's coal-mining frontier. Such approaches can be faulted for discounting the many Central and Eastern Canadians who figured as founding organizers of the party – but they are more fundamentally flawed in abstracting the SPC from the transnational and essential debates within world socialism over the class question. In this different reconnaissance, the SPC emerged as one resolution of a long-standing debate between those who believed that working-class consciousness would emerge spontaneously from working-class conditions (and hence could be well addressed by bread-and-butter, immediate demands) and those who believed that only those with a scientific grasp of the theory of social evolution and Marx's triune formula could be truly conscious of the fundamental significance of class. Partisans of either side were looking for ways of resisting liberal order effectively – otherwise they always had the option of assenting to Liberal rule – but they had very different visions of how to do so. Such leftists debated each other on public platforms, ran against each other in elections, and in subtle ways probably also influenced each other. Some began to dream of a third option, one that combined mixed pickles and militant proletarians.

The revolutionaries, by no means confined strictly to the SLP, could see in the CSL a model of how effectively to reach thousands of Canadians. The gradualists, by no means confined strictly to the CSL, could see in the SLP, RSP, SPBC, and ultimately SPC an answer to their own sense that socialism without a revolutionary theory would bit by bit be absorbed into the surrounding liberal order. As early as 1899 Phillips Thompson had warned that unless "immediate demands" were a subordinate part of the demand for socialism there could be little progress towards a new social order. He warned that radicals were always "liable to be diverted by side-issues and political expedients that promise temporary relief, but do not tend in the direction of socialism."[72] This would become the dominant socialist position, throughout much of Canada, from 1904 to 1911. It was based, in large part, on a shrewd and realistic assessment of the hegemonic strength of liberal order.

For a time, then, the SPC was the most visible organized presence on the Canadian left. Yet it was never unchallenged. The rise and consolidation of labourism, the emergence of anarchism as an analytical alternative to SPC Marxism, and (perhaps most significantly) the rise of "hall socialisms" identified with ethnic minorities meant that this approach to creating a revolutionary working class through scientific education was forever generating sharp debates.

A few years into the first decade of the 20th century, the shine had worn off the Liberal Party. The party increasingly radiated a sense of complacency: its historic compromise with protectionism in 1897 rendered implausible any positioning of the party as the voice of free trade; its historic compromise with imperialism in the Boer conflict deprived it of many of its lingering associations with resistance to imperial impositions; its immigration policies alarmed even its supporters; and its labour policies, ostensibly devoted to pursuing a middle path of reason and negotiation between capital and labour, were when solidified in the Industrial Disputes Investigation Act of 1907 unbalanced in favour of capital. Critics of liberal order had new spaces in which they could constructively work. Moreover, the very success of the liberal experiment meant intensified challenges to it: the very farmers who had been recruited in their thousands with the dream of propertied independence in the West, only to discover some of the region's harsh facts of monopoly and hierarchy, would respond with significant protest movements. The failure of the 1905 Russian Revolution brought to Canada some inspiring new European voices, who strengthened the turn to a more overtly Marxian approach to politics.

Labourism was one halfway house within which disgruntled working-class Liberals could find temporary shelter. Although there had been many "labour" candidates before 1904, many of them were of the "workingman's friend" variety, who quickly became Liberals or Conservatives upon election. Now a new breed of labourism appeared, with candidates swearing to be more independent of the ruling parties. Alphonse Verville of Montreal was one such "new model" labourite. In Ontario, Alan Studholme was elected in Hamilton to the provincial legislature, and would hold the seat for 13 years. Both Ontario and Manitoba saw attempts to build more significant parties. Although, as historian Craig Heron remarks, the labourism of the time remained "for the most part, the direct heir of nineteenth-century working-class liberalism," it upheld a vision of a "decentralized society of small-scale production, where social and political power were widely diffused, where citizens were not far separated in social status, were treated equally under the law, and enjoyed equal opportunities, and where self-reliance, voluntary association, and mutual assistance would be more important than state coercion."[73] Yet after 1904 labourism had a new spirit – a much more assertive sense that "labourites" should organize their own political forces.

Labour parties were ideologically and socially amorphous, and tended to be episodic: they would come to life at election time, and vanish shortly thereafter. In Montreal the Parti ouvrier, which was re-established no fewer than three times after its 1890s debut, was immersed in the distinctive world of labour clubs – at least 20 such clubs were active in the Montreal region from 1904 to 1914 – which played a vital role in social and political life in the city. These clubs, whose membership was open to men of the liberal professions and to small businessmen, undertook the reorganization of the Montreal party in April 1906. The labourist perspective articulated with often surprising candour the fundamental idea that workers had social and economic interests that were radically different from those of other classes, and that to express these spontaneous interests they needed to have representation in politics. As Gustave Francq, one of labourism's most cogent and powerful interpreters, remarked, "It is generally admitted by the labor movement the world over that, whatever may be its own strength in the economic field, it is absolutely indispensable that it should be followed by political action." After all, experience had shown beyond doubt "that most laws are framed, not to help the workingman, but rather for the advantage of the capitalist. The reason for this is very simple: while capital was organizing its forces with all the power of money in order to control the governments – and it must be admitted that they have well succeeded – labor confined itself to the struggle in the economic field only."[74] This labourite position could sound almost Marxist, as indeed could Gompersism, in that it was built upon a recognition of the primacy of class and presupposed that consciousness of class was the reflection of the immediate experience of workers.[75] The labourite assumption was that, because consciousness of workers' true needs arose spontaneously as a natural aspect of their position, and because trade unions were vested with the responsibility of defending those interests in the economic field, the unions should have a privileged position in shaping the workers' political profile as well. Francq, for instance, would increasingly manipulate the rules of the Parti ouvrier from 1908 to 1913 so that a party once open to socialists would increasingly be monopolized by craft unionists – and only unionists recognized by the labour council. It was a concept of a "Labour Party" in which the party would follow "strictly along the lines of trade unionism," in Francq's own words.[76] This approach in essence marginalized socialists and their analytical traditions.

The struggle between socialists and labourites consumed considerable time within the TLC. In the Ontario provincial election of June 1908, a Canadian Labor Party ran candidates in Toronto in seats that were also contested by socialists. At the TLC convention in Halifax in 1908, delegates urged that the Congress endorse independent labour candidates, but encountered stiff opposition from Socialists such as Frank H. Sherman and R. Parmeter Pettipiece. Keir Hardie, the visiting star from British Labour, lamented that the division between the two camps had created a "divorce of interest resulting in permanent injury to both."[77]

Rather than being uniformly hostile or indifferent, the SPC's tone on trade unionism was often more that of a wise teacher confronted by a benighted, confused student. It followed ineluctably from Marx, said the SPC in its authoritative statement on the issue, *Socialism and Unionism*, that "except in one or two favored trades where some vestiges of skill and training are still a desideratum, the successes of the labor unions have been few and far between." The non-success of unionism was the result of "perfectly natural causes which are inevitable consequences of the wage system of production." Since no one could change the economic laws inherent in the wage system, "the efforts of the unions are being ... directed not only against effects, but against effects which are absolutely inevitable. What measure of success can be expected?" Thus ascribing, inaccurately, an "iron law of wages" theory to Marx, the SPC then argued that unions, although they once met the needs of the day, were now less and less likely to do so. Unlike unionists, socialists did not try to "get blood out of a stone, to better our condition within a system whose very existence predicates that our condition must grow worse," the SPC proclaimed. "With the fortitude and tenacity of the working class they are fighting a losing fight. . . . We are fighting a winning one. The more battles they lose, the more recruits we gain."[78]

Socialists sought not to bargain within the wage system, but to oppose it from without: "Their interests lie within the wage system, ours without it." The affairs of labour could thus be dismissed with an almost seigneurial disdain:

To the Socialist Party their internal affairs are of no concern and of but academic interest. Whatever they do, whether they federate or disintegrate, whether, caged in the iron laws of the wage system, they accept the inevitable, or dash themselves against the stout bars, they will do what they do at the stern bidding of necessity. We can neither help nor hinder them. We can but spread our message among their membership as among the membership of our class generally, trusting Time and capital to bring results.

On the side of the trade unions, futility and hopelessness; on the side of the Socialists, the future, aligned with "the slow but unswerving forces of evolution, which make our growth uncheckable, our triumph assured."[79] The division between the SPC and the trade unions was dramatized in 1911 by the *Clarion*'s backhanded endorsement of a call by the Building Trades Council and Trades and Labor Council for a general strike in Vancouver. The strike would be a useful demonstration of the "hopelessness of the struggle in the industrial field."[80]

The rise of a powerful competitor in labour, and one whose conception of class-consciousness was diametrically opposed to its own, did not immediately dampen the energy and confidence of the SPC. The Socialists had, after all, achieved striking results using a single-plank formula that had notable support within the left across the country. It was only by hewing to the revolutionary line that the Socialists in British Columbia had succeeded, Toronto leftists such as Thompson, G. Weston Wrigley Jr., and Simpson told themselves. With just 4,629 well-located votes in 1903 the Socialists had won considerable influence in British Columbia. In 1907 the party's vote exceeded 5,000, and two years later, it topped 11,000 – which was, Martin Robin estimates, about 22 per cent of the vote in the constituencies it contested.[81]

Despite its apparent discipline and accomplishment, the SPC was really a kind of "quasi-party," halfway between the one-time protest movements and labour parties of the 19th century and the full-time national parties that were to come in the 20th. It never did manage to hold a national convention – the closest it came to that was a 1908 B.C. convention, which was held in Nelson (rather than Vancouver, which was the norm) to allow Alberta delegates to attend. Like the CSL – and a telling hint that it was an "educational" rather than a "vanguard" or "mass" party – the provincial party's constitution provided that the site of its annual convention was to be determined by referendum, and that this convention could determine which local would act as the provincial Executive Committee – a notion that mirrored the earlier structure of the CSL.[82] With no regular Dominion-wide conventions, the executive was always located in Vancouver – by virtue of tradition, not a democratic vote.

In other respects the SPC was quite different from its predecessor. The CSL had never enforced any sort of "party line" on its locals. The SPC formally did.

You had to sign on for the "single plank" and the "party pledge" – that is, to agree to the spc's minimalist "Abolish Wage Slavery" platform and to forego alliances, or even (on some readings) appearances on a public platform, with representatives of other parties. This was a reflection of the spc's conviction that it spoke with scientific authority on issues of revolutionary politics. One was certainly free to debate fundamental theoretical issues in the pages of the *Western Clarion*, but the chances of dislodging these firm parts of the party's identity were slim. Although both the single plank and the pledge doubtless caused conflict and hardship for members, they were seen as necessary elements of cohesion under conditions of liberal hegemony, in which the ground was thick with "political speculators" anxious to win over leftists to the Liberal Party. Mackenzie King, for example, kept a sharp eye out for promising socialists who could be "turned" from their convictions and lured into the Liberal Party with promises of fame and fortune. Critics of capitalism could also invest their time and energy in countless ways in various causes, from temperance to public kindergartens, which from the spc's point of view had to be considered secondary to the primary class question. At least in some places, aspiring members of the spc were required to sit examinations in Marxist theory – an idea associated with G. Weston Wrigley Jr. and the Toronto Socialists in particular, who were in many respects more hard-line than many of their B.C. counterparts. This was not a party for half-hearted dabblers, of the sort (an spcer would say) that might be drawn into the various labour parties. Here, the conception of class-consciousness was the polar opposite of that of the labour parties – in that consciousness was properly defined as the outcome of a disciplined scientific investigation, guided by Marxists, into the logical and historical preconditions of capitalist society and its impending demise.

The *Western Clarion*'s masthead proclaimed, "Published in the Interests of the Working Class Alone." The links between militant coal miners – in British Columbia, Alberta, and Nova Scotia – and the spc are plain. Yet, as historian Mark Leier observes, the spc's "upper echelon" was seemingly drawn not from the workers but from the petite bourgeoisie. Thompson studied and practised law before becoming a newspaper editor and publisher; the elder and younger Wrigleys were "middle-class publishers and editors." R. Parmeter Pettipiece ran small-town papers in Alberta and British Columbia before joining with the Wrigleys in 1902 to publish the *Canadian Socialist*. E.T. Kingsley had been a fish merchant, print shop proprietor, and publisher. W.A. Pritchard had worked as a clerk and accountant. Ernest Burns ran a second-hand store and James Cameron a tobacco shop. Thomas Matthews sold real estate and stocks. W.W. Lefeaux was a bookkeeper and clerk. James Boult ran a newsstand and became a real estate agent. James Hawthornthwaite, the spc's star in the B.C. legislature, had worked as a real estate agent, mining promoter, and U.S. consular official.

SPC organizers could make as much as $2 per day, and the party's secretary and editor were paid about $60 per month respectively. Such SPC cadre might be described as self-employed men. Hence, according to Leier, "Collective bargaining and reforms to ease relations between employers and employees [were] equally irrelevant to them."[83] Outside British Columbia many other prominent SPCers were not manual workers – at least not while they were the party's most prominent spokespeople – Alf Budden, James Simpson, Roscoe Fillmore, A.F. Landry, Colin McKay, J.B. McLachlan, William Watkins, W.U. Cotton, Sophie Mushkat, and Albert Saint-Martin, for example. In the *Western Clarion* itself, a Vancouver report referred to a "disproportionately large" business element within the party element and, interestingly, to a "proletariat a large portion of whom expect to escape wage slavery by the real-estate route."[84]

Still, in class position many of these leaders were somewhat betwixt and between – in essence, exemplars of the very "awkward classes" that their orthodox Marxism had so much trouble analyzing. Rather than deliberating on schemes for elaborate state planning from which they themselves would benefit, they more often denounced the very idea of the state, offered bitter critiques of taxation, and fashioned satires on the very idea that government ownership might be a good thing. Capitalism could not be planned – the SPC tells us over and over again – it must be destroyed. It would be put out of its misery not by "experts," but by a working class awakened to consciousness by those who had mastered socialism as the science of social evolution.

For all that Kingsley had been a merchant and could later be considered a self-employed publisher, for example, he was also a man who had lost both his legs in an industrial accident – perhaps formally irrelevant to a strictly Marxist definition of his class location, but not likely to have been personally irrelevant either to him or to his own sense of class identity. For all that McLachlan, the emerging leading socialist of District 26 of the United Mine Workers of America in Nova Scotia, was on some level a petit-bourgeois dairy farmer, he was such because as a mining militant he had been blacklisted by the coal company. For all that McKay was a freelance professional writer, he was also, by times, a wage-earning merchant seaman and, occasionally, an anti-capitalist political prisoner. For all that George Weston Wrigley Jr. was the son of a newspaper proprietor, he was also a trade unionist and working printer. If one were to hazard a different generalization based on the same evidence, it would be that the socialist was often a person who had a past as a worker, a present as a liminal figure, neither fully proletarian nor fully bourgeois, and a sharply uncertain future. In a sense, such intellectuals and activists were forced by the jolting experiences of their working lives into the radical defamiliarization and appreciation of the "constructedness" of the world – occupying positions from which the contradictions of the social order were unusually visible. Because of this, as a rule, they were not especially acting in their own economic interests, or so it would seem, at least from the examples of a few individuals. If Pettipiece hoped to reap a handsome reward from the investment of his savings of $1,600, would he not have been smarter to put it in real estate than in the working-class press?[85] Many leftists – whether Marx, Mikhail Bakunin, or Vladimir Ilyich Lenin in Europe, or Kingsley, Simpson, or Fillmore in Canada – experienced underlying tensions in their attempts to pin down a working-class identity, for themselves or others.

Many of these organizers were, then, workers *and* professionals, would-be self-employed proprietors and salaried employees, men tempted by real estate speculations, men who had lost their limbs in industry. They were against the oppression of workers by capitalists, but they were *for* a world in which such stable and transparent categories were instantly legible, in which the "Interests of the Working Class Alone" could be discerned and defended.

Throughout the spc existed a cultural pattern that was at variance with any strict economic determinism – one captured by Jacques Rancière in *The Nights of Labour*, when he describes the militant universalism of workers who, in their hours spared from labour, were deeply attracted by the possibility of speaking with authority on universal human issues. They carved out, in a society demanding their conformity, freedom to generalize, freedom to analyze, freedom to critique, and freedom to be angry.[86] In both a literal and a symbolic sense, activists of this stripe could feel themselves to be both attached to and detached from the workers – to be a "vanguard of the working class," as U.S. socialist (and future vice-presidential candidate) George Ross Kirkpatrick put it in an spc pamphlet in 1911.[87] spcers in their own minds were the developers and teachers of the most powerful social science known to humanity. They had access to a specialized knowledge most workers did not have, and were responsible for disseminating it. That the paradigm itself might radically change as it engaged with more and more people does not seem to have been part of their outlook. They were like doctors, prescribing a painful medicine. As Alf Budden wrote:

> The acid of criticism must first of all expose the rotting sores before measures for their eradication can be undertaken. The working class must be organized to a point of power where it will be invincible, then, equipped with knowledge, and strong in its self-reliance, it will forge from out [of] the material (happily so plentiful today), that new republic of labor where poverty will be a horrid memory of the evil past.[88]

Socialist Party locals were expected to make the dissemination of the works of socialism a key part of their day to day activities. Every local was expected to have a "literary agent." In 1908 the major "English" (that is, English-language) branch of the SPC in Toronto decided that the chair at public propaganda meetings should announce when and where literature could be purchased; that he single out two books or pamphlets for particular mention; and that the SPC's ward organizers also be considered "assistant literature agents," responsible for having local militants approach all persons known to be interested in the labour question. This vision of "Spreading the Gospel" in essence entailed the SPC becoming a small army of literature salesmen. Like the CSL before it, the party envisaged an "endless chain" of supporters, readers, and enthusiasts of its literature: "It is up to every member of the party to get busy selling literature to his friends and enemies, to strangers as well as to his acquaintances, to everybody who has coin and the intelligence to spare."[89] In its pre-SPC days, *Cotton's Weekly* recommended other approaches to spreading the word about socialism. "The way to spread Socialism is to disseminate Socialist literature. . . . Make out a list of ten barbers in your town, enclose in an envelope with a dollar bill, address to us and *Cotton's Weekly* will do the rest."[90]

In the hours they were not selling books, young SPCers were well advised to be training as speakers. The SPC was so taken with the debating points scored by socialists against their opponents that the *Western Clarion* even carried an in-depth account of a long debate in Manchester, England, pitting the socialist stalwart Jack Fitzgerald, "but a bricklayer," and Mr. G.W. De Tunzelman, B.SC., M.I.E.E., the examiner in physics at one of the universities. According to the report, the poor physicist was no match for the brilliant bricklayer.[91] The ideal SPC speaker could hold his own against hecklers, rival Salvation Army bands, and workers so timid that they would locate themselves at the edge of the crowd and only appear to be listening. Like Jack London's Ernest Everhard, he would be able to silence the opposition by the sheer force of his logic. As Spargo would have agreed, soapboxing was tiring work. Wilfred Gribble, the SPC's star organizer in 1909, was worn almost to exhaustion by his tour of the Maritimes. He described the joys of abandoning an open-air meeting for one held indoors, a venue that was "far easier on the speaker." It was exhausting work, speaking "to the four winds of heaven." If comrades could see their way to advertising meetings indoors, he would be very grateful.[92] Much of the central purpose of the SPC, and core to its strategy for building class-consciousness, was to engage in debate after debate, and win. Indeed, watching the master orator dispose of an ill-informed member of the audience became part of a socialist evening out – so much so that James Simpson, when he was visiting Cape Breton to write on the great coal strike for the Toronto *Star*, posed as an uninformed non-socialist, all the better to be shown up by the formidable Gribble.[93]

In contrast to many of their competitors, SPC activists first received professional training in the science of socialism. Their performances of socialism often took place before critical audiences, including reviewers from their own *Western Clarion*, who were by no means pushovers. Gribble gave top marks to one performer at the regular Sunday "propaganda meeting." It was the 20-year-old comrade's first effort, and he had done very well in his "Analysis of the Process of Exchange." It was all the more gratifying a performance because he had once been so halting and "jerky" a speaker, but was now the epitome of fluency and clarity. Let him be a model, Gribble urged, to other comrades, who too could overcome their deficiencies and become stars on the soapbox. "Your arguments at the Labor Temple won't equip you for this business," he warned, adding: "Some of you would be able to do finely in a short time if you would go the right way about it."[94]

It was part of the yearly cycle: the trees renewed their foliage, and the graduates of the "socialist college" – no fewer than 19 in Toronto in 1909 – were ready to mount their soapboxes. "Labor can accomplish anything. To it must come some day the mastery of the world. And these hustlers, these soap-boxers, with their speeches and pennies and labors, will change the face of the world."[95] So hoped Robert Hunter, imagining a speech he would deliver to the "Red Special" that was launching Socialist orators all over North America in 1908. For Gribble, a willingness to hit the soapboxes was almost a test of one's seriousness as a socialist. "The Socialist Party is a fighting organization and as such has no use for individuals with no fighting spirit," he remarked. The individual who labelled himself a socialist and never came to meetings, never made the smallest sacrifice, and never even distributed literature, "which is the very backbone of our propaganda" – of what worth was he or she? And the excuse that one was "no speaker" did not justify abstention from activism. Yet there were within the party "alleged revolutionists" who always had something else to do when they were asked to participate in some activity or work. They were "shirkers," who could "spin off economic truths like parrots," whereas the better comrades were those "with the fighting spirit," and the best comrades were those with "the economic knowledge and the fighting spirit."[96]

In the SPC, locals were expected to look after their own affairs as much as possible. Most of the activities revolved around open-air meetings and, in some places, electoral struggles. Under the secretaryship of D.G. McKenzie, distant locals were strongly cautioned against pestering the Executive Committee with their problems. Remember, McKenzie urged such rank and file members, that the Executive Committee had to "deal with a population scattered over a vast territory." It could not perform this "stupendous task" if it were constantly hounded by troublesome, fault-finding members.[97] In some ways the SPC model was somewhere between an institutional party with a stable bureaucracy and a loose CSL-like assembly of local clubs. Locals distant from Vancouver might well feel that all that they really got in exchange for their dues was the odd visiting speaker and a good discounted price on Marxist literature. Otherwise they were pretty much on their own – until, that is, they stepped out of line, perhaps by appearing to contemplate an alliance with another left organization, in which case the whole weight of the Dominion Executive Committee (or its regional or provincial proxies), with its ability to expel members, would come down upon them. If the party did not abide by its own teachings about solidarity and democracy, one member wrote critically, it would never be in a position to fill its political mission: "There is no use preaching working class solidarity if we ourselves permit division to be promoted within our own ranks. There is no use clamoring for industrial democracy as long as its most rudimentary principles are not observed by our own organizations."[98]

The world as constructed within the *Western Clarion* was not mappable according to the Fabian precepts of Sidney and Beatrice Webb and other apostles of state planning. It was a different place – volcanic, harsh, echoing with the raucous laughter of refusal. The *Clarion* tried, and tried again and again, to cauterize the wounds of capitalism by pouring upon them the healing acids of criticism. A deep rage burned through the newspaper, a rage that fuelled an almost insatiable drive to command all the resources of Western civilization in a struggle against the bourgeois enemy. "Not People," was the heading of one furious front-page short story, borrowed from the *District Ledger*, on 24 December 1910. "A capitalist mine owner who had not visited his mines for several years went to see them, taking his five-year-old boy with him." Upon seeing the miners for the first time, his child asked: "Who are those people?" "They are not people, son," explained the father. "They are miners."[99]

"One Month's Slaughter," was the heading for a scathing short satire on social progress in the *Clarion* in April 1907. The article pointed to the industrial accidents detailed in a recent *Labour Gazette*: "As an indication of the rapid advancement of the Dominion toward commercial greatness, it is worthy of note that a healthy increase in the number of killed and injured has occurred during the past year."[100]

Few elements of the SPCers and the *Western Clarion* are more controversial than their oft-used strategies to speak to and about workers. In essence, this strategy for rousing class-consciousness through education amounted to an extended campaign of "shock therapy." In the United States, historian Aileen Kraditor spent much of a highly critical book about the American left cataloguing the various terms of abuse that socialists showered down upon the workers.[101] The Canadian left followed a similar pattern. After calling to mind a recent American story of steelworkers heatedly vying among themselves for a few paltry jobs, the *Clarion* decided that it was merely the spectacle of "a lot of hungry slaves fighting desperately among themselves to see which shall secure the coveted master." Or maybe they were more like the suckers at a carnival, taken in by "perpetrators of a clumsy hoax, that would scarce be up to the standard requisite to do credit to a ten-cent show." Those workers taken in by capitalists were "victims ... without brains."[102] Some workers were even dumber than wild animals, Kingsley remarked: "Along the north shore of Lake Superior it is rock and muskeg, a combination shunned by about every animal in the category, except that brilliant specimen, the wage-slave, who would cheerfully go to hell itself, if its brimstone deposits could be used as a means of squeezing a little profit out of his foul carcass for his capitalist masters."[103]

"Comrades," wrote Gribble, "we know it is hard to keep the Red Flag flying in those little towns where there are only a few of you or where there is only one of you perhaps, you feel the want of association with kindred spirits at times. It seems a hopeless fight, the workers seem so stupid, so spiritless." For C.W. Springford, "the human animal is the most selfish alive, give him his hay and oats and he cares nought for his fellows and it is only when he is hungry he starts to think. When he is educated enough by the much despised agitator he will kick but his efforts alone will not count for much."[104]

The popular term "wage-mule" linked the worker with animality, mindless work, and stubborn stupidity: "China is a promising field in which to dispose of much plunder taken from working mules under the wage process of capitalist brigandage," a piece in the *Clarion* pointed out. "If this field, or any considerable portion of it, should be denied to the American brigands (capitalists) they might be compelled to curtail their plundering operations and some of the mules would lose their jobs. And a wage-mule without a driver is a most pitiable object." How, another reader wondered, could one feel anything but contempt for a working class that kept the sensationalistic Vancouver press in business?[105] Workers had almost ceased to be human: "He [the worker] himself has ceased to be a man. He is a machine converting food, clothing, etc., into physical energy. 'Giving off' physical energy into the great machine. Man grinding products into bone and brawn, the machine grinding bone and brawn into products. For that and for that alone he exists, like the machine, and like the machine, when he is worn out he is cast on the scrap heap."[106]

In other passages, the *Clarion* – sounding quite a lot like Spencer on the topic of poor relief – conveyed a sense of working people as needing the goad of hunger if they were to understand the necessity of struggle. "Nothing will help us now but the social revolution. Before us there lies only an era of increasing misery and deprivation. Hunger is a cruel counselor, but none other will the workers heed. The only thing for the man with the six children is to stay where he is and hustle his hardest to help hunger teach."[107] "Wage-mule" not only conveyed a sense of working-class exploitation but also implied, for those exposed to popularized versions of anthropology, a devolution to a lower level of life. Members of this wing of the first formation were professionally committed to a catastrophic and miserabilist interpretation of working-class life.

Such words were also found in *Cotton's Weekly*, supposedly the more reasonable of the two major socialist papers in pre-1914 Canada. Commenting on the absence of socialist members of Parliament in Ottawa, *Cotton's* asked, "When are you workingmen going to wake up? When are you workingmen going to get vexed with your own stupidity? . . . When are you going to get wise to your own interests?" As McKenzie commented, somewhat famously, "We have no concern with the traffic in labor any more than we have with the trade in turnips."[108] Like the Parti ouvrier in France, which was in many ways a precursor of and template for parties of the SPC's temper, the SPC interpreted deskilling as both a harm done to workers, and as a harbinger of "solidarity and a utopian future, once transmuted by the alchemy of socialism."[109]

In *What's the Matter with Canada?* – a pamphlet produced for Frank Sherman, best known as a socialist activist in UMW District 18 but in 1908 running as a SPC candidate in Calgary – the capitalist politicians were depicted as such ignoramuses that any knowledge of the growth and development of human society would be lost on them: "It would be as superfluous as a knowledge of Greek and Latin to an Irish hod carrier." Similar characterizations of the working class were considered veritable *Gems of Socialism* in the eyes of the Lindsay SPC local. "The mule gets his pay in keep, the worker gets his keep in pay. Both amount to the same thing – a meal ticket," was one such gem. "When a workingman has a wooden leg he finds it hard to get along, but he seems to get along all right with a wooden head," was another.[110]

At particular moments, and particularly at times of class conflict, such talk could be especially controversial. McCormack describes instances of Kingsley's expressions of "anti-unionism" in the SPC being contested within the party, with Wrigley Jr. and Burns taking issue with his critique of trade unions, strikes, and boycotts.[111] David Frank notes Gribble's commentary on the Cape Breton miners' strike of 1909: "The majority of the miners are in a state of fatuous confidence as to their success, and are just now unfitted to some extent for listening to the real thing." Trade unions were "no use to the working class," standing as they did "for the present system of industry."[112] Such comments could set local activists' teeth on edge.

For those like McLachlan, Watkins, Simpson, Sherman, Pettipiece, and J.C. Watters, to list just six prominent "Socialist trade union leaders" from Nova Scotia to British Columbia, the SPC's scepticism about trade unionism must have frequently generated some inner, if carefully suppressed, tensions. (Sherman would eventually be expelled from the SPC because of them.) In retrospect, the party paid a high price for its position, as such figures, one by one, became estranged from it. Although Keir Hardie became fair game for the censure of the *Clarion*, the longer-range impact of his example, and both his and Ramsay MacDonald's critique of the "impossibilist" style, strength-ened the conviction of an element within the SPC that unions, sometimes dis-missed as mere "commodity organizations," were actually indispensable elements of the struggle. Such thinkers were in a difficult position, because despite the best efforts of SPCers like Simpson, the TLC was unlikely ever to endorse the SPC as the political arm of labour.

For all its seeming "scientific" clarity, the SPC's answer to the class ques-tion was deeply contradictory. It wanted the working class to take over production, while deriding that working class for its perennial stupidity. Many historians have had no difficulty in convicting the SPC of elitism, insensitivity, and hypocrisy. More subtly, it seems to have sheltered a number of hard-core individualists, self-made mavericks who prided themselves on their freedom to decide on a whole spectrum of issues. They were possessed not only of themselves but also of a substantial cultural capital attesting to their individ-ual attainments. The SPC thus mirrored basic elements of the liberal order that it was sworn to critique.[113]

The relationship between the party and its discourse on class was compli-cated. Enunciated in the context of a liberal order whose official words celebrated the dignity and worth of the individual but whose socio-economic realities treated the individual merely as a unit of labour-power, SPC rhetoric insistently staged socialism as the individual scientist's platform exposé of the existing political order as a fraud and a delusion. Liberals would exude sym-pathy; some would even announce their short-term conversions to sentimen-tal versions of "Socialism." They would announce how far they were removed from the old competitive order. But the soldiers kept shooting strikers. The bodies kept coming out of the mines. Mine disasters called forth the most sin-cere expressions of humanitarian sympathy from people who had not the slightest intention of making them less likely.

The visceral language of the *Western Clarion* cut through the euphemisms and silences that allowed such enormities to continue. SPC-talk regularly, un-forgivably, reconstructed this system of applied liberalism in a language radi-cally foreign to the dominant assumptions – and in ways that clearly chimed with many workers in particular places. It had a liberating cut-the-crap roughness unknown in most of the rest of the Canadian press. In the severe, "gauche" world of the *Western Clarion*, euphemisms and platitudes were ruth-lessly skewered. The *Clarion* worked in every issue to defamiliarize the everyday world. On its every page the *Clarion* preserved that moment of re-fusal that made socialism seem, not an option, but a necessity. "Do these jel-lyfish think they deceive anyone, I wonder, with their manifold and petty excuses?" one writer wondered about the liberal politicians. "This letter will assure them that there is one who isn't fooled, or they can take my word or not, but I can assure them they fool no one else. I know that I am going to be told that I am 'rather harsh,' in consequence of this letter. I have been told so before, and am ready to be told so again, and am also ready with a suitable answer." The writer then succinctly justified his own caustic tone: "There is no room for diplomacy in the Socialist movement. The straightforward way is the best, the only one for us to adopt, and anyone that thinks it isn't has got to show me, and they have not done so yet, and I hereby challenge any posing as revolutionists to do so."[114]

The straightforward way was put to a severe test in rural Canada. If the SPC answer to the class question was the relentless exposure of working-class exploitation, what did this mean for Canada's rural majority, who were not (in the Marxist sense) members of the working class? The SPC developed rural bases in some places – for example, Courtenay, B.C., and Albert, N.B. Johnson reports attempts in Alberta in 1907, through the Society of Equity and the Alberta Trades and Labor Congress, to "socialize" the farmers, with the farmers' representatives resisting the overtures and defending the principle of profit.[115] In 1909 *Cotton's Weekly* defended Spencer's early call for the "nationalization of the land" as "one of the aims of Socialism."[116] Farmers could be forgiven for wondering who would, after nationalization, govern access to, and security on, the farms they had spent so much time and effort developing.

In 1908 Charlie O'Brien confronted this contradiction head-on when he tried to organize SPC locals in the Okanagan Valley (where, perhaps somewhat surprisingly, the SPC did manage to build a base). At Mara, it was noted that Comrade O'Brien had dispelled the false rumour that the socialists wanted to take away the farmers' land and their homes, although another story claimed that the producers continued to cling to this idea, even in the face of all the literature sent to them by the SPC.[117] Were the farmers necessarily wrong in their assumption? The SPC was very good, or at least persistent, at insisting that the farmers were slaves of the soil. It was maddeningly vague in specifying how the soil would be liberated and managed under socialism. After 1910 farmers appear to have distanced themselves from the SPC and subsequently the Social Democratic Party of Canada, moving to listen to more populist and Spencerian voices on the Canadian left. The gap between the language of the socialists and the language to be found in much of rural Canada would be a major theme of the postwar show trials.

Those close to the party were aware of the problem. Will R. Shier remarked in 1909 that socialists were not made "by denouncing other people. They are made by hearing the Socialist philosophy explained. People who can be bulldozed into anything can be bulldozed out of it again. Throwing bricks at people does not educate them." The SPC "went too far," for many, when it broadcast its sceptical views about the trade union movement in the depths of massive strikes. A Russian Jewish merchant in Joggins, the coal-mining town on the shores of Fundy, critiqued Roscoe Fillmore for his "bad language." He told Fillmore that he had shown "too much impatience and aggression in his speeches about socialism," and – tellingly – that he would only anger people if he kept calling them "wage slaves."[118]

Yet somehow an SPC infused with caution and humility would not have been the SPC. Just as the "no party pledge" had benefits as well as drawbacks, so too did the discourses of the *Western Clarion* and many SPCers. Week after week they dramatized the plight of the workers with images drawn from the battlefield, the abattoir, and the slave plantation. Many SPCers earned a reputation for being hard-as-iron stalwarts. They often seemed "impossible" to live with. They also seemed "impossible," most of them, to corrupt – not a negligible quality in a world of foxy and proxy friends and political speculators. They had an appeal to those completely fresh to socialist ways of thinking and acting.

The most colourful, quotable evidence of "impossibilism" also often calls out for a more ironic, theoretically informed reading. When people like O'Brien or Fillmore talked about the "damphool" workers (and the invented word itself was surely self-puncturing) there would have been a thousand visual and verbal cues to indicate that the speaker was himself no plutocrat. This was the down-to-earth language of the barnyard and factory. Those who heard it might well have found it funny, not offensive. It was, perhaps in many contexts, a case of "reverse discourse" – taking a wounding stereotype or expression, and by appropriating it, making it a term of resistance. (The modern record of the word "queer" suggests a parallel.) Spoken within the group itself, a word like "damphool" may not have seemed an insult. The word subverted the hierarchy of class images – by showing that the working-class "fools" harboured an active, "wise" minority. In the *Western Clarion*, with its columns chock full of the latest word on the socialist enlightenment – Aristotle might be front-page news, next door to the "dangblasted" plutocrats! – the whole joke was on those who did not see that the "fools" were fast encroaching on their "wise" social superiors.

In a striking editorial, the *Clarion* proclaimed the working class to be the "Modern Sisyphus." Like Sisyphus, the workers had little choice but to continue to roll their stone up the hill – and to bring the capitalist system to an end. "Capitalism exists for and because of the exploitation of the workers. And there is no power on earth nor in heaven or hell, able to mend it. The workers alone have the power to end it and that is the one thing they can do to it. That they will do eventually because they must."[119] The *Clarion* spoke a hard, truthful language to an established order. Those educated through reading it every week, attending SPC study clubs, and listening to SPC street orators made this language and this "impossibilist" style theirs for a long time after the last light from the *Clarion* was extinguished.

The "resistance through rhetorical rituals" found in the *Clarion* also characterized the SPC in provincial parliaments. Many in the SPC wanted politicians elected on the party platform to be directly answerable to rank and file party members. In other words, they took the "card" of the member of the legislature and saw it being played in a completely different, democratic game. In British Columbia, the demand that he submit a pre-signed letter of resignation helped push Hawthornthwaite out of the party altogether. In this framework members of elected bodies were seen as SPC propagandists who happened to be on the state's payroll – thus allowing the movement the luxury of agitators who were paid for by the very system they wanted so badly to subvert.

In British Columbia the refusal of the Socialists to rise in honour of coal baron cum Lieutenant-Governor James Dunsmuir underlined more effectively than any editorial in the *Western Clarion* the Socialists' resistance to the Crown, to capital, and to the King Coal. It was reported across the country, with the *News* of Toronto particularly shocked by the Socialists' defiance. In a letter to that paper, Phillips Thompson defended the Socialists' gesture as a strategic move in what he called a "class war." The capitalist newspapers' outrage was a measure of the Socialists' effectiveness. If the person speaking for labour interests won approval from the capitalist organs, it was a sign he or she was "either a fool or a traitor." The "one consistent, logical position for a Socialist" was that of "uncompromising antagonism to capitalism and all its ways and works," including the governments that were merely "its servile instruments for keeping labour in subjection." So why, asked Thompson, should socialists pretend to venerate the "ceremonials pertaining to government" that were intended to inspire an awestruck feeling of reverence for class and caste government? Why shouldn't they be "boorish" in the face of such absurdities? And why should they stand up for a man like Dunsmuir?[120]

In the same vein, when Charlie O'Brien made a speech on the Alberta and Great Waterways Railway Company's deal with the government – as described by a SPC pamphlet issued to honour his arrival in the Alberta legislature, the first time that the "interests of the working class had been directly represented" – it was a calculated act of defiance. O'Brien, the epitome of the working-class autodidact, was born in Bangor Hastings, an Ontario hamlet about 50 miles north of Belleville, of "poor, rural, Irish-Canadian stock." He moved from a profound admiration of Laurier (who had first inspired him to read) to the fledgling socialist movement, a transformation evident as early as 1903, when he became local correspondent for the *Western Socialist* and the Socialists' organizer in Fernie, B.C. After being elected to the Alberta legislative assembly in 1909 he spoke at no fewer than 32 engagements in five provinces. According to historian Allen Seager, "O'Brien combined the rhetoric of the Wobblies, the imagery of Jack London, and the prestige of a Debs." He was, one witness remarked in 1911, "broad enough to be friends with everybody and everything except the capitalist system ... and that is probably why the workers like him." He was "particularly free from egotism; he bubbles over with good nature. He would not lay claim to the charm of Laurier, and yet, he is a sagacious old dog at that. Our comrade has that wit and humour known throughout the world as Irish." If all socialists necessarily went through "a period of evolution," O'Brien "had passed the desperate villain stage ... long ago. He is a ripened and mature revolutionist, a sturdy rebel."[121]

When O'Brien stood in the legislature to comment on the railway deal, he gauchely reminded all the members present that they were, consciously or unconsciously, "representing definite material interests," to wit those of the Canadian Pacific and Canadian Northern Railways, among others. He too was representing material interests. "I am here to voice the interests of those who are slaves to the rule of capital." Although he was speaking about a very specific question of subsidizing a railway through government guarantees, O'Brien insisted on connecting this particular issue with a cosmic vision of human history from its beginnings to the present day. O'Brien reminded the increasingly restive Alberta house that he had been elected on the platform of the spc, whose mission it was to "point out the inevitable ultimate collapse of this present commercial system." In its place they would establish production for use and not for profit. In his account of this history, just as he reached the stage of "Civilization" he was almost derailed by members, including future prime minister R.B. Bennett. Nonetheless O'Brien returned to his theme, and in a speech that had an echo of Everhard in *The Iron Heel*, he accused every other member of the legislature of being a "kept man."[122]

O'Brien would earn further notoriety in 1910, when in response to a resolution expressing sympathy for the widow of the late King Edward VII, he moved as an amendment that the Alberta house also extend condolences to the widows of miners recently killed in a mining disaster. Within this framework – elsewhere evident in De Leon's writings about socialists in legislatures – it was not the job of the socialist legislator to help make the system run more effectively. It was his or her job to confront capitalist power with the evidence of its irrationality and depravity, and to broadcast the rival truths of socialism.[123]

Conversely, the spc viewed with disgust attempts to contest "peanut politics" with the bourgeois enemy. Roscoe Fillmore expressed a certain contempt for a socialist movement that was looking only for electoral votes. Speaking of the situation in England he complained, "There are Socialist and labor parties and societies and associations galore. And a labor delegate of approximately 50 in the House of Commons that steadily becomes more a nonentity every day."[124] Revolution would never arrive "as the result of the election of a mayor in Podunk or a whole gross of them," Fillmore warned.

Political campaigns are mighty handy – they get the crowd – therefore, we are on the right track when we get out, put up candidates and force those standard bearers to point out to the workers their slave position and the *only* remedy, *working-class ownership* of the means of life. While we confine our efforts to this sort of work, which is not spectacular and will not get us office for some time to come, we are performing our function as grave diggers to capitalism. Every slave who is persuaded to think of his position is another grave digger. We will have an organization that will be a strong nucleus for the workers to rally around when 'The Day' dawns.[125]

Here, then, was the SPC model – and its indomitable spirit, in all its intransigence and "gaucheness." Those who exemplified it were the real-life Ernest Everhards, except that instead of elegantly trapping their opponents in syllogistic errors, they brusquely interrupted their enemies with the raucous laughter of the oppressed and the harsh rebuttals of the insulted and the injured. In its way, during the heyday of the SPC – from 1904 to 1911 – this defiant discourse often served the party well.

"No Compromise – No Political Trading," proclaimed the *Western Clarion* masthead: no deals with the devil, and let the opportunists select other places to do their business.[126] There was courage, resoluteness, and imagination in the SPC's dialect of socialism that should not be obscured by either its harshness or its practical failings. "The position we hold of no compromise has proved its worth, especially in the province of British Columbia and we are quite satisfied of its inestimable value in Manitoba, as it not only prevents fusion but gives to you a platform which is in no danger of collapsing," argued W.H. Stebbings in the Winnipeg *Voice*. He challenged "our opponents" to "give us some intelligent opposition and criticism," if they were convinced that the SPC position was "not down to bed-rock."[127]

A Maritime Radical: Roscoe Fillmore

Roscoe Fillmore grew up in Lumsden, a government-supported "back to the land" settlement in Albert County, N.B.[128] "The road through the middle of the settlement was straight and bordered by stone walls," writes Nicholas Fillmore in his fine biography. "At his grandparents' place Ross watched Grandmother Elizabeth make tallow candles from scraps of fat after Grandfather John had butchered a steer."[129] In the Spencerian language of the first formation, that early life provided a good instance of primitive homogeneity that had as yet to yield to the sophisticated and integrated heterogeneity of modern capitalism.

At the same time, Lumsden's isolation was somewhat deceptive. The social calendar moved to rhythms set by the Baptist Church, a significant force throughout southern areas of both Nova Scotia and N.B. Some part-time waged work could be found at the local lumbering company, and the nearby Maine labour market beckoned with its higher wages and promise of a better life. In 1893 the Fillmores moved to Gorham, Maine. Then disaster struck: Roscoe's mother succumbed to tuberculosis – an event that "badly confused" people who still believed in divine retribution – and one by one eight members of Roscoe's extended family succumbed to sickness, reducing the Fillmores, on their return to New Brunswick, to objects of charity and virtually destroying the little settlement at Lumsden. In 1898 the Fillmores resettled in the village of Albert, which boasted not only rural artisans – tailor shops, a blacksmith, a carriage-maker – but also a weekly newspaper, whose editor introduced Roscoe to the novels of Charles Dickens and to Thomas Paine's *The Age of Reason*. The social vision of the one and the secularism of the other were to have a lasting impact on him.

Fillmore dropped out of school at 16 and migrated to Portland, Maine, where he worked at a locomotive repair shop and haunted the Bijou Theatre, with its "wonderful stunts, the chorus girls, the tumblers, acrobats, and hypnotists." A key moment arrived when he came across a street-corner socialist orator.[130] He found the socialist's denunciations of poverty and oppression convincing, and became a member of the Socialist Party of America. Returning to Albert, where his family had managed to acquire a nursery operation, he entered Grade 11 at the Riverside Consolidated School, where he "devoured book after book" by such authors as Ralph Waldo Emerson, John Ruskin, the evolutionary theorist A.R. Wallace, John Stuart Mill, Jack London, Upton Sinclair, William Morris, and, of course, Spencer. In spring 1906 Fillmore wrote a long essay for his teacher, in which he made his first declaration of his new-found faith. "We are fighting for a time," he declared, "when there shall be work and leisure for all, when the rich shall no longer live in luxury on the fruits of the labour of the poor; when all the good which is in the individual shall be sought after and encouraged to result in the benefit of all; when no man, woman or child shall go hungry, or live in hovels, whose very existence contaminates society."[131] Fillmore also saw a relationship between socialism and horticulture, and drew upon the writings of Luther Burbank, whose experiments with plants would become world-famous. Burbank's strongly environmentalist views would find expression in *The Training of the Human Plant* (1907).[132] Just as nurserymen like the Fillmores could over time straighten out and invigorate young trees, organic socialists could straighten out the crooked timber of humanity.

Roscoe then travelled to the West, encountering at first hand the vibrant radicalism of British Columbia, selling *The Eye-Opener* on the streets of Calgary, and actively promoting the books published by Charles H. Kerr. He started to read the *Western Clarion*, joined the Socialist Party, and came face to face with death from hypothermia riding the rails. He returned to the Maritimes in 1908 and made his home in Albert. There he built up a small library of the classics of socialism, including the works of Marx and Engels. By March 1908, with the help of his cousin Clarence Hoar, Roscoe had secured the required five citizens of Albert to create an SPC local, New Brunswick's second. They busied themselves opening a Socialist Hall, which had a small library with the latest in socialist literature.

It was not an easy row to hoe. As Fillmore wrote, "We are having a hard time to keep things running just at present. Many of the people would starve us out if it lay within their power." As Nicholas Fillmore relates, on a June night in 1908, as the Socialists were fitting out curtains for their new Main Street headquarters, "they heard a crash against the door. A group of young men and a woman began throwing stones at the building. A window was broken, but no one was injured. Roscoe later found out that the stones had been thrown by the sons of 'eminently respectable citizens' of the village." One especially powerful opponent was the Rev. W.A. Snelling, with whom Roscoe clashed at a meeting called to promote a "Purity League" devoted to cleaning up local politics: "After that meeting Rev. Snelling never missed an opportunity to criticize socialism."[133]

The heyday of Roscoe Fillmore as the Maritime sparkplug of the SPC came in the years 1909–12. A visit from Wilfred Gribble, SPC national organizer, coincided with the 1909–11 strike of the coal miners of Cape Breton and Springhill – the East Coast equivalent of the Vancouver Island coal wars of 1912–13. The arrivals of James Simpson and W.U. Cotton of *Cotton's Weekly* meant that three inspiring missionaries of socialism were operating in close proximity. The region was also generating its own high-powered SPCers, including Springhill's Jules Lavenne, a Belgian-born agitator whose leg had been lost in an industrial accident; Adolphus Landry, who ran as a socialist candidate on the Cumberland Labor Party ticket in 1910, losing the race but carrying Springhill by a two to one margin over the other mainstream parties; Seaman Terris, an energetic campaigner and propagandist in Springhill; Sophie Mushkat, a dynamic Jewish immigrant in Moncton; and Colin McKay and Fred Hyatt in Saint John. Of this dazzling cohort of Maritime socialists, potentially the most significant and influential were the leading activists in the United Mine Workers, including J.B. McLachlan in Cape Breton, who would become the most enduringly famous socialist in regional history, and William Watkins of Springhill, who became District 26's president in 1911. This was a veritable socialist great awakening in the East that paralleled that of British Columbia a decade earlier.

Fillmore played a vital role in it. At a time when the IWW and SPC in British Columbia and the SPC in Winnipeg and Toronto were struggling for the right to democratic public speech in Canada, Fillmore brought this struggle to Saint John, where he too endured arrest from the authorities. The SPC in the region grew to 15 locals, encompassing about 300 members.[134] *Cotton's Weekly* was a regular visitor in many homes – particularly those of coal-mining families in Cumberland and Cape Breton counties in Nova Scotia. A reader of a daily newspaper such as the Halifax *Herald*, the Amherst *Daily News*, or the Saint John *Sun* could easily come away with the impression that "Socialism" was *the* issue of the hour, at least in the region's urban and industrial centres.

As in British Columbia, much depended on the coalfields. In Cape Breton the SPC made important gains and set down roots tough enough to survive the violent crushing of the strikes. McLachlan ran as a Socialist in 1916 with an election leaflet headed *Working-Class Politics* and with vintage SPC rhetoric on the inevitability of socialism.[135] In Cumberland County, and particularly in Springhill, the pattern was somewhat different. Few towns in Canada were as captivated by first formation socialism as strike-bound Springhill in 1909 and 1910. Fillmore was a frequent visitor, as were Mushkat and Landry. As many as 900 people crowded the Opera House for a Socialist evening in February 1910 – a turnout that represented about one-sixth of the town's entire population. Cumberland County, which took in both Springhill and Amherst, became the most *Cotton's Weekly*–friendly constituency in the country, according to the paper's own statistics: the leading organ of Canadian socialism boasted more readers per capita in Cumberland than in any other constituency.[136] Red buttons, red flags, even a red "Socialist Young Guard" organized by Lavenne made Springhill, for a time, a place that recalled the radical bases of France or Italy. "Red, red, red was everywhere," Roscoe exclaimed, describing a major commemoration on 10 August 1910 to mark the first anniversary of the strike. "Red buttons and flags, rosettes, and hair bows. Many of the horses bore red ribbons." The main event was a giant picnic held on a farm outside town and attended by more than 4,000 people from several surrounding communities. "In the morning about four hundred men came down Victoria Street and through the town in a parade led by the town's junior band. . . . As they marched along, a large red flag fluttered in the breeze and many houses along the route displayed red flags."[137]

Fillmore identified wholeheartedly with the model of the SPC as a great force for the scientific education of the working class. He saw the party as one that fought charlatans and hucksters, "more or less interested persons of the 'intellectual prostitute type.'" The capitalists and their lackeys would use all the "side shows and red herrings" imaginable as a way of diverting attention from the core issue – the abolition of wage slavery. "No compromise our motto, and the red flag our standard," he proclaimed. "Let those who will, prate of brotherly love. The facts of existence under capitalism will shortly expose to the workers the hypocritical cant contained in these effusions. Our work must be to educate those of our class, who are ignorant of their slavery[,] to a full realization of it. Vote catching must not enter into the question at all. Educate the workers – make Socialists and the Revolution will come even though no ballots are cast."[138]

This Eastern first formation base, so intensively concentrated in the Cumberland and Cape Breton coalfields, was much more fragile than it seemed. From the distant and dismissive perspective of the *Western Clarion*, the Maritimes were among the "outpost places of the fight," where the socialist agitator was "flying a forlorn hope" and often "fighting single-handed . . . for men who do not know their own interests."[139] In terms of its model of consciousness-raising, the task of a socialist like Fillmore was to expose such ignorant workers to the wisdom enshrined in the party. Yet on a different model of consciousness-raising, many Maritimers had a complex grasp of their own interests and identities, and it was the responsibility of socialists to articulate the revolutionary science of social evolution in a way that was accessible to them. (Had Vancouver been as "red" as Springhill in 1910, it would have boasted a socialist city council.) Yet the *Clarion*'s patronizing prophecy turned out to be self-fulfilling. It was hard to connect the scientific answer to the class question with the life or death struggle of the miners. When the miners of Springhill were defeated in 1911 – a tragic loss less expected, and perhaps more crushing, than that suffered in Cape Breton – the "Red moment" swiftly passed away. The local socialists paid a steep price for their organizational purity. At the apex of their strength, they were able to take over the Cumberland Labor Party in May 1910, but in December 1911 – only a year after the party's provincial candidate had won 1,278 votes, only slightly less than Hawthornthwaite's total in British Columbia in the 1908 federal election – the charter of the SPC in Cumberland County was revoked for nonpayment of dues. Fillmore launched a fierce campaign against any who might be tempted to join the Social Democratic Party, in his eyes the party of the "pseudo-Labour-Socialist-sentimentalists." He denounced "any attempt to 'swap' the movement for the sake of the votes of reformers, single taxers, Orangemen, Christadelphians or vegetarians" and launched a successful campaign to purge the SPC of both Landry and Lavenne. The result was a "steel organization for the workers to rally around when 'the day' dawns."[140]

Thus, rigorously straightened, à la Luther Burbank, the tree of Cumberland socialism had been inoculated against the infection of labourites, trade unionists, Christians, and mere reformers. It was a brilliantly successful operation, in line with the latest insights from the scientific vanguard in British Columbia. Its minor drawback was that the "tree" did not survive it. Fillmore's own account of the collapse of his pre-war project self-defensively stressed the region's religious medievalism, an approach that obviously reflected his own struggles in rural Baptist New Brunswick. His analysis could be supplemented by one looking at both the rapid *rise and fall* of the socialist movement, which had a brief (and in the region unrepeated) opportunity in the depths of industrial warfare to become the "common sense" of a majority of a large coalfield population, but which failed to make the most of its opportunity.

The Emergence of New Voices, 1911–15

Be careful what you wish for: Stebbings' 1908 challenge – "Give us some intelligent opposition and criticism" – was answered by a growing army of new leftists. Many of them believed as strongly as did other SPCers in the scientific answer to the class question – that the true consciousness of class could only arise from a proper understanding of social evolution and Marxian economics. They were as impatient as most SPCers with a notion of socialism as a spontaneously generated and miscellaneous collection of well-meaning working-class demands. Yet as Canadian workers launched a vast revolt from 1907 to 1914 – encompassing coalfields and metal-mining camps east and west, running through the Lakehead docks and transcontinental railways, and culminating in vast demonstrations against the newly visible phenomenon of mass unemployment – many socialists became equally sceptical of the purely scientific answer. They came to argue that class-consciousness would emerge as workers collectively drew appropriate (and scientifically informed) conclusions from their own struggles to change their lives. A powerful system-challenging movement could only arise if socialist theory and working-class struggle were brought together in new forms of praxis. In essence this new answer to the class question, in the framework of "struggle," represented the dialectical transformation of the earlier positions.

The first indications of the advent of this new position appeared in the storms brewing within the SPC as early as 1907, which climaxed in a major split in the party in 1911. The SPC, the dominant left organization in many major urban centres, found itself immersed in complex struggles. On one side it confronted new forms of revolutionary industrial unionism and direct action. On another it confronted a vigorous new left centred on immigrant communities. On yet another front, party stalwarts faced within their own ranks well-informed socialists who argued for new forms of labour politics.

The major schism within the SPC was foreshadowed by a controversy in 1907 over the suspension of Vancouver's Ernest Burns, whose sin was to have extended an invitation to W.T. Mills of Washington, whom the SPC leadership regarded as an opportunist. The vote to suspend Burns, a founder of the party, was controversial and accomplished only through procedural shenanigans. The expelled Burns and his supporters then reconstituted themselves as the Social Democratic Party of Canada, picking up the name both from European parties (most notably that of Germany) and from previous North American experience (the Social Democrats and the *Social Democratic Herald* had been fixtures in the United States less than a decade before).

In a major critique of the SPC, the dissidents argued that it had failed to progress in Vancouver because of its negative propaganda, unnecessarily hostile stance towards unions, sectarian attitude towards visiting speakers, and the iron grip of the provincial executive. The SPC, in reply, said that the Social Democrats had shown that their priority lay with collecting votes, whereas the SPC was in the business of "making socialists." The ironic consequence of the purge was to intensify the somewhat autocratic grip of the very leadership that the Social Democrats had been opposing, precisely at a time, late 1907, when the SPC was drawing into its ranks Polish, Russian, German, Latvian, and Finnish comrades, many of them arriving in Canada with European revolutionary experiences fresh in their minds.

The next major separation involved the Ukrainian branches of the SPC, which began to publish their own paper and demand federated status in late 1907. The Ukrainian socialists became increasingly (although not unanimously) disenchanted with the SPC, and a majority identified after 1911 with the Social Democratic Party of Canada – undergoing, as they did so, two further name changes before they ultimately became the Ukrainian Social Democratic Party of Canada (USDPC).

The split, then, was multi-dimensional and not confined to any one geographical area: Vancouverites, Winnipeggers, North Ontarians, Torontonians, and Nova Scotians all figured centrally in the drama. Many issues were repeatedly raised. One of the elements was certainly a widespread scepticism regarding the SPC's record in the West. Hawthornthwaite's bitter quarrel with his own supporters on Vancouver Island was compounded by business dealings that were arguably inappropriate for a socialist and by allegations of collaboration with the Conservatives. The party's vote dropped below 5,000 in the provincial election of 1912.[141] O'Brien's defeat in the 1913 Alberta provincial election, albeit on the basis of a larger Socialist vote, robbed the Alberta party of its remarkable and likable proletarian philosopher – there would be no more of his punchy exposés of bourgeois depravity in the legislature. The defections of John Place and Parker Williams, once the SPC's standard-bearers among the miners, added to the sense of a movement that had lost momentum and coherence. Dissatisfaction with the absence of internal party democracy ran high.[142]

The foreign-language locals were particularly concerned that the SPC executive had repeatedly refused, on the grounds of expense and revolutionary purity, to recognize calls to join the Second International. Many also decried the isolation and dictatorial habits of the Vancouver leaders, seeing in that executive another example of "boss rule."

The core philosophical issue was dissatisfaction with the single-plank approach. In a cogent letter of 8 April 1909, Vancouver SPC militants Arthur J. Wilkinson and J.L. Pratt focused on a contradiction within the SPC. On the one hand, the party deplored any demands that fell short of "revolution now." On the other it proudly boasted of the significant reforms wrested from the B.C. government by its members. "There is no doubt that imperfect as the work done by our members may have been, and limited as has been their power, they have accomplished definite and permanent improvement in the condition of the workers in whose interest they have concerned themselves," they pointed out. "Why should the party spend its energy in denouncing immediate demands while at the same time it elects members who can do no more than effect palliative reforms of the present system?" After all, what would Herbert Spencer say? "We look upon Socialism as an evolutionary process, a development from a lower to a higher form of life. This implies a struggle, the higher to assert itself and supplant the lower." In this case, "the lower" was "always conservative" and believed in "letting well enough alone."

Like an organ that clung to existence after it had ceased to "fulfil its functions or to answer the purpose for which it came into existence," the SPC's "equipment" was no longer doing the job – which was to rouse the workers to the need for socialism and to channel that consciousness into politically effective directions. "We do not think the best equipment is to be found in interminable philosophical discussions on surplus value, however important that theory may be," Wilkinson and Pratt argued. They also singled out phrases that had become habitual for SPCers but now sounded like "cant" in other ears: "class-conscious, class-struggle, proletariat, bourgeoisie," all of which they judged to be "jargon." Such "meaningless shibboleths" were "freely indulged in by those who style themselves the only Simon pure, clear cut, revolutionary working class," yet their repetition was no longer helping socialists face and change reality. "We believe in taking hold of the institutions already in existence and moulding and shaping them as far as possible to our purpose," they stated. "It is a grand thing to have high and noble ideals, they act as an inspiration and are indispensable, but practical work is just as indispensable – nothing worth while is accomplished without it." The SPC must evolve or it must die. SPCers must resolve to become "living, active, aggressive factors in the life of to-day." The two writers followed with a daunting list of immediate demands for which the party should struggle. The demands echoed many of those found in the Montreal CSL program of ten years earlier.[143]

In Winnipeg the storm within the SPC was also linked to debates and divisions with that city's emerging polyethnic and multilingual left. A turning point came in 1910, when either (depending on who was telling the story) the principled revolutionaries of the SPC succeeded in exposing and defeating an unprincipled fakir, Fred Dixon, a well-known single tax and direct democracy advocate or (and this seemed the more generally accepted version) the party managed to wrest working-class defeat from the jaws of victory by taking votes away from Dixon, thus denying him the electoral victory he deserved. On 24 July 1910 the dissidents resolved to form a separate party, the Social Democratic Party of Canada. As Robin remarks, the reasons advanced for the schism were similar to those earlier advanced in Vancouver: a perceived domination of the party by English-speaking members, the party's aloofness from trade unions, its reluctance to involve itself in municipal politics, and the Dominion Executive's refusal to join the International Socialist Bureau, which it justified in revolutionary terms.[144]

In Ontario the same intense debate was centred on the SPC's refusal to affiliate with the International Socialist Bureau on grounds of expense and revolutionary purity. As the Finnish Communist J.W. Ahlqvist later remembered, there was considerable dissatisfaction in Ontario at the slow provincial growth of the party, with only 600 members by 1908. At a 1907 convention, a program of reforms, inspired by the European example, was overruled by a majority of just one vote. At about the same time, the Finnish locals brought forth a pamphlet called *The Canadian Socialist Party and Social-Democratism*, distributed free of charge to the different locals, which aroused great interest in a different style of socialist politics.[145]

Toronto Local No. 1 passed a resolution to affiliate with the new tendency in July 1909; and it was soon backed up by resolutions from foreign-language locals (Finnish, German, and Lettish). August 1909 saw breathtakingly Machiavellian manoeuvres on the part of the SPC old guard, militantly supported by Wrigley Jr. and Thompson, and implicitly by Simpson, who leveraged the Dominion Executive into purging the Toronto local and then constituting another local as the SPC's Ontario headquarters. The Ontario dissidents affirmed their right to chose their own party headquarters and to resolve their own troubles. The break with the SPC took place on 15 and 16 May 1911, when the Finnish locals withdrew and organized a Canadian Socialist Federation. On 30 December 1911, at a Lakehead convention bringing together the Manitoba Social Democratic Party and the Canadian Socialist Federation, the Social Democratic Party of Canada was born.[146]

By 1913 SDPC membership had doubled, exceeding the SPC's everywhere except in British Columbia. On 19 March 1914, *Cotton's Weekly* reported that the new party could boast 1,142 members in British Columbia, 294 in Alberta, 167 in Saskatchewan, 249 in Manitoba, 2,714 in Ontario, 4 in Quebec, and none in the Maritimes.[147] Even so, in the year or two after the split many of the leftists involved hoped that the two parties could be reunited. They did not perceive the split between them to be one arising from a fundamental ideological difference.

As significant as the new loosely woven organization was the new orientation of the organs – especially *Cotton's Weekly*, which made a transition from an SPC-friendly organ to the voice of the SDPC in 1911. The new party, then, had access to the country's leading English-language left publication. According to Ahlqvist, when *Cotton's Weekly* moved to Toronto in late 1914 its circulation had dropped to 18,700 (from roughly 35,000), and calls came for a clearer party line. It was reborn in October 1916 as the *Canadian Forward*, which would become one of the most dynamic, creative, and persecuted voices of the Canadian left during the Great War. Ahlqvist also contended that the SDPC benefited enormously from the adherence of the Finnish and Ukrainian organizations. "At the beginning of the World War in 1914," he suggested, "the party had eighty-two locals in Ontario, forty-six in British Columbia, forty-five in Alberta, twenty in Saskatchewan, twenty-eight in Manitoba, eight in Quebec, and the total membership was over 5,500."[148] Historian Tadeusz Adam Kawecki characterizes the SDPC as a "loose federation" in which "the locals enjoyed more power than the leadership." The locals controlled policy, the selection of electoral candidates, and could even (if three locals agreed) force the calling of a party-wide referendum.[149] Much of the development of the "mass base" of the SDPC thus devolved onto them. While the SPC had attempted to create a strongly ideological party centred in British Columbia (although in practice this centralism was always more impressive on paper than in reality), the SDPC went in the other direction, creating a structure much stronger in its ethnic components than in its central institutions. The three main foreign-language branches – Ukrainian, Finnish, and Russian – coexisted within a structure that granted them considerable autonomy under Dominion and provincial executives, on which other locals – Jewish, Lettish, Polish, German, and "English" – also had their influence.

During the economic crisis of 1913–15, SDPC activism made inroads among the unemployed in many locations, especially Winnipeg and Ottawa.[150] In late November 1913 the local SDPC in Winnipeg helped facilitate a massive movement of the unemployed, with as many as 2,000 gathered outside Market Square and the employment office; by 26 May 1914, the Social Democrats were prominent in angrier demonstrations against hunger and joblessness that provoked a police riot and the beating of Joseph Dunbar of the Ukrainian SDP, who along with two other protesters, was then hit with assault charges. In Ottawa, out of the downtrodden Rochesterville neighbourhood, a mass movement, in part centred on a new local of the SDPC focused on the Ukrainian, Ruthenian, Austrian, and Hungarian unemployed, and associated with activist Michael Chopowik, mobilized demonstrations of 300 to 400 people to demand work. The SDPC was not "commanding" these spontaneous protests, but neither was it separated from them. In essence it was suggesting the potency of the "third answer" – that of praxis – to the question of class. The SDPC preached much the same maximalism as did the SPC; but it granted much more significance than did the SPC's old guard to spontaneous protests against oppression and exploitation "on the ground."

During the same period the SPC faced a different, but from its perspective arguably even more vexing, challenge from a further split in Toronto, which could be represented as the development of a purified and hardened version of its own strategy. Here SPC Local 24, led by Moses Baritz – who played a stellar role as the scourge of Christian socialism – argued in essence that the SPC's position had been *insufficiently* scientific. In a nine-point manifesto, these activists blasted the SPC's willingness to admit people without a sufficient knowledge of Marxism and attacked the reformist bearing of the party's members in the provincial legislatures.[151] By early 1911 Local 24 had become the Socialist Party of North America (SPNA). Florence Custance, a party militant, later recalled that although restricted in scope to Toronto, the SPNA was the "fire-brand" group in the city. "No other group," she believed, "could function in Toronto as a centre of socialist thought against the S.P. of N.A." She added: "Nearly all its members were debaters, good propagandists and willing workers. Their little hand press was always at work and Sunday morning distribution of leaflets was a common practice. They worked like religionists and the entire party membership was never troubled with the question of personality." A particular emphasis of the party was the members' understanding of the "three fundamentals of Marxism," historical materialism, the theory of surplus value, and the class struggle. Its organ, the *Marxian Socialist*, made it a force to contend with, particularly in its Toronto base. In its consciousness-raising strategy the SPNA placed members in industries – a practical orientation quite different from that prevalent in Vancouver, and (to my knowledge) the first Canadian example of a left party "industrializing" its members.[152]

Each of the SPC's two challengers claimed a superior grasp of Marxian theory, with both upholding the "triune formula."[153] H. Martin, the SDPC's first national secretary, explicitly disparaged reforms, which were "at their best ... but a makeshift, merely patching up, prolonging the system." Another central figure, T. Edwin Smith, welcomed the economic recession of 1913–15 on the grounds that the odds of emancipation got better "when social conditions worsened." The purpose of the party was "to educate the working class, organize it in support of the party, capture the state and change capitalist property 'into the collective property of the working class.'" The "working class needs to be jolted out of its apathy; its false gods need to be destroyed."[154] It was a measure of the continuity between the two parties, and of the SDPC's threat to the SPC's monopoly on theory, that the new party affixed on its banners the same slogan that the SPC had drawn from the European intransigents: "No Compromise, No Political Trading."[155]

Superficially, a core difference rested in the SDPC's willingness to espouse a program combining maximum and minimum demands, such as a reduction in the hours of labour, the elimination of child labour, universal adult suffrage, and the democratization – through such measures as referendums and the popular right to recall members – of Parliament. The SPDC was also willing to work alongside rather than against pre-existing labour parties as parts of broader coalitions, and it welcomed autonomous minority-language socialist groups. Yet, more profoundly, the SDPC's style of activism in the years 1913–15 suggested a different strategy for raising class-consciousness. There was undoubtedly more room in the SDPC for those, like John Queen and R.A. (Dick) Rigg in Winnipeg, who emphasized concrete reforms within the existing capitalist system. Yet there would also ultimately be more room for leftists who would later see in the Bolshevik Revolution a model for the Canadian left.[156]

Albert Saint-Martin

Many of the experiences of Albert Saint-Martin (1865–1947) in Quebec were similar to those of Roscoe Fillmore in the Maritimes, although his life was also shaped by the particular oppression faced by the Québécois, so dramatically revealed in the gallant struggle for free speech in Montreal. Until he was embraced in the years immediately before the Great War by a movement of the unemployed, and immediately after it by people radicalized by the war, Saint-Martin seemingly fought, as Larivière's study suggests, a rather lonely struggle in the province.[157]

Albert Frédéric Rambert dit Saint-Martin was born 1 October 1865 in the working-class neighbourhood of Hochelaga in Montreal, into a modestly positioned family. His father, initially listed as a carpenter, seems to have worked as a kind of "jack of all trades" in construction; he later became a tobacconist, grocery store proprietor, and small merchant. Albert entered an apprenticeship at the age of 15, from which he emerged in 1886 as a member of a modern new breed: a stenographer. Throughout his life he would be fascinated by the politics of language and intrigued by the new possibilities that modern life had unveiled for communications between and among nations. Even the selection of highly unconventional names (by Quebec standards) for his children – one was initially named Hedwiedge Donalda – would appear to reflect an intention to become a citizen of the world. Also notable is that only two of his six children lived to adulthood, a sombre reminder of the life in the "City Below The Hill." His most flagrant declaration of independence from the standards of Quebec society came when he declared that he had "no religion" on a form submitted for the baptism of his second child. In a Montreal that had sent some of its boys to fight for the Pope in Europe, and whose priests weekly contested every sign of deviation from the Catholic faith, this was not a casual gesture. Most of the province's schools, hospitals, and social welfare institutions were influenced, where they were not directly run, by the Church, which also regularly instructed its believers on how they should vote in elections.

Saint-Martin became a socialist sometime around 1904 or 1905. Before that, like so many first formation socialists at the turn of the century, he had been a Liberal and then a labourite. The possibility of either choice suggests a Quebec far more multi-hued than the stereotypical portraits of a backward clerical-nationalist priest-ridden province would allow. Indeed, recent research demonstrates the strength and depth of liberalism in the province – both on the level of popular ideology, where small businessmen were regularly instructed by their press on the timeless truths of individual self-help, and on the level of official politics.[158]

In this distinct society, to vote Liberal, to join a Liberal club, and to discuss liberal ideas were relatively safe ways of indicating a measure of independence from the Catholic Church. (Joining the Freemasons, as many also did, carried a higher price tag.) It seems possible to speak of a discreetly operating, somewhat contradictory hegemonic framework in Quebec, one both Catholic *and* liberal. In that framework such liberal values as private property, order, and patriarchal individualism were meshed with a Catholicism that, on the face of it, might have contested all three of them in the name of "organicism." It rarely did. To sustain their project of liberalizing the northern half of the continent, the architects of Confederation had made far-reaching concessions to the Catholic Church in Quebec, which became in essence a state church within its provincial sphere. Contesting the Catholic sub-hegemony that resulted from the compromise of Confederation often fell, paradoxically, to the local Liberals, descendants of the militantly secular *rouges* of the 1860s and 1870s, who fought, often surreptitiously and subtly, guerrilla warfare on such questions as laicism and education. The Liberal Party, led federally by Laurier, was able to win a majority of Quebec's seats in 1896, despite the Church's endorsement of the Conservatives. The complicated dual hegemony thus allowed the Catholic Church an immense power in some respects, but circumscribed that power in others.

In early on selecting the Liberals as the "party of the left," Saint-Martin was making a common choice of the time, but for reasons shaped by his own cultural circumstances. Saint-Martin spent much of the 1890s and early 1900s fighting for liberalism in Montreal as a way of resisting the power of the clergy. Indeed, little of the "official" socialism of the 1890s, such as the Socialist Labor Party, could touch him – even although, with a cultural sensitivity not usually associated with De Leonism, the SLPers took the trouble to translate their propaganda when they first appeared on the Montreal scene in 1894. The Canadian Socialist League, although it was born in Montreal in 1898, apparently caused not a ripple in his life: it was mobilizing in a different neighbourhood, in a different language, on different issues.

A much less predictable choice, and a fulcrum of Saint-Martin's cultural politics for 50 years, was his choice of Esperanto as a vehicle for his hopes and dreams. Saint-Martin regarded Esperanto as a great liberator, an Enlightenment language that would free humankind from its insularity and narrowness. At crucial points in his life as a socialist organizer, Saint-Martin would pour himself into the struggle for Esperanto, which was a very popular form of linguistic utopianism among socialists throughout Europe.[159]

In Montreal liberalism was not just an ideology but a vast framework of social life – from informal meetings to clubs, associations, and literary societies. It was a society radically distinct from the world of Toronto or Saint John. The clubs and associations were important elements of a liberal world that meant far more to its participants than merely casting a ballot.[160] Saint-Martin's first involvement in experimental politics came within the Chevaliers du Travail (Quebec Knights of Labor). He seems to have been involved in the immensely variegated world of the "clubs" of Montreal, so many of which were organized for workers – the Club Ouvrier, Club Central Ouvrier, Club Ouvrier-Centre, Club Ouvrier Indépendant, Club Social Ouvrier, and Club Indépendant des commerçants de fruits – and popular clubs associated with the Liberal Party – the Club Letellier and Club Geoffrion. It was in this milieu, and three years after the local labour council had recommended expulsion from its ranks for any unionists found guilty of supporting a party of "capitalists," that the Parti ouvrier indépendant was born in January 1898. The Club Ouvrier Indépendant was mobilized in 1899 to denounce the property qualifications for voters laid down in the Montreal City Charter. The same club, on 8 March 1899, demanded explanations from the local politicians who had signed an agreement to fight the trusts. On 12 March 1899, J.-A. Rodier declared, "The only way that workers can ameliorate their position is to create a labour party entirely independent of existing parties." Some three days later he published, on the front page of *La Presse*, a sizzling opinion piece entitled "S'organiser en parti."[161]

On 17 March 1899, at an assembly of the Club Ouvrier-Centre that included members of other clubs, workers decided to found a third party: the Parti ouvrier indépendant. It was not, Larivière remarks, a party gifted with a solid social base. It arrived in the world with no money, no constitution or bylaws, and an organizer, Rodier, who was preoccupied with his job as a labour reporter for *La Presse*. Nonetheless, at its most important public meeting on 27 April 1899, the party drew an impressive 900 people, and 176 remained to sign up their names as members. Then, like so many of the labour parties founded across Canada in the 1890s, it evaporated almost as quickly as it had emerged, leaving behind, after one disastrous electoral outing, a highly "confusing image."[162] In the Montreal case, in addition to conventional Catholic hesitations about workers and labourism, it was hardly helpful that the city was split between two competing labour centrals.

Saint-Martin was in many of his choices in the 1890s challenging liberalism by working within its terms. He was drawn quite closely into the Ligue de l'Enseignement, a body formed on 9 October 1902 and dedicated to the promotion of a new, non-church-centred system of education in Quebec. Here one found Godfroy Langlois, the notorious director-general of the newspaper *Le Canada*, and a reputed Freemason, and a veritable "nest of liberals" who pushed discreetly for a modern system of education in Quebec.[163] Some three years later, with the TLC's 1904 declaration in favour of independent labour politics, the Montreal groups remobilized and decided to run labour candidates in the provincial election. Saint-Martin was mentioned as a possible candidate in Sainte-Marie, but declined; Alphonse Verville, the president of the Trades and Labor Congress, came within 1,330 votes of defeating the Liberal candidate; and the greatly elevated vote given to labour was seen as encouraging. *"Le fer est chaud, il faut le battre"*: Strike while the iron is hot. Montreal's leftists, many of them going in and out of Saint-Martin's place on Rue Saint-Christophe, were quickly mobilizing. In Saint-Hyacinthe, which Saint-Martin frequently visited on stenographic business, the party selected Rodier as its president and Saint-Martin as its secretary. The party's program was widely distributed through 1905, and Saint-Martin played an important role. In Saint-Hyacinthe he conducted a class in political economy, in which he "brought forward the evolution of society from its origins until our own time and offered a glimpse of the future of progress."[164]

In a by-election on 24 March 1905 the Club Saint-Jacques decided to take the unusual step of running a candidate against Liberal premier Lomer Gouin.[165] There was no hope of success; generally such by-elections were mere formalities. But now the atmosphere was different. There was a chance of bringing the message of the Parti ouvrier to a much wider audience. In an interview Saint-Martin brought forward details of his political evolution and discussed the price one might be asked to pay for labour-party activism in Montreal. He remembered his many years as a Liberal, in which he had struggled to have the party adopt pro-labour reforms. To punish him for his political views, he alleged, the government had "deprived him of his functions as an official stenographer for criminal trials in Montreal."[166] At a huge meeting of workers on 29 March 1905, candidate Saint-Martin made a special point of attacking the premier for not delivering on a promise to provide free and obligatory schooling, of which he had not breathed a word since his election. Moreover, Gouin had evidently made a display of his "pro-labour liberalism" by promising to resign immediately if the workers put forward a candidate in the Saint-Jacques constituency.

Even more alarmingly from the Liberal perspective, here was Saint-Martin not only backed by the Club Saint-Jacques and carrying the label of the Parti ouvrier but also supported by the august Alphonse Verville. Saint-Martin made it plain in his address to the voters that, by opposing Gouin in the by-election, he wanted to "force the Prime Minister to render an account of his conduct." He then proceeded to ask a number of sharply specific, "democratic" questions of his powerful opponent. Had the premier not promised to resign if the workers' party put forward a legitimate candidate? Had he not promised to appoint a minister of public education? Whatever happened to compulsory education? And the abolition of the legislative council? Not to speak of universal suffrage? And why the funny business about contracts?[167] Such questions were revealing in that so many of them confronted an orthodox liberal with questions that only a contemporary radical democrat would ask. Saint-Martin played with the image of Gouin, the elite liberal, the powerful premier, covered with titles, promising things he would never deliver, and himself, the working-class man of the people, demanding honest answers. For all that the enemies of socialism liked to talk about their leftist foes as partisans of the "class struggle," in the likes of Gouin they had a living example of somebody who did not preach it, but surreptitiously practised it.[168]

The Liberals promptly launched a vigorous counterattack, pointing out that only one of the two Montreal labour centrals (although admittedly the most representative) had declared its support for Saint-Martin. The Liberals then swamped Saint-Martin's meetings with hecklers and disrupters and – in *La Presse*, supposedly the "friend" of all labour parties – tried to undermine Saint-Martin's credentials as a representative of labour with the claim that the labour candidate was not *really* a worker. (Even *La Presse*'s labour correspondent found it difficult to credit this argument: did one have to be a *manual* worker to be a legitimate representative of a labour party?) They insisted that the workers of Montreal had indeed their own party – the Liberal Party – and that consequently they had no need of Saint-Martin's "politically motivated" candidacy. Gouin refused to debate with Saint-Martin because his opponent was not a workers' candidate. The Liberals' strong and panic-stricken response suggested that they themselves realized that Saint-Martin was asking dangerous questions of them. In the end Saint-Martin won 13 per cent of the vote, with as much as 25 per cent in nine polls and an impressive 34 per cent in one particularly pronounced Montreal pocket of radicalism.

Within the Parti ouvrier itself ideological divergences were opening up between the international unions affiliated with the AFL and the Saint-Martin supporters. In autumn 1905 Saint-Martin organized a Club social-démocrate, which, alongside the organization in January 1906 of a German Working Man's Club of Montreal, constituted an emergent new nucleus of Montreal socialists. There was growing unease with the Parti ouvrier's increasingly obvious socialist orientation. On 18 November 1905, meeting at the Club Espéranto, its executive committee virtually liquidated the Parti, although it would persist on paper and in the existence of numerous local clubs. In February 1906, a revived Parti ouvrier, with a different ideological orientation, would elect Verville to the House of Commons – the first truly independent labour MP. This was, arguably, a development representing a serious challenge to socialists who kept insisting that only they could transform the political system. It seemed to galvanize Saint-Martin to take part ever more intensively in the struggle for Esperanto.

Montreal, now prominently on the map of socialism, attracted the attention of visiting celebrities. Anarchist Emma Goldman, whose way may have been facilitated by Saint-Martin, visited in February 1908. The spc's E.T. Kingsley visited in June. The city's perpetual struggles over the May Day parades, which in some years were broken up by police and in others allowed to proceed in peace, gave socialists a presence in the daily press. Although Saint-Martin (and W.U. Cotton, running in Brome) would do abysmally in the 1908 federal election, Saint-Martin would do a bit better when he ran for the Board of Controllers in 1910 and pulled in over a thousand votes. Although it is uncertain whether or not Saint-Martin officially joined the spc at this point, he did become the public face of the socialists in francophone Montreal. So healthy and active was the spc in the city that a separate section was organized in the working-class suburb of Maisonneuve. Saint-Martin and spc locals in Quebec evidently rallied to the sdp in the course of the great split of 1911, as did *Cotton's Weekly*. On the eve of the war, Saint-Martin threw himself once more into popular struggles – in April 1914 helping to organize massive demonstrations of the unemployed in Montreal, who joined ranks with the socialists on the Champs-de-Mars.[169] Saint-Martin would go on to play a distinguished role in the anti-conscription struggle and persevered as a leftist into the postwar period, suffering grave persecution for doing so.

The Wobblies Come to Canada

From 1907 to 1913 much of the workers' movement in the coalfields, where so much spc support was historically located, underwent vast strikes that placed the party's language of the "damphool workers," and the answer to the class question that it presupposed, under enormous strain. In Nova Scotia a socialist-led struggle to found District 26, into which many workers had thrown their lives since 1907, was conclusively lost by the end of 1911. A strike that same year in Alberta was punctuated by gunfire and a discouraging arbitration award. Perhaps the most tumultuous wars were fought on Vancouver Island, where notorious comments from some spc theorists would not swiftly be forgotten. When George Pettigrew, the umw's international board member, appealed to an SPC branch for declarations of support, he was answered by a former Social-ist provincial candidate who referred to the strike as a mere "commodity strug-gle" and hoped that the workers would be clubbed over the head "good and hard – and many of them – so that the bump on their heads might then hold sense."[170] There was a time and a place for such rhetoric, and this coal war provided neither.

Perhaps the most striking illustration of the SPC's declining ability to "speak for" the miners in any sense was demonstrated by the Miners Lib-eration League, which drew wide support and raised considerable sums to support some 200 B.C. strikers who had been imprisoned by the state, often simply for the offence of arguing for their democratic rights.[171] George Hardy captured some of the atmosphere of this time in his stirring memoir, *Those Stormy Years: Memories of the Fight for Freedom on Five Continents*. Hardy outlined the divisions within the ranks of the Liberation League – between a socialist minority keen to exploit the strike to expose the government and the coal owners, and a right-wing majority arguing for a "cap-in-hand" appeal to release the prisoners. He recalled the negotiations with Conservative premier Richard McBride, in which John Day, chair of the TLC in Victoria, represented the right wing: "We sat around in a half circle." Referring to McBride, Hardy wrote, "This over-fed Tory was a typical representative of big business. He began by saying how pleased he was to hear what we had to say. Pure eyewash. He wanted to soften us up." Then a "pragmatist" made a "sickening appeal" for leniency for the prisoners. "Not a word about the miners being the victims of a conspiracy. No placing of the guilt where it belonged. No challenge to the Government charges that the miners were vicious and violent," Hardy said.[172] At such a time of greatly heightened "spontaneous class-consciousness," the SPC's "scientific" demonstrations of the ultimate futility of commodity strug-gles must have seemed somewhat redundant (and it was also not as theo-retically airtight as it then seemed).[173] "They stood apart, draped in their 'pure socialist' mantle," Hardy remembered, and his views were shared by others in the coalfields. "They would not become contaminated by participa-tion in purely economic struggles! . . . 'Spittoon philosophers' was our word for these 'socialists' who stood aloof while the miners fought for their very ex-istence."[174]

Thus, ironically, as certain industrial situations came more and more to approximate the stark class polarization long envisaged by the SPC, the lead-ership's own "scientific" answer to the class question impeded its ability to ad-dress the issues. It was a contradiction parallelled in many resource industries in which workers, fulfilling the predictions of *Capital* that they would be reduced to being so many anonymous bearers of labour-power in the "free" labour market, nonetheless found that neither spontaneous nor scientific frameworks sufficed.

The Industrial Workers of the World, a significant force from 1909 to 1913, especially in the West, was in many respects a praxis-oriented answer to the class question. At the outset it was by no means hostile to organized socialism – some of the most illustrious U.S. socialists were at its founding convention – but over time it came to constitute a new dialect of first formation socialism, a tendency posing a significant problem for the hitherto dominant voices. Although often interpreted as a U.S. union, indeed at times romanticized as an emanation of the "American Frontier," the IWW's very name emerged because of Canadian complaints that the name initially proposed (Industrial Workers of America) was too nationally limiting. Canadians (F.W. Thompson of Saint John among them) would play leading roles as militants and intellectuals within it; and long after its heyday had come and gone in the United States it was a force to contend with in Canada, particularly in northern Ontario.[175]

The preamble to the IWW constitution, amended in 1908, became a famous manifesto on both sides of the border. It flatly declared, "The working class and the employing class have nothing in common." When hunger and want for the millions were combined with bounty for the employing class, "between these two classes a struggle must go on until the workers of the world organize as a class, take possession of the earth and the machinery of production, and abolish the wage system." Workers had a "historic mission" to abolish capitalism, and their union would prepare them to do so, because "by organizing industrially we are forming the structure of the new society within the shell of the old."[176] The great strikes of the IWW, such as those at Lawrence (1912) and Paterson (1913), would become the stuff of song and legend. So too would the brutal massacres and lynch-mobs with which the IWW was punished. Scholars have often probed the IWW for its resemblances to European syndicalism, the form of leftism that argued against political parties and parliamentary struggles as the road to the new society; it instead championed industrial unionism and the general strike, often with an idealized vision of a post-capitalist society based on a federation of self-governing crafts and industries.[177] The extent to which the pre-1914 IWW was syndicalist will probably always be debated because so many activists perceived no great difficulty in being Wobblies at one moment and Socialists at another. Moreover, trying to nail down the IWW's ideology is an exercise fraught with frustration, given the extraordinary local diversity within the organization. In some locales it seemed to be imbued with an anarchist sensibility; in others it was more like "pure-and-simple trade unionism" with a radical edge. As one critic complained of one part of the *Preamble* presented to the 1905 convention, a conventional unionist could find in it one comforting meaning, a socialist another, and an anarchist a third.[178]

The union's stance towards violence has also occasioned much commentary, then and since. Many were alarmed by the IWW's seeming willingness to endorse dynamite as a legitimate weapon, although scholars who have examined the evidence more closely argue that the union was actually much more often non-violent in its actual conduct. Especially given the organization's non-authoritarian stance, taking one member's comments on violence as a statement of the entire group is a recipe for oversimplification. The hostile media and the state were always delighted to paint a picture of the crazed bomb-throwing Wobbly, who stepped into the role of the demon of the bourgeoisie once reserved for the anarchist.

At times the iww's hostile image was confirmed by its supposed supporters' actual behaviour, although in such cases it is possible that *agents provocateurs* were deliberately steering Wobblies into treacherous waters. Hardy tells the story of a Wobbly in British Columbia who proclaimed at a public meeting that Premier McBride should get someone to taste his morning coffee and "be careful when going out shooting during the hunting season." These remarks were widely quoted to discredit the Miners Liberation League. This same desperado then offered Hardy a job with the government. Hardy concluded that he provided a good example "of how Judases are made in the Labour movement."[179] Leier's fascinating work on Wobbly and labour spy Robert Gosden quotes a remarkably similar speech from his protagonist, who warned "Sir Richard McBride, Attorney-General Bowser, or any of the minions and politicians" that should they "go hunting, they will be very foolish, for they will be shot dead. These men will also be well advised to employ some sucker to taste their coffee in the morning before drinking it if they value their lives."[180] Such theatrical calls for violence, without any consideration of the strategic and tactical consequences of its use, are often associated with labour spies. In this instance, the provocative threat to poison and/or shoot the premier played into the hands of those who were trying to deflect attention from the actual perpetrators of most of the violence of 1913 – the armed forces of the state.

For leftists, a telling indication of the iww's significance was the almost unbelievable level of state and extra-legal violence brought against it. Wobblies were regarded as fair game by vigilante squads, police departments, and the legal system. Some were imprisoned for decades; others were killed. Although the Canadian record on the iww is nowhere near as violent as that in the United States, Leier nonetheless suggests that Wobbly organizers were shot and killed under suspicious circumstances. The secretary of the Kamloops local died, Leier notes, after a severe beating at the hands of the police.[181]

Working from a list of 278 names generated from the radical and Vancouver daily press from 1909 to 1914, Leier argues that spcers, Wobblies, and trade unionists were drawn from markedly different populations. Less than 70 per cent of the Wobblies had British surnames, and 53 per cent were never listed in city directories – convincing indications of the iww's appeal to a much more mobile workforce. A striking piece of evidence on spc/iww difference comes from the *Industrial Worker*'s response to the Socialists' appeal for electoral support in the 1909 election: the IWW newspaper "pointed out acidly that of the five thousand Wobblies in the region, only 75 were eligible to register and vote. Parliamentary socialism cut out significant numbers of workers from the class struggle."[182]

The most famous of the IWW strikes came in 1911–13 as a direct result of the building of two new transcontinental railways, the Canadian Northern and the Grand Trunk Pacific. IWW organization spread like wildfire in the labourers' camps; by March 1912, the ranks of the IWW resistance reached between 7,000 and 8,000 workers. Their demands – such as a nine-hour day with a minimum wage of $3 a day and the enforcement of sanitary laws – were hardly extreme, but the railways fought them ferociously. The strikers established their own form of "peace, order and good government," planning a system of communication between the camps, regulating housing and the feeding of thousands of men, and even administering their own justice system. The strikers enforced collective temperance – "no more than two drinks a day, and no bottled liquor" – and punished infractions with such penalties as chopping wood and helping the cook. When these measures proved only partially effective, they picketed and boycotted the saloons.[183]

The building of the two new transcontinental railways epitomized Canada's age of economic transformation under the aegis of liberal order. The country's borders were opened up to the labour markets of the world. Workers of many nationalities came to the work camps, where they often entered a hellish world of scrimping subcontractors, filthy conditions, and inedible food. Then, having served their function, the workers were simply let go. As described in a fascinating article on the IWW and unemployed activism in Edmonton and Calgary by David Schulze, such cast-off bearers of labour-power then deployed some ingenious tactics in their struggle to survive. In 1913 and 1914 they were pouring en masse into Edmonton and Calgary, desperate for food and shelter. In Edmonton an IWW local that combined permanent town members and itinerant workers formed the Edmonton Unemployed League on 21 December 1914. In the bitter winter cold, they mounted parades with banners that read "We Want Work and Food" and "Midst Christmas Cheer Unemployed Men Are Starving." They demanded of Edmonton Mayor McNamara that the city provide work "for all unemployed regardless of race, color or nationality, and regardless of whether married or single," that each man get enough work that he would bring in $9 a week at a wage of not less than 30 cents per hour, and that in the meantime the men receive meal tickets worth 25 cents. The city, fearing a crime wave, offered terms that the IWW men found reasonable. Yet the city could not afford an extensive relief program, and the province was unwilling to provide one. It cut back relief to 20-cent meal tickets, leaving the workers in a desperate position. As the Unemployed Press Committee put it to the Edmonton public, "These men are hungry and are becoming more hungry every day." Could the unemployed be blamed for preferring the inside of a jail cell, with its warmth, food, and shelter, to the hunger and cold suffered outside?

The Wobblies marched to First Presbyterian Church the next Sunday morning, both to protest their condition and appeal for help. On 11 May 1914, 300 "foreigners" gathered at the iww Hall and voted unanimously "to form an organization of the unemployed." Soon the Edmonton unemployed devised an imaginative new tactic. They planned to go into restaurants, eat their fill, and then exit without paying. Then, once the jail cells filled up, they would recruit more men to repeat the exercise, until the police gave up. The "dine and dash" tactic was modified in practice: 13 men left the iww Hall, ordered meals in three restaurants, then remained seated after they refused to pay.

As strategy, tactics such as meal-ordering and church-invading were performances that highlighted the social relations that not only created hungry people (for there was clearly food for the hungry in the social institution of the restaurant – it was simply being made *artificially* unavailable) but also constructed hierarchies of poor and rich, even within religions supposedly committed to equality of each human being before God (for there was clearly a chasm between the compassionate faith professed in the church and the social relations promoted by actually-existing Christianity). The organization's demand for work rather than charity was of a piece with its Marxist analysis of social reality, and its openness to workers "regardless of race, color or nationality."[184]

The union is deservedly celebrated for its folk songs, poems, salty jokes, and pithy expressions. Writer Philip Foner reports on a little item from the *Industrial Worker* of 15 May 1913: "A brief editorial squib on the death of J.P. Morgan, entitled 'Out, Damned Spot!' ... read: 'A wireless dispatch from Heaven states that Soul Scrubbers' Union No. 1 is on strike in resentment against the impossible task of removing the many foul spots on Morgan's soul." A sample of the same sense of humour was evident in British Columbia when William Taylor, arrested in a major struggle for free speech in Vancouver, "objected to swearing on the Bible, complaining that it could harbour germs."[185] From the iww the labour movement derived its anthem, Ralph Chaplin's "Solidarity Forever," and folk singer and martyr Joe Hill's *Where the Fraser River Flows*, which arose from the union's titanic battles in the B.C. interior.

Yet the iww was clearly also in the business of spreading a specific concept of socialism, one palpably influenced by the social-evolutionary theory of its time. As Salvatore Salerno remarks, "Although the I.W.W. ardently advocated the industrial form of union structure, it is inaccurate to regard the I.W.W. as primarily a labor union in this period."[186] Its locals often functioned more like clubs than like regular trade unions; moreover, much of the iww's time and energy was invested not in fighting employers, but in the people's enlightenment. As John Reed, later celebrated as the man who most vividly described the Bolshevik Revolution, remarked: "Wherever, in the West, there is an I.W.W. local, you will find an intellectual center – a place where men read philosophy, economics, the latest plays, novels; where art and poetry are discussed and international politics."[187] Foner notes the thousands of books, pamphlets, and papers that were disseminated all over the West by the iww. The "union" resounded to calls from organizers for more materials – on improved machinery and methods of production, "discoveries and application of science, general scientific knowledge, discussions of economics and public questions." Foner movingly describes the Wobbly halls, with their dog-eared copies of Marx, Darwin, Voltaire, Tom Paine, Jack London – the *Iron Heel* was a particular favourite – and, but of course, the inescapable Herbert Spencer.[188]

One commentator remembered visiting a Wobbly Hall, and seeing "several shabbily dressed young men reading books taken from the shelves of the library in the room. Others crouched over a makeshift stove brewing a mulligan stew, its ambitious odor permeating the hall. While they tended their supper, they argued some point in economics or religion." Robert Tyler reports a story of a Wobbly who had memorized the entire *Communist Manifesto* – and even as a legend, it is interesting that it would attain currency as a marvel to report.[189] Today the iww's image has been reshaped by more recent countercultures, and it takes an effort of imagination to realize that just as important as the memory of the Wobbly as the down-to-earth battler for workers' rights in bloody strikes is that of the Wobbly as earnest knowledge-pursuing haunter of libraries, many of them constructed at enormous sacrifice and preserved with reverence.[190]

iww theory and practice were interrelated. Historian Melvyn Dubofsky argues that the Wobblies accepted but also subverted the Darwinism pervasive in the climate of their day. Like many contemporaries, they carried the theory of biological evolution into social analysis. Then, like all members of the first formation, they "reversed the discourse" and as "radical, or revolutionary, Darwinists," accessed evolutionary theory as a revolutionary critique – based on the belief that "social evolution differs in no essential respect from organic evolution." As one iww theorist observed, "social evolution" was not always "a direct or simple process, but often a slow, painful, and tortuous course of human development with the wrecks of social experiments scattered along the way."[191]

Rather than being "exceptions" to first formation socialism, then, the Wobblies in many respects were its exemplars. A prime example of their sociology was "Father Hagerty's Wheel," a visual aid that was immensely popular in the early 20th century. The brainchild of Thomas J. Hagerty, still called "Father" long after he had separated from the church, and an activist linked (as Salerno notes) with anarchism, the wheel illustrated his leading organizational principle: that workers would "organize in proportion to capitalist concentrations in industry irrespective of trade or tool." When they had acquired a sufficient degree of class-consciousness in each industry, they would know how to "take over and collectively administer the machinery of production and distribution in the cooperative commonwealth." Hagerty was deeply immersed in European debates over anarchism and syndicalism, and viewed the ballot box as a "capitalist concession. Dropping pieces of paper into a hole in a box never did achieve emancipation for the working class, and to my mind never will."[192]

In essence, the "wheel" was an act of prefigurative Enlightenment science: by raising to the level of consciousness the unseen structure of the industrial world, it also prepared workers to take command of that world after the moment of revolution had arrived. It also revealed how the new society might work once its unnecessary capitalists were abolished and workers were free to run it themselves. Every wage-earning occupation that Hagerty could imagine was placed in one of eight departments, which were then themselves subdivided and subdivided once again.[193] Each Wobbly could thereby situate himself on the wheel, and thus grasp his organic relationship with the whole of the socio-economic order. Copies of diagrams similar to "The Wheel" were treasured by a good number of Canadian radicals. When the political and economic order did indeed seem to be collapsing in 1919, with the workers poised to take over, some – and by no means just Wobblies or anarcho-syndicalists – urgently sought out their battle-worn copies.[194]

The rise of the IWW coincided with the emergence of anarchist circles in Canada. Jewish anarchists enriched the radical cultures of Montreal, Toronto, and Winnipeg. In the case of Winnipeg, as Roseline Usiskin's pioneering research revealed, they established their own "Free Society," which became the dominant group among the city's Jewish radicals in the first decade of the century. In 1915 this Free Society would become Branch 564 of the Arbeiter Ring, a benevolent association and cultural circle guided by an inclusive concept of socialism. If, as Spargo had suggested in 1901, the "anarchist" figured as the irrational other in some early socialist polemics, Emma Goldman – widely celebrated in Canada – presented the tradition in a far different light. In some eyes, praxis-oriented revolutionaries, whether they called themselves anarchists or socialists, shared more common ground with each other than they did with the more aloof executive committees and the "spittoon philosophers."[195]

James Simpson: "The People's Jimmy"

One of the visitors to socialist Montreal who came to a meeting chaired by Saint-Martin in April 1909 at St. Joseph's Hall was a dapper gentleman from Toronto. His first lecture during that stay was on the "Doom of Capitalism." His next, delivered the following day, was a rather more upbeat sequel: "The Inevitability of Socialism."[196]

This was none other than Comrade James (Jimmy) Simpson (1873–1938), a printer, journalist for the Toronto *Star*, ardent Methodist and Prohibition advocate, vice-president of the Toronto and District Labour Council, a recurrent vice-president of the Trades and Labor Congress of Canada (1904–9, 1916–17, 1924–36), school board trustee (1905–10), and controller (1914). He would ultimately become Toronto's first labour mayor in 1935.[197] Simpson – known variously as "Cold Water Simpson" or "The People's Jimmy" – was in turns a member of the Canadian Socialist League, Socialist Party of Canada, Social Democratic Party of Canada, Independent Labor Party in Ontario, and Canadian Labor Party. He would become subject to studies ranging from celebratory accounts hailing him as a pioneer of Canadian social democracy to Communist critiques of a man with a very "dim" idea of socialism.[198] Although generally considered as the reformist opposite of the radicalism associated with the IWW, Simpson might better be understood as another exemplar of a shared Spencerian-Marxist synthesis, and someone propelled into new prominence by a more praxis-oriented movement in the 1910s.

The fervour of Simpson's primitive Methodist faith was, according to Homel, acquired as a stonemason's son in Lindal-in-Furness, Lancashire, and strengthened upon immigration to Toronto in 1888 at the age of 14. Much of the young Simpson's life revolved around the Canadian Epworth League, designed to keep young Methodists within the denomination and strengthen their opposition to the liquor trade and desecration of the Sabbath. Simpson got his first taste of public life in the struggle against the establishment of Sunday streetcar service in 1897. Religious convictions propelled him first into the Social Reform League and then into the Canadian Socialist League. By early 1900 a member of the powerful CSL Local No. 2, Simpson rubbed shoulders with the Wrigleys, father and son, and with Thompson, Mrs. May Darwin, and Dr. H.G. Hargrave, the Local's illustrious president. As a moral reformer and prohibitionist, Simpson was disappointed by the Liberal Party, then governing at both the federal and provincial levels. For him the party's evasiveness on the liquor trade and apathetic handling of industrial problems were signs of a deeper moral decay. At the close of the founding CSL conference in 1901, Simpson was elected permanent chairman, a tribute to his charismatic personality and spellbinding oratorical gifts, which were later nicely described by a Winnipeg journalist: "He is of the whirlwind type of orator, his language following like a torrent and at such a speed that poor hearers can not readily follow him." He was an "eloquential locomotive," reminiscent of the old Methodist circuit riders.[199] Much of Simpson's energy after July 1903 was thrown into the presidency of the labour council. His rise to such a position was a remarkable tribute to his eloquence and personality, because he had been active on the council for only 26 months.

His rapid elevation to a position of leadership also earned him the first of many mixed reviews from his fellow leftists. Thompson, writing in the *Western Clarion*, worried that his comrade might have mistaken trade unionism, with its palliatives, for the political struggle for socialism. Yet under Simpson's chairmanship of the Ontario Socialist League/Socialist Party of Ontario convention in Toronto on Thanksgiving Day, 1903, the 50 delegates heard the key note of "uncompromising socialism" sounded again and again before they adopted the single-plank platform of socialism and the policy of the "party pledge."[200]

Simpson approved of this tactic, in part, Homel observes perceptively, because of his religious background. Primitive Methodism had no use for moral compromises, and "socialism was a moral issue." At the same time Simpson was a political pragmatist, "who liked to win office and accomplish concrete reforms." This "contradiction" between "two facets of his politics" represented, according to Homel, a "lasting characteristic of his career and of the course of Canadian social democracy."[201] In Simpson's case, confronted with the dilemma of being unable, under the terms of the party pledge, to support candidates backed by the labour council he was leading, and facing criticism from some other trade unionists, he offered to resign. Such was his popularity, and the awkwardness of the whole issue of the trade unionists' divided political loyalties, that the matter was allowed to subside. When *The Toiler* remarked that one could vote for Simpson without necessarily being a socialist, it was noting an increasingly interesting aspect of Toronto municipal politics. Many people came to feel comfortable voting for Simpson, even if, as a member of the SPC, he was the sworn revolutionary enemy of the capitalist system.

Simpson's persona also made it difficult to demonize him. Ebullient, articulate, immensely sociable, Simpson was a consummate maker and keeper of friends. Even Goldwin Smith, horrified to the core by some of the class-warfare polemics coming out of Simpson's party, could not bring himself to reject him. Many people believed that Simpson had somehow stumbled into the wrong party. Protestants could vote for him on the school board because he often voted their way. Christian moral reformers could rally to "Cold Water Simpson" as someone who practised what he preached when it came opposing the demon rum. Middle-class Torontonians could abide a socialist who gave every indication of leading a prosperous and moderate life – who could afford, for example, to drive visiting British labour dignitaries about Toronto in his own automobile.

This was nonetheless the same man who preached SPC doctrine with fervour and conviction. Within the TLC, Simpson was a prominent backer of a resolution that called for the "substitution of the competitive system of industry by the common ownership by the people of the means of production and distribution."[202] That resolution was scathingly denounced and obliterated by the TLC leadership – and then Simpson was elected to the position of vice-president.

In the 1905 Toronto school board elections, a well-meaning voter, drawn by the candidate's handsome visage and reputation for moral rectitude, might well have been inclined to vote for Simpson for reasons set quite apart from politics – perhaps because he wanted to vote for an advocate of temperance. The SPC's message to this voter? Get lost. Do not vote for Simpson unless you have well-grounded, rational reasons for doing so. "Don't vote for Comrades Simpson or Thompson because they belong to your union or to your lodge, or because they are 'good men' or popular fellows. Vote for them because they represent Socialist principles."[203] Somewhat remarkably, in the end some 5,930 voters, having presumably satisfied themselves that they were *qualified* to vote for Simpson, cast their ballots for him. (The less eloquent and photogenic Thompson figured near the bottom of the list.)

The SPC also made a point of telling everyone who might listen that Simpson was *strictly* a pawn of the Socialists. The party would vet his every move. "On nights before Board meetings," Homel writes, "the [SPC] committee would confer with him and instruct him how to vote and what motions to introduce." Far from concealing the fact that he was, in essence, the puppet of the SPC, Simpson proudly advertised how often SPC policy had required him to "vote alone." Simpson pursued a socialist agenda on the board consistently and rigorously. He demanded that the board become a major landholder in outlying areas, to prepare for the future expansion of the city. He fought hard for teachers' pensions. More controversially, he opposed a benefit concert in aid of army cadets and bitterly objected to the flying of flags over schools on the anniversary dates of battles dear to the British Empire. All of these stances Simpson defended, in the depths of Tory Toronto, in the language of socialist anti-imperialism. As one reporter conceded, "He ain't no 'Jimmy-beat-about-the-bush.'" When Simpson ran for the board again in the 1907 elections in Toronto, the SPC pointed out to Toronto voters that workers needed to elect as many of their own number as possible, so that "the legalized force of the State will be at their disposal."[204] No fewer than 6,600 voters proceeded to re-elect Simpson. In 1910 Simpson was elected to chair the board.

As *Saturday Night* magazine was eager to point out, contradictions abounded in the life of Simpson the socialist. He was simultaneously a member of the Orange Lodge and on the welcoming committee for the IWW's renowned William Haywood, who used the opportunity of his visit to Tory

Toronto to "take a swipe at King Edward" and proclaim "that when workers could not remove despotism by the ballot, the bullet was justifiable." Playing up the notion of "Jimmy the Plutocrat," the *Telegraph* conceded in 1913 that Simpson might be a nice man, but was nonetheless "a real estate plutocrat who rides to noonday meetings in an automobile."[205] The following year, backed by three daily newspapers, Simpson topped the poll in the elections for the new Board of Control, with 20,503 votes – probably the highest vote count ever achieved in a particular contest by any pre-1915 socialist in Canada.

Given the long-lasting image of Toronto as a God-fearing, conservative city, the spc's impact there, and particularly Simpson's success, might seem surprising. No pre-war socialist in Vancouver or Montreal achieved such a degree of civic prominence. But, according to Homel, Simpson had especially endearing personal qualities and benefited from circumstances that favoured his breakthrough: fractured electorates that allowed a third-party candidate to divide and conquer, the depth of his attachment to a progressive community that cast its ballots not for socialism but for specific reforms, and the popularity of the demand for public ownership and control of such urban utilities as the streetcar service. Simpson was also clearly a master of the modern arts of publicity.

"The victory obviously had little to do with socialism," Homel writes of Simpson's 1914 election triumph. To the contrary, the evidence that Homel himself has so carefully brought together reveals that Simpson was performing a socialism that was as "extreme" in its own way as that of Kingsley, as "propagandistic" as that of O'Brien, and often as unapologetically "Marxist" as that of the irascible *Western Clarion*. It was a form of revolutionary Marxism that was not, as Homel suggests, confined to the "particularist forces"[206] of B.C. politics but was clearly evident in the Ontario of G. Weston Wrigley Jr., Wilfred Gribble, Moses Baritz, Arthur Taylor, Phillips Thompson, and, of course, James Simpson himself.

For eight full years – from 1903 to 1910 – Simpson situated his socialist activism within a revolutionary politics guided by scientific principles laid down by Marx and perfected by Engels and Spencer. Simpson expressed no doubts about Marx and Marxism, nor did he rush to join the general exodus of 1910 out of the party. Rather, when Simpson chaired the first Ontario Socialist League convention in Toronto in 1903 and it adopted the single-plank platform, he greeted the changes "with apparent enthusiasm." He ran municipally on platforms that fiercely derided the "patch-work reformers who are to be found in such aggregations as the so-called labor parties."[207] He apparently never made an effort to join such labour parties.

Scientific socialism taught Simpson that capital and labour necessarily should adopt "diametrically opposed" policies. Simpson's command of Marxist economics, as it was understood in 1909, impressed even Gribble, a hard-liner if ever there was one. In 1908 Simpson was no bashful participant in the SPC's extreme campaign of direct action and grassroots mobilization on be-half of the democratic right of assembly – he was at the very centre of the free speech fight. At the Ontario Socialist Party convention of September 1908, he denounced the Finnish branch for trying to water down the single-plank program with immediate demands. No less an authority on orthodoxy than the *Western Clarion* declared his defence of the SPC program to be "strong and effective."[208]

Perhaps most significantly, when the bitter disputes between SPC locals 24 and 1 broke out into the open in 1910, Simpson stayed with Local 24. While the vast majority of Ontario Socialists rebelled against Vancouver, held unau-thorized conventions, and boldly set sail for the Social Democratic Party of Canada, Simpson hung on and, indeed, held out far longer than did most On-tario socialists. Only in October 1910 was he *expelled* – not because of his di-vergence with the party on questions of revolutionary theory, but because of his role in the Royal Commission on Technical Education and Vocational Training.[209]

Like so many of his contemporaries, Simpson apparently found the revolutionary sociology of the SPC sufficiently persuasive to spend eight years arguing for it. Yet he also steered clear of some of the SPC's more flagrant declarations of hostility to trade unionism, and he quietly sought a way of reconciling the seemingly conflicting claims of trade unionism and socialism. No doubt the break of 1911 signalled, for him, the beginning of a new mo-ment. What may have dramatically changed in the fortunes of Simpson was not his discovery of "social democracy" – which had a very different meaning for most people of the time than it does today – but rather the consolidation of a new and vibrant constituency, destined to play an enormous role in the history of the Canadian left: the ethnic radicals, and most particularly the Jewish leftists, of Toronto, who supplied the foot soldiers for Simpson's dra-matic breakthrough in 1914.

The moment of 1914 demonstrated the possibility of a new historical bloc, fusing ethnic, class, and even gender identities – a left transcending the boundaries of the pre-war world. At his moment of triumph in 1914 Simpson rather uncharacteristically articulated a vision of history. According to Homel, Simpson confessed that he was not "a believer in the great man theory, but rather that I am a creature of environment, a creature of those conditions which have made possible for me my present success."[210] In this triumphal moment, Simpson was thrown back – like so many in the first formation – to the theory of social evolution and to the intellectual authority of the "great man theory" of history, Herbert Spencer.

Undoubtedly there was much that was *sui generis* about Simpson's astonishing career in Toronto, yet it also demonstrated a striking transformation in the "class question" from the 1890s to the 1910s. In the first decade of the 20th century Simpson deftly and unapologetically combined revolutionary "impossibilism" with mainstream campaigns to purify and rationalize politics. In the second decade he was catapulted into even greater political prominence by aligning himself with a new left based on Jewish and Finnish socialists, radicalized trade unionists, and socialist feminists. That he would later come to epitomize (at least in the eyes of his left-wing critics) opportunism and class compromise should not obscure how powerfully he had spoken for the "new left" of 1911–14.

Rural Opportunities and Awkward Classes

These successive dialectical struggles over how the working-class consciousness could be mobilized as a system-challenging force took place in a country with a working-class minority. Even a cosmic theorist had to notice that in Canada from 1890 to 1920 the working class, whether defined narrowly or broadly, was not in the majority. The glaring fact of the matter, as Skelton, that scourge of socialism, took great pleasure in pointing out, was that the agrarian population far outnumbered the urban proletariat, so limiting the possible appeal of any socialism. Skelton considered Marx to have made an "unlucky prophecy" with respect to the imminent proletarianization of the agrarian population. Agriculture's history showed "that the socialist prophecies have been most completely falsified by time. The small farm dominates the situation to-day beyond question."[211]

Yet in the very year his book was published, 1911, Skelton's complacent description of perpetual liberalism was challenged by an unprecedented rural revolt – the first on-to-Ottawa crusade of Western producers, determined to hold the Liberal government to its promises for a better deal for farmers. Across the West, and not just there, the countryside seemed to be echoing to the cries of a rural people's enlightenment. What should socialists do in response? Was this just another version of liberalism? Or something different? In many respects the agrarian question was merely a subset of the class question. It boiled down to the issue of how the proletariat could lead the farmers.

Perhaps the clearest sign of the challenge that socialists faced in rural Canada was the extraordinary rise of co-operativism. As Ian MacPherson notes in his classic account of the movement, in the 19th century there had been retail co-operatives in coal-mining communities and co-operative creameries across Canada. The Farmers' Binder Twine Company of Brantford, Ont., was owned by about 8,000 farmers across the country. Governed by principles of "one member, one vote," neutrality on religious, racial, or political issues, the rule of a low, fixed return on investment rather than a speculative profit, and the distribution of surplus earnings to members on the basis of participation, co-operators came in three varieties: those focused on providing an aid to specific occupational groups or classes (such as the fruit growers of Nova Scotia), those who wanted to address a particular abuse or injustice (such as the efforts to organize retail co-operative stores on the European model as a way of cutting out monopolists and middlemen), and, finally, "those who believed that co-operation could undertake the complete reformation of society."[212]

From 1900 to 1914 this last group was particularly prominent on the Prairies and among the grain producers, who brought a new intensity and spirit to co-operativism. "The spirit of co-operation is in the air and is rapidly spreading throughout the west," proclaimed *The Grain Growers' Guide* on 22 September 1909. "Western Canadians have bowed to corporation rule nearly ever since the country was settled. The time for emancipation has come and there will need to be some able leaders to head the campaign." Founded the year before, the *Guide* itself would open its columns to co-operators of many stripes, including the "mystic co-operators," who, "convinced that laissez-faire economics and Social Darwinism were completely false in stressing the competitive ethic," maintained "that each co-operative society which obeys the laws that it has made for itself constitutes a little world organized in conformity with justice and social benefit, and that it is sufficient to let it develop spontaneously, either by growth or imitation, to realize in the more or less distant future the best of all possible worlds." According to their vision of reality, humanity was naturally co-operative, but (in MacPherson's words) "had been betrayed by corrupt leadership, faulty education, and indulgent individualism." As *The Grain Growers' Guide* maintained on 18 October 1911: "Co-operation is a religion pure and simple. It is something which all your senses recognize and long for in proportion to the good there is in you."[213]

Many co-operators fervently believed in living otherwise. They had come to hate the cutthroat irrationality and cruelty of a capitalist wheat economy. Wheat producers were placed in a very different position than the traditional small farmers who sold their livestock and vegetables to nearby urban markets. Recruited with the promise of individual freedom on the land, they were confronted on the Prairies with the realities of monopolistic railways, distant governments, and predatory banks. The very nature of the wheat harvest itself demanded the organic fusion of individuals into a collective project, that is, one of the largest movements of any material goods on the face of the planet, all necessarily conducted within a few weeks of the year, to the markets of the world.[214] Free-standing individuals in law and theory, wheat producers were in reality functioning parts of a global food economy. A Spencerian discourse of the movement from homogeneous units to heterogeneous and interrelated organisms could easily be related to the producers' everyday experiences.

The "utopian co-operators" who "tried to perceive society as an organic whole and thought that co-operative techniques were ideal for establishing a new social and economic order" were not isolated cranks.[215] Their analyses chimed not only with the latest and best works in social science, but also with many of the on the ground realities of wheat farming. As MacPherson notes, the Grain Growers' Company expanded from 1,800 shareholders to over 27,000 from 1907 to 1912 – or, in terms of wheat, from 2,340,000 to nearly 28,000,000 bushels. E.A. Partridge of Saskatchewan, a key figure in the organizing of grain farmers to protect their interests, became determined, according to MacPherson, "that co-operation was the main weapon an enlightened population could employ against 'the financial buccaneers' to bring about 'an industrial millennium.' "[216]

Agrarian socialists were not the only co-operators. Canada's diverse practitioners of this approach included Quebec's Alphonse Desjardins, whose *caisse populaire* movement became a phenomenal success drawing in powerful Conservative supporters, and Ontario's J.J. Morrison, who championed a more centralized and conservative version of co-operativism, emphasizing the economies of scale and superior management available to farmers as entrepreneurs.[217] But neither were the idealistic Prairie activists isolated and marginal figures. In a Dominion heavily reliant upon the wheat harvest, they combined two characteristics almost guaranteed to create radical resistance to the ruling order – a sharp sense of being exploited and an equally accurate sense of being indispensable. Especially in the West, prophetic co-operators built massive reputations and successful institutions.

When such militants of co-operative living looked around for allies, they often encountered socialists who spoke much of the same language of radical organicism. The ideal of the "co-operative commonwealth" that Gronlund had developed in the 1880s was not essentially about a program for "co-operatives" per se, but about the new social order that would succeed capitalism. In the 20th century the venerable Spencerian term was put to new work to refer both to the ultimate achievement of a socialist society and to present-day measures to bring justice to the rural producers and a greater measure of organic fusion and effectiveness to the economic institutions they most directly controlled: the co-operatives and closely related farmers' political organizations. Because first formationists were not in general focused on expanding the existing state, and many believed as fervently as co-operators did in Kropotkin's vision of existing relations of mutual aid (in the natural and social world) as precursors of a post-capitalist future, they could feel not just a sense of shared purpose with the radical co-operators, but a sense of common identity. In William Irvine's dual career as a theorist of agrarian and socialist revolt, or in Francis Marion Beynon's articulation in *The Grain Growers' Guide* of socialist-feminist arguments against patriarchy and war, we encounter people and positions that challenged contemporary categories of politics.

Rural paradoxes came to the fore in the United Farmers of Alberta (UFA), founded in 1909. The organization began as a non-partisan lobby promoting the interests of farmers, pressured the Liberal government in 1913 to organize the Alberta Farmers' Co-operative Elevator Company, and was a staunch champion of co-operatives, women's suffrage, and a more democratic political order – a stance that by 1920 had won it over 30,000 members. The UFA was closely associated with the outlook of Henry Wise Wood, a Missouri-born immigrant to Alberta who became the organization's director in 1914, vice-president in 1915, and president from 1916 to 1931: "The King of Alberta," some said, in deference to his immense reputation for straight-talking, intellectual seriousness and his devotion to the movement. Wood critiqued the impact of the monopolies, banks, and other manifestations of the new capitalism. He promoted, as solutions, the organization of strong local farm organizations. He became identified as one of the most outstanding figures in the movement of agrarian protest in Canada. He was, to an extent unusual even in this period, immersed in the philosophy of Spencer.

The key to Wood's philosophy was his belief that humanity was guided by social laws. As William Rolph argued in his fascinating biography, although not religious in a formal sense Wood was a deeply spiritual person with "an almost mystical faith in the democratic nature of group action." Like most other radical figures of the period he was strongly influenced by the concept of the social gospel and looked on agrarian co-operation not only as an instrument of political reform but also as a method of bringing about social regeneration. Jesus had shown what these true social laws were and how they could be achieved. Humanity was like a wheat field in which "good" and "evil" were so interwoven that it was impossible to destroy the one by violence without destroying the other, too. Only by building up the wheat or "good" through co-operation with God's will could the tares or "evil" be overcome and "blown away like chaff." As he stated: "My religion and my philosophy of life are founded upon a belief in the scientific development of man, up to an ultimate knowledge of Truth as taught by Christ; and the development of a social system in perfect harmony with Nature's laws, which are the laws of God."[218]

Outlined in a series of articles in *The Grain Growers' Guide* in December 1918, Wood's philosophy was drawn directly from the texts of Spencer, with a particular emphasis on *Social Statics* and *First Principles*. All change, for Wood, resulted from the operation of two social laws: the "false law" of competition and the "true law" of co-operation. It was through co-operation that the animal selfishness of humanity, so illuminated by Darwin, could be overcome. The achievement of the "social state" – to reference Spencer's analogous term – was the only lasting remedy for the ills of contemporary civilization. In Wood's profoundly monist view of the universe, the realization of humankind's struggle to adapt its individualism, integrate its different institutions, and harmonize its economic and social functions was the meaning of life. There were "laws of social development which people can consciously help or hinder," in Anthony Mardiros's apt distillation of the lesson that a disciple might derive from his work.[219]

What might seem today to be matters of mere organizational detail – how to mobilize farmers to make practical changes in their working lives – were, from this left-Spencerian (but not necessarily or clearly socialist) perspective, momentous questions of fundamental, even cosmic, evolutionary significance. Unless the fabric of civilization was reconstructed, humankind itself might fail to survive its evolutionary challenge. That challenge could only be met by replacing the traditional processes of government, with their inherently negative qualities of partisanship, pointless passion, and irrationality, with forms of government based upon the fundamental producing occupational groups, organized to protect their own interests against the claims and interests of other occupational groups. In the co-operative commonwealth, a truly democratic government would be composed of delegates representing all the participating fundamental groups. The way of achieving this grassroots, effective, functional democracy was through organization at the base. If you wanted real change, you must organize groups, educate their members in the philosophy of co-operation, and work every day to put the law of co-operation into effect. Either that, or face a desolate future bereft of prosperity or spiritual integrity, dominated by parties that had only their own selfish interests in mind.

To act locally, to build small anticipatory versions of the co-operative commonwealth, was linked to thinking globally, in terms of a much bigger vision of a co-operative humanity. The local details – whether members of a co-operative should enjoy autonomy, whether they should take up political positions, whether they should form limited-liability corporations, whether they should align with similarly minded workers – were distillations of a global vision: the attainment of Spencer's cosmic vision of the social state, the achievement of humanity's social evolution.

In its dialectical and far-reaching challenge to the liberal order, Prairie radicalism cannot be readily inserted into preconceived and cursorily examined categories – whether "anticipatory social democracy" or "Prairie populism" or "agrarian protest" or "regional unrest." In essence many of its key proponents do not consist of something "regional," "agrarian," "populist," or "social-democratic," but rather of something radically post-liberal, a series of often brilliant if ultimately inconclusive attempts to think outside the categories of a competitive economic and political system. These experiments in reasoning and living otherwise undoubtedly left a lasting mark on the history of the Canadian left, quite out of proportion to the national electoral strength of the officially socialist parties.

How did the more Marx-oriented first formationists respond to this rural radicalism? It posed awkward questions, both because it implicitly elevated farmers to a leadership role and because it seemingly confounded Marxist predictions of the rapid centralization and consolidation of capital. The class analysis of the rural Prairies was complicated by occupational pluralism. As Gerald Friesen notes, "Many thousands of prairie farmers in the pre-war years had been, of necessity, part-time labourers . . . working on larger neighbouring farms as hired hands, by joining itinerant threshing crews, and by heading out for a road or rail construction site, logging camp, or mining town." Even into the 1930s about three-fourths of Alberta's agricultural labour force relied on wage labour to supplement farm incomes.[220] Were they then "capitalists on the land" or "workers who had a bit of capital"? First formation Marxists handled this awkward reality by fashioning two distinct approaches to the agrarian question. One drew orthodox Marxist conclusions and awaited the farmers' integration into the proletariat; the other argued, more in the spirit of the writings of the late Marx, that agrarian producers might themselves be able to force the pace of the democratic revolution. The first position was that of most of the writers in the *Western Clarion*; the second was that of William Irvine, who went so far as to baptise the farmers as the up and coming class-bearers of the democratic revolution.

Although the left in Canada debated the agrarian question intensively, it did not seemingly come up with much original thinking on the subject.[221] To a surprising extent, though, first formation socialism did appeal to many rural producers, who enlisted in its organizations in considerable number. Many were drawn by the deep appeal of the prospect of a popular enlightenment – a rational and progressive alternative to a capitalist modernity that swept up many farmers no less than city-dwellers, whether through the outmigration of countless sons and daughters or the economic burdens shouldered by many farmers, some of whom were more impoverished than most urban workers. In 1900, from Malton, Ont., came a moving description of the socialist enlightenment as it was experienced in a rural area. Canadian Socialist League No. 5 had embarked on a hugely ambitious series of Friday night meetings, taking up such questions as direct legislation, public ownership of public utilities, and banking and currency. "The object of these meetings is not so much to build up a league as to educate the community," its secretary declared, "knowing that sparks falling here and there throughout our country will soon kindle and cause such a blaze that its reflection will pale into insignificance the little halo around anything as narrow as a league. Rural communities want light, and societies like this will soon set them all ablaze. Where will be the next?"[222]

The social-evolutionary paradigm held out a number of possibilities for rural people. A strict application of Spencer suggested that freehold farms were homogeneous and dispersed units, awaiting a progressive evolution into the complex heterogeneity and functional integration demanded by modernity. It followed that, in addressing farmers, one in essence talked to them not as primary producers in the present, but as people destined to be proletarians in the future. Marxists hinted at a process whereby all farm land would be socialized, and focused intently on those things about modern agriculture – the coming of machinery, the intrusions of banks – that looked like modernity everywhere else. Any other approach, the authoritative Karl Kautsky advised, was to struggle to salvage "an archaic form of agriculture, doomed to vanish with capitalist expansion."[223]

Canada was a vast, and unevenly industrialized, archipelago of societies, loosely knit together in the framework of a liberal dominion. As socialists did in Europe, Canadian socialists faced a very mixed population, with a working-class minority, in some regions a small one. If they saw themselves speaking only for and to the industrial working class, they condemned themselves to speaking, for a very long time and perhaps in perpetuity, for and to a minority of the population. If they continued to be wedded to the two-class model, they risked having nothing to say to the world beyond this minority. Yet if they relinquished that model they risked becoming little more than liberals. Only in certain specific settings – the coalfields, some Northern resource towns, some big-city neighbourhoods – could Canadians say that the proletariat as envisaged in classical Marxist theory was predominant. In every province the number of rural primary producers was larger. As Reginald Whitaker astutely observes, "Any attempt to root Canadian socialism in the reality of the Canadian political economy necessitated the recognition of the crucial importance of the rural population and way of life."[224]

Perhaps the most influential attempt to articulate the agrarian question to the class question was Alf Budden's *The Slave of the Farm*, first published in 1914 and reprinted in 1916 and 1918. Budden's book was an early and (for Canada) unusual attempt to apply Marxist methods intensively to a wide range of empirical data. He drew attention to the debate that had unfolded on the agrarian question in the *Western Clarion*. The "older school" had maintained that the farmer stood "in the same category as the wage-worker," with farm machinery analogous to "the carpenter's tool bag." For them, it seemed that the farmers were not selling wheat, oats, or livestock, but rather the "labor-power crystallized into these forms." In this regard Budden was possibly referring to the zeal with which some SPC writers equated the economic condition of the farmer and wage-earner. The campaign literature for Socialist candidate Frank Sherman in Calgary almost suggested their identity of interests: "The wage earner must accept the price fixed by the market for his labor power. The farmer must accept the market price for his products. When either of them purchase goods in the market they are also compelled to pay a price determined by some power beyond their control."[225]

Conversely, the "younger school," according to Budden, maintained that this was a conceptual error. Labour-power referred not to the "release of energy, or energy in motion" but rather to the "latent energy potential in the physique of the slave." So, when the farmer sold wheat, he sold a finished product much in the same way a merchant sold his goods. As for farm machinery, the slightest acquaintance with Marx would surely convince any intelligent socialist that farm machinery, like the weaver's loom, contained within itself the dialectical possibility of transformation from "helpful assistant" to "oppressor." What was true for the displaced Scottish weavers of the Industrial Revolution in the 1820s would probably also be true for the Canadian farmers of the 1910s. Budden argued that the position of the Prairie farmer was analogous to that of the industrial worker. He assembled an array of data demonstrating the mortgage debt under which the Saskatchewan and Alberta farmers were groaning, and he documented the rapid rise to dominance of agricultural machinery, itself burdened with debt. The "whole of the West" was "but one giant factory, whose roof tree is all out-doors."[226]

In another major statement on the question, *Wage-earner and Farmer* [c.1912], the pre-war SPC struggled hard to integrate the farmer who owned his own farm property with the two-class model. "He fancies himself not as a wage-earner, but as an independent property owner and oftentimes as a master, inasmuch as he frequently employs wage-workers to assist in his operations," the SPC pamphlet remarked. "But a careful scrutiny of his case will, however, disclose the fact that in essence his status in capitalist society differs from that of the outright wage-slave in appearance only." The SPC held out, in essence, very little hope for the small farmer, except the reassurance that inevitably all the "expropriators will be expropriated." In other words, all the slaves of farm, factory, mine, and railway would someday be free.[227]

Yet the first formation also included people who, although they argued for socialism as the revolutionary science of social evolution, did so without making primary reference to Marx. They remained at the "Spencer" end of the "Marx-Spencer" continuum. Whereas, in the socialist parties, the balance had subtly shifted from Spencer to Marx in the first decade of the 20th century, in other circles the emphasis remained emphatically Spencerian. Of all the left Spencerians, William Irvine (1885–1962) achieved the most renown as an articulate, original, and controversial activist and thinker. Few could match Irvine in his seemingly effortless and subtle integration of a theory of social evolution into what seemed the most practical and down-to-earth interventions in the socialist movement. Few activists have so frustrated the classifiers, who have pigeonholed him in every category, from fascism to communism. His most famous book, *The Farmers in Politics* (1920), would speak to readers in several very different ways: as a recipe book for the supposed Western regional revolt, an eccentric contribution to an ill-defined progressivism, or even a Hobbesian exploration of political dynamics. But it was also clearly an attempt to fit Prairie social conflicts into left Spencerian categories.

A convert to socialism in Scotland before 1907, under the auspices of a group akin to the Social Democratic Federation, Irvine had studied under Dr. Salem Bland, a towering figure of the social gospel. He also buried himself in Marx, Darwin, Huxley, and Spencer, whose *Synthetic Philosophy* plainly made a lasting impact on him. He would ultimately gravitate to the United Farmers of Alberta and Henry Wise Wood.[228] In his highly original reflections on *The Farmers in Politics*, Irvine was able to make a different case for agrarian radicalism – one that combined a conventional "progressive" enthusiasm for democracy with unconventional "functional" demands for group government and recognition of the farmers as a class, based upon their indispensability to the economy of the Dominion.

Irvine's great contribution to the Canadian left was his critical development of the concept of group government – in essence, an attempt to rethink democracy under conditions of corporate, post-proprietorial capitalism. Group government was a left-Spencerian strategy for dealing with a new capitalism. Each producing occupational group would organize itself to protect its interests; ultimately, largely because co-operating groups would excel in the struggle and those pursuing a competitive ideal would not, the groups would come together to form a co-operative commonwealth, a truly democratic government reflective of the actual functions that each group carried out in society.[229]

Still, a third approach to the question neither waited for the farmers' demise nor exalted their vanguard role. In a bracing submission to *Red Flag* – the heterodoxy of the article drew from the editor the unusual warning that such "contributions on the farmer question" were to be read as the personal opinion of the contributors – C.M. Christianssen argued that farmers could be aligned with socialist workers through an analysis of the labour theory of value. "Farms conducted on a large scale are few and far between, like an oasis in a desert. It may be true that farming on a large scale will become general some day, but at present this possibility belongs to the realm of the speculative and debatable points, and is therefore, more or less of an utopian ideal," he noted. "Yet since our science requires us to take account of capitalism with all its possibilities of development we cannot ignore this point, more especially, since it seems such an easy solution to the farmers' problems."

According to Christianssen, the better approach, and one that could be carried out "without violating a single law of Marxian economics," lay in analyzing the farmers' position in light of the law of value. Because the capitalist system allowed the wage-worker only a small wage, the wage-worker and the small farmer confronted each other on the markets of the world as two producers, "who would gladly exchange products, but are prevented from exchanging but very small quantities, to the detriment of each, by the laws of capitalist production and exchange." With respect to capitalism's penetration of the countryside, Christianssen argued that it could be comprehended "within the meaning of the efficiency phase of the Law of Value." Efficient management and labour-saving devices held out the promise of "lessening the socially necessary labour time required to raise farm products," but any such innovations under capitalism would not benefit the producers. "Just as the butterfly can only develop to a certain stage in the chrysalis, so farming, in all its different branches, can only develop to a certain stage in the chrysalis of the capitalist system."

Christianssen concluded with a poetic evocation of the rural people's enlightenment: "The dark night of capitalism's ebbing life is gloomy enough, especially if one just keeps his eyes on the darkness about. But this night of gloom need not last long. Its length depends on how swiftly the proletariat and the small farmer will go about to overthrow the capitalist system."[230]

From the orthodox Marxist perspective, other classes, strata, and social groups were much less worthy of attention. They essentially had no future. In *The Working Class and Master Class* (1910), the SPC worked overtime to produce a portrait of these "people-in-between" as living fossils, contemptible remnants. It looked at them with an almost palpable impatience: they were the "petty capitalists, in society, little business men and the like," whom Kautsky had revealingly termed "unclassifiable hybrids, belonging wholly to neither class, and partly to both." They were pitiful specimens, their lives a continual worry, "hanging on by the hair of their eyebrows" – and they were historically insignificant, a "negligible factor," since they were bound to be soon sent tumbling into the working class.[231]

Those who were neither capitalists nor proletarians were difficult to encapsulate within the triune formula. They fit uneasily within the labour theory of value and dualistic class analysis, and seemingly stood in the way of progress from one stage of civilization to the next. In talking about them, the socialists generally preferred pseudo-Darwinian hyperbole to a critical realist analysis. Professionals, middle managers, and workers in the service industries were difficult to analyze directly in terms of the production of surplus value. All were often categorized as simply unproductive or as "parasites." As W.E. Hardenburg explained in the SPC pamphlet *What Is Socialism? A Short Study of Its Aims and Claims*, "The small manufacturer sets up a howl loud enough to raise the dead, but he must go. The small shop-keeper lays awake nights worrying over the advent of the big department store and the insidious mail-order house. He, too, is doomed." They were all, this pamphleteer advised, in words that could have been drawn directly from London's *The Iron Heel*, to be trampled into the dust by the "Juggernaut of intensified Capitalism. They have performed their part; their work is over. There remains but the funeral!"[232]

Compared to this unforgiving judgment, Will R. Shier took a far more subtle and compassionate approach, writing fascinatingly about the "people caught between." He too believed that the middle class was becoming more and more endangered, "as their shops and manufactories and farmers [were] absorbed by the all conquering trusts or put out of business by their competition." Yet he also noticed that this development closed doors for workers, who might have hoped for advancement. The "most ambitious members of the working class" could no longer dream of becoming masters; they were now forced to become "mere salaried employees," or else "seek the overthrow of the system which keeps then in economic bondage." He hopefully saw in this new "alignment of forces" intimations of "the final conflict between capital and labour."[233] This analysis, if it did not exactly disagree with Hardenburg, at least strove for a more sympathetic sense of middle-class people caught up in the same heartless processes of capitalist modernity.

The Degenerate and Dangerous Class

The other main conceptual and practical challenge to first formationists as they struggled to strengthen in reality the class struggle that they supported in theory came in the challenge of the unemployed. Darwin, Spencer, Ferri, London, Gilman, and Schreiner, not to mention Marx (at least on occasion), tended to produce a despairing and disparaging sense that the unemployed were unorganizable, a veritable cesspool of degenerates whose sole social purpose was to drag the working class down. *The Communist Manifesto* speaks of the "dangerous class," the "social scum, that passively rotting mass thrown off by the lowest layers of old society." They were here and there possible recruits for the revolution, but far more likely to be "a bribed tool of reactionary intrigue."[234]

Hoboes, transients, the unemployed, and the poor could all be constructed as "parasitical" predators upon the workers, not proletarian allies. *Western Clarion* contributor John Rivers included "those at the bottom of the social pit" among others as he enumerated those "elements in our class" that would be of no help in the struggle. They were "the helpless victims of this system unable to help themselves or assist others. Of course they can't harm us to any great extent, so the best thing to do is just to ignore them." London in *The People of the Abyss* had conveyed much the same idea. Those who were not of the producing classes were parasites who fed off them. As another writer to the *Clarion* pointed out, the "middle and upper classes," unable to read the signs of the times so clearly conveyed by the theory of social evolution, were "degenerate intellectually as well as morally," and ignorant of the system of production they defended. "They prey on the producers, and when sick through gorging themselves they pray to the god of their class for relief." Degenerates (in essence rebels against or outcasts from evolution) and parasites (essentially evolution's freeloaders) abounded in this imagined world. Capitalism, Keir Hardie proclaimed, meant that idle parasites could be found at "both ends of the scale" – as represented by the figures of the tramp and the millionaire. Socialism would do away with both. "The tramp and the millionaire are brothers under the skin," the Lindsay SPC's *Gems of Socialism* stated. "They both live without labor, or rather, live on the labor of others." Socialist parasitology was clearly flourishing in small-town Ontario.[235]

Yet whether they were degenerates, parasites, or (as Marx would more often have said) workers thrown into capital's reserve army, the jobless were increasingly in evidence as the century progressed. Business downturns in the 1890s and 1912–14 generated vast armies of the unemployed. One could respond to this with depictions of them as "lumpenproletarians," or one could look more closely at the Marxist inheritance, in which the "reserve army of the unemployed" is functionally related to the generation of surplus value – and hence a wholly appropriate focus of revolutionary organizing. In the underexplored "Canadian unemployed revolt" of 1912–14, and under pressure from the jobless themselves, socialists combined analyses of unemployment as a symptom of the system's organic decay with activism alongside the unemployed as grassroots allies in the wider struggle. The IWW's campaigns in Edmonton and Calgary were matched by heroic unemployed struggles, often aligned with the Social Democratic Party, in the Lakehead, Sudbury, Hamilton, Ottawa, and Montreal. It would be a scholastic first formationist indeed who failed to see in this uprising of the poor and the jobless a beacon of a people's enlightenment extending far beyond the boundaries of the working class.[236]

Even more than small farmers and the difficult to categorize "awkward classes," the unemployed challenged earlier answers to the class question. Both the spontaneous and the scientific explanations had assumed relatively stable and easily delineated fundamental classes and left little room for (when they did not actively stigmatize) those who fell outside them. The rise of mass unemployment demonstrated, under the conditions of a global economy, how precarious a person's class status could be and how necessary to capitalist development were vast, often transnational, reserve armies of labour – and both of those implications were troubling when placed beside earlier responses to the class question. As they became more and more involved in the struggles of the insulted and injured of capitalism and the liberal order, and grasped the transnational logic of that suffering, socialists in Canada were called upon to articulate a much more expansive leftism. They were challenged, in Gramsci's terms, to articulate an answer to the class question that went beyond the "corporative" interests of the working class, as narrowly and statically defined, to take account of the dynamism and complexity of social world around them.

By 1915, then, much had happened to transform a Canadian left that, in 1907, might have been plausibly interpreted as one in which the SPC enjoyed a measure of dominance. One of the keys to this transformation was an emergent reinterpretation of the class question. In successive periods, "impossibilist"-style theorists had confronted "possibilist"-style labourites and activists. From about 1910 a rising impatience with this dichotomy appeared, coinciding with intensifying social conflicts in the major coalfields, the arrival of new diaspora socialists, and a growing sense of urgency in the face of mass unemployment. The Social Democratic Party of Canada, IWW, and Socialist Party of North America were rival attempts to resolve the class question in ways that simultaneously preserved the vital role of socialism as a science, cancelled its tendency to isolate "expert" practitioners from the rank and file, and, finally, engaged in ever more inclusive and politically effective representations of social reality.

The class question was in part explored in organizations – with regular meetings, minutes, signed-up members, and executives – but only in part. It was as much the focus of organizers – the men and women who threw themselves into the herculean tasks demanded by the people's enlightenment, and who might individually work in trade unions, co-operatives, and social movements alongside (or at times without) a party commitment. It was even more about organs – the publications that carried the message of enlightenment, from *Citizen and Country* to *Cotton's Weekly*, from the Winnipeg *Voice* to *The Grain Growers' Guide*, and of course the inimitable *Western Clarion*. Many such organs were more widely known and influential than the organizations they were affiliated with, and they created communities of contributors and correspondents from coast to coast. In a formation that was so decisively about socialism as a *science*, the shape and size of the party were less important than the clarity and passion with which the precepts of the science were expounded – in print, in provincial legislatures, in the city parks. Indeed, the day of a party-centred socialism had yet to dawn.

The organizers of the first formation fashioned their own distinctive achievements. Their intransigence undoubtedly carried costs, but over the longer term it endowed the Canadian left with some of its most redoubtable and incorruptible fighters. They created a partial but invaluable first draft of a genuine realm of freedom – liberated from superstition, patriarchal respectability, and conventional politics – and one that scientific intransigence made possible for its members. With their motto "No Compromise, No Political Trading" inscribed on their banners, major elements of the first formation could enter the Great War period as a small but quite formidable cadre of believers. If in Skelton's balance sheets the early Canadian socialists amounted to nothing, his accounting turns out to have been quite misleading, as 1919 would shortly reveal. What turned out to be as significant as any election were the considerable achievements in *making socialists* – and those socialists were often confident, lifelong, unbendable, intransigent, and formidably self-educated and self-motivated exponents of reasoning and living otherwise.

In Montreal in 1906, in Edmonton in 1914, and in scores of other places, socialists were doing something new. They were demanding a public sphere in which the class question could be debated and new classless futures projected. In such hidden moments of strength lies much of the solution to the paradox of the early Canadian left – how a movement seemingly so small could, in the six short years from 1915 to 1920, shake the Canadian liberal order so creatively.

Jesus the workingman, as depicted in Rev. Vincent McNabb, *Fair Criticism from an Unexpected Source: Hints for the Guidance of Social Thinkers* (1914), a U.S. pamphlet circulated in Canada. Author's collection.

4

The Religion Question

Raymond, Kans., 1890s. It would go down as one of the most influential questions ever posed in North American religious history. One Friday morning the Reverend Henry Maxwell, the pastor of the First Church of Raymond, a medium-sized U.S. city, was at home trying to finish his Sunday sermon, based upon 1 Peter 2:21: "For hereunto were ye called; because Christ also suffered for you, leaving you an example that ye should follow his steps." He had reached the part of his sermon in which he was going to describe the necessity of following Jesus. Then the bell rang. At the front door stood a shabbily dressed young man, clutching his hat. "I'm out of a job, sir, and thought maybe you might put me in the way of getting somewhere," the tramp said. Rev. Maxwell had nothing to offer except good wishes.

The following Sunday Rev. Maxwell delivered an eloquent sermon full of striking sentences to his comfortable, prestigious church. He spoke "with the passion of a dramatic utterance that had the good taste never to offend with a suspicion of ranting or declamation." Suddenly a man walked into the open space in front of the pulpit. The man turned to face the people. "I've been wondering since I came in here . . . if it would be just the thing to say a word at the close of the service. I'm not drunk and I'm not crazy, and I am perfectly harmless, but if I die, as there is every likelihood I shall in a few days, I want the satisfaction of thinking that I said my say in a place like this, and before this sort of crowd."

The poorly dressed man continued. "I lost my job ten months ago. I am a printer by trade. The new linotype machines are beautiful specimens of invention, but I know six men who have killed themselves inside of the year just on account of those machines." What was a man supposed to do? "I know I never learned but the one trade, and that's all I can do. I've tramped all over the country trying to find something. There are a good many others like me. I'm not complaining, am I?"

It was, of course, the very man who had appeared two days before at Rev.

213

Maxwell's door. "What do you Christians mean by following the steps of Jesus?" He asked them if they meant that they too were suffering, just as Jesus did? He told them that his wife had died four months before, gasping for air – she died in a tenement owned by a member of a Christian church. Had this landlord been following Jesus all the way? His little girl was staying with a fellow printer's family. Now he was hunting for a job. "Of course I don't expect you people can prevent every one from dying of starvation, lack of proper nourishment and tenement air, but what does following Jesus mean?"

The man talked some more. Then he lurched towards the communion table, laid a grimy hand upon it, and collapsed. Three days later, at Rev. Maxwell's home, he died. "You have been good to me," he told his caregivers as he passed away. "Somehow I feel as if it was what Jesus would do."

The minister and his congregation were shocked. On the following Sunday Rev. Maxwell challenged volunteers from his congregation to pledge themselves to ask, "earnestly and honestly for an entire year, not to do anything without first asking the question, 'What would Jesus do?' And after asking that question, each one will follow Jesus as exactly as he knows how, no matter what the result may be."

The results were striking. One church member, a newspaper publisher, started turning away stories about prize fights and advertisements for drink. Another, a woman with a talent for music, rejected a career singing popular songs because her religious music must come first. A third volunteer, a businessman, set up a lunch room for his employees and allowed them the privilege, two or three times a week, of listening to a talk on a subject "that will be a real help to them in their lives." He even became a whistle-blower in his own company when he discovered a "systematic violation of the Interstate Commerce Laws of the United States." Rev. Maxwell overcame his aversion to speaking in front of working-class audiences and ventured forth to a settlement house in Chicago. There he again asked the same provocative question: "What would Jesus do?"[1]

This fictional story is from Charles M. Sheldon's *In His Steps*, a book that since its appearance in 1896 has moved millions of readers worldwide with its plainspoken Christian sincerity. Sheldon himself would go on to become the honorary president of Canadian Socialist League No. 2. More than a century later, his question still echoes in North America. An Internet inquiry reveals that many contemporary U.S. Protestants are certain that they know many specific answers to the question, "What would Jesus do?" In some authoritative U.S. interpretations, Jesus would favour capital punishment, condemn homosexuals, support the latest U.S. war in the Middle East, and – as evidenced by a host of books, such as *Jesus CEO: Using Ancient Wisdom for Visionary Leadership* and *The 25 Most Common Problems in Business (and How Jesus Solved Them)* – promote the values of a business civilization. In fact, in contemporary times, "What would Jesus do?" has been transformed from a burning question into a commodity. In the convenient shorthand form of "wwjd," the slogan is now available on bracelets, anklets, licence tags, licence plate frames, stylish executive-style pens, pewter dog tags, lapel pins, charm necklaces, bumper stickers, and key chains, available in either leather or glow in the dark plastic.[2] Over a century after Sheldon put the question in Rev. Maxwell's mouth, it is still making people think – and buy.

wwjd makes sense today as one sign within a form of evangelical Christianity now extremely influential in the United States. In essence, wwjd calls upon the individual to abide by a particular reading of Christian morality in making personal decisions. Having accepted Christ as one's personal saviour, one need only ask oneself, "wwjd?" and, at an instant, a host of certainties on moral issues might come to mind – from "A" (anti-abortion) to "Z" (zero tolerance for gays and lesbians), all backed up by the inerrant Holy Bible. wwjd seems designed principally as a way of prompting an authoritative interior monologue, as an individual weighs the pros or cons of a potential position or action against the individual example of Jesus. As a brand name for evangelicalism, "What would Jesus do?" functions as a sign of the superior morality of the person who has bought the bumper sticker or key chain. It is, in this sense, a rhetorical question that points the questioner back to Scripture as infallibly interpreted by religious authority.

When placed in a different context – the first formation, for example – the same words can mean something radically different. They combine with other concepts in a particular axiomatic framework, in ways almost completely discrepant at the level of concepts and statements from the reactionary counter-Enlightenment religious paradigm that claims them today. In the 19th century, in sharp contrast to the 21st, "What would Jesus do?" was an invitation issued to a group to think through collective issues of social justice. It was an open question.

In His Steps stresses the class identity of the unemployed printer. He is a worker displaced by new technology. His brief presentation to the church tells tales of suffering and suicide from his trade. The details, carefully selected by the author, connect the worker to a much larger social pattern familiar to most of Sheldon's readers. A century ago the question "What would Jesus do?" was aimed at making people think critically about the hardships caused by a competitive economic and social system and about how they might be addressed. What is now conventionally taken to be a device to help individuals wrestle with personal decisions was then a congregation's challenge to reason and live otherwise. Though individual Christians were expected to struggle with the question's implications, they were being asked to wrestle with them collectively, and not just agree with inerrant and hence authoritative truth. They were expected to engage with social problems, often by joining social action groups, from settlement houses to Christian endeavour societies. In 1896–97, when Sheldon posed it, "What would Jesus do?" was a question about a Christian's *political duty* and *social obligation*. It was, broadly speaking, a radical question – as attested to by Sheldon's elevation to honorary leadership in the CSL (alongside, eventually, the likes of Colin McKay and John Spargo).

Those Christians who asked this question were often haunted by the spectre of socialism. Friend or foe? Or something else? Near the end of the book, speaking at a Chicago settlement house, Rev. Maxwell was talking about the world-changing possibilities that his inquiry had opened up. After some questions, a "large, black-haired, heavily-bearded man" took the floor. The minute he spoke "nearly every man in the hall leaned forward eagerly." It was Carlsen, the Socialist leader, his "great bristling beard" shaking with anger. Carlsen believed that "the whole of our system is at fault," and that "what we call civilization is rotten to the core." Trusts, combines, and capitalistic greed mean "simply death to thousands of innocent men, women and children." When he looked at the "professed Christians," wallowing in luxuries and comforts, and singing their hymns about following the path of Jesus, he was enraged by their complacency. Some of them were good men and women, but if Rev. Maxwell ventured into "aristocratic churches" and put his proposition to them, he would be laughed at as "a fool or a crank or a fanatic." Only a system starting from "the common basis of socialism founded on the rights of the common people" would provide real answers to Rev. Maxwell's question.[3]

The enraged socialist was finally pulled down, yet his speech lingered on in Rev. Maxwell's mind. "Was it true that the church had lost its power over the very kind of humanity which in the early ages of Christianity it reached in the greatest numbers?" the minister later wondered. "How much was true in what the Socialist leader said about the uselessness of looking to the church for reform or redemption, because of the selfishness and seclusion and aristocracy of its members?"[4]

When Charles M. Sheldon came out, so to speak, as a Canadian socialist, it was a matter of celebration on the left and consternation in more conservative circles. When he agreed to become the honorary president of the CSL local, many Toronto leftists were overjoyed and more conservative Christians chagrined. His book had won him a huge international following. When Rev. Sheldon visited Toronto in 1899, men and women "in thousands" came to hear him. He was not a barn-burning evangelical minister. He did not "captivate his audience by his eloquence," reported *Citizen and Country*. He merely spoke "the simple truth of the Gospel." The Methodist *Christian Guardian* grumpily wondered whatever had led Sheldon to the CSL, and the CSL to Sheldon. *Citizen and Country* responded by noting that CSL No. 2 included "nearly a dozen clergymen." It advised the moody Methodists to get on the same page with the progressive Presbyterians who had written to congratulate Sheldon on his decision.[5] For Rev. Sheldon himself, one answer to the question "What would Jesus do?" seemed to be: "Jesus would become a socialist." This answer to wwjd remains curiously underreported in U.S. evangelical circles today.

Throughout the period 1890–1920, many people followed Sheldon's spiritual path to leftism. For many of them, socialism was an answer to the wrenching dilemmas faced by Christians in a capitalist social order. These were not only the obvious problems of reconciling a New Testament gospel that privileged the rights of the poor with a supposedly Christian church dominated by the rich. They were also those of responding to a massive challenge from the left. Rev. Maxwell was indeed jolted from his "dogmatic slumbers" by the unemployed printer who died on his premises. But his moment of refusal – of the middle-class complacency all around him – was intensified by the stark challenge posed by the Chicago proletarians, leaning forward so eagerly to hear the combative rival gospel of that burly and bewhiskered ethnic Other, Carlsen. This Red clearly had a following. The fictional Rev. Maxwell candidly wondered if Carlsen's danger rested in the accuracy of his allegation that the elitist church could not challenge its own privileges. The actual Rev. Sheldon linked his name to the foremost Canadian socialist movement. It was one in which "the Question" was asked again and again.

It was a complicated question that generated complicated answers. One response was that Christianity, more specifically Protestant Christianity, was uniquely charged with providing authoritative answers to social questions. Yet within the first formation were also socialists and workers who demanded that this process resemble, to a large extent, the free deliberations of a new democratic public sphere, with no one person being able to "trump" or silence the arguments of another merely by referencing institutional or doctrinal authority.

For Rev. Maxwell and many of the actual clergymen in the csl, the "Christian socialism" that emerged from this moment would be largely a church-led outreach mission to the working class. They would create temperance movements, Lord's Day observance societies, movements of social betterment. Their social gospel was closely aligned with movements for urban planning and public health. Dozens of mainstream histories of the "Progressive Era" in the United States, or "New Liberalism" in Canada and Britain, document their exploits. Many never left, or aspired to change, a middle-class liberal order that seemed slowly to absorb their ameliorative vision. *Citizen and Country* contained many such voices. This Christianity was of a piece with the missionary endeavours that sent thousands of North American believers, many of them women, to the far corners of the world to spread the good word of the gospel, in one of the largest mass movements of the day. On its face, it seemed a one-sided endeavour – a top-down diffusion of Christian truth to the unenlightened; yet, over the longer term and more subtly, it often awakened in some missionaries abroad and outreach workers at home a sincere identification with the oppressed.[6] Then again, for many who asked Sheldon's question the search for answers could end in a relatively safe place, leaving pre-existing religious and political preconceptions more or less intact. One set of answers was implied by Rev. Maxwell's strategies in *In His Steps*. Jesus would seek the piecemeal purification of the world around him, responding with sincerity and compassion to the social problems as they presented themselves to him. He would join settlement houses, temperance leagues, and Christian missionary societies.

Yet the CSL with which Sheldon affiliated contained many different leftists, and for some of them, Sheldon's question – What would Jesus do? – held revolutionary implications. Carlsen spoke for many – not just in his outrage but in his alienation from the church. Many went further than he did. Some turned against the church altogether and even, in some cases, the faith in God it articulated. They constructed a grassroots critique of the church's implicit monopoly over religious and philosophical discussion. They held that evolution contained revolutionary implications, one of which was the passing away of an anti-Enlightenment church, associated in their minds with irrational medievalism, the public burnings of scientific rationalists, and a bullying arrogance. In essence, they identified with the answers implied by Carlsen. Just as Jesus had driven the money-lenders from the temple, so too would he rise up against the child-killing coal mines and sweatshops, and their supposedly Christian owners. As a revolutionary with a passion for social justice, Jesus would regard with disgust the vast theological bureaucracies and intricate theologies woven around his name. He might well become a non-believer in any religion – or perhaps a believer in Spinoza's "God," the entire cosmos as apprehended through monism. What would Jesus do? He would become, in essence, Karl Marx, and place his resistance to capitalism (and to established religion) on a firm scientific footing.

Perhaps most typically, a good many leftists sought a dialectical resolution of the opposition of believers and non-believers in a new form of left humanism. They would seek to rescue from the church a saving remnant of faith, but they might also express this faith in the new forms of spirituality – theosophy, Spencerian agnosticism, or, more broadly, in the moral authority they discerned in a host of cultural visionaries. Socialism itself might thus be seen as a form of spirituality. They would call not for a rejection of religion, but for revolutionary new forms of religiosity. What would Jesus do? He would build a new church, open to all of humanity, fighting poverty and cruelty in the real world, one that combined what was true in the applied science of social evolution with what was right in the gospel. He would seek harmony and accommodation with other faiths in which the essence of his humanistic message could also be found, even if in a different language – and seek to bring these distinctive religious traditions into harmony with the revolutionary socialist message of Christ.

The "religion question" – could a serious leftist be a Christian, and a serious Christian a leftist, and if so in either case, what were the political and philosophical implications? – was debated in hundreds of polemics in Canada in this period. In the case of every major activist, to be a leftist from 1890 to 1920 necessarily meant having a position on religion. If an activist was sincerely uninterested in religion, he or she would almost inevitably encounter accusations of "atheism," a charge that could be profoundly disabling.[7] During these 30 years few issues on the left generated more commentary, divided people as dramatically, or motivated them as profoundly.

Labour historians often view the "Christian socialists" of this time with a thinly veiled contempt – they are the middle-class meddlers, pious preachers, or at best the mediocre warm-up band for the real revolutionaries who followed them – or simply ignore them. Yet most Canadian workers in this period firmly believed in God, claimed affiliation with a church, and took their religion seriously. They wrote letter after letter to the press. They went in throngs to meetings on religious issues and seemingly could not hear enough about evolution and "free thought" – the ability of men and women to make up their own rational minds about religious questions without state and clerical coercion. They enriched countless polemics with images of Christ the liberator, and fiercely debated religious doctrine with their ministers. Since the 19th century, debates involving religion have both entertained and enraged Canadians en masse. These debates generated hundreds of articles, letters, editorials, speeches, books, and pamphlets.

The more numerous and influential historians of religion – who are understandably, in most cases, religiously minded historians – describe a country that seemingly bears almost no relation to the place described by their labour history colleagues. Their Canada is often, straightforwardly, a Protestant Canada – God's Dominion. (That the largest single denomination was the Roman Catholic Church is a consideration that does not seem to unsettle certainty on this pivotal point.) Within this school of historiography, a big organizing framework for over a quarter of a century has been debate over the "secularization thesis." Did those who sought to regenerate society and build the "city of God on earth" through Christian outreach successfully navigate the social and economic rapids of the *fin de siècle*? Did they almost single-handedly create the modern welfare state? Or, to the contrary, were they the unwitting architects of a secular city in which the Christian message was lost amid the hubbub of secular modernity?[8] Still, both the pro-secularization and anti-secularization camps of religious historians do agree that the main actors in the story were theologians, church leaders, ministers, editors of religious newspapers, and politicians. They also agree that the Christian socialists were, by and large, misguided: from one perspective, because the mainstream evangelicals were doing all the serious work of modernity within the liberal state; or, from another, because with each step these Christian socialists took towards a new religious sensibility, they diminished the particular place of spirituality. Doubters, sceptics, and non-believers – whom they have sometimes reductively figured as "atheists" – are people of little account, quaint and marginal eccentrics in some cases, momentarily influential ne'er-do-wells in others. From one influential perspective, such marginal folk were "beaten back" by an evangelical majority sensible enough to reject their message of social divisiveness and to get on with the job of building a modern state.

The historical evidence suggests, however, that a large number of both working-class and middle-class Canadians followed spiritual paths to leftism; and those who wanted to halt this process at Christian-outreach positions, of the sort congenial to Rev. Sheldon, were persistently challenged by rival forms of Christian radicalism, often articulated in social-evolutionary, Spencerian, and Marxist terms. Those who became Christian revolutionaries were not uninfluential, unsophisticated, or unsuccessful. They made a serious difference to the society in which they lived.

The 19th century bequeathed to 20th-century Canadians patterns of religious affiliation and debate that were slow to vanish. In British North America, both the Church of England in English-speaking British North America and the Roman Catholic Church in Quebec were, in certain respects, state churches. Their sharply different paths under modernity suggested just how heterogeneous was the religious landscape of Canada. Although both churches retained significant (and jealously preserved) privileges in the colonization of the Northwest, and were de facto partners of the state in the attempted assimilation of the First Nations in residential schools and other colonizing endeavours, the Anglicans generally receded as an official church in much of the rest of anglophone Canada, becoming more and more like other Protestant denominations. The Roman Catholics, although often subjected to prejudice in anglophone Canada, became more and more consolidated as a wing of the state in Quebec, with direct responsibility for a vast institutional complex that included schools, hospitals, and charities; and especially after the 1870s, the Church was also significantly imbued with the Ultramontane doctrine arguing for the supremacy of the church over the state. In Quebec, defiance of the Church – whether it meant supporting a library of unapproved books, joining the Freemasons, or backing secular schools – was a serious business. Those who risked it put their social identities at stake. A particular focus of Ultramontane energy was the Institut Canadien, a cultural organization founded in the 1840s that maintained a library of liberal works and disseminated radical ("Rouge") opinion. The Bishop of Montreal placed the Institut under the interdict and denied the sacraments to those who refused to resign from it. In 1869 the Pope himself placed the year-book of the Institut on the Index of Forbidden Books. Into the 20th century the Church would exert itself to keep Montreal free of literature that it did not approve, as suggested by its resistance to the formation of a Montreal Public Library.[9] When the library of Albert Saint-Martin's Université ouvrier was wrecked by members of l'Action Catholique in the 1920s, it was hardly an unprecedented blow against the Enlightenment in Catholic Quebec.[10]

Canada was a country strongly divided by religion, for although the Roman Catholics made up the largest single denomination, only in Quebec could they set the religious tone. More lives were lost in Catholic/Protestant strife in the 19th century than would ever be claimed by the 20th-century labour wars. Particularly inflammatory were the anti-Catholic crusaders, first Alessandro Gavazzi and then Charles Chiniquy, whose cross-country tours sparked incredible turmoil. Although the 20th-century religious disputes were somewhat more pacific, they were still often highly charged affairs. The ultra-rationalist Marshall Gauvin was such an enthusiastic participant in this culture of religious contention that he would send emissaries out to the Sunday morning services of the various congregations, so that in his own Sunday evening meetings he could refute the ministers' sermons point by point.[11] This was often a rambunctious, noisy, indecorous environment.

At the grassroots level the religion and society question was integral to the social gospel, which in Richard Allen's classic definition "rested on the premise that Christianity was a social religion, concerned, when the misunderstanding of the ages was stripped away, with the quality of human relations on this earth."[12] Sometimes the social gospel is imagined in a most measured and stately way, as when concerned minister x looks up from his Bible, notices social problem y, and crafts theological position z. But it more often happened in the way that Rev. Sheldon described: as a response to a sudden, anomalous eruption of one of the multitude, someone demanding redress and constructing a powerful symbolic challenge to denominational leadership that a wise church leader would ignore at his or her peril. Working-class rage, voices of righteous anger, powered much of the debate – the voice that Sheldon captured with the figure of Carlsen. Often the enraged voices we hear in the past were not trying gently to recall the church to its social obligations or regenerate it as a healthy cell within an evolving society. They were calling for divine retribution against child-exploiting employers and gun-toting strike-breakers – as in the case of the wives of strikers in Cape Breton, who were seen kneeling down on the road in 1910 and appealing to God "with genuine fervour to cause the rocks in the pit to fall upon the objects of their hatred," meaning the strikebreakers.[13] Many influential left writers and activists found it preposterous that, when working-class men and women were fighting for their lives, the church would repeatedly exercise its preferential option – for the rich. They saw nothing but hypocrisy in a repulsive institution that had battened on Christ's radical teachings and turned them into an apology for the exploitation of workers and the abuse of children.

The Protestant ethic could, in certain circumstances, be a potent stimulus to the spirit of socialism. The two forces could grow together, competing sharply in many cases over who had the right to speak authoritatively to society, yet also collaborating in other spheres, especially those in which they shared many social-evolutionary assumptions. It was entirely possible that the numbers of people ready to undertake major commitments of time and energy to spreading Protestant ideas and those equally committed to socialism might grow simultaneously. In a climate of deep religious uncertainty, when the pole stars of faith were disturbingly in motion, some people were struggling to construct a "New Christianity" that was not so much about the "social reform" of the existing liberal order as its transcendence by a liberated, egalitarian society.

To many people the realities of life in an individualistic capitalistic order and the ethics articulated by Christ and his followers, no matter how flexibly interpreted, revealed a major contradiction. From the socialist perspective, a capitalist society necessarily requires the systemic violation of Christian ethics. The same point troubled non-socialist but conscientious Christians. As the 19th-century Protestant writer John Clark Murray argued, "Both religious and philosophical imperatives demanded that men and women always be treated as persons and never as things." Yet this was plainly incompatible with any system that necessarily categorized labour-power as a commodity.[14] Capitalism depends precisely upon *not* treating other people as one would like to be treated oneself. A capitalism that did not treat labour-power and its bearers as thing-like "commodities" would not be capitalism.

Much of the existing literature on religious history beautifully captures the radiant intensity of the rise of the social gospel, that extended moment in which prominent and well-read Protestants opened themselves up to Darwin, read the historically informed criticisms of the Bible, and reflected with genuine rigour on the new evolutionary sociologies. Many, including Woodsworth, Mackenzie King, and Salem Bland, poured over Benjamin Kidd on *Social Evolution*, wherein he concluded – via a long argument with Spencer, which Kidd characteristically won only by adopting most of his opponent's contentions – that "the fact of our time which overshadows all others is the arrival of Democracy. But the perception of the fact is of relatively little importance if we do not also realize that it is a new Democracy."[15] Many would also read the work of Henry Drummond, a sensationally popular religious writer who modelled his quest for "natural law in the spiritual world" on Spencer's scientific accomplishments in the secular.[16] In doing so, such thinkers combined a greatly heightened awareness of evolutionary theory with a new emphasis on achieving a deliberative democracy. For many socialists a crucial issue, and perhaps *the* crucial issue, was that of the struggle over authority. Figures such as Salem Bland (1859–1950), Marshall Gauvin (1881–1978), and E.A. Partridge (1862–1931) – three eloquent representatives of the social gospel, the Enlightenment critique, and left humanist positions respectively – provide a useful reminder that these terms, useful as heuristic devices, are not to be taken as names for well-defined and exclusive "schools" of thought. In the lives of each of these men, the religion question was a core element of living otherwise.

Socialism as "Applied Christianity": The First Phase

Throughout much of the 19th century, argues John Webster Grant, most Canadians – at least in English Canada – would have agreed on a number of propositions. God was sovereign, history was the "unfolding of His purpose," Scripture was an "infallible record shedding light on the future as surely as on the past and present," and human beings were sinners by inheritance, incapable of saving themselves. Only if they "responded to Christ in faith and obedience" could they look forward "to an eternity of bliss in heaven." Those who disputed these core truths confronted the prospect of "unending torment" in the hereafter.[17] For many who received such messages every Sunday in church, through the weekend in their newspapers, and perhaps at night from devotional books, an eternity spent in a hell whose fires were a matter of grim and unarguable fact was a high price to pay for the forbidden knowledge of the people's enlightenment. These were not trifling sentiments. Revisiting one's religious roots could mean separation from family and friends, even from earlier versions of oneself. Yet for these people to be a socialist necessarily meant doing so.

Within the largest Christian denomination in Canada, and with some significant exceptions, there would be little movement towards rethinking any of these beliefs until the 1930s. Many – probably most – Catholics staunchly resisted socialism. The Catholic Church's opposition to socialism had been apparent from the mid-19th century. It was reaffirmed in 1891 with the encyclical *Rerum Novarum*, which outlined the Pope's official views on capital/labour questions. A major reason for this opposition was the Church's reluctance to make any space for a rival conception of the world. A subtler rationale for opposition could be found in theology. Many Catholic thinkers saw human beings as inescapably flawed and, following St. Augustine, interpreted the "City of God" as an eternal reality located outside graspable time and space. Catholics carried from their long history a worldly sense of the ease with which fallible human beings would fall into venial and mortal sins. The Catholic sensibility was also wary of allowing unregulated rank and file access to the Holy Scripture, which should be made available on terms acceptable to the hierarchy. Many of the books of the Enlightenment were still on the Index. Faithful Catholics were not supposed to read them.

With a few exceptions most supporters of socialism in Canada in this period were not Catholics.[18] When Skelton cheerfully assembled the reasons as to why Canadians had proved immune to the virus of socialism, the influence of the Catholic Church stood high among them. Some French Canadians announced their sharp opposition to socialism on religious grounds. In 1906 Saint John's numerous Irish Catholics were told by their bishop that any notion of a class struggle between employers and employees was "pernicious."[19] In the authoritative *Catholic Register*, socialism was depicted as a "product of the alcohol-steeped brains of the effete capitals of Europe." The *Western Clarion* returned the compliment, with savage satires on the Pope and his *Rerum Novarum*.[20] Although some leftists looked hopefully to European examples of Catholics in socialist parties, and others found encouragement in the welcome that French Canadians gave to international unions,[21] overall there was not much positive news for the left from the Church. The left in a country like Canada – with a strong Catholic cultural presence undergoing an intensification of Ultramontane clericalism, and importing substantial numbers of conservative priests fleeing from often anticlerical countries in Europe – faced a high hurdle; and when this viewpoint was articulated more and more closely with the identity of the largest single national minority in the form of "clerical nationalism," the left faced a higher hurdle still.

Many Protestant churches would be only a little more welcoming. Any questioning of religious authority, especially in the name of a doctrine of social evolution implicitly holding that religion itself was subject to change, often aroused fierce opposition. Although the wages of theological sin no longer included death, they did encompass disgrace and ostracism. Those who questioned *individualism* in political economy were arguing against the grain of much Protestant teaching, which persistently equated worldly prosperity with God's grace. Those who questioned *liberal order* in general were calling into doubt God's own Dominion. It was an indication of Woodsworth's attachment to the liberal project before 1917 that he praised Protestant evangelism, among other "modernizing" forces, for its potential to break down the ominously collective ways of life of Mennonites and Ukrainians on the Prairies.[22] At the same time the Protestant was often embedded in small communities of believers, monitoring behaviour and shaping the limits of what could be said and thought. Moral offences might be tried publicly before church courts, and offences against Protestant doctrine aired in widely publicized heresy trials through which the community of believers passed judgment on their errant co-religionists.[23] In the residential school system, developed throughout much of the Canadian North for the inculcation of Western values within Aboriginal peoples, the liberal state and Protestant churches worked harmoniously together, and with great success, to break down what were, on both sides, seen as problematic "communistic" cultures.

Yet under conditions of modernity, there was nonetheless a substantial movement for change. In each of the major Protestant denominations – Anglican, Methodism, Presbyterianism, Baptist – many believers argued that the new times demanded new approaches to theology and the "social question." Amongst these churches in particular the Methodists and Presbyterians would prove to have the flexibility, according to Michael Gauvreau, to survive "the encounter with various currents of secular thought," preserving their leadership to some extent. Gauvreau suggests that Canadian Presbyterians and Methodists found Darwinism "troubling" but not "devastating."[24] Given that Darwinism was not a "set meal," Protestants were, for a time, able to believe that they could retain both a belief in the fixed truths of the Bible and the inescapably conditional truths of science. Evolutionary biology was gradually incorporated into the curricula of the universities, and the historical criticism of the Bible was incorporated into theological education.

The Christian socialists who proliferated within the Protestant churches from the 1890s to the 1920s were calling for the extension and modification of their churches. They were not necessarily calling for the wholesale transformation of either institutional or theological structures. Often they explicitly or implicitly argued that the churches should retain their monopoly rights over the abstract questions of value and identity addressed by religion, and used the argument that unless the church changed, it would lose its working-class constituency to revolutionary socialism.[25] Agnes Maule Machar of Kingston, a significant figure in the National Council of Women, acutely sensed the challenge to Christianity posed by the new science. Related by marriage to Grant Allen, and a friend of Kingston-born George Romanes, a colleague of Darwin's, she also communicated with Alfred Russel Wallace on natural selection and spiritualism from her summer home in the Thousand Islands. As Ramsay Cook remarks, Machar was firmly convinced "that Christianity, once brought into line with contemporary intellectual developments, provided the surest method of both comprehending and reforming modern industrial society." Her feminism was grounded in the conviction that "society was an organism with interacting parts." Her belief in a "socially oriented Christianity" was prompted by a fear, Cook argues, that "unless the church took up the issue of poverty the lower classes would naturally succumb to atheistic communism."[26]

It was possible, as Richard Allen has shown, to support conservative, progressive, and even radical variants of the social gospel. The conservatives emphasized "personal-ethical issues, tending to identify sin with individual acts, and taking as their social strategy legislative reform of the environment." The progressives, informed to an extent by contemporary sociology, presented a "broad ameliorative programme of reform," often stressing such measures as settlement houses and such outreach programs as Frontier College. The radicals looked at society in organic terms: "Evil was so endemic and pervasive in the social order that they concluded there could be no personal salvation without social salvation."[27]

The burden of Christian socialism was that moral reform organizations of various kinds would align religious teaching with modern social realities. Belief in a purified, reinvigorated, sociologically aware church was broadcast in many a Protestant assembly and newspaper editorial. In many social gospel presentations, Spencerian sociology was not far beneath the surface – often in the form of references to the work of Drummond. "Within their own sphere the results of Mr. Hebert [sic] Spencer are far from sterile – the application of Biology to Political Economy is already revolutionizing the Science," Drummond explained. "If the introduction of Natural Law into the Social sphere is no violent contradiction but a genuine and permanent contribution, shall its further extension to the Spiritual sphere be counted an extravagance? Does not the Principle of Continuity demand its application in every direction?" The "spiritual laws" were not merely analogous to "natural laws," but were in fact one and the same laws.[28]

Christian socialists often emphasized the social implications of St. Paul's doctrine. In this reading, St. Paul was a *radical* – in essence, an early version of Spencer. Professor George D. Herron proclaimed, and *Citizen and Country* could not help repeating, one of their favourite saint's expressions over and over again: the Pauline gospel that we are all "members of one another." As Herron explained in *Between Caesar and Jesus* (which the socialist newspaper offered to its readers at a discount price), "There is no individual redemption from a social system; only a social redemption will free each individual at last. Society is an organism, and not a certain number of individuals; individuals are members of the social body, and can be healthy only in the health of the whole body." No matter what an individual might wish, he or she was governed by the life of the collectivity. "In the present unity and complexity of life, there is no way for the individual to practise his social ideal, if he have one, until it is realized by society."[29]

Protestantism also posed a certain challenge to liberalism. Protestants sincerely committed to the salvation of the individual's soul could find themselves pitted against a social and political order whose crassness and materialism eroded the boundaries of worthy individualism itself. To redeem the individual, they argued, one must save society. The zeal with which some powerful Protestants impugned the views of the socialists might be perhaps attributed to their own ambiguous position, caught between making a strenuous case against the grotesque materialism and inequalities of the society around them and their commitment to the liberal individualism with which such phenomena were related. The temperance (and later prohibition) crusades, strongly supported by most of the Protestant denominations, perfectly captured the ambiguities of liberal-order Protestantism. On the one hand, the temperance crusaders could be seen making a militant defence of the individual – whose independence, mental clarity, thriftiness, and industriousness were all jeopardized by alcohol. On the other hand, they were also trying to control the individual's right to ingest freely chosen substances. Their very victory might close down competitive industries.[30]

Thus there were those who would answer the question "What would Jesus do?" by saying, "Reinvigorate the church, support its missionary endeavours, and from this base seek to Christianize the social order." The burden of such Christian socialism was that the church itself, and organizations closely aligned to it, would bear the brunt of aligning Christian teaching with modern social realities. "Socialism" was, in this sense, the construction of a Christian commonwealth. A purified, reinvigorated church, having learned about sociology, could be the leader in the moral regeneration of society. "If New Testament philosophy comes to anything it is this," stated Herron, "that no man liveth or dieth unto himself – the same conclusion to which, under different terms, the social sciences are coming. For good or ill, we are bound up together in one human life and destiny."[31]

In the first formation, no name, unless that of Marx, circulated as often and as prominently as that of Christ.[32] For people within the early wave of Christian socialism, the message of Christ was accurately represented by those ministers who spoke in his name. The Sermon on the Mount, the Lord's Prayer, the Golden Rule – here were the texts, some said early on, to be consulted if you wanted to know "What would Jesus do." George Weston Wrigley Sr. would comment in his 1899 overview of "Socialism in Canada" that "The first Socialist sermons were delivered by a carpenter nearly two thousand years ago." They were "known in history as the 'Sermon on the Mount.'" In 1900 Walter A. Ratcliffe of Port Hope, Ont., Canada's "Blind Socialist Poet," extolled the Bible's most widely known text in his "The Socialism of the Lord's Prayer."[33]

The religious left initially saw the churches and the moral and social reform movements closely associated with them as the primary vehicles of progressive change. Many Christian socialists in the CSL adopted aspects of the evolutionary theory that they had learned from Spencer and others. Some were far less sympathetic to, if they even knew of, the triune formula of the Marxists. Within *Citizen and Country* they proudly advertised the gains that socialism had made in recruiting new middle-class, respectable Christians to its cause. They had cause to be pleased: there was an impressive wave of recruits in the mid-1890s to early 1900s, and they could rely upon a large library of Christian socialist works, many from "High Church" Anglicans in Britain who had specialized in this field in the mid-19th century.[34] Tim Buck would marvel at just how tightly interwoven were the ties linking various Protestant groups in his native Britain – Wesleyans, Primitive Methodists, Pentecostals, Bethel – with the partisans of Christian socialism and the leadership of the unions: "There was never any thought in our minds that there was any difference between Christianity and socialism. We were still firmly convinced that true Christianity is the path to socialism and socialism is Christianity in action."[35]

A distinguishing mark of this first phase of the religion question was the enormous authority enjoyed by ministers of religion to stage the discourse on religion and society. In this the ministers were in effect positioning themselves as the vanguard of the proletariat, or at least a vanguard of democracy and social responsibility – people whose professional training, religious calling, and public prominence vested their words on socialism with a great sense of importance. Leading Christians – ministers, writers of theological treatises, and pioneering settlement house missionaries – thus came to define and articulate a "Christian socialism." On 25 February 1901, for instance, the *Globe* reported that Rev. G.E. Bigelow, "one of the apostles of Christian Socialism," had attracted a large crowd to a meeting chaired by Arthur W. Puttee, the newly elected TLC-backed MP from Winnipeg and the founder and editor of *The Voice*. "After a few brief remarks ... and the singing of 'The Holy City' by Mr. G.T. Beales, Puttee explained that he did not really know if he was a socialist or not." According to the newspaper report, "It generally depended upon the man to whom he was talking. Sometimes when he heard socialism ably explained he thought it should be very good Christianity, and, on the other hand, when he heard Christianity ably explained, he thought it should be very good socialism." Rev. Bigelow gave an address on "Socialism in its Economic Aspects." He had no qualms about the "economic basis" of socialism, the idea that the workers as a class must emancipate themselves ("because no upper class ever yielded anything to the class beneath them, except on compulsion"). Citing Count Tolstoy, he denounced the "evil and injustice" of a system that did not pay workers for all the value of what they produced. He ended with a rousing call for the public ownership of all monopolies. Even as late as 1909, one Saint John newspaper could remark that the church was still the "chief agent" moving humanity forward to "saner methods of living."[36]

Citizen and Country brought to its readers news of almost innumerable titles from the world of Christian socialism. From its perspective, the key institutions for building socialism were the churches. "Clergymen! Attention!" wrote Wrigley Sr. in an appeal for money. "You have lost the sympathy of many persons whose confidence I enjoy. They have forsaken the Church because it has been more theological than sociological. I have clung to it, hoping to see it become as much sociological as theological."[37]

As intellectual leaders of their communities ministers were, it was supposed, uniquely capable of discerning and remedying society's most profound social problems. In Halifax H. Cyrus Doull urged ministers to "cry aloud against every form of wickedness which attempts to invade the land he calls his home." To pick up a mainstream newspaper of the day is often to meet up with a galaxy of Christian socialist celebrities – Sheldon, Herron, William Thurston Brown, Walter Rauschenbusch, Charles Stelzle – who were as closely associated with "Socialism" as was any Marxist. "Is it not inspiring, and does it not touch the innermost recesses of your soul, to hear the truth expounded from the pulpit by Rev. J.L. Donaldson?" asked one Haligonian, deeply stirred by a progressive Halifax minister whom others had accused of stirring up class hatred and division. The reader was particularly impressed by the prospect of "a social and industrial system that will put an end to rent, interest, profit, and all forms of usury." Others were equally impressed by Rev. J.J. McCaskill's fiery 1909 sermons in Saint John. Speaking on the theme of "Jesus, the Prophet of Nazareth from Galilee," McCaskill approvingly cited the Italian revolutionary Mazzini: "The next Messiah will be a collective Messiah." He then proclaimed, "The poverty of the toilers is the sin of our age." He even invoked the image of Christ, the scourge of the complacent and the privileged: "If a Saviour returned today, he would come in the name of the unemployed, the factory children, the landless and penniless, and the weary toiling mothers with no food to give to their children. If he would not describe himself as the Prince of Peace, he certainly would as Bringer of Justice."[38]

Once the church itself became "sociological," perhaps it could be the decisive institution in creating a newer, better world. As late as 1920, mainstream newspapers used the image of "Christ as the first socialist" to remind their readers of inherent human sinfulness and the pitfalls of confusing worldly success with eternal verities. A "Practical Christianity" would level class distinctions within and outside the church – not to further any revolution, but to live up to the precise instructions of the Bible. "Practical Christianity would draw a line of demarcation between right and wrong, and help to remedy many existing evils," argued "Old Collier" in the Halifax *Herald*. He supported his position with no fewer than five quotations from Scripture. In this form, Practical Christianity did not entail a substantial investment in a newfangled sociology. It simply meant the application to a changing world of timeless God-given precepts. It meant, Rev. Ralph W. Trotter told the congregation of Calvary Baptist Church in Victoria, that in an age "the trend of which is socialistic," the church had to combine its traditional concern for the saving of individual souls with the redemption of all of society.[39]

For many, both socialism and Christianity came down to the application of the Golden Rule, the Church's answer to natural selection as a social-evolutionary principle. R.R. Osgood Morse of Halifax believed that Christianity meant that "no class of labor will deny to any other class its right to due rewards for its labor," for each class of labour "must learn to recognize the value of the other class in the make up of the social organism." Poet E.W. Wilcox's summation was: "Who on the Golden Rule shall dare insist/ Behold in him the modern Socialist." Many liked to repeat Professor Richard Ely's dictum: "Socialism is simply applied Christianity; the Golden Rule applied to everyday life." Others, like the Lindsay, Ont., socialists, used the equation to answer the critics' charge that socialism was just so much pie-in-the-sky: "Socialism has been tried in about the same way that the golden rule has been tried. This is the reply to the oft repeated statement that 'Socialism has been tried and failed.' "[40] The "economic teachings of Jesus" provided the "only basis on which a better order of society may be built," argued *Citizen and Country*. A woman activist of the Woman's Christian Temperance Union agreed. "Christian Socialism is an all-embracing term," she noted. It extended far beyond the boundaries many wanted to draw for it. "We know that the application to political and business life of the principles laid down by Jesus would bring an industrial millennium. 'Thou shalt love they neighbor as thyself' is a great unexplored continent that is just being discovered." The *Encyclopædia Britannica*'s definition of socialism – "The ethics of socialism are identical with the ethics of Christianity" – was repeated in dozens of different contexts.[41]

One aspect of this Christian socialism was not so easily meshed with the dominant language of the first formation: the representation of Christianity as the treasure house of truth, an institution that superseded both the passage of time and the lessons of the more newfangled theorists. Gauvreau notes one writer who drew a parallel between the social and religious conditions in the Kingdom of Israel in the eighth century B.C. and the present-day menace of trusts and combines; and another, commenting on Bellamy's *Looking Backward*, who advised clergymen to return to the Bible for "the true principles of political economy," in preference to the works of, among others, Malthus, Mill, or Spencer. Tracing the Christian legacy back to ancient history in "Socialism, Its History Ancient & Modern," Rev. Professor Carrothers of Halifax showed that "the Divine plan of government for Israel had been one of beneficent rulers," a plan frustrated only by the unenlightenment of the people. Today's Christian Church called out no less strongly for a "great reformation."[42]

"The social gospel as expounded by the First Socialist is, 'Thou shall love they brother as thyself,' " said *Citizen and Country*. "This gospel is our gospel. Neighbor love, Brother love is the goal, the hope of the world."[43] Yet the very point of bringing forward such authoritative words from the Christian past was to place them in a dynamic relationship with a fast-changing modern world.

The primacy of clergymen in speaking on these questions – and in particular the idea that the church was the best vehicle for social redemption – did not go unchallenged. Certainly some working-class autodidacts believed that they too had a right to speak in the name of Christianity. Colin McKay went to jail for echoing the inflammatory words of one social gospel minister; he himself would audaciously undertake a "higher criticism" of the Old Testament that questioned the authorship of Moses and the scientific credentials of Genesis.[44] In a wide-ranging polemic on "Why Workingmen Distrust Churches" in the Montreal *Herald*, McKay explicitly raised the banner of deliberative democracy in the sphere of religion. McKay argued that while Canadian workers had not advanced as far as workers in Germany, France, and England in becoming antagonistic to the church, "the tendency is towards hostility." He stated: "To many workingmen, it seems that ... the church is more concerned with dogmas than principles." Although it had become more "democratic in form," it was actually "out of touch with the democratic spirit of the age." It continued to preach an individualistic gospel that had "little sanction in the utterances of Christ, and none whatever, from the teachings of modern social scientists." McKay in 1900 was no apologist for the church as he knew it, but he also feared the inroads of Darwinism. "It is impossible to deduce the socialistic doctrine of equal rights from naturalism or materialism," he argued. Drawing from John Stuart Mill and Immanuel Kant, he urged that socialism could not find "sanction in materialism, or any other strictly scientific conception of things. It is based on moral intuitions, rather than natural principles." Both Christianity *and* socialism, in this model, built upon concepts of "eternal justice, absolute, transcendental moral law, and the immortality of the soul." McKay's critique ended with the resounding claim that, while workers and socialists had no inherent quarrel with religion, they were "of the opinion that the church is a rather poor exponent of Christianity."[45]

Complacent responses to McKay's text from George Grant, principal of Queen's University, the Bishop of Nova Scotia, and others, suggested the religious hierarchy's almost complete inability to grasp the point of his intervention or to wrestle with its implications. "And that is the manner of men the majority of the ministers are," McKay pointed out angrily. "They haven't the spirit of Christ in them – the capacity to sacrifice themselves to the good of humanity." Yet even in his anger he could not quite bring himself to dismiss the possibility that the ministers of religion might play their true role as the vanguard of the new democracy: "In Canada, at least, the character of the people is sufficiently elevated to inaugurate socialism, which ... is applied Christianity. All that is needed is reason and knowledge, and we look to the church to throw the light of reason of Christianity on the conditions of life."[46]

McKay's qualified critique – one that condemned "churchianity," the ossi-fied dogmas and institutions of "actually existing" religion, that endorsed Christianity as an alternative to value-free naturalism and hoped that the ministers might yet rise to the occasion – was echoed throughout much of the first formation from the 1890s to around 1907 – by the likes of Reverend Charles Duff of Toronto; by socialist alderman R.N. Price of St. Thomas; and by *The Voice* of Winnipeg, which drew a stark contrast between the recent declamations of a minister who had painted an "extravagant, outrageous travesty" of socialism on the one hand, and the well-reasoned, "kindly and considerate" discourse of W.A. Douglas, B.A., on the other, whose recent ad-dress to the local labour party had pleaded for the "spirit of brotherhood" and the "enthronement of Christ."[47]

Many working-class leaders, rather than stoutly opposing the meddling of middle-class social reformers, were often impressed by such Christian cru-sades to reform the social order. J.B. McLachlan, who fought for temperance both before and after entering the SPC, remarked to the Halifax *Herald*: "I hate the liquor traffic with a whole-hearted hatred because I have seen it used over and over again to dash the hopes of working men when they were on the eve of doing something useful for themselves." In Fort William, Local 13 of the SPC passed a resolution in 1910 that stated: "We want speakers and orga-nizers who come for good of Party, not booze fighters or private bottlers." Before he became a famous SPCer, trade union militant James Simpson cut his left-wing teeth in the Toronto Epworth League, led by the Reverend E.S. Rowe, a Methodist cleric who "not only has ... a theoretical belief, but practices it daily for the benefit of those in the community, always availing himself of every opportunity of ameliorating the ills and woes of mankind.'"[48] In this first phase of the religion question, ministers, churches, and the leaders of the social movements they characteristically promoted were all often seen as "socialists," uniquely endowed with an ability to critique and address the ills of modernity.

The Social Gospel of Salem Bland

The social gospel had its revolutionary left, made up of men and women whose moments of refusal, supersedure, and systematization were the logical outcome of a process of religious awakening. For them, the "social organism" was akin to the Body and Blood of Christ. Among these people was Salem Bland, one of the most articulate, charismatic, and imaginative figures in Canadian religious thought, and a formative mentor to a large cohort of left-wing Christians.

Bland was the daring author of *The New Christianity* (1920), one of the most exciting books produced by the Canadian left in this entire period. He was a Methodist (and subsequently United Church) minister who became particularly well known at Wesley College, Winnipeg, where he taught from 1903 to 1917. It was a college that earned a Dominion-wide reputation as a seedbed of left-wing Protestantism. Like so many in his generation, Bland was drawn to such thinkers as Henry George, Leo Tolstoy, and perhaps particularly John Ruskin – whose condemnations of the inhuman and ugly world remade by capitalism would re-echo in Bland's 20th-century work. In *The New Christianity* Bland presented his readers with a sweeping cosmic vista of evolution, one that seemed destined to bring to humankind an entirely new way of life.

As Richard Allen remarks, *The New Christianity* has the quality of a sermon. It essentially popularized complex theological ideas in a "tract for the many." It also has the quality of a socialist manifesto – so much so that Bland said his publishers were courageous to bring it out.[49] Discreetly structuring *The New Christianity*'s vivid description of the religious struggle for social justice was a complex tradition of Protestant ideas about the nature of God and His revelations in the Bible. The beliefs of an evangelical Protestant of Bland's stripe – a "post-millennialist" – were grounded in the prophetic vision of heaven on earth, a cosmic millennium towards which history was working. Human agency, inspired by providence, could gradually establish the Kingdom of God on earth.[50]

With a gusto worthy of a Vancouver SPCer, *The New Christianity* urged Christians to refuse modern capitalism *in toto*. Capitalism's ethos of competitiveness made its winners selfish and its victims wretched. "Competition for a livelihood, competition for bread and butter, it is the denial of brotherhood. It is the antithesis of the Golden Rule. It is not the doing unto other men as we would have that they should do to us." Christians only defended the system because of the "morally blinding power of the accustomed, the familiar, and, above all, the profitable, which has made Christian men defenders of competition, of war, of the drink traffic, of the opium traffic, and of slavery." Capitalism was inhuman and dehumanizing. To be a Christian entailed *refusing*, root and branch, the capitalist order. "Christianity is a torrent," Bland wrote – he had a great fondness for images conveying sublimely powerful, onward-rushing natural forces, an imagery related not only to the Christian prophetic tradition but also to Kropotkin, who strongly influenced him. "It is a fire. It is a passion for brotherhood, a raging hatred of everything which denies or forbids brotherhood. It was a brotherhood at the first. Twisted, bent, repressed for nearly twice a thousand years, it will be a brotherhood at the last."[51]

If to be a revolutionary in a general sense was to be convinced of the paramount need to abolish capitalism, and entailed an impatience with half-measures, Bland in *The New Christianity* was a doctrinaire, single-plank revolutionary – a hardened "impossibilist." The abolition of capitalism was the necessary prerequisite for "the restoration of right relations among men on earth."[52] Bland conceded that "capitalistic control . . . has, no doubt, played a necessary and useful part in the social evolution." But often rapacious and heartless, and equipped with but a rudimentary moral sense, those exercising such "capitalistic control" now performed few constructive services for humanity. "When the managers on whom it depends desert to the side of the workers, it will be patent how little capacity or service is in capitalism, and how little it deserved the immense gain it wrung from exploited labor and skill." Capitalism meant inequality, a condition that all Christians, committed to a vision of a "deeper, diviner brotherhood," must find abhorrent. It choked genuine human creativity and fellowship. Just as, in a pine forest, no other vegetation could grow under the shade and fallen needles of those trees, so under capitalism, with its fierce business competition, self-absorption, and exhaustion, "little else than business shrewdness, business insight, business knowledge can grow. A thousand seeds of culture, art, music, philanthropy, religion, human fellowship, home, happiness die permanently or fail to germinate at all in the American business man."[53]

Writing in a highly repressive period in which the authorities had recently cracked down on the "subversive writings" of Marx and even Spencer, Bland wondered why they had not also cracked down on the seditious verses in the Bible, such as Luke 1:51–53: "He hath shewed strength with his arm; he hath scattered the proud in the imagination of their hearts. He hath put down princes from their thrones, and hath exalted them of low degree. The hungry He hath filled with good things; and the rich He hath sent empty away." Both "in the name of the brotherhood of Christianity" and "in the name of the richness and variety of the human soul," the church was obliged to mount a "truceless war" against "this sterilizing and dehumanizing competition and upon the source of it, an economic order based on profit-seeking."[54]

Yet, to fight this *truceless war* – a most Gramscian expression – the church itself would have to be ruthlessly purged of the encrustations of the ages. Some two millennia after Christ, the church was riddled with contradictions and paradoxes, Bland declared. Many doctrines hid within the folds of this old religion. Some of them were regrettable, such as St. Paul's "idiosyncratic contempt of marriage and lack of reverence for women." The long, winding path of the church had led through many errors. Indeed, the history of the church demonstrated the dialectical proposition that one arrived at truth – the transcendent truth of human brotherhood, that "passion for equality" that was essence of the "Christianity of Jesus" – only through the "exhaustion of error."[55] As an astonishing report adopted by the General Conference of the Methodist Church of Canada, October 1918, in Hamilton would declare: "We do not believe this separation of labor and capital can be permanent. Its transcendence, whether through co-operation or public ownership, seems to be the only constructive and radical reform. This is the policy set forth by the great Labor organizations."[56] The report represented, in fact, a policy closely linked with the preachings of Jesus. In this form of Protestantism, the betterment of the world and the fulfilment of the gospel were as one. Neither was consistent with private ownership of the means of production, distribution, and exchange.

The enduringly powerful message of *The New Christianity* was that a Christianity able to respond to the postwar social revolution must rapidly adapt itself to these changing circumstances. Two great, unquestionably correct principles, both overflowing from Christianity itself, were transforming the world: democracy and brotherhood. The "disturbance and alarm so widely felt" could be explained by the new regions of life penetrated by these principles, and addressed by developing a new Christianity "adequate to meet the situation." To be a believing and sincere Christian in the 20th century meant struggling for a "democracy of religion, of culture, of politics, and of industry. The inherent dignity of every human soul must be recognized in every sphere of life. Heirs of God, joint-heirs with Christ – how is it possible to reconcile such august titles with servitude or subjection?"[57]

The cosmic scope of *The New Christianity* saw the last 900 or so years in the light of a rising tide of democracy. British democracy was implicit even in the first monastic schools; its deep origins ran all the way back to Henry III. Now, with the House of Commons ascendant and the barriers to adult suffrage broken, democracy seemed like an unstoppable and sublime force of nature. It surged steadily ahead, like the Mississippi, "growing in hundreds of miles from a stream that may be waded to a great river a mile in width and a hundred feet in depth."[58] Those who aimed to "smash" the labour movement were as irrational as those who sought to "smash" a 40-mile-wide Alaskan glacier or stop it from moving to the sea.

"It is a new age the world is entering," Bland argued. "As the determining factor in the social structure of Europe from 800 A.D. to 1500 was feudalism, and from A.D. 1500 to 1900 capitalism, so from 1900 onwards to the dawn, it may be, of still vaster changes as yet undescribed, the dominant factor will be organized Labor."[59] Orthodox Marxists might have quibbled with Bland over the specifics, but this historical schema was essentially not that far removed from that of the early Marx and Engels or from the founding manifesto of the Socialist Party of Canada.

By "an action as cosmic and irresistible as the movement of a great river," democracy was invading the industrial world. No "temporary or makeshift expedients," no mere reforms would "secure equilibrium." Even profit-sharing was merely "a camping place on the journey." To turn away from Christianity now would mean that labour had missed its historic moment: "But it will not. Mankind is in the grasp of divine currents too strong to be resisted."[60]

Bland had come to believe that the rise of labour to world prominence meant nothing less than the opening of a new era in the history of the faith: labour Christianity. Once more taking the long view, he presented a quintessentially first formationist "evolutionary stage theory" of the history of Christianity through its various phases, with a penultimate "Bourgeois" or "Plutocratic" phase (1500–1914) giving way to the "Labour Phase, A.D. 1914 – ." This last phase represented Christianity's adaptation to "the single most important feature of the last hundred years" – the struggle of the proletariat of the Western world for its democratic human rights. The men and women who "did the rough and necessary work of the world" were now rising up against the age-old fate of the "despised, ill-paid, ill-housed servants of the classes who through their fighting power or their money-power could command the services of the toilers." They had made labour "the mightiest organized force in the world."[61]

The New Christianity urged workers to support the labour parties – Bland almost certainly had in mind the British Labour Party. He also urged the full inclusion of "all who contribute to the feeding, clothing, housing, educating, delighting of the children of men." The manual worker and the research scientist, the farmer and those who distributed his produce: all such people functioning within the social order must realize their shared indispensability. Professionals "must cease to regard themselves as other than men and women of labor." Labour would become the master category, "to which all belong who really earn their living and do not seek to 'make' more than they earn."[62]

It was because of the great democratic revolution of the labour movement that a New Christianity was taking shape. There could be no going back. The mighty river of social evolution could not be diverted. Both God and nature could be linked to this providential rise of a collective force of salvation. To turn aside from this majestic social evolution on the grounds of mere convenience or mental laziness was *to mock religion itself*. The left demanded a new social order, and in its demand one saw the hand of God. "To discredit and attack the principle of public ownership is to discredit and attack Christianity," cried Bland, and he went on: "It would seem to be the special sin against the Holy Ghost of our age. He who doubts the practicability of public ownership is really doubting human nature and Christianity and God."[63]

If Bland was in a sense the descendant of Rev. Sheldon, he also showed how much "ministerial socialism" had evolved since the 1890s. In his hands it had become the revolutionary doctrine of social evolution. In Bland's text, with its recurrent cosmic metaphors of vast natural forces, evolving in ways beneficial and necessary for the social liberation of humankind, we sense the extraordinary pull of a social gospel that could take on board the Spencerian Marxist interpretation of history – in a sense, spiritualize historical materialism and (by implication) the labour theory of value.[64] Bland's work emerged as a brilliant synthesis that vindicated 20 difficult years of Marxist/Christian dialogue.

Before writing *The New Christianity*, Bland had in 1917 been dismissed from Wesley College after a financial crisis there was used as an excuse for re-organization. A couple of years later he took a position with a church in Toronto, where he wrote a regular column for the *Star* and continued his political advocacy. In the 1930s he would help form the Co-operative Commonwealth Federation. Given the continuing cogency and influence of Bland and people like him, Canadian Protestantism, tied in a million ways to that of Britain and the United States, could nonetheless retain its own distinctive atmosphere; and the social gospel, whose obituaries have been written since at least the 1920s, would resound, as it still does today, in countless pulpits and programs.

Of Sky Pilots and Medieval Mildew: The Second Phase

Yet, as McKay's 1904 critique of churchianity intimated, coincident with the rise of the social gospel was the growth of religious scepticism on the left, one that would bring about a far-ranging and consequential clash over religion, notwithstanding stalwarts like Bland. In this second moment of the religion question, which overlapped the first, socialists combatively demanded that the church take the workers' side in the many coalfields and other labour wars, renounce its privileges, and, even more radically, simply be brushed aside as an outmoded institution – as so much "medieval mildew," in one cutting expression.[65] Far from being intellectuals vested with a special knowledge and insight from which labour and the left could learn, ministers were, in the discourse of many Wobblies, otherworldly and useless "sky pilots."[66] A central theme of the second phase was the critique of, and in some instances rejection of, the ministers' authority.

In many eyes the ministers were the vanguard no longer. The "left turn" of 1907–13 throughout the North Atlantic left-wing world, characterized by more militant and grassroots industrial unionism, a more insistent emphasis on the class struggle, and a heightened interest in materialist philosophy, was correlated with a far sharper and more critical assessment of religion. The rapidly changing demographic base of the movement also played a part. As left-wing Jews, Ukrainians, and Finns arrived in large numbers, they often brought anti-religious and anticlerical issues of their own into the left.[67]

What passed for a left-wing "common sense" on religious questions in one setting was apt to ignite a firestorm of controversy in another – as activists throughout the Dominion would soon learn. The atmospheric change was noticeable in British Columbia, Winnipeg, Toronto, Ottawa, and the Eastern and Western coalfields. It was associated with a younger generation of socialists, some of whom had come through Christian socialism and were no longer able to see the church as a vehicle capable of playing the central role in the transition to socialism, or see ministers as authorities on the subject. By 1910 John Lyons of Ottawa had to be defending the very idea that Christians might still possibly make a contribution to the socialist movement: "I think that so long as Christians are willing to join our party and work with us toward the desired end, we should be willing to work with them. We have several Christians in our Local here and personally I wish we had hundreds more as good as they are."[68]

Rev. William S. Rowe experienced the pitfalls of this shift. As president of the Ontario Christian Endeavour and a board member of *Citizen and Country*, Rowe had credentials as a Christian socialist. In addition to being James Simpson's mentor, Rowe had played, along with Thompson and Wrigley Sr., a leading role in establishing the Social Reform League, which had in turn evolved into the Ontario wing of the Canadian Socialist League. A measure of his social gospel can be had from a speech enthusiastically reported in *Citizen and Country* in 1899, in which Rowe predicted that even corporations themselves could be regenerated by Christianity. The "Christianization of commerce" would mean that the value of any institution could only be judged by its results. Christianity could replace self-interest as the basis of dealings between people. Hotly denied rumours of a split between Rowe and the movement newspaper he had helped to establish fed on the suggestion that he did not accept the left-wing critique of the Boer War.[69] More decisive evidence of a schism surfaced in 1902, after Rowe moved to British Columbia. Rowe accepted an appointment to act as a member of a federal Royal Commission investigating labour unrest associated with the United Brotherhood of Railway Employees and Western Federation of Miners. The ensuing report was scathingly critical of labour radicalism and alien agitators. Such a stance suggested, said a bitter Thompson, that the "sloppy milk-and-water sermons" and "speeches full of gush and glittering generalities" had all been a waste of time. So much for the leadership of a "numerous class of preachers and professional men" who fondly imagined themselves to be socialists.[70]

After 1907 a growing number of socialists demanded, as an integral part of the people's enlightenment, the right to speak truth to religious power. Some just wanted to question churchianity, the conventional forms of institutional religion that could not contain the urgent challenges of the day. Others wanted to press on to a full critique of Christianity as an outdated and hopelessly compromised faith. Some leftists demanded not the social gospel but the "People's Advent," in essence a revolutionary-democratic religion. In some settings this was not a matter of a secure and powerful Protestant Christendom dealing with squabbling sectarians and irrelevant provocations. It entailed a more gut-wrenching battle over basics. It was not a matter of "secularization," but of "democratization," the pursuit within the sphere of religion of the democratic impulse that socialists wanted to root in politics, economics, and social life.

After 1904 or so, and especially after 1907, the church-centred discourse of the social gospel came face to face with different, society-centred critiques of established religion. This was a theme carried in the voices of righteous working-class wrath. The question "What would Jesus do?" took on a revolutionary aspect. This stream of socialist thought often essentially merged secularism with socialism, creating the impression of a rejection of established religion altogether. With various degrees of intensity, some first formationists argued that there was an inherent conflict between Christianity and socialism. Religion, they said, conflicted with the triune formula: it proposed magical or providential rather than historical materialist ways of understanding society; it was based upon economically parasitical and non-productive strata of the population living off the surplus generated by the workers; and it distracted workers from their true historical mission, the abolition of wage slavery, with superstitions and hocus-pocus.

Now the question "What would Jesus do?" was often asked by a lay socialist agitator, not a minister. It often asked what Jesus would do in response to the repression of popular struggle, the abuse of children in coal mines and sweatshops, and the complicity of churches. It was often answered by images of Jesus as a man committed to a preferential option for the poor, an agitator who chased moneylenders from temples and predicted a heaven closed to the rich. Whatever one said about his divine or earthly status, whether Son of God or human being like the rest of us, Jesus would join the ranks of the social revolution. Sheldon's question had been originally intended as a way of rousing a congregation to a sense of their responsibilities. Now leftists were taking up the question as a way of distinguishing between a true Christianity accessible only to those prepared to be radicals, and the hypocritical and complacent preachings of most ministers. Leftists – and many workers, especially in the socially divided coalfields – were now angrily demanding that the church live up to the example of Christ – which meant a re-evaluation of who had the right to speak authoritatively in the name of a new society. For many writers, the church, having failed miserably to stand by its own principles, could no longer function as any sort of moral vanguard. What would Jesus do? He would leave these "whited sepulchres" (Matthew 23:27) and clerical hypocrites, and seek the liberation of his people elsewhere.

Often the critics sustained Christianity as much as they subverted the authority of the ministers who spoke on its behalf. Paying close attention to the pronouncements of clergy, they lamented the shortcomings of the church, but held out the hope that Christianity itself might nonetheless awaken to its historic task of building socialism. The struggle entailed reconciling what modernity had taught them – that capitalism was a system that risked destroying the social organism – with their prior or persisting patterns of religious belief. Many were struggling, in short, with the quite modern question: How can one reconcile Marx and Jesus, evolution and God? Those who answered the question "What would Jesus do?" with a miscellaneous, well-meaning list of social and moral reform movements occupied a different space than did those who answered, "He would commit Himself, and we should commit ourselves, to the creation of a new religion and a new sociology, in the light of the world-changing labour and socialist movements all around us."

As a Cape Breton "Miner" – a *nom de plume* sometimes used by McLachlan – argued in 1906, with respect to the ministers' talk of a loving Father and tender, forgiving Saviour: "I know all this. Please do not confound Christianity with churchianity. To me they are vastly different."[71] If religion was to survive at all in the age of the new democracy and the scientific enlightenment – and this was now a big "if" for many in the socialist movement – it would have to be taught its place, not at the vanguard of the movement, but in its rank and file. On the day of the people's advent, the social democracy would rouse itself and reclaim all the treasures, spiritual and material, from those who had falsely laid claim to them.

In 1906 "A Miner" (most likely McLachlan) wrote a biting letter to the Halifax *Herald*, which was then immersing itself in the "labour question." The writer imagined a Cape Breton miner confronting the evangelical minister. "See that wife of mine? See these six children of mine?" the miner asks. "Look how thinly they are clad; see how poorly they are fed; see how badly they are housed. Have you any 'Good News' for the poor and heavy laden?" If the minister could not address the miner's "real troubles" – low wages, high expenses – what use was he? After all (and here the "miner" exposed his democratic Protestantism) he himself could very well understand his Saviour on his own. So why should he go to church rather than "spend my Sunday in the green fields and beside the limpid waters . . . especially sir, since the air I breathed all week was filled with powder, smoke and coal dust?"[72]

As the left in parts of Canada – particularly Toronto, Winnipeg, and Vancouver – became more and more polyethnic, not everyone fighting for socialism could be assumed to have (or to have once had) the same religious values. Many Jews were fiercely opposed to religious trappings, to the point of refusing to swear on the Bible when they gave evidence in court. Socialist militant Sophie Mushkat startled a courtroom in Moncton by refusing to swear on the Bible and defiantly announcing her conviction that "she did not believe in the afterlife."[73] Historian Ruth Frager notes a Toronto school action by Jewish children who "went out on strike to protest having to sing Christmas carols in class." They won their point. Pavlo Krat, a socialist intellectual and agitator on the Ukrainian left in Canada before the Great War, penned many bitter polemics against religious authorities.[74] Left Finns became renowned for extending their anticlericalism so far as to celebrate weddings without the presence of ministers. Their vibrant socialist press proudly reported this defiance of religion.[75]

Yet another element in the new atmosphere was the post-1904 general reception of the Marxist classics. What had been a pattern of occasional references to Marx before 1904 became one of pervasive quotations from Marxist classics after that (with a particularly noteworthy turn to historical materialism after 1907). Many Canadian leftists were reading Marxist works intensely for the first time. They were engaged in a massive intellectual awakening, one that made older Christian socialist positions seem sentimental and undertheorized.

It was a pattern found in one major figure after another. When James Cameron established a branch of the Christian Commonwealth of Canada in British Columbia, he was acting on the commonly held conviction that Christian ideals and socialist ideals "were identical and would lead to the restructuring of the entire society." But a stint as an organizer for the Socialist Party of America in Washington state exposed him to "a great deal of Marxist philosophy," and by 1902 Cameron was so staunch an advocate of the single-plank revolutionary platform that he bluntly told the *Western Socialist*, "Any who cannot agree on this plank are not socialists."[76] James Simpson, who came into left politics around 1898 largely because of his commitment to the Methodist social reform agenda, was saying by 1905 that the Methodist Church had little to contribute to the revolutionary socialist politics with which he now identified. Of the four major Marxist thinkers studied by Peter Campbell – W.A. Pritchard, Arthur Mould, Ernest Winch, and R.B. Russell – all except Mould seem to have experienced a sense of alienation from their earlier religious affiliations from 1905 to 1911. McLachlan greatly admired the Covenanters of Scotland, the religious radicals of their day, and spoke quite unselfconsciously of the Creator and the Son of God, yet organized religion seems to have lost much of its meaning for him in this period. One telling moment in his disillusionment seems to have come with the decision of the church elders of St. Andrew's Church hall in Sydney Mines to bar the way to the renowned British socialist and Christian Keir Hardie.[77]

McKay's case was particularly telling. The same man who in 1900 had been worried about the post-Christian naturalistic implications of Darwinism in 1913 wrote a decidedly lukewarm review of Walter Rauschenbusch's epochal *Christianity and the Social Crisis*, a statement from one of the key U.S. figures of the social gospel. McKay was sceptical about the "scientific value" of a book that hoped so fervently "that the social message of Jesus if consistently heeded, would work a revolution in industry as complete as that desired by the socialist." He nonetheless held out some faint hope that the revolutionary working class might yet have the "blessing of the church." McKay would later round out the rejection of his earlier social gospel politics even more emphatically when he asked: "Is the labour movement any stronger today, or the working class any nearer their emancipation from the wage system, because . . . Charles Sheldon wrote *What Would Jesus Do?*"[78]

Many on the left now scoffed at the hope that Sheldon and the other ministers of the church would lead a revolution. As D.G. McKenzie put it in the vintage language of the *Western Clarion*, socialists should operate "not merely to the exclusion of Christianity but also of Atheism, Theism, Buddhism, Hypnotism or any other ism. Worship what god you will elsewhere, but let that altar be consecrated to the goddess of Revolution alone." Or as Roscoe Fillmore remarked in 1909, "We care not what God ye worship, as long as ye do not worship Mammon."[79]

Such comments were inflammatory and bound to stir up controversy. Neither comment, obviously, was "atheistic" – in fact, McKenzie included "atheism" among the "isms" to be excluded from socialism. Yet, given the strong, abiding religious beliefs upheld by many, perhaps most, Protestant Canadians, such critiques could easily be stereotyped as atheism in the polemical exchanges they invited. Baiting clergymen made for exciting journalism and riveting soapbox performances. The term "atheistic socialism" would lodge itself in the discourse of the times and be repeated by scholars thereafter. Yet socialism was only "atheistic" to the extent that in the realm of freedom it envisaged and partially constructed, atheists would be free to hold and express their opinions. Some socialists, by most measures a minority, used this greatly expanded democratic public sphere to express atheist convictions. Many used it to advance arguments for a socialist Christianity, and others for forms of radical humanism. Socialists in Canada were instrumental in creating, not a groundswell for atheism, but a climate of religious modernity.

The term "atheism" was, in this context, a wonderfully effective polemical weapon for right-wing propagandists eager to paint the entire left as a marginal, divisive force. It had, and perhaps still has, the added attraction of being a "bullying word," which if successfully applied as a label, essentially places the target beyond the pale of civilized discourse. "Atheistic socialism" had at best a minor role as one thread in the many religious discussions on the left, but it played a major role as a bogeyman in frightening people away from reasoning and living otherwise. As a misleading slur it could hobble the movement in much of a country of which it was said that only two things – politics and religion – were taken with deadly seriousness. The socialism = atheism equation could be read into many of the anticlerical outbursts of leftists, as some of them mistook Voltaire for Marx, and the local minister for the ruling class.

Leftists themselves do not seem to have fully appreciated the minefield into which they were walking. Many seemed to think that they could simply revisit such classics of free thought and rationalism as the works of Col. Robert G. Ingersoll, which had a strong impact in 19th-century Ontario. Some in Quebec may have identified themselves wholeheartedly with secular education and even rallied to the Freemasons. Some, like British immigrant Gertrude Richardson, may have had a substantial attachment to the secularist traditions associated with F.J. Gould.[80] The interests of the left – with its emphasis on the building of a democratic society in which people would be free to pursue knowledge and freedom without fear of reprisal – clearly overlapped with conventional 19th-century rationalism and anticlericalism. Yet in and of themselves, such viewpoints did not lead to counter-liberal propositions.

The scope of this struggle was extraordinary. In a country that took its religion seriously, even a small minority of agitators could rouse a massive response if they brazenly challenged the authority of religion. The Toronto *Globe* and many other papers devoted full-length editorials to the religious views of a small band of Marxists. Challenging religion was news. Baited and derided as atheists, leftists often returned the favour with diatribes on the implausibilities of the Bible – the "digestibility of Jonah" providing a favourite trope[81] – and the inconsistencies of the clergy. The many editorials and pamphlets put out by the left were often couched in terms seemingly designed to defeat rather than to persuade the enemy. At other times they suggest a much more profound and thoughtful questioning of religious belief.

Some leftists argued that the people's enlightenment required free thought. Indeed, they sometimes implied that this stance towards religious authority defined socialism itself. As J.H. Burroughs observed in a provocatively titled 1912 spc pamphlet, *Religion Thy Name Is Superstition*: "The 'divine right' of kings of all descriptions, whether they be of dynasty, or of mine, rail, and soil, is . . . but the might of the strong to oppress the weak. The spell of creeds and litanies is vanishing, and the disinherited are getting ready to measure their might against that of the Lord's anointed."[82]

What would Jesus do? In this period Jesus would be urging the ministers to take up their proper place beside those fighting for justice, and align the church with their struggle. Even John Spargo, the once fervent Methodist who in his speech to the csl's 1901 Toronto meeting had seemed to be such a hard-core agnostic, entered the fray in 1907 in a polemic with Goldwin Smith. "I have asked myself constantly while studying your letter," Spargo wrote reprovingly to Smith, "Would Jesus have said 'Seek the Kingdom of God and His Righteousness – but seek it not too earnestly or with fervor'?" Eugene V. Debs would consciously emulate Jesus Christ, whom he interpreted as a radical political leader, the forerunner of John Brown, Abraham Lincoln, and, of course, Karl Marx.[83] What would Jesus do? Confronted with mounting evidence of the radical evil entailed in any conceivable capitalism, he would join the revolution – as one revered man within a much greater democratic wave.

And maybe he would even pour scorn on the church and its traditions. The *Western Clarion* rarely passed up a chance to take a shot at Christianity. Even Christmastime brought out the newspaper's trademark sarcasm. In 1908 the editor offered his impressions of Vancouver: "It is an exceedingly fortunate thing that the Redeemer had a birthday," he began bitingly. Then he rhymed off all the dubious characters – this "gang of traders, peddlers, hucksters, charity mongers, Salvationists and other riff-raff too numerous to mention" – who were profiting from Christmas. "To them the birthday of Christ is no legend. It is a fact, clearly demonstrated to them upon each recurring anniversary of the occasion. They not only know the Redeemer was born, but also that 'the Redeemer liveth in the hearts of men,' for do not the net receipts of the Christmas season clearly prove it?" Two years later the *Clarion*'s Christmas message was equally dire. The editor wrote about bumping into an out of work young man panhandling on the street, to whom he gave 20 cents. The down and out man should not be downhearted, though, for "there is consolation at this gladsome period." He could just go down to "P. Burns & Co.'s shop and gaze enraptured upon the robust swine there gaily bedecked, in holiday attire. . . . Maybe he will be rewarded by a glimpse of actual cash being paid for a real turkey. Then he will surely cogitate on the bountiful blessings showered upon the Lord's children."[84]

A great amount of time and energy was spent disputing the authority, and often the integrity, of those who stood for organized religion. In his pamphlet Burroughs drew attention to the ensemble of ideological instruments aimed at the young. Once the "superstitious chloroform" had worn off, the ruling class turned to such "holy and patriotic institutions" as cadet corps, Boy Scouts, and the militia, all for the "preservation and protection of the God-ordained dispensation of capital and human slavery." As street-corner and city park competitors, Salvation Army bands were frequent targets of socialist wrath and satire. The Army was involved, charged the socialists, in the shady business of importing immigrants for low-wage jobs. It was also implicated in drowning out the socialist message. Wilfred Gribble said of one of his Maritime engagements in 1909: "There was a bunch of bosses . . . and as soon as I started to speak, they began talking and laughing loudly, in order to convince me. They got theirs alright and soon subsided. Then the Salvation Army arrived and showed their Christian spirit by starting a meeting close by, thumping the drum and howling something like 'Oh, you must wear a collar and a tie, Or you won't go to heaven when you die.' "[85]

The socialist/Christian conflict came to a boil when religious revivalists showed up in town. When the hugely successful evangelists John E. Hunter and Hugh T. Crossley came to Victoria in 1907, one of them declared that he would rather vote for the devil than for the socialists. He was subsequently "bearded in his den" by two socialists, who commemorated the event with a wry description of the evangelical good life – beautiful carpets, flowers and plants, a trilling canary in a cage – and of the evangelist Hunter, who "immediately informed us that he was a Socialist – but. Had he not taken his hat off upon several occasion to working men; did they not give part of their proceeds to the worthy poor, etc. etc." To him the *Clarion* editor responded, "just as gently as my angelic temperament allowed," that charity was "distasteful to the average man," and that "all people desired was to proceed down life's highway unmolested, with the fruits of their exertions."[86]

In 1898 the most prominent socialist organizations had been concerned to court the favour of Protestant clergymen, and they had been delighted when one or two showed an interest. By 1908 many socialists and some workers could be heard mocking the "sky pilots" who clung to antiquated religious beliefs in the scientific, class-conscious, democratic new Canada that the left was bringing into being. After P.F. Lawson came across a piece in the *Christian Guardian* that had proclaimed, "Let us . . . banish all jealousy of the rich, and all oppression of the poor," he simply questioned the writer's scientific credentials: "I presume his environment has been bookish, his teachers orthodox and his whole training such as would lead him and others to throw upon God and the church the settlement of the labor problem." How on earth, Gribble wondered in the *Western Clarion*, could so clever a Marxist as London's Henry Ashplant, the renowned standard-bearer of the SLP and the author of a treatise on economics, ever mix up "a material science like socialism with Christianity . . . considering the economic knowledge he possesses"? McKenzie argued in the *Western Clarion*: "The propaganda of Socialism has for its foundations solid ascertained facts. It needs not the uncertain prop of faith, creed and dogma. It is too much like wheeling Hercules around in an invalid chair."[87]

Even more brusque was the *Western Clarion*'s treatment in 1908 of a letter written by Rev. J.G. Shearer, a prominent Presbyterian, head of that church's Board of Moral and Social Reform, and secretary of the Lord's Day Alliance. Shearer wrote, rather in the manner of Rev. Sheldon, that as "pastor of a church of workingmen" he had "learned to know and respect and take a large interest in their problems and struggles. I longed to be worthy of their friendship and confidence." He proudly noted the election of Port Arthur SPC member Frederick Urry, who had joined the likes of Mackenzie King on the Board for 1908–9. "It is worth while for the workers on their part to encourage and appreciate this [Christian] interest, never so clearly manifested as now," Shearer concluded. A decade earlier Rev. Shearer's announcement might have been greeted with enthusiasm. Now the *Clarion* was curtly dismissive. "We . . . hope that the 'Department of Moral and Social Reform' will have more success in the future than it has had in the past two thousand years," the editor remarked. "If Mr. Shearer is sincere in his longing to be worthy of the friendship and confidence of the workers, the best thing he can do is to investigate carefully the causes of the ills that afflict the workers. If he does that . . . he will find that there is but one class of people that can help the working class and that is the working class of people."[88]

Echoing the critical spirit of Grant Allen, Burroughs guided his readers back to "primitive man," who, surrounded as he was by an unpredictable and life-threatening world, "naturally" ascribed flood, fire, and earthquake to some "powerful, malignant individual." Every step since taken by humankind along "the pathway of knowledge" had "increased skepticism as to the existence of a supernatural devil," and logically should engender a like incredulity before a beneficent god: "The light of scientific research has been turned on the dark places, and God and the Devil are rolling their blankets." Similarly, the Western Clarion spoke of the god Jupiter as "a hoax, a senseless fraud," just like "all the rest of the mythological and speculative phantasmagoria of the ages." All such gods were simply products of the imaginations of "the world's most cunning knaves and unscrupulous rogues."[89] Both responses to religion seemed to draw back to 18th-century rationalism more than to the historical materialism of Marx.

At the same time, following Engels more loyally than Marx, and Jack London more faithfully than either, SPC authors often fashioned an image of Christianity as the world's first international socialist movement. "There are many pious souls, even more ignorant of the religion they accept than the Socialism they reject," argued Vancouver SPCer W.J. Curry. "They are not even acquainted with the historical fact that primitive Christianity was a working class, revolutionary movement." Yet it had since degenerated into a "ruling-class religion," opposed to "the onward march of freedom and truth, represented by the Socialist movement." As one Alfred J. Gordon said, rehearsing an aperçu of Karl Marx in 1847, "We have had the name of Christ and Christianity held before us for over eighteen centuries, but with it all, the condition of the working class has not improved to any great extent."[90]

"In general," remarked Cotton's Weekly, summing up its version of the Enlightenment critique of religion, "religious experiences are a composite of blind emotion and irrational mental processes." It cited as evidence Salvation Army meetings and Methodist revivals, as well as the "repetition of creeds in a solemn and unctuous manner." All of this showed that in religion, "reason is held in abeyance and emotion holds sway." Curry suggested that anyone who could be talked into believing that the "great object of life" was that of staving off damnation "by our loving Creator" after death was not going to be much good in the class struggle: "If one's mental structure can be sufficiently twisted to accept this proposition it is evident that the victims can never be much force in the social regeneration of mankind, and this is exactly what the ruling class desires."[91] Countless editorials drove home the message that religion and reason were opposed.

Some ambitious articles and pamphlets went in for elaborate anthropological explanations of and historical disquisitions on religion. Paul Lafargue – whose locally reprinted 48-page *Causes of Belief in God* must have represented a considerable SPC investment – built explicitly on the arguments of Grant Allen. Other socialists merely indulged themselves in slighting comments in the "medieval mildew" vein. "The world is for the living and should not be ruled by rules, laws and customs, formulated by dead men," counselled the Lindsay socialists in their *Gems of Socialism*. Percy Rosoman, a fire-breathing Ottawa socialist, likened socialism and metaphysics (that is, religion) to oil and water in a December 1910 *Clarion* piece. "Give 'em the pure dope every time and let the [religious] ignoramus squirm," Rosoman concluded.[92]

In the same month *Cotton's Weekly* put the point a trifle more graciously. Implicitly contrasting the socialist to the Christian moral reformer, *Cotton's* observed, "We no longer preach against hypocrisy. We no longer thunder against the evil doer and appeal to his better nature to do better." Rather than such pointless moralizing, "We busy ourselves with the economic structure of society. . . . We work for the coming of that mode of production and exchange under which the self preservation of the one will coincide with the preservation of all." When in 1919 the *Red Flag* rapturously acclaimed Ernst Haeckel's work in its lengthy obituary of him, it especially singled out the theorist's capacity to unsettle believers: "Haeckel has perhaps roused the ire of the orthodox more than any scientist of the last century; and his 'Riddle of the Universe' created more than apprehension in the sheep fold of the Lord. . . . No child ever contented itself more with make-believe than does your orthodox Christian!"[93]

Some socialist writers affected a complete disinterest in religion – although in doing so they usually took care to disparage Christianity. In this version of the people's enlightenment, believers were examples of evolutionary throwbacks. "They are . . . a little lacking in reasoning powers and generally sickly emotional and sensational," said the irrepressible Rosoman of his religious fellow-citizens. "They are generally very good at catching on with the ignorant crowd, who are used to reading fiction and also hearing it preached from the pulpit and whose minds therefore have been fed on, and grown up on, this kind of food." For Brandon's Edmund Fulcher, any talk of human beings having both "spiritual" and "physical" parts was "medieval rubbish." Any scientific consideration of the facts of human conception would discredit any talk of "spirits."[94]

Religion was not only medieval, but mendacious. From Revelstoke came a vicious satire on one Rev. Day, who had come to town with a sermon on the Christian orphans of Macedonia. His tales were moving, but his real agenda was to sell young immigrant orphans to grasping middle-class people. "'Christian' labor-skinners are smooth," the satire concluded, "but their game somewhat coarse and vulgar from a working-class standpoint." From *Cotton's Weekly* came a similar verdict: "The plute Christian gets down on his knees and thanks the Lord for putting him [in] a position where he can plunder the work of his fellow men." The poet Robin Adair asked, "Do you hear the workers toiling in the murky shaft of Fate?" and continued: "Heavens! Listen to the thunder of the sound/ Of a million whispered curses; a million thoughts of Hate,/ A molten dream of anger – underground. Do you see the miner sweating, reeking naked to the loin,/ Oh, you pious bible-thumping man of God?"[95]

"Who but an abject, ignorant slave of the belly-crawling type would in these days pray to an idol of imaginary form 'for thine is the kingdom, the power and the glory, for ever and ever'[?]" asked Rosoman.

> It is that kind of dope pumped into children by their fond but ignorant parents before the children are weaned; and continued through after years by the priests and clergy for the sole purpose of keeping the people tame and easily robbed that makes it so hard for Socialists to get the working-class to reason things out correctly. We cannot make good Socialists of them till we knock out this accursed religion, this belly-crawling, master and slave, religion.[96]

Rosoman's anathema, curiously reminiscent of the fire and brimstone denunciations of his clerical enemies, concealed, as did many socialist polemics, a point more central to the enlightenment tradition that the first formationists sought to defend. The point was not that religion should be abolished. It was that the questions it raised and the positions it proposed should be part of a democratic public sphere, open to rational debate, and not enforceable by the confessional, the heresy trial, or the coercive power of the state. Implying that socialism meant just *one* such position, and a bullying tone of voice that shamed those who did not hold it, were hardly fulfilments of the ideal of deliberative democracy in the sphere of religion. Some of those who exercised this freedom of religious thought might choose atheism, others (like Thompson) theosophy, and others (like Simpson and Ashplant) evangelical Christianity. Yet others (like McKay and McLachlan after 1907) simply relegated Christian beliefs to the sidelines without, it seems, explicitly ever renouncing them.

Yet the form of discussion put forth by Rosoman (and many others) presented believers with a socialism that in essence *replaced* religion as the true exponent of the Golden Rule. A socialism that cried out that it *was* religion was not one that was going to co-exist easily with institutions that claimed to speak *for* religion. In the down-to-earth language of the soapbox and socialist newspaper column, the veneer of conciliation barely concealed the core of harsh critique. If providing for the poor and lifting up the oppressed were really "injurious to the religion of any man," Fillmore stated in a December 1909 article in *Cotton's Weekly*, "then the sooner mankind says goodbye to such a religion the better." In the piece Fillmore focused on the "Problem of Evil" – God's apparent willingness to allow injustice and poverty to flourish in a universe that He supposedly controlled. Would God have really given the coal seams to the robber barons, with the proviso that the miners be crushed in the mines? Or lakes of oil to the Rockefellers, with the understanding that their old and worked-out employees would be thrown on the scrap heap once the moguls had finished with them? Did he say to the robber barons, "Don't be particular about safety appliances for lo! the slaves multiply like rats and will over run the earth if you don't kill off a few occasionally"?[97] If Christian businessmen used religion to cover up their crimes, then that brand of religion was opposed to the interests of workers. Church and state were just tricking the workers with "shell games and red herrings," all to serve King Capital.[98] "That vulture, the church, the prostituted intellects of countless cowards of the press, public platform, university and school – in short, any and every means at the disposal of the masters, has been used, and successfully so far, in the effort to kill all revolt in the slaves," Fillmore would later write.[99]

Class and religious issues were interwoven in Springhill, scene of the epochal 22-month strike from 1909 to 1911, and a place where socialists had made considerable headway. As early as 1908 the Cumberland Labor Party – a major gathering point for socialists – was drawing flak for its supposed atheism. In his extensive polemics in the Halifax *Herald* against the activities of the socialists within the party, a correspondent writing under the name of "Probus" drew special attention to the extent to which religion had formed "such an extensive portion of the socialistic propaganda." Assuring "Mr. Workman" that he was not about to argue for or against the existence of the Creator, a matter "better left to the innermost conscience of the individual," Probus nonetheless called attention to the supposed Christian/socialist argument about God's existence. Since workers were able to make up their own minds, why were socialists or Christians trying "to force their opinion on you"? Better to leave the settlement of religious questions to the privacy of the home.[100]

The Springhill employer J.R. Cowans was a man notorious for his reactionary anti-union policies. The East Coast's answer to British Columbia's Dunsmuirs, he was also a staunch Presbyterian, whose ostentatious Sunday offerings were the stuff of Springhill song and legend. The coal miners had overwhelmingly endorsed in a democratic vote the United Mine Workers of America over the Provincial Workmen's Association. Cowans had stamped out their union before, in the 1890s, and he was not the least reluctant to try to do so again, as witnessed by the outrageously offensive letters he wrote targeting the workers and their union.

For the left this struggle combined all the bitterness of a civil war within the working class, with crushing displays of state violence and repression. For many believers, in this struggle there was only one correct path for the church, and that was on the side of the people against a coal company that had historically been careless with the lives of its workers. Yet the church prevaricated. The local Presbyterian minister – with historic ties to both Cowans and the members of the older, now discredited union – came down against the left. The result was a sharp sense of betrayal among some believers in Springhill. Cowans called himself a Christian, said the socialists – quite the contrary was the case. His insults to Brother Watkins, the socialist leader of the UMW, revealed that he was not a good Christian. "I accuse you," shouted one polemicist, "of using Satanic means to keep the miners of Springhill in subjection." Another writer likened capitalists such as Cowans to "devils." Perhaps they went to church, gave alms, and built colleges and asylums – but "they are robbers, devils. Their wealth is made from the robbery of the workers. Their generosity is founded on injustice."[101]

The public meetings called to support the strikers inspired some, but the intemperately irreligious words spoken at them offended many others. At one point the socialists imported H.H. Stuart, lay minister and socialist from Newcastle, N.B., to allay fears of atheism.[102] Even so, according to Fillmore's own analysis of the collapse of Cumberland County socialism, the forces of "religious superstition" had undermined the left: "The old fables and the 'Divine right of kings' are explicitly believed in by a very large majority of the people."[103] The atmosphere persuaded him (and the SPC's Maritime executive) to resist any attempt to make the SPC officially anti-religious. Memories of the SPC's (and especially Fillmore's) irreligion lingered for decades in the town.

In Toronto a similar tension pervaded the religion question. Many influences – the historic intransigence of the Toronto SPC, the arrival of many new diaspora socialists, and the emerging SPC/SDPC split – were at play, yet so too was the intellectual force of the "harder materialism." Among the Toronto Finns, J.W. Ahlqvist remembered, the "Ingersoll anti-religious booklets" were regularly debated in the "Big Shop," a collective tailoring establishment in which many leftists could be found: "The issue of religion got a thorough treatment in its time. If there was someone in the Shop with religious ideas, it did not take long to beat them out of him."[104] Tim Buck would remember the visit to Toronto of evolutionary theorist Arthur M. Lewis as a formative moment in his youthful abandonment of Christian socialism for "materialism." Echoing German philosopher Ludwig Feuerbach, Lewis proclaimed: "It is no longer God and Man, nor even Man and God, but Man only, with God an anthropomorphic shadow, related to man not as his creator, but as created by him. God and Man are not 'two,' but in reality 'one.' "[105] Lewis, a merciless critic of all religion, would not abide any position, like those advanced by some thinkers in the Second International, that suggested that socialists and religious believers might co-exist in the same movement. "To seek to impose upon the modern mind the petrified blunders of primitive men, is as hopeless a task as would be the administration of a great modern city by the regulations which prevailed two thousand years ago in a Syrian village," he argued. "The theological concept and the evolutionary concept are irreconcilable enemies, and either can only live in peace by the extermination of the other."[106] For Lewis, one could *not* simultaneously be a revolutionary socialist and a Christian – a viewpoint that seemingly came close to that of Fillmore himself, and which was in 1915 a mandatory theme of spc propaganda.

Here were the materials for a conflagration, in a city that not only had a rapidly expanding socialist movement but was also the headquarters of many a Christian church and publishing house. The controversy in Toronto was sparked on 21 September 1910 when Rev. S.D. Chown made some interesting comments at a Social and Moral Reform Conference held at Elm Street Methodist Church. The event's theme was "Downtown Social Problems and the Relation of the Church Thereto." Noting that the parables of Christ were full of "socialistic teaching," Chown bluntly declared: "The Church of Christ does not stand for competition. How could a Church stand for competition that believes in the Golden Rule?" Socialism itself was founded on the principles of Jesus. The church stood for certain principles, and if the application of those principles required smashing competition, then that was the way it was. In any public sphere in which religion was discussed, the church had the right to an authoritative voice.[107] So said Chown, one of the social gospel's mightiest voices.

It was too much for Moses Baritz, who was at the time the self-described "accredited organizer for the Socialist Party of Canada for the Province of Ontario." For Baritz, possibly stimulated by the appearance earlier that year of *Socialism and Religion,* a British delaration of socialistic atheism reviewed in the *Western Clarion,* the correct position, founded upon science, pure and simple, had nothing to do with the teachings of Jesus. Responding to a report of Chown's talk in a letter to the *Globe,* Baritz pointed out that socialism was "opposed to all religions, which we maintain were products of given social conditions." Baritz predicted that, with the establishment of a socialist regime, "Christianity, Judaism and all supernatural ideas clinging to mankind will be abolished." For good measure, he also condemned the "unscientific worship of Christ, Buddha or Mahomet," arguing that socialists "cannot believe in any supernatural God. If they do they are not Socialists.... The Church will find in us their unrelenting foes. Christianity, with its superstitions, must be submerged before the workers obtain their complete emancipation." In case the reader had drifted off and somehow forgotten his thrice-repeated point, Baritz ended his letter by making it once again: "A Christian cannot be a Socialist, and a Socialist cannot be a believer in Christ or God."[108]

The cat was amongst the pigeons. The feathers flew on schedule. The liberal *Globe* was moved to respond to Baritz with an editorial endorsing Chown's articulation of the social gospel and expressing its astonishment that someone like Baritz could speak with the authority of the Socialist Party of Canada on the matter. "If he does, and the Socialist party is avowedly anti-Christian, there is need for vigorous action on the part of the Churches in the direction of combating its progress," the editorial argued. "The world can do without Socialism; it cannot do without Christianity.... Keir Hardie, M.P., says that he first learned his Socialism in the New Testament, where he still finds his chief inspiration. Between Keir Hardie and Moses Baritz there is a great gulf. On which side of it does the Canadian Socialist party stand?"[109]

No fewer than 12 correspondents to the *Globe* promptly responded with their own views. One single taxer applauded Baritz for conclusively demonstrating that the "fundamental principle of Socialism" was "necessarily atheistic." Single taxers had been saying as much for years. Those Canadians who did not want to deny the goodness of God should now realize that their future lay with the single taxers, not the socialists. Several letters came from steadfast socialists who could not stomach Baritz's position. "I am a Socialist of many years' standing, casting my vote always for Socialists," said William Joyce of Toronto. "But Baritz I do not know. Jesus I know, and prefer him even to Moses. Jesus taught me Socialism – a Socialism that would make of this poor groaning earth a veritable heaven."[110] W.E.S. James of Casterville, Lincoln County, Ont., opined that some spcers in British Columbia and some writers in the *Western Clarion* shared Baritz's opinion, "though in a much milder and less antagonistic form." Only "a very small percentage of them would say that a Christian cannot be a Socialist nor a Socialist a Christian." All spcers were now obliged to take up a position with regard to their organizer's inflammatory comments.[111]

Phillips Thompson weighed in with a categorical denunciation of Baritz's position. "The dictum of Comrade Moses Baritz ... that 'a Christian cannot be a Socialist and a Socialist cannot be a believer in Christ or God,' cannot be too strongly or promptly repudiated as an official utterance," he argued. "It is altogether unauthorized, either by the constitution, the platform, or the pledge taken by members of the party, in none of which can a word be found to justify such a contention." No such question with respect to religion could be raised "without violating the constitution and the hitherto accepted principles of the party."[112]

In response Baritz challenged Thompson to appear at the next meeting of the Toronto local and test the opinions of the SPCers gathered there. Then, with the panache of a veteran soapboxer, he deflected Thompson's challenge by repeating his initial argument even more fiercely. "Religions are products of the ignorant. Socialism stands for scientific knowledge, and that means the abolition of the God-head idea." Thompson shot back that Baritz had not answered his constitutional objection. He dared him to produce one official document that "expressly or by implication bars Christians or other religionists from membership."[113]

The last word, it would seem, went to Baritz, who in a soapbox address near the corner of University Avenue and Queen Street drew upon Marx, Spencer, and Lewis Henry Morgan, among other scientific authorities, to show that "society has been a gradual growth from epoch to epoch, and that social and ethical ideals and morals had been not the result of religion, but the outgrowth of social conditions." Socialism had roots that went back a thousand years before Christianity, which was nothing more than a "plagiarized version of Buddhism." In 1915 the SPC's Dominion Executive, denouncing "laxity in matters of importance affecting working-class philosophy," declared the anti-religion stand taken in *Socialism and Religion* to be official social policy.[114]

What would Jesus do? Curry thought he discerned "between the lines . . . the records of a man born twenty centuries before his ideals could be realized. Were he here today . . . He would be found marching with his comrades under the red flag which symbolizes the blood ties and brotherhood of man." For Curry, the question of religion had to be at the top of the socialist agenda because "if the Socialist Party is to capture the citadel of state it must conquer the strongholds of theology which lie between it and success."[115] Jesus, in this version of first formation religious thought, would have to agree that he was just one participant in a democratic public sphere in which he enjoyed only rational and political, not magical or supernatural, rights to free expression.

Marshall Gauvin: Autodidact and Atheist

Perhaps the most ardent and famous of all who plumped for the socialism = irreligion perspective was Marshall Gauvin (1881–1978), born in Fox Creek, near Moncton, N.B.

Gauvin was a proud autodidact. One of his lectures asked, "Is a College Education Worthwhile?" Gauvin answered, in essence, "Not really."[116] Notwithstanding his francophone ancestry and surname, he was raised as a Baptist and later recalled the frequency with which his minister had referred to the works of Col. Robert Ingersoll, long the *bête noir* of Christian believers. Like many a teenager since, Gauvin, baptized in 1899, succumbed fully to the pleasures of the fruit so emphatically forbidden him. After the young Marshall got his hands on the texts of the renowned U.S. rationalist, he was overpowered by the arguments made. In some respects Gauvin can best be understood as a man who inherited Ingersoll's legacy.

There began a career and a building of a reputation that continues to this day. His "Did Jesus Really Exist?" text, still readily available on many Internet sites, became as widely and fiercely debated a text as any generated by a Canadian first formation intellectual throughout this entire period.[117] In many ways, if Bland's great vision of one evolution sweeping all before it recalled Kropotkin at his most cosmic, Gauvin's much more limited sceptical appraisal of religion suggested the continuing legacy of Grant Allen (upon whom Gauvin directly drew). In the twilight of his career Gauvin estimated that he had delivered 800 lectures, including 240 in Minneapolis and 560 in Winnipeg. He would become a fixture in Winnipeg from the 1920s, a Prairie Voltaire who delighted in making life difficult for clergymen. Measured simply by the number of his works and his impact upon the North American reading public, Gauvin must be considered one of the most enduringly significant of the first formation autodidacts.

Gauvin established his reputation as a contrary-minded intellectual in socialist and labour circles in Moncton, where he worked as a carpenter in the Intercolonial Railway shops. He used his spare time to learn all he could about the history and teachings of Christianity. One of his first lectures, influenced strongly by Ward's *The Ancient Lowly*, was entitled "Historical Reflections on the Labor Movement." The local left-wingers thought so highly of Gauvin's effort that it was reprinted in no fewer than four issues of the *Eastern Labor News* of Moncton.[118] The local left thought no less of Gauvin's lectures on "The Eight Hour Day" and "Socialism, the Destiny of Democracy," a presentation he recycled for the benefit of a rationalist meeting in Boston in 1910. Gauvin's fellow workers had no problems in honouring with a farewell dinner their ultra-rationalistic comrade whose impromptu lectures on free thought had enlivened many of their lunch breaks.[119] In Boston Gauvin established contact with *The Truth Seeker*, a prominent U.S. free thought publication. In June 1912 he moved to Toronto, and in 1913 to Indianapolis. He would return to Canada after the Great War, eventually settling in Winnipeg in 1926.

An Appeal for Truth in Religious Teaching, Gauvin's first publication on the theme of free thought, was based on a lecture delivered in Moncton in May 1909 on behalf of the Moncton Truth Seekers Association. Audience members were promised a two-part presentation, the first "scientific, historical and critical," and the second a discussion of "Bible criticism as it is taught in the leading universities and seminaries." In its review, the *Eastern Labor News* proudly played up Gauvin's labour identity – here was "a member of the Carmen's Union of this city" – and noted that the subject had been "handled in a way that did credit to the speaker and aroused much interest to the large audience present." Notwithstanding the religious focus of the talk, the *News* noted "many points of interest to organized labour," including the eight-hour-day question.[120]

The text is a militant declaration of the secular enlightenment.[121] "Truth is man's most valuable intellectual possession. Truth is intellectual light. Without truth, our minds would be shrouded in the darkness of ignorance – we would be savages groveling in the abyss of primal degradation." Truth explained why humanity had risen above cannibalism and ritual religious sacrifices. Truth explained the wonders of an age of railways, modern architecture, and awe-inspiring ocean liners – marvellous "cities on the waves." (Gauvin might have put that hymn of praise to technological progress just a bit differently had he been speaking two years later, *after* the sinking of the *Titanic*.) "It was Truth that had given us all there is of value in philosophy, in science, in poetry, in literature." The science of evolution was the epitome of what truth could achieve. The geologists had discovered that the Earth was millions of years old. Then came the great biologists, who, "by weaving together and explaining an ever-growing multitude of facts," had built up "the wonderful science of evolution." This science had proved beyond doubt that all the creatures on earth and sea were related, and that the higher forms of life had evolved from the lower over millions of years. (Interestingly, like many leftists, Gauvin makes no mention of Darwinian natural selection, and actually seems to have harboured doubts about it.) Then came the astronomers, who showed that planets had evolved from nebulous material. Next came the social scholars, who studied "the evolution of tribes and nations, of manners and customs, of religions and laws and morals, of literature and art and science. Evolution, therefore, is the secret of the universe, the earth, man and civilization. It leaves nothing untouched – it explains all."

When religion was brought before the bar of Gauvin's truth of evolution, it was exposed as little more than an ensemble of cruelties, superstitions, and lies – a mélange, in short, of science-destroying errors. Like J.S. Mill and Fillmore, Gauvin could not get past the difficulty of reconciling cruelty in the world and in the Bible with the image of God the loving father. "What father would dream of slowly burning his child to death?" he asked. "What mother is there who does not love her wayward boy the best? Can it be possible that God will forever hate the object of a mother's love?" If we would harshly judge a father who tortured a child he loved, what were we to think of a God harbouring "boundless love" for humanity, who would "burn eternally the populations of a thousand million worlds?" It was a "falsehood so false that compared with it every other falsehood is gloriously true!"[122]

The Christian doctrine of Hell was just one instance of the problem with religion. Like Fillmore, Baritz, McKenzie, Gribble, and Rosoman, among others, Gauvin declared his opposition to a cruel Christianity that opposed, at every turn, the progress of humanity. It was by definition a force of the counter-Enlightenment. It caused "fears and heartaches and cruel separations." It even minimized the importance of living "a clean, moral life."[123]

A high point in Gauvin's North American career in free thought was the publication of *The Illustrated Story of Evolution*, brought out in New York in 1921. True to his time, Gauvin argued that *nothing* escaped from the paradigm of evolutionary theory. It offered a mastery of the entire universe. With echoes of Spencer, he suggested that a "creating God" was a mere guess, "unthinkable in quantity or quality, [bearing] no conceivable mark of reality." Into God's place stepped "Man the builder," truly the "Master of the Universe." He was now free to shape his destinies "in a world fashioned to his choice." And what wonders were now possible, thanks to this grand enlightenment of humanity: "The desert has been made to blossom like the rose; cities of solid masonry have arisen from the noisome swamp; industries supplying a thousand human wants now occupy the sites where wild beasts once filled the jungle with their savage roars." Added to these socio-economic achievements were the splendours of a people's enlightenment: "Invention, art, discovery, have tapped exhaustless stores of wealth and culture; literature, the press, schools, disseminate intelligence; and, rising above earth, man now solves the secrets of the stars and calculates with precision their changing movements. Man, Nature's gifted son, is Nature's conqueror!"[124] Gauvin's was a utopia far exceeding in its hubris and certainty Marx's "metabolic" vision of humanity's place in the natural world, not to speak of the empirical scruples of Darwin. In Gauvin, evolution had clearly become its own secular religion.

Significantly, by so elevating cosmic evolution, the explanation for everything, Gauvin now no longer had much need for Marx, the explainer of only some things. Gauvin's thought insistently left social history behind altogether and journeyed to the outermost heavens. Such a class-free, cosmic evolutionism was, and remains, a popular scientistic message to bring to North Americans – yet, seemingly, it had less and less to say to the socialist movement.

Left Humanism and the Spectre of "Atheistic Socialism"

Were Baritz, Fillmore, and Gauvin correct? Was it true that to be an apostle of the people's enlightenment and a proponent of free thought, one necessarily had to champion atheism?

As early as 1908 the socialism = atheism equation was so generally distributed that we find in the "Answers to Correspondents" column in the Halifax *Herald* this reassuring reply to "Socialist (Sydney)": "All socialists are not atheists." The association of the left with atheism gave the movement's enemies a heaven-sent weapon (so to speak) that they could use to bludgeon those who doubted the Genesis account of creation or the divinity of Jesus. W.A. Pritchard would pay dearly at his 1920 Winnipeg show trial for an off the cuff remark at the famous 1918 Western Labour Conference in Calgary: "The worst enemy of the working man today is the late lamented Mr. Christ." In Nova Scotia, Pictou County's John McKay was hauled over the coals for "sneering at the church" and deriding "the words of holy scripture and the teachings of our Saviour," for comments that (on their face) would seem to have simply made the point that Jesus was a carpenter who often spoke about the material needs of working people. So dire was the menace of this supposedly potent mix of socialism and atheism in the eyes of the Ottawa Literary and Philosophical Society that it took the unusual step of disbanding itself and then immediately regrouping under the new name of the Arts and Letters Club – a manoeuvre, historian John Taylor remarks, designed to shed "heterodox" members alleged to be trying to "turn the society into a means for the propagation of a species of Atheistic Socialism."[125]

Yet on the left as a whole this tendency towards atheism was relatively minor; the evolutionary theory central to the first formation was not necessarily atheistic. The socialist positions of the time on religion showed a remarkable diversity, with hundreds of sincere Christians, socialists, and those who aspired to be both leaving a vast amount of evidence to this effect. Any straightforward equation of socialism, even revolutionary socialism, with atheism therefore comes up against a much more complicated reality.

Those who did equate socialism with atheism could justify themselves in part with words from Marx that from the 1840s to the 1940s were often associated with this position. Marx's famous aphorism from his *Contribution to the Critique of Hegel's Philosophy of Law* – "*Religious* distress is at the same time the *expression* of real distress and also the *protest* against real distress. Religion is the sigh of the oppressed creature, the heart of a heartless world, just as it is the spirit of spiritless conditions. It is the *opium* of the people" – is often read as a critique of religious belief (although astute close readers of the passage have noted both that opium had a different medical connotation in the 19th century than its recreational drug-taking image suggests today, and that Marx was not likely to have been wholly unsympathetic to any expression of, let alone protest against, *real* distress).[126] Less familiar today, but probably more commonly cited in the period of the first formation, is Marx's historical critique of Christianity. Christianity's social principles had, said Marx in 1847, "justified the slavery of antiquity, glorified the serfdom of the Middle Ages and are capable, in case of need, of defending the oppression of the proletariat, even if with somewhat doleful grimaces." Every first formation socialist who read *The Communist Manifesto* would have encountered Marx's satire on Christian socialism as nothing "but the holy water with which the priest consecrates the heart-burnings of the aristocrat." The many who were also grappling with Marx's concept of the commodity in *Capital*, volume 1, would have encountered Marx's conviction, developed out of the work of Feuerbach, that "The religious world is but the reflex of the real world."[127] Grant Allen, Lafargue, and Kautsky were three who struggled to interpret religious phenomena as reflections of social realities.[128]

As David McLellan shows in a masterful study, the youthful Marx and Engels, upon arriving in Paris in 1843, were aghast that their "intended crusaders-in-arms agreed with most of their ideas but that the one thing they could not stomach was their apparent atheism." Among the Parisians, "the dominant, if rather simple, view was that communism was just Christianity in practice and that Jesus Christ was the first Communist." Yet, as McLellan observes, almost all of Marx's comments on religion are delivered en passant. All of his followers, ranging from those who had no difficulty combining Marxism with religious belief to "those whose materialism ruled out any religious statements as *a priori* false," could find "*some* support in Marx himself."[129] As Michael J. Buckley remarks, the conviction that religious belief was no longer possible became for Marx "more atmosphere than argument, much more part of the air Europe is to breathe than a conclusion seriously demonstrated by him."[130] Over time many Second International thinkers came to argue that Marxism as a science and religion as a body of normative judgments could coexist, because the religious believers could hardly take exception to a "mere science of society," nor could Marxists object to "a religion that was irrelevant to scientific socialism."[131] In essence, they proposed that in this sphere socialists could make use of a division of cultural labour.

Marx and Engels would both have probably agreed to call themselves "atheists" – certainly Marx in 1844 identified humanism and atheism, and implicitly hailed the progressive implications of both. Yet, crucially, neither writer provided a sustained argument that the socialist movement should be, let alone must be, atheistic – that is, that it should aggressively promote atheism or envision a socialist state that actively represses religious expression. We find, in fact, precisely the opposite point of view. For socialist human beings the mutual interdependence of human beings and nature was what was essential. Abstraction "from the existence of nature and man" had no meaning. As Marx argued in the *Economic and Philosophic Manuscripts of 1844*, "Atheism is a *negation of God,* and postulates the *existence of man* through this negation; but socialism as socialism no longer stands in any need of such a mediation."[132] In other words, because religion was the fantastic projection into heaven of the real problems and sufferings that people endured on earth, once socialism had abolished those oppressive conditions religion itself would fade away without socialists needing to accelerate the process. Focusing on atheism as a core principle of socialism itself was in error.

On questions of religion Spencer was cited more often, and more extensively than Marx, and across a broader spectrum of Canadian left opinion.[133] Spencer's *First Principles* had an extraordinary impact on leftists – it was into its fourth U.S. edition as early as 1886 and cited again and again by leftists as a definitive statement on religion.[134] In many respects *First Principles* is a generous endorsement of religion as a contribution to human knowledge.

In *First Principles* Spencer insisted that the war between religion and science should cease. It was a conflict based upon a crude misconception of their proper spheres. Science's successes were obvious, but religion was no antithetical realm of delusion: "Religion, everywhere present as a weft running through the warp of human history, expresses some eternal fact." A consistent evolutionist, in the face of the near-universality of religious belief, confronted two choices. He or she might argue that humankind was "directly endowed with the religious feeling by a creator; and to that creator it designedly responds." Or this evolutionist might conclude that there exist "in the environment certain phenomena or conditions which have determined the growth of the feeling in question." In either case, any "Theory of Things" was required to treat the religious sentiment with respect: "these two great realities are constituents of the same mind, and respond to different aspects of the same Universe, there must be a fundamental harmony between them."[135] Positive knowledge would never be able to answer every question – it was impossible to think of a universe of limited space, for instance, and equally impossible to imagine a limitless universe. All questions led to more questions, all explanations resulted in something further to be explained. The very existence of the universe defied final explanation, and all attempts to find one created further mysteries. Human beings were incapable of absolute knowledge, and those who claimed otherwise did a disservice to science and religion alike. Religion met demonstrated social-evolutionary needs, and its central position – the impossibility of ever knowing the unknowable – was impregnable. Science could never solve the questions of existence that were unsolvable, and that was the great truth of religion.

For the scrupulous and theoretically informed first formation socialist – someone who followed Marx, Engels, and Spencer among the heavyweights, and such writers as Grant Allen among the popularizers, socialism required that religion generally, and Christianity more specifically, be explained in evolutionary terms as a socio-historical phenomenon. It did not, and for most should not, dismiss religion as meaningless. Scientific socialism did not necessarily, and for many should not in principle, actively work for a godless future – for to do so would be to retrogress to a struggle no longer essential to the achievement of a better world.

Religion and Left Humanism: The Third Phase

Baritz's uncompromising "atheistic socialism" was seemingly not a widely diffused position on the Canadian left. Yet the general equation "socialism = atheism" was widely reported and, in local settings like Springhill, highly damaging to socialists. In response, many socialists struggled to develop a third position. In essence, drawing upon such writers as Spencer, some of them emphasized the emergent European (and Socialist Party of America) position that religion was a strictly individual concern. John Spargo – who had laced his 1901 address to the CSL with sceptical asides about God – became an important North American proponent of this orientation.

Spargo returned to the much-travelled path of Christianity's historic record as a religion of the oppressed, and re-posed the question, "What would Jesus do?" He imagined that the "Carpenter-preacher of Galilee" would be received well by a "few Socialists," but "the majority of church-goers would shun him and pass him by." Both Christianity and socialism were movements for universal peace and brotherhood. In both were to be found a "defense of the poor and the oppressed, the same scathing rebuke of the oppressor, that we find in Judaism."[136] Spargo – having travelled a long way in ten years from his rather dismissive 1901 presentation – now championed those who approached socialism "from the religious approach." Rather than deriving socialism from religion, he sought to work out an environmental argument for socialism that would appeal to religious believers. "Religious life is impossible under capitalism," he argued. "Everywhere, at every turn, the spirit of capitalism kills Religion. He tries valiantly to live up to the great ethical precepts which constitute the heart of his religious inspiration, but he is constantly baffled and repelled. In the maelstrom of capitalist society he is tossed about as a cork is tossed about by tempestuous seas."[137]

Spargo thus sought to counter precisely the polarization created by the more flamboyant socialist declarations against religion. If, a few years previously, "the average Socialist would dogmatically assert that Socialism and religious belief of any kind were absolutely incompatible," such a position was now no longer tenable or necessary. Echoing the sentiments of Spencer, Spargo remarked, "In every age, and under all kinds of governments, men have looked at the stars scattered through the upper deep and asked themselves whence they came, wondered whence and why the lightning's flash, and whence and why and whither the first movement of life in the void and blackness of the unremembered and unrecorded Beginning." Some answered this mystery with an intelligence named "God," and others with an inevitable process called "Evolution." Having dropped their former hostility, the socialist parties of the world now recognized religious belief as a "private matter."[138] Christians and socialists could move forward together.

No less than a personage than James Hawthornthwaite, MLA, told a

Nanaimo audience that the socialism = atheism slur was baseless. "It is perfectly true that many atheists are Socialists, but so are many Liberals and many Conservatives," he remarked, adding – with a nod to Spencer's "law of equal freedom" – "the basic principle of Socialism is absolute justice to all, absolute freedom to all, bounded only by the equal rights of every other individual."[139] A Halifax socialist agreed: "A man's religion – that is his own personal matter – between himself and his Creator." Writing of British socialist Robert Blatchford's notoriously irreligious *God and My Neighbour* in the *Western Clarion*, Morrison Davidson was aghast at the author's "Jamesonian Raids into the domains of Theology and Metaphysics – where, to say the least, he is by no means at home." He feared the famous writer's irreligion would lead all socialists to be condemned as "atheistic and immoral." Davidson called himself a "theist." Blatchford went under the name of "atheist." What did it really matter if they could both agree on "collectivism"?[140]

"Is Socialism opposed to religion? No!" proclaimed *Cotton's Weekly*. "Socialism is a working class political movement that has nothing to do with a man's religious beliefs." Many Christians, including clergymen, belonged to the SPC, it claimed. It accurately pointed out, *contra* Baritz, that the SPC platform contained not one word opposed to religion.[141] In essence, having tried out the position that the church could pronounce the authoritative word on socialism, and then the position that socialists must seize the ideological terrain occupied by the church, many on the left seemed to be reverting to a position upholding the individual's freedom to do whatever he or she liked in the sphere of religion; it had nothing to do with socialism.

Yet this "separate spheres" argument was a compromise that went sharply against the grain of first formation sociology, which was forever struggling to connect every function and every institution within an evolving "social organism." Many searched for a more positive approach – forms of spirituality that would accommodate both Enlightenment scientism and respect for pre-existing religious traditions. It was not an easy assignment. Caught between the ideological juggernauts of theism and atheism, religiosity and scepticism, early 20th-century socialists found it difficult to arrive at a coherent middle position. Many religious leftists were not able either to affirm or to deny the religious beliefs that most of them had learned in childhood.

Therein lies the reason for the intensity with which so many tried to enlist Christ as the "first socialist," in contravention of every sensible dictum of serious historical research and of all the insights of social-evolutionary theory, whereby it was just as likely that he would have been the first Rotarian or the first shoe salesman. They replaced, in other words, the figure of Christ the Son of God with a no less metaphysical one of Christ the Son of Socialism. And they did the same thing with St. Paul, who was aggressively repackaged to be, not a largely unknowable figure from a culture radically unlike that of 20th-century Canada, but the Herbert Spencer of the ancient world. Whatever it was that Paul had meant when he originally wrote the words that were eventually translated as "We are members of one another," the leftists projected back on to this opaque phrase a meaning that echoed Marx: "From each according to his abilities, to each according to his needs."

Many Protestant forms were adopted quite consciously by socialists. As Linda Kealey shows, the Church of the Revolution in Toronto, which functioned after 1907, played an important role in the organization of the Women's Social Democratic League and helped in the creation of a reading circle.[142] Rather like Gauvreau's many 19th-century evangelicals, whose elasticity allowed them to take on evolution and the higher criticism without lasting trauma, some socialists could absorb unresolved, and most likely forever unresolvable, debates about theism and atheism without necessarily believing that such struggles placed all of their fundamental categories at risk.

For many, socialism was itself a broad, all-encompassing, and "cosmological" outlook – even, in essence, a form of spirituality. Fillmore implicitly invoked Spencer's concept of "evolution" as a kind of deity in an appeal to his "religious friends," whom he would go on to alienate so badly in 1911. "You say you believe in a Supreme Power. So do I. I call that Power Cosmic Evolution, you call it God," he urged them. "Cosmic evolution" was a force that dwelt "within you and I, in fact within everything. The phenomena of Nature are the clothing of it. It is everywhere visible. Surely you can go thus far with me."[143] Fillmore, along with others, was gesturing towards a cosmic sensibility discernible in Engels and Spencer and arguably traceable back to Spinoza.[144] The first formation revealed many other indications of such a sensibility. Members of Winnipeg Local No. 1 of the Socialist Party of Canada treasured a copy of Engels's *Anti-Dühring*, which they possessed as one of the "Landmarks of Scientific Socialism" in its 1907 Charles H. Kerr edition, and in which they could explore concepts of infinity. Riverdale Local No. 87 of the Social Democratic Party of Canada enshrined *The Physical Basis of Mind and Morals* by Michael Hendrick Fitch, in which the author launched into a considerable although also admiring critique of Spencer's writings on "The Unknowable." Bernard Sinclair, a B.C. novelist who wrote about the lives of fishermen and loggers, remarked in 1921, "If I were so constituted that I had to have a religion . . . I think I should bow down to worship before Herbert Spencer's special god, the unknowable."[145] While a "religion" by convention requires a supernatural being, a "spiritual" perception of the unfathomable scope of the cosmos and a sense of humility before it do not. Evolution itself could become a sort of religion.[146]

Margaret Haile and Gaylord Wilshire of the CSL were inspired by this same "cosmic socialism." For Haile, the true socialist was one who saw "an inconsiderable planet swinging in the immensity of space, divided by Nature

into certain great divisions more or less suitable for the abode and maintenance of human life; and upon it a race of beings who have come out of God
knows whence, who tarry a while and go back again to God knows whither,
without wish or will of their own in either case."[147]

For Wilshire:

> The greatest exaltation that can come to the spirit of man is to realize himself at
> one with the universe. This can only come when men are as perfectly related to
> each other and to humanity as a whole as are the cells in the living body related
> to each other and to the body as a whole. Men must be united to humanity in
> an organization at once perfectly democratic and perfectly autocratic.

By this he meant that "All humanity will be at one with God and every man
will be a god." This was the "glorious ideal which spurs on the Socialist and
which enthuses him with a religious ecstasy comparable with no emotion
which has ever hitherto stirred the world."[148]

What room was there for ethics in so limitless a universe? In search of answers to questions of ethics, many of this generation turned with remarkable
zeal to new humanist saints. Walt Whitman was revered as a poet of nature
and democracy; an interesting cult grew around him in Bon Echo, Ont., and
in London, Ont., his foremost Canadian disciple, R.M. Bucke, made no bones
about this religious devotion to the "great cause."[149] Thomas Carlyle, rather
surprisingly given his association with the "Great Man Theory of History"
that socialists were almost honour-bound to denounce, was nonetheless
widely reverenced for his ethical resistance to the cash nexus. McLachlan was
very much taken with Carlyle's dictum, "We must all toil or steal, howsoever
we name our stealing," and as late as 1920 was citing Carlyle's *French Revolution* in discussions of the great postwar democratic ferment.[150] Yet towering
even higher than Whitman or Carlyle in the cohort's moral imagination was
John Ruskin, who appealed deeply to those whose moral and aesthetic sensi-
tivities were wounded by capitalism, and who felt betrayed by conventional
religion. Ruskin saw in the pillage of labour by the rich the key to the severe
social problems of 19th-century England. Socialists and scholars will forever
debate whether Ruskin was on the left or on the right, because many of his
political prescriptions combined authoritarian paternalism with radical outrage. Leftists would pick up from him the ideals of co-operation and of educating the workers in politics and economics, and also many ideas about the
beauty and order of the natural world. He gave them an inspiring example of
anti-materialism, selflessness, and critical independence. To those who could
appreciate his often difficult prose, Ruskin seemed the prophet of a new, post-
materialist age of co-operation, beauty, and unity with the cosmos.[151]

For Fillmore in 1915, borrowings from the likes of Ruskin, Emerson,

Carlyle, Bellamy, or Tolstoy were fine for the "middle class sentimental asses" who had a strange need for "old concepts . . . old ideas, relics of the days when we believed in heavenly spooks." They should stay out of the Socialist Party. In his hard-core materialist philosophy, the only morality worth discussing was "that of revolting slaves. . . . That which helps us in our fight is moral and right from our viewpoint." From his perspective, when the slaves rose up against their masters, "the fellows with the well-manicured hands" with their talk of "Law, Religion and Morality" would count for little. It was a law of nature that "They may take who have the power and they may keep who can."[152]

His hard-boiled instrumental ethics was not characteristic of the first formation, even his own SPC. Across a wide spectrum leftists were searching for a way of distinguishing right from wrong that did not reduce to "right makes right." It was a time of great searching. Some who were attracted by socialism formally joined theosophical, Unitarian, or labour church groups – the experimental forms of spirituality in their day. Theosophy won renown especially among Toronto leftists, who saw in it a way of transcending both the parochialism of their Protestant environment and the individualism characteristic of liberal order. The Toronto Theosophical Society, chartered in 1891, could boast of the membership of Phillips Thompson and his fellow leftist Felix Belcher, as well as feminists Dr. Emily Howard Stowe and Dr. Augusta Stowe-Gullen.[153] Theosophy, founded by Helena Petrovna Blavatsky and institutionalized with the founding of the Theosophical Society in New York in 1875, was in some ways the forerunner of the new age philosophies and religions of our own time. One can see why it might deeply appeal to a Spencerian Marxist like Thompson. As explained by Madame Blavatsky in *The Key to Theosophy*, theosophy was not a religion but a "Divine Knowledge or Science." It aimed to "reconcile all religions, sects and nations under a common system of ethics, based on eternal verities."[154] Theosophy chimed with radical organicism in its calls to its disciples to transcend individualism and embrace a cosmic pattern of evolution in which the best of the human spirit was released from a crass world of greed and selfishness.

In his satire of utopian communities in *Heavens Below: Utopian Experiments in England, 1560–1960*, W.H.G. Armytage describes one utopian community in England where the typical male resident was "clad in knickerbockers and, of course, sandals," kept two tortoises as pets, prized his volumes of William Morris, H.G. Wells, and Tolstoy, and proudly displayed the works of Madame Blavatsky. A photograph of Madame Blavatsky would even have pride of place on the mantelpiece.[155] In British Columbia the Finnish utopian community at Sointula associated with Matti Kurikka was significantly affected by its leader's commitment to defying religious authorities – Kurikka's ringing manifesto *Uudelle Uralle* (New endeavour) fiercely condemned the clergy who had besmirched the noble morality of Christianity

– and by his attachment to theosophy.[156] It was a philosophy, writes Kevin Wilson in his deeply interesting study of the experiment on Malcolm Island, that Kurikka used "to deride symbols of structure and reason in European society (at one point pairing science with organized religion as two symbols of false authority), but to promote a true Christianity based on simple love."[157] Kealey points out: "In contrast to the organized churches which promoted marriage and monogamy, Kurikka interpreted theosophy as a spiritual force that stressed harmony, non-coercive relationships, and the power of spiritual forces."[158] For Thompson, there was nothing in the "truths of Theosophy" that cast doubt on his own position as a "class-conscious socialist from the ground up."[159]

Others turned to Unitarianism. A material and social precondition of much of William Irvine's creativity in the 1920s was the support of the First Unitarian Church in Calgary, whence he travelled with his family in 1916. Unitarianism flourished in Canada from 1890 to 1920, and a good number of its adherents were left-wing Christians no longer able to abide orthodoxies that required them to believe the unbelievable. Other leftists, it seems, were reluctant to pin themselves down to any one particular expression of spirituality. They respected the perennial human need for spiritual experiences, deeply distrusted the institutional attempts to provide them, and believed in a socialism that could provide human beings, if not with a sense of certainty, then at least with a community in which such philosophical questions could be freely discussed. They would come to think of the state as something more than an essentially profane and limited institution, but rather as the expression of the community – though here again, since it was so much the prisoner of capitalist interests, they would alternate between periods of great hope and despair when they thought of rescuing it for its higher social-evolutionary purposes.

The period also saw a new openness to non-Christian religions. Left humanism raised the possibility of socialists speaking, not just to Protestants and Catholics, but to the growing numbers of Canadians who were neither – to members of experimental religious groups, to Jews, to Muslims, and to others inspired to oppose the cruelty of capitalism on spiritual grounds. Writing to *Cotton's Weekly*, in somewhat uncertain English, Mikuno Ikeda of British Columbia first congratulated the paper, and then explained his position. "Please excuse me. I also be a socialist. I be a Buddhist for the next life but I want socialism for this life indeed." He pointed out to *Cotton's Weekly* that "socialism be not one piece grander for the Christians than for the Hindoos, Bhuddists or Hottentots. None of these religions are whatsoever to do with socialism at all." He speculated that "if Buddha and Jesus were alive like us now they would join the Socialist Party I be sure." If so, "each could teach his religion. All nations disagree on religion; same; all agree on socialism." His pointed conclusion: "Christians do not own socialism no more than all other religions. Please take example from your Buddhist socialist and restrain from confusing religion and politics." But Christian ownership of socialism was not easily challenged, as suggested by the headline attached to the letter by *Cotton's Weekly* – "A Jap Speaks Out" – and by its decision to run the letter complete with its grammatical errors.[160] At the same time it did register the Buddhist's politely worded challenge to the left's cultural limitations.

Others filled conventional Christian imagery with a humanist content. Instead of simply jettisoning the Christian legacy, they wanted (like Vancouver's Curry) to enlist Christ as the first socialist, and the church as an early anticipation of the Socialist International. Instead of signing on to a wholly naturalistic Darwinism, which offered them no rigorous reasons for fighting for one future over another, they wanted to find a meaningful pattern in the evolution of the cosmos that could sustain personal values and collective identity. Neither conventional Christianity nor positive science sufficed. Various forms of left humanism – a term only some would have recognized – affirmed the equality and dignity of human beings, argued against the literal interpretation of the Bible, and largely adopted Spencer's position in *First Principles* that both science and religion could impart important truths, even if the final answers to the deepest questions would always prove elusive.

William Irvine recalled how he used his Methodist post at Emo, in Ontario's Rainy River district, to present his congregation with a new version of their faith. "I was preaching sheer humanism," he remembered. "The supernatural had vanished. There were no miracles, no virgin birth, no atonement and no resurrection. . . . It took nearly two years for it to dawn on the people of Emo that I was not preaching to get people into heaven but that I was much more interested in getting heaven into people." When he was charged by his church for heterodoxy, Irvine explained to his accusers that the Bible was not the Word of God, but a "heterogeneous collection of writings derived from ancient peoples." Rather than seeing history as the "Fall of Man," Irvine suggested instead that it provided a record of humanity's evolutionary ascent. "This kind of religion cannot be kept out of politics," Irvine proclaimed. "Being inseparable from life it permeates its every department, and extends the domain of the sacred to what have been called material things. The line between the sacred and secular is being rubbed out . . . everything is becoming sacred." He envisaged the day when the "land by which we live" would be as "sacred as the little plot in which we bury our beloved dead."[161]

On the East Coast McLachlan may have been drawn to a position he attributed to the poet Robert Burns – half-agnostic, half-universalist. When he wrote of Burns's vision of the "world to come," reserved for the "just, the amiable, and the humane," McLachlan echoed his hero: "Would to God I as firmly believed it as I ardently wish it!" For Saint John Fabian W. Frank

Hatheway, the eternal message of Christian love far outweighed debates over theological issues. Theological debates should be left to "the schoolmen ... we have not the time to waste. Erasmus is dead, Luther is dead. Their souls know the falseness or truth of their beliefs. Why, therefore, need we quarrel over consubstantiation or transubstantiation?" Hatheway called out for preachers to follow in the footsteps of Christ, who was the partisan of "the worthy poor, not ... the indolent rich." What would Jesus do in Edmonton in 1914? asked the city's unusually socially conscious Mayor McNamara: "Instead of looking on sarcastically from the hotel windows and scoffing while the I.W.W. parades were going past, I believe Christ would have been in the parade and probably carrying one of the banners."[162]

The socialist-feminist Alice Chown (1866–1949) beautifully summed up her own disillusionment with conventional Christianity and her persistent search for human purpose and meaning in her autobiographical novel *The Stairway* (1921). "I had gone through all the stages," she reflects. "I have led prayer meetings, been zealous in all the good works of the church; I have visited the sick and the poor; I have spoken to the stranger within the gates. Every church activity has some time in my life found in me an earnest exponent." Yet she had been left feeling spiritually empty. "I used to laugh and say that my past was a graveyard of buried enthusiasms. ... The truths that once meant life and growth, force and virility, having been accepted as an end instead of a beginning, had killed the life of the spirit." Now conventional religion "seemed to me a dead organism existing by augmentations of number and institutions – a faith in external things.[163]

Her fellow socialist-feminist novelist Francis Marion Beynon (1884–1951) filled much of the opening chapters of her brilliant novel *Aleta Dey* (1919) with a sustained, scathing critique on institutional religion in Canada – an attack all the more effective for being placed in such an accessible, autobiographical form. Some of the novel's most vivid moments come when a young Aleta encounters the Bible in her classroom. She is full of questions. "How did God learn to use such beautiful words?" she asks. A hush follows her question, and the teacher leads the children in gales of laughter. "Already the public school had taught us to titter when authority laughs, which is one of its great functions in society." Gradually Aleta's doubts about scriptural authority extend to the character of the Almighty. When she asks her teacher, "Does God ever change his mind?" her teacher responds, "Aleta, you are a very irreverent little girl. ... God doesn't love little girls who are irreverent." When the local minister pays a visit and leads the family in prayer, she sees "his face was shining with a strange light. He had opened a pathway to his God – a narrow-minded, bigoted, dogmatic God, it is true, for his very limited intelligence was not capable of drawing a great and splendid picture of God – but his God." In an entire chapter devoted to "Socialism or Christianity," Aleta and her socialist friend Ned, taking some time out from their on-again, off-again romantic interest in each other, shut down the novel's narrative engine to argue over whether Christianity can be salvaged from "churchianity." "Found a new church," Ned predicts, "and inside of fifty years it will have become as much the tool of capitalism and the policeman of authority as is the old one."[164]

What is most apparent in this fictional reconstruction of a real-world, widespread discussion is a sense of deep disillusionment, whether sadly or angrily expressed, with a church that had seemingly betrayed its people. And this state of mind is evident not just among working-class militants, but in middle-class novelists like Beynon and Chown. When the children were dying in the mines, and when the machine guns were mounted in church steeples, where were the voices of the supposed followers of Christ? Many of them could be found singing the praises of the rich mine owners whose profits had been squeezed from the bodies of vulnerable little children and broken old men, and who had the gall, like J.R. Cowans, to lecture the workers on their lack of Christian sentiment. On the day of the People's Advent, the social democracy would rouse itself and reclaim all its treasures, spiritual and material, from those who had falsely laid claim to them. The scribes and Pharisees, the theologians and professors, the capitalists and their learned accomplices – would all scatter to the winds. Humanity would be free.

At its most ambitious, left humanism itself sought to become a new religion, purged of the supernatural and anti-scientific. Socialist meetings and religious revival meetings often resembled each other. A lone (generally male) minister or orator, who had often trained in speaking techniques for months, unburdened his soul before a mass audience. Like evangelists, the socialist soapboxers faced the occasional hecklers. The difference between them lay in the nature of the authority they had at their disposal. As John Webster Grant reports: " 'Smite him, my God!' an early Methodist preacher exclaimed when a mocker interrupted his meeting." The man in question "was soon writhing on the floor in agony."[165] A socialist orator might achieve roughly the same effect with a cutting display of superior economic logic.

Very much like religion, much of first formation socialism entailed the construction of a myth-symbol complex that located the adherent in history and helped explain his or her mission. From 1890 to 1920, left discourse often returned, again and again, to the list of the saints of science who had given up their reputations, and in some cases their lives, to the cause. Copernicus, Galileo, Bruno – all were re-created with a vividness and intensity missing in the typical reconstruction of other historical subjects. Robert Blatchford, widely read in Canada, liked to remind his Christian readers that, even as they prepared to persecute him for infidelity, they should remember that they themselves would have been so charged a few centuries before. "Are you not aware, friend Christian, that what was Infidelity is now orthodoxy?" he asked. "Heresies for which men used to be burned alive are now openly accepted by the Church. There is not a divine living who would not have been burned at the stake three centuries ago for expressing the beliefs he now holds. Yet you call a man Infidel for being a century in advance of you."[166] This emphasis on the church's victims worked both to tar the clerical enemy with the brush of the Inquisition and to remind the socialist faithful of those exemplary Enlightenment heroes who had gone before. It was a strategy familiar to anyone raised on John Foxe's *Book of Martyrs*.

Also like religion, much of first formation socialism was a matter of summoning up an intangible spirit through words and acts. Contemporaries marvelled at the sheer number of socialist meetings that took place in the years before the Great War. "Millions of meetings are held every year, in every civilized country, all with that one object of converting the people to the belief that collective ownership is the only cure for the ills which society suffers from to-day," the Saint John *Globe* remarked. The newspaper marvelled at the thousands of books and pamphlets, the zeal with which people poured themselves into translations, the quest for knowledge. "But it is not its literature, it is not its meetings, that are responsible for the growth of socialism," it added. "It is the intense enthusiasm of the whole of its adherents. An enthusiasm that today is often likened to the early days of the various churches." The true convert to socialism was obsessed with a new vision of the world: "In the workshop, at the dinner hour, in the street, anywhere where he can get a man to listen to him, he is forever talking socialism, socialism, socialism, morning, noon, and night."[167] Socialists, like evangelicals, did so much talking because they wanted to share their breakthrough to a new way of seeing with as many other human beings as they could. Only then, they said, could new converts acquire the backbone necessary to withstand the ridicule, isolation, and (quite possibly) persecution coming their way, just as the martyrs of the scientific Enlightenment had braved the Christians' Inquisition in days gone by.

If the left's constant repetition of Enlightenment martyrs was theatrical, it made a serious point. *Cotton's Weekly* drew, from an institutional analysis of how churches had evolved, the lesson that "the sanction of the Divine Being" was the construction of the people who had coalesced to form a church.[168] The socialists' critique of churchianity pointed out the narrowness of church debates, so often punctuated in this era with heresy trials and terminated with invocations of unquestionable authority. This churchianity was merely another form of autocracy with little place in a democratic age. Many left humanists saw themselves as the carriers of a new form of faith that placed the emphasis on "socialism" and drew freely upon Christian allegories and narratives as ways of grounding ethical and political insights not directly derived from religion.

An increasingly large number of socialists shared this quest for a new humanism in a relatively quiet voice (compared to those who wrote epistles on religion and pamphlets on atheism) that represented neither an embrace nor a rejection of Christianity. In Canada, as early as 1900, members of the Canadian Socialist League Local No. 5 in Malton were saying: "We are expecting something, suspecting something, anxiously looking ahead for some idea, some principle or philosophy that is to teach absolute purity in the relations that should be maintained among all sentient beings. This – religion, if you will – is unquestionably Socialism." The Lindsay Socialists filled their *Gems of Socialism* with such nuggets as "Sin against the human . . . is the only sin that can be committed."[169]

In *Cotton's Weekly* in 1909 J. Stitt Wilson offered his ideas on the road that needed to be followed. "I want a race of Comrade-Souls," he wrote, "not whining religionists, not cadaverous priests, not the good whose virtues are a vice." No, he wanted socialists who were "courageous, frank, ingenious, hospitable, hearty, full of laughter, not afraid of danger or death, knowing that Death introduces still greater worlds for Life and Love. I would have them royal, princely, dignified, proud and powerful." These new socialist men and women would be a "race of intellectual athletes."

> Not for show – not to write books, or to paint pictures, or to carve the stone . . . for the plaudits of the people. But, each for his own sake in intellectual self-sufficiency. To perceive Truth, that is the luxury. I want for every child the culture of mind that will release his own original powers to original action and expression. As I want him not blind of eye, but perfect in vision, just for his own sake, so I want his mental eye live and penetrating and creative.[170]

In this "Morning Meditation," Wilson thus treated the Canadian left to a symphony of democratic humanism worthy of Walt Whitman, very likely one of his sources of inspiration.

Although in retrospect it might be tempting to see the intensive socialism vs. religion debates of the early 20th century as a great misallocation of time and resources – consuming many miles of newspaper columns and undoubtedly taking attention away from other questions – they did make sense in the context of the time. Christianity, in both its Catholic and Protestant forms, often reinforced a liberal order whose anti-democratic narrowness and conventionalism the first formation was dedicated to opening up. Religion's hegemonic influence had to be challenged, even if the cards in this symbolic-political game were always stacked high against any leftist who tried to do so. Questioning religious doctrines in this period could and did lead to burned libraries, heresy trials, and public condemnation at the hands of the true believers – but the question itself was not an unimportant aspect of the people's enlightenment. It opened up spaces of rationality and democratic openness that had not previously existed. In this climate it took enormous courage to insist upon the right to reason and act *otherwise* in the sphere of religion.

Given much of the left's deep investment in Darwinism and social-evolutionary theory, many concrete political and ethical positions – on gender equality and on race, to take two prime examples – were evaluated according to whether or not they would assist or impede evolution. Following that path could lead to eugenics, race segregation, and right-wing appropriations of Darwinism; but most Canadian leftists did not move in those directions. They tended instead to carry within themselves a counterbalancing, thinly secularized humanistic concept of inherent human worth – a concept that could not easily be reconciled with the ruthlessly utilitarian and functionalist language of pure and simple Darwinism (or, indeed, with some emergent and many existing forms of Marxism and liberalism). Ultimately, the powerful legacy of revolutionary Christian activism and socialist humanism might well have been to save the Canadian left from the excesses of right-wing Darwinism that, in the liberal United States as well as Nazi Germany, would engulf much of social and political thought in the 1920s and 1930s.

The various responses to the religion question – in the forms of the social gospel, non-belief, and humanism – cannot readily be placed in a linear narrative. All three currents had their ebbs and flows. Nevertheless socialists within the first formation regarded the religion question as an urgent priority, and many of them saw in socialism itself a movement infused with the best human qualities. This was a value-saturated socialism that aimed at the redemption of humanity. Much of it was suffused with a pragmatic, humanist utopianism – the earnest hope of a better, more rational world.

Cotton's Weekly, more apt to walk on the sunny side of the street than was the acerbic *Western Clarion*, captured this spirit beautifully in 1910. In attempting to put into words just what it was that socialists wanted, it perceptively recaptured their often confusing inward experience of questioning that preceded the moment of supersedure. "The Socialists propound questions, very frequently, like little children," the editor remarked. They asked, why were there slums? Why such inequalities? But these questions led them not to despair over humanity but to celebrate what humanity could accomplish and enjoy. "Socialists are Socialists because they are human creatures and have so much human nature in them. They want sunlight and laughter. They want leisure and rest. They want the pretty things of life. They do not like to live in rented rooms. They want homes of their own."

Socialists were those who thought a world of grimy factories and desolate lives could be transformed into a world of beauty and harmony matching that of nature itself. "The Socialists do not want barricades nor bloodshed. But the Socialists, with the spirit of humanity in their hearts and the love of freedom red in their veins, are bound to win the social revolution."[171]

Idealism and the Cosmic Process: E.A. Partridge

Perhaps the most beautifully worked out expression of this left humanism came in the writings of Saskatchewan's E.A. Partridge (1861–1931), a legendary figure in the history of the co-operative movement on the Prairies. His book *A War On Poverty* (1926) stands as one of the greatest monuments to first formation idealism. Gauvin and Bland, writing at the crest of postwar radical optimism, projected into the near future contrasting utopian visions of a regenerated world. Partridge, writing somewhat later and in a less optimistic time, was much more interested in Christ as a moral exemplar, a heroic figure in the liberation struggles of producers, than he was in evolution. Perhaps, writing as the first formation was past its heyday and the left on the defensive, he was more inclined to invest in a somewhat static vision of utopia than to place his hopes in a cosmic process of evolution.

Partridge was, in historian Louis Aubrey Wood's words, "a big man, of restless demeanor and flashing eye" who "became the seer of the Canadian plains-folk."[172] Born near Barrie, Canada West (Ontario), in 1862, he became a remarkably successful builder of lasting institutions. After travelling west with his brother Henry in 1883 he settled in the country east of Sintaluta, Sask. Teaching school while he homesteaded, Partridge became active in the Patrons of Industry and, later, in the early 20th century, threw himself into dramatic legal battles with the CPR over the allocation of grain cars. Both he and his brother won renown for having symbolically bested the CPR in court. In 1905, buoyed by the reputation he achieved through this struggle, Partridge was sent to investigate the workings of the Winnipeg Grain Exchange. He emerged deeply disturbed by how the system worked to the disadvantage of farmers. Through the skilful blending of wheat of very different qualities, the capitalists were able to pass off as "No. 1 Hard" wheat that did not make that grade. In response Partridge organized the Grain Growers' Grain Company, which would ultimately become one of the largest of its kind in the world. Partridge was its first president and a driving force behind the organization in 1908 of *The Grain Growers' Guide*, which consistently argued for a state-managed grain-marketing and delivery system. The publication became a major voice of the Prairie left. After a series of business and personal adversities, Partridge returned to Sintaluta. He was involved in the "No-Party League," which argued for the complete radical transformation of a bankrupt-party system. After the Great War Partridge re-emerged as a major agrarian leader and came to play an important role in inspiring the Farmers' Union of Canada.

The true measure of Partridge's leftism, which combined anarchist and socialist themes in a down-to-earth, accessible vocabulary, emerges from his brilliantly visionary *A War on Poverty: The One War That Can End War*, which was shaped by pre-1914 social theory even though it appeared in 1926.[173] *A War on Poverty* is renowned among some historians of the West as an early call for an independent Western state, to be called Coalsamao. The name represented the amalgamation of the four names of the Western provinces: British *C*olumbia, *A*lberta, *S*askatchewan, and *M*anitoba, with the concluding "o" for a slice of Ontario west of the Lakehead that was also to be amalgamated, one assumes voluntarily, into this new Western "co-operative commonwealth." Unlike later right-wing projections of Western separatism, Coalsamao was an egalitarian projection into the troubled present from an imagined radiant Bellamyite/Spencerian future.

No other book in the Canadian left tradition is quite like *A War on Poverty*. None (at least until we get to Pierre Vallières in the 1960s) is so unrepentantly "utopian." None, save Bland's *The New Christianity*, is argued so passionately. No other Canadian socialist, to my knowledge, ever committed to print such a detailed blueprint for the "realm of freedom" that would follow the dark ages of capitalism. The classical Marxist texts warned about trying to offer blueprints of the future. The non-Marxist Partridge risked ridicule in daring to spell out, down to the smallest details, what the socialist/anarchist utopia would look like once established in the Canadian West.[174]

Partridge's book clearly suggests the impact of the thought of Ruskin, who, as he did for so many of Partridge's generation, figured as the moral authority of a new humanism. For Partridge, Ruskin had brilliantly highlighted the hypocrisy of Victorian capitalism. Partridge loved how Ruskin, in talking about liberal political economists, likened their sterile abstract reasoning to a science of gymnastics worked out by intellectuals who assume that human beings have no skeletons. The science is logical and elaborate, and the intellectuals' conclusions follow infallibly from their premises – yet their plans simply had no application to the real world of gymnastics. Modern liberal political thought was guilty of no less fantastic a distortion of human reality. As the politically polymorphous Ruskin was constructed in Partridge's text – he is referenced no fewer than eleven times, often at length – he is the spiritual scourge of a system that systematically degraded and defrauded the poor. Ruskin, inspired by sources as diverse as the Bible and the pioneer Welsh socialist Robert Owen, argued that a world of abundance was possible, if only the resources adequate for life were justly and efficiently distributed. "Old John Ruskin," a.k.a. the "peerless old knight," would be the patron saint of Coalsamao, and his great moral lesson, that a selfish political economy would "ruin . . . the Economy of Heaven," would be engraved on the hearts of its citizens. In contrast Partridge spent remarkably little time on Canadian political realities or conventional socialist analysis. He brought forward a few Canadian authorities – Sir Andrew Macphail, Edward Porritt, John Bourinot – but only in brief. *A War on Poverty's* imagined homeland is not Canada but a mid-Atlantic New Moral World.

The book, like most first formation work, contained remarkably little empirical analysis. It was not a scholarly examination of the problem of poverty in line with the supposedly "objective sociology" being developed by J.S. Woodsworth. Rather, it was an impassioned call for revolutionary action now – "for a great 'Cromwellian Clean-up in Canada.' " The Anglo-Canadian readers would have been aware that Partridge was praising the revolutionary responsible for the beheading of a king.

Partridge, writing on the margins of the left's core constituencies, expressed a complete disinterest in Darwinian evolution and, except for a critical dig at the theory of "proletarian dictatorship," left Marx by the wayside. *A War on Poverty* was playing a different, arguably more innovative, language game than did most first formation texts. Most of them, in one way or another, earnestly established their scientific credentials and roots in the Enlightenment tradition. In this text, Partridge, by contrast, often seemed to be horsing around – to be indulging in fabulous wordplay and experimenting in a much more direct, personal style of writing. Today Partridge would have a blog, a web-page, and a list-serve.

Yet like other first formation thinkers Partridge did have a reverence for evolutionary sociology as the new science of a new world. *A War On Poverty* was a hybrid, something evolved for life on the Canadian Prairies, combining Bellamy's *Looking Backward* and Spencer's *First Principles*. Drawing on Ward's neo-Spencerian *Dynamic Sociology*, Partridge saw sociology as the one science indispensable for progress, and he demanded its dissemination through the general population, "which can be achieved only by a properly socialized system of education." Showing a Bellamyite influence, Partridge has his New World organized into army-like camps, with an equal sharing of the burden of labour and a beneficent state (although, unlike the first version of Bellamy's, the state is very much answerable to the grassroots communities).

In the argument against the private ownership of land, Partridge's theoretical mainstay is clearly Spencer's *Social Statics*. At a decisive moment in his "Concluding Address," the author reflects on the ultimate meaning of his vision and on its religious significance. The "wise man" would not disregard the faith within him. He would view it as the "supreme authority to which all his actions should bend." It was not the mission of such an intellectual to tailor convictions to the time, but to "fearlessly utter" the "highest truth conceivable by him." If he did this and then played his appointed part in the world, he would know that, "If he can get done the thing he aims at – well; if not – well also, though not so well." These are the very words that Spencer uses to bring to a stoical conclusion his own reflections on the unknowable in *First Principles*.[175]

For all its Ruskinian instrumentation, then, the underlying harmonies of *A War on Poverty* are profoundly Spencerian. It is Spencer's theory of evolution that will kick-start the maddeningly slow progress of actual evolution – London's Ernest Everhard had precisely this same intuition – and for this to happen, a vanguard or an "intellectual aristocracy" is necessary. "Ah, the unassisted progress of old Evolution is too slow – generation by generation we die while we wait," Partridge exclaimed. "He, Old Evolution, like everybody and everything in this scientific age must have artificial assistance. We have used Science for every purpose save to make men sensible and sociable. We must make experiments in the field of social science as well as in the physical." A scientific "aristocracy" would overthrow all that was archaic and irrational in the hold of mildewed customs and expose the sinister manipulations of the rich and powerful.

Although Partridge professed to "know little, and care less, about the Darwinian theory," his long utopian manifesto was organized throughout by Spencer's closely related, and more cosmic, evolutionary vision. "We are all entangled," he proclaimed, "inextricably, I think, and, at present, most of us, very uncomfortably – in the 'web of life.' " The web was evolving in its own way within a vast changing cosmos. Humanity, located on a "rather lightweight planet," could gaze at the heavens and become "conscious of kinship and kindly disposed towards one another." A sense of being one small part of an evolving species, in turn set within a vast evolving cosmos, should be one of humility and mutual aid in the face of the unknowable and compassion towards each other – in essence, a scientific understanding of the universe could be the precondition of a new humanism. In Partridge's hands, Spencer's unknowable was transformed into a principle of humility and solidarity in the face of the universe's limitless expanse.

In many respects Partridge appears to have been in the grip of an existential crisis as he wrote his book, struggling to maintain, in the face of the seeming indifference of the universe, that sense of purpose he had once derived from evolution and the farmers' movement. In company with Alice Chown, Beynon, Irvine, and Woodsworth, Partridge found it extremely difficult to reconcile belief in an all-powerful and loving God with the sheer irrationality and cruelty of capitalism and the liberal order. He movingly described his own evolution, from unquestioning belief to doubt. Like Gauvin, he found repulsive God's "threat of post-mortem vengeance on unbelievers," the maker's "acts of hate-inspired violence directed against the work of his own hands." He could no longer respect, much less love, "the personality thus portrayed," or believe in the accuracy or the "wisdom" of the book in which He was described. Yet at the same time, the coherence of the world around him, the existence of human values, the possibility "of knowledge, and system, and sequence," led him back to a certain faith in humanity. Partridge's was a vision, like Spencer's, that was both lyrical and stoical, mystical and scientific. The integration and consolidation of humankind foreshadow the end to competitiveness, war, and capitalism.

Here, in his mind, was the cosmic justification for the co-operatives that he had helped to organize in Saskatchewan, indeed for his entire lifetime of thought and activism. They would become the "cells" of the new co-operative organism, growing out of the dying husk of private property as evolution's next step forward to a perfection of humanity. Co-operatives were important in and of themselves, as Partridge, an organizer of down-to-earth institutions for the Saskatchewan wheat farmers, knew well. Co-operation was also, and more importantly, a transcendent ideal, only partially realized in co-operatives. Co-operation was a program of national salvation, a prescription for an entirely new social and political order. Partridge's "co-operative commonwealth federation" was by no means, then, a bland, middle-of-the-road reformism. It was, on the contrary, a vision of a world transformed. There was a direct line from Partridge's utopian vision to the discussions among Saskatchewan producers that would help to create the Co-operative Commonwealth Federation, which began its momentous consolidation the year after Partridge committed suicide in Victoria in 1931.

Partridge was proud of never having joined a political party, and reserved some of his strongest condemnation for the parties that purported to represent the Prairie farmers. Like Spencer, he found the contemporary state contemptible. Parliamentarians? They were simply "pimping politicians and puddling pap-fed publicists," who continued "to exhale flatulent predictions of prosperity and exude oily optimism while the country is going to the devil head-foremost economically and morally right before their eyes." Nothing they said could be trusted. Even when they spoke of "confidence," Partridge smelled a "confidence game." As for the regulatory state, not even Spencer himself matched Partridge in his categorical judgments against supposedly beneficent governments. They were in the business of cajoling ordinary people to forget their actual interests and invest their loyalties in "The State," whose deep-seated corruption was correlated with its insatiable appetite for passing laws: "the more laws, the more lawlessness," was his succinct distillation of the smothering of ordinary people under obligations and legislation. Individuals needed to combine at the grassroots for their mutual aid, and ignore those who deafened ears and sickened souls with their "clamorous appeals from press, platform, pulpit, professorial chair, and the floor of parliament." These passages could have been lifted, word for word, from Spencer's polemics against the state or Kropotkin's calls for mutual aid and anarchism.

Although the detailed plans for Coalsamao – its dress codes, dietary restrictions, and architecture – are quaint in retrospect, as all old utopian schemes are apt to be, they do their damnedest to reconcile grassroots democracy with Bellamy's unappetizing vision of industrial work armies. If *A War on Poverty* was a foreshadowing of forms of political activism and dialogue that would only become feasible in the age of the Internet, Coalsamao was Partridge's version of the "temporary autonomous zone," a humanist "realm of freedom" against which the drab and exploitive world of Prairie capitalism could be measured. "My readers," Partridge wrote, "may regard themselves . . . as listening to an inhabitant of the new autonomous political entity, known as Coalsamao, describing it and its institutions to an interested foreigner."

The constitution of Coalsamao defined the new state as "a Co-operative Commonwealth" – Gronlund's evocative phrase that Partridge helped keep alive, as a glowing vision, in Saskatchewan. This commonwealth would be a grassroots anarchist federation in which humans combined to survive and prosper, collectively supplying common needs and furthering common interests. Unlike Bellamy's vision of utopia, Partridge's Coalsamao would be made up of a federation of co-operatives, each as self-governing as possible, in which both everyday affairs and general political decisions would be subject to a participatory democracy, with its motto "Each for all and all for each." Human nature had not been altered overnight – in common with Marx, Engels, and most of the tradition, Partridge did not question that "human nature" existed – but, thanks to the rapid diffusion of the "new-old sociological discovery of the absolute solidarity of human interest on the higher level of living," individuals in the future had come to understand that the happiness of each was dependent upon the happiness of all.

What would Jesus do, asked Partridge, if he visited 20th-century Western Canada? "Would He, metaphorically speaking, have been using His whip of small cords on Communists? Or on Capitalists?"[176] His answer was different from Sheldon's. In Partridge's leftism, Jesus would bring down his whip upon the "bunch of boodlers – bankers and the like." Jesus would inscribe on his banner, "You shall know the truth, and the truth shall make you free." How could forgetful followers live with themselves, when all around them, in a region overflowing with natural resources, there festered oppression and poverty? Had they not read the unqualified command of Jesus, "Do unto others as ye would that they should do unto you?" It was "manifestly the duty of Christians to seek to bring in the 'Kingdom' in the form of a Co-operative Commonwealth." The hour demanding the performance of that duty fast approached: "My friends! Let us bestir ourselves! The Millennium, the Kingdom of Heaven, the Co-operative Commonwealth, different names for the same blessed State, is at hand – ours for the taking."[177]

As Martin Buber would explain, "all the force of dispossessed Messianism" often enters into such utopian projections. Partridge's scheme could be said to originate "in a kind of abstract imagination which, starting from a theory of the nature of man, his capacities and needs, deduces a social order that shall employ all his capacities and satisfy all his needs." In essence, Partridge (in Buber's words) "does not believe in the post-revolutionary leap, but he does believe in revolutionary continuity. To put it more precisely: he believes in a continuity within which revolution is only the accomplishment, the setting free and extension of a reality that has already grown to its true possibilities."[178]

Partridge's brilliant experiment, a kind of playful eschatology, projected Coalsamao into the drab realities of Canadian politics as its democratic antithesis – and did so with an engaging sense of humour. His book is now obscure, his name generally forgotten, and his vision of the co-operative commonwealth sometimes mocked – but there was, in Partridge's remarkable text, a burning coal of righteous justice to be passed on to the new socialism taking shape under that vast Prairie sky wherein he saw face of God.

Margaret Haile, as captured in *The Social Democratic Red Book* (1900) and also seen in *Citizen and Country* (Toronto), 16 May 1902. The portraits of S.A. Corner (below left) and John A. Kelly (below right) appeared in the same issue of the paper.

5

The Woman Question

*T*oronto, 16 May 1902. "The Socialists" of the city, *Citizen and Country* told its readers, "have nominated candidates to contest the constituencies of East, West, North and South Toronto, in recognition of the fact that no matter how many issues may be raised by capitalist politicians to confuse unthinking minds, there is but one real fundamental issue before the workers of Canada to-day – that of SOCIALISM VS. CAPITALISM."

On the one side, the notice explained, were the Liberal and Conservative parties, and on the other, the "Socialist Party," which stood for the replacement of the present "competitive warfare" by the "principle of co-operation." If you voted for the Socialist Party, you were voting for a "clearly-defined policy regarding the liquor traffic, viz., that as long as this traffic exists it should be under public ownership and control." If you voted for the Socialist Party, you were voting for a party that would fight for democracy, and not for class rule. If you voted for one of the old parties, on the other hand, you need not be surprised "if Factory Acts are unenforced, sweat-shops multiply, women and children are allowed to work long hours in unsanitary conditions, and if such acts as old age pensions, adopted in other countries, are unheard of here."

Atop the notice was a large portrait of the famously dapper James Simpson, the Socialist candidate for East Toronto, wing-collared and handsome, looking for all the world like a young Wilfrid Laurier. At the bottom were portraits of three other Toronto candidates. S.A. Corner and John A. Kelly looked statesmanlike in their suits. Corner was on the left, with a modern American-style collar, receding hairline, broad forehead, neatly trimmed moustache, and a look of sincerity and earnestness. Kelly was on the right, a rugged Abe Lincoln look-alike, his fiery eyes and pugnacious chin seeming to pass a harsh judgment on the ills of the world. In the middle was Margaret Haile. "We trust that no advocate of woman suffrage in this district will fail to record his vote in favor of the first woman candidate for the legislature in Canada." In this provincial election, a vote for the CSL candidate was not only a vote for the full enfranchisement of women – it could mean actually voting for a woman candidate.[1]

In an example of extravagant gender radicalism in this, the very first general electoral outing of the Canadian Socialist League, not only was a party running a woman but it was also proudly placing her front and centre in the campaign. Her visual representation emphasized a strong, forward-thrusting chin, broad shoulders, and a cheerful but determined demeanour. Even she wore an Edwardian collar and a bow tie – as if the pamphleteers were wrestling visually with the gender-bending implications of the CSL's brash deed.

No woman had ever before run in an election for a Canadian legislature. Small wonder: women could not even *vote* in elections for Canadian legislatures. Some said, inaccurately (though not by much), that it was the first such female candidacy in the entire British Empire.[2] It was a highly controversial move, associated in many minds with the rise of George Weston Wrigley Jr. and his ultra-radical ilk to a position of influence within the CSL. "The League platform demanded universal adult suffrage," Gene Homel remarks, "but nominating a woman for the legislature was much too scandalous for all but a few Toronto minds."[3]

Why was it so "scandalous"? Because women were, by the rules of Canada's well-established liberal order, at best *probationary* individuals. The demands of both nature and society – their supposedly frail constitutions and their responsibilities for child-rearing – precluded them from being free-standing individuals. Many liberals would wonder if women could sensibly manage the burdens of suffrage. Although they had earlier been enfranchised in parts of British North America, however unevenly, they were progressively removed from the vote through the 1830s and 1840s. In 1895, during one of the six attempts in this period to enfranchise Nova Scotia women, J.W. Longley, attorney general, "progressive liberal," and undoubted authority on women (having written an entire book on *Love*), proclaimed that women filled four functions in life: bearing and bringing up children; creating homes and the beautifying of home life; "to charm men and make the world pleasant, sweet and agreeable to live in"; and "to be kindly and loving, to be sweet and to be cherished, to be weak and confiding, to be protected and to be the object of man's devotion."[4] Longley was unusually candid, but not uncommonly sexist, in his social theory. In the classical liberal order as it had evolved in Canada since the 1840s, women were not the equals of men – in law, politics, or society. Vast libraries of liberal common sense "proved" the point, and the tendency was little rocked by the feminist protests of a John Stuart Mill or a Herbert Spencer. The Canadian Liberals and their Liberal-Conservative opponents did not disenfranchise women, or maintain the host of other disabilities under which women laboured, in a fit of absence of mind.

For the CSL to take advantage of a legal loophole and nominate a woman candidate in 1902 was thus a brilliant act of defiance. Predictably, the reaction to this move was stormy. Haile's opponents tried to prevent her from speaking. *The Toiler* refused to endorse her. Later and lesser sisters have buildings named after them; there is even a statue on Parliament Hill to the five women who originated the famous "Persons Case" in the 1920s (notwithstanding some doubts about the racism of at least one of them). To this day Haile's singular achievement has gone largely unacknowledged, and her sophisticated reflections on party-building and left-wing culture have been overlooked.[5]

The difficulty with Margaret Haile is that she was a revolutionary socialist whose feminism was structured in large measure as a challenge to the liberalism that still dictates the shape and content of what can be counted as legitimate history. Her legacy also disturbs many of the assumptions of contemporary liberal feminism. She was a mould-shattering first formation intellectual who both grasped the paradigm in its post-liberal essentials and wrote brilliantly on the "problem of the party" within socialism.[6] Indeed, the period in which she was active witnessed a remarkable flowering of socialist feminism – partly evident in such activists as Haile, but even more in powerful cultural and political work outside the formal institutions of the left – in literature, grassroots organizing, and peace activism. A reconnaissance of the first formation in all its diversity would argue against allowing the sexists in the institutional left to monopolize the discussion of what contemporaries liked to call "the woman question" – an umbrella term that covered everything from women's paid labour to the politics of sexuality.

Haile's writings on the theory and practice of the Socialist Party, published as the U.S. party was emerging as a powerful electoral force, make compelling reading. She wrote them as a woman who had already developed a substantial reputation in the United States. She was one of two women members on the nine-person executive board of the Social Democratic Party of America. A 1901 article published in the *Social Democratic Herald* on "Theories of Party Organization" subtly sought to weave together different proposals for the new Socialist Party then emerging in the United States.[7] The article, ambitious in its scope, came at a pivotal time in the institutional history of U.S. socialism, when the Social Democratic Party (fd. 1898) and dissidents from the De Leonite Socialist Labor Party were debating the terms of their possible consolidation within the emerging Socialist Party of America (fd. 1901). Haile defended the SLP's revolutionary objective – "the total abolition of the capitalist system and the institution of the cooperative commonwealth through the agency of political action on the part of the organized wage-earning class" – but not its ideological rigidity, which she thought had been imposed upon it far too early in its evolutionary development.[8] She carried her Spencerism lightly but unmistakably.

"A heap of separate and independent grains of sand is not an organization, nor is a heap of stone," she argued, invoking Spencer's pivotal argument about the inherent evolutionary drive from simple homogeneity of dissociated elements to the complex heterogeneity of interrelated ones. "To move and act, there must be a body, with different members performing different functions, but actuated by one will and moved by one muscular system." When these Spencerian insights were applied to the concrete tasks of building a new political party, they suggested that rather than indulging in rhapsodies on "the beauties of abstract unity," socialists should be focusing on the evolutionary imperatives of how best to organically combine the necessary functions of a socialist party in a new political structure. This task would require a realistic study of the terrain and disciplined reflection on what it was that the socialists wanted the new instrument to accomplish. "Just as a scientific farmer analyzes his soil and supplies in fertilizers the constituents it lacks for raising the particular crop he wants," Haile remarked, "we must study our great field of labor – the United States – analyze the soil and intelligently apply whatever is needed to raise a bountiful crop of socialists."[9]

Haile's principled practicality came through in her proposals for the emergent party. "Let us get down to business," she said. Undertake a *realistic* assessment of the possibilities open to socialists. Submit the proposed union of the various organizations to the light of practical reason, noting all the advantages and disadvantages of the various proposals, to arrive at a definite plan of reorganization. The work in each state, and across the whole country, required an intensive labour of "mapping." It was a mission of reconnaissance that would require money, to be generated through a regular and democratic system of dues, "so that, all paying equally, each may feel that he has as much voice in the conduct of affairs as every other."

This approach implied a national, centrally located headquarters, a network of branches each aware of its local and general responsibilities, and – this above all – a well thought out program of education. Do not confuse the *party* with the *socialist organization*, Haile cautioned. The mere political machinery should be subordinate to, indeed merely the instrument of, the wider body of socialist volunteers. Otherwise, it might fall into the hands of "professional politicians." The fundamentally important work of the organization should be education. Just as the socialists should examine their soil and their fertilizers, so too should they examine the groups they wanted to reach and the language of the messages they were transmitting to them. Haile believed, like Jack London, that at the end of the day there would be a giant "tug of war" between capitalists and socialists. To win it, the socialists needed the support of the majority of the people. So they must mount an effective and realistic program of propaganda, geared to each group. Farmers, miners, railroad men, factory workers – all needed to hear the message put in a language that they could understand.

Yet Haile did not believe that education alone would do the trick. Finally, the socialists would have to make a "giant stride forward" and take power. Putting her own model of accessibility into action, Haile used a pleasant organic metaphor familiar to every farmer: "We must remember that socialism is not inevitable unless we do our part, and that promptly and wisely. The chick develops inside the shell, but unless he has life in him and ability to peck the shell open he remains inside it and dies." The socialist organization of the future would necessarily have to be prepared to "peck its way through the enclosing shell of capitalism when the proper time comes." She could have said, "Smash the State" – since once the chick is hatched, its former shell is indeed left in pieces – but how much better, for her purposes, to demonstrate the necessity of an active, aggressive party without resorting to disturbingly violent imagery.

Like Lenin, Haile believed that in the era of trusts, which she analyzed acutely as a new form of capitalism, socialists needed to refashion their instruments of struggle; yet she arrived at strikingly different conclusions based upon the very different conditions prevailing in North America. Like the "sewer socialists" of Milwaukee (or the "gas-and-water socialists" of Great Britain) she esteemed the practical, but unlike them she warned against confusing local political successes with the great movement for a new kind of politics – they might even infect militants with "political fever" and distract them from "the great work of national education." Like the SLPers, she wanted a *scientific* socialist politics, but not one immersed in destructive, soul-destroying polemics, and not one that confused theory with practice. "System without energy stagnates. Energy without system and wise direction dissipates itself fruitlessly," Haile argued, and she drew this tactical conclusion: "No more random firing, hit or miss; but every shot directed at the point where it will accomplish most."[10]

The woman running in Toronto in 1902 thus had a major claim as one of the prominent thinkers in the reconstruction of socialism then happening in the United States – the former state secretary for Connecticut of the SLP, state secretary for Massachusetts of the Socialist Party, and one of eight women delegates (out of 128 in total) at the Socialist Party of America's historic Indianapolis Convention in 1901. She was perfectly suited to be a legislator, a party leader, even (it was indelicately whispered) a premier.[11] Why not? *Miss* Margaret Haile was put forward by the CSL as a tough-minded professional – and not as a *mother* embarking on a grand housekeeping operation at Queen's Park. There was not even a hint of chivalry or coyness in the presentation. The 81 votes ultimately cast for Haile came from men who had been warned, in words and images, and in no uncertain terms, that the Toronto Socialists aimed to transform the position of women in politics and society.

Haile's journalism in *Justice* (Providence, R.I.), the *Social Democratic*

Herald (Chicago), and *Wilshire's Magazine* (at the time, in Toronto) provides clues that reveal her brand of socialist feminism. She certainly identified herself as a "new woman." According to Haile, the Woman of Tomorrow would transcend the roles of wife and mother to become a much more well-rounded individual. "She feels her individuality more than her sex. . . . Her intellect trained, her tastes educated; and all her mental and physical powers developed. She does not believe that life is over for her when she stands at the altar. . . . The new woman believes in being herself right down to the end of life, living out her own personal life." On another occasion she remarked, "Woman's sphere is just as big as she can make it. Her nature must be perfectly rounded out in all directions, mentally, morally, and physically."[12] She had been converted to socialism by Frances Willard, the legendary moving spirit of the Woman's Christian Temperance Union and noted Bellamyite, and spoke with some of her mentor's emotion about temperance and the disappointed hopes and broken hearts of wives and mothers. Yet she was also a sharp-eyed political economist, a scathing critic of the "Morganization of the world" and the creeping culture of consumption. She was an astute observer of the "capital unions" that were emerging as businessmen united to fight labour. She was an early analyst of the dynamics of imperialism, which she linked, as did other prominent theorists, to capitalism's inherent tendency to produce far more than it could market, leading to a cutthroat struggle with other countries. The capitalist system was about to collapse. Only socialists, with their "world-wide view," their understanding of diverse fields, their commitment to the entire human race, their sense of deep social-evolutionary time, and their appreciation of the interconnectedness of the global economy – only socialists could guide the country and the world through this perilous hour.[13]

To call her a maternal feminist would seem a reductionist description of her multifaceted, wide-ranging theory. On the basis of the turn of the century texts, Haile would seem, rather, to be someone who only incidentally weaves maternal themes into her arguments for socialism. What emerges far more forcefully from these texts are the words of a revolutionary militant who combined a rigorous understanding of political economy in general and U.S. imperialism in particular with a vigorous appreciation of the aesthetic and ethical mission of the socialist movement. Margaret Haile was a Marxist feminist – no Heritage Moment for her.

The Ambiguous Legacy of Socialist Feminism

In her book *The Feminist Challenge to the Canadian Left, 1900–1918*, Janice Newton notes the existence of a "small but significant contingent of feminists who were active within the ranks of the socialist movement, proving that socialist feminism has a heritage that dates from the turn of the century in Canada." This small core, she says, "accepted maternal feminism and turned it to radical ends, making the home a primary site for radical socialist transformation to enhance the autonomy of women." Rather than scorning the domestic sphere, the women integrated it into their conception of a socialism that might transform "both the private and public worlds: the home; relations between men and women; and the waged-labour relationship."[14]

Newton argues, however, that this "radical feminist voice" did not prevail because it came up against men's domination of politics in general: "Socialist women were vastly outnumbered and sometimes silenced by their male comrades." Not only that, but they were further excluded and marginalized by the dominant male culture and its sense of camaraderie: the men's smoking, heckling, and general vulgarity were of a piece with a movement that was often hostile towards women. Because men dominated party executives and editorial positions, Newton writes, "they infused masculine dominance into the social atmosphere of the left."[15]

In *Enlisting Women for the Cause: Women, Labour, and the Left in Canada, 1890–1920*, Linda Kealey covers something of the same terrain and time frame, arguing judiciously that Canadian women "mounted an opposition to the inequalities inherent in industrial capitalism and, sometimes, to the inequalities in the very movements they so closely identified with." Only a small vocal minority was able to withstand this opposition. Generally, within the movement, women "experienced a gendered division of labour much as they did in the labour market." "Socialist opinion," remarks Kealey, à propos of both European and Canadian movements, was "divided on the question of equal rights for women and the desirability of separate women's organizations, usually associating them with the 'bourgeois' women's movement." Kealey points out in her nuanced and empirically rich account that the parties were not necessarily monolithic: both the SPC and SDPC were divided "on the question of separate women's organizations and activities."[16]

These critiques of the organized left are accurate, and in the case of the *Western Clarion*, perhaps understated. Certainly, within the SPC and other parties of the time many women did experience a rough passage into the political left. Some SPC critiques virulently attacked women's suffrage, and editorials and patronizing commentaries in the *Western Clarion* disparaged the significance of the cause.[17] The SPC rejected demands for the transformation of domestic labour, as Newton points out, because many men, as privileged members of the household, did not consider women's work within the home an issue relevant to socialism.[18] In the SPC, according to Kealey, activists such as Wilfred Gribble considered women to be "unsuited for certain kinds of political activity that were defined as male," such as soapbox oratory.[19] The SPC also exhibited a certain hostility to the cause of prohibition, which was, according to Newton, "one means by which women could exert influence over masculine behaviour." When women raised issues that we would now roughly bunch together in the realm of "sexual politics" and that at the time were pioneering efforts – birth control, the "White Slave Trade," sexual autonomy, censorship – they tended to be sidestepped if not rebuffed. In their discussions of the sex trades, some socialist men manifested a basic concern about preserving their sexual access to working-class women.[20] They might have supported calls for an end to prostitution, but they refused to examine their own sense of sexual entitlement and privileges that contributed to women's oppression. They promised that socialism would transform society, but that transformation stopped short at the domestic realms they ruled. Socialist men used "science" to sustain male privileges and their powerful positions within the party to marginalize women. Kealey notes the impact of evolutionary theory, which sent "confusing messages" to "women in the movement."[21] In general, throughout the socialist parties, male socialists were at best ambivalent about their women comrades.

Though they have marked differences in approaches, in their books both Newton and Kealey leave a distinct impression of the obstacles that made socialist feminists an often beleaguered minority in the broader left. Newton's story in particular is largely about the suppression of leftist women, whose voices were "stifled in the nascent stages of building the socialist movement."[22] Her narrative is organized around a dualism, with men/socialists/science at one pole and women/feminists/maternalism at the other; and the first is above and dominates the second. Yet, although many of the critical points about the "male left" have substance, a reconnaissance of this terrain provides a somewhat broader framework, one that does not so readily minimize a range of socialist-feminist achievements – in organizations, minority groups, socialist fiction, advice columns, peace activism, networking. A reconnaissance, without denying the opposition confronting socialist feminists, opens up the possibility of restoring more complexity and agency to the first formation's gender politics.

Rather than being relatively airtight and opposing ideologies – with the second defying or challenging the first – "socialism" and "feminism" were to a considerable extent interwoven, often in surprising ways. Many women *and* men were at the same time both socialist and feminist. Of course, a recognition of this tendency depends partly upon definitions. If a feminist is a person who believes men and women are inherently equal in worth and entitled to respect, and that obstacles in the way of such equality should be eliminated, and if a socialist feminist is a person who combines these goals with that of struggling for an egalitarian society in which class divisions have been abolished, there were many socialist feminists in early 20th-century Canada, both men and women. Although it is nowadays conventional to assume that femi-

nists are women, such was not always the case – in some earlier left formations, many feminists were men. This was markedly the case in Germany, but
even in England in the 1880s, when debates on the woman question were furiously waged, it was sometimes even assumed that feminists were men.[23] In
Canada consistent and outspoken male feminists included George Weston
Wrigley Jr., Phillips Thompson, Ernest Burns, William Irvine, E.A. Partridge,
and W.U. Cotton. Over the course of the 1890–1917 period the woman question became progressively articulated more and more by women themselves.

A pivotal point here relates to *context*. In a liberal order in which the exclusion of women from political rights was the tip of the iceberg of an entrenched and pervasive ideology of gender, one minimizing the extent to
which women were in any real sense "free-standing individuals," the first
formation consistently pushed the gendered boundaries of the established
order. If we want to explain the significant transformation in the political possibilities open to women in the early 20th century, we cannot ignore the
activism of socialist feminists of both genders. A narrow focus on the institutions of the left has, ironically, historically marginalized a much more interesting, original, and boundary-busting socialist-feminist movement.

Gender, Sexuality, and Social Evolution

Apart from the excessively quoted editorial columns of the *Western Clarion*
and positions enunciated by SPC Dominion Executive members, especially
from 1908 to 1911, pro-feminist positions were orthodoxy on the Canadian
left. In theory, socialists were expected to favour the equality of women. Not
to do so flouted canonical works and, for many, conflicted with the essential
purpose of socialism itself.[24] Knowledge of and respect for certain approved
texts on the woman question were generally expected. For those at the
Spencerian pole of the continuum, core texts included *Women and Economics*
by Charlotte Perkins Gilman and *Woman and Labour* by Olive Schreiner; for
those at the Marx pole, *Woman under Socialism* by August Bebel – Daniel De
Leon's unfortunately mistitled translation of *Die Frau und der Sozialismus* –
and *The Origin of the Family, Private Property and the State* by Friedrich Engels. A properly read first formation activist would in theory have an understanding of both literatures, and be able to articulate the woman question
in a scientific and egalitarian framework.

Theory and reality often collided. Many movements within the left were
almost exclusively male – the IWW in the lumber camps, the UMW in the coalfields – and at best episodically expressed support for the equality of women.
More subtly, in a society in which "men's spaces" and "women's spaces" were
often carefully set apart from each other, at least in middlebrow respectable
society, the male-dominated organizations often met in taverns – there is even

some suggestion from Alberta of UMW District 18 meetings being held in a brothel[25] – and allowed for public smoking, setting up imposing barriers for all but the most defiantly unconventional of women. Socialist parties and trade unions did not invent these patterns, nor did they often clearly challenge them.

Socialist feminists often supplemented Marx with up to date readings in evolutionary theory. That they drew extensively upon Spencer will occasion surprise, because of the Master's well-known views, broadcast in *The Principles of Psychology* and *The Study of Sociology*, on women's supposed natural inferiority to men. Many Spencerian Marxists, especially in Italy, used Spencer to bludgeon the demands of women – they even considered women's waged work to be "counter-evolutionary." (In this they were seconding the opinions of many Canadian doctors.)[26] Trying to draw feminist approaches out of such a body of evolutionary theory might seem rather like trying to make a silk purse out of a sow's ear.

Yet such was the inescapable assignment confronting socialist feminists in the heyday of social-evolutionary theory. Starting from the 1880s they took it up with imagination and courage. Some turned to the radical feminist writings of the young Spencer, whose passion for women's equality was more thoroughgoing than that of his fellow liberal John Stuart Mill.[27] More often they turned to the implications of radical organicism – to the concept of the "physiological division of labour" and to socialist parasitology. Socialist feminists could argue that to confine women to an artificially delimited separate sphere meant a perverse attempt to stunt the natural growth of individuals and to impede the course of evolution itself. Discrimination against women confined them to a parasitical status that was imprisoning for them as individuals and damaging to the entire social organism.

These interrelated evolutionary themes would echo powerfully among Canadian socialist feminists, especially after 1907. Why, asked these feminists, if a measure of a society's evolutionary advance was progress in the division of labour, increasing specialization, *and* the greater integration of functions, should this great all-encompassing evolutionary process halt at the doorstep of the domestic sphere? Why, when every other part of the economy was being rationalized and harmonized, should the household be left as an unassimilated "little ganglion of aborted economic processes?" – to quote Gilman's acerbic critique of the 1890s.[28] Why cling to patriarchal myths of a supposedly sacred "private sphere," when in fact sociology showed that the whole social world was interconnected – that the "public" and the "private" were intermeshed? By disregarding some specific Spencerian positions and focusing on the implications of his holistic sociology, socialist feminists could plausibly argue that they were simply applying Spencer to topics that the writer himself had not fully appreciated. When Wrigley Jr. referred to the U.S. publication

Socialist Woman as a good resource for those concerned to make socialism a "two-sex working class movement," he was recommending a publication with a clear left-Spencerian agenda: that of looking to evolutionary theory for arguments against the subordination of women.[29]

Socialist feminist theory – like historical materialism and evolutionary theory but perhaps even more so – was hardly a fixed meal in this period. After enthusiasts had digested the "big books" and then many of the "lesser works" on the woman question, the issues raised were still open for debate and discussion. These were highly interpretable texts. The most famous ones, those of Bebel and Engels, were opposites in style and, in a sense, competitors in approach.

August Bebel (1840–1913), although by no means as prestigious a name as Engels, exerted perhaps as much influence over North American leftists when it came to the woman question. He was both a product of and contributor to a German left tradition of male feminism. There was, according to writers Anne Lopes and Gary Roth, a core of "several tens of thousands of men who [would] in varying degrees help organize women workers, campaign for women's legal and political equality, support women's suffrage, financially back women's newspapers, and sanction the election of female delegates at all-women meetings to counteract gender bias in ostensibly gender-blind elections."[30] *Die Frau und der Sozialismus* was Bebel's life-work. He revised and expanded it six times after 1883, each time updating the empirical research and in some cases changing his position.[31] Canadian women's study groups consulted De Leon's flawed translation, a hefty volume of some 379 tightly packed pages. They were in good company worldwide. More than 140,000 copies of Bebel's text were in circulation in Germany, and it was translated into more than 20 languages. As Richard J. Evans remarks, Bebel's work "formed the theoretical basis for the social democratic approach to female emancipation in every country where socialism existed."[32] It remained a controversial book well into the late 20th century, damned by some feminists for appropriating the voice of the women's movement (although, when he wrote it, there was not much of a German women's movement in evidence) and hailed by others as providing a scientific evolutionary answer to Mill's idealistic writings on the question, notably *On the Subjection of Women*.

Based on their close examination of Bebel's text, Lopes and Roth see the German theorist as someone who turned socialist theory against gender privilege – even the gender privileges enjoyed by socialist men. As they provocatively observe, thanks largely to Bebel the socialist movement drew attention to such feminist issues as sexual harassment and suffrage decades before they were picked up by other feminist groups. "Feminism was as much a men's as it was a women's movement," they argue. Moreover, the "men's feminism" they describe was not just a force among men: they document cases of women whose lives and outlooks were transformed by the book, which was read out loud in many women's circles. Much of the book's appeal lay in its sympathetic and detailed evocations of everyday life. As one seamstress remembered of the book: "Because everything was so new it took considerable effort to come to terms with Bebel's views. I had to break with so many things that I previously regarded as correct."[33]

"It was more than a book," the renowned feminist and socialist Clara Zetkin said of *Woman under Socialism*. "It was an event."[34]

For many other socialist feminists, the key event was provided by Engels's much shorter, yet more cosmic, rendition of the question – *The Origin of the Family, Private Property and the State*. As Lopes and Roth remark, one of the enduring ironies of socialist history is that Engels's book, which began as a mere pamphlet on recent anthropological writing and vaulted into the socialist canon with the virtual deification of "Marx and Engels" that occurred in the Soviet Union, overtook the likes of Bebel's much more encyclopedic study. Of a piece with Engels's passion for the telescopic cosmic approach, *The Origin* locates the beginnings of women's oppression in a very early stage of human social evolution – essentially, in the transition from "savagery" to "barbarism." Engels's theory was to the Marxist theory of women's oppression "what *Capital* is to Marxist economics," as Varda Burstyn would later remark. Certainly some left Canadians thought so – an energetic Toronto study group, formed in 1908 and ultimately influential within the Social Democratic Party, focused specifically on it.[35]

Canonical or not, *The Origin* is an odd book, half sober-sided Victorian armchair anthropology and half a quietly hilarious send-up of the dire tedium of heterosexual bourgeois marriage.[36] The first, "serious" side of the book has not fared well as science. It is a vintage Victorian production, drawing heavily and reverently on the work of Lewis Henry Morgan (1818–81), hailed improbably by Engels as a thinker in the same league as Darwin and Marx himself.[37] Morgan's account of the overthrow of "mother-right" (the legal and political predominance of women, particularly mothers) recalls the grander cosmic speculations of Spencer, and Engels's own narrative of the supposed downfall of "mother-right" provides the rationale for "*the world-historic defeat of the female sex*."[38] Analytically, as Juliet Mitchell remarks, Engels's solution to the origin of women's oppression was schematic and economistic, rendering it merely an aspect of the rise of private property.[39] Paradoxically, it could be (and by some was) read as a text justifying the marginalization of women's issues altogether – since, being little more than the reflection of property relations, they would automatically solve themselves once the property question was resolved.[40] On the other hand – and there is often an "other hand" with Engels's texts – the work nonetheless did bring women's agency into the core of historical materialism. If the "female sex" had suffered a "world-historic defeat," could not this same historical agent contemplate a "world-historic victory"? More generally, the cosmic significance that Engels bestowed on the woman question meant that it became something that had to be incorporated into Marxism. The importance of being Engelsian meant that even when Canadian commentators seemed to be talking about conditions in the present day, they might actually be glossing the work of the Founding Father.[41]

The enduring value of Engels's work lies in its utopianism and unbridled humour. It reconstructed, out of very ambiguous data, an image of a golden past, and projected from that an image of a radiant future; it also indulged in a series of explosive *bon mots* calculated to startle its Victorian readers out of their leather armchairs, in a freewheeling, almost campy satire on bourgeois marriage. It subjected that most sacred institution to a series of lethal putdowns. Long engagements? Merely a guarantee, snorted Engels, that men will go to the brothels more often. "Till death do us part?" In Engels's depiction of the bourgeois world, both husbands and wives slept around, the wedding vow was a dead letter – and all that "Protestant monogamy achieves, taking the average of the best cases, is a conjugal partnership of leaden boredom, known as 'domestic bliss.'"[42] Most bourgeois marriages were merely disguised forms of prostitution. Much as many good socialists rejected the claim that socialism aspired to destroy marriage and the family, there was in Engels's text a playful dismantling of ideals that most respectable Canadians took very seriously.

Like many satires, Engels's is founded on firm preconceptions about the normal state of affairs – which will return once the class question is settled. For all his convention-challenging squibs about monogamy, Engels never doubts that "family duties" are the natural province of women.[43] Once they enter the world of full economic equality, both women and men will become spontaneously and happily monogamous – at every age group and in every setting. (It is heteronormatively assumed throughout, of course, that only male/female couplings are natural.) What would disappear from monogamy under socialism were "all the features stamped upon it through its origin in property relations; these are, in the first place, supremacy of the man, and, secondly, indissolubility. The supremacy of the man in marriage is the simple consequence of his economic supremacy, and with the abolition of the latter will disappear of itself." In the future men and women would enjoy monogamous, intense relationships. Once those partnerships palled, as the worldly Engels thought very likely to be the case for men, the individuals involved would move briskly on to the next relationship, without suffering poverty as a result.[44]

Engels's text was open to many different readings. Problematic as *The Origin* is, both politically and scientifically, as yet another utopian text it opened up a new realm of freedom. It suggested the real-world possibility that the hypothesized age of mother-rule might some day be restored.[45] It projected an ideal in which women *as a sex* were beings not just with reproductive functions to fill but collective historical interests to defend. "The family" had a history; family forms were historically variable and socially constructed; women were not, and should not be, powerless; and equality between the sexes, having once existed, was a real-world possibility. Many socialists in Canada were quite comfortable with the text's stage by stage narrative of inevitable development, yet some male first formationists managed to miss the main point of Engels's text – that all such stages had different implications for men and women and for the structure of the family.[46]

The "canonical" literature of Bebel and Engels was deceptively "scientific" in its certainty and ambiguous in its implications. Apart from sceptical asides, neither Bebel nor Engels "criticized the sexual division of labour itself," as Karen Hunt points out in her study of the woman question within the British Social Democratic Federation.[47] Engels makes the woman question a central part of socialist analysis – after all, "the first class oppression coincides with that of the female sex by the male" – yet, as Hunt remarks, "the nature of the original sex antagonism is not made clear; it merely slides into one of class antagonism." The sex/class analogy remains a "remarkably muddy" concept – "Was women's oppression to be understood in theoretical terms as a qualitatively distinct kind of oppression from that of class?" Hunt asks. "Women were to be integrated into the heart of socialism, its class analysis, through the sex/class analogy; yet that analogy precluded the emergence within socialist thinking of any developed understanding of women's oppression. All too often, the woman question found a socialist 'answer' by disappearing into the class, or 'social,' question."[48]

Within the left, one response to the work of Bebel and Engels was the idea that social evolution, through an inevitable process of differentiation, led to the two sexes drawing ever nearer together, and a conviction that socialism would mean the marginalization if not erasure of inequalities. Gilman, Willard, and an entire school of "socialist feminists" in the United States, and prominent socialist feminist Mary Norton of British Columbia, were deeply attracted by utopian visions of a future in which men and women were equals – a vision powerfully sustained by the young Spencer's ardent feminism. Another response suggested that the truest socialist feminist was the class warrior, because without the abolition of capitalism all talk of sexual equality was simply hot air. In this response, raising women's consciousness meant the close articulation of the woman question with the workers' movement and an acceptance of many aspects of conventional heterosexuality, including monogamous marriages and even restrictions on women's employment. Otherwise the left would become distracted from the primary historic task of scientific education upon which the fullest emancipation of women itself depended.

These two responses clashed, with the result that, after about 1908, a third position began to emerge and gain adherents. This approach suggested that the development of consciousness on the woman question depended upon a synthesis of the first two positions – yet one in which they were subtly transformed. This "new woman question" – significantly, it figured prominently among women feminists – entailed the concrete achievement of political tasks (such as suffrage, unemployment relief, war resistance) in ways that both welcomed women as equal class warriors *and* acknowledged the deep-seated evolutionary reasons as to why their historical trajectory was necessarily linked to, but distinguishable from, that of men. Although there were misogynists and sexists on the left, none of these three positions would have reflected their point of view – in essence, all three positions (utopian, class-centred, and praxis-based) were ways of thinking through "socialist feminism."

As Hunt suggests, on the left in general the woman question could be seen, paradoxically, as both crucial and marginal. The question was obviously important enough for groups like the SLP (and SPC) to invest time and energy in publicizing and debating it. They could denounce capitalism as having destroyed once-happy proletarian families, forcing thousands of men to tramp the country in search of work. Capitalism had forced children into the labour market and created "arduous toil" for women. Yet what was to be done? U.S. SLPer Olive Johnson counselled a prospective activist against becoming a "ridiculous, over-bearing and domineering" proponent of women's rights (although she thought only the most "pig-headed" chauvinists would resist enfranchisement), largely because doing so would divert time and energy from the first priority of the socialist woman, the "battle of education" for the salvation of the entire working class. Proponents of this position protested any insinuation that they were against demands for the "rights of women," because in their analysis such demands would only be fulfilled with the abolition of wage slavery.[49]

Critics often drew upon conventional ideas of motherhood to bolster their critiques of capitalism. John Spargo, who extended his almost pontifical omniscience to the woman question, wrote an opus on *Socialism and Motherhood* (1914) that developed this position at extravagant length. Socialists, said Spargo, demanded "equality of opportunity" as the "birthright of every child." Men might assent to this proposition on one level, but "a woman . . . especially if she be a mother," would really understand that this demand "voices the most revolutionary aspiration ever born of human hopes and nurtured by human hearts." Therefore, to be a true revolutionary, one had to defend the most traditional domestic arrangements. It was a crime that "women had to leave their families to go to work," and even if motherhood was not for all women, it was "surely woman's highest and holiest mission." A "curse" rested upon any social system that tore "millions of mothers away from the cradles of their babies" and forced them into "factories, workshops, stores, counting-houses and other women's kitchens to labor while their children are neglected."[50]

Some socialists, Gilman most notably, would follow Spargo whole-heartedly into the world of eugenics, "the study of the agencies under social control that may improve or impair the racial qualities of future generations, either physically or mentally," in the words of Francis Galton, its founding father. Karl Pearson would draw upon socialist parasitology to substantiate his racist eugenicism in 1905: "The stability of the nation depends essentially on the fitter stock being given sensibly greater fertility than the unfit stock."[51]

Significantly, the work of Olive Schreiner both allowed for an intensely realistic engagement with the question of women's work *and* scientific justification for a politics that rejected women's economic marginality not merely on "idealistic" grounds, but because such "parasitism" was counter-evolutionary and regressive. For the adherents of this position, socialist-feminist consciousness was neither the realization of a utopian politics of equality, nor the subordination of the woman question to the class question (albeit in a way that made the resolution of the second the precondition of solving the first). Rather, it was a matter of an arduously acquired awareness of the concrete history, present circumstances, and plausible future trajectory of actual women's struggles. This approach entailed a transition in *who* was "talking socialist feminism." After 1908 it might well be a woman speaking from a location outside the formal party structures, from one of the autonomous new socialist-feminist organizations, or perhaps outside the formal institutions of the left altogether. This position sought to combine evolutionary feminism and Marxism in a way that not only afforded a new springboard into theoretically informed activism, but also challenged the assumptions of both liberal feminists and Marxists. This position too might entail "maternal" arguments, but would cast them in a very different key than that found in Spargo and other such thinkers. The solution to the victimization of women in sweatshops was not to get them back into their kitchens but to agitate for effective and inclusive trade unionism, effective state inspection and regulation, and heightened social awareness through union label campaigns.[52] The proper socialist-feminist response to elevated women's unemployment, then, was to hail the entry of women into non-traditional roles as being essential to social-evolutionary progress (for without it "the race" ran the risk of degenerating) and to demand that women, like men, were in need of relief, both from the state and from other workers. *This* socialist feminism implicitly challenged the male "breadwinner" protectionism of most of the trade unions, the hypocrisy of the church, and the class prejudice of the mainstream suffrage movement.

Thus, although the first formation had a great deal to say about the woman question, and invariably tried to link it to evolutionary theory, its arguments did not add up to one consistent or coherent party line, but several.

It was provocative in its analysis and elusive in its prescriptions. Provocative: in its relentless drawing of links between marriage and prostitution, wedded bliss and women's oppression, monogamy and changes in the mode of production, romantic love with economic calculation – all of them analogies and parallels that could quite easily inspire skittish souls to discern in socialism the most monstrous modernity of all, one that threatened to smash their most intimate and necessary relationships. Yet also elusive: at the end of the day, were socialists "for" or "against" marriage, "for" or "against" suffrage, even "for" or "against" the far-ranging cultural revolution that would place male privileges, those of the "leading comrades" included, in the trash can of history? Whatever would become of London's Ernest Everhard if, instead of a future full of thrilling debating victories against emissaries of the ruling order and a domestic relationship in which he was free to reprogram his wife, he instead had to change diapers and do the dishes?

Putting the Utopian Tradition into Practice: Alice Chown

Of all the major figures of the early Canadian left, Alice Chown ranks with E.A. Partridge as one of the great Canadian exponents of utopian forms of living otherwise. Growing up in Kingston as the only surviving daughter of Edwin Chown and Amelia Anning, Chown was unusual in this cohort in having gone to university and in coming from an impeccably middle-class background. A relative of the eminent Methodist minister S.D. Chown, she made a considerable reputation as an activist within the Canadian Household Economics Association, wherein she argued that the level of women's emancipation could be gauged by their progress within the home. The death of her mother in 1906 liberated her from having to manage care for the older woman. "Today I am free. My first day of freedom! It is my new birth!" she exclaimed (through a thinly veiled autobiographical character) when released from this bondage, in an almost shocking defiance of the conventions of maternalism.[53] Now she was free to travel the globe in pursuit of her dream of the regeneration of the social world and more particularly of a thoroughgoing revolution in the relations of men and women, if they could but be released from forms of marriage that sacrificed the autonomy of women.

Chown played a significant role in the 1912 strike at the large clothing factory of Toronto's T. Eaton Company, a place long notorious for its low wages, long hours, unfair supervision, and vicious child-labour practices. A reporter in the city, she mobilized support for the strikers and even (unusual in that day and age) raised the issue of the sexual harassment of female workers by male foremen.[54] She was arrested with the strikers. The experience of the strike brought Chown face to face with the cramped conventionalism of middle-class feminism. "I tried to interest the various women's clubs," Chown remarked, "but I was amazed because they had no sympathy with the strikers, unless I had some tale of hardship to tell." They seemed uninterested in the "everyday longings" of the workers. To retain their interest, Chown had to tell, over and over, stories "of the bosses who favored the girls whom they could take out evenings, girls who had to sell themselves as well as their labor to get sufficient work to earn a living."[55]

Chown went on to describe this moment in a barely disguised description of the Equal Franchise League, thinly fictionalized as the "Woman's Political League." A woman representing the strikers' side of the dispute had been sent to the meeting to speak to the League. She made a "very wise and illuminating speech." Yet for all her eloquence, as Chown relates, the labour representative aroused a great deal of "hard feeling amongst the zealous suffragists, who were afraid that their pet cause would be hurt through being linked with an unpopular one."[56]

Chown came face to face with the difficult truth that class and ethnic divisions could often trump appeals to a common sisterhood. She had taken up a position that, Diana Chown observes, "was to distance herself effectively from the established society from which she sprang." She left Toronto for New York in 1913, once again to support striking workers. The people she found there – who would all be considered "so abnormal" in Kingston – were exploring "the coming ideas." Everywhere, she noted, people were reading Carlyle, Morris, and Ruskin.[57]

Out of these and many other involvements would emerge *The Stairway* (1921), another must-read book of the early 20th-century Canadian left. *The Stairway* takes the form of a diary in which the protagonist, whose life closely resembles that of Chown herself, reflects on her experiences on the left from a socialist and feminist perspective. The very title suggests the "onwards and upwards" ascent of our hero, who gravitates to utopian communities of assembled dissidents seeking a new way of life – "socialists, single-taxers, syndicalists, communistic anarchists, Tolstoyans, and people against private ownership." The purpose of this climb up the stairway of "evolutionary consciousness" was to achieve the one great objective in her life: the "emancipation of women."[58]

In *The Stairway*, men and women are alike engaged in thinking through and implementing a more rational design for living together – and, it must be said, male gurus figure far more centrally than do female authorities in articulating this vision of gendered enlightenment. What is strikingly modern about *The Stairway* is that although the narrator is ascending the stairway of evolutionary knowledge, she is always part of a collectivity. Chown's book is an early-20th-century pilgrim's progress through the places and times in which a collective living otherwise seemed wonderfully, tangibly real. Equally striking is the extent to which the narrative form allows the fictional Alice Chown to try out and discard successive solutions to the woman question, without ever really settling for any one of them.

In the diary entries, extending from 28 May 1906 to 10 June 1919, the protagonist moves from "Lakeside" (Kingston) through New York, London, and Toronto, ending up at "Hearthstone" (near Boston). "My Utopia exists!" the hero exclaims when she visits Letchworth, a visionary "garden city" north of London. "It was the procession of the great democracy – the democracy that includes women as well as men," she says of a march for political rights for women in London.[59]

The major intellectual influence on Chown's developing position on sexuality was Edward Carpenter (1844–1929), author of *Toward Democracy* (1883) and *Love's Coming of Age* (1896). Carpenter, cohabiting openly with his lover George Merrill and living in accordance with a vision of socialism that included a joyful celebration of same-sex love, was in many ways Spargo's and Schreiner's worst nightmare.[60] By selecting Carpenter as her intellectual beacon, or even (in her somewhat jarring words) one of her "gods," Chown was setting some distance between herself and the sexual mores of her native Kingston. Chown deeply admired Carpenter, in part because he had so completely defied "all conventions which men deem necessary, and which in return choke their souls." He had spurned "all appearances, all customs, all artificial needs, all false relations with people."[61]

The turn to Carpenter made sense in the context of Chown's intrepid and distinctive search to find a sexual order that conformed to socialist-feminist principles. An attractive aspect of her book, especially when it is set beside the first formation's more didactic texts, is its willingness to take a position on one page that is transcended 20 pages later. The protagonist's perspective on love, marriage, and sexuality evolves through the book. We can see her climbing step by step to a secular-humanist, sex-positive position similar in many respects to that developed by Emma Goldman, whose work Chown deeply admired and whose speeches tempted her to join with the New York anarchists.

Chown traces her hero's seven steps through the marriage question. The first (September 1906) constitutes an indignant refusal that one could live with a man without marrying him, sparked by a knowledge of visiting celebrity Maxim Gorky's widely debated "free relationship" with his partner: "It is incomprehensible to me that any one who has any claim to good morals should consider, for one moment, the possibility of a man and woman living together without a formal ceremony of marriage," Chown declares with bourgeois Kingstonian outrage. Then come discussions with her friend Norman, a scathing socialist critic of the bourgeois hypocrisies involved in compulsory monogamy, and a heart-warming if discreet representation of life *chez* Edward Carpenter, a man "truthful only to himself ... who saw clearly the coming time when men shall all be brothers, and who chose to live in the coming democracy here and now." (To be much more candid than that would have probably resulted in the banning of the book.) Next – the third step – our hero receives a missive from a proponent of Marxism, who advises her that the "sex question is changing on account of economic changes." Sexuality shall henceforth be a merely "natural function."

Then our hero, although deeply attracted to one of her suitors, is reluctantly obliged to decline him, on the eminently first formation grounds that they have incompatible "theories of sex relations." Taking up the position of Gilman, she now believes firmly that "sex relations must be limited to reproduction." (How this fits in with her esteem for the blatantly nonconforming Carpenter is not clear.) She follows that with an intense session with a Freudian in Toronto, who "pulled me up a big step to where I was willing to know the facts of sex as they are ..." Now she repents of her earlier judgmentalism: "Henceforth I hope I shall be brave and not try to cover over my own or any other person's sex experience with some moral platitudes." The sixth step comes when, on visiting Ariel Colony, a Ruskinian experiment in England, she has a moment of epiphany in being confronted with a scandal. A married man has left his wife and gone to live, openly and unrepentantly, with a new lover. Their cohabitation poses a moral challenge to the colony, but in Chown's new view, closely aligned with that of Grant Allen, if the two were actually in love and living in open honesty with themselves and each other, "the colony has justified itself."

Finally, after yet another conversation with another male "god," on 21 September 1915 she is jolted out of her complacency by his thought that, in the future, unions between two lovers, once no longer enforced by law, would be suffused with a new spirit: "We shall go on cherishing the same old ideals of human conduct, but with new motives and new inspiration." Free love would hence be a great boon to humanity. Our narrator finds that these remarks give her another "rude jerk upward." With their help she further ascends her stairway. And where will her complicated if upward journey end? "I have built my stairway, and from the top I can see the level road of security and certainty stretching ahead. I have gained the faith that will illuminate the road. I shall march serenely. 'The future I can face, for I have proved the past.' I shall go singing all my days, 'I know what I have believed.' ... I have won my freedom."[62]

The Stairway is a didactic and unrealistic novel – did any actual individual ever spend this much of his or her time obsessing over the sex question? – and the succession of male gurus becomes somewhat tedious, yet its passionate earnestness, its sense that there must be, at the top of the stairway, a *right* way for men and women to live and love, is a great redeeming quality. Few Canadian books convey quite so vividly the early 20th-century utopian search for a solution to the vexed question of how one should best live one's life under the perplexing conditions of modernity. Compared to what is by now a large library of left books prescribing sure and certain positions on the personal and the political, Chown's novel vividly reminds us that there was no sure and certain feminist position on a host of questions that socialism had to confront.

Chown left posterity with one of the most fascinating first formation texts, a veritable catalogue of old utopianisms. "Step by step my faith in laws, institutions, customs, enforced on me by some external authority, whether of church, state, or Mrs. Grundy, had to be destroyed, to be replaced by faith in the life within me," Chown wrote, describing a sense of an "open sexual modernity" characteristic of many in her cohort. "Through my contact with others I had to learn that in them as in myself was the craving for freedom to express the love, the life, within them. Alike we have traversed arid roads of selfish individualism, self-will, egotism, that we might rid ourselves of the garments that choked the life within us."[63]

The Political and Social Democracy Question, 1890–1915

For the majority of first formation leftists, women's suffrage was simply a non-negotiable demand. The left's democratic idealism emphasized the free discussion of a host of issues normally kept out of the limelight in Canada, and it also translated into the massively supported demand across virtually all segments of the left for complete women's suffrage – with the glaring exception of the SPC, whose single-plank platform did not allow for it (or indeed any other "immediate" demand). Certainly, well-documented polemics written by McKenzie, Fillmore, and Kingsley served as examples of the arrogance of male socialists and their indifference to such a basic democratic demand. Yet the overall record of most of the first formation, apart from such SPC figures, was clearly on the other side of this question.

The honour of running the first socialist women candidates evidently belongs to the SLP in Ontario, which from 1899 on ran several women in its forays into local politics. Full adult suffrage was written into the founding program of the very first CSL branch. As Wayne Roberts remarks, outside of the SPC, "every current of the socialist movement was a forceful advocate of the suffrage," including *Cotton's Weekly*.[64] That paper supported not only the peaceful acquisition by Canadian women of the right to vote but also the turn of British suffrage militants to violent direct action – the smashing of windows, the forcible disruption of their opponents' meetings, and other acts of defiance against the liberal regime in the motherland. "We do not want to have to coax for a thing that should be ours by right," Mary Wisdom [Cotton] urged readers. "We are going to insist upon having a vote. When that day arrives we will see to it, that some of the infamous man-made laws now in force are abolished in short order." She added: "We are pledged to work, study, speak and write towards this end, for we are heartily sick of being governed, ruled, judged, sentenced, imprisoned and even hanged by men and man-made laws."[65]

When the SDPC split away from the SPC, it inscribed women's political equality on its banners with unusual eloquence: "To remove the bonds that hold the working woman in double slavery, to combat the crying evils that today make woman's work a curse instead of a blessing, to give women political freedom as a means of winning economic freedom, it is for this that the Social Democratic Party demands votes for women." Many of the male feminists in Canada were outraged by the political disempowerment of women, "the greatest crime of the century," in the words of Colin McKay.[66] They would find themselves not only writing letters on behalf of women's enfranchisement, but also becoming militants within such organizations as the Men's League for Woman's Suffrage.[67] William Irvine even wrote a play, *The Spinsters' Convention*, as a work of propaganda for the cause. He would subsequently be instrumental in the election campaign of the first woman parliamentarian in the British Empire.

If socialists raised concerns about specific suffrage proposals, they generally did so because the mainstream suffrage movement was sometimes willing to preserve anti-democratic property restrictions in the envisaged new political regime.[68] Moreover, even the SPC was on balance pro-suffrage rather than otherwise – since, repeatedly, Socialist MLAs James Hawthornthwaite and John Place fought tenaciously in the legislature for the enfranchisement of women. As was the case in other respects, the organization and its organ did not always follow the same line. The *Clarion*'s cultivation of a scandalous style, which was of a piece with its equally hubristic certainties about coal miners, may also have reflected the possibility of down-to-earth advantages in sales and notoriety. The paper plainly did not speak even for the party with which it was most closely identified. On suffrage, the record of the early Canadian left was more consistent and democratic than that of many of its far grander and more sophisticated European counterparts.[69]

Synthesizing Socialism and Feminism: Francis Beynon

If Alice Chown was in some ways caught up in "male feminism," one in which male authorities on socialism and sexuality enlightened the woman pilgrim from Canada, Francis Marion Beynon, the author of *Aleta Dey*, suggested how the discourse on a new world for women would start to look, once women themselves began to appropriate it.[70]

Beynon was the second-youngest of the seven children of two devout Scots-Irish-Canadian Wesleyan Methodists. When her father was 54 and her mother 42 they moved their farming family west to a homestead near Hartney, Man. Many troubles ensued. Her mother died of cancer in 1898; her father failed in business and died in 1906. Beynon, who had trained to be a primary school teacher, left the rural hamlet for good in 1902. She eventually chose work in the advertising department of a large Winnipeg store. Her elder sister Lillian was a journalist with the city's leading Liberal newspaper, the Manitoba *Free Press*. Both sisters became prominent journalists and front-ranking members of the pro-suffrage Political Equality League of Manitoba. Beynon became the women's editor of *The Grain Growers' Guide*, and from 1912 to 1917 she informed a wide readership on topics ranging from suffrage to sourdough.

Beynon was a remarkable journalist, and her page in the *Guide* stands as one of the most powerful explorations of contemporary socialist-feminist themes. Under her inspired direction, the pages devoted to "The Country Homemakers" brought into the conventional "women's page" a much fuller recognition of modernity. Even the page's appearance was designed to be "free from all the fussy little curly wurlies with which it is commonly deemed necessary to ornament the heading of a woman's page."[71] Beynon was quite conscious of having taken a mildewed and patronizing tradition – "It was only yesterday that women's pages used to be filled with prescriptions for making furniture out of boxes, beauty hints and instructions for the young girl as to the words in which she should bid adieu to her gentleman caller" – and changing it beyond recognition: "Within the last few years we have advanced a revolution or two."[72]

The humble women's page was, in Beynon's mind, part of a world feminist revolution, which she (like Engels) traced to forces of social evolution stretching back to the prehistoric age. "It seems to me that this is proof positive that there is something fundamentally wrong with their present position," she argued. "No movement spreads like an infection all over the world as this has done without there being at the bottom of it a great human need."[73]

As an ardent disciple of Schreiner, Beynon clearly wanted to introduce a much more exacting, unsentimental, and modern tone to the discussion of what she herself called the "Woman Question." To do this first required a great refusal of the indignities, humiliations, and cruelties borne by Prairie farm women. Here lay Beynon's most unusual contribution. In essence, she used insights derived from Schreiner to initiate a women's consciousness-raising group in print. In a shared "culture of correspondence," mediated by Beynon, a general publication oriented mainly to male grain growers became the site of a feminist revolution.

In the pages of *The Grain Growers' Guide* women found a place to speak new words of rage about their position of dependence upon men. One of the most widely noticed letters came from "A North-West Woman," who wrote in

1912 to the *Guide* to describe her plight as "A Tight-Wad's Wife." As "North-West Woman" told the story, once she had dreamed of raising a happy family on a prosperous farm. In her family of origin she had never been obliged to ask for anything. Her parents had happily provided the best they could afford. Then she married the wrong man, someone from a very different background. They began homesteading at the bottom rung, on poor land, without experience or management skills, and almost no surplus cash. She believed it was wrong to spend money on herself when they had children to clothe, whereas he thought they should spend money on pleasurable excursions. Soon he stopped asking her to accompany him on those outings.

Now, in somewhat more prosperous times – they owned six quarters of land, with good crops, stock, and machinery, buggies, and covered cutters – she found herself poor and oppressed. The mould had been set: he had all the money, and she had none. "Why should a wife have to ask for money?" she asked. "Has she not as good a right to it as her husband? . . . Oh! it makes my heart ache when I think of so many sacrifices a woman makes and then is told he is the only one who is making a dollar when he has sons working on the farm, so that he has not had to hire a man for years, and when the boys ask for a few dollars he cusses and asks what they want with money."

Her husband believed himself entitled to leave the farm and visit distant hotels, but his wife and sons were humiliatingly begrudged every penny. "I feel I have a perfect right to a share; I at least might have a hired girl's wages, for I know I work too hard to save every penny I can, and we are not poor. If I want to go anywhere or for a drive, I'm told they are tired of driving, they would rather lie on the couch and smoke and sleep, while I do my work. Now, thank God, every man is not like this. Maybe it is my fault, for I always felt I should be used liked a helpmate in place of a slave."[74]

Other women soon joined in these explorations of the personal and the political. "I would like to take the opportunity to express my experience about men," wrote "A True Friend of Unhappy Wives." Her hard-working woman "friend" – if it was not the writer herself – had worked long hours to keep her family clothed and fed while her husband paid for the land. She had even laboured outside as a farmhand, to spare the expense of hiring one. Yet all her sacrifices had earned her a hard, bitter life. "He has always been mean to her, abusing her, and now when he is well-to-do tells her she has got no share in the place whatever." Her husband even told their boys that she had no claim to the property. Her only "rights" were "to work and say nothing." Although generous to his boys, he would give her no money for clothes or medicine, and stopped her from selling eggs and a chicken to raise the cash herself. Here was a portrait of "humiliation."[75]

Even more compelling was the tale of "A Sufferer," who was convinced that "you city people" knew "nothing of the hardships on a farm and being deprived of necessaries." She began with the widely shared homesteader experience of beginning in a one-room cabin, with almost no money, horses acquired on credit, and a pile of additional debt on the building and equipment. She too had helped outside when they were too poor to hire a man. But a degree of prosperity for the farm had brought no benefits to her. Her husband's relatives, not her, seemed about to benefit from all their joint labour. And then, broaching a more difficult issue, she exclaimed: "Another things is this, that wife-beaters should get the lash in the West. If a man wants to fight, why does he not fight a man instead of fighting his wife? He is a coward and is afraid to tackle a man." So he abused her, and if she did not like it, she could always leave – with nothing. So said the law. "Is life worth living when it is only hell on earth and wives are to have nothing when they are old, after years of toil and deprivations?"[76]

There followed many additional letters on the plight of farm wives: "It certainly seems to me there should be a law of some kind to protect such wives," remarked "Mother of Three," continuing: "and not every law be made for the protection of the men who can be kind or otherwise just as they chance to feel and the woman has nothing to say. If the woman does not get the chance to vote the laws should be made to make her at least a partner in the home and land instead of a slave."[77]

A "North-West Woman" wrote in again in January 1913 to defend herself against those who had questioned her meek submission to her husband, and to defend the reputation of her sons (whom some correspondents had demonized along with her husband). The moral of her story, she now realized, was plain: "Now I look back I see I should not have let him put himself first and me last; but I did not want to fight for my rights. I wanted him to grant them of his own free will, but he never has yet. Some women can stand up and demand what is right, but I want what is right given willingly and freely or not at all."[78]

Were such individual stories of hardship and tragedy experienced by many Prairie women or only a few? According to *The Grain Growers' Guide* itself in 1913, they spoke of systemic conditions that oppressed farm women. It argued, "Many farmers' wives have gone to early graves through over-work and too little care in the struggle of pioneering, when a little more relief from heavy burdens and a little more recreation would have spared them to their children and their husbands for many years."[79] The *Guide* also noted a widely reprinted story revealing the national debt that Canada as a whole owed to the suffering Prairie wife. "It is hardly possible to exaggerate the limitations and difficulties of her life. Going from the East, where social privileges are many, and taking up her task amid the solitude of the prairies, she faces a life that no one can understand who has not experienced it." A recent visitor in Edmonton observed, on two occasions, women driven insane by the isolation and hardship of homesteading being placed on Eastbound trains. It was "fair warning" to the "women of the East" who imagined Prairie life as "a golden picture of waving grain, framed in blue sky and varnished by sunshine."[80] On the contrary, it could be grimly isolating and oppressive for women.

Beynon, whose own life had taken her from a struggling homestead to the lights of Winnipeg, understood very well the false promises of modernity. She wrote with great power and sympathy about the rural girls who flocked to the city in response to its Exhibition, gazed upon "the gay streamers, and the prettily decked shop windows, and in the evenings the theatres and moving picture shows and brightly lighted streets," and resolved to abandon their old farm haunts and come to the city to live. Yet when they arrived they were often confronted with cold, brusque employers. What seemed like rudeness to them was simply the new business culture of the city: for the employer, the new arrival from the West was "only an atom, a single unit in a great system," regarded as being little different than "the office fixtures and the typewriting machine."[81]

Beynon was particularly disgusted by how the legal system treated violence against women. One "human wretch" was not only "an ordinary wife-beater but his chief pastime, when under the influence of liquor was to beat up his wife and children and then kick them out of doors." One of his children had died from this treatment. His punishment for a repeat offence? Six months in jail. "If he had stolen a lace collar or a handful of jewelry from one of the department stores he would probably have been sent down for a year or two," Beynon remarked. It was just one example of the injustices piled on women by a system that discriminated against them. She urged men, many of whom shared her indignation, to join the movement to right such wrongs, to unite with progressive women to sweep out the cobwebs of tradition.[82]

A "New Man," she said, was emerging as the complement of the "New Woman." Half of the executive of the Political Equality League in Winnipeg was made up of men, and the membership was "pretty evenly divided between the sexes."[83] The "New Man" of the feminist movement would be as "different from the tyrannical licentious man of ancient days as the modern woman is from the weeping incompetent wife of David Copperfield." Taking notice of the numerous male feminists, Beynon exclaimed that many of the "new men" were "more anxious for the enfranchisement of women than the women themselves and would willingly open to them the gate leading into every field of employment." Such profoundly enlightened men wanted their wives to be, not drudges or slaves, but comrades. They would readily see that the "laws have been made for them," and that women had done the housework they had no interest in doing. Although many would defend their privileges, Beynon found it "very praiseworthy" that so many had been willing to give up those benefits "in the interests of a square deal." New women and new men would together unite in egalitarian marriages, in which there would be no boss and no underlings: "There is no 'boss' in this household. It is a partnership where each one does his share of the work and the profits are shared equally whether large or small."[84]

For Beynon, this new world of women could be best grasped by those who had read Schreiner's masterwork, *Woman and Labour*. This "splendid book" was sold by the *Guide*'s own book department for $1.25, and Beynon wanted her audience to be inspired by it: "Read it. It will do you good." It was undoubtedly "one of the greatest books on the Feminist Movement." For Beynon, Schreiner was simply "one of the greatest women of this, or any other age." For her readers on the farm, some of whom may have been perplexed by their sudden immersion in the first formation's speculative anthropology, Beynon summarized at considerable length *Woman and Labour*'s metahistorical argument. Sparing her readers Schreiner's lengthy disparagements of parasites of various descriptions, Beynon captured the evolutionary feminist's core position: "It is one of the inexorable laws of nature that a hard-working motherhood is necessary to the growth and expansion of the race."[85]

Beynon herself had seen proof of this pattern with her own eyes. She knew of a brilliant man who had unaccountably married a woman "with the most primitive mentality" and had consequently left the world with a legacy of seven stupid, inefficient offspring. Yet even this grim fate was kinder than that of the lazy women of the ancient world, whose pampered indolence had led to generations of "fops with scented hair and showing a decided tendency to mental degeneration." A race could be "no greater or more virile than its motherhood" and would only thrive "when it has a hard-working womanhood."[86] A pampered or slovenly womanhood might create monsters – dandies and degenerates.

For Beynon, Schreiner's theory offered an avenue to a systematic understanding of the position of 20th-century women. With wars, famines, pestilence, and high infant morality becoming things of the past, women were no longer required by evolution to bear large numbers of children. Moreover, machines were making such large families redundant and the expenses of educating children had become so high that parents could no longer afford large families. Then what, Beynon asked, was to become of women? "Are they to fritter away their lives at bridge parties and pink teas and shopping and gossiping because men stand at the break in the hedge of convention, which has enclosed them for years, blocking every path that leads to useful toil?" Not if they followed the lead of a heroic few women who were already "bobbing up serenely" as doctors, lawyers, mayors, and delegates to political conventions. "These women are the breakers of new trails, the leaders in a great movement that is stirring all womankind." The men who argued that such pioneers were endangering "the future of the race" had it exactly wrong: such women, by refusing pampered lives of privilege, were combatting patterns of indolence whose outcome would be degeneration.[87]

What was most remarkable about Beynon's journalism in *The Grain Growers' Guide* was how she brilliantly adapted the 19th-century journalistic conventions of the "readers' clubs" made famous by the *Family Herald and Weekly Star* to the requirements of feminism. The page, with its "nice cosy sort of name," often seemed an incongruous mixture of feminist outrage and the location of recipes for such "delectable meat dishes" as Baked Ham, Roast Goose, Chicken Pie, and Beef à la Mode (to cite the offerings of Christmas day 1912). An impassioned, critical dialogue with her readers was part of the "new order of things" that she wanted her page to prefigure.[88] As an apt student of Schreiner, and arguably reflecting her status as a successful middle-class journalist, Beynon often urged her desperate women correspondents to take militant personal steps.

Power relations within the home mirrored the interests and ideologies of men outside it. As Beynon wondered, subversively, where did the saying "Woman's place is in the home" come from? "Some man said so and it was echoed around the world because most men felt so. They decided that woman's place was the home, because they wanted her to stay there. I never yet knew a man who had any fondness for washing dishes and scrubbing floors, so they think it is the ideal work for a woman." Even leaving beds unmade or dishes unwashed, or investing time in fluffing hair and polishing shoes, could be interpreted as emancipatory acts, if they were understood as such. To the "North-West Woman" with her "bitterness," Beynon was blunt: "I hope you will forgive me if I say that I think you are to blame for your condition, not because you feel you should be treated as a helpmate, but because you do not insist upon that kind of treatment. . . . It is time that husband of yours was jerked up short and made to right about face." Rather discounting the woman's account of her own personal poverty, she recommended that she take an extended trip away from home and "make a point of getting some fashionable clothes while you are away." Such direct personal action would help her family understand how hard she worked. To the woman whose "true friend" had endured a spiteful ungenerous husband and his grasping relatives, she said, "I'm sorry for your friend, but nevertheless I think she is a simpleton to put up with it. When she can make money by working for others why doesn't she either bring her husband to his senses or leave him?"[89]

It followed from this sometimes harsh critique of deferential or timid women that Beynon, echoing Schreiner, would construct a post-romantic stance on modern marriage, one focused upon the economics of the relationship. Beynon was exacting in her critique of seemingly chivalrous men who were oblivious to the deeply structured economic realities of women's subordination. She was once told of a wealthy man who had refused to give his wife an allowance. The husband's position was that his wife could already spend freely – simply by asking him for whatever money she needed. In Beynon's eyes, this only *seemed* like generosity. " 'In order to make a good fellow of himself,' I said, 'he is subjecting his wife to the life-long humiliation of having to ask for every cent of money she spends.' You may depend on it that she wouldn't keep asking for an allowance if she didn't want it."[90]

Many wives worked 12-hour days; their labour added to their husbands' wealth. Why were they then different from workers? Did managers of businesses believe that they were performing a charitable act when they paid their employees at the end of the week? Yet even this analogy understated the case, Beynon urged. Wives should be full partners, entitled to half the profits. Yet, flagrantly, they were denied their rights. The male farmer typically invested money in machinery, disregarding the slavery of his wife: "I have seen it hundreds of times," Beynon said. "The woman slaves early and late for fifteen or twenty years while John tacks on another quarter section on the east and an extra half on the west and builds a new barn on the home place and at last, just as they are about to move into the new house about which she has been dreaming all these years, she dies." Whatever the official cause of death, Beynon would call it *Landitis*, "a fatal ailment peculiar to western farmers' wives."[91]

Without a clear economic understanding between the contracting parties, marriage could be a death sentence for Prairie women. Without a scientific concept of housework, allowing for the efficient calibration of means and ends, financial resources, and family objectives, "domestic life is a muddle culminating in a deficit." Without enlightened education, disseminated through the *Guide* in such pamphlets as *The Most Beautiful Story in the World*, *How to Teach the Truth to Children*, and *The Nobility of Boyhood*, the children of the family would remain mired in ignorance and conceivably suffer, as in the case of boys, "the terrible consequence to the young man of impurity of thought and deed."[92]

How could this program of women's enlightenment be extended beyond the confines of the household? Prairie women especially needed to cultivate a "broader outlook on life."[93] One of the most ambitious of Beynon's schemes was the creation of a network of clubs wherein women would combine the practical discussion of homemaking issues – "the preparation and uses of foods, care of poultry, making and marketing of butter, care of children and sanitation come naturally to mind" – with "municipal, Provincial and Dominion questions – homesteads for women, Direct Legislation, suffrage or any other matter of great moment which interests them."[94] In this variant the suffrage struggle was not so much a mild-mannered "maternalist" campaign to houseclean the political system as it was an aspect of a far-reaching struggle to change the totality of women's lives.

In all of this Beynon had gone well beyond the conventions of her time in so candidly linking the personal with the political. Some men worried that, by publishing letters from angry women, Beynon was opening up the floodgates of bitterness. "I think if such letters would not be printed or written it would be better," remarked one male reader, "because there are a number of girls who read our page and it makes them feel hard towards men, even their father and brothers. Now, I'm talking from experience." *The Grain Growers' Guide* itself, in an editorial in April 1913, generally supportive of Beynon's positions, nonetheless took care to discourage any perception that it was seeking "to encourage friction between man and woman."[95]

Beynon – who in much of the pre-war period inhabited a political space at once "new liberal" and "socialist" – created a discursive zone wherein a feminist enlightenment might be imagined. The vulnerability of her audacious experiment, dependent as it was upon the wider commercial and ideological world of *The Grain Growers' Guide*, became increasingly obvious as the Great War passed from rumour to reality. When Beynon thought about war, she again drew heavily upon Schreiner. Countering traditional "separate sphere" arguments that defined war as an exclusively male zone, Schreiner argued that "woman alone knows the cost of human life" because only women supplied "the primal munition of war – the men who are slain on the battlefield." Compared to the sufferings of women in pregnancy and child-rearing, "the most trying march of the soldier seems comparatively easy." Women knew "the agony and danger that must be faced every time a woman goes down into the valley of the shadow of death to bring a man into this world."

Consequently, as women's influence grew, so too would more peaceable ways of settling international disputes. Yet even if war did persist in the modern world, modern technology meant that women were just as capable of waging it as men. A woman could take aim and fire as effectively as a man, and women were intrinsically more patient than men, as demonstrated by "the women on the farm who rise at four in the morning and are on the go until eight or ten at night and all the time having half a dozen things that want doing at once." Most men "would do something desperate" if they were condemned for days and years to the routine of the average farm wife, with "baby shrieking and Molly trying to tip over the pan of boiling water and the potatoes needing to be drained and the table to be set." Both arguments helped Beynon make her point: "If war should prove to be a necessity of our modern life, instead of a relic of barbarism as we think it," women should not be shut out of public affairs.[96]

It was, perhaps, one thing for the "Women's Page" to advance arguments specific to women. It was, in 1914, a far different matter for Beynon to criticize the war. As early as 1912 Beynon's sceptical appraisal of militarism was drawing the hostile notice of her more jingoistic readers.[97] In league with her sister Lillian, Beynon resisted the majority of the feminist movement within Canada and the British Empire more generally by opposing the war. In 1917 the Beynons' lives were disrupted when Lillian's husband was relieved of his *Free Press* position after approving of an anti-conscription speech. Shaken by the fiercely militaristic climate of Winnipeg, both sisters moved to New York, where Francis wrote her important book *Aleta Dey*, an unforgettable portrait of one socialist feminist's response to love, war, and marriage.

The novel follows Aleta from her childhood through her career as a feminist and suffrage advocate to her untimely demise as an opponent of the war. She is a questioning woman, politically and socially alert – not unlike Schreiner or the writer herself. Published to some critical acclaim (even winning a favourable review in the august *Times Literary Supplement*), the book vanished from sight until its reclamation as a radical-feminist text in the 1980s. It stands as a classic description of, and often a polemic against, its time and place.

Aleta Dey might easily be dismissed as a romance – as a girl-meets-boy, girl-drops-boy, girl-meets-another-boy story, lacking anything a 21st-century reader would identify as a probing analysis of the human condition. It often recalls a sermon in its earnestness and heavy-handed didacticism. Everyone, even Aleta on her deathbed, delivers improbably well-crafted speeches that will test the credulity of most 21st-century readers. But it is as a work of politics that *Aleta Dey* stands out. Read as a Schreinerite political manifesto cunningly disguised as romance, *Aleta Dey* is explosive. It is one of the most astute and engaging portraits of what the Great War meant for a major socialist-feminist thinker of her time.

The story traces free-thinking Aleta's life through the storms and travails of a rigid Christian upbringing, her relationship with a Tory patriarch whose opinions run diametrically against her own, and her violent death at the hands of a soldier who is part of an atavistic Winnipeg mob.[98] Read against its own romantic grain, it yields political insights into its time, which was – as Schreiner so astutely noted – one in which women, lacking easy access to other forms of authoritative discourse, often put their critical and creative energies into fiction.[99] It traces a "left pilgrim's progress" through the pre-war socialist enlightenment struggles over religion, to the consolidation and crisis of the left in the depths of the Great War. The "moments of refusal" that dominate the early pages of the novel include Aleta's pointed critique of religious orthodoxy, a visceral rejection of the educational system, and an attack on the conventions of the patriarchal family.

Her critique of the established order does not focus exclusively on men, although admittedly its most powerful moment occurs when Aleta's father beats her, inspiring this evolutionary insight in the young Aleta: "There is no more horrible spectacle than that of a human being drunk with the desire for victory over the body of another human being. The revolting thing is that in reverting himself to the emotions of the jungle he drags his victim down with him to the level of a beast of prey." In the family, Beynon argues through Aleta, are learned the habits of submission to authority that would be carried over into employment into the capitalist world: "Between them they succeeded so well that now when my employer rings for me my first sensation is always fear."[100]

From the novel's moments of refusal emerges a much more all-encompassing moment of socialist-feminist supersedure. Aleta (and, we must imagine, Beynon) begins to see connections between seemingly disparate forms of oppression, and she realizes that her true vocation lies in resisting them. Her father's rigid political views, his violence towards his children, and his stern religious orthodoxy are all knit together in a critique of a man who personifies patriarchy. Like Schreiner, Aleta decries parasitism. In the posthumous letter she sends her lover, she denounces, in words that might have been spoken by Schreiner herself, the "loathsome cancer of the social body, which breeds fear and suspicion and prepares the soil for violence and scandals and every conceivable form of evil thinking and doing." She cites a philosopher who proclaims, "A miasma exhales from crouching consciences."[101] This "cancer of the social body" is the fear and conformity pervading a war-torn world. In her moment of supersedure, she realizes that the church, school, and family are profoundly integrated aspects of an oppressive system. How should this system be contested?

In answering this question the novel tries out three tentative solutions, without ultimately deciding which should take primacy. The first is clearly that of a conventional "maternal feminism." For all her complicity in oppressive life, Aleta's mother emerges as a more compassionate and integrated person than her father; she is a "guardian angel" in the jungle of bourgeois family life. Aleta discards Ned as a potential suitor because he believes she will have to abandon her life outside the family upon marriage. She is a firm advocate of suffrage and speaks on its behalf in public meetings. Before 1914, Aleta epitomizes the mildly progressive suffragist, alert to a range of social issues, intent on resisting the evils of drink, determined to avoid the fate of "parasitism" that Schreiner had feared would overtake womankind if they did not resist subordination.

Yet, unmistakably, Aleta cannot stay with this understated feminist position. Aleta and her sister Pauline argue fiercely over the socialists, who had fired questions at Aleta about the "capitalist system," which she felt unable to answer. "They make me sick," declares Pauline, who hates hearing from "ignorant beggars" such expressions as "class conscious workers" and "capitalist system." As a good first formationist, Aleta responds: "There's more to Socialism than that, Pauline. . . . Some of those people are poor because they have been so weakened by malnutrition in their youth, and so hampered by the lack of an education that they haven't a chance in the struggle for existence." Aleta finds mainstream liberal feminism too narrow: " 'Have you no imagination,' I asked indignantly, 'that you seem incapable of sympathising with any injustice except this matter of woman suffrage, which touches you personally. Do you intend to go through life saying, "I don't believe it" about everything it would make you uncomfortable to face?' "[102]

Increasingly, Aleta comes to believe that the feminist and socialist struggles are irrevocably intertwined. Despite having (somewhat inexplicably) fallen in love with the reactionary McNair, Aleta cannot restrain her critique of his politics, for he has not realized that "for one person to act as the proprietor of another is a crime. It is a local expression of all the intolerable tyranny in the world."[103] Aleta persistently goes to meetings in the Labour Temple, critiques feminism's class-blind politics, and sympathizes with socialist Ned, persecuted for his anti-war opinions.[104]

Yet Beynon is also not quite sure about socialism. As a contributor to the SDPC's *Canadian Forward*, soon to be in hot water as an agent of sedition with the Canadian authorities, and an ardent exponent of the conscription of wealth, she had undoubtedly lived and breathed the air of the far left of Canadian politics. Still, as someone earlier drawn to the feminist writings of Mill, and arguably still something of a liberal sojourner among socialists, she was uncomfortable with an emergent revolutionary movement. In an unusually direct foreword she denounced that stream as an emergent tyranny. She feared that the socialist commonwealth as defined by Ned would, in its narrow materialism and its greatly expanded state, oppress minorities and individuals, that it would "be a new kind of hell for anyone who happens to have an original mind."[105]

Beynon could not follow Schreiner wholeheartedly in a naturalistic presentation of sexuality – this was, after all, a novel set in Canada – but she hinted that, compared to the brawny Scot who won Aleta's heart, with his glinting eye and masculine pipe, Ned was sexually unattractive for our protagonist. "McNair caught my hand in his and held it firmly, and he looked long and tenderly into my eyes, so that I forgot about feminism and democracy, and remembered only that my hand lay in the clasp of the man I loved." For all his progressive politics, Ned is a bit of a weed, a "drab medium-sized man," whom we glimpse in young middle age as "discouraged and saddened by his social isolation, but going doggedly on, impelled by some unknown law to follow the stony path of resistance."[106] So strong is Aleta's attraction to McNair that she even considers – in pre-war middle-class Winnipeg – the possibility of a common-law (and bigamous) relationship with him. The sexual allure of McNair survives the shattering revelation that he enjoys the bottle and therefore runs a serious risk of degeneration. Socialism and sex are working at cross-purposes.

The Great War forces all of these tensions to a new level of intensity, and from it emerges the outlines of a new kind of systematization. *Aleta Dey* argues passionately that the Great War was a moral and political disaster – a shocking regression to an earlier, pre-enlightenment epoch. Beynon pushed strongly for a radical democracy – a strikingly courageous thing to do in the poisonous postwar atmosphere. As Barbara Roberts remarks, Beynon argued for "a referendum rather than a series of Cabinet orders." Beynon suggested that "the draft should be applied universally to married as well as to single men" and that "Great Britain should have to renounce her imperial ambitions before Canadian men were conscripted to fight on her behalf." Moreover, "if there was to be equality of sacrifice, wealth as well as men should be conscripted." In her view, "the financial pinch of the war" should be more evenly shared.[107]

In *Canadian Forward*, in *Aleta Dey*, and in her private correspondence, Beynon was struggling to refuse and to resist the Canadian political order as she found it in the war. Aleta Dey was the subject of surveillance by the police. So would be many actual Canadian leftists. "Since when had Canadians relinquished the right to discuss unmade legislation? Was this Prussia or Canada in which we lived?"[108] Beynon was disgusted by the aggressive right-wing squads of vigilantes who broke up left-wing meetings. She used her novel to register her disapproval of the new political climate, right down to the killing of the charming Aleta by a soldier at a protest meeting.

Was there, then, no salvation? Aleta professes a continuing faith in humanity, without which she could not have coped with the dark years of the war. At Aleta's funeral the biblical text was drawn from *Isaiah*, often read in this period as a text of rebellion.[109] Aleta's own funeral verses combined the message of the transitoriness and vulnerability of human existence with a triumphalist sense of God's return to Israel, in a triumphant moment "that bringeth the princes to nothing" (Isaiah 40:23) – take warning, o ye Pharisees, warmongers, and profiteers – yet endows the true believers with such strength that "they shall mount up with wings as eagles" (40:31). Aleta enters the novel as a self-proclaimed "coward" and exits it, albeit posthumously, as a brave triumphant eagle. She is a feminist – and a socialist – hero.

Socialism and Sexuality

If for Chown and Beynon left feminism meant that the personal was the political, to a surprising extent theirs was not an unusual viewpoint. Some leftists were pushing the boundaries of gendered "common sense." Many things that contemporary leftists now take for granted – the advisability of sex education for the young, the importance of contraception, the significance of sexuality in the lives of individuals and hence the need to safeguard rights to its expression, within the broad limits of the equal rights of others – were (to put it mildly) not generally accepted. (Even advertising contraceptives contravened the law.) What is striking is how radically and consistently some socialist feminists, and not only Chown and Beynon, pushed the boundaries of liberal order by demanding a democratic sphere in which "private life" could be debated publicly.

Bebel, Engels, Gilman, and Schreiner all, in their different ways, raised explosive questions about sex and marriage. In general they left radically undetermined the "right answers" to those questions. Was socialism "for" or "against" the family as it was typically found in the society around them? Was socialism about the "restoration" of "traditional motherhood" – with no more women in jobs that should be held by men, and women embracing motherhood as a duty to society and the nation?[110] Or was it about the equal rights of men and women in the labour market? What would parenting look like in the socialist world of tomorrow? Did socialists stand for "free love" – and what exactly did that mean? Limitless sexual experimentation with a host of different people, or the right to leave a loveless and abusive marriage without having to pay a brutal economic price? Or, as socialist-feminist Grant Allen had demonstrated in his novel *The Woman Who Did*, did it mean the principled *rejection* of marriage as a relict of a barbaric and oppressive age?[111] Or were socialists partisans of a modernized variant of the conventional marriage, minus its domestic violence and plus a sense of comradeship? What was the correct socialist position on the sex trades? Were socialists in favour of revolutionizing or preserving the ideas of masculinity and femininity that they absorbed from the world around them? Or did they simply repeat the conventional gendered truths of bourgeois society? Debates over "family values" are not of recent invention. They echoed and re-echoed throughout the first formation.

For many anti-socialists, *here* lay the supreme danger of the agitations and questions unleashed by the movement – and a most tempting target for vitriolic polemics. Even such a cool-as-a-cucumber critic of socialism as Skelton lost his academic composure when it came to socialism and marriage. Skelton knew for a *fact* that "the *inevitable* result of the establishment of the socialist régime would be the universal breaking-up of the family relation." It would "*inevitably*" be the case that "the family would be crushed between individual selfishness and state interference, the care of children would more and more be made a state affair, family life would be emptied of its responsibilities as well as its privileges.[112] Charges of atheistic socialism paled in their effectiveness beside those of "free love" and "family-smashing." Vote for the socialists, and wait for the moral maelstrom.

Many leftists were thrown on the defensive. "The vitality of this hoary libel is remarkable," Spargo complained. "Refuted thousands of times, it still appears in every attack upon Socialism. In spite of protests, denials, explanations and programmes there are still many persons who honestly and sincerely believe that Socialism aims at doing away with the family and turning over all its functions to the State." Even the *Western Clarion* felt obliged to answer the charge of free love. " 'Socialism would destroy the home.' Of course it would, repeats the non-thinker, cos Mr. Wisehead says so," went one of its lame responses to the allegation.[113]

"Socialism will preserve the family instead of destroying it as is the way with capitalism," ran one of the more assertive of the Lindsay SPC's *Gems of Socialism.* "Socialism is not a social reform or a sex reform movement," the *Western Clarion* argued. "It makes no attack upon marriage as an institution. It no more criticizes matrimony than it criticizes eating peas with a knife." Newton underlines the left's disinclination to pursue the issue of birth control and notes Moses Baritz's attack upon its proponents as "small breasted women and fat headed men."[114]

Yet Skelton clearly had a point – which was backhandedly conceded by *Cotton*'s frank acknowledgement that the movement sheltered some who were unorthodox in their "domestic arrangements." As a political and cultural movement – outside the official organizations and organs – the first formation was bubbling over with dissident thoughts about sexuality and marriage. The socialist feminism influential through much of the movement created, at the very least, the sense that well-established conventions and institutions – marriage, the male breadwinner, male suffrage – were transient, potentially malleable forms. In essence, much of its politics was, at least tangentially, about a form of sexual modernity. Many of its most hallowed authorities, such as Bebel and Engels, proposed that among the "solids that had melted into air" were such fixed and fast certainties as the relations between men and women, husband and wife. Even a passing acquaintance with its literature would confirm that it often turned sexual and gender certainties into questions.

That questioning was particularly the case with respect to the sex trades, which for some leftists represented the most visible and disturbing signs of a social order in crisis. Indeed, a casual reader of the secondary literature might jump to the conclusion that first formation leftists in Canada were peculiarly obsessed with "prostitution." Yet in some ways they were themselves caught up in a larger North Atlantic media frenzy around the so-called White Slave Trade, a press sensation that manufactured out of meagre evidence a vast moral panic about the safety of young White women, said to be the targets of decadent and designing Asian men, hell-bent on tricking them into prostitution.[115] This panic almost required leftists to take a position – which, armed with Bebel and Engels, they believed themselves uniquely qualified to do. They could respond to the issue in a way that both demonstrated the evils of capitalism and the rigorous beauty of social-evolutionary theory – and, perhaps not altogether incidentally, sell newspapers and fill lecture halls. For some inexplicable reason, sex invariably attracts more of an audience than does the labour theory of value.

Certainly, Bebel, Engels, Gilman, and Schreiner all talked about prostitution at length. Bebel devoted the third chapter of *Woman under Socialism* to "Prostitution, A Necessary Social Institution of the Capitalist World." For Engels, "prostitution" revealed the present-day dimensions of the world-historic defeat of the female sex, but it was also a trade that "degrades the character of the whole male world."[116] Gilman was predictably far less nonchalant: for her, prostitution was "a racial wrong, productive of all evil." Prostitution was counter-evolutionary, because it defied the natural laws that necessitated that both parents devote themselves to their children. It dramatically revealed the craven dependence of females upon males, and demonstrated how unnatural human life had become. Human beings were "the only animal species in which the sex-relation is also an economic relation."[117] In *Moving the Mountain*, those prostitutes still remaining in the new social order were advised to shuck their old lives as "over-sexed female animals" and embrace their new, more rational lives as celibate women, to join the "great moving world of service and growth and happiness."[118]

Schreiner essentially agreed. "Prostitution can never be adequately dealt with, either from the moral or the scientific standpoint, unless its relation to the general phenomenon of female parasitism be fully recognized," she argued. Aligning herself strongly with Engels, whose arguments were well-known to her, Schreiner believed that only the finest of lines separated the prostitute from the married woman. "Probably three-fourths of the sexual unions in our modern European societies, whether in the illegal or recognized legal forms, are dominated by or largely influenced by the sex purchasing power of the male."[119]

A significant tension existed between two poles in this almost canonical literature – with Bebel and Gilman seeing prostitution as bestial degradation and Engels and Schreiner viewing it more functionally as part of the social system. For casual, and even not so casual, readers of Engels and Schreiner, the unsettling implication was that many marriages were no more to be revered or respected than was the implicit contract between a prostitute and her customers. Far from being a haven in a heartless world, marriages *were* that heartless world, thinly camouflaged with sentimental persiflage and deodorized with the holy incense of the wedding ceremony.

Some socialists believed that social evolution would gradually draw sexuality into the orbit of rational planning and "socially evolved" conduct. In this social-evolutionary concept of the realm of freedom, human beings would enjoy a greater *freedom from sexuality*, which, like electricity, would gradually be harnessed and turned to constructive purposes once integrated into a new way of life. The "beast" of "selfish, egotistic, sexual lustfulness" would be collectively and individually subdued by a socialist movement that demanded the transformation of sexual relations between men and women, with men, as writer Lucy Bland puts it, taking "responsibility for changing the oppressive aspects of their sexual behaviour."[120] As this more rational and enlightened future inevitably unfolded, prostitution would evaporate. (This was very much Gilman's scenario.)

For some who affected the "impossibilist" style, the entire debate was outside the remit of the socialist movement. For Arthur Bullard, it was just one more case of adding redundant "reform" planks to a revolutionary platform, simply to "catch votes." "Of course we would like to see these reforms granted. But we would like to have everybody clean their teeth regularly, we would like to see better taste in municipal architecture," he remarked, before adding, with typical "impossibilist" insouciance: "We would not object to the elimination of prostitution."[121]

For B.C. socialist-feminist Amy Campbell Johnston, "White Slavery" and "Wage Slavery" were analogous. Just as the working man was being "ground down by capital," his daughter was being "lured away to supply this traffic" and his son steered into "the army to protect the capitalist." He needed to come to his senses and realize that the suffragist whom he had been taught to despise was in fact his "truest friend and sympathizer."[122] Yet he might be given pause by other feminist critics of prostitution, who bluntly blamed "men" in general for the phenomenon. "Men carry this disease to their innocent wives and children; men spread the disease through hotels and restaurants, and men in the first place infected the white slaves," went one argument.[123] Others theorized that the sex trades, which antedated capitalism, must have more complex roots than simply the mode of production. Wilfred Gribble, who claimed to have treated hundreds of cases of venereal disease when he was in the navy, argued that men who visited prostitutes were acting on the basis of "a demand that is insistent, irresistible, older than the wage system, older than society, old as the human race and older . . . the demand for species perpetuation."[124] Brothels were deeply enmeshed in the early 20th-century history of the Canadian North and West, and the men who spoke out on this issue sometimes clearly raised the suspicion that they themselves had visited them – which might be taken either to reveal blameworthy evidence of their chauvinism or a new willingness to speak frankly about a well-known but little acknowledged part of Canadian society.

Novels that circulated within the left readership sought to address the question by attempting to put the reader in the shoes of prostitutes. Estelle Baker's *The Rose Door* (1911) depicted Yiddish-speaking Rebecca enticed into "the life" because she desperately wanted to return to her homeland. It was a brave stab at socialist realism, undermined to some extent by its author's penchant for interrupting her gripping account of her hero's predicament for rather less absorbing slabs of Spencerian sociology. "Even where a monogamic form of marriage prevailed, polygamy has always existed; also cases of polyandry," mused one of her key characters at a particularly dramatic point. "But with the conception of private possessions came the desire that one's own children might inherit these possessions; therefore the custom of one man taking one woman to be exclusively his own."[125]

If the treatment of prostitution suggested a means of once again framing a burning public issue within the scope of social-evolutionary theory, homosexuality led to a different set of challenges. Such a phenomenon could not be easily grasped within its evolutionary categories. Many first formation leftists had certainly heard about homosexuality – the Oscar Wilde trial of 1895 had implicated a British socialist well known in Canada – but the upshot of considerations on sexuality was the stigmatization of any sexual activity outside heteronormative relationships – a pattern that would persist long after the movement's heyday.[126]

Thus, despite his credentials as a notorious apostle of free love, the Finnish utopian Matti Kurikka could not think beyond the male/female polarity that shaped sexual thought. He likened sexuality to electricity. "Man" represented the "positive" (striving forward), women the "negative" (accepting). Having set up this duality, Kurikka candidly acknowledged that it did not encompass everyone – there were active women and passive men – but such anomalies against the basic laws of nature "for that very reason" became objects of derision.[127]

The major socialist-feminist theorists all tended to pathologize same-sex love, or indeed many sexual expressions outside the reproductive sphere. Bellamy was even severely dismissive of "celibates," who were "almost invariably men who have failed to acquit themselves creditably in the work of life."[128] In Spencerian theory, which viewed the body as a closed-energy system, homosexuality could be construed as an abuse of organs intended by nature for other purposes, and consequently an unwise depletion of an organism's finite energy reserves. Interestingly, homosexuals in Bebel's evolutionary account were constructed more as overly sensual men who had gone through so many sexual experiences (presumably with women) that they became *roués*, needing increasingly "special irritants" to arouse them, "excess" having "deadened and surfeited them." And thus: "Many accordingly, lapse into the unnatural practices of Greek days. The crime against nature is to-day much more general than most of us dream of: upon that subject the secret archives of many a Police Bureau could publish frightful information." Even among women, "the unnatural practices of old Greece come up again with force. Lesbian love, or Sapphism, is said to be quite general among married women in Paris." Bebel painted a picture of the big cities of Europe thronging with "disciples of Sappho."[129] It was another item in the lengthy indictment of capitalist modernity.

Eleanor Marx and Edward Aveling, decrying the separation of the sexes, said of "the effeminate man and masculine woman" that "these are two types from which even the average person recoils with a perfectly natural horror of the unnatural." Both were "diseased forms due to our unnatural dealing with the sex relations."[130] Allen, although pressured by a friend to endorse the goings-on of the "uranians," or homosexuals, could not do so, because, as a Spencerian, he could not countenance "unproductive sex." In his books, it seemed, heterosexuality was the key to a happy and successful life – even among flowering plants.[131]

In Gilman's socialist-feminist thought, homosexuality – "perversion" in her blunt sexual language – could be grasped through the evolutionary concepts of excess and degeneration. Sex-attraction, like hunger, was designed by evolution for certain purposes, and not for others. Nature gave humanity hunger to spur the organism to secure its food. Sex-attraction was simply an essential factor "in the fulfillment of our processes of reproduction." Anything over and above that – such as non-reproductive sexuality – was excessive and damaging because it bore "no relation to the original needs of the organism." If carried to excess it would tend "to pervert and exhaust desire as well as to injure reproduction." Surplus male sexual energy, prostitution, unnatural vices, and non-monogamous and non-permanent sexual relationships all derived from an evolutionary division of labour that had removed women from free production and confined them to roles subordinate to men. A relation that produced "abnormal development" could not be permanently maintained. The "limitless exaggeration of sex-instinct" would find expression "in the unnatural vices of advanced civilization." In her utopian novel *Moving the Mountain*, those afflicted with "excess sexual energy," although they might not be weeded out with quite the exterminating zeal evident in her handling of degenerates and "real perverts," would still be candidates for medical, perhaps surgical, treatment.[132]

Schreiner was less graphic but no less emphatic. Parasitism bred perversion, and the perverts were, under conditions of modernity, seemingly ubiquitous. She vividly called up the image of the degenerate, imagining "the curled darling, scented and languid, with his drawl, his delicate apparel, his devotion to the rarity and variety of his viands." His "severest labour is the search after pleasure." Even hunting, once upon a time an "invigorating and manly toil," had become for him "a luxurious and farcical amusement." The history of the ancient world, where admittedly the perverts had proliferated, was simply evidence of the deep danger those misfits posed to Western civilization. Having reduced their women-folk to parasitism, that is, to "comparatively ignorant and helpless females," the upper-class males turned to each other, and soon pleasant conversations were transformed into something much worse. "Man turned towards man; and parenthood, the divine gift of imparting human life, was severed from the loftiest and profoundest phases of human emotion." Hence, from the time of ancient Greece the race was decaying at its core. True, it had been temporarily rescued by Alexander the Great, the "son of the fierce, virile, and indomitable Olympia," who, thanks to the Lamarckian inheritance of acquired characteristics, was able to knock some temporary sense into his unhealthy fellow-Greeks – but their true redemption would await the arrival of the Goths, "a branch of that great Teutonic folk whose monogamous domestic life was sound at the core."[133]

As for more up to date degenerates, Schreiner spoke with scientific certainty about their impending demise. "The loss of a small and unhealthy section will be the gain of human society as a whole." Shed no tears for "the undesirable, the residuary, male old-maids of the human race." They were the parasitical consequences of modernity itself, and evolution itself would take care of the matter. The perverts were slated for an extinction as complete as that which had swept away a comparable "body of males" in ancient Rome. No, whether the pervert was spotted in "the later Roman Empire, the Turkish harem of to-day, or in our Northern civilizations," this male, "more repulsive than the parasite female herself, because a yet further product of decay," was the symptom of a profound evolutionary disorder. "He is like to the bald patches and rotten wool on the back of a scabby sheep; which indeed indicate that, deep beneath the surface, a parasite insect is eating its way into the flesh, but which are not so much the cause of disease, as its final manifestation."[134]

Gilman's and Schreiner's analyses of perverts and male old maids were echoed throughout the Canadian left. Some Canadian socialists paid attention to Edward Carpenter and others enthused about Walt Whitman, but the sexual politics of the first and the homoerotic sensibility of the second did not provoke sustained Canadian commentary. Evocations of ancient world sexuality stressed degeneracy, not diversity.[135] In all succeeding Canadian socialisms until recent days, the homosexual was by definition a symptom, not a comrade: a "degenerate" outside the normal progress of social evolution. Much of this emphasis can be traced back to evolutionary theory in general and Spencerian theory in particular.

Conversely, being a socialist man meant being able to take it like a man, shout down hecklers, and rejoice in the bare-knuckled, rock'em-sock'em, cut-to-the-chase arguments that took up so many columns in the *Western Clarion*. Marxist masculinity meant straight talk and straight shooting. It meant firing down opponents in the "O.K. Corral" of Marxist theory. Socialist styles of polemical warfare, in which strong debaters went after each other without fear or favour, were often Everhard-like demonstrations of masculine prowess.

Many first formationists echoed Jack London in his rapt admiration of manly, free-standing, tough, and assertive men. When one of Phillips Thompson's critics suggested that he had a "nature as gentle as a girl" and would spend the entire day "trying to figure out how to get to work without stepping on a potato bug," he was not paying this male feminist a compliment for his refined sensibility.[136] As early as Spargo's 1901 speech to the Canadian Social-ist League, the true manliness of the socialist was counterposed to the contemptible, non-manly, effeminate Other – these *decadents* of bourgeois political economy. It was monstrous, Spargo told his Toronto audience in 1901, that "a pale-faced curate in New England" or "some old maiden lady in the South of England whose only 'labor' is the fondling of her tabby cat" profited from investments in places they had never seen. Why it should have been any less problematic if a ruddy-faced farmer or a vigorous young woman in the North of England had been clipping the dividends was never made very clear. Under socialism, reasoned another leftist, the abolition of inheritance and the reversion of all wealth to the commonwealth would mean that "every man would have to stand on his own industry and so be a man."[137]

Colin McKay, a lifelong bachelor, did discreetly question this cult of man-liness in his sea stories – one of which has a delicate and dapper "Mate from Maine" settle the nerves of hard-bitten but panic-stricken fellow workers as they undergo one of his almost too frequent fictional storms at sea. The neatly dressed mate, with dainty hands and delicate manner, prevails through his logic and science where the rough and tough Jack-London-style seamen lose their heads in booze and brawling. It was a clever rejoinder to London, if that was what it was meant to be – but nobody seems to have noticed it, in a North America enraptured with London's hypermasculine adventurers.[138]

Thus, barring such isolated if interesting voices, and despite the sexual modernity implied by some of its authorities, much of the first formation, and especially its official parties, tended to revel in mainstream gender conventions. Why should Vancouverites voting in the school board elections vote for the SPC candidates? Not only, said one SPC candidate, to support the replacement of capitalism by socialism, but to institute manual training for boys and domestic science for girls in the local schools. After all, girls would "in the natural order, become the wives and mothers of the succeeding gener-ations," and so a "knowledge of house-keeping, cooking and raising babies is more essential than the correct pronunciation of mere words or the rules of grammar."[139]

"Be men; be women!" exclaimed the *Western Clarion*, with the subtext that the meaning of the exhortation would be obvious to all who, in the natu-ral order of things, unambivalently occupied the only two valid adult subject-positions. Such gender conservatism extended to the rituals and customs of the movement. When well-known SPC activist John Mortimer perished in

1908, the press published condolences to his partner, who was identified as "Comrade Mrs. John T. Mortimer." "This heroic woman," it remarked, "is braving it all with a resolute spirit in keeping with the noblest traditions of her sex." As Gribble put it in his poem "The Break of Dawn": "By your parents' arduous lives,/ By your toiling, careworn wives./ By each soul which bravely strives,/ Rise! Be men, be free!/ Now the hope within your view – / All the world a nation new/ To yourselves and class be true/ Rise! For Liberty!" The coming of class-consciousness meant the "dawn of true life, of true manhood," W.J. Curry remarked. "What are you doing to emancipate yourself?" asked *Cotton's Weekly*. "Are you content to be a slave and crawl through life at the beck and call of a boss who has been placed over you as a slave driver? It is up to you workingmen of Canada to achieve your own liberty? Have you the manhood to do it?"[140]

Yet, alongside the stereotypical exhortations to "Be men!" were some interesting reflections on the social-evolutionary reasons as to why "Being a Man" had become a tricky business. The fate of the male artisan, for example, suggested that the liberal model of the male individual, captain of his fate and master of his craft, was a thing of the past. Once a "most important person," now his job could be performed by anyone, Alf Budden said, "pulling a lever or turning an electric switch." References to the suicides of male workers – such as the self-inflicted death of a young sailor after his public degradation in a flogging – suggested the outmoded, irrational brutality of the society in which they lived. "The sailor in question must have been especially thin-skinned to have felt that any humiliation was attached to the part he played in it," said the *Western Clarion* in its deadpan, almost film noir, style. "Such touchy people are entirely unfit for military or naval service."[141]

First formationists, confronted with Skelton's charge of grave gender and sexual irregularities, could reply with an honest righteous indignation that their movement was precisely designed to uphold traditional values and make such irregularities wither away. The more they were attacked on this point – and it would be a rare anti-socialist who would not have recourse to the critique – the more fiercely many of them would retort that the left was as committed to monogamous marriage and patriarchal family values as everybody else.

Still, just having such debates in public, and in this often unsentimental and scientific language, portended a dramatic change in the cultural order. Skelton had smelled out a valid point: there was a subtle logic within socialism that did lead to surprisingly far-reaching reconsiderations of questions that contemporaries often swept under the carpet. Just by asking the woman question, these writers and activists unsettlingly made certainties into debates, rock-hard truths into contingent positions. This was in itself a moment of socialist modernity.

Free Love and the Politics of Sex

First formationists who talked about marriage and sexuality frequently became embroiled in the polemics surrounding socialism's supposed support for "free love." Rather than a plethora of short-term hookups with dozens of sex-partners, free love generally meant, as Allen demonstrated in *The Woman Who Did*, that both partners in a relationship were independent, uncoerced by convention or clergy, and free to leave the relationship when they felt they had to. (It was, then, not all that far removed from the norms of many 21st-century young people who try living together before they get married and, without being financially and socially ruined, will separate if things don't work out.) Free love also meant candid discussions of sexuality, contraception, and the sexual rights and responsibilities of men and women, within a framework that held sexual expression in high esteem. In the United States free love advocates were prominent (if not numerous) from the days of utopian socialism. Anarchist figures such as Ezra Heywood and Emma Goldman were closely identified with free love. In Britain, Canadian-born Stella Browne participated in socialist debates prompted by the sexological researches of Havelock Ellis.[142]

Kurikka launched a free love debate at Sointula in early 1904, driven in part by his association with the Finnish feminist and socialist Minna Canth and his deepening attachment to theosophy with its emphasis on freely chosen harmonious relationships. As he argued: "Once private ownership is abolished, the family becomes unnecessary and marriage recognized as fornication, what could be purer than what is already seen in uncorrupted nature." It was a position premised on resistance to the subordinate position of women within marriage and linked to his vision of communal child-rearing. Early in 1904 he launched a campaign in the pages of *Aika* against the "chains of marriage," arguing the case for free love from a feminist standpoint: "Natural sexual drive did not have an opportunity to develop within marriage because husbands had turned the marriage contract into a licence to rape." The community was sharply divided on this question, and ultimately the issue contributed to its disruption. As Kurikka wrote to his daughter: "The main reason for this split . . . is female emancipation. As a result of my writing [in *Aika*] many wives started to oppose the passionate advances of their husbands and the latter became angry and jealous and in the end started to believe that their wives had fallen in love with me and for that reason had betrayed them."[143]

Perhaps the most significant socialist-feminist advocate of free love was Dora Forster Kerr – who, contrary to Newton's suggestion that the left barred its doors to sexual radicals, also played a significant role within the B.C. movement. As early as 1902 Kerr's article "We Women," which recommended the work of sex radicals to the Canadian public, was published in the *Western*

Socialist. (Eventually her articles on "Sex Radicalism" in the U.S. journal *Lucifer* would lead to the banning of *Lucifer* from the Canadian mails.)[144] In 1905, under the name Dora Forster, she brought out *Sex Radicalism as Seen by an Emancipated Woman of the New Time*, a remarkable and engaging manifesto calling for a radical sexual enlightenment. Under what Forster called a "new and rational sex system," women would be relieved of their sexual frustrations, which stemmed from their oppression within marriage. Finally, said Forster, women were able to speak to each other about their dissatisfaction with the "weaknesses of men," one of which was their lousy love-making. Present-day marriages were often sullen with sexual discontent, and men could look to themselves for some of the reasons why. They were prone to enjoy sex in the same way that "some of our northern barbarians drink, – he tosses off the wine of life in one fierce draught, caring only that it quenches thirst, instead of sipping its delicious fragrance."

Yet by discussing amongst themselves the sexual and other inadequacies of men, women needed to be mindful that such problems were rooted in an oppressive system that had reduced women to economic and sexual dependence. What was to be done? Spread the sexual enlightenment through the education of children and the radical reform of marriage, for "knowledge and thought are always bracing and helpful; ignorance is demoralizing." Break the power of the church, that cruel upholder of "sex slavery." Open up marriage so that both partners were free to express their sexual natures. At that point, Forster – who up to then might have been sounding like someone of our own time – reverted to her context in the first formation. The point of giving women this added sexual independence was not only because so many were miserable in stale and oppressive marriages, but also because doing so would block the degeneration of the race. By restoring to women their full Darwinian powers of sexual selection, they could reassert a level of reproductive quality control that otherwise might be threatened by the overproduction of the deficient offspring of the poor and biologically unfit. Forster and her partner R.B. Kerr (who added this last suggestion) thus positioned the sexual liberation of women as a panacea for the supposed "crisis of degeneration."[145] Given this framework, and notwithstanding her "sexual radicalism," Forster unsurprisingly did not go near the issue of homosexuality.

If B.C.-based Forster probably attracted few Canadian readers with her pamphlet, which was aimed primarily at a U.S. audience of sexual radicals, free love in the general sense of an enlightened sexuality was far from being her own peculiar hobbyhorse. As Kealey notes, sex education was advocated by Bertha Merrill Burns, one of the founding figures of the B.C. movement. "This is not socialism, perhaps some will say," Burns remarked, anticipating "orthodox" critiques. "No, but it is no less important than socialism. . . . So long as we look upon the origin of life – the fusion of sex force – with contempt and shame, so long will life itself be held the cheapest and lowest commodity in the universe."[146]

In Port Arthur, Finnish leftists were put on the defensive in 1913 by accusations in the city's *Daily News* that they combined three traits: "socialism, atheism, and free love." It was not an entirely baseless accusation. Among the Finns common-law relationships were sometimes dictated by necessity, but others, according to Varpu Lindström-Best, "were a deliberate political statement by Finnish socialists who refused to sanction the authority of the church." Such "free unions" between men and women went back to at least 1902, with examples found in many Finnish communities, where there were at times intense debates over free love and the abolition of marriage. Many Finnish socialists supported "free unions" between men and women and proudly advertised their defiance of the prevailing system. Prominent notices in *Vapaus*, a leading Finnish socialist newspaper in Sudbury, announced that no "black cloth" or "sky pilot" had been present at a recent wedding. The Port Arthur Finns, having been targeted by the mainstream press, quickly amassed 461 people to reply to the charge of living outside the accepted moral code. They noted that in Canada each person had the right "to care for his soul according to the dictates of his conscience." Socialism was not illegal in Canada, they observed. Rebutting the daily newspaper's free love accusation, they argued that at least the Finns were against the common Lakehead practice of men paying prostitutes for "love." For advocates of free love in the Finnish community, "marriage without love," Lindström-Best observes, "was seen as a form of prostitution for women."[147]

"Why should a man and a woman ... have to go through a ridiculous ceremony mumbled by a priest or preacher before they can live together? If they love and love purely, that is sufficient," Emma Goldman urged a Winnipeg audience.[148] Even in Halifax, perhaps not universally renowned as a haven of sexual radicals, the publication of part of a book called *Woman's Wild Oats: Essays on the Refixing of Moral Standards* provoked a firestorm. The author, British Fabian C. Gasquoine Hartley – who had earlier revealed *The Truth about Woman* to a waiting world – dedicated her book to her husband and her son. She aimed her polemic against the "*laisser faire* system," which in the realm of marriage was "as false ... as it is in industry and economics." She denounced the "monstrous sham" of "much of our civilisation ... more dangerously indecent because of its pretence of decency." Disturbed by the chaos and confusion of modern life, and energized by Freud's revelations, Hartley denounced a "worm-eaten" and "musty" social and sexual order. She proposed "some kind of fixed recognition for every form of sexual relationship between a woman and a man." Men and women who did not want children, or "the bondage of a continuous companionship," could nonetheless have the security of some form of written partnership, which might for some be a kind of trial marriage. She concluded, "We have to re-make the world."[149]

"*Not on our watch!*" came the massed voices of outraged conservative Nova Scotians, including the Bishop of Antigonish. "What is the world coming to?" asked Mrs. Donald Shaw, a leading figure in the Halifax women's movement. "There seems to be a mad desire just now on the part of a large number of people to tear down and cast aside all the creeds, rules and laws that have in the past built up moral and stable nations." Hartley's proposals amounted to a prescription for "race suicide," the "morals of the dog kennel and poultry yard, a cold-blooded scheme of temporary wives and husbands." Sin and disease were synonymous terms, she argued, and "promiscuity between the sexes is a sin which carries its own natural punishment."[150]

What was perhaps most troubling to mainstream critics was not that most socialists lived and breathed free love – such was patently not the case – but that they had transformed certainties into questions. Socialists allowed themselves to wonder whether men and women *had* to live according to the conventions of their society. Much contemporary socialist discourse on sexuality and gender was premised on the idea that the relations between men and women could be made better – more rational, orderly, and dignified – if only they were placed in an evolutionary context. Little discussed and rarely politicized topics had become questions for debate.[151] First formation discourse did not generally draw the line between the personal and the political that would later characterize left politics. Canadians studying Bebel, as many did, would have heard words candidly celebrating, among other things, sexual fulfilment for both men and women (always provided, of course, that the relations were heterosexual): "*The satisfaction of the sexual instinct is as much a private concern as the satisfaction of any other natural instinct,*" Bebel wrote. "None is therefore accountable to others, and no unsolicited judge may interfere. How I shall eat, how I shall drink, how I shall sleep, how I shall clothe myself, is my private affair, – exactly so my intercourse with a person of the opposite sex." Abolish prudery and affectation, and one would see a "more natural intercourse of the sexes than that which prevails to-day."[152]

Such open and serious reflections were unusual in a Canada otherwise transfixed by social purity crusades and masturbation scare campaigns. Instead of just repeating an unthinking naturalism – although admittedly there was more than a little of that – some first formationists created a democratic public sphere in which sexuality could be explored and debated. They reconstructed in a new way conventional sexualities as problematic and potentially changeable aspects of social reality. By making a politics of such questions, and struggling to connect that position to wider social patterns, the early socialists were at least reflecting on – if not coming anywhere close to resolving – the problems faced by heterosexual men and women as they came to realize the unattainability, both in economic and personal life, of the self-possession and individualism that the liberal order held out as its ideal.

Often they speculated what it might be like if sex virtually disappeared as a shaper of human destinies. A common theme in left feminist work on sexuality, including thinking within the free love movement, was that men's aggressive sexual behaviour was anti-social and counter-evolutionary. Men enjoyed a destructive sexual freedom under the notorious double standard. The atrophying of their sexual drive was seen as the next step in social evolution. Gilman's *Herland* presented a woman-friendly future largely freed from the burdens of sexuality. In Partridge's imagined Prairie utopia of Coalsamao, sexual life in the co-operative commonwealth had been purified, thanks in part to a "marvelous simplification of dress." By common consent, people had done away with the "wearing of feathers, fur, and fantastic fabrics of all conceivable variety of shade and diversity of pattern, with buttons, and beads, and buckles to match," with the result that all who served in the "Army of the Common Good" were "comrades, not competitors." Why was it possible to so change the rules of fashion? Because now, in Coalsamao, there was no more sex war. Freed from capitalist bondage, a woman no longer need worry about "making herself sexually attractive to some male possessed of wealth sufficient to supply her needs," because making an "advantageous sale" of her own body is no longer necessary for her survival.[153]

Many socialist feminists, like Partridge, saw the socialist future as one in which humans would enjoy freedom from sexuality. Yet other texts gingerly advanced a free love proposition that sexuality might be an end in itself. Allen's writings in defence of what he called a "new hedonism" could be interpreted that way (although only for those who followed the heteronormative script).[154] Goldman could also inspire her many Canadian listeners with thoughts of a much freer sexuality – in her case, an ideal she would eventually extend to homosexuals as well. It will probably forever be impossible to say with certainty where most Canadian socialists located themselves on this asceticism-hedonism continuum, but what is remarkable is the success with which the first formationists had created a political and cultural space within which such issues could be openly debated.

From Man's to Woman's Feminism, 1908–1915

A marked sea-change occurred in the discussion of the woman question after around 1908. Essentially, the "question" gradually became much less one that was asked by men, often pitched at a high level of abstraction, and more one asked by women as they sought ways of framing and transforming immediately pressing political and social issues.[155] This transition in the discussion of gender politics had a certain parallel, then, with the transition noticeable in the discussion of class-consciousness. There was a sharpened impatience with the scholastic and often mischievous "impossibilist" tone of the SPC polemics, and a much more concerted attempt to find theorists and practices that would transform gender politics in the actually-existing world. Women showed a marked tendency to organize autonomously of men and to undertake their own appropriations of left feminist theory.

An example of a new spirit came in Ontario with the emergence, initially within the spc, of the Socialist Women's Study Club (fd. 1908). This weekly meeting group launched its reading program with Engels's *Origin of the Family, Private Property and the State*, and its members contributed funds to buy other books.[156] The group also co-operated with the Canadian Suffrage Association to lobby the Ontario government to extend the ballot to women on the same terms as men. The semi-autonomous Toronto Women's Social Democratic League, Kealey notes, was formed in September 1914. Attached to but not subordinate to the Social Democratic Party, it aimed "to aid in propaganda and educational work among women in the socialist and labour movements," and to become the nucleus of a province-wide socialist-feminist movement that would embrace "every town and city in Ontario." Socialist feminism within the sDP showed a new intensity; the party's new manifesto decried the "double slavery" faced by working women.[157] In Montreal, as Kealey points out, Mrs. R.P. Mendelssohn of the sDP participated as an activist in the newly established Equal Suffrage League of Montreal. In British Columbia women's branches of the sDP emerged, in line with a party policy requiring women's organization committees. The branches were sufficiently numerous by fall 1913 to require their own provincial secretary.

Ukrainian communities showed active support for women's rights. The writings of Yavloha Prynduse in the widely read Ukrainian left newspaper *Robochyi narod* (Working people) revealed a holistic feminism linking "child-rearing, cooking, and cleaning to larger political questions, such as the need for involvement in schools, municipal health, and even issues of national importance, such as tariff policies."[158]

When a woman socialist campaigned as a candidate for the Toronto Board of Education in 1913, backed by the Independent Labor Party (ILP) and the labour council, she mustered almost 2,000 votes.[159]

This remarkable surge of socialist-feminist institution-building was combined with a new insistence on *difference* as well as *solidarity*. Some debates sponsored by the Toronto Women's Social Democratic League were women-only events.[160] The Toronto Women's Political Club, associated with Helen Cunningham, combined Georgeite economics with appeals to Pankhurst-style "militance."[161] When she was interviewed in later years, Mary Norton did not remember any sex discrimination within the sDPC. Rather, she noted the separate women's meetings in the party and the "aggressive spirits" of the socialist women.[162] At least one spc local banned smoking at its meetings, as did the spc's Ontario convention of 1907.

One major component of this transition was the arrival of large new groups of socialists associated with specific non-Anglo cultural communities. Although the Finns had been arriving in numbers since the 19th century, it was only after 1905 or so that their presence became unmistakable on the left.[163] In Finland the Social Democratic Party, although founded only in 1899, was within a decade the largest political party in the country. Women had been involved since the beginning, and as Lindström-Best relates, "By 1906 about a quarter of the card-carrying members were women." The year after Finnish women won the vote, 19 women were elected under the auspices of the SDP, a powerhouse in European and world terms. From 1890 to 1920 thousands of Finns – probably a good many more than the 21,494 noted by the 1921 census, given the frequency of trips to and from Finland – came to Canada, sometimes as sojourners and sometimes as permanent settlers. No fewer than 44 per cent of these immigrants were women, and as many as 60 per cent of the women were single.

Finnish socialist women began to organize autonomously as early as 1894. In North Wellington, B.C., according to Lindström-Best, the temperance society Aallotar underwent a "process of transformation from a religious to a socialist society," completed only in 1896: "The minutes reveal that, unlike the church councils, women sat on the socialist temperance society executive . . . they exercised their right to speak at socialist meetings years before the first Socialist Party in British Columbia was founded." The left publication *Toivo* published many articles on "women and socialism" between 1902 and 1904, including translations of Engels. It painted Finnish socialists in Canada a picture of a future in which woman "will no longer be a slave but stand beside a man, totally free and in charge of her own happiness.'"

Yet theory and practice did not easily mesh. In 1905 a Port Arthur woman complained that women were in effect "pieces of furniture" hidden off "in the corners" of meeting halls, that they were "taken for granted, or worse yet, ignored" except when they could be used "for practical purposes." Nonetheless, among the Finnish immigrants, socialist feminism attained a mass base and a degree of sophistication not equalled by many other Canadians. Finnish women may have made up as much as 30 per cent of the membership of the left-wing Finnish Society of Canada (FSOC). In Toronto, where tailors formed a significant nucleus of the Finnish left, such eminent socialist leaders as Frans Syrjälä, who had attended the founding meeting of the SDP in Finland, brought with them a strongly Marxist articulation of socialism. A library and reading room were established early in the 20th century. Women, who made up nearly half the membership, "were invited to participate, encouraged to speak, debate, and attend all meetings," Lindström-Best observes. About half of the 146 Toronto Finns ousted from the SPC in 1910 were women.[164]

As Ruth Frager revealed in her study, Jewish socialist women were also becoming more prominent. The Jewish community in Toronto grew from about 3,043 people in 1901 to 31,709 in 1921, and, like Finnish women, Jewish women brought with them gender patterns dissimilar to those normally associated with Canada. The economic sphere was seen to be as much the domain of women as that of men; consequently, a Victorian "cult of true womanhood" was not really in effect. "Although Jewish women were considered intellectually weak," Frager notes, "East European Jewish culture did not view women as too fragile for venturing outside the safety of the home. . . . Indeed, in a culture where religious scholarship, not physical strength, was valued in men, Jewish women were not seen as particularly fragile." In Eastern European Jewish culture, Frager remarks, "it was the woman, not the man, who was associated with the material as distinct from the spiritual world. Thus the notion of women being too pure for this world was entirely foreign to East European Jewish tradition," which tended to associate women with practical sense and men with other-worldliness. In one important Toronto strike in 1905, fought by about 125 female and 75 male Russian Jews, women picketers played a decisive role, which suggested that "the women workers were not necessarily just following along after male militants."[165]

Still, women workers confronted a union culture that was in many respects also a male culture. As Mercedes Steedman reveals, in both Montreal (1910, 1912) and Toronto (1912) women militants, many of them Jewish immigrants, fought spiritedly not just against their employers but also to some extent against the male workers, who could draw upon gendered conceptions of skill to defend pay levels that were as much as twice as high as those of women workers doing equally demanding jobs. The plight of women workers in both cities often led to chivalrous calls for the exclusion of such "angels" from the workplace altogether, and to declarations of their work as being a threat to the moral fibre of society.

In Montreal anti-Semites sometimes presented French-Canadian women workers – the "midinettes" – as the helpless victims of their rapacious Jewish employers, and the women themselves reported reservations about mixing with organizers drawn from outside their own cultural milieu. In Toronto the cutters, mainly English Canadian, resisted joining the Amalgamated Clothing Workers of America (ACWA), in part to avoid mixing with immigrant Jews. The International Ladies' Garment Workers' Union (ILGWU), often a hotbed of socialist activism, was largely organized by Jews in both Montreal and Toronto. Divided on the grounds of gender and ethnicity, the industry was no less complicated in its class structure. A good number of small employers, many of them fellow Jews, shifted in and out of paid employment and served as ethnic and trade union leaders. Jewish women often preferred the larger factories to the small neighbourhood shops because in the small shops, with their family-like atmospheres, women were expected to be dutiful and self-sacrificing.

Remarkably, even given these formidable divisions, the workers launched powerful strikes. Inspired in part by events in New York City, such as the "uprising of the 20,000" in 1909 and a massive cloak-makers' strike in 1910, and driven by 60-hour workweeks, low wages, and miserable working conditions, the workers launched the industry's first general strike in Montreal in February 1910. By the last week of February a strike that had started out as a wage dispute in one small shop had escalated into a strike involving 27 shops and over 1,000 workers. Suddenly lines of division between French Canadians and Jews, and men and women, seemed to have been bridged. As Rose Henderson, a prominent suffrage militant and socialist in Montreal, explained, it was in the class interests of men that women be organized. Yet after the strike, despite their prominent role as militants, the women were not represented on the key bargaining committee, and the union's requests for a French-speaking organizer were disregarded. Some two years later the United Garment Workers of America (UGWA) launched an even larger nine-week general strike in the men's clothing industry, bringing out over 4,000 garment workers, many of them from Eastern Europe, drawing inspiration from the socialist movement and provoking jingoistic attacks on "radical aliens."

In Toronto, as Steedman shows, the Eaton's strike of February 1912 pitted the ILGWU against the company. Provoked by a seemingly minor issue of men being given "women's work" in the giant factory's cloak-making department, the dispute prompted a massive sympathy strike, which, in organizer J.B. Salsberg's words, became "the first big strike in which the Jewish tailors struck 'in defense of *undzere shvester* – our sisters.'" As in Montreal, the more radical elements of the women's movement, typified by Alice Chown, threw themselves into the struggle. Although Eaton's eventually won out (with owner Timothy Eaton insisting that the workers sign a statement renouncing their reasons for the strike and even apologize for the hurt feelings they caused him), the strike would long be retained in memory as a watershed moment for the city's radicals and Jews. "The strike changed the face of labour in Toronto," Steedman concludes, "and its demonstrations and marches marked a turning point in Toronto's labour history."[166] The strike also, Frager notes, underlined the creative ways in which an industrial dispute could take on the dimensions of a broader struggle – with an ambitious boycott campaign bringing the struggle home to consumers across the country, some of whom mailed back their Eaton's catalogues in protest.[167] Yet in this instance as well, while male workers had shown solidarity with women workers, it was a phenomenon that corresponded to their own self-interests, and the action did not necessarily unify Jewish and non-Jewish cloak-makers. Although both strikes revealed the "elasticity" of gender and ethnic categories, in their wake powerful gender, ethnic, and class interests pushed for business as usual.

In both Montreal and Toronto the diaspora socialists had created some of the most dramatic and remembered strikes in Canada, and in both cases socialists, inside and outside the labour movement, had played central roles. In the end, socialist internationalism and ideals of gender equality could not prevail over deep-seated divisions. Yet the new diaspora socialists strengthened the position of socialist feminism, and arguably changed its character. For many, it no longer seemed adequate merely to genuflect to Engels and Bebel, or to the inevitable socialist revolution, or to treat "women's issues" as subordinate to, or even easily separated from, class issues. As women themselves took greater possession of the woman question, they transformed it from one of abstract science to one of revolutionary praxis.

The Practical Socialist Feminism of Helena Gutteridge

If in her journalism and her fiction Francis Beynon revealed how abstract feminist theory could influence a much more down-to-earth engagement with local issues and actual women, Helena Gutteridge (1879–1960) provides an even more telling example of how leftist women were struggling to effect a practical politics based upon a combination of socialism and feminism.[168]

Gutteridge, one of the most remarkable of the socialist feminists of the time, was born in London, England. She was for a time a journeyman tailor who became an activist in the Women's Social and Political Movement (WSPU), led by the dynamic Pankhursts, to which large middle-class movement she brought a distinctive working-class perspective. As biographer Irene Howard suggests, Gutteridge was very much influenced by Sylvia Pankhurst, who, unlike her sister, mother, and much of the rest of the movement, considered the education and organization of working-class women an essential part of the feminist struggle.[169]

The five years following Gutteridge's arrival in Vancouver on 21 September 1911 witnessed her rapid elevation as a leader in the labour and socialist movement. Gutteridge joined the cutters' union in 1913 and was soon president of Local 178 and a delegate to the Vancouver Trades and Labor Council. She also quickly gravitated to the Vancouver branch of the British Columbia Political Equality League, which was holding "parlour meetings" almost every day to educate women about newly acquired civic voting rights and to press for a general provincial suffrage for women, a demand that had been put forward in the province since the 1880s. She became an important voice of women workers within the B.C. Federation of Labor, mounted a passionate campaign for women's suffrage, and established an imaginative program for the relief of unemployed women.

Underlying all these activities, and documented in her editorship of the "women's suffrage page" in the *British Columbia Federationist*, the province's new labour newspaper (edited by R.P. Pettipiece), was her firm conviction in a scientific Marxian feminism that combined Gilman, Schreiner, and Marx. It was a framework defended not only in her own writings but also in those she presented to the readers of her *B.C. Federationist* column. As Howard astutely observes, through Gutteridge's work many B.C. women evidently became familiar "with the sexual philosophies of the leading feminists."[170]

Much of Gutteridge's outlook shone through in her review of Helen Keller's *Out of the Dark*, in which the famed blind and deaf woman related her love of the red flag and her diligent absorption through Braille of the socialist writings of Karl Kautsky: "It is no easy and rapid thing to absorb through one's fingers a book of 50,000 words on economics. But it is a pleasure, and one which I shall enjoy repeatedly until I have made myself acquainted with all the classic socialist authors," she quoted Keller as saying. Gutteridge remarked: "Her investigation of blindness led her into the industrial world. 'My darkness had been filled with the light of intelligence, and behold the outer daylit world was stumbling and groping in social blindness.' What a rebuke to us who imagine that we see!"[171]

As it was for Keller, so it was for Gutteridge. The "light of intelligence" could illuminate the "social blindness" of the capitalist world. For Gutteridge, if "the story of the progress of the human race is the history of the birth of moral ideas which attain their fruition in society by one or two means – evolution or revolution," the great "new idea" of the day was that women are "an equal half of the human race." This idea was manifested "in a demand for human equality in the body politic." It meant that "men and women are equal as touching their humanity," and it could only result in a refusal of "the claim of men to rule women without their co-operation or consent by the divine right of masculinity." Indeed, "In the newly awakened women lies deep the divine call of evolution." If this idea met with "only the normal obstructions," then it might gradually emerge as part of "the social inheritance of humanity." But if it was blocked or oppressed, revolution would follow. Because of evolution, women had a right to motherhood – not just as individuals, but because they could express an idea of "race motherhood, that the children of all may be cared for and happy."[172]

For Gutteridge, it was important for deluded romantics and traditional moralists to realize that "we live in an age of hard facts, not an ideal dream land, we have to deal with conditions as they are and not as they should be."[173] Her comrade-in-arms Bertha Burns described the socialist/feminist relationship wittily in an article, "Women and Socialism," based upon a paper read to the Social Democratic Party, in which Burns served as the provincial secretary of women's organizations. Burns remarked that, on being solicited to speak "on the relation to socialism of the feminist movement," she had been reminded of an "Irishman named Patrick O'Brian," who when asked if he was any relation to Mike O'Brian, replied that he was a "distant relation," since he was his mother's first child and Mike was her thirteenth. "Just so 'distantly' is the question of woman's emancipation related to the question of the emancipation of the working class," she said. In fact, as the story implied, the two struggles were organically connected – even if, at times, they seemed far removed from each other. At the same time they were not to be falsely equated, as in the case of socialists who denied the very existence of a "sex war" and argued that, once the working class acquired the means of production, each working man would be able to support one or more women, "and that everything will then be lovely."[174] Such male socialists needed to remember their own Marxian analyses of class society. The supported creature was never really a free creature, and until women were economically independent they would not really be free.

For Burns, the "sex struggle" was rooted in the politics of the family. It began "when the baby girl wheedles nickels out of her reluctant father's pockets by her pretty smiles and coaxing airs," and continued until, "as the grown daughter, she sulks when she cannot obtain all she wishes, or all she believes her father might give her." The same wheedling characterized many marriages, and was degrading for both men and women: women because they were reduced to pauperism and powerlessness, and men because they were continually labouring under the pressure to live up to their wives' expectations. "It is a sex struggle, unnatural, but based on economic law," Burns argued, in words that both Gilman and Gutteridge would have warmly endorsed. "How many men struggling to support a family feel the slavery of it all – a slavery into which they have been entrapped by the sex lure and from which sex antagonism must arise. And the woman, feeling the failure of her husband, her supporter, to give her that support she needs, how she, quite as logically resents and questions the tie that binds them."[175]

Gutteridge was an enthusiastic promoter of Gilman, an invaluable inspiration in her eyes for struggles against prostitution. Her Spencerian analysis was combined with a Marxist critique of political economy, which identified the systemic reasons as to why starvation loomed for working people as soon as business entered a financial crisis. In one vintage first formation paragraph, Gutteridge went from describing the "billions of white blood cells" contained in the bloodstream to the problem of unemployment in modern society. Just as poor blood evidently allowed germs to enter and propagate, so too did poverty and malnutrition. Just as physiology had discovered the beneficial powers of white blood cells, so too should socialists, through the propagation of their knowledge, seek to illuminate "our social and economic disorder," of which tuberculosis and decayed teeth were only symptoms. For Gutteridge, the images of these white blood cells helped her shape her critique of prostitution, which she argued could only be eliminated if the business interests that profited from brothels were punished.[176]

For this Marxist feminist, the "harsh reality" of women's work was "the grim fact, against which women are increasingly inclined to revolt, that an immensely disproportionate share of the unpleasant drudgery of daily life, a great deal of the dangerous work, and most of the monotonous and semi-automatic work is done by women." In manufacturing centres, even if a man and his wife both worked in a factory, the woman was left to do all the housework. Women were increasingly being rendered "unfit to bear and care for their children efficiently. . . . The country is beginning to reap the harvest of women's economic inferiority in a sickly, degenerate race born of the mothers who try to fulfill the triple duty of worker, wife and mother, and the children of a nation are its greatest asset."[177]

Gilman's and Schreiner's essentially Lamarckian arguments permeated the B.C. Marxian feminists' analyses that Gutteridge promoted in her women's page in the *B.C. Federationist*. Any leading nation, Amy Campbell Johnston argued, necessarily recognized that men and women played separate biological roles and consequently had divergent interests. Nations that squashed women paid the price in the diminished capacities of women's offspring. "If the mother's intellectual faculties are cramped and starved through lack of freedom to express herself," she argued, "then will the children inherit dwarfed faculties, and it follows that a nation with such mothers can never be fully enveloped, or mentally balanced enough to retain a permanent footing as a leading nation." When man tried to rule woman, he simply demonstrated his need for self-glorification. "The foundation of man's development has not been strengthened as woman's has, by the many sacrifices of motherhood, and the indispensable attention to the many details of daily life," she observed. "The dense materialism enclosing man, his self-centered blind egoism has been a barrier to the highest development of any nation beyond a certain point." Woman had evolved along "higher human lines," and were one to envisage a perfected human race, it would be one in which "the human and humane instincts of the woman" would be freely expressed, with the result that war and its attendant evils would vanish as well.[178]

The "woman's point of view" was that all life was sacred, Ida Douglas Fearn argued, in a close paraphrase of Schreiner. The "man's point of view" was demonstrated by the callousness with which men poisoned milk for babies, and "man-made laws" punished them for it with only a small fine. "That is the value men put on the child that has cost the mother so much anguish and so much care." Exclusion from active political life meant that women were prevented from paying the debt they owed to the community, Mrs. Ernest Lloyd remarked in another article owing much to Schreiner. This implicitly cast her in a parasitical role, which meant both that her "desire for self-expression which is her right as a human being" was stifled and that her "debt" to the community went unpaid: "Therefore she suffers and the community suffers with her – the structure is incomplete."[179]

Gutteridge, renowned as a suffrage activist, played a large role first in the Political Equality League and then in the Vancouver-based Pioneer Political Equality League that split off from it in 1913. But she gradually became dissatisfied with the snobbery and class bias of the suffrage campaigners, whose "afternoon parlour meetings" by definition excluded working women. Gutteridge rejected the implicit paternalism of the League and created a working-class alternative, one that entailed soapboxing on city streets, campaigning in local unions, and the creation of the B.C. Woman's Suffrage League. She won official support for the cause from the B.C. Federation of Labor, a host of unions, and the *B.C. Federationist*, although before the final victory of the campaign on 5 April 1917, Pettipiece, the *Federationist*'s guiding spirit, Gutteridge's one-time comrade, and famed SPCer, withdrew his support. Gutteridge unabashedly admired the Pankhursts, and discreetly threatened the province's recalcitrant government with the idea that the Pankhursts' tactic of direct action might be adopted in British Columbia. Her suffrage struggle was inspired not only by the ideal of the democratic transformation of the public sphere, but also by a sense that women's enfranchisement was predetermined by the profoundest currents of social evolution. Only if women were empowered, she wrote, would there be a "new and effective form of government," one that would allow its citizens "to develop the best in them," create a "contented happy people," and desist from manufacturing criminals, weaklings, and degenerates. When mothers, who were "called upon to supply the basic ammunition," were truly free, the result would be that war (and here Gutteridge directly echoed Schreiner) "will be held in abhorrence by all."[180]

While Gutteridge's trade union activism opened doors for her as a suffragist, her commitment to working-class struggles went far beyond pragmatic considerations. Women's suffrage and feminist consciousness-raising, trade unionism, and class-consciousness were not, for her, warring tendencies. They were necessarily combined in one unified struggle for a more enlightened and emancipated world. A Woman's Suffrage League statement – most likely "the voice of Gutteridge" – declared: "The woman's movement and the labour movement are the expressions of a great revolutionary wave that is passing over the whole world. . . . The woman and the worker stand side by side."[181] Gutteridge was a stalwart supporter of the Vancouver Island coal miners in their long war against the coal companies, and in summer 1913 spent three weeks working at a fish cannery near Steveston to learn first-hand of women's work and wages on behalf of the B.C. Federation of Labor. "Our demand as suffragists is for deeds not words," she cried, when a labour commission exposed low wages paid to women and girls – an evil best combatted, in her mind, with an effective minimum-wage law.[182]

Suffrage, socialism, and social legislation were all non-conflicting aspects of one and the same struggle for enlightenment and progress. She was overjoyed when others interpreted reality in the same way. She hailed the "splendid spirit" of the women of the Vancouver Island coalfields and hailed the 500 citizens of Nanaimo, many of them striking miners and their wives, who, at a mass meeting held under the auspices of the Social Democratic Party, unanimously supported the parliamentary franchise for women. The "excessive sentences" passed on the miners revealed just how much women needed their full political freedom.[183]

Perhaps Gutteridge's most original contribution to early Canadian socialism was as an innovative anti-poverty activist. Early in 1914 the *B.C. Federationist* hailed the activism of Rose Henderson, who as a crusading probation officer in Montreal had described in gripping detail the degradation and filth of the slums, from which would issue "insane, diseased and mis-shapen human beings, destined to fill our penitentiaries and asylums."[184] Closer to home, a serious economic recession had swept hundreds of Vancouver women into dire economic straits in 1913–14. In the trades familiar to Gutteridge – tailoring, dressmaking, millinery – women's unemployment reached devastating levels.

Gutteridge threw herself into her newly formed Women's Employment League. The League, recipient of $2,000 in relief money from an obviously wary city council, established a registry for women seeking employment, and by the end of October 1914 had registered some 600 of them – roughly 400 single women and 200 widows, deserted wives, and women with unemployed husbands. Some of them were set up in temporary housing until they could find work, and many received meal tickets and groceries. The situation brought home to Gutteridge the urgency of a more socially responsible state. "It is so easy, under normal conditions, to admit the justice, logic and actual need for certain specific reforms, and do nothing," she reflected. "But with others weeping bitterly as they explain that they have children to feed and clothe with money earned by themselves, and a husband dead, or having gone away to look for work and not heard of since, the need to do something, as well as admit the necessity, becomes obvious." The crisis revealed the pitiful economic dependence of women upon men, Gutteridge suggested. One young woman, a charwoman, about 23 years old with one four-year-old child and another expected shortly, had returned home from work so tired and sick that she could not eat the food she had laboured so hard to provide. Her desperate husband thereupon left the house, swearing he would find some job to keep them going. After three months he had still not returned. With a young baby, the mother was unable to find work. Should she give up her children? Beg for charity? Or watch her children starve?[185]

What was to be done? Theory was indispensable, but without practice it had no purchase on reality. Women needed to organize their own anti-unemployment struggle. Taking over an empty 33-room house on Robson Street, the League established a workshop for unemployed women. Although most of its workers were untrained, the workshop aimed to create dolls for the Christmas market. When the *B.C. Federationist* visited in late November, its reporter found 130 women and girls working in an atmosphere of industriousness and calm. "No flurry, no bluster, but just smooth running efficiency under the quietly business-like direction of a mere handful of tireless women, obviously content in the assurance that they are helping as many of their sex as they can to make the best of a bad situation," the reporter noted. It was a socialist, self-generated women's project that went well beyond the normal bounds of charity work. The wider feminist implications of the fledgling institution did not escape the reporter's attention: "Any man obsessed with the idea that capacity for organization and management is an aptitude confined exclusively to his sex, can have his conceit knocked into a cocked hat."[186]

Gutteridge's career as one of Vancouver's most prominent radical voices reveals a number of conundrums: the fragility of the feminist/labour alliance, especially when it seemed that women would start to compete for men's jobs; the pervasiveness of labour racism – for Gutteridge and much of the Canadian labour movement turned on Asian immigrants when it seemed expedient to do so; and the class tensions within feminism itself, which in the 1920s and later would deny Gutteridge recognition and credit for the huge suffrage victory that she was important in achieving. Yet her career also illustrates another, perhaps less noticed, aspect of the socialist movement, and that is the practical significance of theory. Throughout her journalism *and* activism, Gutteridge was performing a specific kind of socialist feminism, one that she had acquired first-hand in England and which then became rooted in British Columbia. Far from being an oddball proponent of an alliance between Marxism and feminism, she was working within a network of like-minded people, all committed to bringing a socialist-feminist enlightenment to British Columbia.

The Extraordinary Diversity of Socialist Feminisms

A socialist feminist – as we've seen in action here – is a person who holds that any society founded on the subordination of women is unjust; that more egalitarian relations between men and women can be established; that the relations governing gender and sexuality, like those of production, distribution, and exchange, should be restructured in the light of reason; and that the preconditions for such a gender revolution are also to be found in the actual world around us.[187] It is possible to imagine many different ways of being a socialist feminist: for example, approaches that stress the inherent differences between men and women, calling out for action on behalf of women; approaches that argue for the essential similarity of conditions experienced by men and women, which makes all the more objectionable the vast body of discriminatory rules and regulations; and approaches arguing that a central oppression shaping the relations between men and women stems from the oppressive regulation of sexuality.

In their studies of women's political roles in this period, both Kealey and Newton see a connection between the turn to science and the sidelining of feminist concerns in the SPC and other organizations. Kealey's study suggests that evolutionary science was a poisoned chalice for women; in its Lamarckian and Darwinian versions it sustained a naturalized vision of gender differences and intensified the movement's shabby treatment of minorities, reduced, as were women, to the status of less developed children. As Kealey remarks, "Canadian socialists subscribed to these very ideas, sending confusing messages to women in the movement."[188] Yet many women also enthusiastically subscribed to such theories, especially those of Spencer, Gilman, and Schreiner. They saw in those ideas a way of providing a scientific foundation for their socialist feminism. Rather than providing arguments as to why women were unsuited for left activism, they fuelled a sense of urgency for that militancy. Many socialist feminists creatively and cogently used Schreiner, Gilman, and Engels, and the evolutionary analysis of women they provided, to argue for a new world for women, both within and outside the official movement.

In itself, when applied to the woman question, the evolutionary-scientific framework provided a space within which far-ranging assaults on patriarchy and capitalism could be launched. Socialist feminists – and, as the period progressed, more and more *women* socialist feminists – could themselves be enlighteners, bearers of theoretical insights that merited respect because they generated powerful insights into reality. Thus, as the project of socialist feminism proceeded, it discernibly became less a question of men (or male theorists) instructing women, and more one of women engaging in conversation with fellow women and even, if they would but listen, their socialist brothers. The reductively named "woman question" became a series of questions that actual women posed to capitalism – and to their often sexist comrades. In this new way of questioning, women shared significant interests and, potentially, a new conception of hegemonic struggle. At the same time the continuing impact of evolutionary thought in general, and Schreiner and Gilman more specifically, led some activists to posit women as the decisive evolutionary force. Their liberation from patriarchy and potential power over sexual selection meant that they were now guardians of the future well-being of humanity. Moreover, women, by virtue of their having suffered so much to bring children into the world, would prefer peace to war – a point that became a vital argument of the emergent women's peace movement. Women, that is, were seen as having an actual or potential biological investment in peace that transcended the more fleeting and inconsequential commitments of men. In resisting such phenomena as the sex trades and alcohol abuse, as well as workplace hardships and unemployment, women could now rely on scientific, and not merely religious, arguments: militant resistance was scientifically mandated because of women's particular evolutionary role. Finally, all of these convictions were integrated into what seemed to contemporary feminists, both male and female, to be the overwhelmingly convincing case for women's suffrage – the largest single extension of democratic rights in 20th-century Canadian history, to which the left made a great contribution.

Given the various lives of socialist feminists, and the panoply of causes, from suffrage to free love, that engaged left women, Kealey's valid argument with respect to women in socialist parties – that their roles were "largely confined to support activities" – does not apply to women across the whole of the first formation.[189] The most creative, long-lasting, and significant work carried out by socialist feminists took place in a left public sphere that the socialist parties did not monopolize. Here was a socialist-feminist moment that generated the first woman to stand for legislative office in Canada (and one of the first in the entire Empire), significant interventions in debates over sexuality, the first autonomous women's socialist organizations and parties, and (ultimately and in part) the most dramatic extension of the franchise in Canadian history, with a progressive woman running on a left-wing platform – Louise McKinney in Alberta in 1917 – being the first in the British Empire to attain public office.

Socialist feminists brought into play the country's first autonomous working-class women's anti-poverty and anti-unemployment mobilizations. Breakthroughs were registered in one field after another – whether it be Margaret Haile's candidacy and political theorizing, the initiation of feminist counter-hegemonic peace networks, the beginnings of new forms of consciousness-raising in journalism, or (perhaps most surprisingly underreported) the beginnings of a vibrant socialist-feminist literary tradition. Socialist feminists opened up, in highly original ways, issues of gender identity and sexuality, masculinity and femininity. As a result, for leftists and people outside the left, previously taken for granted aspects of the lives of men and women – marriage, the regulation of sexuality, the existence of sexual minorities – became at the very least subjects of discussion. Although many of these achievements fell far short of the New World for Women that many leftists of this time had dreamt of, given the enormous legacy of liberal patriarchy they were truly impressive. The socialist feminism of this period was successful in rooting the woman question in Canadian politics.

What is most apparent in this period is the existence of a formidable socialist-feminist cultural moment that generated influential debates about sexuality, inspiring poems, highly political novels, and lasting interpersonal networks. Many women came together to raise their voices against the bleak realities of isolation, dependence, and abuse. To stand up as a woman and speak truth to power demanded tremendous reservoirs of courage. These were not theories elaborated in a seminar room for the edification of a chosen few. These were ideas that were meant to change the world. Some were erroneous, but in this case, as so often, the error was a moment of the true. The very willingness to use evolutionary theory as a way of making the everyday world look strange was in itself a kind of truth, quite apart from the specifics of the science and its methods of application. For this cohort of first formation feminists the personal was (even then) the political. Margaret Haile was not an aberration. She was a forerunner.

"Will the Dyke Hold?" imagines the precisely demarcated properties of the Dominion of Canada as threatened by the liquid menace of the Eastern Other. *Sun* (Vancouver), 26 June 1914.

6

The Race Question

Vancouver, 23 May 1914. The vessel crept into Burrard Inlet shortly
before three o'clock that Sunday morning – a weather-beaten,
average-sized, rusting old thing, scarred with its 24 years of hard
labour on the oceans of the world. Just another working ship, in a worldly port
well used to them, a casual observer might have said. Yet as darkness yielded to
dawn, crowds gathered on the waterfront, some in hope and others in anger,
gazing expectantly out on this unprepossessing vessel anchored in the stream,
well away from the bustling wharves and docks of the awakening city.

Appearances were deceiving. Once this British-built vessel had been called
the *Stubbenuk*. Later, working the North Atlantic as part of the Hamburg-
American Line, it had gone by the name of the *Sicilia*. Now it was owned by a
small Japanese company, Shinei Kishen Go Shi Kaisha. It had sailed under
Captain Yamamoto, with a Japanese crew. Just under 330 feet in length, with a
gross tonnage of 2,926 tons, it had been chartered for the Hong Kong–Vancouver run, in part to carry a shipment of Japanese coal. Yet for some reason,
in the words of the Vancouver *Province*, this "sea-grimed vessel" had "suddenly jumped into the spotlight."[1] For the vessel once known as *Stubbenuk*
and *Sicilia* – and now as the *Komagata Maru* – would leave its name in history
as the very epitome of the explosive politics of race and immigration.[2]

Well before it ventured into Vancouver harbour, the ship had become a
matter of concern among officials who worried about the British Empire's
future in an age of inter-imperial rivalry and nationalist resistance. For weeks
Ottawa, Hong Kong, Victoria, and Vancouver had been abuzz with rumours
about the Japanese ship. In addition to the coal it carried "some 700 Hindus,"
the Shanghai *Mercury* of 16 April 1914 had stated. Perhaps these "Hindu
Invaders" were sick, some people worried. Perhaps they were armed, others
warned – if not with weapons, then with seditious ideas. Perhaps, like earlier
South Asian immigrants, the passengers would arrive impoverished and poorly
dressed – although the Victoria *Times*, the first daily on the scene, reported that
some of the travellers wore European clothes. Some wore riding-breeches and

helmets. Some had "Mohammedan red caps pressed tightly down on their thick black hair." Some were in "native costume," and quite a few were in the khaki uniforms of the British army. "They stand very erect, and move with an alert action," the story reported, in a tone of mild surprise. "All their suits are well pressed, and their turbans spotlessly clean. The most of them know a little of the English language, and some of them converse in it remarkably well."[3]

The 376 male passengers on board the vessel – 12 Hindus, 24 Muslims, and 340 Sikhs, all of Indian origin, and all but 20 of them newcomers to Canada – now found themselves to be at the centre of an immense transnational political and cultural storm. For the vessel was entering no tranquil city, but one that over the past decade had become a byword for the exclusion of Asians from Canadian shores – the epicentre of what writers Franca Iacovetta, Michael Quinlan, and Ian Radforth call the de facto "White Canada Policy."[4] Earlier, in September 1907, stirred by the agitations of the Asiatic Exclusion League, Vancouver rioters had inflicted over $36,000 worth of damage to Chinese and Japanese property. Now, almost seven years later, anti-Asian sentiments had not subsided. In the depths of an economic downturn came renewed calls for the exclusion of Asians, and even the dismissal of Asians employed in the city's restaurants and hotels. The *British Columbia Federationist* noted that Japanese fishermen had actually driven "white fishermen" off the Fraser River near New Westminster. "The seizure of the fishing grounds up river by the Asiatics is regarded as a very serious matter by all the residents and the New Westminster board of trade." The same issue published a long list of Vancouver hotels and restaurants employing "Japanese and Chinese on their staffs," with the suggestion that their dismissal would free up 400 positions for Whites.[5]

As the days turned into weeks the vessel remained anchored at a distance from the shore, and in Vancouver the police and immigration authorities struggled to stop access to it. While its passengers wrestled with such material challenges as heat, hunger, and thirst, and probably experienced alternating waves of hope, anger, and despair, Vancouver's citizens threw themselves passionately into debates about race, national and imperial identity – about the very future of White Canada. The passengers on board the *Komagata Maru* confronted no fewer than three laws that might prevent their admission to the country – but would those laws hold? Or, as had been the case the year before, when a remarkably similar vessel had landed, would the laws be overturned in the courts? Might the "Hindus" be planning a surreptitious landing? Meanwhile, what should be done with the passengers? Should they be given food and water, or should that decision be left up to the charterers and assignee responsible for them? It was as if, entrapped in a metal cage, the passengers had a dual existence: one as actual suffering human beings, and the other as symbols of a tide of modernity, portending a monstrous future of disintegration and degeneration.

Almost a month into the crisis, on 21 June 1914, supporters of the trapped men gathered at Dominion Hall in downtown Vancouver for a protest meeting called by Hindu and Sikh societies. The participants – according to the *Sun*, 800 "Hindus" and 200 Whites – passed a resolution denouncing the immigration authorities for preventing the passengers from consulting with their legal advisor, blocking provisions and water, and "making their lot on board one to which cattle would not be subjected." Such "brutal and unlawful treatment of British subjects" would not be tolerated in India. They urged the authorities to remember the golden rule – "do unto others as you would have them do unto you" – and to deliver "the Hindus . . . from the high-handed action of the immigration department."[6] Copies were sent to Prime Minister Robert Borden and the secretary of state for India.

Two days later Dominion Hall rang to the sounds of a very different meeting. It was called by Vancouver's self-important mayor, Truman Smith Baxter, to give voice to the "unqualified objection of the citizens of Vancouver to the landing in British Columbia of the immigrants now in the harbor on board the steamer Komagata Maru." The Nanaimo politician Ralph Smith denounced the Hindus as "anarchists." The mayor proclaimed the Hindu to be "not a desirable citizen, and when I say that I am backed up by public opinion." Undeterred by this hostility, 40 or 50 courageous "wearers of the turbans" showed up at the mass meeting. When a resolution calling for the exclusion of all "Hindus" was put to the crowd, these "Hindus" bravely raised their hands against it. Nonetheless, the mayor pointedly declared the resolution "unanimously carried by the citizens of Vancouver." He placed special emphasis on the word "citizen," to underline the point that the turbaned dissidents were nothing of the kind.[7]

If the law-abiding Vancouverites confronting law-disrespecting "anarchists" were on such solid ground, why not simply take the matter to the courts and let the law in its majesty punish the evil-doers? Revealingly, and in sharp contrast to the "absolutism" of his rhetoric, Mayor Baxter and many other White Canada proponents were not really sure that the law would back them up. From the perspective of the virulently nativist Vancouver *Sun*, recourse to the courts was undesirable, and it would be better if the "Hindus" were blocked from them altogether: "If the cases of the Hindus get before the courts the matter may end, after the long legal strife which will follow, in the undesirable Orientals gaining admission to British Columbia after all." Mayor Baxter warmly agreed. The "Hindus" must be stopped from "taking action in the courts to force their presence upon us." He had in mind a more vigilante form of justice, in which a couple of tugboats would be ordered to hitch on to the *Komagata Maru* and "haul her with her load of undesirables out to sea."[8]

It was a direct-action tactic that many seemingly found attractive in Vancouver that June. "I will give $250 towards a movement to hire a tug, cut the cable of the vessel with the Hindoos aboard, and tow the ship outside the harbor with a warning to its officers to depart and never return," one wealthy man reportedly told James H. McVety of the Socialist Party of Canada.[9] Even Vancouver MP H.H. Stevens, who had bellowed out a long enumeration of the "anarchistic" and other sins of the Asians to the House of Commons, thought that the best course might lie in a quite unparliamentary direction – that of having a steamer tow the *Komagata Maru* outside the three-mile limit, so that the "Japanese can take charge of her and work her back to Hong Kong."[10]

There were laws that formed a seemingly "solid" dike against the flood of Asian immigrants that many people imagined was symbolized by the *Komagata Maru*. One order-in-council required passengers to carry $200 with them; another of 1908 imposed the "continuous passage rule," excluding anyone who did not make a direct journey to Canada (and the country had no direct steamship connection with India); a third, rushed through early in 1914, barred "labourers and artisans" from entering via British Columbia.[11] All of the orders delicately preserved the appearances of a colour-blind liberal universalism while working surreptitiously and effectively to "Keep Canada White."

Yet these and other solid-seeming barriers had in the past melted into air when challenged in the courts. In 1913 a Japanese company, the Nippon Yusen Kaisha, began to issue tickets to South Asians, and a total of 46 South Asians subsequently arrived in Victoria on board the *Panama Maru* in autumn of that year. Of them, seven, previously resident in Canada, were admitted. The other 39 were ordered deported by Immigration officer Malcolm Reid. They appealed for a writ of habeas corpus, and when the case reached the B.C. Supreme Court they obtained a judgment in their favour, on the grounds that the relevant orders-in-council departed from the wording of the Immigration Act. The decision thus seemingly rendered null and void the sole legal means of excluding South Asians. It suggested that, if individual immigrants could successfully appeal for a writ of habeas corpus, they stood a fighting change of admission into the country on technicalities, especially if their cases were heard by the right judge.

This 1913 decision was deeply alarming to advocates of a White Canada (and as deeply inspiring for Sikhs awaiting news from Canada in Hong Kong). Although the orders-in-council were quickly redrawn, the upshot of the 1913 case was to offer hope to South Asian immigrants. Individually, they could apply to one judge after another, and if only one judge would rule that they were being illegally detained, they could go free. In this context, who could be sure that he or she stood on "solid ground" when arguing that the voyage of the *Komagata Maru* was "illegal"?

From the standpoint of Robie L. Reid, the agent of the minister of justice on the scene, there was a very real chance that the immigrants might success-fully work the system: "We would not consent to any course which would permit of any *one* Judge giving a decision which would admit the applicant into Canada, and this without any appeal to a higher Court."[12] Hence the ex-traordinary precautions taken to isolate the vessel – its enforced distance out in the harbour, the close restriction of access to its passengers, and the intense surveillance of the Shore Committee of South Asians struggling on behalf of its imprisoned passengers. Legal counsel were even obstructed in attaining access to their clients. As Eric Wilton Morse, no friend of South Asian immi-gration, conceded in a 1936 masters thesis, "The Indians possibly had grounds for believing that at first there was obstruction of justice. During all the time that the cases were being tried the immigration authorities took the greatest care that no communication should take place between the passen-gers and either their solicitors or their countrymen on shore." The passengers' solicitor, SPC member J. Edward Bird, wired Prime Minister Borden on 23 June to inform him that he had been prevented from boarding the ship to take instructions from his clients. They were being kept imprisoned on a vessel on very short rations; the charterers had refused to supply food or water to them.[13] Was Immigration officer Reid upholding the law, then, or was he him-self obstructing it – as he had a year earlier when he had unceremoniously deported a priest in defiance of a writ of habeas corpus? As historian Rajini Srikanth remarks, Reid "openly flouted the process of justice prohibiting the passengers from appearing before the Board of Inquiry, where they hoped to test the validity of Canadian immigration laws." There was more than a whiff of vigilantism in Reid's use of food and water, sometimes withheld for as long as three days, as bargaining weapons, and in his attempts to have Captain Ya-mamoto to declare the passengers mutinous as a pretext for the authorities to board the ship.[14]

Reid's actions, possibly motivated by his own need to "settle the score" for his legal reversals over the previous years, thus contradicted the rhetoric of legal certainty with which partisans sought to draw solid, fixed and firm lines between the "orderly" inside and the "disorderly" outside. Although, in a sense, three different orders-in-council stood in the way of the South Asians entering Canada, the lawyers had substantial reason to worry about whether this exclusionary dike was really as solid as it seemed. It was only when the ap-peal for a writ of habeas corpus was refused, and a Court of Appeal upheld the orders-in-council and Section 23 of the Immigration Act (which shielded immigration officers from the judiciary) that the last ray of legal hope was ex-tinguished for the passengers, many of whom had invested everything they owned in the venture.

A Liquid Modernity

From 1859 to 1914 British rule in India posed complicated problems of reconciling liberal theory with imperial practice – as exemplified perfectly by the collective works of James Mill, who authored a seemingly authoritative multi-volume work about an India he had never visited, and John Stuart Mill, who wrote so many inspiring words on imperialism's capacity to uplift, violently if necessary, the benighted inhabitants of the subcontinent to the standards of liberal rationality that he so consistently championed.[15] Insurgents were emerging in many of the subcontinent's new universities and schools, and by the early 20th century, from Switzerland to the United States, émigré radicals were articulating new, increasingly militant, visions of independence.[16] Vancouver would become one of their most significant gathering points in the years leading up to the Great War, and a centre for publications produced locally and aimed at the homeland.

The Liberals (and after 1911 the ideologically very similar Conservatives under Borden) were acutely consciously of the need to maintain a delicate balance on questions of immigration. If immigrants were drawn in large numbers from outside the British and French communities, they might disturb an already fragile equilibrium between the two major linguistic groups and the two dominant forms of Christianity. With respect to the *Komagata Maru*, the governing elite confronted an acute dilemma. Simply to exclude or to remove South Asians risked accelerating and radicalizing the independence movement in India itself, and carried serious implications for the very concept of the British Empire. Moreover, it called into question the "Honour of the Crown," which had declared in 1858 that Indians would enjoy equal rights with other British subjects in any part of the Empire.[17]

The case of the *Komagata Maru* threw into sharp relief the paradoxically fluid identities of Canadians in 1914. Rapid immigration had created hundreds of thousands of new Canadians, drawn from many quarters of Europe – but among these were huge numbers of Britons, who in 1914 still made up the single largest group of immigrants. At that time Canada was, for a vast number of people, particularly those within the hegemonic liberal mainstream, in a strong sense "Greater Britain," culturally, diplomatically, and economically united with its motherland. When war arrived in August 1914, there was no doubt about Canada's active involvement at Britain's side. Elite Canadians cherished British culture, subscribed to British magazines, kept up with the latest British news, jockeyed for British honours – one of them (Bonar Law) would even become the British prime minister in 1922, and another (Max Aitken, later Lord Beaverbrook) parlayed his windfall gains in Montreal finance into a seat in the House of Lords. Their Canada was in essence a White settler society, and the nationalism of the majority of its population was a British nationalism. This Canada was, if the term is taken in its fullest cultural sense, a grand experiment in "whiteness," an imagined community founded upon the British occupation of the northern section of North America. The "Great White North" was a term that did not just call up "snow" to the mind. (In truth, if "snow" was to be a fundamental criterion of Canadian-ness, Vancouver and Victoria were in a spot of trouble.) To be a true Canadian was to be White, English-speaking, and Protestant – with some allowance made for French-Canadian Catholics, provided they were deferential to the Empire. This was not necessarily sub-servience – a Canadian nationalist like Prime Minister Borden would insist that Canada merited a place at the table when big decisions were made – but neither was it "independence," which in this period carried an overtone of disloyalty to the Crown.[18]

"It is hard to say what conception these people have of British institu-tions," exclaimed the *Sun* of the passengers aboard the *Komagata Maru*. "They did not appear to be capable of grasping the fact of this country's sovereign rights, but look on it as another India. Asked why they expected to be allowed to enter Canada, they said it was because they were British subjects, but they would explain it all in the courts."[19] White Canadians, then, had the right, indeed the duty, to reject such immigrants.

As the secretary of the Victoria Trades and Labor Council explained, "The people of India, in common with all Asiatic races, are reared and nurtured in and under the influence of civilization and environments that seem to be, in principle, totally opposed to the civilization and environments under which we of the Western civilization are born and reared." Within this reading of Canada, the "people of the Western races" had settled and developed the country, and aspired to control its future; the admission of the supposedly less evolved and very different Hindus "would threaten and even make impossible the realization of such hopes." The "unrestrained mixing of the races on this Coast," advised the local Methodist monthly, "would lead to economic disas-ter and ethical demoralisation."[20]

The India Office incurred the displeasure of local commentators for seeming to imply that the Dominion should accept immigrants it did not want, and the *Times* of London supported "Canada's" attitude as necessary to her self-preservation.[21] As O.D. Skelton shrewdly observed, the responsibility for exclusion of South Asians from the full benefits of Empire was shifted on to Canada – from Britain, which ruled India, to a Dominion that Britain did not fully rule.[22]

Hence, in responding to a local event – the appearance of the *Komagata Maru* off their shores on 23 May – Vancouverites were directly confronted with, and contributing to, a crisis of global dimensions. Everything about the *Komagata Maru* turned out to be transnationally intricate. The ship's owners, who played a discreet behind the scenes role in the drama, were Japanese, as were the captain and crew.[23] The "Hindus," although apparently all originating in the Punjab, had been picked up by the vessel in Hong Kong, the China Coast, and Japan. Gurdit Singh, the voyage's key promoter, was an affluent businessman who had made much of his money in the railroad industry and rubber plantations of Malaysia. Fluent in Malaysian, he was as much at home in Hong Kong, India, and Singapore as in India.

Far less visible to the public, yet of direct significance to the unfolding of the struggle, was the unsolid identity of one of the key protagonists in the struggle to exclude the South Asians from Vancouver. As Andrew Parnaby and Gregory Kealey reveal, William Charles Hopkinson (1880–1914) was officially hired to a permanent position in the Immigration Department in 1909 and assigned to the Dominion Police. He was also paid $100 per month as an interpreter of and spy on the South Asian community. Thus, although he might appear to be a "Canadian" working in a "Canadian" context, he was just as much an "Imperial" working in a "world" context. His activities, initially concentrated on southern British Columbia, soon encompassed territories extending all the way to northern California. Even his public identity was ambiguous. As an Immigration officer he could "admit, reject, or initiate deportation proceedings against new immigrants,"[24] and hence was often in the public eye. Yet he was also spying on their meetings, reading their publications, and reporting to superiors in Ottawa and ultimately in Calcutta. Hopkinson, the Indian-born son of a Brahmin mother and a British army officer, resident on the subcontinent for over two decades and fluent in Hindi – was he any more essentially "British" than the "Hindus" he was so keen to exclude?[25] Did his uncertain "racial" status add to the vigour with which he went after his fellow South Asians?

By bringing the *Komagata Maru* into the waters of Canada, promoter and financier Gurdit Singh meant to send a message to Britain. His secretary wrote out a statement and gave it to the correspondent of the Vancouver *Sun*: "The main object of our coming is to let the British government know how they can maintain their rule in India, as the Indian government is in danger nowadays. We can absolutely state how the British government will last in India forever." If the Hindus were admitted, all would be well for British rule, but "otherwise then there will be trouble."[26] Singh was clearly interested in making a point about British rule in India, although his motives in themselves were difficult to read. As a businessman, he was plainly intrigued by the possibilities of trading coal for timber and engaging in a movement of passengers to and from Asia and Canada. As a Sikh patriot he was, it was said, deeply upset by the plight of Hong Kong Sikhs awaiting acceptance in Canada, where they might join their relatives and friends. Was he anti-British? His activism in 1914 may have reflected an attempt to overcome the legacy of 1857, when Sikhs had helped quell the rebellion of Indian army officers. Was he consciously defying the law – that is, having been forewarned that the ship would not be allowed to land at Vancouver, had he decided to make the exclusion of its passengers a symbol of British racism? Or was he inspired by the recent legal victories of South Asian immigrants, and by the possibly favourable silence on the part of Canadian authorities in response to telegrams from the governor of Hong Kong?[27]

It took little time for the *Komagata Maru* to become a topic of international debate. As the *Province* remarked, "The history of the Hindus' struggle to enter British Columbia has been published all over the world." Theosophist Annie Besant, writing in the *Daily Chronicle* of London, was among those well known to the international left (both Phillips Thompson and Helena Gutteridge could be numbered among her admirers) who denounced the colour bar, and warned that both British Columbia and Australia risked pushing the Indians into a drive for outright independence. The Royal Colonial Institute's official journal deplored the Vancouver incident, placing the event in a global context. "Until the Russo-Japanese war it was held as an axiom that no Asiatic nation could successfully challenge a White one. That illusion gone, the White nations are obliged to reconstruct their international obligations to include the possibility of powerful rivals whose citizens are refused entrance to countries under the British flag." India would "vent her discontent" not upon Canada or South Africa, but Great Britain. R.B. Angus, director of the Canadian Pacific Railway and formerly general manager of the Bank of Montreal, reported that the viceroy of India himself had conveyed his worries about the exclusion of the Hindus from British Columbia. Speaking in the House of Commons in 1926, Henri Bourassa, the *nationaliste* MP, remembered being in London in 1911 and asking a high official of the India Office what best contribution Canada could render to the Imperial cause. "If you could bring B.C. to open her doors to Hindu immigration," was the reply, "that would be worth all the dreadnaughts you could build in ten years."[28]

In Vancouver itself the transnational dimensions of the crisis posed a dilemma for the most fervent imperialists – for if, on the one hand, the White Canada policy favoured their interests, it also carried the risks of imperilling the Empire. "It is feared," proclaimed the *Province*, "that should this shipload of Hindus return to India there would be violent demonstrations against British rule there and the consequences would be serious." As Morse remarked in 1936, "The situation would have to be handled with the greatest delicacy. Ottawa was uncomfortably situated, between London and Vancouver."[29] The *Komagata Maru* drama, unfolding on a Vancouver stage, was being closely watched by an international audience.

It was a play, in large part, about race[30] – in which the race of "Whites" was pitted against the race of "Hindus." What came to be called the "race question" combined separate strands of "nation," "colour," and "ethnicity" in highly problematic ways. In essence, when people asked the race question they were posing three questions. What is Canada – what great purpose should it be serving? Who is Canada – what sorts of people are fundamental to the project, and who should be allowed to join them? And where is Canada – is it a free-standing state within North America or an organic component of a world-girdling Empire, the vital link between the British motherland and its overseas possessions? To these three questions, the dominant *fin de siècle* answers were: "Canada is a British Dominion, whose purpose is to create a political and social order founded upon Christianity, liberalism, and capitalism"; "it should be run by and primarily populated by White people biologically predisposed to share these ideals"; and "Canada is part of *pax Britannica*, commercially linked to the United States, but by virtue of its intrinsic Britishness, separate and distinct from it." The race question was about Canada as an imagined community in the world.

As Patricia Roy, the leading scholar on British Columbia's anti-Asian agitations, remarks, "A White Man's Province" became one of the most popular slogans in B.C. politics. It was warmly endorsed by Conservative premier Richard McBride, a sworn opponent of the "Asian menace."[31] The slogan, linked with British imperialism, had been recently highlighted by Rudyard Kipling, whose depictions of the mysterious East and the "White Man's Burden" were extremely popular in this period. In his visit to Canada in 1907, Kipling had presumed to tell Canadians that the West cried out for immigration, but only immigration of the right sort: "You must have labourers there. You want immigration, and the best way to keep the yellow man out is to get the white man in," he advised. "If you keep out the white then you will have the yellow man, for you must have labour. Work must be done, and there is a certain work to do which a white man won't do so long as he can get a yellow man to do it. Pump in the immigrants from the Old country. Pump them in . . ." To act "White" was to act in accordance with principles of British fair play and decorum, and "Speak White!" became a well-known taunt to throw in the face of French-Canadian *nationalistes*.[32]

Whiteness in Canada was an expression of confidence in British geo-political might and cultural pre-eminence – and haunted by an ambient dread that both might be lost in the twinkling of an eye. It was both anti-modern, based upon notions of blood, soil, and military valour, and ultra-modern, mobilizing up to date technology and drawing, so it was thought, upon the latest word in evolutionary theory. It gloried in the steel rails and steamships that bound the Empire together, and visualized a future in which the backward and benighted peoples of the world would be redeemed and reordered through their exposure to their racial and cultural superiors. This volatile contradiction of certainty and fear explains much of the extreme response to the "Hindus." On its face, the *Komagata Maru* "crisis" was an improbable overreaction to a minor kerfuffle. There were scarcely 5,200 South Asians in

British Columbia, and had British Columbia been confronted with ten times that number the whole of them would still not have come close to forming 10 per cent of the population. Even in the terms of the racialist arguments popular at the time, many South Asians were not exactly "non-White." Many of them were, in terms of one popular racialist mythology of the day, "Aryans." A good many, especially among the Sikhs, had sacrificed life and limb for the Empire.[33]

Even for ardent exponents of the White Man's Burden, the Sikhs were a tricky borderline case, having borne such a large part of that supposed burden in helping to crush the sepoy revolt in India in 1857 and having then played an indispensable role in the "Great Game" of the Empire in Afghanistan. "It seems to me," remarked one of the champions of the South Asians, "that these Punjabis are entitled to official recognition and protection. Hundreds of these men have been soldiers in our Army and wear medals for their services in the field. They are the subjects of our Empire, and are yet denied the rights of citizenship by a large proportion of their fellow subjects." Yet, as Rajini Srikanth remarks, it was the very legitimacy of the Punjabis' claim that was so terrifying for partisans of White Canada, because it removed most of the conventional grounds on which the Other had been excluded from the Dominion.[34]

The language in which the "White" denominated the "Other" in this struggle was deeply suggestive. The nomenclature itself – "Hindoos" or "Hindus" – was neither accurate nor innocent. Most of the passengers were Sikhs, not Hindu. Some commentators said they used the term "Hindu" as a way of referencing "Hindustan," a term once popular as a way of designating the entire Indian subcontinent.[35] Others said they used it as a way of distinguishing between "Indians from India" and "Indians in North America." Yet it was a term that exoticized the South Asian immigrants, firstly implying that their stable and essential identity was founded on a complex set of religions that few North Americans understood, and secondly by fixing them in an identity-category drawn from a pre-modern world. (Throughout the whole moment of the *Komagata Maru*, the opposite of "Hindu" was rarely "Christian" – it was "White.") The term allowed people to "talk race" without seeming to be "talking race," because – if challenged about their colour prejudice, which even in 1914 many Canadians were skittish about explicitly defending – they could always argue that they were merely talking about geography (merely denoting a native or resident of "Hindustan," an archaic term for India) or about climate (referring to a person who came from the hot, tropical "South") or about religion (denoting an adherent of Hinduism) or about culture (to more loosely describe a pre-rational specimen of pre-modern humanity). All five connotations – colour, country, climate, cult, and culture – were confusingly at play in 1914, with the paradoxical consequence that the "Hindus" themselves, who curiously also used this word to designate themselves, remained virtually unknown people to the citizens most anxious for their removal. The grounds for excluding them could thus be shifted from one heading to another, depending on circumstance, including the argument that people from the hot, tropical South could never survive in the climate of the North. In his book *Strangers Within Our Gates*, after dismissing the Hindus' costume as "grotesque," J.S. Woodsworth goes on to say: "They are very slow, and do not seem capable of hard, continuous exertion. Their diet is light, and physically, they are not adapted to the rigorous climate of Canada."[36]

"Race" was a protean concept, and if it suggested the hidden essence or logic underlying phenotypical and cultural differences, it did so in a perpetually mystifying way, one that defied any possible "scientific" refutations. Race-thinking was a "tangle of quarrels, a confusion of assertions, a knot of facts and fictions that revolt the intellect and daunt the courage of the most persistent. In its mazes, race-thinking is its own best refutation," remarks Jacques Barzun. "If sense and logic can lead to truth, not a single system of race-classification can be true." Yet, adds Robert Young in his brilliant exploration of *Colonial Desire*, "the very perversity of the logic of race theory also makes it hard to refute. If it simply erected essentialist, biological categories that could be deconstructed, then matters would be simple." Its inherent complexity "allows it to survive despite its contradictions, to reverse itself at every refutation, to adapt and transform itself at every denial."[37]

Even the most courageous critics of Vancouver's toxic racism of 1914 seemingly worked on a conceptual terrain in which "Hindus," "Whites," and "colour" all were self-evidently accurate words for fixed and firm realities. "They are of a different color," remarked one favourably disposed clergyman, "but in spite of their color, they belong to the same great Aryan stock from which we, ourselves, have sprung. Their literature is one of the greatest in the world. They are a temperate nation."[38]

The constructed image of the "Hindu" was that of a harbinger of a monstrous wave, the first symptom of a deluge of Asian difference that would sweep all the cherished things of everyday British life into a vast tsunami of disorder and ruin. A 26 June 1914 Vancouver *Sun* cartoon, "Will the Dyke Hold?" captured this dynamic in striking fashion – suggesting, in its bottom half, a happy "Canada" (without any representations of human beings) – a tidy farmhouse, with a friendly verandah, smoke billowing from a chimney, and a well-positioned shade tree, all located on a carefully squared-out lot – with its "Immigration Laws Dyke" about to be besieged by a "Flood of Oriental Labor." The ogre-like figures shown in this transnational flood appear to represent an endless succession of humanoids, emerging like so many frothy emanations from the waves. Underneath the sinister glowering eyes of the central ogre is, very vaguely, a somewhat Sikh-looking beard, but perhaps more obviously the figure is a generic "Eastern" jinni – summoned out of the *Thousand and One Nights* to perform as a shape-shifting, liquid terror. He threatens to undermine everything good liberal Canadians should cherish about their fair Dominion – property, individualism, peace, organization, prosperity – in an awful wave of liquid modernity.[39]

Drawing from back files of the *Canadian Magazine*, E.W. Morse unearthed startling comments about the "Hindus." One "Vancouver city-father" remarked that he would "rather see a Hindu immigrant die of hunger and cold before his eyes than succour him." Another sneered derisively at the British military medals worn by the Sikhs to honour their service to the Empire as "tin-pot ornaments," and another ingeniously adopted the tropes of another race-based campaign when he urged that the true meaning of "Sikh" was "a member of the lower class. . . . Those who have no set aim in life. . . . They are the coolies of Calcutta."[40] Even before the *Komagata Maru* arrived, the *Sun* was certain that the Hindus were "very secretive." When at last the vessel was in view, the newspaper observed Hindus gathering on the waterfront in "excited groups, talking in low voices, as if plotting schemes to aid their countrymen on the Japanese steamer to get ashore." The imagined Hindu was primitive and simple, yet, perplexingly, also intensely legalistic and given to public argument: "With the bent of the Hindu for litigation they are evidently set on a legal fight," remarked the *Sun*, "and they would probably be much disappointed if they did not get it." They were childlike and somewhat cowardly – according to the *Province*'s headline, "Ready to Surrender Rather Than Chance a Fight" – yet also warlike and dangerously anarchistic.[41]

Were they even fully human? As the imprisoned passengers on the *Komagata Maru* suffered for want of food and fresh water, the *Sun* ran an article by the improbably named columnist Pollough Pogue on "The Canned Hindus" – "The two hundred swarthy tribesmen of the earth's lost tribes," whose sufferings were probably faked and whose claims to a shared British identity were dismissed. That the imprisoned passengers risked death from lack of food and water was, from some perspectives, not a public responsibility. "The owners of the steamer have already been put to great inconvenience and expense by the delay of the vessel here and they care nothing if the Hindus starve or die of thirst because they only chartered the ship to Gurdit Singh," reported the *Province*. "If he does not care to feed his countrymen, that is his lookout." From the not altogether Christ-like perspective of the Immigration Department, hunger and thirst were useful negotiating tools, not elements of human suffering. The "Hindus" were "just as hungry and clamorous as ever," complained the *Province*, as though writing of an irritating flock of pigeons, and not starving and thirsty fellow human beings, trapped in a metal prison in full view of the city.[42]

Yet, notwithstanding such dehumanizing racist tropes, there was a delicate liberal skittishness about referring too explicitly to skin colour as the grounds for exclusion. Again and again, by ingeniously calling upon one of the many connotations of "Hindu," the exclusionists urged with a straight face that their campaign had "nothing to do with colour," but was rather about "culture." Canadians fancied themselves quite different from Americans, whose overt habits of racial segregation and lynching they often deplored (while often sending their own children to racially segregated schools and maintaining colour bars in taverns and trade unions). "It is not a question of color," Pogue remarked. "Some of the hillmen from the pine forests of the Himalaya mountains are almost white." (He then rather spoiled the rhetorical effect by adding: "The Sikh people say that they were white once. If this is true, some one must have muddied the strain.") It was not colour, but that deep mysterious essence, that unbridgeable chasm that set the British West against the Enigmatic East (Pogue had obviously been reading his Kipling). "It is that we do not think as Orientals do," argued the *Sun*'s correspondent. "That is the big reason. That is why the East Indians and the other Asiatic races, and the western white race, will always miscomprehend each other." Even the "complex and quite unaccountable" Sikhs, although the "least objectionable of the East Indians," were ominously reminiscent of another not quite White people: these "remorseless politicians" and "disturbers" were "like the worst of the Irish raised to the Nth or the fourth dimension." The *Colonist* declared them to be "a case more apart even than the Chinese. Their habits of life are unsatisfactory. They do not bring their wives with them, and will not make homes or rear families. They are totally unfitted for a white man's country."[43]

Rather than speaking openly about objectionable skin colour, the exclusionists preferred to speak, ever so compassionately, about the disabilities confronted by Southern people in the climate of the North. As Mackenzie King argued in his *Report* on "Oriental" labourers: "The experience has shown that immigrants of this class having been accustomed to the conditions of a tropical climate are wholly unsuited to this country and that their inability to readily adapt themselves to surroundings so entirely different inevitably brings upon them much suffering and privation."[44] The Sikh veterans of wars in Afghanistan would, so the story went, be entirely perplexed by the extreme rigours of a Vancouver winter.

The Question of Race

"Race" – along with its cognates "racism," "racialism," and "racialization" – is a contested concept.[45] The history of the word goes back to the beginning of the 16th century. Originally used, according to Michael Banton, to "denote lineage, a line of descent, as in 'the race of Abraham,'" race also came to be loosely used to denote what would now be called nations or ethnic groups –

such as the Gauls and Saxons in France and Britain respectively. At the end of the 18th century race began to be used by some writers, Banton says, to denote "a class of creatures with common characteristics, making it synonymous with either species or subspecies in modern classifications."[46]

In the 18th and 19th centuries, in parallel with the European peoples' conquest of much of the world, the concept provided, according to Constance Backhouse, a "convenient justification for their right to rule over 'uncivilized' peoples, a rationale for the creation of colonial hierarchies."[47] By the 1850s, even before Darwin's *Origin of Species*, some anthropologists argued that human races were distinct species with "different capacities and inherent antagonisms toward each other." "Typological doctrines" suggested that the differences between races was akin to that between lions, tigers, and leopards – all different species within the genus *panthera*, kept distinct by nature through genetic inheritance.

Many Canadians used "race" in a much more expansive way. When André Siegfried brought out his interesting *Race Question in Canada*, and Abbé Lionel Groulx his *L'Appel de la race*, they were talking about the country's French-English divisions, not about race issues pertaining to what we would now call people of colour.[48] Many thought of Jews, Ukrainians, Finns, Russians, and the British as constituting "races." In much of the country outside the three largest cities, and particularly through the North and West, racism and the project of liberal order were profoundly complementary projects. In theory the freeborn Briton might not necessarily be a White man. In the practice of liberal order from the 1840s to the 1910s, and especially with the diffusion of forms of evolutionary theory after the 1850s, the intelligence, independence, and self-possession of the "individual" pertained to White men alone. Herein lay the liberal ideological justification for the subordination of Native peoples, the imposition upon them of Indian agents and residential schools, and the denial (to all but those who were certified as "civilized") of the franchise down to the third quarter of the 20th century.

Even among those whose origins were in the British Isles, racializing distinctions were drawn throughout the 19th century, creating a hierarchy with Anglo-Saxons at the top and some Celts at the bottom. Edmond Demolins's *Anglo-Saxon Superiority: To What It Is Due*, written to wake up his French fellow citizens to the ever-increasing gap separating them from their English competitors, was typical in finding racial explanations for the most diverse phenomena, from the cleanliness of farmers' homes to the Britons' supposed lack of snobbery. In the 19th century the Irish were often considered a "race apart," and "inferiorized, denigrated, and simianized in racial terms." They were, as David Roediger remarks, noted to be "*low-browed* and *savage*, *groveling* and *bestial*, *lazy* and *wild*, *simian* and *sensual*" – all insulting terms applied to antebellum Blacks.[49]

If the Irish gradually became White, groups identified as actually or incipiently hostile to British liberal order could become "Black." Russians in the 20th century were gradually coded as dark people. They were "simianized," as the extent of their revolutionary challenge, first posed by the Russian Revolution of 1905 and then by the revolutions in 1917, became clear. Germans were also subject to different racializing strategies. Benjamin Franklin even regarded the "swarthy" Germans as insufficiently pale when he dreamt of the United States as a land of "White People."[50] The differences between Blacks and Whites, Gauls and Franks, Protestant Irish and Catholic Irish, and Anglo-Saxons and Celts were held to be no less deep-seated.

Many groups of Eastern Europeans, nowadays considered "White," were then considered racially "Other," intrinsically "foreign" to Canada. In the bush camps, Edmund Bradwin noted in his pioneering sociological work *The Bunkhouse Man*, the "Whites" always included the "Canadian-born, both French-speaking and English-speaking, as well as the new arrivals from the British Isles, and Americans from different states of the Union," as well as the Scandinavians (although the Finns were a borderline case). The men accepted as their equals would also win the classification. The "foreigners," that is, the "non-Whites," were everybody else – including many Finns, and vast numbers of Southern and Eastern Europeans – even if, to an eye untutored in race theory, their skin colour might appear as "white" as that of many of the British. Irene Howard reports a striking extension of the concept of "whiteness" in 1911, when in British Columbia "a school board member visiting the little Swedish-Canadian settlement of Silverdale turned to the teacher at the front of the class and in the full hearing of the students asked, 'Have you no white children in your school, only Swedes?' "[51] Even Newfoundlanders, who migrated in large numbers to work in the steelworks in Sydney, N.S., were viewed as Others – "miserable half starved pirates" and "devils." Race, in short, was often the complicated articulation of class.[52]

By the turn of the century many argued that a Darwin-derived "race science" confirmed the separate and unequal existence of races.[53] In that era of "scientific racism," races were categories that "accurately described and identified discrete groupings of the human species."[54] The subsequent modern history of applications of the race concept, in eugenics, Nazism, and Islamophobia, was horrific. For decades, for most Canadians who thought about this subject, the races were undoubtedly organized in a hierarchy, according to how closely they approximated to the British ideal, the very apex of human evolution. As Mariana Valverde notes in her path-breaking study of moral and social reform, "The slippery term 'race' allowed Anglo-Saxons to think of themselves as both a specific race and as the vanguard of the human race as a whole." It was obvious that as Anglo-Saxons progressed or declined, "so would the world." The privileging of White European ethnicities and the marginalizing of those of Asian or African descent were just "common sense." In the words of James W. St. G. Walker, "It did not need to be examined or proved, for it was self-evident." Races, according to Walker, were assumed to be "evolutionary units, fixed in their physical and behavioural characteristics," although some thinkers expressed the possibility that they could slowly change over time. Yet, as Nancy Stepan remarks, "The very scientific methods that produced races led to an undermining of the concept of race." Even before the 1920s, some writers demonstrated a growing scepticism about race – especially given that the number of "major races" found by major theorists differed dramatically from one to the other. It was a category "built upon shifting sands," in Backhouse's evocative words.[55]

If the messiness of the "Hindu/Sikh/Indian/Asiatic/Oriental" category in storm-tossed Vancouver in 1914 seemed acute, it was not unusual. Even measured and comprehensive lists of the "races" of Canada were hopelessly confused. W.G. Smith's widely read 1920 study on Canadian immigration listed 40 "countries or races," including no. 15, Hebrews, no. 22, Negroes, no. 23, Newfoundland, no. 39, United States, and no. 40, West Indies – a miscellaneous jumble of religious, "racial," colonial, regional, and national identifications. The list defied common sense as well as science. What was one to make of a "Hebrew" who emigrated from Newfoundland, for instance? Or a West Indian of African descent who immigrated to Canada from the United States?[56]

At its most narrow – as reflected in the Canadian census of 1901, for instance – race meant "skin colour," of which there were only four: "*w*" for White, "*r*" for Red, "*b*" for Black, and "*y*" for Yellow. (Putting in an additional "*b*" for "Brown," a colour often linked with race – indeed, the one most often applied to the so-called Hindus – would have meant two "*bs*" and thus posed the grave risk of bureaucratic untidiness.) "The whites are, of course, the Caucasian race, the reds are the American Indian, the blacks are the African or Negro, and the yellows are the Mongolian (Japanese and Chinese)," Backhouse observes. "But only pure whites will be classed as whites; the children begotten of marriages between whites and any one of the other races will be classed as red, black or yellow, as the case may be, irrespective of the degree of colour." So constructed, the census categories generated a representation of Canada with a White population of 96.2 per cent, Reds at 2.4 per cent, Yellows at 0.41 per cent, and Blacks at 0.32 per cent. The distinguished few who defied all such powers of racial description figured at 0.66 per cent.[57] Obviously, human beings then, as now, did not actually come in any of these colours, and their application to population statistics creates an unscientific official fiction. Yet, however arbitrary the categories and absurd the statistics, they had a powerful effect once they entered general circulation. In this instance, they "proved" that Canada was White.

Through the process of racialization, what were thought to be both common sense and scientific observations of skin colour were transposed from one context to another after another – moving from supposed evolutionary science to religion, culture, politics, aesthetics, and everyday life. "That is very 'white' of you" was something a person might say appreciatively of another's good deed. Race became an all-purpose abstraction – so all-purpose that its exact meaning was often quite unclear. As Karl Kautsky remarked in his discussion of Darwin, although humanity had been studied more closely than any other organic species, even the simple question, "How many races has humanity?" might generate answers ranging from 2 (Virey), 4 (Kant), and 8 (Agassiz) to 16 (Desmoulins) or 63 (Burke).[58] However fictional such races were later shown to be by 20th-century science, which demonstrated that there is more genetic variation within races than between them, as they were repeatedly used by scientists, written into laws and conventions, and repeated in the popular press, the "races" became non-fictional realities. As Roediger remarks, "For all its insubstantiality race is a very powerful ideology." In Canada, Backhouse reminds us, "The roots of racialization run far deeper than individualized, intentional activities." Institutions, intellectual theory, popular culture, the law – all resonated with the idea and practice of race. "Racialized communities were denied the right to maintain their own identities, cultures, and spiritual beliefs," Roediger states. "Education, employment, residence, and the freedom of social interaction were sharply curtailed for all but those who claimed and were accorded the racial designation 'White.' "[59]

In the crunch, for those who fell on to the "wrong" side of the White/non-White binary – as in the moment of the *Komagata Maru* and countless other cases – things could go badly indeed. A dramatic example of this process was exemplified by the Aboriginal peoples of Canada. When functioning as indispensable partners in trade and Empire, the country's initial inhabitants could be regarded as knowledgeable, militarily powerful, and (to a point) worthy of a certain respect. After 1820 they came increasingly to be patronized. Anthropology played an important role in developing a "niche" for Aboriginals as a dying, primitive race, which would be the hegemonic construct under which residential schools, treaties, and legislation against potlatches and sun dances would all be justified.[60] Conversely, Jews, often seen as a distinct (and problematic) race in the 19th century – the "Jewish Question" would be *the* major international focus of socialist discussion about race and racism in this period – increasingly came to be regarded as "White" in the 20th.[61]

Radical Responses

Ideas become material forces under specific conditions – and in Vancouver in 1914 people were driven to say and do many things based on the conviction that they were defending the White race. Many saw in the *Komagata Maru* the menacing, alien face of "the Orient," and constructed a virulent version of what Edward Said would later call "Orientalism." Even without meeting them, they knew how to categorize and evaluate the human beings on the vessel – as so many primitive or negative versions of their own "White" culture. They *racialized* the vessel and its occupants by transposing into this new context an already evolved framework of understanding, in which skin colour, language, and religious difference functioned as signs of irremediable Otherness – mysterious, dangerous, inferior.[62]

Thus, when the passengers' supporters held a protest meeting, a Vancouver journalist described the atmosphere as echoing with the "weird music from strange Hindu musical instruments."[63] When five Sikhs were allowed off the *Komagata Maru*, they were described as spending "a pleasant hour sunning themselves on the wooden buoy in the harbor to which the coal hulks tie." Dubbed the "lonely Singhs," they "squatted on the bare surface of the buoy and abstractedly speculated as to the theory of transmigration of souls and the possibility of indulging in their favorite pursuit – a lawsuit."[64]

Although the *Komagata Maru* apparently arrived without any women on board, that did not deter commentators from speculating about the plight of both Sikh women and women in general. The Sikhs' perspective on females in general was "the most bestially hateful thing you could imagine," advised the *Sun*'s columnist. "Once in Vancouver a white woman married a Sikh. If I were not under some repression I could tell you something that would be of interest. But if I told what I know about the Indians in Vancouver the result would be a riot." Public-spirited Mayor Baxter was considerate enough to pass along a letter from an Englishwoman in India, who urged Canada "to be firm and not admit the East Indians." That, she argued, would be the "earnest wish and prayer of every English woman and man who knows India and its vilely low, common inhabitants!" Were they not "to keep all Orientals out of their domains, within five years, if not a lesser period, there will not be a corner of the globe for the white man or woman to exist in," thereby allowing the "Oriental . . . such a low, filthy-minded brute" to treat women in Canada as they were treated in India – "no better than dogs." As Malcolm Reid – charged with official responsibility for handling the question – explained: "Without their women here they will only make their own race worse. They will come here by the thousands. Keep them out."[65]

Childlike, cruel, barbarian, anti-women, superstitious, half-naked – here were "savages" who, like countless others before them, called out for the tough love and developmental guidance of the "civilized," through concepts and models well elaborated over six decades of liberal order – such as residential schools, reservations, and restrictions on the free practice of religious beliefs.[66] Yet, most ominously, these supposed savages were now making common cause with the sworn enemies of liberal order itself, in moves that seemed to presage the disintegration of the fair Dominion into an unfathomable anarchy. As the India Sedition Committee would later be informed, at a Vancouver meeting in December 1913 a poem was read from a Ghadar Party newspaper urging the expulsion of the British from India. From the standpoint of MP Stevens, the "Hindu" community was fast becoming a hotbed of anti-British "anarchism." He sustained his argument in the House of Commons by providing quotations from the type of literature they were reading.[67] The "Hindus," then, have the honour of being among the first of many socialistic ethnic menaces to haunt the 20th-century liberal imaginary. Hence the need to repress them, through both pre-emptive strikes (excluding them from Canadian shores) and the vigorous application of deportation, which was to become a stock anti-radical tactic of the 1920s and 1930s.

At the 21 June protest meeting at Dominion Hall, some speakers had "raised the red flag" and called the superintendent of Immigration "an oppressor and a despot." As the *Sun* exclaimed, "Sedition and treason were openly and frankly preached." Their "cloven hooves" (in the *Sun's* telling metaphor) were clearly on display.[68] The hostile commentators were observing an important development. In the face of cruelty and oppression, a genuine radicalization was underway among the South Asians, and it was taking aim at the liberation of India from British rule. As Parnaby and Kealey remark, the "continuous journey" requirement enraged members of the South Asian community. It not only cut them off from family and friends, but also underlined "the emptiness of the Crown's claim that all British subjects were equal before and under the law."[69] Radicalism was suffused with an emergent struggle for national and spiritual liberation and for the overthrow of the British Raj.

As Peter Campbell demonstrates, in that struggle the Socialist Party of Canada and South Asians achieved a kind of common front – fragile, partial, and, given its context, remarkable. Some of the East Indian publications in Vancouver had been produced with SPC assistance. An example was *Free Hindustan*, published by celebrated activist Taraknath Das and based in Seattle but, according to Parnaby and Kealey, "printed locally with the assistance of the Socialist Party of Canada."[70] The radical London-based publication *Indian Sociologist*, to which the SPC itself later subscribed, was distributed through a small store run by Guran Ditta Kumar, "a self-described 'Punjabi Buddhist' and 'Worker in the cause of Temperance and Vegetarianism.'" The "gravest aspect" of the 21 June protest meeting," the *Sun* reported, was the participation of "white Socialists of the extreme type," one of whom exhorted the protesters "to return to their own country and throw off the British yoke, and become masters in their own land," and "spoke of the governments of Canada and England, in fact of all governments in a taunting and contemptuous way." Such extreme views were upheld by Balwant Singh, the priest of the Sikh temple, and by Hussain Rahim, whom the newspaper identified as a man notorious for "spreading mischievous doctrines among the East Indians here."[71] Rahim (earlier known as Chagan Khairaj Varma), an SPC member, was for a time integrated into the party leadership and, perhaps even more dangerously, had won a stunning legal victory over the Immigration Department four years earlier. His arrival on 14 January 1910 had signalled a major political change, especially after efforts to deport him were defeated. Rahim had come to Canada via Honolulu as a tourist before the passing of the Immigration Act, 1910. The authorities wanted to deport him, but they were up against a tenacious opponent. Rahim defeated them on a technicality, and they resented him for it.[72]

Radical resistance had a focal point in Rahim. The Immigration Department's Hopkinson, for one, keenly recognized the issue: "The failure . . . of the Department to deport Rahim from Canada has so bolstered up his position in the Hindu community here as to make him a leader and a counsellor in respect to all matters concerning their community." As Campbell remarks, what the South Asian militants derived from the radicalism of an activist like Rahim was not so much "Marxism or socialism per se," but rather the intensely idealistic conviction that the Indian people through their own efforts could overthrow British imperial rule.[73]

The Vancouver Socialist-Sikh alliance of 1914 went flatly against the long-standing objections of the labour movement, both nationally and locally, to Asian immigration. The *Industrial Banner* of Toronto deemed "unrestricted immigration" to be the "great menace that looms so threateningly over the dominion today" – "nothing short of a national crime" and an "insane and criminal policy." For the *B.C. Federationist*, the exclusion of the East Indians on board the *Komagata Maru* was not a question of colour or nation, but strictly one of wages: "The organized labor movement is opposed to Asiatic immigration because Asiatic labor is cheap labor. It is not essentially a question of whence it comes or what its name or color is. The point is that it is cheap, and as such is a menace to the wages and standard of living which the organized white workers are spending money and effort to try and maintain." J.H. Hawthornthwaite had likewise defended Asian exclusion in a speech on 13 October 1907, with warnings that Asian workers would swamp the local labour market and threaten Western civilization.[74]

Oxford graduate Dr. Sunder Singh, editor of a Hindu newspaper on the West Coast, had been warmly received at the Empire Club in Ottawa and the Canadian Club in Toronto – the "leading citizens" of the latter even passing a resolution in December 1911 urging the government to redress the South Asians' grievances. (Echoes of this earlier campaign could be heard in 1914 as well: one Montreal clergyman declared that the treatment of the Hindus violated Christian principles and British fair play.)[75] Yet the appearance of warm-hearted understanding was undermined by labour and socialist activists. On 4 January 1912, the Toronto and District Labor Council passed a resolution condemning any relaxation of the immigration laws "in favour of any particular section of the Hindu race." The labour council explained that the introduction of "Asiatic races" would mean the reduction of moral and social standards throughout the country. James Simpson warned the churches that if they did not reconsider their supposedly pro-Asiatic position, organized labour would "fight them to the finish." J.W. Bruce of the Plumbers' Union, claiming a first-hand experience of residence in Australia and South Africa, insinuated that Sunder Singh was merely voicing the views of the Canadian Manufacturers' Association, and warned that if East Indians were allowed to bring their families in, their children would attend public schools – which would mean that the children of Canadians "would become contaminated by all the vices of the Orient."[76]

At times, labour and socialist exclusionists sometimes tempered their anti-Asian comments with intriguing suggestions of an ironic awareness of their own contradictions. James H. McVety, the well-known Vancouver SPCer and former editor of the *Western Wage Earner*, pointed out, in a column that was otherwise firmly onside with Asian exclusion, that bourgeois proponents of South Asian exclusion were curiously indifferent to their own employment of Chinese servants, and were also departing from Christian ethics. In conversation with an ardent proponent of vigilante justice against the Hindus, he "mildly suggested that [the man's] language hardly befitted a follower of the Lowly Nazarene and one who was a staunch believer in 'British justice.'" Labour in Canada "has always been opposed to the Asiatics, for many other than competitive reasons," wrote McVety, but it had not found many allies among businessmen. Why should workers now become "hysterical, either over the ravings of men who have fleeced labor to the extent of millions of dollars, or on account of any injury they could possibly receive through a further influx of Hindoos, the must useless of all the Asiatics who are here?" McVety also predicted that, if rioting broke out, workers would be held responsible for it. That concern was echoed by others. As one of the delegates to a meeting of the Trades and Labor Council in New Westminster put it, if any trouble started over the landing of the Hindus, "the unions would be blamed for starting it, regardless of who were the actual perpetrators."

As the situation on the *Komagata Maru* heated up, the *B.C. Federationist* mocked "Britain's Glorious Empire," which had implicitly promised the Hindus that they belonged to it as completely as any worker did to his union, only to have shown its loyal subjects "the travesty of it all when the British empire came forth last Tuesday to drive them back with cold steel. If they did nothing more, they at least succeeded in demonstrating just how much imperialism is worth." What a revelation it must have been, to come to Vancouver, and find a "fellow Britisher" confront them "with bullet and bayonet welcome." The *Federationist* even provocatively drew a parallel between a Scots collier arriving in Nanaimo and being confronted with the bare bayonets of his fellow Scots, and the South Asians who had arrived in Vancouver to face the weaponry of their fellow British subjects.[77]

On 18 July the authorities made a concerted effort to retake the *Komagata Maru*. The Immigration officers were applying intense pressure on Captain Yamamoto to leave at once, under penalty of a fine of $500 for each passenger on board, if his passengers, who had seized general control of the vessel, were not immediately taken outside the three-mile limit. The captain made a formal application to the police to help him regain command of his ship. The attack on the vessel was to be made by 120 policemen and 40 special Immigration officers, accompanied by the gallant, indeed Napoleonic, Stevens, MP, all of them setting off in the *Sea-Lion*, a Vancouver tugboat. Although it might seem that any struggle between burly well-fed Vancouver policemen and starving, thirsty, and exhausted prisoners would be stacked against the prisoners, the forces of law and order overlooked an important tactical consideration of naval warfare: the question of the height of the vessel in the water. The deck of the *Sea-Lion*, which was doubtless as valiant and inspiring as a Vancouver tugboat could possibly aspire to be, was some 15 feet lower than the deck of the *Komagata Maru*. The passengers resisted the assault team with a hail of coal, bricks, and scrap-iron, among other things. The forces of law and order were repulsed. It was reported that some 20 of the police and officials had to be taken to hospital with wounds and broken bones.[78] The Battle of Burrard Inlet would not go down in Canadian military song and legend.

Were the policemen who had struggled to take the *Komagata Maru* really such heroes? "We would like to see this hero business mixed a little more," the *Federationist* remarked. Radicals who had had their heads broken by police in Vancouver's recent free speech fights might find a certain satisfaction in the spectacle of police officers suffering the same fate at the hands of the passengers of the *Komagata Maru*.[79] There were small but evident cracks in the seemingly solid surface of labour racism, fissures that some socialists were determined to widen.

In 1907 the *Western Clarion*, for instance, had used the words "virulent" and "bestial" to describe "racial prejudice" as "one of the meanest in the category and the least founded upon reason" – a decisive objection to it. Often the most interestingly heterodox attitudes were found among those who affected the most "impossibilist" style. In 1909 D.G. McKenzie had hailed the decision of the spc-influenced United Mine Workers convention at Leth-bridge to admit Chinese and Japanese workers with the remark: "A 'White Canada' will no longer serve." On the subject of Japanese immigration, the *Clarion* suggested that "the little brown man" was only following the precedent of "the white man throughout all history," and added, in puckishly "impossibilist" style: "The white man, however, is chiefly remarkable for the ability to preserve his equanimity when he is a winner and squeal like a stuck pig when a loser."[80] It was as if the very "abstractness" and "distance" for which leading spcers are so often critiqued, especially when it came to ex-plaining to coal miners the triviality of their "commodity struggles," also made it possible for these socialists to treat the local labour movement's latest racial crusade with a certain distanced irony.

Vancouver socialists even began to deconstruct the concept of race itself. The Court of Appeal heard the passengers' socialist solicitor, Bird, develop an argument more suggestive of Kautsky than of Kipling. Bird challenged the sci-entific status of the racial definitions written into Canadian law. What, he wondered, could the "Asiatic race" possibly mean? If there were, according to the commonly accepted definitions of race, no fewer than three races in Asia, and if the East Indians were in fact "Aryans" just like White Canadians, how could they possibly be excluded on racial grounds? His sophisticated argu-ments went to the heart of the official liberal race theory of the day – which was probably why the province's press mocked them as so much arcane, legal-istic hair-splitting.[81]

The South Asian socialist Rahim, whose career Campbell deftly re-constructs, epitomized the transnational anti-imperialist struggle – what a later generation on the left would call a movement of national liberation. "You drive us Hindoos out of Canada," Rahim told Hopkinson, "and we will drive every white man out of India." He was centrally involved in the temperance struggle and took a leading role in the iww free speech fights.[82] With the *chutzpah* that recalled the csl's running of Margaret Haile as a can-didate in 1902, at a time when women were not even allowed to vote, Rahim signed up as a scrutineer in the 1912 provincial election at a time when Asians were excluded from the franchise. Not only that, but he also jauntily cast a ballot. The result, notes Campbell, was dramatic: "When William Hopkinson found out about Rahim's activities, he tracked him down and had him ar-rested, then had his house searched. The search turned up a substantial quan-tity of spc and iww literature, a newspaper clipping dealing with the preparation of bombs, and evidence that Rahim had solicited more than $100 from South Asians for the Socialist Party and iww."[83]

As Campbell notes, Rahim may even have been responsible for putting the indispensable but ailing *Western Clarion* – which went out of publication between November 1912 and March 1913 – back on its feet. He provided the

SPC with space and free rent at the offices of his Canada-India Supply Company, where the Dominion Executive Committee held its meetings until late in 1914. Hopkinson would later report that Rahim and 12 other South Asians "had formed a local of the Socialist Party of Canada in order to translate SPC and IWW literature into Indian languages."[84]

It was a short-lived and uncertain breakthrough – it is not certain if the local ever functioned, and Rahim would soon leave the SPC's Executive Committee in the violent aftermath of the *Komagata Maru* struggle[85] – but it was nonetheless apparently the first time a significant Canadian political party welcomed into its leadership a person of colour. (And, just as Haile's breakthrough of 1902 has been erased in official liberal historiography, so too has Rahim's socialist defiance in 1912.) In the Vancouver context, the SPC – arguably because its style of Marxism allowed it maximum freedom of manoeuvre from the local working class – was able on this issue to show dramatic, if revealingly ill-remembered, leadership.

Much of the complexity of the Socialist–South Asian encounter surfaced in the meeting held on the afternoon of 21 June in Dominion Hall. Bird, speaking as both a solicitor and an SPCer, remarked, in phrases that showed how difficult it was for anti-racists to avoid the discriminatory entanglements of the language of race: "I believe there is no finer race physically or mentally than the Sikh. . . . Physically they are our superiors and mentally our equals." Were the visceral fears aroused by the Sikh the product of fear of competition? Was not talk of a "white man's country" simply prejudice? H.M. Fitzgerald remarked that he knew of no "collection of human society" that "did not have an Asiatic origin." Yet at the same time he urged the South Asians to go back to their own country and renew the struggle against the Empire there. As Campbell notes, one of the most surprising elements of the SPC involvement in the moment of the *Komagata Maru* was its restraint on the question of religion. Much of the anti-racist resistance of the moment of the *Komagata Maru* was shaped by the Sikh religion, elements of which could be aligned with socialist ideas. SPC comments on the "Hindus" were "remarkably free of attack on Sikh religious beliefs."[86]

For well-informed friends of the Empire, much depended on the Vancouver struggle. According to Campbell, the existence of a "socialist propaganda" in Vancouver had earlier caused Lord John Morley, who became secretary of state for India in 1905, to fear the "consequent danger of the East Indians being imbued with socialist doctrines." Morley's concerns had been borne out by items in the *Western Clarion*. The Vancouver SPC local took out a subscription to the *Indian Sociologist*, and listened to speakers depict the British conquest of India as a disaster for humanity. One evening in 1908 the speakers had been the well-known South Asian activists Taraknath Das and Suren Bose. In "well chosen words and remarkably clear English," they told the SPC of the nightmare consequences for India of British colonialism.[87]

In keeping with the prevailing fears, Col. E.J. Swayne, the governor of British Honduras, apparently offered up his colony as a possible solution to the "Hindu" problem in British Columbia and the Empire's "Spanish" problem in Central America. Swayne believed that South Asian immigration to Canada should be closely controlled. He presented two compelling reasons for this approach. The first was geopolitical: the Empire's temperate zones should be reserved for the "surplus white population," leaving "full scope to our Asiatic subjects in the more tropical zones of the Empire." The second related to the threat of radicalism: "Socialists of a very undesirable type have made it their business to tamper with the East Indians in Vancouver." When the Sikhs returned to the Punjab, they might bring back with them, along with a more clear-eyed understanding of the limitations of White labourers, "new, ill-digested socialistic ideas." It was a pattern that could only work "to the detriment of British prestige."[88] The tiny and divided SPC in Vancouver was thus, perhaps to an extent its activists themselves would have found surprising, considered a force to reckon with by influential figures in the British Empire.

Images of battle, invasion, and insurrection saturated Vancouver during that summer of 1914. Fed by the looming conflict in Europe, and by a sense of panic over the fate of an Empire in which so many had invested their sense of being part of a globe-girdling "imagined community," war fever lent an apocalyptic air to the crowds and the headlines. Even the very opening days of Vancouver's encounter with the *Komagata Maru* were framed in the language of war: here were the "Hindu Invaders" who had sailed right into the city's harbour. It was a vessel, a *Province* article advised in mid-June, "seething with an insurrection."[89] "Hindus," being the sort of people they reportedly were, were thought capable of the most "desperate measures." One report indicated that the passengers had armed themselves with "kerosene bombs," and another that the enraged "Hindus" had thrown four Japanese sailors overboard – both unfounded "wharf rumours" that added to the "Great Fear" gripping Vancouver. "The refusal of the Dominion to permit the landing of the Hindus in Vancouver may mean a war," Malcolm Reid remarked on 6 July. "There are three hundred millions of Indians who may possibly be led to extreme offense by reason of the actions of the officials of British Columbia." A couple of weeks later the *Province* exclaimed, "Not since the anti-Asiatic riots of 1907 has Vancouver been so worked up as over the threatened battle of Burrard Inlet."[90]

Yet the great battle did accelerate the drive to achieve, through a cunning combination of consent and coercion, a resolution of the crisis favourable to those defending the hegemonic construct of White Canada. "Consent" was personified by the intervention of the Hon. Martin Burrell, minister of agriculture and the emissary of the prime minister. Burrell addressed the question of whether anyone would be repaid for the value of the cargoes transported by the ship – cargoes left stranded in the harbour just like the passengers – and promised to wire the prime minister to ask him that the claims be thoroughly and impartially investigated, on condition that the passengers refrain from violence, return control of the ship to the captain, and agree to return to the port from whence they came. Some on the *Komagata Maru* were under the impression that more had been promised verbally, and later on they would say that they had been duped by the government, from whom they had expected to be repaid for the money invested in the charter. They believed they had bona fide assurances from Burrell, and on that basis only they had eventually agreed to allow the *Komagata Maru* to leave Vancouver.[91]

The "coercion" element in the Burrard Inlet drama was provided by the HMCS *Rainbow*, a vessel in the new Canadian navy. One Montreal newspaper would sardonically remark that the "Hindus" had "done the Canadian people a service," by providing "some kind of work" for the service's otherwise underutilized vessels. As Skelton saw it, the scene revealed a harsh irony: the nucleus of the new Canadian navy, intended to be a gesture of Canada's support for the Empire, was being used to prevent the landing of British subjects on British soil.[92] On board the *Rainbow*, all was in readiness for a violent clash. According to the local press, even chemical weapons that would have "reduced the insurgents to submission in short order" were at hand.[93] Two militia parties, carrying rifles with sword-bayonets but with no ammunition in their magazines, were poised to bound over broad gangplanks thrown across to the *Komagata Maru* as soon as the *Rainbow* was alongside. The primary weapon against the "insurgents" was to be the ship's firehoses, which were to be used with full force "in the face of anyone on board the *Komagata* who attempted to obstruct the operations, or the passage of the troops on board."[94] After the passengers finally agreed to leave, none of these weapons proved to be needed.

Rear-Admiral Walter Hose, then commander of the *Rainbow*, would later remember the sight of the *Komagata Maru* as it lay at anchor on that morning of 22 July, after it had become overwhelmingly clear that the passengers now had no option but to give up their struggle to enter Canada. All of the passengers had crowded onto the upper deck. An "old white-bearded fellow" stood on the bridge and made a "perfectly executed" semaphore signal to the *Rainbow*. His message read: "Our only ammunition is coal!"[95]

At 5.10 a.m. on the morning of 23 July 1914 the Japanese steamer sailed for Hong Kong, taking with it the South Asian passengers whose presence in Vancouver since 23 May had caused such an uproar. Even at such an early hour, great crowds once more lined the shore and housetops, and troops lined the docks, to witness the departure of the *Komagata Maru* under the escort of the HMCS *Rainbow*. The smoke rising from the ship's funnel was interpreted as evidence that the "Battle for Vancouver" had been won and the "Hindus" were departing.[96]

The passengers on board the *Komagata Maru* would, after six arduous months, finally reach India on 27 September. Their experiences in Vancouver, and intensive discussions on board the vessel, had brought them to a different level of political consciousness. As Rajini Srikanth states, "The British government's refusal to intervene in Canada's exclusion of the *Komagata Maru* passengers strengthened the resolve of many Vancouver Indians to join forces with the revolutionary Ghadr party members in California and heightened the fervor of anti-British rhetoric and action in North America." Many Ghadarites would return to India following the outbreak of the Great War to join the struggle against British rule.[97] The SPCers, Campbell suggests, may have actually influenced the Ghadarites with their emphasis on popular enlightenment and insistence on the possibility of a revolutionary transformation of the existing social order – as well as by their schematic notions of how to put that change into effect. In the Punjab, perhaps, the SPC emphasis on education lived on in a way that it did not elsewhere, even in Canada itself.[98]

Once in India, some of the Sikhs wanted to place the Guru Granth Sahib (also known as the Adi Granth), the revered holiest scripture of their faith, in a Gurdwara (temple) in Calcutta. For their part, the British authorities wanted them to board a train for Punjab. Attempting a march to Calcutta, the Sikh party was forced back to Budge Budge, where it was fired upon by troops, who slaughtered 20 of them.

Meanwhile, the bitterness and division in Vancouver persisted. Several of Hopkinson's informants were murdered, and on 21 October 1914 Hopkinson himself was assassinated. Stevens, an enthusiastic front-line participant in these exciting events, had looked forward to "a stroke against the unwelcome immigrants that must be absolutely successful."[99] If the arrival of the *Rainbow* was such a master stroke, and if over the medium term the tactic was "absolutely successful" with respect to preservation of the exclusionary logic of liberal order, in the longer term the *Komagata Maru* would fortify very different political strategies, with serious implications for the Empire as a whole.

The events of 1914 are now commemorated by a plaque at the Gateway to the Pacific in downtown Vancouver. The message briefly enumerates the "British Subjects" on board the *Komagata Maru*, deplores "that unfortunate incident of racial discrimination," and "reminds Canadians of our commitment to an open society in which mutual respect and understanding are honoured, differences are respected, and traditions are cherished."[100] In 2008 the federal government issued a belated apology for the incident. Yet as so often in official liberal history-making, "remembering" often constitutes a complicated form of forgetting – in this instance, it means erasing the role of the Sikh-socialist united front. Even more tellingly, the official memory effaces both the complicity of the mainstream parties in the decades-long continuation of the racist project of a White Canada, and the determined agency of vulnerable, trapped, and hungry people – whose most appalling crime, when one came right down to it, was their desire to become Canadians.

White Canada: Racialized Liberalism and Its Others

The moment of the *Komagata Maru* threw into sharp relief the contradictions of the project of Canada – of instituting a liberal White settler colony, modelled on Britain, in northern North America. It revealed the emergent outlines of the first organic crisis of the Canadian state, one that would unfold in the years of the Great War. The paradox is that it did so when liberal political economy, liberal statecraft, and liberal culture were at the forefront in the homeland and in the Dominion. So why the panic? What conceivable harm would one boatload of South Asians do to the project as a whole?

On their face, the facts of Canada's turn of the century demographic revolution suggested a regime confidently astride the great progressive currents of history. The government made a concerted effort to increase the numbers of immigrants. The efforts had only modest results at first, with levels barely over 40,000 in 1899 and 1900, but the following years were far more successful; in 1907, as many as 272,400 immigrants arrived on Canadian shores. To an unprecedented extent the state itself became a promotional agency, selling Canada throughout much of Europe. It also expanded recruitment efforts in Eastern and Southern Europe. From 1903 to 1914 more than 20 per cent of the immigrants were drawn from continental Europe, with a marked increase in the numbers of Poles, Italians, Ukrainians, and other Eastern and Southern Europeans.[101] As Ninette Kelley and Michael Trebilcock note, between 1896 and 1914, "Canada experienced six of the ten largest annual immigration levels ever registered." Between 1896 and 1914 this country with its fast-growing economy – railway mileage more than doubled, mining production tripled, and wheat and lumber production increased tenfold – drew roughly three million people to its shores, twice as many as were recorded to have come within the preceding 30 years. The annual intake rose from roughly 17,000 in 1896 to over 400,000 in 1914; the country's population in 1914, now almost 50 per cent urban, was 30 per cent higher than in 1901. Although the largest single group of immigrants (38 per cent) continued to be from Britain, by 1921 fully 15 per cent of the population was of neither British nor French descent.[102]

The carrot of inducement was combined with the stick of top-down discipline. Immigration acts passed in 1906 and 1910 provided a stable legal framework that lasted into the post-1945 period. At the core of this legal regime was the principle of sovereignty. As Kelley and Trebilcock point out, "The executive branch of government was free to determine – unencumbered by judicial or parliamentary scrutiny – those who would be permitted to enter the country, those who would be accorded citizenship, and those who would be excluded or expelled."[103] The outlines of the authoritarian liberalism that was to dominate interwar Canadian politics were already visible in the prewar immigration regime.

Each year as many as 70,000 workers were drawn to the railway construction sites – and when the three major railways requested the admission of immigrant workers "irrespective of nationality," they got what they demanded. The coal mines, metal mines, steel mills, and lumber camps of the Dominion were crowded with immigrant workers. The newcomers also went to work on farms across the nation. From 1907 to 1913–14, the percentage of unskilled workers in Canada's immigrant uptake increased from 31 to 43 per cent.[104]

Both the Liberal and Conservative (formerly Liberal-Conservative) parties were in essential agreement on the grand design of Canadian immigration policy. Just as Liberals had long crusaded against the evils of John A. Macdonald's National Policy, and then, after gaining power in 1896, had preserved almost all its features, the Conservatives denounced Liberal immigration policy in opposition, but after finally gaining power under Robert Borden in 1911 they too preserved its essential characteristics. More immigrants were admitted in 1914 than in any previous year in Canadian history. The only significant departure from previous administrations was the 1914 closure of Western seaports to immigrant labourers, in an effort to stave off an invasion of the sort of South Asians represented by the *Komagata Maru*.

Both parties followed ideologically coherent and consistent immigration policies deeply rooted in liberal ideology and implemented with care and ingenuity. When several hundred Black Oklahoma farmers thought they might try their luck at farming on the Canadian Prairies, they ignited a firestorm of public controversy. The Liberals, with Minister of the Interior Frank Oliver taking a leading role, drafted an order-in-council prohibiting the landing in Canada of "any immigrant belonging to the Negro race, which race is deemed unsuitable to the climate and requirements of Canada."[105]

Liberals, in struggling to clarify and codify just what it was about so many immigrants that fell short of the standards of individualism, became caught up in a logic of essence and types that could only undermine the very category of the "individual" that they were sworn to uphold. At bottom a turn of the century Canadian liberal believed, first, surely, in *liberty* – in the *freedom* of the individual, religious, intellectual, cultural, and economic; second, in universality and equality, especially before the law; third, in progress and science – and, more particularly, in a rational and progressive social and political order in which individual people were treated with dignity and respect, an order based on Spencer's law of equal freedom, which dictated that individuals had the freedom to do all that they will, provided that they do not infringe upon the equal freedom of any other; fourth, in the moral superiority of the British state and civil society – in the majesty of the British constitution, whose measured and organic development stood in stark contrast to the demagogy and uproar of the republican experiment to the south and the distant but menacing possibilities of social democracy on the European continent; and, finally, and perhaps most definitively, in *property* – in the natural or God-given right of individuals to hold and enjoy their property (always provided that doing so did not infringe upon the law of equal freedom). A mainstream liberal believed in the prosperity and progress uniquely possible in a business society in which the state's economic role was primarily one of facilitating the accumulation of capital in private hands – and not in the aggrandizement of state planning or social welfare programs, for instance; and in the efficacy of a propertied respectability as an index of the worthiness and propriety of the individual. Each of these seemingly banal and tightly intermeshed elements of liberal individualism were aspects of the current common sense. Yet, when applied to the transnational world of the new capitalism, and to the politics of immigration, these tendencies generated one ideological and structural contradiction after another.

A consistent argument of liberal theory is that humanity is made up of rights-bearing and morally autonomous individuals. By recognizing the rights of others, the good liberal safeguards his or her own rights and freedom. What divides us as members of racially distinct groups is less significant than our shared individuality.[106] Yet, in the moment of the *Komagata Maru*, "individual" Hindus were dissolved into their race. They were categorized on the basis of racialized signifiers – skin colour, turbans, dress, deportment, language – that worked, in essence, to de-individualize them. They became the Djinn-like forces of nature, threatening to cascade over the dikes of middle-class Canada.

With a disregard for material realities that was very characteristic of classical liberalism, the law of immigration appeared to treat every individual equally. The same law applied to the Dominion Iron and Steel Company and to the Newfoundlanders pulling a 12-hour shift in its mills. But in practice, as scholars have shown, the government repeatedly deferred to the priorities of employers, who were rarely overruled on immigration issues of fundamental significance to them.[107] Moreover, the immigration regime meant the importation of thousands of workers who lacked basic human rights. Notwithstanding an official commitment to recruiting farmers and an official reluctance to import guest workers as virtual short-term serfs of labour contractors, in actually-existing liberal order such pronouncements only went so far. Were "individual" workers under armed guard, sweating in their closed boxcars in 1914, really the equals of the corporation executives who had brought them to Canada? For the trapped passengers in Vancouver in 1914, or those fighting for their lives in the remote and unknown labour camps, liberal order entailed illiberal unfreedom. The Austrian consul general in Ottawa complained in 1907 that the treatment of Ukrainians and Bulgarians by Montreal-based labour agencies was so cruel and abusive that his blood had curdled. Here, then, was an emissary from one of Europe's most brutally repressive empires expressing shock about conditions in the Canadian North.[108]

For many new immigrants, Canada had the feel of an experiment in applied Darwinism. Socialist organizer Fred Hyatt described a "struggle for existence" in Calgary in 1909, when a "crowd of men of all nationalities" scrambled to win jobs excavating a city sewer. Initially the British had seemingly won the contest, but the "foreign element" ultimately got the work because they were cheaper and had political connections. The scene encouraged Hyatt to remember Spencer's pithy distillation of the theory of natural selection: "The state of affairs is competition for jobs with a vengeance; in fact, it is the survival of the fittest (?) and to the devil with the rest. All this took place in a supposed Christian community."[109]

A number of the liberal order's most resilient and talented democratic critics would emerge, not surprisingly, from the rugged and often brutal confines of the Northern resource camps. Like the children who had graduated from the coal mines, they were superbly located to measure the order's claims of universality, liberty, and equality against an everyday world of oppression, poverty, and abuse. "Rights fade at the last frontier town," Bradwin said pointedly in *The Bunkhouse Man*. "They disappear entirely when the end of the steel is passed." "Trespassers" could be forced out of the camps and "rebels" denied food and lodging. The work contractors were the potentates of the north – "not unlike the Tartar chieftain, the larger contractor bestrides his realm."[110] From the Western Federation of Miners to the Wobblies to the One Big Union (OBU), organizers would repeatedly rediscover the harsh truth that liberal theory was one thing and the labour camps another. Out beyond the city limits was another realm, where the rule of law was often an easily disregarded fiction.

Perhaps the most fascinating contradiction of liberal order with respect to immigration was that to consolidate the country's extension into the West and promote a business civilization – to build a prosperous and British dominion founded upon the rights of private property – the Canadian state facilitated the arrival of thousands of actual or potential *critics* of private property. Some group settlements – the Hutterites and Doukhobors most obviously – entailed the arrival of settlers with communitarian property regimes, which on religious grounds they were committed to preserving. Thousands of other immigrants re-created in Canada many of the collective solidarities they had first experienced in Europe.

Immigrants were solicited by candid appeals to their individual self-interest and, most especially, by the lure of almost free land. Yet they were also often imported en masse and in ethnic blocs. Around the turn of the century, Liberal Frank Oliver, for one, was worried about this pattern, as he commented on his fellow Albertans' resentment against Slavs in general and Galicians in particular. Here were people "who have no ideas in regard to our system of government or our social life, who have no ambitions such as we have, who are aliens in race and in every other respect." They posed a "danger to our social system, our municipal institutions and our general progress."[111] Some two decades later W.G. Smith was no less pessimistic. "The fact that there are colonies of Hutterites, Mennonites, Doukhobors, Ruthenians, Scandinavians, Germans, Mormons, and others, scattered throughout the Western Provinces renders the work of bringing these people into the activities of public-spirited citizens well-nigh impossible," he complained. "They are disposed to retain their mother tongue, maintain old customs, harbour ancient prejudices and make little educational progress."[112] Whole nations-within-the-state arrived in a few decades, testing, at times overwhelming, the assimilative capacities of the liberal order.

The challenge to that order went well beyond such collectivities. Karl Polanyi has famously described the "double movement" of the 19th century. On the one side, he observed, was "the extension of the market organization in respect to genuine commodities," and on the other "its restriction in respect to fictitious ones." On the one hand, markets were spreading over the entire globe, with the quantity of goods growing to "unbelievable proportions." On the other hand, policies and measures were emerging "to check the action of the market relative to labor, land, and money." A "deep-seated movement sprang into being to resist the pernicious effects of a market-controlled economy," to mobilize against "the perils in a self-regulating market system."[113]

Individuals and collectivities recruited to be part of a vast experiment in liberal state-building found themselves exposed as never before to the power of capitalism and market relations. Where that relationship was most unmediated, in the Canadian West, for instance, was often where national and class movements of grassroots solidarity were set in place to shield human beings against its brutal force. "Collective bargaining by riot"[114] in the camps – and only sometimes did the immigrants' brave revolts against their plight reach the newspapers – ceded place, eventually and after ruthless resistance on the part of employers, to enduring labour movements. Bradwin, no enemy of liberal order, worried about the contribution of the labour camps to Canadian radicalism: "Men sit nightly in such groups with avidity, by the glimmer of a candle stuck in a bottle, or from the light of a borrowed lantern whose cracked globe has been patched with flour and paper, pamphlets and circulars cooked to inflame, not tempered with saneness," he anxiously noted. "Only the influences closest at hand most determine whether there is evolved a Lincoln or a Lenin."[115]

Driven by combined but conflicting logics of accumulation and sovereignty – the need to make money from public and private investments in the West and to keep the Americans from grabbing the territory – the liberal state imported thousands of people, some already radicalized by oppression in their homelands, and many to be further radicalized by their shoddy treatment in Canada. Immigrants were recruited as so many anonymous units of labour-power. Their arrival had everything to do with the energy that their bodies were capable of releasing into the capitalist machine. Yet once here, hurled into a strange experiment in radical individualism, many people banded together and created new instruments of protection and empowerment. To the monopolies they opposed co-operatives, to the bosses they opposed unions, to the liberal parties they opposed the concept of democracy, and to ignorance, superstition, and illiteracy they opposed the people's enlightenment.

One of the richest contradictions in Canadian left history is that the West, the region most massively reshaped by the modern Canadian liberal order, should have generated so many of its most intrepid and impassioned critics. This was, then, the ultimate contradiction of a racialized liberal immigration policy: in the furtherance of a society based upon private property and individualism, it necessarily encouraged forces and tendencies that systematically subverted those goals. Liberalism's punishing contradictions were socialism's radiant possibilities.

Woodsworth: "Strangers Within Our Gates"

Perhaps the best-known, and most curiously misrepresented, books exploring the cultural contradictions of turn of the century liberal order were J.S. Woodsworth's *Strangers Within Our Gates* (1909), with contributions from Winnipeg *Tribune* journalist A.R. Ford, and *My Neighbor* (1911).[116] Intended as awakeners of the Christian conscience and primers in the new urban sociology, with their precisely ordered, eminently Spencerian grocery lists of racial and ethnic groups, enumerated according to their desirability, these pre-war writings proved to be in effect liberal theorizations of race, bringing to the surface many of the underlying contradictions of the project of White Canada.

Woodsworth's preoccupation with maintaining a British racial order can be traced back to the legacy of his Ontario-based family, which migrated to Brandon, Man., in 1885. His father's 1917 book on the Canadian Northwest celebrated the victory of "British rule" over "disaffected half-breeds and rebellious Indians." Woodsworth Sr., as Kenneth McNaught remarks in his biography of Woodsworth the son, had seen his own "mission in the West" as one combining commerce, agriculture, and the "moral precepts of Methodist Christianity."[117] J.S. Woodsworth was profoundly shaped by his father's expectations, anguishing – even into his thirties – about making choices that might disappoint his watchful parent. The evidence that he had internalized a deep sense of himself as a defender of "British" values in a fast-changing West is overwhelming.

At the same time the formation of the Methodist subject meant that Woodsworth was required to be a free-standing spiritual entity, endowed with free will, temperate, rational – someone who exemplified the concept of "individual" in its purest, most abstract form. "For the individual," McNaught writes, "Woodsworth thought that honesty, a belief in progress, and the spirit of bienfaisance, implemented by the willingness to work were the prime requirements."[118] Many of Woodsworth's early political positions – such as opposition to separate schools on the grounds that they impeded character-formation, national cohesiveness, and religious individualism – indicate someone who fully identified with Canada as an expansive, thoroughgoing, and future-oriented project. In 1907, as "an observer" of politics (as his daughter put it), he expressed regret that the Liberal Party – which he said "stood for temperance, better school laws, clean politics" – was "so badly defeated" in the Manitoba election.[119]

In a way, the title *Strangers Within Our Gates* says it all. The book is a worried assessment of White British Canada's ability to absorb the "waves" of immigrants descending upon it. The standard that Woodsworth applies to each people is that of the capacity of its units to become the self-sufficient individuals of liberal social theory.[120] As befitted a Methodist social activist, the choice of title had sound biblical roots, although the eight scriptural passages from which it was seemingly drawn are not unambiguous in their sociological import: on one reading, they might either be an invitation to immigrants to the Canadian feast or calls for their more stringent moral regulation.

The title also sets the book's essential thesis in a dramatic frame, and encapsulates its major themes: (1) *Strangers* – those Others – are peculiar, uncanny, unfamiliar people, whose essences remain disturbingly beyond our grasp; (2) *Within* – and yet, in all their terrifying otherness, they have come inside us, bringing the danger of infection as well as the possibility of economic growth; (3) *Our* – the most important word here – you and I are a "we," because, sharing the Bible, Britishness, liberal individualism, and the morality that stems from all three, we cohabit a universe of assumptions that "they" do not as yet share; and (4) *Gates* – suggesting both an opening and a barrier, biblically the entrance of an ancient city but also, given the pervasiveness of the book's water imagery, the floodgates of a dam or dike, and, in any event, "the strangers" are on land that is *ours*, not theirs.

The sense is of a threat that must be regulated and controlled. The text proceeds to juxtapose, against the solidity and tradition of the "gates" and assumed "walls," the terrifying sublimity of the "flood." "Our" gated walls confront unstoppable rivers, oceans, rivulets, springs, and streams. The "castle-like" solidity of the one is set against the ominous liquid modernity of the other.

Woodsworth constantly reminded his readers that, like people confronting the waves of the ocean, they can barely grasp the power and majesty of the demographic changes sweeping the world. This great leaderless force, "like a mighty stream," finding "its source in a hundred rivulets," is invading Woodsworth's world. "In tongue it is polyglot; in dress, all climes, from pole to equator, are indicated, and all religions and beliefs enlist their followers. There is no age limit, for young and old travel side by side. There is no sex limitation, for the women are as keen, if not more so, than the men."[121] Modern immigration is a vast and terrible wave, majestic and world-changing, sweeping aside all certainties, melting away in its awesome insistence even such seeming solidities as the difference between men and women.

This vast human tide is a world movement based on economic interest and the pursuit of individual freedom. With Woodsworth as a tour guide we may pause before the items carried forward by this majestic flood. "What a field for study!" the writer exclaims. An artist in search of "picturesque groups" will be deeply rewarded by a passage on an Atlantic ocean liner. "Here they are – Galician peasants in their sheepskins – fair-haired, clear-skinned Swedes – dark-eyed, eager Italian children. Here a withered old Russian woman in her outlandish dress with her old-fashioned little grandchild – a diminutive copy of herself; there a bent-shouldered Jew; yonder a young Syrian pedlar." In this swarm of humanity, the artist might find "something more than forms and colors. He will find the lights and shadows, the gladness and tragedy of life."[122]

The point of view here is that of the roving shipboard artist, someone not directly implicated in the lives of those he paints and, not altogether unlike *Sun* columnist Pollough Pogue, appreciative of their quaint appearances. Yet what lay behind these pleasing impressions? The Syrian might be colourful, but what was he concealing? The diseases that the text tells us are particularly associated with his kind? And then, what of the subtler, yet perhaps no less dangerous, political viruses that might lurk behind the pleasing surfaces of the colourful immigrants? After all, many of "our immigrants" were Jews and "Socialists, some of them of the most extreme type," driven against their individualistic natures to such a strange religion-like faith by the intolerable conditions of Eastern Europe. Yet, said Woodsworth in 1909, reaching a conclusion remarkably similar to those reached by Skelton two years later, in Canada, where conditions were so different, "the extremists cannot secure a large following, and the general tendency seems to be to adapt themselves to actual conditions and take an active part in the political life of the country."[123]

A decade later Woodsworth himself would be judged just such an "extremist."[124] What the book powerfully conveys is the shock of a man fully invested in "our Canada" – a British White Canada permeated by Protestant culture – as he confronts the massive sea of anonymous immigrants whose waves threaten to overpower the liberal society he so fiercely admires.

Strangers notes the imperative need to *liberalize* those who have seemingly arrived at our gates bearing aliberal notions of civil society and the state. Under this heading, a Protestant of Woodsworth's generation might think first of the benighted Catholics, with their unreformed and unprogressive church. "If we are to help these Catholic peoples, two courses seem open," Woodsworth argues. "Either we must try to make Methodists of them, or we must help them to work out their own salvation. The first is easiest to attempt, but seems to us doomed to failure. The second is most difficult, but seems to be in accord with the laws of spiritual development." This last phrase suggests that Woodsworth had bought into some of Henry Drummond's analogies between semi-parasitological organisms and adherents of the Church of Rome.[125]

My Neighbor: A Study of City Conditions, published two years later, reveals a transition from a liberal moment of refusal to a tentative and partial moment of supersedure. Woodsworth had moved to a more organic "sociological," though still not "socialist," conception of modern city life. In this book, over and over again, he takes us through cases in which the narrator comes face to face with the surprising fact of social interconnection – a first formation theme that, perhaps more than any other, made a deep impression upon the writer. Woodsworth imagines a middle-class, "modern man" eating breakfast. Presumably from his morning newspaper, he learns that ten workmen have been maimed or killed in a workplace accident. "Well," asks Woodsworth, "what is that to him? He hardly pauses as he sips his coffee." His eye quickly passes to other items – a rise in the price of wheat or the story of a great horse race. Even if he owns stock in the company, he feels no responsibility for the accident. "Countless legal and moral questions complicate the situation and confuse the moral sense," Woodsworth remarks. "But the groaning of these men has gone up to God. If through indifference or selfishness we protest, 'Am I my brother's keeper?' there comes the inexorable reply: 'The voice of thy brother's blood crieth unto me from the ground.'"[126]

It is a vignette highly reminiscent of Jack London's *Iron Heel*, published three years earlier. Elsewhere the text invokes St. Paul, including 1 Corinthians 12: 26 – "Whether one member suffer, all the members suffer with it; or one member be honored, all the members rejoice with it" – which was a passage that had also excited Colin McKay 12 years before. Not surprisingly, then, Woodsworth finds that "the city is not a mere aggregation of independent individuals, but rather a certain type of social organism." Indeed: "The physical city must be considered as a whole and the various parts must be subordinated to the whole – yes, that their highest welfare is dependent on that of the whole."[127]

The following passage vaguely intimates a sort of Mackenzie King–like 1890s-style "socialism": "We hold firmly that personal morality is the basis of public morality and yet admit that the morality of the community, as expressed in its customs and institutions, is the most potent factor in determining the morality of the individual." Even more plainly: "We dream of a socialistic state." Yet, Woodsworth says, quoting John Graham Brooks, a contemporary social critic, this "Mecca of the Co-operative Commonwealth is not to be reached by setting class against class, but by bearing common burdens through toilsome stages along which all who wish well to their fellows can journey together."[128] This "socialism" embraced neither the triune formula of the Marxists nor the rigorous evolutionary reflections of the Spencerians.[129] In the famous texts of 1909–11, Woodsworth knew what he refused, but not exactly what he could meaningfully affirm.

"What a jump," Woodsworth reported in *Strangers*. "We have entered a new era in our history. The immigrants are upon us! For good or ill, the great tide is turning our way, and is destined to continue to pour in upon us."[130] There was much that was "ill" about this future (especially as noted in the chapters contributed by Ford, who was an even more enthusiastic generalizer than Woodsworth). The book's readers encounter the supposed races of the East – the "little brown men" from Japan, the "Hindu" from India (who, in an anticipation of the amateur anthropology in the Vancouver press five years later, "cannot work with men of other nations"), the dodgy Macedonians ("a simple, sluggish people"), the Slovaks of Northern Hungary ("distinctly a lower grade," at least when weighed against the Bohemians) – and the conclusion: "We confess that the idea of a homogeneous people seems in accord with our democratic institutions and conducive to the general welfare."[131] Confronted with the sublime terror of the waves of immigrants, Woodsworth reached, as did so many of his contemporaries, for seemingly solid criteria of evaluation: grocery lists of ethnicities, sorted conveniently by their position on the evolutionary scale; unquestioned notions of peace, order, and good government; and firm theories about the centrality of precisely regulated rules of property in the achievement of the liberal Dominion.

Woodsworth's text is profoundly *racialist* – that is, it works within a framework in which "races" are thought to be tangible, efficacious conditions. Perhaps those conditions were hereditary, perhaps environmental, but in both cases the principle of collective coherence underlay the picturesque peculiarities of the individual. The text is only in places *racist*, in the sense of arguing that some races are inextricably inferior to others and that they should be kept separate or treated differently on that account. Woodsworth allows that *some* groups might progress. At the same time, those associated with different skin colours are not likely to do so. As in the case of the *Komagata Maru*, just how these "races" were constructed was of dire significance for those who fell within a maligned racial category.

"Who are we?" is Woodsworth's governing question, and he is of two minds on this. He celebrates an "inclusive" we. Of the past decade, he writes, "a national consciousness has developed – that is, a nation has been born." At one time Canadian-born children called themselves "English, Irish, Scotch or French" – "Natives" were not included in this enumeration – but now they happily call themselves "Canadians," and "the latest arrivals from Austria or Russia help to swell the chorus, 'The Maple Leaf Forever.'" Although a "fixed Canadian type" had not yet emerged, *something* was uniting Canadians. "Our hearts all thrill in response to the magical phrase – 'This Canada of Ours!' We are Canadians." Yet almost all the "racial habits" itemized in his book belong to people outside the Anglo-Celtic mainstream. The contradiction is nicely exemplified by his multinational chorus belting out "The Maple Leaf Forever," which is a hymn of praise to the British acquisition of Canada through General Wolfe's force of arms. The objects constructed by the text of *Strangers Within Our Gates* – the "strange Doukhobors," the "withered old Russian woman in her outlandish dress," the "picturesque figure of the Habitant," the no less "picturesque" Hindu, the out of place Sikh, the promiscuous and unsuitable Negro, the fanatical Catholics of Eastern Europe – can all only be seen from the panoptical tower of the implied liberal narrator who shares none of these characteristics.[132]

Woodsworth in essence made his readers into tourists, detached individuals brought in to savour, or to shudderingly reject, the sights and sounds of a startlingly polyethnic city. Then, in an uncanny anticipation of the official liberal multiculturalism of the post-1970s period, he had each imagined group provide a kind of folkloric performance in the text. The implied reader is a person who shares Woodsworth's system of weights and measures, his tourist guide's sense of what makes for a pleasing social sight, and what, on the contrary, assaults the eye. This was, then, not just a text illustrating the bad old days of ethnic prejudice and racial exclusiveness in a long-ago Canada. Rather, it highlighted certain lasting proclivities of the liberal order that conquered and resettled the West according to a program of rapid economic growth. It was an order that demanded "resourceful and enterprising" farmers and not the "failures" of English cities. His liberal critique of Mormonism – in Woodsworth's mind, a dread menace to Canada, illustrated by an octopus stretching out its tentacles from Utah, a foreshadowing of the many spiderweb charts illustrating economic and social networks that would crop up in Woodsworth's future – was not just that with Mormonism might come polygamy, but that its extension into Canada would mean the "utter surrender of personal liberty, and the acknowledgement of the absolute authority of the priesthood."[133] Woodsworth's was a deeply liberal response to the "liquid modernity" implicit in a period of record-breaking immigration.

Woodsworth was a compassionate man, and would never have been caught standing on the docks of Vancouver, howling abuse at the *Komagata Maru* (although he too was firmly of the conviction that the "Hindus" were "sadly out of place" in Canada).[134] Yet his underlying convictions in 1911 were not all that different from those of the White Canada militants in British Columbia. As he came to identify more and more closely with a Canadian nationalism, he would carry into it many of the categories and values that informed the Britishness of *Strangers* and *My Neighbor*. Canadian nation-building, as Adele Perry has persuasively argued, was strongly identified with attracting White immigrants – preferably British.[135] Many Canadians, and not just those in elite positions, found their answers to the troubling political and social questions of the day in a kind of Canadian imperial nationalism – one that glorified British civilization and yearned for the time when Canada itself would be a "Britain Beyond the Seas," perhaps even the new centre of the entire Empire.

Race and Labour

As suggested by the favourable reviews given his work in the labour press, Woodsworth's sense of the race question was also not all that different from the view of organized labour, whose position on immigration would prove enormously significant for the left.

The sojourner phenomenon – the arrival in Canada of thousands of guest workers whose labour was essential for the country's second industrial revolution – posed a substantial challenge to trade unionism, whose traditional craft structures were not well adapted to meet it. In many spheres – lumbering, coal and metal mining, railway construction, steel, agriculture – Canadian business had discovered the profit-making magic of migratory labour. Capital profited richly from the sojourners who would take almost any job, provided such employment gave them money to send back to Europe; for, rather than seeing Canada as their new home, the sojourners often laboured to maintain struggling families in Europe and to return to those families as soon as they could. On the lookout for cheaper and tractable labour, a company such as Dominion Iron and Steel, the largest of the Nova Scotia steelmakers, recruited in such distant places as the Ukraine and Barbados and even talked to Ottawa about importing Chinese labour. By 1910 Europeans and Newfoundlanders made up half its employees. Italians, Poles, Ukrainians, and Hungarians were recruited for "less skilled labouring jobs in the yards and around the blast furnaces, coke ovens, and open-hearth furnaces." In Hamilton in 1918, "foreigners" were said to do " 'practically the whole of the heavy and laborious work' in the city's iron, steel, and metal-working plants."[136]

Around the steel mills and coal mines, the sojourners would crowd the "foreign colonies," overwhelmingly male. Many resided in boarding houses, often run by fellow expatriates. Often the beds would never grow cold, as one shift of workers would simply be replaced by another. As historian Craig Heron observes, one 1913 report from Hamilton found 17 such boarding houses in the shadow of the smokestacks, housing no fewer than 232 men (213 of them single), 19 women, and 12 children. In Sydney's working-class and immigrant neighbourhood of Whitney Pier, 331 Poles and Russians lived in 19 houses; another block of 19 houses was home to 257 residents, mainly Italians.[137] The sojourning phenomenon helps explain why Sydney and Hamilton, to pick two examples, were not the centres of the left in 1890–1920 that they would become in the 1930s and 1940s: for it was only in those later decades that the population of sojourners and guest workers had been largely replaced with a permanently rooted proletariat.

Across the country – from Sydney to Montreal and Toronto, from Windsor to Sudbury and Port Arthur, from Winnipeg to Vancouver and Victoria – well-known urban neighbourhoods provided immigrants with culturally specific institutions, while, in the more rural areas, sojourners could be found in hamlets of flimsy tarpaper shacks. Often these neighbourhoods were dubbed with unflattering racialized names – one district in Nova Scotia's rural Joggins coalfield, although populated primarily by Eastern Europeans, was revealingly called "The Hottentot."[138]

Canadian unionists, as David Goutor notes in a path-breaking study, critiqued immigrants not only for depreciating the cost of labour but also for failing to behave as proper consumers. As the Nanaimo Knights of Labor argued, the Chinese were not so much wage workers as "parasites" who drained the country of its natural wealth because such a high percentage of their earnings went back to China. The serf-like "Chinese coolie" was imagined to be the exact opposite of the free-standing, respectable, organized workingman. As the *Industrial Banner* explained, "Trade Unionism Stands for a High Type of Civilization." Countries in which trade unionism was strong stood "at the highest in the scale of civilization." They could be contrasted with a land such as China, where the "coolie accepts his lot and is content with his position. He has no aspirations; he is an animal."[139]

For British-Canadian nationalists who believed themselves to have reached the apex of social evolution, Chinese immigration constituted a complicated imaginary threat: on the one hand, as the docile creatures of monopolists, the Chinese provided a worrying glimpse into a future in which capital had destroyed workers' organizations and crowded out the labour movement; on the other hand, as a less civilized people, they could not be integrated into a modern, progressive Canada. As Goutor perceptively points out, from the labour leaders' point of view the Chinese were "models of industrial wage slaves." For the movement this was, not surprisingly, something to be bitterly opposed. "We will shed blood before we become slaves," proclaimed one speaker at an anti-Chinese union meeting in Victoria. "An intelligent population is the best safeguard against the tyranny of capitalism," stated the Victoria *Industrial News*. "This is why monopolists and syndicates are endeavoring to force servile Chinese coolie labor on this community."[140]

To resist the entry of the Chinese was to save liberal freedoms and labour rights from an enemy that was both past and present rolled into one, the worst of the medieval ages and the worst of modernity. Chinatowns came to be seen, according to Goutor, as "the primary source of the evils of modern industrial urban centres, particularly drugs, gambling, prostitution, and diseases such as leprosy."[141] In Halifax, crusades against the supposed evil of Chinese restaurants culminated in vicious anti-Chinese rioting in 1918.[142] Others sought to link the Chinese with the sex trades – "They bring no women with them but for those brought for the vilest purposes," was one claim advanced at a Victoria working-class rally – and feared that they would seduce White women in their opium dens or even in the booths of Chinese restaurants.[143]

The *Palladium of Labor* lamented that British Columbia had been "so tamely . . . given up to Chinese slave labor and Chinese lust and leprosy," and argued, "Chinamen breed invariably a moral and physical pestilence in the white communities into which they intrude." Others even blamed the Chinese for condemning many men to lives of celibacy, because by setting up such trades as laundries they took away jobs from White working women. The Chinese were thought to exemplify the lascivious behaviour that some Knights thought a symptom of capitalism itself. Effeminate yet a peril to womankind, indolent yet capable of astonishing amounts of work, rich money-hoarders who could live on practically nothing: these contradictory images were, Goutor remarks, "hopelessly untenable," but they served to turn Asians into caricatures of "fully dehumanized tools of capitalism." As in Vancouver in 1914, many believed that the Asians, few in number as they were, were taking over whole branches of industry. Many members of the labour movement held no hope that the deeply embedded differences between the races could be altered. As Goutor points out, union leaders mainly embraced existing stereotypes and ideas, rather than creating them themselves. Organized labour identified the Chinese in particular as instruments of the National Policy, most visibly exemplified by the Canadian Pacific Railway. Labour's critique focused on the "large contractors and other monopolists" who squeezed immense profits out of the public and then turned around and brought in "Chinese laborers by the shipload."[144]

Racialization meant the transposition of race into new spheres. In the case of labour, this entailed the shifting terms of the Other to be resisted, which evolved from "Chinese" to "Orientals" and then to "Asiatics." By the early

20th century the line separating Asian and other immigrants was drawn more sharply. In 1906 a committee reporting on immigration to the TLC's convention included "a general demand for exclusiveness based on ethnicity and character." Another plank singled out the "Chinamen, Hindus and all other Asiatic peoples" as "classes that are not desirable" and announced its support for the head tax and the complete exclusion of Hindus. According to Goutor, the statement "did not specifically request the exclusion or even restriction of eastern and southern European immigrants."[145]

The anti-immigration fervour of the 1900s and 1910s, in some places a veritable mass movement, bears the marks of many moments of refusal of capitalism: for many workers apparently saw in the "Coolie" and "Chink" and "Jap" not only the figures of their future enslavement, but also, in White Canada, the emblem of the supersedure of troubling transnational realities. In some cases, racism emerged as an ultimate systematization, in the form of a seemingly scientific set of concepts that could explain the fast-changing visible world and in institutions such as the Ku Klux Klan (which was to enjoy substantial growth in Canada in the 1920s). Worldwide and in Canada, the socialist movement had met in nationalist racism a dangerously plausible competing formulation. It was an approach that did not require, as socialism did, a wrenching break with liberal definitions of social and political reality.

Foreign-born leftists walked warily in a society prone to typecast them as aliens and deport them if convenient. John A. Cooper, writing an early critique of socialists in Canada, decided that the leftists were agitators and dreamers, who shared "the wild revolutionary spirit" of the "off-scourings of Europe, who, hunted from their native lands, have fled for refuge to the United States, where all men are citizens." Such types might come to Canada, or they might infect Canadians themselves who had gone to the United States and then returned to the Dominion with "new and devilish ideas." Mary Wisdom Cotton reported on a friend's response when she told her she had attended socialist meetings. "She asked me in real earnest if I was not afraid that 'some of those foreigners would stick a knife in me.'" The postwar Halifax *Herald*, never inclined to judicious understatement, focused on the "Cancer of Foreign Influence," which could be blamed for "nine-tenths of the discord, the industrial and social strife, the insidious, cowardly, nation-betraying, that is going on in the diseased minds of the spawn of countries that are anything but white and British."[146]

As Allen Seager remarks, even in the ethnically diverse Crow's Nest Pass coalfields of Alberta the labour leadership only gradually ceased to be a "British preserve." By 1914 the movement still had only a handful of "ethnic" leaders. The "Whiteness = Britishness" equation culminated in the uproariously enthusiastic response among Anglo-Canadian workers to the call to British arms in 1914. Just three days after the British Empire entered the war on 4 August 1914, the coal towns held a "monster demonstration," complete with fireworks and volleys. Between 15 and 20 per cent of the coal miners enlisted. Trade unionists in Blairmore, centre of the regiment, served on patriotic committees, sold war bonds, and – most divisively – agitated against the employment of so-called "enemy aliens," fellow miners who originated in parts of Europe that were now officially at war with Britain. At Hillcrest mine, "patriotic workers" took advantage of the war to have their Ukrainian fellow workers fired and even helped to get them interned.[147] The Ukrainian left paper decried such divisive actions but also counselled patience: "We will survive this misfortune and not only will we remain faithful anti-militarists but we will try to teach those workers who have gone crazy over chauvinism."[148] In Springhill, N.S., equally patriotic coal miners went on strike to force "enemy aliens" to wear specially designed lamps, so as to preclude an anti-British suicide bombing; the precautionary measure was widely regarded as payback for some of the "aliens" having arrived as strikebreakers in the strike of 1909–11. Such currents of working-class imperial nationalism would persist after the war; in Hamilton in 1919 a crowd estimated at 10,000 people demanded the deportation of "enemy aliens and other undesirables."[149] In these cases, imperial nationalism had trumped class solidarity.

The nativism within the labour movement did meet with some misgivings and reservations. As in the moment of the *Komagata Maru*, some worried that riots against foreigners would be pinned on organized labour, with injurious consequences for its image. As early as 1903 the Western Federation of Miners suggested organizing Chinese coal miners, although nothing came of it.[150] Yet the radical WFM was not the mainstream of the labour movement, and in that mainstream nativist sentiment ran high – bolstered as it was by the traditional, profound feelings of British patriotism and bread and butter issues of economic well-being.

Socialism: "No Vaccine against Racism"

Many socialists of the time saw relatively little need to engage in a battle with this ideological juggernaut. Much of the left, particularly its most moderate and labourist elements, would not have identified with any critique of the Empire. Canada was part of the most successful Empire in the world. Many of its citizens were more fully informed about events in Britain than in other parts of the Dominion. After all, a good proportion of them were first- or second-generation immigrants from Britain. For them, "Canadian independence" might well carry a taint of disloyalty to Britain. The leadership of the Canadian left was crowded with newly arrived Britons: J.B. McLachlan, William Watkins, James Simpson, Arthur Puttee, W.A. Pritchard, Tim Buck, Gertrude Richardson, and Helena Gutteridge, to name a few.

Socialists were by no means immune to British-Canadian nationalism, which in essence meant that they were rarely critical, or even conscious, of the division of the country into two predominant linguistic groups – what the outside world often called the "Race Question in Canada." Under the headline "Nationalism of Lower Canada. Will Quebec Ever Be Anglified?" *Citizen and Country* gave great play to a piece, originally published in the *Presbyterian Review*, by the Rev. John E. Duclos, who drew upon the case of Norway and Sweden to suggest that no such amalgamation of races could occur. "Canada can never become a consolidated nation so long as there exists two official languages," he argued.[151] W. Frank Hatheway of Saint John contented himself with recycling historian Francis Parkman's vague thesis that the chief difference between French and English colonists was that "while the English at once set about to establish laws and govern themselves, the French were content to be governed by those of whom they had not the choosing."[152] W.U. Cotton rarely noticed the French Canadians, even though *Cotton's Weekly* was originally published in Quebec's Eastern Townships.

Glimmerings of more substantive appraisals did appear. Colin McKay, whose journalism and militancy had brought him in closer touch with Montreal francophones, and who could at least read texts in the French language, wrote to the *American Federationist* in 1902 to defend the French Canadians' reputation as trade unionists and to caution anglophone labour organizers not to be condescending in their treatment of them.[153] Merely by describing himself as the "Chef du Parti Socialiste du Canada, Section française," Albert Saint-Martin implied a two-nations position not universally appreciated, and not generally recognized, in either the SPC or SDPC. Yet as late as January 1908, the SPC lacked a French-language section in Montreal. (None is listed in the report from Comrade Otto John, secretary, Local Montreal, who dutifully enumerates the city's English-speaking, Jewish, Italian, and Russian branches.)[154] Although Saint-Martin did play a dramatic role in Montreal's May Day struggles, he seemingly spent more time on Esperanto than on *la question nationale*.

A characteristic pose of the leftists was to poke fun at the pretensions of Empire. Kipling's "White Man's Burden" was forever being satirized. Even the *Western Clarion* spoke of the "British Vampire," whose imperial projects in India and Africa it mocked. *Citizen and Country* published a caustic cartoon showing Uncle Sam and John Bull forcing alcohol upon their recently conquered subject populations.[155] Substantial sections of the left opposed the Boer War – the Canadian Socialist League, highlighting Thompson's ardent anti-militarism, lost some of its middle-class Toronto supporters because of its stance – and in New Brunswick Martin Butler used *Butler's Journal* and *The Canadian Democrat* to denounce "The Dragon of Imperialism."[156]

Still, a chasm existed between these ironic treatments of imperialism and a full-blown critique of White racism and Canada's position as a colony of White settlement. The *Clarion* studiously avoided discussing race oppression in a serious manner, even when it was reporting on questions that seemingly could not help but involve it. One article "On the History of Slavery" somehow managed to omit the transatlantic African slave trade altogether. Another on bridge-building in Central Africa overlooked both the racial dynamics and the imperialist logic of the enterprise. A piece on the Suez Canal said nothing about the thousands of lives lost in its construction. Another article contented itself with heavy sarcasm when describing the plight of Martinique canal workers suffering and dying as they dug the Panama Canal.[157] These ironic jibes stood in marked contrast to the *Clarion*'s treatment of oppression dished out to Whites in other places, such as Russia, the "prison-house of peoples" under the czarist regime that most everyone on the left regarded with particular revulsion. *Clarion*ites were assumed to be familiar with the details of English history – the Magna Charta, Cromwell, the Glorious Revolution – but not with those of the world beyond the Anglo-American North Atlantic world.

Even the utopian projections of E.A. Partridge, whose Western-separatist utopia was seemingly furthest removed from official Canadian nationalism, contained such themes as British superiority, British Canada's inherent right to occupy an "empty" West, and, conversely, the erasure of the First Nations. However separate from the Dominion Coalsamao might have been in its communalism and radical democracy, it was never that far removed from the universe that celebrated the "British bulldog breed." As late as 1928, William Irvine, writing in *Co-operative Government*, unselfconsciously assumed that his readers were "We of the British race."[158]

These patterns of nationalism had profound implications. Hegemony is powerful: when linked to the myth-symbol complexes of nationalism it can sweep away the most prudent calculations of personal and class advantage. Liberal order generated at one and the same time contradictory and powerful images: of perpetual progress, of a sweeping cosmic vision of a British imperium settling and civilizing the world, of extraordinary monarchs under whose beneficent regimes a vast family of races and nations could be harmoniously gathered; and, simultaneously, of the "dark" worlds that it was struggling to enlighten, of the barbarism and incivility of the non-British world, of the tangled irrationalities, oppressions, and impoverishment of that benighted majority that yet lacked British Protestantism, British institutions, even British manners. For Hatheway, in whom were combined the seemingly contradictory roles of Tory tea merchant and crusading Fabian social reformer, identification with the "new nationality" arising in Canada meant cheering on the Empire's troops in South Africa and around the world. Like the participants in the *Komagata Maru* affair, he was keenly attuned to the wider fortunes of the British Empire. Upon his return from a trip to Australia and India in 1910, Hatheway was bitterly critical of Keir Hardie, whose speeches had allegedly turned the Indians to rebellion.[159] In this period, then, one distinct strand of thought on the race question – a strand that flourished unhindered within much of labourism – consisted of leftists who simply assented to the racialized imperial nationalism of "White Canada," which they theorized in a form of "social-evolutionary nativism."

The theorists upon whom the first formationists so often relied did not provide unambiguous guidance on the race question. Darwin's *The Descent of Man* (1871) had notoriously advanced the view that non-Europeans and women were at a lower evolutionary stage than were European men. Spencer's sociology also considered some races "lower" than others on the evolutionary scale. The echoes of this kind of "evolutionizing" of difference can be discerned in Woodsworth's laundry list and especially in his discussion of peoples of colour. The Marx-Engels theoretical pole could certainly inspire a general resistance to talk of nation and race – "The workingmen have no country," said *The Communist Manifesto*, in what was perhaps more of a statement about the hoped-for future than a realistic assessment of the world in 1848. After the 1870s, socialists sang "The Internationale," which promised that the workers of the world would one day become the human race.[160] But both Marx and Engels often did generalize about whole peoples in ways that also sorted them into hierarchies, although Marx was frequently more subtle, and on the Irish question brilliantly anticipated contemporary theories of racialization and whiteness.[161] Neither Marx nor Engels provided first formationists with a means of easily constructing a working alternative to the hegemonic politics of White Canada.

From Lewis Henry Morgan, and particularly his key work, *Ancient Society, or Researches in the Lines of Human Progress from Savagery through Barbarism to Civilization*, came important insights into race. Marx's ethnological notebooks suggest Morgan's profound impact on him.[162] Engels's *The Origin of the Family, Private Property and the State* was crucially dependent on the U.S. scholar. Indeed, the "Marx-Morgan" framework attained the status of orthodoxy among many North Americans, including De Leon, and found one of its fullest (if oddest) expositions in the SPC's foundational manifesto. In Canada W.A. Pritchard singled out Morgan's works on ethnography as the "epoch-making" achievements of the "one man in America who has been recognized by the Universities of Europe as a real scientist." McKay's many forays into patterns of social evolution drew directly from Morgan.[163] Yet the implications of Morgan's thought for the politics of race were ambiguous. On the one hand, and this can be plainly seen in McKay's thought, he predisposed socialists to view with interest and sympathy the history of the First Nations as one of "primitive communism," whose ethics of solidarity were greatly superior to the capitalist societies of the present day. On the other hand, as Mark Pittinger remarks, Morgan's predetermined stages – savagery, barbarism, and civilization, each associated with distinctive forms of property, technology, and kinship – allowed some U.S. socialists to reduce Native Americans to "obstacles on the path of Euro-capitalist progress."[164] To be "earlier" in the more determinist constructions of anthropology was inherently to be inferior: "Our forebears were rude, unlettered, unorganized, unintelligent and totally lacking the first principles of cohesion and organization," pronounced the SPC in *Socialism and Unionism*.[165]

Truly alert socialists might have picked up on more contemporary theoretical developments on the left. On the Darwinian side, they might have noted that Sydney Olivier, a British Fabian who served as governor of Jamaica, wrote an interesting treatise on *White Capital and Coloured Labour*, published as part of Ramsay MacDonald's "Socialist Library," in which Darwinian and Spencerian categories were used to further an argument against "negrophobia" and the "colour line."[166] On the Marxist side, Kautsky, responding to the dramatic rise of anti-Semitism and racial theorizing in Germany, and drawing on a youthful allegiance to Darwinism that conditioned much of his subsequent Marxism, very usefully critiqued the entire concept of race. In a classic discussion, beginning with a learned disquisition on the animal kingdom before finally reaching the particulars of human history, Kautsky disposed of the notions of racial purity and the inherent antagonism between particular races; and he foreshadowed the turn against scientific racism within anthropology that was to take hold two decades later. Kautsky underlined the recent conclusion of Franz Boas, that "the absolute persistence of human types" was an untenable theory. "There is no Semitic race, there is no Aryan race," Kautsky argued. "The Aryan race is not a primitive race, but merely an 'invention of the closeted scholar.'" Races were in a constant state of flux, and no "dominant race" could meaningfully boast that its "present superiority was based on its blood." The concepts of racial purity and a "natural" hostility between races were delusional. In a sense Kautsky's pioneering text anticipated modern deconstructions of race, and perhaps even bettered them in closely studying the biological evidence. Given Kautsky's stature as the "Pope of Marxism," his position was an important one – although until the 1926 appearance of *Are the Jews a Race?* his followers in the English-speaking world necessarily relied on fragments of the position he had disseminated in Germany in 1914.[167]

The international tradition as a whole, then, offered enigmatic and often unhelpful pointers. Some who had influential voices within it, such as Ferri, London, Schreiner, and Gilman, wrote on race in ways that were notoriously both "racialist" *and* "racist."[168] In a certain strand of the race question on the left, there were few weighty arguments that first formationists could raise against the pervasive conflation of anti-capitalism and race-based nativism.

What might now seem to be blindingly obvious facts of colonialism and oppression were then often invisible. For example, when he reached for an expression to describe Canada before capitalism, Alf Budden evoked a time and place when there "were only Indians and gophers." E.T. Kingsley would describe as "worthless" the region north of Lake Superior. Here was a land "shunned by about every animal in the category, except that brilliant specimen, the wage-slave." That much of this land was the established territory of Aboriginal peoples apparently never occurred to him.[169] In British Columbia socialist writers tended to stick to stereotypical images of "the Indians" and their carefree lives and were rarely able to find any other narrative place for them, such as, for example, that of fellow workers.[170]

With respect to Afro-Canadians, many socialists followed the labour movement in expressing general sympathy and support for Blacks and disdain for U.S. racism.[171] As Goutor notes, the labour press offered some expressions of sympathy for Aboriginals and Blacks, with the *Palladium of Labor* even promoting the works of Frederick Douglass on the position of Black workers. In Halifax John Thomas Bulmer, a Labor Reformer and in some books a socialist, actively campaigned against segregated schools. Yet, at the same time, both Phillips Thompson and Fred Dixon, to name two prominent examples, felt comfortable with "darkie humour," conveyed in a dialect that they found amusing.[172]

On the question of immigration, there were certainly some non-racializing socialist critiques of the crash program of capitalist accumulation that the Liberals had initiated in the country. SPCer John Mortimer wrote to Clifford Sifton to complain of the "hundreds of thousands of dollars" that had gone towards aiding immigration, which he said were "extorted principally out of the laboring classes in order to make the price of labour cheap, to inundate and slaughter the labor market." Yet many socialists defended the anti-Asian policies and even derided the Chinese as a people. The pioneering United Socialist Labor Party of British Columbia, defending "a true democracy of happy workers," placed an anti-Asian plank in its platform in 1900 – which was, according to researcher Ross Johnson, the first and last time the socialist party would do so. SPC members in the B.C. legislature did not consistently fight anti-Asian legislation and sometimes not only acceded to the prejudices of their time but also accentuated them. According to Johnson, the socialists repeatedly attempted to attach provisions for "all-White" labour to railway bills coming through the legislature. The SPC even tried in 1910 to amend the Public Schools Act to allow the Board of Trustees to "exclude any child or children from the school or schools on the ground that owing to racial or other differences it is deemed to be inadvisable to the best interest of the majority of children to admit them."[173]

However pioneering she was on the woman question, Helena Gutteridge followed the mainstream in urging discrimination against Asians. Irene Howard reports an incident that occurred in early 1915:

> [Gutteridge] appeared before the Board of Licence Commissioners at Vancouver City Hall to plead for Oriental hotel workers to be replaced by white women. "I have no color prejudice," she claimed, "but I think in this case and in the interest of efficient white female labor in this city the board might put a white labor clause in the granting of hotel licenses, so that work being done by Chinese help to-day may be done by white women who are now out of employment.[174]

A point that Leier sagely makes about the Vancouver SPCers – that "socialism was no vaccine against racism" – could be extended well beyond Vancouver. In the Maritimes McLachlan referred to the "calamity that an industrial China will bring on the western world," and looked forward to the day when workingmen would "get round the ballot box and send men to parliament." Then the "rat fed Chinaman run mad over the world with a product that he himself has created but refuses to use" would desist. "Our comfort would teach him also to vote for socialism and China and all its wealth for all the Chinese." Both the vivid dietary detail and the sense of the Chinese being "taught" socialism by the non-Chinese suggested the string of racial associations awaiting even a confirmed anti-racist. McKay, who in general made no consistent use of the concept of race in his work and fought anti-French Canadian prejudices, could nonetheless write of the "pigtail pest" when describing Asian immigrants in 1900. For its part, *Citizen and Country* reprinted without critical commentary the supposedly radical *Rossland Miner*'s declaration that "While the people of this province are as loyal to Imperial connection as any part of the Dominion," they could not endure without serious protest "having their country overrun and their industrial prospects ruined by the influx of Oriental laborers."[175]

Assumptions about racial characteristics also extended beyond the question of Chinese immigration. In the *Western Clarion* in 1908 W.J. Curry reported on a steamboat cruise up the Skeena River, where he noted the "manner in which the Indian, Jap and Anglo-Saxon responded to the demands of modern industry." He found the Japanese worker to be "small, but agile, tough and strong," and "energetic, versatile and a great imitator." The Chinese worker functioned "like a Waltham watch. Start him right, keep him sound and oiled with material and wages and he never varies." (This detail confirmed the ominously "modern" aspect of the imagined Chinese menace.) The Indians lagged behind their Asian competitors. The White workers came in last. What did this mean, then, about their relative positions on the evolutionary scale? "Anglo-Saxons" were degenerating, "intellectually as well as morally," ignorant of the system of production they defended and blind to "the stupendous significance of the Asiatic invasion of America." But the White workers were also "on a higher level of mentality than that occupied by either the Indian or Jap," because they had become conscious of their class interests, and alone could save Western civilization from being taken over by the "virile barbarians" of the new age. The ultra-socialist Curry and the not-yet-socialist Woodsworth were thus united in drawing up hierarchies of races. Both, if pressed, could have had recourse to Spencer's "Descriptive Sociology" series, which ranked groups in hierarchies much in this manner.[176]

In "Socialism and the Survival of the Fittest," published over many issues of the *Western Clarion*, we meet the "timid New Hollander," the "vivacious Celt," the "stolid Chinaman," the "warlike Red Indian," and the "philosophical Hindu," all in a narrative apparently designed to offer a scientific rebuttal to the Book of Genesis.[177] Linda Kealey shows how thoroughly attitudes of "Anglo-Saxon superiority" permeated even an article designed to show support for Jewish cloak-makers and shirtmakers in Toronto: *Cotton's Weekly*'s blared forth a denunciation of strikebreakers who were "not Chinese, blacks, or other foreigners but 'WHITE GIRLS AND MEN OF BRITISH BIRTH ... CANADIAN GIRLS ARE HANDED WORK THAT JEWISH GIRLS REFUSE TO DO.'"[178]

An Abstract International Universalism

In a second strand of the race question on the Canadian left, a theme that had been implicit in many early treatments became more and more pronounced. All forms of nationalism and patriotism, including those that were racialized, were instances of false consciousness and delusion. The race question was not so much answered as abolished.

This position had been anticipated as early as 1899 by Henry Ashplant. Writing under the name of "Heterodox Economics," Ashplant denounced socialists swayed by the anti-Asian agitation. "The Socialist Labor Party of Canada recognizes in a British Columbia Chinaman a brother man, the victim of Canadian and British capitalists," he declared. "The Chinaman in Canada introduces more than he receives from Canadian employers, and receives nothing until he has earned it." In the *Labor Advocate* Phillips Thompson indicated serious misgivings about Chinese exclusion, and while not calling for a reconsideration of labour's policies, still declared it silly for the TLC to be worried about the arrival of "a few washeee-washee men among us."[179] The wording of his declaration suggested limitations in its ostensible universalism.

"Socialism is not patriotism," advised the Lindsay socialists. "Under patriotism the people have nothing to say. Under Socialism the people have all to say." They added, for emphasis, "The capitalist flag has but three stars, rent, interest and profit." In *The Socialist and the Sword*, an SPC pamphlet of 1912, George Kirkpatrick of the American Socialist Party denounced the "hate-filled madness called patriotism" that had "paralyzed and blinded each new generation of the working class, rendering them the easy, self-slaughtering dupes of a crafty ruling class. Thus have the workers been duped and stung till now." The "class line can only be clearly drawn between those who own and those who do not," the SPC argued in *The Working Class and Master Class* (1910). "It can only be drawn on property lines. It can not be drawn on organic lines, for all members of the human species are organically the same. It can not be drawn on lines of color or race, as we have Anglo-Saxon capitalists, German capitalists, Chinese capitalists, and negro capitalists; we have Anglo-Saxon workers, German workers, Chinese workers and negro workers. There are capitalists of all races, and workers of all races."[180]

The *Western Clarion* agreed. With reference to the "Oriental Problem" in the West, it remarked, "This race question is being agitated by the master class in order to delude the workers into participating in a trade war for their masters' benefit.... The longer that the hope of betterment by emigration is before the workers, the longer they will be in discovering that their one common hope of betterment lies in the overthrow of the wage system." Now recanting (without seeming to acknowledge) a decade of SPC pronouncements in the B.C. legislature and labour movement, "We are slaves here," the *Clarion* declared in 1913. "We are slaves in China or Japan; so our condition can be changed but slightly while the capitalist system lasts." The SPCers of Lindsay maintained, "Socialists do not recognize any race problem." They emphasized: "It is the class interest that determines the action of any class, not any race division within the class."[181] In essence, the new position was that race was an irrelevance.

Posited at a time when lynching and race riots were on the rise in the United States, the Lindsay SPC's maxim, "Socialists do not recognize any race problem," seems unintentionally revealing. Abolishing the race question in theory did not, of course, mean abolishing racism in reality – and not addressing the reality led to other difficulties with the approach. "In the south," a piece in *Cotton's Weekly* pointed out, "men are lynched for robbing women of their virtue. What of a skunk who would rob decent men of their honor?"[182] Yet it was not just "men" who were being lynched in the South, but (primarily) "Afro-American" men. First formation discourse echoed and re-echoed with talk of "wage slavery" – yet to make slavery a "colour-blind" proposition was to miss a core contradiction of North American history since the 18th century.

Perhaps the noblest exemplar of this abstract international universalism was the Industrial Workers of the World. If uncharacteristic of much of the Canadian labour movement in warmly embracing the unskilled and the isolated camp workers, so many of them recent immigrants, the Wobblies did share a general first formation turn away from nativism in the 1910s. In the well-reported words of one Prince Rupert Wobbly: "When the factory whistle blows it does not call us to work as Irishmen, Germans, Americans, Russians, Greeks, Poles, Negroes or Mexicans. It calls us to work as wage workers, regardless of the country in which we were born or color of our skins."[183] The IWW, with its low initiation fees and dues, transferable membership cards, and grassroots democracy, was well adapted to the migratory lives of the foreign workers, so often compelled to wander from one workplace to the next. Its ambitious educational program and libraries must have appealed to many foreign workers, who often came from European countries where the level of radical discourse was far above that attained in North America. The Vancouver *Sun*, with its characteristically crude focus on the ethnic dimensions of every situation, clearly sensed that something new was up in the IWW: it urged the provincial government to quell this "invasion of the most despicable scum of humanity" and "drive these people out of the country."[184] Many of the movement's roughly 400,000 members across North America in 1913 were immigrant workers who found in the IWW their first champion of a better life.

This change in socialist discourse can also be tracked on the local level in UMW District 18, in which, as Seager notes, socialists would be influential throughout much of this period. The original District 18 constitution, adopted in 1905, barred Asiatics. The district even urged that the international union write such a policy into its constitution in 1906. Frank H. Sherman, the founding figure in District 18, argued strenuously that "Asian immigration . . . is a most serious menace. . . . Every effort should be made to stop this class of immigration from coming to our shores." Such words found a receptive audience among many coal miners. As Seager remarks, the coal miners of the Western interior regarded themselves as a kind of "Maginot line against the Oriental menace," with Albertans leading the agitation to exclude Asians from membership. Yet, in 1909, wracked with Bright's Disease, Sherman in a fiery convention speech not only demanded a "left turn" towards public ownership of the mines and industrial democracy, but also "convinced the delegates to extend an invitation to the small minority of Chinese and Japanese in the district to 'unite with the union to better the moral, material, and intellectual conditions of the toilers.'" District 18 did not long preserve this spirit. According to Seager, when a few Chinese workers employed in the Banff district walked out in 1911, "all the union men could say (through their *District Ledger*) was: 'Conditions Pretty Rotten When Slant Eyes Refuse to Work,'" and the racially inclusive policy was rescinded after Sherman's death. But it was nonetheless an indication that one significant socialist had come to a different position on the politics of race, and had been able to convince other workers to share it.[185] There was much more fluidity and movement within the working class than a bald declaration that it was "racist" will allow.

At the same time, although such abstract internationalism and anti-racism was obviously an improvement over the left's earlier uncritical accession to the liberal politics of racialization, and was defended heroically against entrenched opposition by Wobblies and some other progressives, it sometimes carried the imprint of the "impossibilist" style favoured by much of the SPC. Racial theories of society were as overblown and fictional as Kautsky had shown, yet this did not mean – as Kautsky himself emphasized – that their consequences were any less real or oppressive for those who suffered them. "There is surely nothing more absurd than the theory of the 'natural' hostility between races," Kautsky wrote, "but unfortunately it is not one of the theories that may be killed by laughing at it. It arises from interests that are too strong, it serves too well the purpose of facilitating the demagogic exploitation of ancient prejudices and errors." Propounded endlessly and perpetuated through countless institutions and traditions, "race hostility" had come to be seen as a "self-evident truth, imparting to it ever new accessions of vitality."[186] Simply announcing that socialists on scientific grounds could not see colour did not make "race" vanish as a potent "self-evident truth" of daily life. Racism was real in its consequences, if unreal in its science.

Challenging Anglo-Canadian Imperial Nationalism

Yet a third strand of the race question emerged, implicitly, from the new diaspora socialisms that began to become prominent after 1907. These diaspora socialisms were created among immigrant groups who had left their homelands at times of conflict and who often found, over time, that it was difficult to return to them (as opposed to sojourners, who might readily winter in Europe). This third position responded to the high costs for the left of the ethnic and racial divisions within the working class, yet did not seek to abstractly "abolish" those differences as being unworthy of the attention of scientific socialism. Here the somewhat "abstract" critique of racialism of the second strand was made more concrete by an emphasis on the real-world divisive consequences of racialized divisions. What marked this movement was a growing hostility to racializing discourses and their successful manipulation by employers and politicians. In a sense, this third position began to develop something like the approach of Marx in his analysis of the Irish question in Britain in the 1870s, with its subtle blend of economic structure and national identification. It was all the more remarkable an achievement given the often unpromising materials in social-evolutionary theory with which first formationists had to work.

A little-noticed turning point in the history of the Canadian left, and certainly a major moment in the transformation of the race question, was the early 20th-century crisis of the Russian Empire. Russia's defeat in the Russian-Japanese War of 1904–5 and the Revolution of 1905 delivered two messages: that a non-European power could best one of the major countries of Europe in a military struggle; and that Russia's peculiar combination of czarist abso-lutism and capitalism was vulnerable to revolutionary change. If the Canadian left was always a transnational phenomenon, it became even more so with these events because they – and an oppressive political order rapidly descend-ing into chaos – sent to Canadian shores three distinct groups of immigrants whose diaspora socialisms would, over the long term, permanently change the landscape of left politics: Finns, Ukrainians, and Jews.[187]

Yet, contrary to much of what we think today about Canada, and also contrary to the "America" whose image circulated far and wide in Europe, Eu-ropean immigrants were not fleeing to a liberal democracy, but to *another em-pire*. They came not to a republic, in which governance in theory stemmed from the people, but to a dominion, a British colony held by right of conquest. Here too was a ruling order wielding the powers of exclusion and deportation. In this empire, too, it seemed, especially after the passing of the War Measures Act in 1914, that the civil rights of minorities could be abrogated as easily as they were granted. As in Russia, entire "peoples" could be declared suspect. Even the public use of entire languages could be prohibited. If there were no actual "serfs," as there had been in Russia down to the 1860s, there were nonetheless in Canada tens of thousands of workers bound to labour contractors, working in the woods and mines without any of the social or legal protections of citizens – suffering, in a figurative sense, a second kind of serfdom. In the contradiction between the hopes for freedom nurtured by refugees from the Russian Empire and the grim and oppressive realities they en-countered in Canada lies much of the original inspiration of the Canadian left.

In short, yearning for freedom, many diaspora socialists found in Canada something far less ennobling; and many brought with them ideals of the radi-cal enlightenment and advanced understandings of socialist theory that allowed them speedily to grasp these New World conditions in sophisticated ways. Certainly many political leaders sensed early on that something alarm-ing was afoot. Winnipeg mayor J.H. Ashdown, for example, feared the worst from a 1908 visit from the famous anarchist Emma Goldman. "We have a very large foreign population in this City, it consists approximately of 15,000 Gali-cians, 11,000 Germans, 10,000 Jews, 2,000 Hungarians and 5,000 Russians and other Slavs and Bohemians," he wrote. "Many of these people have had trouble in their own country with their Governments and come to the new land to get away from it, but have all the undesirable elements in their character that created the trouble for them before." They were just the "right crowd" for an agitator of Goldman's revolutionary ilk.[188]

The immigrant socialists, although diverse, did share commonalities. They generally paid rapt attention to events in their recently departed homelands. As Bradwin observed, the Bulgarians and Macedonians on construction gangs in 1910–11 would re-enact Balkan conflicts in the backwoods. They besieged any newspaper-carrying visitor for news from the homeland, and melted away from the camps on the outbreak of war.[189] Many immigrants also arrived with a proud sense of their own theoretical and cultural achievements, and had little time for well-meaning but patronizing Anglo-Canadians. Many foreign-born Marxists considered themselves more knowledgeable in socialist theory and practice than the leftists they encountered in the host society and, in the privacy of their own newspapers and in their own languages, could vent their frustrations. As the Ukrainian left newspaper *Robochyi narod* observed of Canadians, "All of them are literate, that is true, but after scrutiny, they are worse than illiterate. They aren't interested in a single progressive thought – the only thing they know is the dollar." They had "no class consciousness and their social democratic movement is very weak, greatly weaker than the Ukrainian."[190] Only intermittently and slowly did these cultural and linguistic barriers begin to fall.

Jewish socialism would find its most dramatic expression in Montreal, Toronto, and Winnipeg, with Russian Jews developing an especially sterling reputation for socialist zeal. The Jewish branch of the SPC in Toronto was making itself known as early as 1905. By 1908 Jews were prominently involved in pro-SPC "free speech" fights. Distinctive Jewish institutions were rooting themselves; in Winnipeg, as Gerald Tulchinsky points out, the establishment of the Yiddisher Yugend Farein (Jewish youth organization) in 1905 led to the foundation of a National Radical School in 1914, representing a move towards a more radical and internationalist position. Under the name of the Peretz School, this would long be a significant force in the Winnipeg Jewish left. In Toronto the Jewish National Radical School was so zealous a partisan of the radical enlightenment that it generated turmoil within its own larger community, with opposition from Toronto's Jewish religious establishment.[191] By 1911 the Jewish socialists had organized a socialist Sunday School and by 1916 a Young Jewish Workers' Club, which, as Linda Kealey notes, "combined physical culture and mental and moral development with debates and fundraising for strikes and political campaigns."[192]

"They are always at it," marvelled Wilfred Gribble. "It is their life. . . . Most of these have not been long out from Russia. 'These are they that have come out of great tribulation'; but they know, not believe, think, or have an idea, but *know* that the rule of the dominant class here, though milder than there, is the same old rule, differing only in degree."[193] In Montreal the SLP had substantial ties with the Jewish Community, and the SPC seems to have used the Jewish Socialist Hall for meetings of various branches.

Of particular significance for the Jewish diaspora socialists in big-city Canada were the Arbeiter Ring (Workers' circle) organizations, which supplied both mutual aid and education for Jews. Just six years after its initial North American appearance, the first Canadian branch was set up in Montreal in 1906; a branch in Winnipeg was established in 1907; Toronto followed suit in 1908, and Hamilton in 1910. In Winnipeg, Roz Usiskin shows, the Arbeiter Ring soon had three branches reflecting cleavages in the Jewish radical movement: Branch 169 was for the "Revolutionary Marxists" or Bundists; Branch 506 was for the "Nationalists" or Socialist Territorialists; and Branch 564 was for the anarchists. All three were distinct, yet when circumstances demanded it, they could also pull together.[194] As Usiskin remarks, "United by their strong commitment to socialism and to the development of a progressive, secular Yiddish working-class culture, the *Arbeiter Ring* became a vital, social and cultural force in the Jewish community, bringing to it a level of awareness and dedication unequalled in the general Jewish population." Merely by existing, "The *Arbeiter Ring* was able to legitimize radical ideology as an acceptable alternative."[195]

As Ruth Frager demonstrates, other elements in the labour movement and the left treated Jews with some wariness. Among some Christian socialists Judaism was associated with an Old Testament religious regime that needed to be overcome.[196] Even a seemingly non-threatening step like addressing a Jewish audience in a synagogue caused Woodsworth to look over his shoulder, wondering at the likely response of his fellow Methodists. As the flamboyant atheism of Moses Baritz suggested, scepticism towards Judaism was widely diffused among socialist Jews, many of whom seemed much more anti-religious than their Christian counterparts. In middle-class hands, the critique of Jewish religious faith shaded over into anti-Semitism, typified by restrictive clauses forbidding the sale of properties to Jews, prejudicial hiring practices, and even discreetly discriminatory admission policies in universities.[197]

Unlike the stateless Jews, Ukrainians had an actual European homeland they could look to, albeit one largely under the thumb of the Austro-Hungarian and Russian empires. Many looked for inspiration to the Ukrainian Social Democratic Party, founded in Galicia in 1890. They could also derive inspiration from the Russian Social Democrats' promise in 1910 of a future republic based on "full equality of all peoples and languages."[198] For them, national liberation and socialist struggle were not antithetical but complementary objectives, although how to balance these goals would be the subject of protracted debate.

As Peter Krawchuk points out in his informative 1979 study, among the earliest activists for socialism was Kyrilo Genyk, who before arriving in 1896 had been a member of the Russo-Ukrainian Radical Party in eastern Galicia and imprisoned for spreading socialist propaganda. In North America his work appeared in the U.S. publication *Svoboda*, and in 1903 he organized the Shevchenko Reading Society, named after Taras Shevchenko, the national poet of Ukraine. In 1906, after assimilating a Ukrainian freethinkers' club, that organization became the T.H. Shevchenko Scientific Society.[199] Towards the end of 1906 Ukrainian leftists in Nanaimo formed a socialist circle named "Volya" (Freedom), and others also founded SPC branches in Winnipeg, Portage la Prairie, and Nanaimo in 1907 – which came first is unclear – and in November began to publish *Chervonyi prapor*, the first Ukrainian socialist paper in North America.

Soon the left Ukrainians' presence in Winnipeg was made dramatically obvious in mass demonstrations – as many as 10,000 people thronged the city's May Day celebrations – and in agitations around issues in the Ukraine. For instance, they marked the assassination of the czar's representative in 1908 by Myroslav Sichensky, mounted a mass campaign against his death sentence (complete with a petition signed by 7,915 sympathizers, including many non-Ukrainians), and rejoiced when he escaped from jail. By 1910–11 the Ukrainian left in Winnipeg could boast of a labour temple, socialist publishing association (which brought out a translation of Bellamy), the Workers' Drama Club, the Socialist Propaganda Club, and a co-operative society – a level of institutional development unparalleled in the rest of Canada.

Outside Winnipeg, Ukrainian branches of the SPC were organized in Edmonton, Calgary, Hosmer, Phoenix, Brandon, Montreal, Vancouver, Cardiff, and Kenmore.[200] Such rapid growth created tensions. Some Ukrainian leftists spoke of "chauvinistically-inclined English comrades, who try to push us aside without regard to the fact that we pay, just as they do, a 10c membership fee every month." Those funds, they said, were used "exclusively on propaganda and literature for the English community, though thousands of our people live in illiterate darkness."[201] In November 1909 disgruntled activists decided to hold a convention, open only to delegates from Ukrainian SPC branches, and this "first Socialist Convention of Canadian Ukrainians" resolved to create "one autonomous, centralized organization," the Federation of Ukrainian Social Democrats in Canada (FUSD). It appealed to the SPC's Dominion Executive Committee to recognize its jurisdiction, but it also criticized the Executive Committee's stance on affiliation with the Socialist International, the equality of women, and trade unionism.

The FUSD held its first convention in August 1910 and by 1913 had amassed 23 branches with over 600 members, in sometimes fierce competition with the SPC-affiliated Federation of Ukrainian Socialists (FUS). On 31 January 1914 in Montreal, an Ontario-Quebec conference of the FUSD resolved to change the name to the Ukrainian Social Democratic Party (USDP), which as a wing of the SDPC down to 1920 would be the predominant (but never the only) organization of left Ukrainians. It had more than 2,000 Winnipeg members to its credit in 1918, and could boast the leading role in the construction of the city's striking Ukrainian Labour Temple, initiated at a mass meeting of the USDP in May 1918 – making the group there one of the largest, most concentrated, and most prominent "lefts" in the entire country. The USDP also developed a large base among Ukrainians in Eastern Canada, notably in Montreal, Toronto, Hamilton, Welland, and Ottawa.[202] In retrospect, what mattered as much as any of these institutional complexities and factional struggles were the achievements of the Ukrainian left that surmounted them – its sophisticated newspapers, mutual-aid networks, and book publishing program. From 1907 to 1918 the Ukrainian socialist movement had, through many splits and mergers, become one of the strongest left forces in the country.

Many of the newly arrived Finns also brought with them advanced socialist ideas, and established Canadians hostile to these ideas laboured to "orientalize" the newcomers, emphasizing their *Eastern* Europeanness as opposed to the *Western* Europeanness of the Swedes, Danish, Dutch, and Norwegians.[203] W.G. Smith reasoned that the Finns came in two varieties: the "Good Finns," educated, commercially oriented, industrious, law-abiding, and respectable; and the "Bad Finns," the riff-raff that the Good Finns judged had been "recruited from the most ignorant and immoral of all the emigrants from Finland." This variety of Finn, Smith said, was uneducated, unpatriotic towards Canada, and deplorably hostile towards "established institutions, political and religious." The bad lot had crept in under the wire of the country's lamentably lax immigration laws. Bradwin dwelt at some length on the "racial divergences" that explained why the Finns were quite different from the Swedes and the Norwegians.[204]

Of the diaspora socialisms to emerge from the crumbling Russian Empire, that of the Finns was the most striking, certainly when contrasted to the comparatively small size of the group (only about 21,494 in 1921, according to the census). Finland would not gain its independence from Russia until 6 December 1917. Before that, and for most of the previous century, the Finns had been part of the autonomous Grand Duchy of Russia. In the early 20th century they were in essence fighting a national liberation struggle against Russia – a struggle that split the country into Reds and Whites. Russia's failure in the war with Japan provoked a general strike in Finland, characterized by stark armed conflict between the two sides. The introduction of universal suffrage in 1906 – Finnish women were the first women in Europe to win the vote – created a massive base for the Social Democrats, which became the strongest social-democratic party in Europe, paradoxically still under the tutelage of the czar, the "Grand Duke" of Finland.

Left-wing Finns might, no less than the Ukrainians, have well regarded themselves as having lessons to teach Canadians in how to create a successful socialist movement. They were coming from a country whose left party had achieved high levels of strength; and in British Columbia, the Lakehead, and Toronto, Finns did become powerful figures on the left. They often identified strongly with Finnish-language institutions, including the newspaper *Aika* (Time), *Työkansa* (which became a daily before its bankruptcy in 1915), and the famous *Vapaus* of Sudbury.[205] In Toronto many Finnish immigrants congregated at the "Big Shop" established by Jaakko Lindala. It was a workshop in which tailors, as many as 50 at a time, could rent table space and tools at a weekly charge, thus avoiding the expense of establishing their own places.

J.W. Ahlqvist's warm description of the Big Shop suggests how the Finns reinvented in downtown Toronto the artisanal traditions of an older time. In the shop, they could arrange for work, buy ship tickets, send money to Finland, locate a translator, and find companionship. Finnish-language newspapers and books were circulated in the shop; sometimes the material was read aloud by readers hired for the occasion. It was a favourite place for agitators and other "promoters of enlightenment." Any new currents of socialist thought that emerged in Finland would soon make their appearance in Toronto, and the Big Shop, according to Ahlqvist, would become "an everyday forge whose fire was stirred up." Debates over the big questions of the left could go on for days, sometimes for years. When a discussion got out of hand, approaching a "riot," the shop elder would shout "One at a time," and order would eventually be restored. When the workers heard that Finnish left papers outside Toronto were in dire need of money, they would send donations. In one case, according to Ahlqvist, when the U.S. newspaper *Raivaaja* (Pioneer) got into financial difficulties, the Toronto Shop hustled and in less than two days raised $1,000.[206]

Out of this and many other halls would emerge the Finnish Organization of Canada, founded in Port Arthur, 19–23 March, 1914, as the consolidation of many already functioning local halls. For the next half-century, this "hall socialism" and the Finns would be a dynamic force on the Canadian left, radiating a rare solidarity and militancy and often giving extraordinary amounts of money to the English-speaking movement. By Ahlqvist's calculation, the Finnish Organization gave $12,013.72 to the Social Democratic Party of Canada from 1911 to 1918 – a vast sum, in its context – and it also was instrumental in propping up *Cotton's Weekly* in the same period.[207] The ascent of the Finns was evident in Toronto when Jaakko Lindala ran for the mayoralty in 1908 and the Board of Control in 1910 – racking up votes that scared the daylights out of Toronto's mainstream newspapers, and far exceeding those attained by individual SPC candidates in British Columbia.[208]

These diaspora socialists were different from other immigrant groups in that, by and large, they contained a sizable number of people committed to fashioning new lives in North America – overwhelmingly so among the Jews, preponderantly so among the Finns and Ukrainians. Many of them also shared a common enemy in the Russian Empire, epitomized by its hateful czars and Siberian hellholes. At the same time these three pivotal groups had distinct profiles. The Jews were primarily urban and concentrated in Montreal, Vancouver, and Winnipeg (with smaller communities in other centres). Notwithstanding their Toronto and B.C. exploits, the Canadian Finns were to a great extent a cross-border, Minnesota/Northern Ontario population – so much so that the Canada-U.S. border may not have registered nearly so deeply as an identity-marker as did a Finnish sense of being a minority nationality in North America as a whole. The Ukrainians, an enormous demographic presence on the Prairies and in Winnipeg, were also to be found in the camps and resource towns of the North and industrial cities of the East.

Still, the diaspora leftists' piety towards their own cultural traditions and ancestors, or conversely their energetic contestation of them, often served to limit their leftism to the cultural confines of the given group, and arguably made it difficult for them to share in the heroes and traditions of others. As Ahlqvist remembered, the Big Shop was a tremendous asset for the left, but it did have one significant drawback: "We isolated ourselves from our English-speaking comrades; in consequence we did not learn English which would have been so necessary for the advancement of our activities."[209] Did any of the Finns know of the left heroes of the Jews, or the Ukrainians of the great moments of the Finns?

Yet these groups were nevertheless able to come together and form the Social Democratic Party of Canada in 1911, largely at the urging of the Ontario Finns. This federal structure of language-based parties was able to put forward coherent positions on such life or death issues as the Great War. It represented a model that replaced top-down "assimilationism" with "sovereignty-association," with each language-defined party free to conduct its own political and cultural activities, but within a framework of solidarity and common purpose with the others.

In this strand of thought and activism on the race question, then, the leftists involved did not accede to or apologize for Anglo-Canadian imperial nationalism, nor did they abstractly pronounce race and patriotism non-issues: instead they sought, implicitly in the very act of organizing such a vast array of national left institutions, to challenge these established tendencies. Implicitly the new synthesis was the first sustained experiment in Canadian multiculturalism – replacing the sterile, elitist, and inherently racialist concept of the mosaic with the dynamic, mutually respectful, and dialectical concept of a polyethnic movement. Still, evidence of a general rethinking of racial categories that corresponds to this institutional mutation is highly qualified and ambiguous, arriving in the shape of isolated perceptions rather than in manifestos or clear statements of position.

Some of the most intriguing indications of this new synthesis emerge where one might least expect it – from the biography of the man whose writings would become closely identified with the nativist denigration of "foreigners." Although Woodsworth's radicalization occurred in the context of his war resistance and his direct experience of proletarian life on the docks of Vancouver, to a considerable extent he was also tutored in the realities of racial politics in Canada by the Finns of Gibson's Landing, B.C., where he had been exiled from Winnipeg. He was at first rather bothered by these "materialistic socialists," some of whom had once been associated with Finnish utopian communities in the province. He thought their teachings helped keep people away from church.[210] Yet gradually he and his partner Lucy were drawn into the life of the Finnish community. At regular Friday night community meetings they would participate in great debates on issues of the left – Pritchard of the *Western Clarion* was a speaker at one of them in 1918. They were meetings, Woodsworth reported, in which "prejudices were broken down." Sometimes the Finnish socialists would do battle with a "British outpost of Empire." The debates would go on until late at night, and then "in every direction could be seen the little 'bugs,' homemade lanterns made with a candle set sideways in a lard-pail, bobbing along the trails like tiny stars, guiding the tired folk home to bed."[211] It was during this time that Woodsworth's reading and writing began to turn sharply towards the rigorously defined scientific texts of the first formation.

As reconstructed by Peter Campbell, the life and work of James Alexander Teit (1864–1922), an SPCer who spent most of his life at Spence's Bridge in the southern interior of British Columbia, also suggested how merging abstract universalism with concrete struggles could yield interesting results. Teit achieved some renown as an anthropologist, although primarily as a collector of data and translator more than as a theorist. A collaborator and correspondent of anthropologists Franz Boas and Edward Sapir, Teit was concerned about salvaging Aboriginal lore before the elders who remembered it had all died. He was competent in the language of the Nlaka'pamaux and could also speak Lillooet and Shuswap; he compiled vocabularies of other Salish dialects. As he remarked, Native meetings were often subject to a feeling of gloom surrounding the issue of survival: "The belief that they are doomed to extinction seems to have a depressing effect on some of the Indians. At almost any gathering where chiefs or leading men speak, this sad, haunting belief is sure to be referred to." Teit's theoretical orientation undoubtedly drew on the unilinear models of social evolution pervasive on the left since Morgan, and, as Campbell notes, his correspondence, "with some exceptions, is remarkably free of moral condemnation of what has happened to native people." In a general sense, he shared the first formation conviction that the destruction of "primitive

communism" was the necessary, if tragic, prelude to capitalism and ultimately socialism.[212] Yet he repeatedly went beyond this abstract position in
his involvement with the mounting Aboriginal struggles in British Columbia
over land rights, which extended back to the 1870s and had attained a new
visibility with the presentation of a petition to King Edward VII in 1906.[213] He
drew upon social-evolutionary theory, for instance, to defend the traditions of
the potlatch against oppressive regulation by Ottawa: "You are aiming a blow
at their life, and if the blow is effective, it means their demoralization. Any
white race powerful enough would fight to the bitter end against this." Echoes
of first formation evolutionism can be heard in his characterization of the
conscription of Natives as a form of "enslavement," which he predicted would
be "forcibly resisted and probably cause bloodshed."[214] Teit thus took pro-Na-
tive positions that are not normally associated with the early Canadian left.
They were paralleled in post-1918 statements in SPC-affiliated newspapers
about the significance of the Afro-American struggle for socialists across
North America.[215]

In general, though, the first formation was as yet in no position to
generate a compelling new vision of race and nationality in so vast and heterogeneous a country. The immigrant socialists especially were evolving institutions and activists that could start to transform the race question into the
"Canada question." The Communists who would undertake the first sustained
and serious left analyses of the Canada Question in the 1920s would not be
starting from scratch. At the very least many of them understood that their
very own movement, into which so many of the Jews, Finns, and Ukrainians
had moved, was inescapably required to balance equality with difference, abstract economics with particular circumstances, the dream of a universal humanity against its particular manifestations in distinct peoples, languages, and
customs. In this respect the first formation would leave, in the shape of cultural and political institutions that would last for many decades, a precious
legacy to its successors.

Diaspora Socialism: Trailblazers and Homebodies

When he was asked in 1913 about Canadian affairs, the Finn A.B. Mäkelä
(1863–1932) responded: "You could hardly find a less suitable person. What
do I know about Canada? What do I care about Canadian affairs? . . . I get
some Canadian papers, and reading them I have followed *their* affairs to some
extent, but while always feeling they do not touch me one bit."[216] Mäkelä
might have been speaking for scores of newcomer leftists in Canada, whose
lives as activists were devoted to developing socialist ideas among their own
people. Events in the homeland would resonate far more powerfully than anything outside their ethnic enclaves.

Matti Kurikka (1863–1915) followed much the same path: essentially, a form of political engagement primarily geared to the European homeland or to fellow expatriates in Canada.[217] Kurikka re-enacted in 20th-century Canada the utopianism of Robert Owen in the 19th. Born in Ingria, not far from St. Petersburg, Kurikka attended Helsinki University. Like many of this generation, he was deeply impressed by Tolstoy and gravitated to the Tolstoyan salon maintained by the feminist Minna Canth at Koupio, northeast of Helsinki. Gifted with a magnetic personality and unbounded self-confidence, Kurikka rose quickly in the Finnish left, becoming editor of the leading newspaper of the labour movement, *Työmies* (Worker) in 1897. He became convinced that the salvation of the Finns lay in utopian communities on other continents. The first choice was Queensland, Australia, where the idealistic Finns found themselves stuck in squalid sugar plantations. Then a letter from British Columbia arrived, from Finns who had worked in the coal mines. They had heard about Kurikka from fellow countrymen who had left Australia for Canada early in 1900, and they wanted him in person as they themselves searched for an alternative to the mines. Kurikka's reply hinted at his own sense of class distinction: "I am prepared to do work of any kind since I have discarded all the mannerisms of the upper class in Helsinki. Now I have hands as calloused as anyone, which is the lot of the working man." To his daughter in Finland he wrote: "A servant of the people must not look for peace and quiet, but most go where the darkness is deepest and give the people consolation and keep up a torch of fire."[218]

His fare paid by the B.C. miners, Kurikka arrived in the province in October 1900. He organized a company called Kalevan Kansa, a name that referred to the *Kalevala*, the Finns' national saga and central focus of their romantic nationalism. "We are the only living people among humanity," Kurikka boasted, "whose revered cultural past exists in insurpassable verse. Incomparable, for there is no other work equivalent in value and stature to the *Kalevala*, a magnificently preserved record of happiness saved for present humanity." Throughout Kurikka's career in "spring-like America" the goal was to begin a new era for the Finns' "superior culture." Of British Columbia, he said, "This is where the new Finland is going to take shape.... Maybe in Finland, the Finns will be slaves to the Tsar, but in this new country they will live as a free people." Even with this specific aim, Kurikka drew upon many of the familiar thinkers of the first formation. His library contained works by Spencer, Ingersoll, Darwin, and Bellamy.[219]

After negotiations with the provincial government, the Finns chose Malcolm Island, about 200 miles north of Vancouver, for their New Finland project, which they called Sointula. Kurikka wrote that the community of Sointula ("Harmony") was to be "a Nazarene's light in Europe's darkness," a beacon of literature, music, and shared philosophical ideals.[220] This light was to shine in literature, music, and philosophy. Its site was close to shipping lanes, suitable for agriculture, yet remote enough to allow the Finns to develop their project undisturbed. Kurikka advertised the scheme in lectures in the United States and correspondence to Finland. Under the terms of its agreement with the government, the Colonization Company was to settle 350 people on the island; Kurikka himself dreamt of transplanting all of working-class Finland, indeed "the entire Finnish nationality." It was to be a version of Finland abroad. As J. Donald Wilson notes, "The essential Finnishness of Sointula was never in doubt. The colony's flag even reflected this: the white shape of Malcolm Island on a blue background with a golden *kantele* (the traditional stringed Finnish folk instrument) centred on the island."[221] All the settlers were to be, it was hoped, Finnish.

The first group of settlers settled on Malcolm Island on 6 December 1901; and by the following spring nearly 100 Finns, primarily from southern Finland and the United States, had settled. There was prosperity for much of 1902, but in 1903 the community was hit by calamities. A fire killed 11 people and left many others homeless. Agriculture proved a dicey proposition, given the poor grazing lands and distance from markets. Lumbering beckoned as an alternative, but Kurikka had no real head for business and signed bad contracts. He seems to have poured much energy into the newspaper *Aika*, which publicized the benefits of the new lifestyle without devoting the same care to practical matters. It was in the pages of *Aika* that Kurikka launched the campaign for free love, which probably played a part, along with poor business deals and a deadly fire, in the demise of his experiment.

In the wake of a split among the colonists, an embittered Kurikka left Sointula, but proceeded immediately to become secretary of a new colonization scheme, Sammon Taokjat, a name once more derived from the *Kalevala*. Ultimately the colony would transform itself into a co-operative enterprise, but well before that point Kurikka had returned to Finland, where he participated in the country's great General Strike of 1905. Over time he emerged as a mercurial, deeply idealistic man, castigated by some (such as the satirical journal *Väkäleuka*) as a man of a "hundred faces ... not one of them the same." Among the Finnish socialists, the collapse of Sointula in 1905 was a warning about utopian schemes: "Those who deviated from orthodox Marxian socialism were often labeled 'Kurikkas' or their schemes were denounced as 'another Sointula.'"[222]

Mäkelä, although Kurikka's friend and comrade in the early years of Sointula, later became his critic. Familiar, like Kurikka, with Canth, *Työmies*, and (on Kurikka's invitation) Sointula, he was of a radically different cast of mind, far more oriented to building a scientific movement and an effective revolutionary presence. He opposed Kurikka's concept of free love on doctrinal and practical grounds (moreover, his own partner left him during the controversy).

He had no use for theosophy, which he wryly denounced as "the seventeenth form of religion they have tried to force upon me in my lifetime." He saw the history of Sointula as an exemplary case of how not to perform socialism. As Wilson remarks, he frequently critiqued "the people who tried to make the stumps lay eggs" or who, like Kurikka, were perpetual motion machines. Their determination was admirable but their strategy misguided. They overlooked the extent to which any revolutionary "must always be prepared to relate to the 'outside' capitalist world."[223]

Mäkelä also returned to Finland, but found re-entry difficult into his old political circles. Nonetheless, he was a pivotal player in Finnish social democracy. He joined the "Northern underground" of both Finnish and Russian revolutionaries struggling against the czar, and was even elected to the executive of the Finnish Social Democratic Party in 1907. Like many who made the Atlantic passage, Mäkelä found the crossing had left him without a secure base on either side of the ocean. When he died on 28 February 1932, *Vapaus* hailed him as "one of the most faithful members of the Communist Party of Canada."[224] He exemplified the often difficult journey from sojourner to permanent resident that so many diaspora socialists experienced.

The Ukrainian left generated an army of memorable figures whose names would long be cherished within the tradition – Kyrilo Genyk, Myroslav Stechyshyn, Myroslav Sichensky, Vasyl Holovatsky, Roman Kremar, Toma Tomashevsky, Ivan Hynyda, and Mathew Popovich – yet the life and work of the revolutionary poet and activist Pavlo Krat (1882–1952) is perhaps the most revealing of the contradictions and possibilities of diaspora socialism. As Nadia Kazymyra demonstrates, when he arrived in Canada in September 1907 Krat brought years of revolutionary experience with him, notably a deep involvement in the Revolutionary Ukrainian Party, which had an emphatically nationalist orientation.[225] In 1902–3, two of Krat's revolutionary poems – *Hodi terpity* ("We can no longer suffer") and *Oi vzhe chas* ("The time has come") – came to be greatly esteemed as protest songs by peasants who were rising in revolt. Deeply immersed in the socialist literature of the time, Krat became dissatisfied with the existing balance between nationalism and radical political activism, and along with dissenters at Lviv University he formed the Ukrainian Social Democratic Union of the Russian Social Democratic Party, which came to be known as the Spilka.

After involvement in an unsuccessful peasant uprising in the Kiev region, Krat immigrated to Canada, partly inspired, it seems, by issues of the promotional *Kanadyiskyi farmer* (Canadian farmer), which he encountered in Europe. Thus, when he arrived on the Prairies, Krat was already seen as a radical who had earned his reputation in the movement, someone who could induce in his followers a sense of "hypnotic euphoria" as he made them believe that the promised land was within grasp. Both for them and for him, radical politics also entailed a program of national redemption. In the Shevchenko Educational Society, and as the writer of a history of the Ukrainian language, *Gramatyka zahalnoi ukrainskoi movy* (A general Ukrainian grammar book), Krat did what many 19th- and 20th-century nationalists set out to do: provide a national community with a sense of an immemorial past and a glowing future. "In order," writes Kazymyra, "to prove to Ukrainians that they did not belong to an inferior race, Krat wrote a history of the Ukrainian language, tracing it to a common ancestral form of before the fourth century A.D. He concluded that the structure of the Ukrainian language was more complex than ancient Greek." Much of Krat's time and energy were taken up with attempting to unsettle the cultural authority of the newly imported Ukrainian Catholic and Orthodox churches, which he satirized mercilessly. One special target was Bishop Nykyta Budka, appointed by the Vatican in 1913 to oversee the Ukrainian Catholics in Canada. Krat welcomed the Bishop with a satirical gazette, *Kropyto*, in which the eminent clergyman was depicted as a toady of big business and an underling of the French Canadian bishop.

A fiery presence in the FUSD and the USDP, editor of *Chervonyi prapor* (Red flag) and promoter of the Tovarystvo Samostiina Ukraina (Society for an Independent Ukraine), modelled in part on the Chinese Nationalist League in Vancouver, Krat would become a highly controversial figure in the war years because of his collaboration with the press censor's office and his conversion to Presbyterianism. His most interesting contribution to the left was his book *Koly ziishlo sontse: opovidannia z 2000 roku* (When the sun rose: a tale from the year 2000), which he brought out in 1918.[226] Scholar Walter Smyrniw suggests that this was the first Ukrainian utopian novel, which Krat wrote to show that "the communist state should be based on love and high education and other virtues." In some ways it was highly derivative of Bellamy's *Looking Backward* – it too is set in the year 2000, and features a hero who is roused in the distant future from a state of suspended animation by a doctor descended from the woman he loves – but in other ways it strikes out on a new path. In this case, the hero is not a well-bred man but a poor Ukrainian immigrant, Petro Ivanchuk – who is not an insomniac but a proletarian figure who sacrifices himself to the cause of enlightenment and entrusts his fate to a scientist at the University of British Columbia. The imagined Vancouver of 2000 is not, like Bellamy's Boston, a grand metropolis, but a veritable garden community of parks, orchards, and low-lying buildings.

As Smyrniw suggests, in some ways Krat's green utopia more closely resembles that of William Morris in *News from Nowhere*, although in its reliance on air transportation (individuals have access to flapping wings) and anticipations of the Internet – Krat imagines "bibliophones" that can record sounds and images and "dictographs" that can transcribe speech into written messages and send them over wire, all part of a global communications and transportation network – this imagined Vancouver tends towards a more technological version of heaven on earth. (Krat even develops a relatively novel emphasis on solar power.) The book centrally addresses the questions of race and nation. Although Krat's novel savours of the "abstract universalism" of the SPC – in his utopia there will be no states, only people – it also wrestles with the actually-existing cultural divisions of humanity. Not only does our Ukrainian hero have an Anglo-Canadian fiancée, but she turns out to be passionately devoted to the future of Ukraine, which in 2000 flourishes with marvelous folk songs, a thriving language, and abundant happiness. In Canada itself, Krat imagined a land in which each national group was recognized, with a special place reserved for the Native peoples. He envisaged multicultural festivals featuring displays from all corners of the world, and collective marriage ceremonies. Krat was clearly struggling to balance equality and difference in his utopian vision of the future of the race question.[227]

Sanna Kannasto, born in Yli-Härmä, Ostrobothnia, Finland, in 1878, was similarly a "household word" in her community, as suggested by Varpu Lindström-Best's path-breaking study of Finnish women in Canada. Immigrating, probably alone, to the United States in 1899, she attended the Finnish People's College, joined the Socialist Party of America in 1905, and set to organizing the Finns for socialism. She migrated to Canada in 1907 in the company of J.V. Kannasto – she adopted his name but, in the Finnish radical style, never legally married him – and in 1908, at the Ontario SPC convention, became "the first paid political organizer for the Finnish socialists." She seems to have been a remarkable speaker and organizer. According to Lindström-Best, Kannasto crisscrossed Canada five times and made "countless shorter journeys." Whenever possible, she held meetings for women, looking not only at such "organizational" issues as women's role in socialist society, but "also discussing the more intimate issues of marriage and birth control." In summer 1913 the Finnish Socialist Organization of Canada reported 562 women members – which would make it one of the largest single forces for left feminism in Canada.

Kannasto was widely seen as one of the most knowledgeable socialists of her time, no small feat among the Finns. For her own people, she became, in Lindström-Best's words, "the radical Finnish heroine." In a telling, down-to-earth description of her selflessness, Lindström-Best notes an apologetic letter she sent to the FSOC headquarters in Toronto, explaining that, "for the first time in my life," she had travelled in a sleeping compartment – for, otherwise, she would have been too tired even to speak. Often suffering from "exhaustion, cold, and lack of shelter," on monthly expenditures of around $150, cadging lifts on buggies and later in cars, and even walking from one meeting to the next – Kannasto was performing socialism with a zeal that outmatched many of her male comrades.

Like all good Canadian radicals, she ran afoul of the law. Arrested by the RCMP while travelling by train to Manyberries, Alta., she wrote that she had "charmed her captors" to the point of being allowed to use the warden's typewriter. She confessed that her English-language skills were "short," to the point that she could not quite make out what the interrogations of her had been designed to elicit. Yet, Lindström-Best observes, she was proud of her own strength in this situation. "What makes them [police] most upset," she wrote, "is that they don't succeed in making me angry or nervous and thereby in making me cry and confess. I am as if made of iron, I never knew how much I could endure." Five days later she remarked: "I am not nervous. . . . I have not yet shed a single tear, although I have been in cruel cross-examinations. Despite everything, I am happy and I try to joke and keep up the humour with my prison guards."

Kannasto exemplified the sheer courage so often displayed by diaspora leftists, struggling simultaneously with an often intolerant society, significant language barriers, widely dispersed communities, and at times hostile fellow expatriates; and women soapboxers probably paid a higher personal cost for their party work than men did. Her free marriage brought both children and a much lower political profile. A terse note in the 1914 FSOC annual report indicates some of her troubles: "Sanna Kannasto would be the ideal person to send for these agitation tours but J.V. Kannasto strictly forbids it."[228]

A rather different pattern of diaspora socialism emerged in the case of Sophie Mushkat (1887–1954), born into a secular Jewish family in Warsaw, Poland, then part of the crisis-ridden and oppressive Russian Empire.[229] Immigrating to Canada around 1903 or 1904, Mushkat settled first in Moncton, N.B., where her family was associated with a small dry-goods store. Here, with the founding of a socialist party around 1908, the Mushkats, Fanny Levy, and perhaps Marshall Gauvin came to comprise a small but influential left movement. Mushkat first surfaced in the socialist press in July 1909 when she spoke in Moncton on behalf of the local Socialist Party of Canada, a branch she had recently helped to found. Roscoe Fillmore, who lived not too far away in Albert, was delighted to receive a letter from this mini-group responding to an advertisement he had placed in the Saint John *Sun* asking Maritime socialists to get in touch with him. "The girls are thoroughly well read," he wrote approvingly to his friend H.H. Stuart. "They beat any women I have ever met in the movement. No silly talk about hats, ice cream, etc. They are the genuine article and no mistake."[230] Fillmore considered Mushkat a "Russian revolutionist true blue." Her repertoire of speeches included "The Class Struggle," "Socialism and Trade Unionism," "The Materialist Conception of History," and "On Woman's Place in the Socialist Movement."

What stands out about Mushkat is her utter fearlessness and conviction. Her lecturing style was tornado-like. Large hostile crowds were silenced by her intense zeal and how she punched the air with her fists. Arrested in Moncton as a result of her soapboxing, Mushkat refused to swear on the Bible, expressed her scepticism about the afterlife, and proudly declared her allegiance to the SPC. In the Springhill strike of 1909–11 she was a star performer, greatly valued for her ability to speak to some of the strikebreakers in their own languages. Then, like many others involved in that débâcle, Mushkat moved west around 1911, and by 1913 was organizing for the SPC in the mining towns of Southern Alberta and British Columbia. She spoke at no fewer than 33 English and 10 Polish meetings between 28 April and 10 June 1913. In 1914, after a journey back to New Brunswick, she addressed as many as 14 meetings on the hardships of homesteading and the farmers' relationship to the working class. By the fall of 1914 she had settled in Calgary and was earning her living as a teacher and acting as provincial secretary of the SPC.

On the eve of the Great War, as Linda Kealey relates, Mushkat immersed herself into work for the Unemployed Committee in Calgary. Her voice rang out in a conference on the unemployment crisis in November 1914. The government needed recruits, she noted: "Where are you going to get them if you are going to starve them?" In August 1915 the *Western Clarion* reported that the SPC, in a strict application of its rule against sharing platforms with non-socialist parties, had expelled Mushkat for taking part in a prohibition campaign in Alberta. She had long been interested in the issue of prohibition, speaking out on the topic in Newcastle in 1910 and later in Saint John. Her position, predictably, had been that only the coming of socialism would ultimately solve the problems that the prohibition campaign was attempting to address. Most likely, however, Mushkat also connected this "ultimate" demand with a more pragmatic and immediate sense of the urgency of temperance as a socialist-feminist issue for women confronting dwindling food budgets and drunken husbands. Her "expulsion" did not mean an end to her SPC activism. In its very next issue, the *Western Clarion* was noting Mushkat's work on behalf of socialism in the Alberta coal towns.

After the war RCMP spy reports would leave behind a stirring impression of Mushkat as an intrepid radical: "She stated that history was repeating itself and that we were now at the point where we would have to show whether we were real revolutionists or just a party of social democrats, that is a party that was scared to defy constitutional authority. SHE is a real menace."[231] She was so most of all, perhaps, because she worked to combine the issues specific to foreign-born communities with wider struggles on the woman question and against unemployment.

For some diaspora socialists, then – and perhaps especially the Finns – the homeland exerted a phenomenal pull, one that would (at later points) influence the very nature of the left-wing movements they favoured: they were, perhaps, already prototypes of "transnational socialists." For others, the new continent quickly became the focus of politics – although in the case of the Jews the emergence of a Zionist movement in the 1910s would create an as-yet hypothetical new homeland somewhere in the world, and some of these diaspora leftists would gravitate to it. For Finns and Jews in particular, the unusually elevated status of women carried over into the possibility that women could be inspiring leaders and speakers, to an extent not characteristic of other groups. Each diaspora shaped its own socialism, yet first in the Social Democratic Party, and then in the Communist Party and later in the Co-operative Commonwealth Federation, each would also find its distinctive way of contributing to the larger movement.

* * *

To many of us today, the early 20th-century focus on race may seem unforgivable. Against such moments of cruelty as the *Komagata Maru* and the head tax, later to be followed by deportations and forced migrations, the first formation certainly did not speak with a unified or clear voice – and it is hard not to wish that it had done so. It spoke with many voices, some of them racialist and even racist. Still, positions did shift over time. This period saw significant breakthroughs around the race question, if not so much in theory then in practice, with the emergence of the language-based movements and parties, the rise of at least some minority socialists to positions of authority, and the generation of a framework of new diaspora socialisms both connected to and autonomous within the wider formation. Wrestling more decisively with the questions of race, ethnicity, nation, and indeed "Canada" would await the second formation.

The Frozen Breath of Bolshevism

If Bolshevism comes to Nova Scotia it will do here what it has done in Russia and what it seeks to do in Germany.

LIBERTY will be destroyed, because Bolshevism means that one class shall rule over all other classes.

PROPERTY will be confiscated without payment to its owners. Your house, your household belongings, if you do not own a house, your savings in the bank, your Liberty Bonds—you will lose all these.

FOOD will be put beyond the reach of all except those who can seize it by brute strength, for Bolshevism takes the farmer's land, eats the food that is in sight, and makes no provision for to-morrow.

LAWS will be annulled and the whole social system thrown into chaos. There will be no courts to adjust wrongs; no punishment for wrong-doers.

GOVERNMENT will be transferred from the elected representatives of the people into the hands of committees, or soviets, without any central authority—without legislatures, parliaments or premiers.

WOMEN AND CHILDREN will be the property of the state. One of the soviets which set the fashion in Russia—the Soviet of Vladimir—has already decreed that all women over eighteen must register at a bureau of free love and there hold themselves subject to the will of any man who may order them to follow him.

RELIGION will vanish when respect for law and for women and children vanishes. Bolshevism worships not the God of our fathers, but License.

Russia, after her months of Bolshevism, is almost a desert, with millions of her people dead and other millions dying of famine; her industries paralyzed; her government in the hands of ruthless assassins; her law-abiding men and women either murdered or living in hiding, stripped of everything they possessed.

The Canadian idea guarantees every man a free and open opportunity to share in prosperity and happiness. The workman of to-day may be the capitalist of to-morrow. Labor to be efficient and productive, must co-ordinate with capital; both must live under the laws which are made by the elected representatives of all the people.

Our greatest bulwark against Bolshevism must be the intelligence, the thrift and the patriotism of the Canadian workman.

This Article is one of a Series—Be sure to read them all—Canada First Publicity Association.

BULLETIN NO. 1

"The Frozen Breath of Bolshevism." Readers of the *Herald* (Halifax), 23 May 1919, along with newspaper readers coast to coast, are warned of the counter-evolutionary dangers of Bolshevism by the Canada First Publicity Association. Library and Archives Canada.

7

War, Revolution, and General Strike

Toronto, 8 January 1918. One does not expect too many surprises from the *Mail and Empire*, the voice of Toronto Toryism. The Empire is good, and its struggles are right. Business sense is common sense. Foreigners should watch their step. The certainties rolled on relentlessly, year after year. Yet on this day the columns of the venerable newspaper contained the surprising opinions of an angry Jewish journalist temporarily residing in the Bronx. In an article printed side by side with an advertisement for Dodd's Kidney Pills, he had a great deal to get off his chest.

The whole globe was caught up, the writer declared, in one unprecedented crisis. "All talk of the present bloody clash being a work of national defence is either hypocrisy or blindness," he said, referring to the Great War, which was still being fought on the battlefields of Europe. "The real, objective significance of the war is the breakdown of the present national economic centres, and the substitution of a world economy in its stead." This "collapse of the national states" signalled the crisis of the old forms of socialism, organized on a national basis – those old forms could no longer contain the "revolutionary idea." Social Democrats in Europe had sealed their own fate by surrendering to the policies of war-making governments. Those in Germany had collaborated with a brazenly reactionary and aggressive state, in part because they were so keen to preserve their printing presses and their bureaucracies. The proletariat – the readers of the *Mail and Empire* were advised – could pit "its revolutionary force against imperialism," but only if it took "to the battlefields of Social Revolution."

Social democracy, appealing only to the "upper strata of the proletariat," had built up a formidable array of organizations, the writer said, but it had gradually lost its way in routinism and institution-building. Now a vast new army was transforming the landscape of the left. "With the weapon in his hand that he himself has forged, the worker is put in a position where the political destiny of the state is directly dependent upon him," he argued. "Those who exploited and scorned him in normal times, flatter him now and toady to

417

him." Moreover, this worker now had a greater familiarity with armed strug-gle: "He crosses the border, takes part in forceful requisitions, and helps in the passing of cities from one party to another." The "revolutionary epoch" was at hand. With it would come "new forms of organization out of the inex-haustible resources of proletarian Socialism, new forms that will be equal to the greatness of the new tasks."[1]

So claimed someone who, rather like John Spargo 17 years before, had been living the precarious life of the socialist writer and agitator. Just about a year before the article was published this journalist, living in a cheap Bronx apartment with his small family, had been writing for the left press in New York and taking speaking engagements here and there, wherever he could get them. Born in the Ukraine, part of the Russian Empire, in 1879, he had as a young man become heavily engaged in political activities and for many years was on the move through Europe before his anti-war activities led to his de-portation from France to Spain to the United States in December 1916.

After a brief stay in New York City, and months before his stories were splashed across the *Mail and Empire*, this obscure writer had moved on to bigger and better things. By May 1917, inspired by the February 1917 revolution in Russia, he had made his way back to that seething country, where he was to play a major role in the October Revolution of that same year. By early 1918 this man – Leon Trotsky, with his seemingly wild vision of a world teetering on the brink of an unfathomable vast crisis – was serving as the foreign minister of the new Russia.[2]

This was not the *Mail and Empire*'s standard up-with-Britain fare, but then these were not standard times. Most likely many a bewildered Toronto businessman was spilling his tea in disbelief over the uncensored proclama-tions of the zealous Russian revolutionary. Many thought him, as the edito-rialists of the paper themselves did, a "scoundrel," an apostle of terrorism and hate, and (unknowingly or otherwise) an agent of Germany.[3] Or was he a statesman? Or something else? Suddenly many of the fixed categories of bour-geois life were disturbingly in motion. Such were the times that the spectre of revolution could not be politely ushered off the Canadian stage. All that was solid, and certainly much that was czarist, had melted into air.

The *Mail and Empire*'s decision to bestow such prominence on the writ-ings of Trotsky was undoubtedly about selling papers as much as providing information. But it had at least one unexpected result. Reading the paper that day was a left-leaning 19-year-old student, a graduate of Humberside Colle-giate Institute now enrolled in modern history at the University of Toronto. The *Mail and Empire* articles opened his eyes to a new way of thinking about the world. He would remember the moment vividly more than four decades later. "Every time I saw one of his crystalline phrases there it really sent a thrill through me." Here was something different from the other socialists he had encountered – "They were just *talkers*. . . . Here was a genuine leader . . . a genuine man of action, and a great thinker."[4] Trotsky revealed the possibility of fusing talk and action. The *Mail and Empire* would play a pivotal role in the making of one of Canada's foremost socialist thinkers and activists of the following decade.

At the same time as Trotsky was thundering in the columns of the *Mail and Empire*, a storm was also breaking out at the University of Toronto. A letter in the *Varsity*, the student newspaper, closed with "Yours for revolt and in revolt" and was signed "Karl Marx." It called for the "Resurrection of International Polity Club." The letter argued that the "war weariness now manifest among the European belligerents is the dawn of the return to sanity." The day of narrow nationalism was over: "Our intellectual sympathies must permeate the barriers that have been erected between people and an attempt must be made to forget the immediate past so as to build for the future. Our first task is to realize a speedy peace." The "sagacious British policy of compromise" should overrule the demand for victory. A resurrected International Polity Club could help "organize the consciousness" of students regarding "this change in world-sentiment regarding the war and its aims."[5]

The undergraduate's letter sparked an outcry in the university and consternation in the offices of the chief censor in Ottawa. E.J. Chambers wrote to the university president to tell him that under normal circumstances he would have simply suppressed the paper but he hesitated to do so given its affiliation with so eminent an institution. "I hope you will agree with me that an example should be made in this case," he urged. He wrote to the editor of the *Varsity* outlining his grievance. The letter was "a very distinct and open denunciation of the policy of the Empire and its allies as regards the prosecution of the war." It might rouse dissatisfaction with His Majesty and "prejudice His Majesty's relations with foreign powers." It was therefore in "open and flagrant contravention of the Consolidated Order Respecting Censorship, a copy of which reached you by registered letter shortly after its having received the assent of His Excellence, the Governor General." The censor cordially warned the manager of the paper's printer, University of Toronto Press, that "anyone concerned in any remote way with the printing of 'objectionable matter' is liable to a fine of $5,000 or a term of imprisonment of 5 years, or to both such fine and imprisonment, and any plant engaged in the production of 'objectionable matter' may be seized and held indefinitely or for such period as the Secretary of State of Canada may direct."[6]

A young Maurice Spector (1898–1968) was both the *Mail and Empire* reader and the author of the letter to the *Varsity*. Spector, destined to become a major Canadian Marxist theoretician and a leader of the Communist Party, would devote much of the next two decades of his life to making Trotsky's vision of a world revolution a reality. Already in January 1918 the precocious teenager was immersing himself in the world of the Social Democratic Party of Canada. Isaac Bainbridge, the party's dynamic and embattled general secretary and newspaper editor, regarded the student as a protegé. Bainbridge persuaded Spector to read Lenin's *Soviets at Work*, a pamphlet stressing the practical tasks confronting the new revolutionary administration in Russia. Eventually Spector would become a member of the executive committee of the Communist International, an organization designed to fulfil one of the predictions that Trotsky had made in the pages of the *Mail and Empire*: the creation of "new forms of organization out of the inexhaustible resources of proletarian Socialism."[7]

Every "wide awake, practical man," used to "dealing with the hard realities of life" rather than "mooing around" in a "queer dream-world," knew that such things could never happen, mused an eloquent columnist in the *Mail and Empire*. Yet they did happen. In the space of just one year, a man could hardly be transformed from a wandering, penniless journalist in New York into "one of the central political figures on earth."[8] But he had been. One of the oldest, most revered, and most detested monarchies in Europe could hardly vanish overnight. But it had. As the *Mail and Empire* pronounced wonderingly of the czar, "He and his dynasty were abolished with less resistance than has attended the cancelling of a liquor license in Toronto."[9] If that was possible, what else might happen? Could Canada itself have a revolution? Who would support it? Surely it was impossible that the sane and solid Canadian working class would mount any such thing?

Yet suddenly that kind of event did not seem so impossible. In 1919 a vast revolt unfolded in Winnipeg, with "Revolution on the Red River" making headlines from Turin to San Francisco. Just eight years earlier, O.D. Skelton had pronounced Canada to be the land most likely forever to be insulated from the virus of socialism. Now, impossibly, the country itself seemed to be teetering on the brink of a great transformation.

The Fevers of War

For a time it had seemed that the moral absolutes of war precluded any such possibility. Patriotic fervour caused some workers to go on strike against the "enemy aliens" in their midst, and others to demand the rounding up of foreigners. Recruiters were successful in working old ties of community and neighbourhood into life-changing enlistments in the Armed Forces.[10] Dalhousie University's president was delighted that one out of three male students had enlisted, and praised the professors for their patriotism-inducing lectures.[11] "Business as usual" meant a liberal state that collected no income tax, influenced but did not presume to plan the economy, and ceded even such vital issues as shell manufacture to the businessmen, who unsurprisingly pursued their own interests. Had the war ended in early 1916, the whole event would have posed few challenges to liberal order.

Not that socialists were asleep at the switch: both of the larger left parties denounced the war (whereas across much of the rest of the international left, division and confusion reigned: even Kropotkin was moved to endorse the war against autocratic Germany). "The rude god of war gallops across the world in a saddle of steel and sneers and laughs in savage glee," proclaimed the Canadian Social Democrats. "He wades in blood. His own sweet music is the rattle of rifles and a million sobs and groans from broken hearts." The war exposed the falseness and moral enormity of capitalism, which, one writer said, "stands bankrupt and ragged before the world, mockingly murmurs a prayer for help, and grinds its sword for the throat of labor."[12] After one significant pro-war slip in the *Western Clarion*, the Socialist Party of Canada followed suit. Some of its best-known activists, including Wilfred Gribble, were arrested for their war resistance.[13] At a time when more than 600,000 Canadians entered the armed forces, with 50,000 more in other allied armies – in all, as Craig Heron and Myer Siemiatycki note, "roughly a third of the male population of military age enlisted"[14] – such socialist voices were largely drowned out in a wave of patriotic sentiment. As casualties started to mount – nearly one in ten of these Canadians would not return from Europe – the political and cultural costs of opposing the war also rose. At such a time of trauma and bereavement many Canadians, as Jonathan Vance suggests, found meaning and solace in the belief that the Great War had been a crusade for human decency and democratic values. In the emergent "high diction" of the war, those who died were "the Fallen," who had sacrificed their lives for Canada.[15]

Initially the Great War solidified pre-existing conventions more than it destabilized them: it confirmed local notables in their roles, underlined ties of ethnic allegiance and weakened those of class, and demonstrated the power of religious institutions. Moral absolutes flourished in wartime. Radical questions about the war's purpose, strategies, and emergent outcome were readily silenced by appeals to God, country, and civilization. Mass torchlit rallies, exalted celebrations of blood and soil, and the selective targeting of foreign influences all contributed to a British-Canadian discourse of imperial patriotism. Even the Germanic name of the province of New Brunswick was attacked, and the loyalties of Lunenburg fishermen came under suspicion (though their 18th-century ancestors had arrived not as "Germans" but as "Foreign Protestants"). In Ontario incautious partygoers who drunkenly called into question His Majesty's motivations and competence found themselves facing charges of sedition.[16]

Yet gradually after 1916 the mood shifted. Having committed himself to the principle of voluntary enlistments, Prime Minister Borden returned from an eye-opening visit to France to announce his conversion to the cause of military conscription. Across the country, the measure was controversial, especially among francophones, both in the Maritimes and in Quebec. On the left, conscription was constructed as a kind of ultimate outrage – a violation of the liberal freedom of conscience, of possession over one's own body, and of the rights of minorities. Some, like Gertrude Richardson, refused to believe that such a tyrannical measure could ever be tried in liberal Canada. It was a form of "Prussianism" through which conscripts simply became the "property of the State." In early spring 1918 attempts to enforce the Military Service Act provoked three days of riot in Quebec City's working-class suburbs; four civilian lives were lost after the federal government sent in a Toronto batallion to quell the disorder.[17] In British Columbia the killing of war resister Albert "Ginger" Goodwin sparked a massive strike on 2 August 1918, a vast outpouring of grief and anger in a tumultuous funeral procession, and lingering doubt over the role of the state in disposing of a respected radical.[18] Although the December 1917 election strengthened a Union government made up of Conservatives and prominent pro-conscription Liberals, the disenfranchisement of many "enemy aliens" and the Tory campaign allegation that Laurier Liberals were really Bolsheviks in disguise were also sharply polarizing.

From 1917 to 1920 a climate of fear and suspicion gripped much of North America. The monstrous figure of the "Hun," a barbarian bereft of British morality and decency, was easily combined with that of the "Bolshie," in essence an updated version of the crazed, bomb-wielding anarchist. With its Chicago headquarters raided in 1917, and its activists subject to hostage-taking and mob violence in Washington and Montana, the IWW was in particular singled out. Montana Wobbly Frank Little was lynched and castrated for his anti-war activism; in Washington a similar fate was meted out to Wesley Everest. Church publications endorsed mob violence, socialists elected to legislatures were denied seats won in open elections, and police raids resulted in masses of leftists going to jail (one of them was Alberta's former MLA, Charlie O'Brien).[19] Although the Canadian Red Scare did not attain the dimensions of its U.S. counterpart, it was no picnic. Armed with laws against sedition and seditious libel, the ability to rule through order-in-council under the notorious War Measures Act, hurriedly passed in 1914, and extensive powers to deport troublemakers, many of the most senior leaders in the liberal state believed that their entire system was in danger. As Borden would remember in 1938, some Canadian cities had seen a "deliberate attempt to overthrow the existing organization of the Government and to supersede it by crude, fantastic methods founded upon absurd conceptions of what had been accomplished in Russia" – all of which explained his repression of such movements "with a stern hand." More religious writers expressed the same intuition. The Catholic Church press in general thought that Canada confronted an immediate and real revolutionary menace, as countless workers – fatally attracted by the three "isms" of Bolshevism, socialism, and anarchism – raced down a shortcut to doom and destruction.[20]

"Bolshevism" was the new name of the monstrous Other. As the Toronto *Globe* so usefully put it, "Bolshevism" was a label for "any act or tendency which happens to offend our beliefs or prejudices." For one writer to the Halifax *Herald*, both unreasonable employees and their unreasonable bosses might be thought of as two tribes of "Bolsheviki," one the "just common reds" – the "lower class" – and the other the "more select scarlets" – the "upper class." Both were troublemakers, and "the chief trouble they make is ... hurling fire brands at each other." An address to the Halifax Commercial Club on "How to Combat Bolshevism," a "Menace at Home That Now is Tearing Russia in Pieces," advised that the answer lay in the "wonderful possibilities" and "good deeds" of "the Boy Scout movement." A writer in the *Mail and Empire* provided the most glaring example of "Bolshevitis" when he equated Bolsheviks with Bad Drivers. He began his article "Bolshevism on Wheels," rather grandly, with a high-flown theory of the word "Bolshevism," which for him meant an "utter disregard for the rights of other people, carried often to the point of plundering and killing them." But he moved swiftly on to the case in point: the discourteous driving of Toronto motorists during a recent police strike.[21]

The "Bolshevik" was a rude and unreasonable person. He or she was also "non-white," in the contemporary sense of "non-British." Depictions of "Bolshies" made them appear swarthy, unkempt, and dark. Peter Wright, one of the earliest and most intrepid of the anti-Bolshevik crusaders in Canada, called the Bolshevik the "wild man from Borneo," who respected neither mankind nor God. Reviewing E.J. Dillon's *Eclipse of Russia* in October 1918, a *Mail and Empire* contributor saw the Russians in terms of Kipling's description of primitives about to become the White Man's Burden – "Half Devil and Half Child" – and hailed the writer for showing "hundreds of instances which prove the Russian to have all the virtues and vices of human beings, plus a good number of vices which we supposed belonged to the lower orders of creation." Visual representations of the swarthy crazed Bolshevik, often accompanied by his trusty industry- and home-destroying torch, helped readers grasp the "dark otherness" of this strange Russian creature. It was past time, said critics of the Russians, for Canada to take a hard look at its immigration policies.[22]

Others touched on the Jewish question. Some hoped Jews were temperamentally disposed to supporting more moderate parties. Others urged that Bolshevism simply *was* Jewish – it was the outcome of a few agitators of Jewish birth, "some of them on the pay-roll of the imperial government of Germany." They had mixed themselves among the wage workers of Russia and were preaching certain doctrines that were "anarchistic" and dangerous to the "old noble soul of Russia." In a November 1917 editorial on "Jews and Socialism," the *Mail and Empire* drew on recent New York City polemics that sought to dissuade Jews from supporting the Socialist candidacy of Morris Hillquit. It went on to issue a warning. "It is of vital importance," the paper observed, "to the Jews in this country that they should not permit themselves to be regarded as Socialists, for Socialists, who are too often pro-Germans and pacifists, are going to have a rough time in Canada when the war is over."[23]

The other nationalities associated with the left also gradually came into focus. Only slowly did the mainstream press register the dimensions of Finnish radical socialism. Those Finnish leftists they did finally notice were not *really* White. They were "not properly Europeans, but belong to the Mongolian race. They have intermarried with the Swedes since early in the Thirteenth century, when they were Christianized." As for the Ukrainians, they were actually just "Russians," in the somewhat myopic eyes of the *Mail and Empire*. Although the newspaper had once held out high hopes that Ukrainians would stand up against the Bolsheviki, these hopes had been dashed. After they declared peace with Germany, "We then came to the conclusion that, while the Ukrainians might not be like other Russians, they differed merely for the worse."[24]

Yet, however strange and troubling such nationalities, there was an even more ominous menace contained by the Revolution. It seemingly presaged an internationalist future beyond the nation itself. The *Mail and Empire* was thunderstruck by Trotsky, who in *The Bolsheviki and World Peace* had proudly declared himself to be a citizen of the world. "Trotzky makes no boast of being a patriot," the *Mail and Empire* noted perceptively. "Rather does he proclaim himself a man without a country." Having published the "ravings" of this man at great length, the newspaper's editor would seem to have been caught in a performative contradiction. Nonetheless, he persisted in his sharp critique of his sometime correspondent. The peculiar horror of the Red flag, recently banned in New York City, resided, he argued, precisely in its internationalist significance. "The red flag is the banner of Socialism, but it is also the banner of Bolshevism, the I.W.W., and anarchy generally," he observed. "It does not stand for a Government or a nation. When it floats it is a signal defying all Governments, all law and order except what the mob may choose to establish." He generously allowed that Socialists might have a right to recommend improvements to the government, but "those whose flag is the red one" were "calling . . . for a return of the ape age."[25]

Stephen Leacock thought a degenerating disease of violence was gripping the entire North Atlantic world, afflicting Social Democrat and Bolshevik alike: "All across Europe the plague spreads. And in front of it, even across the

Atlantic runs the fear of it – the instinctive, psychological collective fear as of a thing that threatens all society with a common ruin."[26] In the most vivid right-wing discourse, Bolshies were depicted as animals – snakes, parasites, and especially wolves. In one widely distributed image that recalled London's *Call of the Wild*, as set in some peculiar parallel universe, the wolf of Bolshevism breathed his cold death-like breath upon the factories of the nation, in an arresting image that cleverly combined wolfish Russianness, cold-blooded rationalism, and a counter-evolutionary "reversion to type." Building on techniques of propaganda perfected in the Great War, the Red Scare projected on to all the leftists the trends in modernity that liberals feared and distrusted. In the first massive coast to coast anti-Red campaign in Canadian history, the ruling order sought to reconstruct the symbolic representations emanating from civil society.[27]

On 25 February 1918, as it became clear that Trotsky's Russia had backed out of the Great War, the federal government issued an order-in-council banning a medley of organizations for the duration of the conflict. The "A" list suggested the limited intelligence upon which the state was operating, since some of the groups probably did not exist and the names of others were distorted. It included the Industrial Workers of the World, Social Democratic Party, Russian Social Democratic Party, Russian Revolutionary Group, Russian Social Revolutionists, Russian Workers' Union, Ukrainian Revolutionary Group, Ukrainian Social Democratic Party, Social Labour Party, Group of Social Democrats or Bolsheviki Group of Social Democrats or Anarchists, Workers International Industrial Union, Chinese Nationalist League, Chinese Labour Association, and "any subsidiary association, branch or committee" of these groups. Some big radical groups were missing, such as the Socialist Party of Canada and the Finnish Organization of Canada, but their members could be nonetheless arrested and harassed under a further provision that outlawed "any association, organization or corporation which, while Canada is engaged in the war, should have for one of its purposes the bringing about of any governmental, political, social, industrial, or economic change within Canada by the use of force, violence or physical injury to person or property, or threatened such injury in order to accomplish such change."[28]

Such measures won general applause from the mainstream media. "Any demonstration of Bolshevikism in this country ought to be put down at the point of the bayonet," advised the *Mail and Empire*, rather forgetting the month-long demonstration it itself had provided in the shape of Trotsky's writings. *Saturday Night* recommended the "firing squad" for Bolsheviks encouraging unrest or strikes. Looking ahead, Sir James Aitkins, K.C., the president of the Canadian Bar Association, meeting at the Ritz-Carleton in Montreal, advised his elite audience that "new positive law" would be needed "controlling conduct in the many phases of Socialism accentuated and developed by the war." One obvious place to start would be a tightening up of the laws respecting immigration and asylum.[29] Most of the religious papers supported the deportation of subversives deemed to be responsible for Bolshevik activity.[30] As the inimitable Vancouver *Sun* advised on 5 July 1920, "The man who preaches Sovietism in this country should be promptly deported or sent to jail." Even Leacock, who usually argued that leftist ideas were best undermined if brought out into the light of day, was urging, "If the Bolshevik begins to 'bolsh' in the open streets as he did at Petrograd, shoot him."[31]

Contradictions of Liberal Order

The events of 1915–20 can best be interpreted as an organic crisis of liberal order, in which the terms of hegemony shifted dramatically. To a considerable degree, social groups became detached from their traditional parties – and the liberal parties themselves became "non-traditional" (first with the formation of the pro-conscription Union government, an unprecedented attempt to create a national coalition of the Liberals and Conservatives, and secondly with the rise of the primarily rural Progressives, most of whom made it a point of principle not even to *be* a party). In such a situation the ruling class or group must be perceived to have failed, in Gramsci's words, in some major undertaking "for which it has requested, or forcibly extracted, the consent of the broad masses (war, for example), or because huge masses (especially of peasant and petit-bourgeois intellectuals) have passed suddenly from a state of political passivity to a certain activity, and put forward demands which taken together, albeit not organically formulated, add up to a revolution."[32] In the Canadian case, the rulers of liberal order had not overtly failed in their primary project – the Germans had, at a massive cost of Canadian lives, been defeated; and in retrospect we can see that certain elements, such as a strongly unified left and a fragmented regime, were missing from this "revolutionary situation." Yet many Canadians believed that the state had plainly failed to "save democracy." At the time, too, some of the most intelligent and well-informed minds within the federal state, fed with alarming intelligence from the country's burgeoning security apparatus, saw revolution as a real possibility.[33]

In its first years the Great War seemingly confirmed the efficacy of a traditional liberal political economy and the profound loyalty to Empire of Canadian working people. The Canadian Great War was initially conducted in voluntary ways – through recruitment drives that left it up to the individual to enlist, through public/private structures that devolved the planning of the war industry on to entrepreneurs, and in a "business as usual" environment that encouraged citizens and householders in the belief that their everyday lives would not be unduly unsettled by the war. As one Maritime business publication put it, "The discovery has been made that it is possible to carry on war and do a profitable business at the same time."[34]

Before 1916, "business as usual" meant a liberal state that collected no income tax, influenced but did not presume to direct the economy, and relied upon the voluntary principle to secure such objectives as raising an army. After 1917 "business as usual" meant a liberal state that collected an income tax, directed increasingly large swathes of the economy, had incurred massive public debts, and relied upon coercion to meet the manpower objectives of its army. One telling example of the "new normal" came in official attitudes towards food. In 1914 the hoarding of foodstuffs by middle-class families was considered as so unobjectionable that stores advertised they would keep extended hours in order to assuage the demands of consumers. As the war dragged on wartime policies encouraged, even to some extent compelled, a collective husbanding of food under the Canada Food Board. Similarly, in March 1918 the individual's right to drink was now curtailed by the enactment, under the War Measures Act, of federal "bone-dry" prohibition. As historians Ramsay Cook and R. Craig Brown so deftly put it, in trying to preserve the pre-war social order "the government of Canada had changed it almost beyond recognition."[35]

One of the political order's primary contradictions lay in the acute tension between those acts and words that presupposed a transcendent, noble purpose for which one should be glad to make sacrifices, and the individualism inherent in a liberal and capitalist society. The blood of the "Fallen" of Flanders and France sanctified the Canadian crusade against the enemy. "Canadians," remarks Vance, "never lost sight of the fact that November 1918 marked a victory over the forces of barbarism."[36] "In Flanders Fields," one of the war's most famous poems, brilliantly combines a humanistic celebration of soldiers as human beings (in its first two stanzas) with a stirring recruiting-hall speech in the third – a strong argument against any negotiated peace with "the foe."[37] For many Canadians, questioning the war meant questioning the integrity of the men and women who died in it. "The sanctity of the fallen ... was paramount," Vance concludes. "No truth was so important to discover, no fiction so important to puncture, that it could justify calling into question the sacrifices of the dead."[38]

The high diction of the Great War could thus play into a new conception of the state as the organic embodiment of the finest traditions of the Canadian people and attached by blood and soul to the core project of the nation. Yet this elevated discourse of blood and belonging did not necessarily play out easily or automatically for the established order. It could also mesh with evolutionary theory and work effectively for the order's radical opposition. Indeed, the belief that the state should live up to the noblest ideals of patriotism and sacrifice was the springboard of powerful critiques against it. The left had its own high diction, and in many ways it made much more sense and was just as popularly rooted as the right wing's imperial-nationalist cult of blood, soil, and death.

The contradiction within liberal order was palpable with the many scandals that rocked the government. Business activities normal in the *fin de siècle* capitalist economy – buying cheap and selling dear, on the fine old principle of "let the consumer beware!" – suddenly took on a different hue when their front-line consequences were rotting boots, lame horses, and defective rifles, all palmed off on a too-credulous and patronage-ridden government. Selling nickel to the highest bidder took on a different cast when that higher bidder manufactured it into arms to shoot at Canadian soldiers. The SDPC in Ontario would draw attention to this shocking anomaly and present what it believed to be the patriotic and sensible solution to the problem: the nationalization of nickel, along with "every means of production and distribution – land, mines, factories, railroads, food supply, etc."[39]

The glaring evidence that some were doing very well out of the war and others were suffering was ruthlessly satirized by the Winnipeg SPC in a 1918 pamphlet, *All I Possess*. The text, originating in *The Liberator* magazine, published in New York, was said to have been written by a young U.S. conscript, John T. Goolrick Jr., in response to a card urging him to enlist in the "Unconditional Surrender Club" and to pledge "to make whatever sacrifice I may be called upon to make to the end that the Central Powers may be brought to realize that only an unconditional surrender will be acceptable to me and my country."[40] Although Goolrick said he was more than willing to nobly lay down his life for his country, he also urged the patriotic campaigners to send the appeal to others who were not going, who would also doubtless be anxious to give all they possessed – men such as John D. Rockefeller, H.P. Whitney, and J.P. Morgan Jr., of New York, Thomas T. Lawson of Boston, and a "Mr. Swift, care of Swift &. Co., Chicago, Ill." All that these plutocrats would be asked to do would be "to give up all their surplus and unused property and incomes, which surely they will be willing to do if I am willing to go to France to save them." They might also come out personally to work on the farms, to raise food for the soldiers.

> Some night, when I am out there looking up at the crimsoned sky, which tomorrow night I may not see, I shall be thinking of you . . . my partners in this great sacrifice. I shall dream, there, on that ensanguined soil, of the ideals for which I fight and the Justice and Liberty for which you and I are laying aside each our possessions, our loves and our friends and for which I am going nine steps further and offering my life.

But imagine the bitter thoughts and deeds that might arise if the rich did not do their part! "I fear," said Goolrick, "that if I returned to find that you have not kept your pledge to 'give all that I possess' as I have kept mine, I should turn on you and with the bayonet that has pointed to brave men who fought, strike at you."

Driving the lesson home, the Winnipeg Socialists concluded: "It is not for the Coal, the Milk, the Bacon, the Milling or Munition Barons, who have become rich while you have been pouring forth your blood and your sweat. The issue is now up to you. In your councils you must formulate your demands for your own protection. Remember the promises which were made to you – are they being kept?"[41] The SPCers had been reading up on the rhetoric and underlying logic of militarism – as evidenced by a well-thumbed copy of Karl Liebknecht's eloquent analysis of its German and international dimensions that some of them obviously treasured in their socialist library.[42]

The political contradictions of liberal order were evident in the December 1917 federal election. In bringing a new Unionist formation to power, it opened the door to other, more far-reaching and permanent mutations in a party structure that had been remarkably stable since the 1860s. The highly racialized language of the election and the demonization of French Canadians who were resistant to conscription meant that the national question was raised during the Great War with a rigour that placed in question the project of Confederation. Runaway inflation and rampant profiteering led to demands for comprehensive wartime planning in which the rich would pay their fair share. "Dictatorship of the bourgeoisie," an occasional slogan of the pre-war left, had a new plausibility when orders-in-councils banned strikes, loafing, the public use of enemy languages, and even the possession of such books as Spencer's *First Principles*.

Leftists buried their libraries under floorboards, in back gardens in the case of J.S. Woodsworth, and in that of Bainbridge, "under the coal in the coal bin."[43] A police spy reported that Jacob Penner (1880–1965), a sparkplug for decades in the Winnipeg movement, had "made a bonfire of his Socialist Literature some time ago for fear that his house would be raided."[44] In January 1919, UMW Local Union 2299 passed a resolution condemning the federal government's prohibition of entry into Canada of the Charles H. Kerr books, "our main source of the classics of working class philosophy."[45] In the historical memory of the Winnipeg left, the attack upon the libraries was linked with assaults upon the family home. Over and over again, first formation leftists presented the war on the libraries as an extraordinary outrage. It went to the heart of the autodidact culture that they had so painstakingly built up over three decades of patient inquiry and determined polemic. Sometimes it almost seemed that the book-burning and book-banning offended them more grievously than did the assaults, imprisonments, and deportations meted out to human beings. In Winnipeg the raid on the house of SPCers George and

Helen Armstrong, for example, was condemned as an outrage on learning it-self: "Then the door was opened and armed with a blank search warrant, they proceeded to investigate every nook and corner of the house – gathering up books, papers and periodicals – the valued sources of knowledge – knowledge of the truth, which shall eventually set men free."[46]

Equally reprehensible was the state's censorship of publications.[47] In January 1919, surveying the secret censorship of the mails and the intimidation of radicals, the spc's *Red Flag* remarked, "This action of the postal officials seems specially designed to seriously impede and cripple this party, both as an organization and in its business of supplying its customers throughout the country with literature on economics, history, sociology, and a range of sciences." A couple of months later the *Red Flag* reported the heavy costs incurred by the Alberta provincial Executive Council of the spc, whose treasury had been heavily taxed "for the defence of comrades charged with sedition or being in possession of banned literature." One spcer, charged with having the banned *Western Clarion* in his possession, had paid out over $300; another faced prosecution for possession of *Class Struggle*. At least 70 socialists had been arrested in 1918 in Ontario alone, charged with being members in unlawful associations (mainly the sdpc and affiliates) or for having seditious material in their possession. Only six were ever brought to trial. If, as *Red Flag* would later announce, "Marxian knowledge is all powerful for the international proletariat," the Canadian state was clearly complicit in preventing its growth and development.[48] Socialists turned with almost obsessive interest to histories of counter-Enlightenment persecution, projecting on to past martyrs of science their own sense of being targeted by an irrational and knowledge-hating regime.[49]

One Big Union? The Changing Questions of the Left

Notwithstanding all this repression, the Canadian left turned out to be a beneficiary of the high diction of wartime sacrifice and the "low politics" of wartime planning. The war provided a way in which the various elements of socialism could be merged into one overarching project. In essence, the four great questions of the Canadian left – class, religion, gender, race – were fused into a fifth: peace. Although many socialists had long been critical of war as an aspect of capitalist society, the Great War gave anti-war radicals a much higher profile than they had ever had before.[50]

In this respect the Canadian pattern diverged markedly from that in other countries. In Germany, France, and the United States, the war was bitterly divisive for the parties of the left; the epochal split between Social Democrats and Communists dates from this time. Canada's socialist parties, which lacked similar ties to organized labour, institutional depth, and political significance, had no such dramatic splits. Within the sdpc, always a loosely knit party to begin with, the war did undoubtedly intensify divisions among the groups, especially given the federal state's skilful application of a divide and conquer policy of treating the "foreign radicals" differently than the English-speakers. The *Western Clarion* showed a momentary lapse into patriotism, and, of course, many socialists themselves responded to the call to arms. Most essentially, there was a split within the labour movement, with significant elements of the TLC supporting the war and conscription. Still, compared to Europe or the United States, the socialist movement emerged from the war without the burning, divisive memory of bitter internecine feuds over the voting of war credits or cheerful collaboration with conscription.

In contrast to other countries, in Canada the Great War was the making, not the unmaking, of a more organically unified left – and one that was not lumbered with the heavy burden of having entered a partnership with bourgeois parties in wartime. There was in Canada a more deep-seated left consensus, emergent after 1916, that the war was mistaken, its profiteers criminals, and its apologists deluded. Roscoe Fillmore put a general disgust with the betrayal of the Second International parties in his customarily pungent form:

An ever-increasing number of us believe that the time has come for a house-cleaning. The truth is the only salvation for the Socialist movement today. We must find the seat of the trouble and cut it out. Halfway measures are of no use. Mistaken ideas of gratitude will not save us. When we find a traitor he must do his dirty work on the *outside* from now on, whether he be a traitor from lack of knowledge or from the fact that he has secured a more elaborate meal ticket, and even though his work in the past has been good. Individuals don't count – *results* do. How are we to save the movement and make it a powerful weapon towards the freedom of the workers?[51]

No more "peanut politics!" No more mild reforms! Even Woodsworth, in his heart a moderate and a centrist, declared, when he came to visualize *Reconstruction from the Viewpoint of Labor*, that his objectives were "frankly 'revolutionary,'" aiming as they did at the "complete turnover in the present economic and social system."[52] To be a leftist in the atmosphere of 1917–1920 was to breathe a very special atmosphere, one in which a top to bottom reconstruction of society had seemingly gone from being a utopian dream to a real possibility.

Having brought into being a new kind of state, obsessed with the shaping of public opinion, the war also resulted in a new, more powerfully focused left. Rather like the *Mail and Empire* inadvertently inspiring someone who would become the leading Canadian Communist of the 1920s, the wartime governments, by governing through orders-in-council, heightening the official discourse of patriotism and sacrifice, and effacing many of the traditional lines dividing government from business, inadvertently fused the many paths of left-ism. Abstract soapbox appeals for the overthrow of capitalism were now necessarily combined with concrete demands for the end of the War Measures Act and of dictatorial government by orders-in-council. Conscription, wartime economic planning, and the massively enhanced state propaganda drives gave the state much more concreteness. The war prompted leftists to start to think hegemonically, both holistically and specifically, and to notice, in some cases for the first time, that they were operating within a very particular Canadian context.

The Great War transformed the labour movement and with it prevailing left-wing conceptions of class-consciousness. Workers who had been pushed beyond endurance mounted a series of little spontaneous strikes, some of which they called "holidays." In the four years down to 1920, roughly 350,000 workers participated in strikes in Canada, with 457 strikes in 1920 alone. Perhaps one in five workers was now organized in a union – an all-time high.[53]

Yet a potent contradiction of the late war and the early peace was that this rapidly expanding labour movement enjoyed only marginally more influence over crucial events than before. One early indication was the TLC's path-breaking decision in 1913 to mount a determined campaign of resistance to conscription, even threatening a general strike on the issue. When the TLC executive later backed down before the government (playing an equivocating role reminiscent of the European social-democratic parties), it confronted a large, angry minority within the labour movement. The formation of the Canadian Labor Party (CLP), represented by candidates in the 1917 federal election, was an attempt by the leadership to steer this anger away from resistance via the general strike to a quieter, political channel. It soon became apparent that the government concessions granted the labour leadership, including consultations with cabinet ministers and representation on state regulatory bodies, did not amount to a genuine attempt to meet the demands of labour. Indeed, in 1918 labour's accommodationism seemed to lead to even more aggressive acts of repression – bringing Western Canada to the brink of a general strike over the demands of letter carriers in the summer of 1918, and to discussions at the Labor Party convention in Quebec of the advisability of armed resistance.

Throughout the country, workers connected these many issues to the existence of a system that only a more rationally designed, unified, and comprehensive labour movement could challenge. Leftist unionists, sensing that they had been betrayed by their leaders, denounced the established leadership in 1917 and 1918 and embarked on a path that led to the One Big Union, the remarkable experiment in revolutionary industrial unionism that seemed destined at the time to become the leading labour organization of the

Dominion. The OBU was initiated on 13 March 1919 at the Western Labour Conference in Calgary, when the assembled delegates called for a referendum among Canadian union members on secession from the American Federation of Labor in favour of an organization of a new type, a scientifically designed revolutionary industrial union uniting all the workers in a given area. The terms in which delegates viewed the secession reflected the significance of evolutionary and functionalist concepts: the "vital trades," like vital organs, were those which, if they ceased work, would compel others to cease "by virtue of the fact they cannot carry on without them." As Jack Kavanagh remarked, "Sure it is force, nothing but force in existence," but "unless you are aggressive no other element counts."[54]

Such "evolutionary functionalism" was expressed in more picturesque detail with the revival of Father Hagerty's Wheel, the immensely intricate chart of the "One Big Union." The scheme, initially associated with the IWW and echoing in plans put forward by the Australian OBU, was now revived on the pages of the *Western Labor News*, where it was misleadingly presented as reflective of the Soviets. As David Bercuson points out, the "plan" was by no means unanimously accepted. R.B. Russell, one of the OBU's organic intellectuals, thought it at best a way of educating workers to think about what a Canadian plan might ultimately entail.[55] Built into the OBU, and manifested in these drives to produce plans, was a conception of a scientific trade unionism that could express a systematic counter-hegemonic vision to both capitalism and the existing labour movement. The OBU won many supporters in the West, Northern Ontario, and in pockets of Nova Scotia (where the Federation of Labor itself had strong OBU tendencies). It may have had as many as 50,000 members at its peak in 1920, which made it by far the largest homegrown left-wing organization found in Canada in the entire period 1890–1920.

What the OBU promised within the labour movement – an integration of structure and function within a much larger and more radical central – the demand for the "conscription of wealth" suggested more generally. The slogan, adopted from Britain, was deceptively straightforward, but fiendishly subtle. It was open to many interpretations. Succinctly and memorably, the slogan suggested that "wealth," no less than actual human beings, was a "social entity" called upon to make a contribution to the war. Just as "The Fallen" in Flanders testified to the noble sentiments of true Canadians, so too should the "Conscription of Wealth" testify to the noble sentiments of truly rich Canadians. Corporate "individuals" – banks, pork-packing companies, railways, and the people who directed them, all intrinsically connected together in the social organism – should be grateful of the chance to help civilization face down barbarism in Europe. The slogan cleverly played "commodity fetishism" against the system itself and appealed to widely shared sentiments of fairness and equity.

As Rev. A.E. Smith, a prominent Methodist and soon to be a major architect of the postwar labour church, explained, "All the wealth of the nation is the result of some community action. . . . No one should be able to increase his bank account at the expense of the people in the form of war profits."[56] The "conscription of wealth" thus ingeniously worked to subvert the unifying "myth of the war" while seemingly agreeing with it. It was of course "utopian" to think that every Canadian, fired by patriotism, would surrender his or her "bankbook" – that is, happily court poverty in the cause of the people. But was it really any more "utopian" than high diction itself? If the government war propaganda was sincere, why shouldn't all classes of citizens chip in to the best of their ability? The conservative *Canadian Annual Review* quite rightly sniffed a socialist smell about all the damnably "wide and loose talk" going around about the "Conscription of Wealth." It did not deny that this "openly seditious" slogan had developed serious traction, including support from the widely distributed Toronto *Star*.[57] Gestures towards the demand were even included in the Unionist platform of 1917, and in severely watered-down form the idea found its way into the first income tax of 1918.

The demands for a conscription of wealth from above eventually became demands for conscription of wealth from below. One pamphlet described in the *Mail and Empire* exhorted the returned soldiers specifically and citizens generally to "rise and seize what is rightfully yours!" If revolution prevailed, and the government resisted, the people were importuned "to take the law into their own hands and 'wade in blood up to the knees, if necessary.' "[58] If the paper was describing *Peace and the Workers*, distributed in Southern Ontario in November 1918, it was embroidering considerably on the documentary evidence. The pamphlet condemned in relatively standard first formation terms the "crew of parasites" and painted a portrait of the bourgeoisie that calls to mind the fine hand of Moses Baritz:

> Many millions of women and children have died of starvation while fat capitalists have rolled in luxury and have accused you of squandering your miserable wages. Their fat and silk-clad women have urged your overworked wife to "conserve food" – you must know that you have been forced to "conserve" all your life and yet you kept silent under the sneers of these people who rob you of nearly all you produce! You have gone through all this for what?[59]

The Regina Trades Council drew upon vivid organic imagery to paint the profiteer as a creature "fattening on our soldiers' blood." Conservative politicians on the ground warned Prime Minister Borden that they had never in the past quarter-century encountered "such wide spread *rage* over any other scandal" as that associated with the profits gleaned by pork-packer Sir Joseph Flavelle.[60] In the left's rendition of the high diction of wartime sacrifice, if the fate of the entire social organism was really in the balance, obviously the needs of the collectivity must, in the name of patriotism, take precedence over the conventional profit-making of the individual.

Even apart from the OBU a new spirit of "quasi-syndicalism" was emerging. This was not syndicalist in the narrow sense of believing that the general strike and revolutionary unionism represented the royal road to socialism, but it drew from many of the same inspirations in arguing for grassroots democracy, the removal of skilled/unskilled barriers, the formation of more integrated and unified bodies capable of bargaining for large masses of workers, and a favourable attitude towards general strikes as one of labour's legitimate and most powerful weapons. In the Spencerian terms of the day, the labour movement was going beyond a primitive homogeneity of simple units to attain a complex heterogeneity of forms and functions. These new forms were hardly the monopoly of "the West": in November 1918 the Amherst, N.S., Federation of Labor was formed as an industrial-based organization for workers excluded from craft unions, and in the following June its members voted, by a startling number of 1,185 to 1 – one rather wonders who the one dissident was – to affiliate with the OBU.[61]

The OBU-style organization had broad support – solidarity across the lines of industry and class, unified collective bargaining, and general strikes – that found expression within the established trade union movement. Instead of standing by tried and true craft-union methods because of parochialism and traditionalism, Maritime workers, influenced by the United Mine Workers' J.B. McLachlan and the AFL's C.C. Dane, an Australian boilermaker and self-proclaimed "Bolshevist," developed a Maritime variant of syndicalism.[62] They poured this new wine into old AFL bottles, but the modestly named "Districts," "Councils," and "Federations of Labour" did effectively group masses of workers together in large and politically active bodies. In Pictou County, Amherst, and momentarily in Sydney Mines, "Federations of Labour" and not individual craft unions were the principal organizing mechanisms; in Halifax, councils of unions in the building trades and the shipyards carried out collective bargaining. Most crucially, under the left regimes that predominated from 1918 to 1923 in District 26 of the UMW, a powerhouse with its roughly 13,000 workers, came a serious attempt to reconcile the miners' grassroots democracy with the demands of district-wide collective bargaining. By 1920 at least 40,000 Maritimers had signed on as union members – more than four times the number reported in 1915. "Casting the mind's eye over the Canadian field of labor," wrote a contented commentator in the *Eastern Federationist* in 1919, "in no part does it look more bright than in Nova Scotia." The writer observed, "The entire province is organized . . . and they are all affiliated in the Provincial Federation so that no union stands isolated."[63] The class sensibility of 1915–20 was that once-separate workers and units should be organically fused: responding to the newly consolidated capitalism, labour organizations should reflect a new class solidarity; and in their new organic fusion, they should generate a consistent program of overturning the class structure. The class question was transformed by the war.

Woodsworth Revisited: From Social Work to Socialist Work

A similar transformation in socialist thought can be charted among those for whom socialism was primarily the reflection of a religious critique of capitalism. Here Woodsworth, the one-time liberal interpreter of immigration, serves as something of an archetypal case. In the abundant and deeply interesting writings about him, he is a puzzling figure. Kenneth McNaught's classic biography discerns in him a common-sense, abstraction-distrusting, stubbornly individualistic "prophet" who opposed "the futility of 'scientific socialism' as applied in a Canadian context" and hence became the scourge of the Marxists. Allen Mills's more recent Woodsworth is something of a "paradox," a bundle of largely unexamined contradictions, yet nonetheless a vigorous and consistent anti-Marxist. Above all Woodsworth was a deeply middle-class man. As Maurice Spector observed in a by no means mean-spirited assessment, "the language and the practice of the class struggle" were not Woodsworth's mother tongue.[64]

What is most apparent is that Woodsworth was roused to change his political course and engagement by the experience of the Great War. In 1911 he was fascinated by the worldwide connections drawing people to Winnipeg and the invisible patterns that explained how they behaved once in the city. He was regarded as a "progressive" clergyman with slightly left-of-centre views, which is why he could advance in national social work circles without causing serious alarm. His was the voice of meliorative social work. Had the war not intervened, his life might have remained fixed in a Mackenzie-King-like pursuit of moderate measures on behalf of the working class. The war closed those options, and opened others. On deeply held religious grounds, Woodsworth had to refuse this war. From 1915 to 1920 Woodsworth transformed himself from an evolutionary liberal into an orthodox first formation socialist, working quite comfortably with its Spencerian and Marxian concepts and arguing for revolution as a greatly accelerated process of evolution – a position not well captured in the dichotomies of later scholars.

On 4 October 1915 Woodsworth went to an army recruiting meeting at St. James Methodist Church in Montreal. "Really Lucy," he exclaimed in a letter to his wife, "if I weren't on principle opposed to spectacular methods, I would have gotten up and denounced the whole performance as a perversion – a damnable perversion, if you like – of the teachings of Jesus, and a profanation of the day and the house set apart for Divine Worship." Woodsworth was disgusted by the spectacle he saw there, of a pastor stirring up a spirit of hatred and retaliation. He was horrified by the argument that any young man who did not enlist was "neither a Christian nor a patriot." He was appalled by the announcement that recruiting sergeants were stationed at the doors. "I felt like doing something desperate – forswearing church attendance – repudiating any connection with the Church."[65]

In June 1918 Woodsworth decided that he had to break with the Methodists, and he submitted his resignation to Rev. A.E. Smith, president of the church's Manitoba Conference. In a long letter to Smith he outlined past conflicts with the church – conflicts that had more than once put him on the verge of resignation. But previously he had been convinced to stay within the body of the church, working first at All People's Mission in Winnipeg and later as secretary of the Canadian Welfare League and then director of the Bureau of Social Research of the Governments of Manitoba, Saskatchewan, and Alberta. In 1917 he had ended up in British Columbia, where he worked on a "little coast mission field" at Gibson's Landing. Years earlier, he said, "I had been led to realize something of the horror and futility and wickedness of war." Now, in his resignation letter, Woodsworth wrote that, according to his "understanding of economics and sociology, the war is the inevitable outcome of the existing social organization with its undemocratic forms of government and competitive system of industry." Those who fastened on some other factor – the assassination of Archduke Ferdinand, the invasion of Belgium – as the "cause of the war" were guilty of "ignorance, or a closed mind, or camouflage, or hypocrisy." Those in the church who preached the gospel of war had pitted themselves against the "teachings and spirit of Jesus." He had been with the Methodist Church for 22 years. "This decision," he said in the classic accents of supersedure, "means a crisis in my life."[66]

It also meant the end of his social work in Gibson's Landing and the beginning of his time as a working-class sojourner in Vancouver. Woodsworth's reflections on his new status – a renowned social worker with a Canada-wide following now working as a manual labourer on the docks – offer the measure of the man: both tough and whimsical at the same time. "Fancy lifting trunks all day long! Fortunately they did not rush the work but it made me sweat just the same. I have a new theory as to why the men describe themselves as working *stiffs!*" he exclaimed. Grace MacInnis remembered being shocked at the thought of her 130-pound father turning into a manual worker. "Mentally, I recognized that men in overalls were just as worthy of respect as men in white collars; emotionally it was a shock when my father took off the collar and put on the overalls. His letter makes it apparent that it was something of a shock to him as well."[67]

Moderate in most things, Woodsworth was a revolutionary extremist in his hatred of war. As his daughter put it, Woodsworth's hatred of war was a "burning, passionate thing that flamed more fiercely every day he lived."[68] The Great War conflicted with his Christian conceptions of right and wrong. War also violated his core belief in social evolution and progress, which he emphasized more and more. During the war years Woodsworth was noticeably more critical of capitalism than he had been in his books of 1909 and 1911. From 1902 to 1916 he had rejected militarism publicly and privately. He had sensed the tension between conventional British patriotism and his deepest convictions – his refusal of militarism and all the symbols and practices it entailed. Yet over those years he had, even if with difficulty, managed that tension in such a way that it did not catapult him out of the norms and comforts of middle-class life. Even in the first years of the Great War, he had persisted in his course. What forced him into a moment of refusal was the political demand that he himself take part by participating in a survey for military registration. Yet, once embarked on this path of resistance, he was pushed forcibly out of one context – Winnipeg, dominion-wide "social work," the company and esteem of middle-class professionals, and the Protestant political and religious elite – and into another – British Columbia, increasingly radical "socialist work," the company and (qualified) esteem of working-class radicals and longshoremen, and the decidedly radicalized socialist movement. Once he had connected his opposition to war with the underlying system of economic and social power, and had determined to live out the consequences of that moment of supersedure, he found himself to be required both to live and to reason otherwise.

He was on the slippery slope to internalizing the already well-developed system of concepts of first formation socialism. Woodsworth's "socialism," as it developed after this crisis of his life, was as much war-derived as it was an inevitable product of his Christian faith. A path that had been entered in a religious resistance to war might lead to a formation shared with people whose paths had been started in resistance to capitalist employers or ethnic oppression. Once on this path, he could revisit earlier concepts – such as the structural-functional theory of society provisionally at work within *My Neighbor* – and translate them into a newer, more combative dialect. After 1917 the triune formula generally absent from the immigration books is plainly at work in Woodsworth's activism and writing. Woodsworth now came to believe in revolutionary evolution. His socialism of 1917–20 accepted Marx as an authority. He shared with the likes of W.A. Pritchard and Colin McKay the dream of a people's scientific enlightenment. Driven by his unyielding hatred of war and revulsion against those Christians who sang its praises, Woodsworth became a revolutionary – that is, a supporter of radical anti-capitalism, general strikes, and independent socialist politics.

In an article published in the *Western Labor News* in October 1918, Woodsworth offered praise for British Columbia's new Federated Labor Party, which, he said, "leaves the 'scientific orthodox' group and the 'revisionist' groups to fight out their theories, but takes the great underlying principle stressed by Marx, viz., the collective ownership and democratic control of the means of wealth production. Men may differ widely in theory and yet unite to fight a common foe."[69] In registering resistance to the sectarian debates between SPCers and "revisionists" – significantly, Woodsworth appeared to back off from supporting either side – he was also saying that he approved of a party that took up the "great underlying principle" of Marx.[70]

In a later article Woodsworth described his introduction to the Vancouver work world: "I had to stand outside on the steps of the Longshoremen's Hall, awaiting the chance of a casual job. Here one began to realize in all its nakedness and ugliness the workings of the competitive system." He discovered the numbing monotony of dock labour, the importance of meetings in which collective grievances could be discussed, the manual worker's yearning for self-expression in work, and the working-class demand for a radical social democracy. "In the course of some months it began to dawn upon me what the workers mean by class consciousness," Woodsworth wrote. "Here were we, the workers, doing the work of the world, the employers reaping the dividends. We read in the papers of the huge profits made during war times by some of the employers, and bitterly compare this with the meagre sums which barely suffice to keep our own families at the low standard of living. Thus rebels are made." The experience of working on the docks grounded and radicalized Woodsworth's earlier insight into the "social organism." He now recognized the importance of class analysis, the labour theory of value, and historical materialism in ways that had earlier escaped him. The "tourist" of *Strangers Within Our Gates* had changed his epistemological position. He now felt, in good measure, as though he shared the same position and destiny as the people about whom he was writing.[71]

Woodsworth's sociology remained highly positivistic, his Christian moral absolutes undertheorized, and his sense of Canada enduringly Anglo-centric – he was no Bolshevik, and the label "revolutionary" will never fit comfortably on him. Yet what he gave the movement was a sense that the mastery of the sociological facts led inextricably to a realm of freedom, that a religious modernism could respect the traditions from which it descended without consenting to elitism and irrationalism, and that it was simply a matter of common sense that Christianity and the co-operative commonwealth were inextricably intertwined. Was it not a bit harder for people to believe that socialists were plotting to burn down their churches and murder their priests if Woodsworth was out there, backing up every one of his positions with a suitable gospel quotation? Like Salem Bland, William Irvine, and E.A. Partridge, he drew significantly from the deep wells of evolutionary theory – but he did not do so in the immediate postwar period to argue for a gentle, purely parliamentary path. Like most of the first formation, his eye was on the long-term, thorough-going, cosmic transformation of the social order.

Gertrude Richardson and the Transformation of Socialist Feminism

Brought to life in a remarkable work by Barbara Roberts, the career of Gertrude Richardson (1875–1946), a prominent member of the new generation of leftists of the 1910s, demonstrated striking parallels with that of Woodsworth. Nearing her forties when the Great War burst upon Canadian leftists, Richardson brought with her a background rich in struggle – for freedom of thought, for pacifism, and for women's suffrage. Under the pressure of anti-war activism her work came to encompass a more general critique of capitalist society. As a middle-class radical and feminist she experienced the Great War, that festival of patriotic unreason, as a devastating blow, and the heightened gender essentialism of the war years played a large part in this experience.

Much of the Great War was constructed and understood as a vast demonstration of gender ideals. In the emergent myth of Canada as described by Jonathan Vance, women were constructed as the bereaved "mothers of the race," and men as its valiant, fearless warriors. When the men died, they became "the Fallen," and they were redescribed through high diction as Christ-like figures animated primarily by the highest ideals of Christianity and nationhood.

Yet many men returned from the war embittered about Britain, disgusted by wartime profiteering, angry at those who had not shared their hardships, and (in many cases) psychologically traumatized by their experiences at the front. Although Vance makes some allowance for dissident voices in the 1930s, he rather overlooks those who even as the myth was being articulated were fiercely critical of its elitist bias, including Will R. Bird, whose war memoirs have given him a posthumous reputation as one of Canada's most perceptive war writers.[72] McKay, although in some books a war hero, summed up his experiences with a daring satire on "In Flanders Fields":

> In Flanders' fields the poppies droop,
> And dead men rising, troop on troop,
> Go stumbling thro' the dismal rain;
> Grim, mangled horrors, mad with pain
> And angry that they cannot sleep,
> In Flanders' fields.[73]

In this left version of the myth of Canada, the ordinary Canadian soldier had "fallen" so that the rich and privileged – the corrupt landlords, the price-gouging munitions manufacturers, the parasitical purveyors of rotten pota-toes, lame horses, and defective boots – might "rise." In the interwar years the turbulent disaffection of thousands of returned soldiers, many of whom looked with jaundiced eyes upon the political and social order that they had sacrificed so much to defend, contributed to another way of thinking about the country they lived in.

Both right and left versions of the myth of Canada could be articulated in ways that responded to the veterans' perceptions. The right could play on hos-tility towards foreigners, imperial patriotism, the irrationalist cult of blood and soil, the masculine honour of the soldier. Yet for its part the left could ad-dress the veterans' sense of alienation from state authorities, the profiteers who had cleaned up in their absence, and their new demands for work and wages. Early in this propaganda struggle, it became clear to the right that the returned soldiers would be a decisive group in the shaping of the Red Scare. Under the headline, "An Eloquent Testimony to Loyalty and Patriotism of Home-Coming Troops, That They Are Willing to Help Suppress Anything Like Attempted Revolution," the Halifax *Herald* saluted a Great War Veterans' manifesto: "We have borne with very creditable patience many irritating delays, and a long list of exasperating scandals. We have our share of private and public feuds and a full measure of repatriation difficulties, but our first duty, as veterans with a proud record of service behind us, is to Canada and her interests." The veterans proclaimed their determination to rid Canada "of the foul brood who preach and teach anarchy" and to guard Canada against the "invasion" and "devastation" planned by the followers of Lenin and Trot-sky. The *Herald* did not linger on the same veterans' sharp critique of the "profiteer who encourages revolution," but, turning a worried eye upon the returned men as a potential source of revolutionary agitation, the paper perceptively observed that the alternatives were clear: thoroughgoing reform or complete social revolution. "Delay in dealing with the 'new order' now de-manded may easily bring about revolution by force." The most uncertain link in the "infamous chain" that the radicals were forging was "the attitude of the returned men. Every effort is being centred on winning them over to the 'cause.' "[74]

As Heron and Siemiatycki note, "By the end of 1917 returning soldiers had become the loudest and most belligerent critics of the employment of 'in-terlopers' and 'enemy aliens,' terms applied loosely to Europeans of many dif-ferent backgrounds. . . . Early in 1919 there were violent assaults on eastern European immigrants in Calgary, Drumheller, Winnipeg, Port Arthur, Sud-bury, and Halifax. Employers also felt the wrath of the workers, who de-manded that the 'enemy aliens' be fired."[75] For the left the issue was particularly dangerous. If the soldiers could be talked into smashing up left meetings and attacking ethnic radicals, they would destroy much of what the movement had achieved through the Great War. In Francis Marion Beynon's *Aleta Dey*, the returned soldier, ultimately responsible for killing off the book's protagonist, figures as the embodiment of an out of control masculinity.

Gertrude Richardson experienced in activism much of the turmoil that Beynon described in her fiction. Born into a working-class family in Leicester, England, Richardson came with her sister to Canada in 1911 to join her home-steading brother Fred, who had settled near Swan River, a small community about 800 kilometres northwest of Winnipeg. She carried a century's worth of Leicester radicalism, secularism, and feminism with her to Canada, and throughout the war years she stayed in close contact with that city's immensely creative left. In Canada Richardson became the hub first of a network of women and men fighting for suffrage and then of one fighting for peace and socialism.

Richardson lived in northern rural Manitoba, and never ran in municipal, provincial, or federal elections, organized a strike, or built a trade union. Yet she also lived in a North Atlantic world of activism and debate. She wrote weekly columns for the socialist *Leicester Pioneer* and the *Midland Free Press*. Like so many in her cohort, and arguably in an even more sustained way, she had an outlook shaped by religion. She moved from Baptist evangelicalism to Unitarianism to the Leicester Secular Society, whose star, F.J. Gould, looms large in the history of free thought in the North Atlantic world; his "Church of Humanity" would prefigure the religious innovations of postwar Manitoba. Her vigorously unorthodox Christianity added a new dimension to reasoning otherwise, allowing her to go beyond a "narrow rationalism" to a kind of "moral ferocity" inspired by the figure of a Jesus awful in the terrible wrath he "poured forth on all oppressors."[76]

Richardson's take on feminism was (for her) exemplified by C.K. Ogden and Mary Sargant Florence's widely read *Militarism versus Feminism: An En-quiry and a Policy Demonstrating that Militarism Involves the Subjection of Women* (1915). Ogden was a maverick Cambridge freethinker and professor, Florence a prominent British artist and militant; and their work brought to Canadian feminists a highly theorized justification for feminist opposition to the war. It was the "practised eye" of Spencer, said Ogden and Florence, that had in 1876 detected, in the first volume of his *Sociology*, how militarism was reviving in Britain. Spencer had also revealed the "superior position of women amongst such peoples as are not addicted to war." The great lesson of Spencer, the text declared, was that international hostilities were "the most dangerous enemy of emancipation with which women have to struggle."[77]

Closely following Olive Schreiner, Richardson initially placed the war within a maternal feminist perspective. The war was the creation of men. "No woman has been consulted as to the provisioning and clothing of the troops, though in their thousands they are working on their comfort, and toiling to relieve the distress caused by the paralyzing of ordinary life and work, as well as all the other havoc caused by the carnage and horror."[78] Yet this was a version of Schreiner with an emphatically anti-capitalist overtone. Women with "mother-hearts" should understand that "this war was arranged and is dominated by the blood-stained Capitalists of the world, not by any means of one nation only."[79] She would remark in 1916: "Surely there was never a time when the maleness (if I may use the word) of the world-systems was more apparent than this. . . . From Houses of Legislature, from pulpit, from platform, rostrum, and Press of every land, thunder forth to-day the gospel of dominance, of righteousness of force, the holiness of compulsion. Progress and retrogression go hand in hand."[80]

In Richardson's anti-war activism – which fused rationalism, feminism, and social-evolutionary theory – socialist women comprised a progressive vanguard fighting against a masculinist retrogression to barbarism. "Do not let us content ourselves, dear women, with merely caring for the physical needs of our dear brave soldiers," she wrote in 1915. "Let us work for a reconstructed world, where war, with all its attendant horrors shall never more find place, the new world of brotherhood, the kingdom of God on earth."[81] These "mothers" of the nation were not visualized as sock-knitters but as militant activists, rising up (as Schreiner had predicted) in wrath against men who would destroy the children they had laboured so hard to bring into the world.

Still, even amidst the atmosphere of the Great War, when so many women were called upon to serve as symbolic mothers – knitting socks, shaming pacifists in "White Feather" campaigns, sustaining the fighting men through work in canteens and in fundraising campaigns – socialist feminists in rural Manitoba and around the world came to see their anti-war struggle not so much as one pitting "maternal love" against "paternal violence" but rather as the fight of both men and women against the emergence of "militant societies" that everywhere endangered the progress of all. By 1917, fired by the menace of conscription, inspired by the example of anti-militarist men, and discouraged by the example of pro-militarist women, Richardson had moved beyond a narrowly maternalist reading of women's enfranchisement and empowerment.

In this approach Richardson was part of a much bigger pattern. Helena Gutteridge, Rose Henderson, Becky Buhay, Francis Beynon, Alice Chown, and Laura Hughes constituted something of a "new generation" of socialist feminists in Canada, whose activism and thought were significantly more grounded in practical issues of struggle and activism than in the more abstract feminisms of an earlier period. Hughes and Chown in particular figured prominently in the anti-war struggle. Together, in the Women's Peace Crusade (fd. 1917) – the Canadian version of the Women's Peace Party, an organization initiated in the United States in January 1915 by social reformer Jane Addams – they mounted a courageous campaign for peace on the basis of a model for continuous mediation between the hostile parties designed by Julia Grace Wales, a Canadian teaching at the University of Wisconsin. The party, later called Women's International League for Peace and Freedom, marked a significant step in the crystallization not only of the peace movement but also of feminist political struggle. It "based its program for a new international order," according to historian Thomas P. Socknat, "on the reforms outlined at The Hague, including compulsory arbitration, universal disarmament, and the establishment of a league of democratic nations."[82]

Richardson brought significant feminist credentials to this struggle. Utterly convinced that "Woman has always been the equal of man," she was elected in 1914 to a third term as the Roaring River president of the Political Equality League and visited Winnipeg to meet with the key leaders of the suffrage movement. As Roberts remarks, her arrival in "the inner circle of feminist writers in Canada" was signalled by her invitation to become a regular contributor to *Woman's Century*, published by the National Council of Women of Canada.[83]

Women activists now found in the unyielding "impossibilist" language of peace a way of articulating a new dialect of socialist feminism to other forms of struggle. Richardson's columns, some of which drew directly upon the horrible abuses suffered by her brother from right-wing vigilantes and prison authorities, were among the newspaper's most powerful. In Winnipeg, unevenly matched pro- and anti-war forces clashed. J.W. Dafoe, editor of the Winnipeg *Free Press*, long regarded as the very epitome of Prairie liberalism, worked tirelessly to discredit the anti-war campaign. The *Tribune* printed thinly disguised calls to violence against the left critics of the war. Attempts by the Anti-Conscription League to rent hall space were repeatedly frustrated, and its meetings disrupted. R.A. Rigg, secretary of the local trades and labour council, Fred Dixon, MLA, and City Councillor John Queen were among those threatened with violence.

In 1917, inspired by models in Britain, the United States, and Australia (where conscription had been defeated), Richardson launched the Women's Crusade. She urged women to consider two tactics. One was boycotting all jingoistic newspapers. The other was a more daring act of civil disobedience. Whenever a minister or priest abused his pulpit by preaching the gospel of war in the name of Christ, anti-war women should simply rise up and leave "as a protest against the blasphemy."[84] As Roberts suggests, Richardson's primary commitment was no longer to the "women's movement" narrowly defined, but to a more radical socialist-feminist anti-war crusade. Her affinity groups were increasingly made up of the Independent Labor, Social Democratic, and Socialist party activists who were mobilizing in Ontario and the West. In Ontario, anti-conscriptionist Laura Hughes became an important leader in the ILP. In Manitoba, Richardson turned to the Social Democratic Party, and after June 1917 she published regularly in its well-circulated flagship newspaper,

Canadian Forward, the Canadian left's most interesting paper in the period of the Great War. Indeed, in the pages of *Canadian Forward*, under Isaac Bainbridge's inspired editorship, an increasingly large and diversified movement – Quakers, French Canadians, socialists, labourites, left liberals – debated the vital issues of peace, war, and class.

In league with her women allies Richardson crafted the ringing 1917 manifesto of the Crusade. It was written against the cobalt night of a terrible time. "Mangled, torn, blinded, maddened, slain, are the victims of this inhuman strife. Europe is a vast charnel house, yet still the Molochs of War cry out: 'More men; more of the flower of earth's manhood,' and still the monster is insatiate," it declared.

> We, members of the Women's Crusade, believing that the men and women of all nations are the brotherhood and sisterhood of the great Family of Humanity, assert our opposition to all war, conscription and slavery. . . . We desire social and political purity, the world for the workers (to whom it belongs), the true religion, which is the fulfillment of the Golden Rule, the creation of a safe and happy world for the unborn.[85]

In the atmosphere of 1915–20, gender ideals were magnified in the now highly propagandistic state apparatus. Those who questioned the state found themselves increasingly demonized for stepping outside the norm. Shortly after the war ended the link between the woman's question and other forms of socialist activism epitomized by Richardson was also dramatized by the widespread attempts to demonize the Russian Revolution by a campaign against the Bolsheviks' supposed "nationalization of women," a far-fetched but effective propaganda campaign against the revolutionaries' struggle to achieve gender equality.[86] The sorry plight of Russian womanhood became a stock theme of anti-socialist propaganda for decades. Newspapers delivered chilling portraits of the "typical, short-haired, leather-jacketed women who are so numerous in the ranks of the Reds." They were "Utterly Devoid of Humanity."[87]

In those years what might have earlier seemed insuperable barriers – between spc-style scientific rationalism and Christian radicalism, or between the Marxist revolutionaries at *Canadian Forward* and socialist-feminist poets and pacifists – were lowered. In creative moments of fusion and resistance the war was seen, from these and other perspectives, as the epitome of a cruel and irrational political and social order. Richardson thus exemplified a wider movement on the socialist-feminist left. She showed how one activist, rooted principally in the woman question, could come to realize that the issue could only be addressed within a larger movement of movements. "She had abandoned the women's movement as the carrier of women's traditional values of peace and nurture to the world, lost her hope that when women got the vote, evil would beat a hasty retreat," Roberts notes. "Although she now pinned her hopes on the brotherhood and sisterhood of the new humanity, she had relied on the pacifist remnants of her years of suffrage sisterhood one more time, in reaching out through socialist circles for support for her Women's Peace Crusade." Her appeals were still pitched to "Sister Women," but – as suggested by the influence of *Militarism versus Feminism* – she now embraced a socialist-humanist ideal based on "preservative lore" rather than a "female universal" predicated on motherhood.[88]

Renovating the Race Question: Isaac Bainbridge and the Social Democrats

Isaac Bainbridge (1880–1932) became one of the most visible, and certainly most hounded, of the socialist critics of the war – and is one of the most significant of the many little-remembered figures of this formative era in the history of the Canadian left.[89] His story exemplifies the transformation of racial and ethnic politics under the repressive conditions of the Unionist government.

Bainbridge had played a heroic role in standing up to the Canadian state throughout the Great War. A British immigrant from Westmoreland County, and trained as a stonemason, he came to Canada in 1907, joining his brother John in Winnipeg. After experiencing numerous hardships he returned to England before coming back with his wife and two children to Canada in 1911. He finally settled down in Toronto. He was the first (and evidently only) editor of the monthly *Canadian Forward*, and became the dominion secretary of the Social Democratic Party – which, significantly, had grown to a membership of roughly 5,000 by 1918 and was seen by at least one commentator to be one of the most effective (and dangerous) of all the socialist movements.[90] He would later be represented as a moderate socialist, but his wartime writings and activism suggest otherwise. A letter of his surfaced in a Red Russian newspaper, *Krassnoya Znamys*, in Vladivostok, hailing the Revolution as a great moment in the history of freedom.[91]

Bainbridge was in good company: many radicals found fresh purpose and a new visibility in the revolutionary atmosphere of 1917–20. Anarchists, hitherto rather quietly sequestered in their ethnic enclaves, came forth with public declarations and manifestos. In 1920 *The Awakener* – "issued unperiodically by the Anarchist Groups of Canada" – thundered in its May Day issue against the lickspittle labour fakirs, treacherous socialists, and right-wing politicians. "Instead of participating in elections," it advised working-class Canadians, "start General Strikes, Uprisings and Revolutions!" They should remember that "The Destructive Spirit is Creative Spirit," and take inspiration from nature itself:

On the First of May nature Awakens, and everything in that sphere blossoms forth in full bloom. Why then, should we human beings – the toilers – be worse than the dumb trees and plants that start giving out their beautiful smells and fruits, or the birds who begin to sing their enchanting melodies?

Can not we be at least as wise as the animals and trees and once in our history, also begin to Awaken, and blossom forth by REVOLTING against the entire present society, until we replace it by the Anarchist Commune Society?[92]

The "Anarchistic Communists" proscribed by Canadian law were unrepentantly bringing their message to the country, and some authorities and editorialists were convinced this newly visible tendency, linked in their imagination with Lenin and the Bolsheviks, posed a palpable threat to law and order. Little could they realize that behind *The Awakener* was a small group of Yiddish-speaking anarchists, centred in the United States, or that all its articles were written by only one man, Romanian-born Marcus Green, writing under the pseudonyms of the anarchist martyrs of Chicago. And, after all, in this upside-down world, was it not possible that the "Soviet anarchist" revolutionaries might find an audience, even in Toronto?

The overthrow of the czarist "prison house of peoples" especially breathed a new revolutionary energy into the Finnish, Jewish, Ukrainian, and Russian leftists in Canada. The numerous and highly visible Finns caused special alarm. In a learned paper on "Socialistic Propaganda in Canada: Its Purposes, Results and Remedies" delivered to Montreal's St. James Literary Society in December 1918, C.H. Cahan, K.C., drew particular attention to the resurgence of the Finns within the SDPC, wherein Finnish children were being taught "to sing Bolshevist songs imported from Russia."[93] In Windsor on 5 July 1918, the police arrested Andrew Bobank, allegedly the co-conspirator of John Perchuda, and declared that they had uncovered evidence of "a continent-wide plot to overthrow lawful authority and establish a similar regime to that instituted in Russia by Trotzky and Lenine." Later on letters to the "Union of Russian Workmen" in Montreal and other Canadian cities were introduced into the court. In these documents local authorities were denounced as "parasites," and socialists were encouraged to fight against militarism. Bobank had incriminatingly signed off with "Yours for anarchism and communism," which, said the interpreter, was "the slogan of the official organ of a Russian group of anarchists in America." Books containing minutes of secret meetings held in a disused schoolhouse in Ford City (a section of Windsor) were entered as evidence. The upshot of the Windsor raids was a trial concluding on 17 December with fines totalling $2,750.02 imposed on 24 Russians. Some of the men had, when arrested, been carrying copies of *Free Daily Russia*, a Russian-language publication from Chicago. The prosecution alleged a booming business in cross-border sedition.[94]

A Toronto Bolshevik, Constantine Goshuik, received a three-year term in Kingston Penitentiary and a fine of $1,000 in the police court for the weighty offence of having objectionable printed matter upon his person, to wit the minutes of a meeting of the Social Revolutionary Society of Bolsheviks, held in the Occident Hall. The accused had lived in Toronto for five years and, as the organization's secretary, was not even really the author of the objectionable anti-capitalist words. Magistrate Kingsford believed none of the arguments made on Goshuik's behalf. In sentencing him to Kingston Penitentiary Kingsford brought up the wholly unrelated case of the murder of a British subject in Petrograd.[95] It seemed that Goshuik was being held personally responsible for events half a world away – but in 1918, such happenings were experienced as though they had occurred just next door.

There was also evidence in 1918 of a growing left mobilization linking Canadian centres. In Montreal in July 1918, one inflammatory circular in Yiddish, denouncing any attempt to crush the "freedom and self-ruling of the Russians," brought down the weight of the Dominion police upon the local Bolsheviks. A raid on a meeting at Prince Arthur Hall, said to have drawn an audience of 700 Russian and Jewish Socialists, who were to have heard addresses in both Yiddish and Russian, resulted in 14 arrests.[96] In October 1918 one of the "biggest onslaughts on organized Bolshevism in the City of Toronto" brought the police to the doors of the Russian Revolutionaries (552 Queen Street West), the Finnish Society (214 Adelaide), the Social Democratic Party (185½ Queen Street West), and the Chinese National League (105½ Queen Street West). The raids netted 44 members of the Chinese Nationalist League, 22 members of the Social Democratic Party of Canada, and others from hazily named groups denominated as the Democratic Party of North America, Russian Social Revolutionary Party, Ukrainian Socialist Party, and Finnish Socialist Society.

Bainbridge was among those arrested in the raids. Others included the proprietor of a Ukrainian bookstore on Queen Street; two leaders of the Russian Social Revolutionary Party; and the editor of an allegedly revolutionary Chinese newspaper. According to the newspaper report, the police seized "Much Booty" – that is, supposedly seditious literature.[97] After all the thrilling exposés of wild-eyed Bolsheviks and bomb-wielding militants, some dummy rifles used by the Chinese nationalist group for military drills provided the most concrete evidence of a supposedly vast left-wing armed conspiracy.

The political party most closely associated with this multicultural moment of the Canadian left was the Social Democratic Party of Canada. In mid-November 1918, "Secret Service Men" announced the discovery of "an extensive, well organized" Bolshevik propaganda machine, run "mostly among foreigners." It had made "startling progress" in the past year, as "certain anarchistic foreigners" had infiltrated the Social Democratic Party and "camouflaging their real purpose with a politico-economic platform, have been printing and circulating literature of the most seditious, criminal and revolutionary character," stated a report in the Halifax *Herald*. "Bolshevik printing presses in Toronto and Montreal have been seized." Despite the vigilance, no fewer than 18 branches of the SDP had been formed among the Russians, Finns, and Ukrainians. "In Winnipeg it was discovered that certain Russians and Finns had formed a regular Soviet committee." These were not merely socialist organizations; they constituted a "menace" that threatened "the very basis of Canada's social and political existence."[98]

What did so many revolutionaries see in the SDPC from 1916 to 1919? The party had a history of allowing autonomy to the national groups operating within it, as the powerful Ukrainian Social Democratic Party and the Finnish Socialist Organization of Canada demonstrated; for it to provide haven and leeway to Russian, Lettish, and other groups was in keeping with its tradition. Yet, just as important was the party's honourable record in the war. Through Bainbridge's *Canadian Forward*, from its first issue of 28 October 1916 to its last in 1918, the party announced an undeviating resistance to the war. As a spokesperson of the USDP remarked, "It can truly be said of the Social-Democrats of Winnipeg that we have led the way in condemnation of the war and in education of the working class as to its cause and folly."[99] It was a resolute statement, given the noxious climate of fear and intimidation that the government was generating around immigrants in general and the Ukrainians in particular. *Canadian Forward* became a place in which feminists, "foreign radicals," anti-conscription activists, disgruntled trade unionists, and ever-more-candid Marxists could voice their outrage at the war and develop a shared understanding of how to oppose both militarism and capitalism. Bainbridge's work as editor exemplified this common front against the war – and brought down upon his head the hammer of state repression.

On 18 April 1917 police raided the publication's offices at 363 Spadina, and Bainbridge was charged with seditious libel, to wit, the publication of an argument by Fenner Brockway of Britain's Independent Labour Party against conscription. Bainbridge had not only placed the article on the front page of the newspaper but had also circulated it independently as a pamphlet. He initially pleaded not guilty, but changed his plea and on 1 May 1917 was found guilty with a suspended sentence. He was out of court in enough time to address a May Day rally of over 1,000 people. With a characteristic sense of internationalism, he used the opportunity both to draw attention to his case and to launch a protest against the recent outlawing of trade unions in the West Indies.

He was rearrested on 12 September 1917, once again for the publication of certain materials in the *Canadian Forward*, this time "The Price We Pay," an anti-conscription tract by Irwin St. John Tucker, which the SDPC again distributed as a pamphlet.[100] Between the time of his second arrest and his trial on 22 November 1917, the Bolsheviks had come to power, and the earliest indications of the Red Scare were perceptible. In the interim, the Crown had changed the indictment against Bainbridge and added new materials, including entire issues of the *Canadian Forward* from 10 September and 24 July 1917. Of particular interest from the first issue were letters from Becky Buhay and Hazel Halliwell. Buhay's letter cried out: "If ever there was an earnest time in Canada that time is now! If ever the chances of propagating our principles were good, it is now!"[101] The jury found Bainbridge guilty on 22 November 1917, with a strong recommendation to mercy; instead, on 28 November, the judge gave him nine months at the Burwash prison farm. He was subsequently released after the Supreme Court of Ontario, on 1 March 1918, overturned his conviction on a technicality.

On 27 May 1918, Bainbridge appeared once again in the Assize Court, this time because he was taken to have violated his previously suspended sentence. He was sentenced to three months' imprisonment. Bainbridge found this spell of imprisonment particularly wearing, experiencing lice-ridden bed linen and filthy cells. After an extensive protest from the socialist and labour movement, he was released on 29 June, after a month and two days in jail.

In September 1918 two orders-in-council suppressed the foreign-language press and outlawed a series of left organizations, including the Ukrainian Social Democratic Party, Russian Social Democratic Party, and Finnish Social Democratic Party. Those found guilty of membership in such parties, or of possessing banned literature, could be fined as much as $5,000 and imprisoned for as long as five years. On 3 November 1918 the state followed up with a "divide and conquer" policy of lifting the ban on the SDPC in general, perhaps in response to the considerable support it received from the labour movement, but maintaining its list of SDPC affiliates and extending the blacklist to include the Finnish Social Democratic Party, Revolutionary Socialist Party of North America, and Ukrainian Revolutionary Group. The decision to ban non-religious meetings conducted in such "enemy languages" as Russian, Finnish, and Ukrainian, and restricting publications to the French and English languages, followed the same Machiavellian logic.

Early in October 1918 Chief Censor Chambers was able to have the *Canadian Forward* banned altogether. Even the simple possession of a copy of the *Forward* could be grounds for imprisonment under Order-in-Council 2384. Bainbridge was caught up once again in the series of police raids across Ontario on 20 October 1918. This time he received a suspended sentence. The Russians and Ukrainians were jailed.[102] In effect, the authorities in both Ottawa and Toronto had identified Bainbridge, the SDPC, and the *Canadian Forward* as extremely dangerous and had repeatedly used the legal system to impede their work.

To his sympathizers and even to those who merely cared about consistency in the application of the law, the persecution of Bainbridge was a prime example of the new authoritarianism and arbitrariness of the political order. Why imprison and harass Bainbridge, when Henri Bourassa, the notable French-Canadian nationalist, was saying many of the same things about conscription, and in a much more charged language? For that matter, if spreading revolutionary opposition to the war was a crime, why wasn't the editor of the *Mail and Empire* in jail for disseminating the work of Trotsky, couched in words far more revolutionary than anything in the *Canadian Forward*?

Although the precise reasoning behind all this effort to silence Bainbridge may never be known, the general case for it can be discerned in the comments of Cahan and Chambers. Bainbridge and the SDPC were important because they blurred the lines between "loyal citizens" and "aliens" that the state was trying to draw. So much could certainly be inferred from a fascinating piece of writing by Bainbridge on the race question in the *Canadian Forward* on 28 October 1916. Here the SDPC's dominion secretary put forth quite original ideas. His little-noticed article was one of the first attempts on the Canadian left to theorize race and ethnicity in a non-essentialist and non-racialist way. It was also one of the first efforts to conceptualize a multicultural Canada in terms dramatically different from those of imperial nationalism.

For Bainbridge, the "race problems" of Canada were "interlocked with the exigencies of capitalism" and called out for general, not local, solutions. "The Socialists of Canada," Bainbridge argued, "can point with no small measure of pride to the splendid organizations which embrace men and women from Finland to Bulgaria, from Scandinavia to Russia, from France to Austria, from Italy to Poland." The party's success in addressing Canada's "race problem" lay not in its "creed and hope of universal brotherhood," but in its analysis of "the economic aspect of society." Canada was, Bainbridge remarked, truly "cosmopolitan." It was a land in which "Teuton vies with Saxon and Anglo-Saxon, Mongolian with African, each of which contributes to this complex society their quota of human evolution tinged with divergent traditions, histories and religions." How this "heterogeneous mass" could be welded together was a problem that baffled "statesmen, politicians, religions, doctrinaires, and social reformers of every type."

The socialist, who "views this question in the same light as he views all other questions – the economic aspect," understood that national identities were not stable but fluctuating, as shown by the shifting alliances of peoples in Europe. "The history of the past hundred years goes clearly to show that racial antagonisms can change within a generation. It is not a deep-rooted, ineradicable part of our nature." At a time when professors, preachers, and editorialists were drumming into Canadians the idea that Germans and Britons were intrinsically opposed to each other, Bainbridge was observing that the differences between "the Saxon" and "the German" were "greatly outweighed by the community of likenesses." It was the members of the ruling class who, when it suited them, magnified the differences between such groups. The "racial instincts of the peoples" were historically a "lever used by the rulers."

Such ruling-class designs had the unintended effect of eroding each nationality's innate belief in its superiority. The pursuit of cheap labour had inadvertently created the possibility of a new universalism in Canada. The workers themselves would cast off the old particularist paraphernalia, "with all the grace of one who discards a worn-out ill-fitting garment, joyfully accepting the new vestment of human brotherhood and equality woven in days of bitter experience and ungrudging toil." Many of the "wonderful traits of character" seen in "the different races of mankind," Bainbridge argued, could be traced back to the age of barbarism. But now that barbarism was happily a thing of the past, socialists could envisage a time of mutual tolerance and co-existence: "Suppose we were to practice living with each other instead of living on each other! Could we not by the adoption of such a principle more readily hope to achieve that harmonious relation which is the consummation and desire of all intelligent human beings!"[103]

Not surprisingly, then, a liberal order under siege saw itself as being particularly threatened by Bainbridge and the SDPC. For here was essentially a Kautskyite position on race and ethnicity, a position acknowledging the depth and tenacity of such categories while also arguing that they were contingent, historically specific, and transcendent within a socialist movement. Apart from Krat's utopian vision of Vancouver in 2000, Bainbridge's argument was unusual in the Canadian socialist movement in the generosity and internationalism of its outlook – in identifying "racial" diversity as a positive aspect of modern life, and (despite the topical reference to the "melting pot" in its title) essentially sidelining any agenda for top-down cultural assimilation. In essence, it would be through class struggle that the various "races" would come to identify common objectives and overcome their long-standing prejudices against each other.

Bainbridge's analysis and activism occurred during an intense period in which the federal government had taken up the device of labour camps and made it an effective instrument of state formation. During the war about 8,000 "alien" prisoners were held in camps and stations across the country. As historian Bill Waiser points out, "the majority of the internees" – technically prisoners of war, and detained because of their supposed attachment to enemy powers – "were unemployed or destitute Ukrainians from Galicia and Bukovyna in the Austro-Hungarian Empire."[104] In other words, they were workers who had been drawn to North America by the prospect of jobs, and many of them were unlikely to have identified with the Austro-Hungarian Empire. Having massed in the cities and (in alliance with the SDPC) launching significant movements against unemployment – marching 2,000-strong in

Winnipeg in 1914, for instance – they represented a challenge for the ruling regime. Under the terms of the federal government's policy on alien registration and internment of 28 October 1914, those aliens living in urban centres were thus required to appear before a local registrar. As Waiser found, any aliens who "lacked 'the means to remain in Canada' were to be interned in work camps as prisoners of war." At the same time, the Dominion Parks Service, keen to make the parks of Banff, Jasper, Yoho, and Mount Revelstoke accessible to the automobile-driving public, was on the hunt for a source of cheap labour. Tourism promotion was thus combined with imperial patriotism: by using the prisoners as a source of coerced labour, the Canadian state met the demands of local nativists (some of whom wanted all the "aliens" rounded up, even those who were naturalized Canadians), park developers (who in the end benefited handsomely in new roads and other facilities), and local authorities (who feared the unemployed masses and the demands they might make on civic order and budgets). As Waiser remarks, "The real reason behind internment . . . had nothing to do with charity or relief. . . . The simple truth of the matter is that Ottawa was haunted by the spectre of public disorder and was determined to control the number of unemployed immigrants pouring into urban centres."[105]

Violating the rules of the 1907 Hague Convention on prisoners of war, the Canadian government saw internment as a chance to halt urban protests, punish supposed enemy aliens, *and* tap a source of cheap labour to achieve a nation-building project. The unintended consequence of state repression was a new sense of pride and identity among its victims. John Thompson observes that while before the war "peasant migrants from Galicia and Bukovyna had only a weakly-developed concept of themselves as Ukrainians," their "resentment of unilingual education, internment, and disenfranchisement aided a small nationalist intelligentsia to encourage a growing national self-consciousness," a movement heightened with the Ukrainian National Republic's unsuccessful bid for independence after 1917.[106]

The construction of the inspiringly picturesque – such as the motor road from Banff to Lake Louise – would thus be undertaken by the dispirited and the downtrodden. Those who had committed no crime were treated like traitors. They were forced into compulsory labour, working six-day weeks at 25 cents a day, a rate less than that of enlisted men and, Waiser notes, "far short – in some cases by as much as $1.00 – of what the workers had secured during the prewar boom years, even for the most distasteful jobs." As one prisoner wrote in 1915, "The conditions here are very poor, so that we cannot go on much longer, we are not getting enough to eat – we are hungry as dogs." Prisoners were punished (according to one Canadian general) by being "hung by the wrists" and, according to a description in the Ukrainian Social Democratic newspaper *Robochyi narod* of 28 October 1915, by being "mercilessly driven" at bayonet point, chained, and "fed bread and water for insubordination." They were poorly clothed: as one major lamented, "Some prisoners have boots with their soles half off . . . and nearly half of them are in rags." Strikes and escapes ensued, as did shootings of prisoners. In the closing years of the war the remaining internees – about 2,200 of them, mostly German by that time – were joined by 130 socialists. By the end of February 1920, according to Waiser, "Over 1,900 men and some 60 women and children had been deported."[107]

To create an inspiring emblem of modernity – a modern park system within easy reach of the flows of the tourism trade – the liberal state had resorted to the reinvention of serfdom, complete with starvation, torture, and shootings, all based on the imprisonment of people whose only apparent crime was to have been poor immigrant guest workers. At a time such as this, Bainbridge's socialist theorization of an enlightened stance towards cultural difference was profoundly courageous.

From Ottawa's perspective, what was undoubtedly far more alarming than Bainbridge's path-breaking outline of left multiculturalism was how this vision was being realized in practice. The SDPC was by design a multinational and multicultural party, a quilt of semi-autonomous parties united by their general pursuit of a socialist agenda – and after 1914 by their adamant rejection of the war, although there were probably still some patriots lurking, especially in the party's English-speaking sections. But the different members were not forced to submerge their identities as they pursued their shared objectives. (It is telling that Jewish Maurice Spector, to become Canada's most gifted Marxist theorist in the 1920s, was recruited to socialism by none other than Bainbridge.) In the 1910s Bainbridge was an exemplar of a new politics of race on the left – and the implementation of that politics called out for forcible suppression by the guardians of official order.

At no time were the horrific costs of chauvinism and prejudice more obvious than in the war years. Never before had the extraordinary divisiveness of such issues for labour and the left been more evident. Yet the left responded with creativity in the elaboration of new positions and organizations. The pattern of 1915–20 on the Canadian left was thus one of a "fusion of the refusals." Woodsworth, Richardson, and Bainbridge were quite dissimilar in the shape and substance of their radicalisms, but under the duress of war their anti-militarism led them into similar postures of resistance. From the social gospel, socialist feminism, and the SDPC's implicitly transnational radicalism would flow activists, models, and inspirations that would ultimately reshape much of the Canadian left.

Revolution and Reaction, 1917–20

In May 1918 the SPC's Vancouver offices were raided by police on the hunt for seditious literature. In August the censor warned the *B.C. Federationist* that its enthusiasm for Bolshevik writings had placed it in violation of the law. On 4 October the *Western Clarion* was banned. Following a cat and mouse strategy soon to be tried again in the Winnipeg General Strike, the socialists changed the publication's name to the *Red Flag* and then, when that was also banned, to the *Indicator*. Alas, such name changes did not fool the state: once publications were denied access to the mails, their readerships were greatly reduced.

Yet if the government intended to quell the sense of revolutionary enthusiasm that was abroad, it signally failed to do so. Even the SPC, not known for its warm-hearted approach to left-wingers who did not completely subscribe to its platform, sent a letter of congratulations to the Central Committee Council of Workmen's and Soldiers' Delegates, Petrograd, expressing its pleasure that the committee had decided to adhere to the classic teachings of Marx. The SPC even added, reassuringly, "We have yet to notice an error of tactics or a violation of revolutionary working class principles."[108] In Vancouver, a keen leftist could spend many nights of the week at large left-wing meetings in the downtown halls, listening to such increasingly famous speakers as Pritchard, Woodsworth, and W.W. Lefeaux.

Socialists had long maintained that revolution was simply a moment in an evolutionary process. The Russian Revolution was no different. "The class struggle is a war inherent in the capitalist system due to the fact that the capital class live by robbing the working class. This class struggle is a process and passes through evolutionary developments as everything else within this universe," explained an article in the *B.C. Federationist*. "The class struggle reaches its final phase of development in what is called a revolution. The revolutionary period is determined by the total impossibility of further property relations existing alongside of the productive forces of a given society. The revolution breaks [out]. The war of the contending classes comes clear to the surface."[109] The *Canadian Forward* viewed the Bolshevik Revolution as "the first of a series of social revolutions (not necessarily violent) that will transform the present chaos into world peace and order based on international brotherhood and economic liberty."[110] Figures of speech suggested that the Revolution was something like a mighty, natural event, such as a tidal wave or an earthquake. The Winnipeg *Voice* indicated that it showed "socialism is coming upon us at a breakneck speed, and the gates of the capitalist hell cannot prevail against its mighty surge." Its successor, the *Western Labor News*, argued that the Russian revolutionaries were "evolving a civilization that must finally be accepted as the guiding star of the world's destiny." It was, said another labour paper in Vancouver, "the approach of Freedom's dawn," and "the complete negation of all that exists under this civilization."[111]

The *Soviet*, published by the Edmonton SPC, reported on 18 April 1919 that twice in recent days Toronto had "awakened to find its doorsteps decorated with printed four-page messages addressed to soldiers and workers, explaining the principles of Bolshevism and calling upon the population to rise and throw off the shackles of capitalism." Tens of thousands of the circulars were said to have been distributed. Toronto, the newspaper reported with some satisfaction, "is nervous."[112] On 30 April 1919 Communist Party of Canada leaflets appeared in mailboxes in Toronto, Hamilton, Brantford, and St. Catharines. This underground organization put forward a seven-point program, starting off modestly with the "forcible seizure of the governmental power and the establishment of the dictatorship of the proletariat," in the interests of a society that would be run "in the interest of the worker alone."[113]

The more conventionally electoral left was also mobilized. Even in Quebec, where the Catholic Church and Gustave Francq were mounting strenuous campaigns against the Bolshevik menace, a highly energetic Montreal SDPC and the Quebec section of the Labor Party were sparkplugs in a general mass mobilization. The Montreal Labor Party endorsed the OBU, which enjoyed some local successes, and when he ran for civic office in 1918 Michael Buhay won some 38 per cent of the vote in a ward located in the heart of the Jewish garment district. In 1919 May Day was again greeted by a large crowd, this time of some 3,000 people, marching down Ste-Catherine Street.[114]

The most surprising of all the victories came in Ontario. In 1918 and 1919 Toronto seemed, in some experienced eyes, to be as explosive as anywhere. In autumn 1919 workers and farmers, in the form of the United Farmers of Ontario, were swept to power in the provincial legislature, placing the province, as James Naylor suggests, "in the vanguard of labour electoral action." The victory represented a remarkable transition over the space of just three years, from marginality to power – one that recalled the turn of the century transition in the B.C. left. The Independent Labor Party claimed 78 branches in the province and was powerful in the unions. It mounted an ambitious cultural program, including "monster picnics," one of them drawing as many as 2,500 people, and educational and literary evenings and lectures by famous foreign socialists. ILPers were not, says Naylor, merely "reformists." As he explains, "The Independent Labor Party presented itself not as a mere party of reform, but as the party of a new, reconstructed social order." ILP stickers declared, "Every Vote for Labor is a Vote for Democracy."[115]

Yet, as the SPC learned in British Columbia, and other farmer-labour organizations were forced to grasp in Nova Scotia and New Brunswick, entering into the conventional political world posed the risk of serious compromise. Just over two years old, the ILP received 124,654 votes in the 20 October 1919 Ontario provincial election, which translated into 11 seats – an unprecedented level of popular support for a left-wing party in Canada. It joined the 45 elected members of the United Farmers of Ontario to form a coalition government. But with their minimal program, relying on an alliance with a farmers' party that had only the barest understanding of or sympathy with working-class positions, and captive to parliamentary processes and political personalities over which they could exert little control, socialists within the ILP found themselves without much room to manoeuvre. As Naylor concludes: "Labourism's uncritical acceptance of parliamentary institutions was very much its hallmark. Indeed, the ILP considered its task to be the defence of these institutions against the profiteers and patronage machines. As a result, the party remained blind to the individualist premises of the political system."[116] It was slowly digested by the very system that it had sworn to contest.

The war destroyed and divided, but it also created and consolidated. New "fused" forms of struggle had emerged from the institutions and the militants that the authoritarian liberals tried so brutally to repress from 1915 to 1920. Bolshevism was on everybody's lips, as an indication that they were alive to the revolutionary spirit of the day. Many Canadian leftists said that the Revolution had recharged the batteries of the left. After the years of repression and persecution, it gave them a renewed sense that history might be on their side after all. And, for once, society's rulers were listening to what workers had to say with a new respect.

"Bolshevism," said the *Red Flag*, was not the same in Canada as in Russia. It was really "a spirit of revolt against high-handed action and merciless exploitation. That 'Bolshevism' is growing rapidly. It is perhaps . . . safe to say all labor men and a great many more are Bolshevists." Even SPC sceptics who thought the Russian Revolution premature also considered it invaluable. Even if they had considered the collapse of capitalism inevitable and the achievement of socialism the logical outcome, socialists were, before the Revolution, haunted by the sense that the success of their project was "considered vague and was a matter of speculation," mused a writer in the *Red Flag* in June 1919. "Although Socialism is not the system of society in Russia, the workers have gained control, and control through the form of organization, namely, the Soviet. The success of the Russian workers has certainly acted as a stimulus to Socialists the world over."[117] In 1918 and 1919, many leftists saw Lenin as a great democratic liberator, and his revolution as a turning point for all of humankind. Speeches on the Russian Revolution and the Canadian state's campaign of repression often reminded listeners of the left's historic mission to uphold the values of the Enlightenment.[118]

As one writer in the *B.C. Federationist* explained, the Russian Revolution demonstrated that mastery of certain laws had put both "master" and his "fellow worker" in a different position. Before the Revolution, both master and wage slave were the unwitting victims of their own ignorance of "the laws of production, distribution and exchange." But now "my class has found out those laws and they propose to establish a new order of things that will tend to keep society living in harmony with those universal laws instead of, as in the past, living in opposition to them." There was shining in Europe "a beacon light showing the road to Freedom." As Woodsworth exclaimed in Vancouver before one of many overflow crowds soaking up the revolutionary message, "Ignorance and indifference were the pillars of the present system, and they must expound the truth till people see it. After all, it was not the message of a party or an organization, it was the message of a new day for all workers." That message, for Woodsworth as for the SPCers, was that "exploiters were doomed to be overthrown."[119]

For a time the Russian Revolution became a unifying symbol of all that the first formation leftists had traditionally hoped to achieve. W.A. Pritchard made the case for the Revolution as an experiment in democracy. Speaking in Vancouver's Empress Theatre in February 1919, according to one report, he "based his argument on the concrete achievements of Bolshevism in Russia, 'open diplomacy,' 'restoration of the land,' education, and the fact that they have remained in power up till now through the expressed will of the majority of the people." At its Winnipeg convention in March 1918, the Social Democratic Party of Manitoba not only voted its support for the overthrow of the capitalist class in Russia, but also called for unity with the Socialist Party of Canada on the basis of the "Bolsheviki programme." In Montreal in December 1918, the Quebec section of the Labor Party at its second annual convention – with 175 delegates "representing, they claimed, 16,000 organized workers, some Socialist societies, the People's Power League and various labor clubs" – carried by a "big majority" a resolution demanding that the federal government release political prisoners and lift the ban on the socialist press. The *Mail and Empire* reported, "Resolutions praising the efforts of the Soviets and sending greetings to the Soviet Government of Russia and the revolutionaries in Germany, were passed by a large majority."[120]

In later years Crown attorneys and some historians would paint as dramatic exceptions the meetings in Winnipeg that had been suffused by the same revolutionary atmosphere. They seized on this comment and that gesture as evidence of criminal conspiracy. Yet a revolutionary spirit was on display very generally throughout urban Canada in 1918 and 1919. Diligent investigators could have multiplied by a thousand the damningly "revolutionary" quotations that were flourished in the show trials after the Winnipeg strike. For example, even though his electioneering materials now downplayed his socialist ties, James Simpson found it necessary to adapt to the pro-Bolshevism of his left audiences. He aroused much enthusiasm from a huge audience at the Monument Nationale in Montreal by declaring his fervent support for Lenin and Trotsky and stating that he would rather participate in a Bolshevik government that had nationalized banking institutions than be part of a British House of Commons that allowed aristocrats to retain their big estates while the people stood in lines to obtain meagre quantities of food.[121]

Still, for Canadian leftists, even the pro-Bolsheviks, the implications of the new model had yet to be fully assimilated. Sometimes leftists conceded that there was much in the Russian situation that could not be grasped by old models. "Russian Bolshevism, Tyranny or Freedom?" asked Bessie Beatty in a reprinted article in the *B.C. Federationist*, and she concluded: "The most essential thing in understanding the Russian situation is a realization that it cannot be judged by any of the old measuring sticks. We have here an experiment in government which has never before been made in the story of the race." In the United States, Louis Fraina, a prominent revolutionary theorist, argued that in "the proletarian revolution in action" there could be no compromise between, on the one side, "moderate Socialism," with its "petty bourgeois ideology," its "compromising tactics and opportunism," its avoidance of "the real industrial struggle" and rejection of "mass action," and its illusions about great change happening through the mechanisms of "the bourgeois parliamentary state," and, on the other, a revolutionary socialism that rallied to the cause of the overthrow of the bourgeoisie worldwide. In Canada, Vancouver's Jack Kavanagh strongly agreed. A certain kind of socialist "evolutionist" would have to go because "each system must kill the ideology of the preceding."[122] The argument was a foreshadowing of the fundamental struggles that would ensue on the left, particularly after 1920.

There was a tremendous yearning, in a suddenly enlarged and vigorous left, for practical engagement with the world. Leftists had learned from their opponents that the mere exposure of the evils of capitalism was insufficient. As Peter Campbell puts it so tellingly, in a comment on Pritchard: "The problem was that exposing the hypocrisies and brutalities of the capitalist class did not lead in a straight line, or even circuitously, to worker organization and the eventual creation of a socialist society."[123] Reasoning otherwise and hastening the actual ability to live otherwise were related but separate projects in much of first formation socialism. The Great War pushed them much closer together. Many leftists waited impatiently for their complete integration.

Winnipeg 1919: The Revolutionary Practice of the People's Enlightenment

For some political activists, that moment of an inspiring socialist fusion arrived in Winnipeg in 1919. From 25 May to 25 June 1919, workers and their supporters took control of Canada's third-largest city. The images of this event, of the Winnipeg General Sympathetic Strike, as it was initially known, are burned into historical memory: the nattily dressed crowds crowding Victoria (or "Liberty") Park; the placard "Permitted by Authority of Strike Committee" displayed on bread and milk wagons; the thundering charge of the Mounties and special police down Main Street on Saturday, 21 June ("Bloody Saturday"), the horses a blur of violence, a crumpled body on the sidewalk; a lone overturned, burning trolley; phalanxes of club-wielding "special deputies"; machine-gun-laden cars careening around corners.[124]

The Winnipeg Revolt began in earnest on 15 May 1919, when between 25,000 and 30,000 workers answered a call from the Winnipeg Trades and Labor Council to support workers in the building and metal trades in their struggle for the principle of collective bargaining, better wages, and improved working conditions. The following two weeks were marked by an uncanny calm. A Central Strike Committee, made up of delegates elected from unions affiliated with the Council, bargained with employers and co-ordinated the provision of such essential services as bread and milk deliveries. In stifling heat, workers often met at Victoria Park, under the auspices of the Labour Church.

Pitted against the strikers was the Citizens' Committee of 1000 – the descendant of an earlier Committee of 100 – which grouped together some of the city's important middle-class professionals and businessmen. They portrayed the strike as a Bolshevik uprising. This view of reality was constructed in the Winnipeg *Citizen* and sustained to a considerable degree by the state, especially in the actions of the municipal, provincial, and federal governments. The strikers, for their part, argued that they were only trying to win collective bargaining rights, a living wage, and an assurance of reinstatement in their jobs. This alternative view was presented in the *Western Labor News*, "Special Strike Bulletin," which explicitly renounced "1. Revolution. 2. Dictatorship. 3. Disorder,"[125] and in countless speeches and demonstrations in Winnipeg and throughout the country. Uneasily positioned between these two emergent poles of opinion were the hundreds of soldiers newly released from the Great War, who in the spring and summer of 1919 were still returning from overseas and might be recruited for one side or the other. Historian Chad Reimer points out: "Their political sympathies were less clear than the strike leaders claimed. The veterans were both men of order, 'comrades' within the community, and men of action, agents of violence and disorder. They could do battle against 'foreigners' and forces of the Left, or join with them against the police."[126]

In the major disturbance on "Bloody Saturday," sparked by the veterans' announcement that they would hold a mass silent protest, twenty-four civilians and six Mounties were injured, and one protester was shot and killed. Shortly afterwards the strike was concluded without achieving any of its declared objectives. Many of those leftists and workers held responsible for it were arrested and tried. Some of them received penitentiary time after trials held later in 1919 and in 1920. Just what happened in Winnipeg 1919 has been hotly debated ever since: whether it was an apprehended revolution (the point of view particularly of those who were critical of the strike, especially those involved in its forcible suppression); or whether it was simply a matter of sincere if naive strikers peacefully attempting to achieve limited objectives.[127]

Was it a "Children's Crusade" – with the strikers and their leaders chasing revolutionary rainbows when they should have been going after real things like better wages and secure unions? That was certainly among the first of the bourgeois responses to the strike. After all, in his commission's *Report* on the strike Judge H.A. Robson decided that in it gullible people had been led astray by "turbulent persons." In the eyes of the Winnipeg *Telegram* of 28 June 1919, perhaps 90 per cent of the strikers deserved to be treated as naughty children, "misled, deceived and stampeded by windy oratory" – rather like a flock of bleating sheep in a thunderstorm, perhaps. Some had been "cruelly intimidated" into acting in ways "detrimental to their interests and abhorrent to their sentiments." If they were truly repentant, these souls could be welcomed back into the liberal fold: "Let us treat those misguided strikers as if they were bad boys and girls returning repentant to the discipline of our laws and institutions." As for the people who had misled them, "They should be permanently black-listed. They should be made to wander abroad. . . . This will be simple justice."[128]

Or was the strike, perhaps not so simply, a revolt of Westerners against Easterners, with the West, as David Bercuson (writing with Kenneth Mc-Naught) argues, being *literally held in subjugation* by the traditional, conservative leadership of the Trades and Labour Congress of Canada and the American head offices of international labour organizations"? The theory is that these subjugated Westerners, forced by their small numbers, poverty, and isolation to "succumb to policies forged by others to suit very different conditions," finally rose up in revolt, both against their employers and against the Eastern labour bosses.[129] Yet another theory would posit that it was a *regional manifestation* of a much broader Dominion-wide and international labour revolt, with Winnipeg as the "storm centre" of a vast Canada-wide storm, which was itself connected to the turbulent international weather system.[130] Indeed, there was undoubtedly something unusual about Winnipeg in 1919 that allowed it to become, for a time, the epicentre of left revolt in Canada, much as Cape Breton would be a storm centre in the 1920s, and Toronto and Montreal in the 1960s.

In the end, though, as the available evidence shows, Western workers did not rise up angrily either as children on a crusade or essentially *as Westerners* to demand the resolution of slights and injuries inflicted upon all the people of their region by people in the rest of Canada. The resolution that got the One Big Union rolling in Calgary, after all, was not "Do you agree to throw off your subjugation by the Eastern bastards and rise up as a proud Western worker against the effete labour bureaucrats of Ontario?" or some such. Rather, it was: "Are you in favour of scientifically reorganizing the workers of Canada upon the basis of industrial organization instead of craft unionism?"[131] Many workers across the country liked the idea of "scientifically reorganizing" themselves. In Montreal and Toronto, for instance, a good number of the members of the British-based Amalgamated Society of Engineers, at that moment withdrawing from North America, embraced the OBU concept with enthusiasm. Although the regional pattern of pro-OBU voting is not clear-cut, neither were the ultimate bases of support for the new labour centre – which was at times Manitoba-based, at other times disproportionately popular in Northern Ontario, and at yet others heavily invested in recruiting the miners of the Maritimes.

Historians have praised Judge Robson's report for its wise objectivity, whereas the strikers have been marked down for the "emotional tone of their appeal" and the "primitive and narrow evidence they supported to support their case."[132] Yet in *"Saving the World from Democracy,"* their own history of these events, based in part on the reporting of the *Western Labor News*, the strikers provided both a wry and detailed account that blended in evidence from hostile anti-strike sources, reprinted primary documents, and created a richly textured, multi-perspectival view of the event – an unusual achievement given that, as Norman Penner points out, much of the book consisted of material written or published during or soon after the strike and before the official strike trials were concluded in April 1920.[133] That the Winnipeg leftists were sufficiently organized and committed to bring out this pioneering work of labour history at all – possibly the first major book-length statement about Canada from socialists in Canada[134] – is significant in itself.

The tone of patronage and forbearance in discussion of the event was enshrined in the motif of the Children's Crusade. In this liberal interpretation, Winnipeg 1919 was a *Crusade* because of the unbridled passion and religiosity of many of its participants – and, more profoundly, because the Winnipeggers were acting in a particularly untimely way, bringing up ancient forms that pertained to a superseded era of society. They were fired by "a sense of holy mission" incongruous in a modern 20th-century society.[135] It was a *Crusade* because, like its prototype in 1212, it was bizarre, unaccountable, outside the norms of church and state, a grassroots happening – in fact, not a *proper* (Church-authorized) exercise at all. It was a moment of Spring Madness, happily short-lived and put to rest, thanks to the wise and temperate measures of the liberal authorities and conscientious capitalists.

Perhaps for some commentators the most unsettling anomaly of Winnipeg was that the workers seemed able, for a time, to take over and run a major Canadian city. The Strike Committee, in the words of McNaught and Bercuson, was "assuming functions which tended to make it the *ad hoc* government of Winnipeg." Winnipeg became the site of mass teach-ins on economics, spirituality, and the science of social evolution. As Bercuson perceptively remarks, "Once the workers began to assume a partial administrative responsibility for the maintenance of water, heat, light, power, and food distribution, their position in society was radically altered and their power greatly enhanced. They were now as important to the everyday directing of society as was capital and they began to rival capital's power to exert leverage on the government."[136] The city became a temporary autonomous zone. Winnipeg 1919 was only in part a strike over concrete demands. Most radically, Winnipeg 1919 might better be described as a "revolt" than as a "strike." What was most extraordinary about Winnipeg 1919 was how the events functioned as a prism that captured, intensified, and (to a certain extent) integrated long-standing debates about class, religion, gender, race, democracy, and the people's enlightenment.[137] In particular, the concept of the One Big Union, an idea inextricably interwoven with Winnipeg, was not simply an attempt to regularize "collective bargaining" as a normal routine of capitalism, but rather an experiment in living otherwise, a model of a "war of position" wherein workers would wrest ever-increasing amounts of economic and cultural power from their rulers: a working-class revolution taking place through the logic of social evolution.

Winnipeg 1919, although undoubtedly sparked and enriched by labour struggles, cannot be reduced to them. Many, perhaps most, of the visible participants in Winnipeg 1919 were not employees, and a large number of the events associated with this moment cannot be read simply as direct responses to bread and butter trade union issues. Winnipeg 1919 was also, and for some participants primarily, about *other things*: about the construction of a new form of Christianity, or the achievement of women's equality, or the rights and privileges of Britons. In Winnipeg 1919 were interwoven the key questions of the first formation, all raised to a higher power, debated with a greater intensity and brought together in new and potent ways. Winnipeg represented an imminent fusion of moments of supersedure, as the customs and questions particular to one historic community of the left were functionally integrated with those of another. In this it was akin to a more recent event: Paris 1968 was in part, but only in part, about student fees and workers' wage rates. Winnipeg 1919 was in part, but only in part, about structures of collective bargaining and the cost of living.

Certainly the events of Winnipeg 1919 were shaped by the underlying realities of class and power in the city. Class divisions grounded in economic life were written into the city's social geography. "The social elite, mainly Anglo-Saxon and Protestant," writes Bercuson, "gathered themselves in certain well-defined bastions of affluence: Armstrong's Point, Wellington Crescent, and River Heights. The working population, laced with new immigrants, lived in parts of Fort Rouge, northwest Winnipeg, and the 'north end.'"[138] These "two Winnipegs," with their separate "headquarters," encountered each other in 1919. On one side, according to McNaught and Bercuson's description, were the "grubby quarters of the Labour Temple," the "small front parlours or kitchens of north-end houses," or the "coffee-stained tables of inexpensive cafés." On the other were the comfortable quarters of the Industrial Bureau, "the officers' mess of Osborne barracks, the Board of Trade building, or the sumptuous Manitoba Club." In these more refined settings, the self-proclaimed "citizens" exchanged confidences with "the mayor, the premier, the city police and RNWMP [Royal North-West Mounted Police] commanders, the principal judges, and visiting ministers from Ottawa."[139]

The city had long been important to Canadian leftists. Arthur W. Puttee had carried the seat federally as the first "Labour" MP in 1900 (although preserving substantial ties, as was the custom of the day, with the Liberal Party). The socialist left had been active in Winnipeg at least since 1894. Henry Ashplant, the SLP dynamo from London, had visited the city in 1895. James Cameron of the CSL had organized in the city in 1902. On arriving in Winnipeg in 1904, Jacob Penner, later a legendary figure in the city's Communist movement, searched in vain for fellow socialists until, finally learning of Vancouver's *Western Clarion*, he organized a meeting of some seven or eight SPCers and in 1906 helped organized the Winnipeg branch with about 50 members.[140] Throughout much of this period, the *Voice* was one of the best left and labour papers in the country, with columns representing perspectives ranging from anarchism to liberalism. By 1914 the Winnipeg left – now having swung fairly strongly over to the SDPC, to the point that the city's SPC local temporarily passed out of existence – had succeeded in sending one Social Democratic member (Dick Rigg) and a single taxer (Fred Dixon) to the provincial legislature.

Every tendency found elsewhere in Canada, from the CSL to the Independent Labor Party to the SDP, had its moment in Winnipeg. At times the factional warfare was fevered. There were fierce words when the Socialist Party of Canada played the "spoiler" role and robbed Dixon of a seat that he would otherwise have carried for labour in 1910, and equally harsh words between SDPC "splitters" and continuing "SPCers" when the former moved in numbers away from the latter's party. The Jewish left contained anarchist, Labour Zionist, and social-democratic factions. From 1916 to 1918 Winnipeg leftists mounted one of the country's most effective campaigns against conscription. As early as July 1917, J.M. Bumsted points out, the commanding officer of Military District 10, which included Winnipeg, identified men such as Rigg, Dixon, John Queen, A.A. Heaps, and George Armstrong as candidates for prosecution under the War Measures Act.[141] Yet such old leftists and their quarrels were fused in the atmosphere of 1919 with new leftists and new energies. There was something about Winnipeg 1919 that allowed for the development of a left that combined a striking heterogeneity of forms with a striking unanimity of purpose.

One, rather paradoxical, element in Winnipeg as the emergent epicentre of the postwar revolt was the city's massive immigrant community. Over barely two decades immigrant groups had crafted astonishingly varied and successful communities of resistance in Winnipeg. The Jews of Winnipeg, for example, established one of the most dynamic and complex radical communities in the country in the early 20th century; indeed, they were organized before the SPC itself. The three Winnipeg branches of the Arbeiter Ring, although nurturing a profound sense of their separateness, could also interact with fellow Jewish leftists on questions of common interest. Liberty (or *Freiheit*) Temple, the home of the Arbeiter Ring, was a "centre" not only for many different tendencies, but also for the poets, musicians, dramatists, and novelists who could speak to the socialism they shared.[142] Yet Winnipeg was also the capital of the Ukrainian left, whose hall socialism was manifest in a magnificent new structure opened in the midst of the postwar turmoil. As researcher Ernest Chisick points out, a Ukrainian socialist organization could be found in the lower North End of Winnipeg as early as 1903.[143]

Thus, in a city that exemplified the promise and achievement of the liberal West – the home of the Winnipeg *Free Press*, Grain Exchange, and J.W. Dafoe – were also some of the most theoretically alert and well-organized critics of the political and social order. It was also a city on the rise: the population had increased every decade since 1891, from 25,639 in 1891 to 42,340 in 1901, and from 136,035 in 1911 to 179,087 in 1921. From the eighth-largest city in the country in 1891 it had grown to become the third-largest in 1921.[144] The locus of Portage and Main was drawing the masses of the world, and their labour-power was creating more and more wealth for a flourishing business class. Yet the city also exemplified an obvious contradiction of liberal immigration policy, which was that in order to achieve its goals of capitalist accumulation, the Canadian state facilitated the arrival of hundreds of thousands of immigrants who were re-creating in Canada many of the collective solidarities they had first developed in Europe. In Winnipeg were "manifested," then, not only the "continuing class divisions" of Prairie society, but also the cultural contradictions of transnational capitalism. Making up about 15 per cent of the total population, Central European immigrants were overrepresented in the working class and in particular neighbourhoods, of which the North End was the most famous. Long would this neighbourhood be a shining inspiration to the left of the entire country.[145]

Could this multinational left come together to achieve any one big purpose? A Winnipeg leftist c.1911 might have been sceptical. True, there had been impressive moments of cross-ethnic and cross-tendency unity, such as the successful 1910–11 campaign to prevent the deportation of Savaa Federenko, a Russian revolutionary accused by czarist authorities of the murder of a village policeman — an event that foreshadowed the Defense Committee that campaigned on behalf of the Winnipeg strike prisoners in the aftermath of the strike.[146] Yet there were many divisions. However much outsiders might lump them all together as "foreign radicals," these activists themselves had their own separate identities, not all of them easily harmonized; even among the Jews, it would be misleading to assume that the left Zionists, Bundists, and anarchists made up one big happy family. All the cantankerous debates of the left on non-ethnic issues – the struggles over the single-plank platform, the place of free thought and atheism within the left, and so on – were fought out in Winnipeg with a passionate intensity. Nor might we find more optimism in a leftist in the time around 1916, given the ethnic divisiveness of the Great War, the imprisonment and persecution of many Ukrainians, and the complicity of certain Anglo-Canadian workers in their predicament. Yet at the same time the Great War climate illustrated how imperative multinational unity was for leftists: like so many others, foreign radicals were forcibly jolted out of the contemplation of their own distinctive issues and traditions by the urgent necessities of the situation itself.

The first window opened into early Canadian socialism by Winnipeg 1919 is onto the attempts by the left to construct a meaningful answer to the class question – how can workers arrive at a consciousness of their position, and how can they unite with others to launch a counter-hegemonic struggle? As Reimer observes, just such a "counter-hegemonic dynamic" can be discerned in the *Western Labor News* masthead, which proclaimed: "We must control all we produce – We produce all." Although not an exact distillation of Marx on value, or of many of the more sophisticated first formation theorists, this was nonetheless a slogan that captured much of the message that soapbox orators and socialist journalists had been proclaiming for three decades. It took value theory and combatively projected it into the future.[147]

For many, a strike is a strike is a strike – and undoubtedly, in large measure, Winnipeg 1919 was merely one such event, on a larger scale. It pitted strikers against employers, the Citizens' Committee, and the state, in pursuit of class objectives determined by the economic base. For the strikers and their supporters the issues were rising living costs, low wages, the non-recognition of unions, a labour shortage, and the craft workers' resistance to the entry to their trades of other "unskilled" workers. Ottawa had recently implemented increasingly draconian labour legislation: P.C. 1743 decreed that there should be no strikes or lockouts in war industries; in October 1918 P.C. 2525 forbade strikes or lockouts in industrial disputes – a measure reversed one month later.[148] The growing polarization in the ranks of labour between partisans of the OBU and those of the craft unions was conditioned by this adverse climate.

Why a general strike and not some other response? As historian A.B. McKillop once suggested, the "general strike" became the crystallization and fusion into one form of many pre-existing interests and forces. If on the right it epitomized an inherently revolutionary proposition, on the left it might be taken to be one of a number of appropriate weapons to be wielded by the labour and socialist movements, but probably not one that would definitively settle the fundamental problems of social evolution.[149] The general strike had been abstractly argued for in countless IWW publications. No less an authority than Jack London had imagined how the general strike would unfold in *The Dream of Debs: A Story of Industrial Revolt* (1909), a futuristic work read by many of his fans in Canada. London's point seemed to be that a general strike, as a powerful weapon in labour's toolbox, could force the ruling class to its knees, although his story did not explore how workers could exercise power in the period of the general strike; and it envisaged a "return to normal," albeit with a closed shop for trade unionists, after the strike was finished.[150]

Although the Winnipeg General Strike was, then, at least in part about labour issues, certainly many of them could have been handled without a general strike. But a key to the use of this new tactic was the rise of a new social-evolutionary sensibility within the labour movement. Since the September 1918 TLC convention in Quebec City, the dream of a "scientific" organization of labour had won over many adherents. They confronted craft unionists with evidence that their trade unions were outmoded relics, trapped in the slow lane of evolutionary change. Discussion became even more polarized after the Western Labour Conference in Calgary in 1919, when the plans for the separate and more "scientific" One Big Union were placed before the trade unionists of the Prairie West. There was a new and passionate conviction that a more scientific and enlightened form of labour organization was at hand. As Tom Mitchell and James Naylor point out, as of 1918 Winnipeg had already moved towards a general strike on no fewer than four different occasions. That summer, as many as 17,000 Winnipeggers had joined in an "escalating strike movement in support of the newly organized civic workers."[151] By 1918 the "general strike" had come to be regarded in Winnipeg as merely "another and more effective" weapon in the working-class arsenal.[152]

The labour theory of value was, in this setting, not just the hobbyhorse of a few overly abstract intellectuals. The SPCers and other organic intellectuals of the strike could draw upon the rich reserves of socialist parasitology to hammer home the point that the "profiteer" was the "parasite" against

whom both soldiers and strikers could unite. Value theory provided an ideological basis upon which one could imagine a historical bloc made up of
strikers and soldiers. Like the parasites critiqued in Henry Drummond's theological tracts and Olive Schreiner's socialist-feminist texts, these capitalists
were *useless* impractical parasites, who had lost their ordinary survival skills.
The striker-historians used both the *Western Labor News* and the history
based upon it to regale readers with the pitiful spectacle of the "Millionaire
Volunteer Fire Brigade, using their hands to break glass instead of using
their hatchets," just as might be expected from impractical, unhandy, effete
aristocrats. Such men were *leeches*, but afflicted with guilty consciences – the
knowledge that their hands would be forever stained with the blood of the
soldier-workers whose labour and lives they had sacrificed.

> The rich, who have become rich on war profits, know that this is the price of
> blood. The gold that has touched their palm has left its stain both there and in
> their conscience, and they cry: "Out damned spot," but it will not out. They live
> trembling at the thought of the future. They are afraid of retribution. They live
> in fear today and dread tomorrow. They feel deep down that there is a day of
> reckoning.[153]

Such passages appear to have been haunted by London's angst-ridden Avis Everhard, with her fervid visions of the blood-drenched homes of the elite.

Implicit in the construction of the striker-soldier, so radically contrasted
with the bourgeois strikebreakers, was a creative transformation of
conventional class analysis. Whatever their "class origins," the returned soldiers of 1919 were *not* proletarians, unless they had in fact returned to their
waged jobs. In essence they were liminal figures; and so, conversely, were
many of those who *were* proletarians, but whose positions of relative privilege
prompted them to desert the movement. As the *Strike Bulletin* mused on 4
June 1919, the railway running trades, when they betrayed the cause by signing an agreement with their employer, had become the "old Tories of the labor
movement."[154] In Winnipeg 1919 class lines were, under the pressure of
events, redrawn in ways unpredicted by a reductionist Marxian sociology.
Even the roles of striker and strikebreaker were not so easily distinguished. As
Bercuson insightfully points out, the strike forced upon many workers a type
of performative contradiction. To fulfil their pledge to keep the city functioning, they had to perform many services. This very performance enabled the
bourgeoisie to shield itself from the consequences of the conflict. In effect, the
workers themselves, by keeping essential services functioning, served as the
chief strikebreakers.[155]

At bottom the Winnipeg General Strike was not just an industrial dispute
aiming at reconstructing collective bargaining in Winnipeg. Many of the most

numerous participants in Winnipeg were not strikers in this sense. At the very least, many thousands of the most visible and militant among them were *striker-soldiers* – soldiers who sympathized with the strike (but many of whom as yet had no jobs from which they could withdraw their labour-power). Women in the domestic sphere – the "strikers' wives" – also participated. Other participants were drawn from the petite bourgeoisie, people such as Samuel Blumenberg, a Jewish store owner, or Rev. William Ivens. Many people went on strike in general sympathy for the demands of other workers. Support also came from beyond the city limits.[156] The Winnipeg General Strike was at least partly an attempt to form a new historical bloc – to expand a vocabulary (and identity) based on the working class, and articulate to it a variety of other identities and interests, terms and values, that were as yet not fully the property of one side or the other.[157]

The Winnipeg model also suggested a deeper practical answer to the class question. In most of labour's major pre-war struggles, with the exception, perhaps, of the Vancouver Island and Nova Scotia coalfield strikes immediately before the war, socialists had been on hand as orators to lend their support to the cause and provide a wider context for the workers' struggle. In Winnipeg 1919 socialists were organically linked to the strike. An earlier fastidious withdrawal from the working-class movement on the part of some was now transformed into a new conception of class and class-consciousness, with socialists playing a central role in motivating and interpreting the struggle. How else could the working class survive as an organism if not through a socialist strategy, both defensive and offensive, that could help it adapt to the enveloping reality of capitalist consolidation and state centralization? Winnipeg 1919 represents the culmination of changing relationships between socialists and labour already evident in the unemployment struggles of 1912–15.

The Religion Question and Gender Politics

Although Winnipeg 1919 unfolded in large part as a massive class struggle, many of its greatest single moments occurred in religious settings, as spiritual leaders put their beliefs into practice and performed highly political liturgies not just in prayer meetings but before mass crowds. In a sense the strike became a defining moment of the "Christian Revolution."

The evidence of working-class religiosity in 1919 was widespread. The most massive strike gatherings in Winnipeg 1919 were those orchestrated by the Labor Church, which was established at the Labour Temple in July 1918 as "an independent and creedless Church based on the Fatherhood of God and the Brotherhood of Man."[158] As A. Ross McCormack suggests, the Labor Church was part of a long history of religious innovation. Fred Tipping, Dick Rigg, Arthur Puttee, Salem Bland, and J.S. Woodsworth all made Winnipeg a centre of religious experimentation. Nowhere else, McCormack states, "was there collected such a group of brilliant and energetic radical churchmen." Rev. William Ivens, the most prominent Winnipeg-based advocate of revolutionary Christianity, made sense within this pattern. Some saw him as a crazed fanatic, others as a "tremendous egotist," a characterization that gains plausibility from his tendency to list his degrees and include his photograph with many of his articles. "His faith was basic and direct," say Winnipeg writers Harry and Mildred Gutkin.[159] At the time the right-wing press was particularly frenzied in its attacks on "Ivens the terrible,"[160] who was regarded by some as the Methodist Church's answer to V.I. Lenin.

The Labor Church operated with both fervent intensity and fierce pragmatism. Within it the form was, in large measure, the content: the erasure of boundaries separating discussion of pay envelopes from the God of mercy was in and of itself the enactment of a theological position. Gradually the Labor Church meetings grew larger and larger. By June 1919 no building in Winnipeg could hold the swelling congregation. Its membership had grown to around 4,000 (possibly making its Winnipeg base as large as the entire Canada-wide membership of the Socialist Party of Canada). It was, by one reckoning, the fastest-growing church in Canada.[161] On the second Sunday of the strike the church moved its services to Victoria Park, and from these massive meetings emerged some of the strike's most memorable visual images – not of workers being crushed by force of arms, but of the working class as a people in quest of enlightenment. These massive teach-ins reached a large percentage of the city's population – performances of socialism on a scale never before witnessed. They were both festivals of the downtrodden and mass pedagogical exercises of the oppressed.

Rather than fitting the "muddle-headed ministers" stereotype, these spiritual leaders served a practical, down-to-earth purpose. With an attendance of well over 5,000, the collection at the first service in Victoria Park came to about $500. The following Sunday, again at the park, drew an attendance of over 10,000 and a collection of $1,504.10.[162] These were large sums to add to the workers' treasury, especially when the right-wing enemy could draw upon the seemingly limitless resources of capital and the state.

In what may well have been the largest left-wing demonstrations in the entire period of 1890 to 1920, brilliant orators – Ivens, Woodsworth, Pritchard, Roger E. Bray (a returned soldier but also for six years a Methodist lay preacher) – would, in meeting after meeting, introduce massive crowds to the socialist approach to reasoning otherwise. Ivens, recently removed from the pulpit of McDougall Methodist Church largely on account of his anti-war views, invited a wide range of social gospellers to address the audience. Many were Methodists.[163] Even more tellingly, in the summer of 1918 Ivens was elevated to the editorship of the *Western Labor News*. Some Marxists, such as the writers at the SPC organ *Red Flag* in Vancouver, minimized the "stone age mumbo jumbo" of Ivens's previous church and suggested that he would be better off without it. "Ivens will be no worse for being 'unfrocked,'" it remarked. "A frock is no garment for a man in the twentieth century."[164] As the Labor Church expanded to as many as 19 churches in Canada – eight in Winnipeg alone, plus churches in Edmonton, Brandon, Calgary, Vancouver, and Victoria, all except the Edmonton church organized by A.E. Smith – Marxist dismissals grew sharper. In Edmonton in June 1921, as Richard Allen shows, P.F. Lawson convulsed the local church with declarations that recalled the earlier pronouncements of Baritz: "Anyone who believed in a God helping the workers accomplish their emancipation was a traitor to the working class."[165]

Winnipeg 1919 thus witnessed a radical reworking of the religion question, in essence under enormous pressure reconciling Marx with Christ for thousands of members. Instead of the traditional church service, directed by the minister, the *form* was often a mass meeting or discussion group, with much opportunity for interplay between crowd and speaker, and with room for grassroots initiative around topics for discussion. The Labor Church, in a nutshell, spoke of the power and creativity of the people, not their benightedness. And the *content* was not the gently ameliorative or the briskly positivistic social science of the pre-war Woodsworth, but something more like a theology of liberation. Within the Labor Church the left could debate all manner of new ideas – anarchism, Bolshevism, women's rights. What would Jesus do? In Winnipeg, 1919, Jesus would empower his followers to undertake the people's enlightenment.

On the first evening of the strike, a large Labor Church audience focused on the core issues in question. As Masters paints the picture:

> Ivens opened the service with prayer, and an earnest, closely reasoned address was delivered by James Winning. "The strike," Winning insisted, "was caused by the inadequacy of the pay envelope to last to the end of the week. . . . The profiteers refused to recognize the men's organizations, and were unwilling to give him a living wage, though they admitted the justice of his demands. . . ." It was a political meeting held in a religious setting.[166]

Then again, it might be said to have been a religious meeting in a political setting. In the words of Methodist radical A.E. Smith, the strike was "just as religious a movement as a Church revival."[167]

In a sense, the Labor Church could still be assimilated into the social gospel paradigm – as a primarily Methodist outreach to the working class. In another sense, amply confirmed by the expulsions of radicals that punctuated Prairie church conferences in 1919, it was the transcendence of this social gospel paradigm, because both in form and in content it essentially reversed the received vision of religious enlightenment. What had once been the education of the benighted by faithful missionaries was transformed into its opposite: the scientific and spiritual enlightenment of society as a whole by that universal class which alone held the key to the new moral world.[168] As Joanne Carlson Brown notes, the Labor Church had deep roots in forms of dissident Methodism – similar to, for example, G.S. Eby's Toronto Church of the Revolution of 1909 (which played a creative role in nurturing socialist feminism within the Social Democratic Party). She notes Woodsworth's strong sense that the church was "essentially in line with the teachings and spirit of Jesus."[169] For Ivens the creation of a new religion was no mere camouflage. As the Gutkins point out: "In his sermon notes and in his public pronouncements, [Ivens] insisted again and again that a belief in God was the driving force of socialism, that the emancipation of the masses must begin with the rebirth of truth within the soul of the believer." In his presentations to the Labor Church, Ivens conceptualized the working class as a collective Christ. Speaking in Victoria Park on May 16, the ex-minister exhorted the masses: "If you will but stand firm for a short time, we will bring them cringing on their knees to you saying: 'What shall we do to be saved?' "[170]

Winnipeg 1919 was also a showcase for the transformation of the woman question. The strike leadership was overwhelmingly male – unsurprisingly, perhaps, given the prominence of male-dominated building and metal trades unions in its genesis. Much of the women's activism was structured in ways reminiscent of women's domestic work in the home. *"Saving the World"* is replete with many choice passages of "proletarian chivalry." For example, after the Committee of 1000 prevented the strikers from getting access to the Industrial Bureau for the church services, the leaders charged the Committee with indirect responsibility after "several women" fainted "from exhaustion due to the heat and the prolonged standing" in the park. The striker-historians also indicted the agents of the state with the even graver offence of intruding upon the domestic sphere. Speaking of arrests that took place on 16 June, they wrote with shocked disapproval about how the search party had barged into Roger Bray's home, upsetting his children and not even giving the man and his wife a chance to get dressed. Their heterosexual normality contrasted sharply with the policies of those whom Bray himself called the "spineless emasculated ninnies at Ottawa," or with the evident perversion of the special police billeted at Gladstone School, who spent their time with "obscene books" and sketching racy drawings on the blackboards.[171] As the Gutkins observe, when Woodsworth addressed the Soldiers' Parliament on "Ladies' Day," he predicted a day "when women would take their place beside men, not as dependents or inferiors, but as equals, and that better relationship would result, based on equality and love." Yet his subtext was clearly that "for any woman, working outside the home under any circumstances was most unfortunate."[172]

At the same time certain elements of the uprising did not fit the chauvinist script. The arrival of a new generation of socialist feminists had much to do with this. In Winnipeg 1919 Helen Armstrong, the descendant of an illustrious radical family with roots extending back to the Knights of Labor, showed just how brilliantly a certain style of "impossibilist" intransigence could work in a concrete situation. Her activism in the women's suffrage campaign, SPC, Women's Labor League, and the Retail Clerks' Union, and her strike support work, made her a leader of the Winnipeg left. She was so intrepid that when the Tories staged a Next-of-Kin Committee rally at the Walker Theatre in December 1917, Armstrong brazenly intercepted people as they arrived, "condemning their disgraceful display of ignorance, exhorting them to recant, handing out pamphlets."[173]

Her direct role in organizing workers echoed that of Helena Gutteridge in Vancouver. In April 1918 Armstrong was elected president of the new Hotel and Household Workers' Union. She attended the founding convention of the OBU in Calgary. She organized meeting after meeting for working women in attempts at union-building, and took part, according to Linda Kealey, in "information and strategy-planning sessions."[174] Her role in the strike was qualitatively different from the supporting roles generally reserved for left women. Indeed, she proved to be instrumental in the very first moments of the strike, from the time that the initial strikers – 500 telephone operators – punched out at 7 a.m. on 15 May. As Mary Horodyski notes, Armstrong's role as a prestigious and significant leader in the strike comes out especially in the story of two young women, Ida Krantz and Margaret Steinhauer, who went to the Labour Temple one day during the strike to seek her out. In late June 1919 Armstrong was committed for trial for "inciting" Krantz and Steinhauer "to assault two *Tribune* office employees who were selling newspapers on the street." The two women charged with the assault got off with a fine of $5 plus costs each, but Armstrong was detained, and "two days later, the *Tribune* reported that Armstrong was still in the provincial jail 'owing to the refusal of the authorities to grant bail.'"[175]

To have a woman in this powerful position, not as a grassroots "supporter" of a male-dominated strike but as an active "mobilizer" of fellow female militants was unprecedented on the Canadian left. (Even Gutteridge's somewhat similar role in Vancouver was rather more reminiscent of progressive social work than such direct class struggle.) A prime example of the organic fusion of the abstract and concrete, once again traceable back to Armstrong, can be found in the Women's Labor League kitchen, designed to provide women strikers, or indeed any women in need, with meals. Men were also welcome, but they were expected to pay – if they could not do so, they needed a ticket from the Relief Committee.[176] The kitchen may have served as many as 1,500 meals per day.

Women were also involved in many of the acts of grassroots direct action through which district organizations enforced pro-strike solidarity. One reason why the bread delivery drivers might well have welcomed the controversial placards giving them permission to deliver their goods was because some of them had been threatened by women militants. According to Horodyski's findings, "One of the women warned a driver: 'We will murder you if you attempt to make deliveries in this district again.' The driver observed, 'And they look as if they mean real business.' "[177]

The prominence of women in Winnipeg 1919 underlines the difficulty of reducing the event to a strike, even a very big strike.[178] So many non-unionized women joined the ranks of the rebellion that it can hardly be seen as an event monopolized by male trade unionists. Armstrong's kitchen served many women who were waged "workers" only in one short-lived aspect of their lives. The very existence of so large an operation, and its specific focus on *women*, suggested a creative, new left awareness of the centrality of women's domestic labour. In Winnipeg 1919 the achievement and the limitations of the first formation on the woman question were plain. The achievement could be found in the public militancy of women, the unprecedented centrality of a figure like Armstrong, and the possibilities for sweeping hegemonic challenge contained in a specific moment of class struggle. Drawing upon many of the intellectual and organizational resources of the first formation, activist women were able to change the very terms of the woman question.

Still, very much like the garment strikes in Montreal and Toronto in 1910 and 1912, or Sophie Mushkat's role as a compelling speaker in the Eastern coalfield strikes, such moments of "gender elasticity," in Frager's apt words, proved short-lived. Traditional roles "snapped back into place" once the "particular contingencies" had been dealt with.[179] Once the revolutionary atmosphere of Winnipeg 1919 dissipated, traditional gender conventions were there to be reinstituted, and there was no powerful body to preserve even the memory of socialist-feminist breakthroughs. The Strike Council included just two women among its roughly 50 members, and the strike-historians, all male, constructed an account of the strike that largely excluded women except as victimized helpmates. When Armstrong died in 1947, she did so in obscurity – in contrast to some of the male martyrs who became legendary figures, both in Winnipeg and beyond.[180]

The Struggle for Class, Not Race

In Winnipeg 1919 lines of race were also sharply drawn on both sides. The glaring weaknesses and subtle strengths of a first formation that had drawn heavily upon evolutionary theory were on full display.

In the city's crucial construction trades, for instance, many workers were of

Slavic origin; and in the years leading up to 1919, as Don Avery shows, such workers had been increasingly well organized and militant. A large, forceful construction strike in July 1917 resulted in the arrest of 23 strikers; those identified as "enemy aliens" were interned in camps. Nonetheless, their spirit was not broken. The immigrant construction workers, with Mathew Popovich playing a key role, faced down the Builders' Exchange. In 1918 strikers at the Manitoba Gypsum Company were said to be "of alien nationality, many of them not naturalized." Security officials and the Citizens' Committee worried that organizers like Oscar Schoppelrie were managing to build solid links between returned soldiers, strikers, and the ethnic organizations.[181]

When immigrants ceased to be "abstract labour," so many units bearing a commodity purchasable in the world market, and turned into "rights-claiming citizens," they threatened the principles of ethno-racial hierarchy and economic discipline central to the entire liberal project. Dafoe would argue that the best way of destroying the strike movement was "to clean the aliens out of this community and ship them back to their happy homes in Europe which vomited them forth a decade ago."[182] These were not just the panic-stricken words of one Prairie editor; they came close to epitomizing the official line of Prairie liberalism, which consistently sought to blame the strike on the foreign radicals, victimize any of those whom it could plausibly connect to it, and continue the use of labour camps and deportation as useful weapons in the struggle for whiteness.[183]

Such well-placed spokespeople had a mass audience for their nativism. The ethnic tensions of the postwar period – with returned soldiers bitterly resentful of the "foreigners" who had evidently, at the behest of the state, taken their jobs[184] – poisoned the atmosphere. Both Jews (often Russian Jews) and Ukrainians (associated in the public mind with Russians) could easily be stereotyped as Russian Bolsheviks. The blaming of "foreign radicals," though, could only go so far. Most of the prominent strike leaders were, it was said, of "Anglo-Saxon" (more properly Anglo-Celtic) origins – only the Jewish member A.A. Heaps stands out as a prominent exception – and no one with an Eastern European surname became numbered among the leaders enshrined in the memory of the left. As Masters took pains to point out in 1950, of the 234 delegates to the Calgary Labour Conference, "only 11 had names that were not obviously Anglo-Saxon or Irish and 7 of this 11 were in the Alberta delegation of the United Mine Workers. The Winnipeg delegation did not contain a single 'foreign' name."[185]

In the Winnipeg events of 1919 many leftists were clearly working with concepts of whiteness entirely at one with the society around them. Dixon regaled his Labor Church audience with a "darky joke," complete with accent. Commenting on the "yellow contract" – itself a racially loaded expression – that the city wanted to force upon police officers, the *Western Labor News* called it an "abject pledge of subservience" and cried, "ONLY A SLAVE COULD SIGN IT. A FREE MAN, A WHITE MAN – NEVER!" The radicals in Winnipeg 1919 often seemed to be tiptoeing on a racialized minefield, acutely conscious of the damage that their enemies could inflict with the "alien" card. The Strike Defense Committee countered charges of "aliens" in its ranks by challenging the Citizens to compare their personnel with its own.[186]

Although much remains to be learned about the relations between native-born and immigrants in Winnipeg 1919, new evidence qualifies Bercuson's claim that there was "little intercourse" between foreign-language radical groups and the Strike Committee.[187] The many reports compiled by the police from 1919 to 1921 about Jacob Penner – of German-Russian-Mennonite extraction, and linked by marriage to the Jewish community – suggest that he was fully engaged with the strike and played a role in both the German and English socialist locals; he also took a strong part in the subcommittees that made arrangements for workers' meetings. He was deeply involved in the Labor Church (he "cares nothing about religion except the creed of Rev. Ivens," the spy noted disapprovingly) and would later be active in the workers' alliance combining Jewish, German, and English socialist groups, which met at times in the Ukrainian Labor Temple. His subsequent stature on the left would be affirmed by his role in the Defense Committee, and later as a candidate for office. With all due caution with respect to the veracity of stool pigeons, we can conclude that these interesting reports draw a portrait of Penner at variance with too marked an insistence on the isolation of the "radical aliens."[188] On a practical level, it would have been difficult to maintain the strike without drawing upon the expertise and energy of radical leaders with roots in ethnic communities, given the demographic composition of the city.

The best known instance of the returned soldiers' anti-immigrant violence came in January 1919, when a crowd of soldiers gathered at the Swift Company meat-packing plant to protest the employment of alien workers. Mayor Charles Gray urged the soldiers not to destroy the property. Significantly, as an upholder of the established liberal order, he also endorsed their sentiments and legitimated their viewpoint: "We want to get the aliens out and I am with you in that, but let us do it constitutionally. Go back to the city and if they don't do it, then is the time for reckoning." The Austro-Hungarian Society and the Socialist Party of Canada offices were wrecked. In the case of the SPC office, a piano was shoved through the window; books from the library were piled high; and the crowd set both on fire. On Main Street, foreigners, or people who looked like foreigners, were set upon. Samuel Blumenberg's establishment was trashed, and his wife was publicly humiliated by being forced to kiss the Union Jack. Repeatedly through 1919 soldiers raised an anti-alien cry in Winnipeg. Their objectives were displayed on various banners: "Britons Never Shall Be Slaves," "Down With the

Profiteers," "Deport ALL Undesirables," "We Stand for 35,000 against 1,000." Particularly notable was "We Fought the Hun Over There. We Fight the Hun Everywhere."[189]

Rather than condemning the acts of book-burning and violence, the mainstream press contrasted the manly soldiers with the craven aliens.[190] Naylor and Mitchell underline the message: "The leadership of the Great War Veterans' Association, the *Winnipeg Telegram*, and the mayor backed the veterans' actions. Authorities made no attempts to restrain the crowd, and those who had attacked immigrants and their property were not arrested or punished. The lesson was clear: extra-legal violence had official sanction."[191]

The left faced a truly delicate situation. If mishandled, it risked bringing armed violence and mass arrests down upon vulnerable people and indispensable allies, including countless Jewish and Ukrainian comrades. Many of the ethnic parties were illegal. The issue was similar to that faced by the Vancouver left in 1914 at the time of the *Komagata Maru* crisis, but with a notable difference. In 1914 some Vancouver socialists had expressed their general support for the Sikhs and their struggle against imperialism, but with only slight exceptions there was little sense that the two movements were organically connected. In 1919 the Winnipeg socialists were in a palpably different situation. In their case the "foreign radicals" were not moored offshore, but were, rather, located at the very heart of the struggle; without their support it could not succeed.

To be sure, leftists of all stripes often played a difficult hand with considerable finesse, balancing somewhere between adroitness and exclusion. They worked hard to defeat a resolution by the soldiers' executive denouncing all the "revolutionary doctrines and propaganda" associated with "the undesirables, enemy aliens and others," who were said to be debasing the labour unions. They preferred a resolution sympathizing with the aims of the general strike and pledging every effort to maintain law and order. The vexed question of deporting the "enemy alien" could wait until later (and the category itself was left tactically undefined). The Strike Committee seconded the Soldiers' Parliament in calling for the deportation of "undesirable aliens" – precise meaning left unclear – and a restriction on further immigration.[192] As Mitchell and Naylor remark, "Concerns over the crucial issue of maintaining the support of most of the returned soldiers meant that the strikers were often defensive about the multi-ethnic character of their struggle."[193]

That the foreign radicals were willing to accept the leadership of the Anglo-Celtic Strike Committee may be construed as a symptom of their marginality and subservience – or as a politically shrewd move, on both their part and that of the strike leadership, to obtain the maximum effect of solidarity without feeding the Red Scare or endangering the immigrants' lives.[194] Avery underlines the point that immigrant workers must have been willing to follow the leadership of the Strike Committee: "Ukrainian and other Slavic workers faithfully followed the guidelines of the Central Strike Committee even though the membership of this Committee was exclusively Anglo-Saxon. Moreover the strong sense of community among Ukrainian workers helped to transform the strike into something more than a mere economic conflict; it became a life and death struggle in which any deviance from the ethnic norm was branded as traitorous."[195]

Certainly, without the "aliens," such a large strike would not have been possible. But any Eastern European radicals who took a leadership role in the strike would have been asking for trouble – if not from bigoted fellow Winnipeggers, then from the Immigration agents wielding the awful powers of deportation, or from bosses determined to protect "their" workers from Bolshevik leaders. As writers in the *Western Labor News* were keen to point out, the members of the Citizens Committee of 1000 were themselves dependent upon the labour of "aliens."[196] "*Saving the World*" proclaimed: "The bosses have no quarrel with the rich alien, no quarrel with the unorganized alien. The only aliens they complain about are those who have had sense enough to join the ranks of organized labor and therefore cannot be used to scale down wages."[197] Drawing on the organic language of parasitism, *Western Labor News* writers sought to underline the employers' hypocrisy:

> But alien is one – of class, not race – he has drawn the line for himself;
> His roots drink life from inhuman soil, from garbage of pomp and pelf;
> His heart beats not with the common beat, he has changed his life-stream's hue;
> He deems his flesh to be finer flesh, he boasts that his blood is blue.[198]

For many of the Winnipeg activists in 1919, "home" was not necessarily a geographical location on the Red River. Home was where the red flag flew.

The most influential left – the left that spoke through the *Strike Bulletin* and the Strike Committee – was crafting a hegemonic challenge to liberal order, and in doing this it had to achieve two seemingly antithetical objectives. On the one hand, it had to reclaim the high discourse of patriotism, wartime sacrifice, and "the community" from the bosses and the government, at a time when the state machinery of image-production was still working in high gear. On the other hand, to remain faithful to any notion of "scientific universalism" and "rationality," it had to nurture the seeds of cross-cultural socialism. Elements of anti-alien discourse could be incorporated into the left's conceptual system only if they were first translated into the language of abstract universalism. Hence the ringing resolution from the Calgary convention: "That the interests of all members of the working class being identical, that this body of workers recognize no alien but the capitalist; also that we are opposed to any wholesale immigration of workers from various parts of the world and who would be brought here at the request of the ruling class."[199] As Reimer notes, the emergent left position, reflected in the *Western Labor News*, was that "it was class, and not race, that really mattered. The immigrant, then, was viewed as a fellow worker and striker, while the employers were attacked as hypocrites."[200]

Practically speaking, such a stance might mean downplaying the role of immigrant speakers at the Labour Temple, while insisting at the same time that "British Justice" be made equally available to all, no matter what race or ethnicity.[201] As *"Saving the World"* put it: "Labor unions here, for years, have fought the Government of Canada on the matter of wholesale immigration of peoples from Central Europe, brought in by large corporations for the purpose of breaking strikes, and generally to reduce the standard of living of the Canadian worker, but all to no avail." So, now that the "strangers" were well and truly "within the gates," it was time to treat them as fellow workers. Unionists thus faced a kind of ultimatum: "They had to turn round and organize the foreign speaking workmen for their own welfare and advancement, and now refuse, and rightly, to turn against these men at the behest of the same powers and interests that were the most active in bringing the so-called alien into the country in the first place."[202]

If we adapt Frager's term "gender elasticity," perhaps a certain kind of "racial elasticity" was coming into play. At some moments issues of race and ethnicity were confronted in transformative ways, only to be succeeded by other moments in which the old hierarchies and conventions snapped back into place. *"Saving the World"* epitomizes this pattern. On the one hand, the "alien" – or "so-called alien" – was never really given much prominence in the text. In a different universe of discourse, Michael Charitinoff, former editor of *Robochyi narod* – arrested for possession of illegal literature, sentenced to three years' imprisonment, hit with a substantial fine, and very much a focus of the famous fiery meeting of 22 December 1918 – might have been constructed as one of the heroes of Winnipeg 1919. He showed up at this notorious meeting but, revealingly enough, remained silent.[203] His visible silence conveyed a rich meaning, speaking of his liminal position, neither "fully us" nor "fully alien," just as his textual presence in the strikers' history suggests an "alien" who was also "one of us." He made an appearance. He was not granted status as an authority.

Similarly, Samuel Blumenberg might have been constructed as both a major speaker at left meetings and a martyr to the cause of justice. He was given exceptional treatment in *"Saving the World"* – he was the one immigrant granted paragraphs of text clarifying his positions. He was the man who seconded a Walker Street Theatre meeting's resolution calling for the withdrawal of the Allied troops from Siberia, and who wittily dissected the Manitoba *Free Press*'s twists and turns in its coverage of Karl Liebknecht and the

German Revolution. Given that his shop was smashed up by the returned soldiers and his partner humiliated on the streets, he certainly could have been developed as one of the major victims of vigilante violence. He wittily "performed" his Jewishness at the Walker Theatre meeting by attacking a daily newspaper for refusing to disclose his nationality. The striker-historians reported: "Laughter followed his statement that such a question was entirely unnecessary since the map of Palestine was written on his face, and on his nose was the mount of Zion." Yet unlike Woodsworth, Pritchard, and their ilk, Blumenberg was never placed in the pantheon of strike heroes. Nor, as Bumsted remarks, was Moses Almazoff, despite his "impassioned speech of defence before a special deportation committee."[204]

Yet on the other hand there was also in 1919 – to an extent unusual for the first formation – an outraged left critique of ethnic discrimination. *"Saving the World"* asks its readers (who are by implication Anglo-Canadians) to put themselves in the shoes of one Verenchuk. He had been arrested along with the other supposed ringleaders, but in fact he was just a boy who had tried to fight for his country, and against whom the state had no concrete evidence. As the text put it, he had in 1915 "volunteered to help 'make the world safe for democracy'; was wounded and recovered and passed through all the stages of hospitals, convalescences, retraining and another draft for France, where he was wounded the second time and shell-shocked on the Somme in those terrible days of 1916." He was honourably discharged in Canada in 1917, and no warrant for his arrest had been issued. So why was this wounded boy imprisoned? And why, in dropping the charges against him, did the prosecutor offer no apology, but advised the boy's admission to a mental hospital – to railroad "a perfectly sane and innocent man to a lunatic asylum"?[205] That the authors of *"Saving the World"* do not seem to have known Verenchuk's full name is surely rather revealing. He too is a liminal figure, not quite fully there in the text. Yet we should not minimize the extent to which we are invited to walk in his shoes and imagine the world through his eyes. This item struck a new note of inclusiveness on the left.

Penner was not the only one named in the Mounties' reports, which were very interested in the activities of the foreign-born in distributing propaganda.[206] Yet their treatment by the authorities provided eloquent evidence of the risks of their activism. As Avery observes, the "aliens" arrested on Bloody Saturday were especially singled out by Winnipeg Magistrate Hugh John Macdonald, who ordered them to an internment camp at Kapuskasing, Ont., for "safe-keeping." Over labour protests, they were then secretly deported. Macdonald's motivations were suggested in a letter he wrote to Arthur Meighen, the acting minister of justice, on 3 July 1919: "As Police Magistrate I have seen to what a large extent Bolsheviki ideas are held by the Ruthenian, Russian and Polish people, whom we have in our midst . . . it is absolutely necessary that an example should be made." Fear, he added, was the only agency that could be employed with success: "If the Government persists in the course that it is now adopting the foreign element here will soon be as gentle and easily controlled as a lot of sheep."[207]

Avery makes the crucial and easily overlooked point that, by calling in the armed force of the state, the enemies of the strikers were implicitly conceding that "the existing conflict could not be ended by playing the veterans off against the foreign workers and their Anglo-Canadian allies."[208] Although the strike did not readily dissolve all "the barriers of color, race and creed," few instances of inter-ethnic violence within the ranks of the strikers themselves were reported; and in the aftermath of the strike, the non-Anglo-Saxon Penner could take on a leadership role within the Defense Committee.[209] The strike suggested a new level of inter-ethnic contact within the left, in this case not as a matter of abstract universalism but of practical necessity.

The Democratic Challenge

Perhaps the most impressive achievement of Winnipeg 1919 was its successful demonstration of new forms of power – forms that a later generation would call "participatory democracy." In the course of the 41-day strike, according to one estimate, a total of 171 mass meetings were held. "Whatever its limitations," Mitchell and Naylor remark, "the strike was an exercise in mass participation that represented a dramatic departure from workers' marginal role in liberal democracy."[210] It was, to put a slightly different spin on it, a *prefigurative performance*, a performance of future possibilities, as people wrestled – in Victoria Park no less than in the Strike Committee – with the pragmatics and poetics of a truly democratic society.

It was of a piece with a new intellectual confidence and organizational capacity on the part of the Canadian socialists. Given the official restrictions on Charles H. Kerr books, the SPC, assisted by a bequest from a charity, commenced an ambitious publication program of its own, bringing out (for instance) its own editions of *The Communist Manifesto* and *Capital*. In Winnipeg the Great Strike of 1919 initiated the Great Publication Program – the first of its type in Canadian left history – of 1919–25.[211] Many of the articulate leaders of Winnipeg 1919 saw one major theme of their cause as the defence of the working-class movement's intellectual achievements – as exemplified by publishing programs, libraries, and study groups.

In what Mitchell and Naylor usefully call the "strike or revolution paradigm,"[212] those writers "sympathetic" to the strike argued that it was indeed "democratic," that is, it respected the rule of law, abjured revolution, and adhered to the "constitution." Its critics maintained that it was anti-democratic because it was "revolutionary," that is, it aimed at the violent overthrow of the established government as a means of establishing an alternative, anti-democratic form of rule on the banks of the appropriately named Red River. But in essence Winnipeg 1919 was an experiment in radical democracy; it aimed to empower and educate the people. The strike was orderly; and the strikers left behind them no convincing evidence that they maintained armed camps and secret caches of dynamite, or that they harboured concrete plans to mount a frontal assault on the Canadian state. To some degree the Strike Committee even co-operated with city council and the Citizens' Committee. The *Strike Bulletin* of 5 June, urging the workers in huge capital letters to "DO NOTHING" and "KEEP OUT OF TROUBLE," added this piece of advice: "Continue to prove that you are the friends of law and order."[213] Yet simply to argue, as they did, for democracy in a post-1915 Canada of detention camps, arbitrary deportations, rigged elections, mass disenfranchisements, and dictatorial government *was itself revolutionary.*

Leftists cited the Magna Carta so often that some naive listeners must have wondered if these radicals had written the document themselves. Throughout Winnipeg 1919 radicals would invoke the proud history of the British constitution at the drop of a hat. They never tired of reminding listeners that the rights and freedoms of the British subject – now gloriously if ambiguously rolled into the concept of the citizen – had been purchased at the price of the head of Charles I. The Glorious Revolution of 1688 was remembered as though it had happened on the banks of the Red River – and constituted a bona fide revolution. "The British-born are asking if Canada is really under British law," the *Western Labor News* asked. "If not, well they have been nurtured in British tradition and they will not surrender a freedom guaranteed them by the Magna Carta and the Bill of Rights." After the midnight arrest of ten strike leaders on 17 June, the strikers' newspaper demanded justice for them based upon the "great body of common law and precedent from the Magna Carta on down that guards the personal liberty, not only of British subjects, but of the meanest slave that sets foot on British soil."[214]

"*Saving the World*," drawing on the *Western Labor News* of 16 May 1919, explained that the workers were *not* revolutionists. Yet the publication continued: "They want the control of industry in their own hands as soon as possible so that they can get the full product of their toil and eliminate production for profit. But they will wait until this is accomplished by constitutional processes."[215] In short, the political activists could be "constitutional" and "revolutionary" at the same time.

Winnipeg 1919 entailed an intense debate over political and intellectual rights. By identifying themselves so forcefully with the myths and legends of the Whig interpretation of British history, the working-class intellectuals implicitly cleansed themselves of any taint of being foreigners, while also condemning their opponents for their constitutional ignorance. They attached themselves to a reading of their political lives that saw them as unfolding within a historical time and place defined by British precedents and traditions. As Pritchard explained, "The workers stood for open discussion and decision by ballot. That was how this strike was called."[216]

Leftists characteristically interpreted government by order-in-council as an insult to British liberties – "a subversion of political democracy and civil liberty," declared Ontario members of the International Association of Machinists – and an affront to the Enlightenment: "Trial by jury is not permitted and sentences that are an outrage upon human decency are imposed upon them for the possession of literature in which are expressed the greatest thoughts of the liberators of mankind." George Armstrong of the SPC, generally considered a fine old-fashioned "impossibilist," nonetheless warmly praised duly constituted authority and warned against the subversion of the British Constitution. Political authority in Canada, he warned, had "passed from that position where it derives its power from the Government of the nation to where it maintains itself by physical force."[217]

Demands for freedom of the press and freedom from arbitrary arrest were stock stipulations in 1919. *"Saving the World"* repeatedly expressed shock and anger at the actions of the police – at how they barged into bedrooms, confiscated libraries, and overpowered their victims with a spectacle of unbridled menace. "Open the door or we shall break it open!" was followed, in the newspaper's description, by the intrusion into private space of policemen, "each packing his gun and loaded riding whip, bedecked in sombrero, top boots and spurs, whilst in the first light of early dawn could be seen a big high-powered car in charge of a chauffeur, who kept his engine running." Why these and other measures were necessary to apprehend pyjama-clad citizens, only the Mounties could say.[218]

An almost philosophical incompatibility existed between the "criminal conspiracy" model plainly predominating in Ottawa and within the police on the one side and, on the other, the left's vision of Winnipeg 1919 as a moment of "democracy" – that concept which, though only recently elevated to a hallowed status by being integrated into the reasons as to why Canadians were fighting the Great War, had long been suspect in the minds of many traditional Canadian liberals. Even "collective bargaining" was by no means a straightforward description of a stable regime of recognized unions, regularly renegotiated collective agreements, and grievance procedures. In 1919 the term clearly worried those who saw it as carrying a sense of workers' control – the steady and debilitating encroachment of employees on the rights and privileges of the owners. At the time it also might have implied the more radical, and dangerous, meaning of bargaining through more inclusive labour bodies so structured that they could speak for a generously defined *collectivity* of workers (who would thus not be organized on a narrow craft basis). As the

Western Labor News remarked, "We have a historical mission to perform. We have no choice but to go forward. Our basis of organization must broaden still further, and develop until it embraces all who perform a useful function in society; until it eliminates the wages system with all its resultant evils of wealth and poverty, and establishes in its stead a system where usefulness and not profit will be the basis of production."[219] If this was "collective bargaining," it was more a synonym than an antonym to "revolution."

Certainly, revolutionary ideas and publications, including Lenin's influential *Soviets at Work*, were abroad in Winnipeg, and many powerful figures in federal government had at least some reason for their fears that a revolution was taking place there. Yet within the first formation "revolution" generally meant a rapidly accelerated period of social evolution. As Pritchard remarked, "Revolution means a change which comes at the end of a line of growth or evolution, and the scientist, insofar as I can see, when he looks into the world of material things around him, does not distinguish evolution from revolution. That is growth from change."[220] Revolution did not necessarily mean bloodshed or violence. It meant the successful application of the science of socialism – the end of wage slavery, the coming of the next stage of social evolution, the triumph of enlightenment over superstition and ignorance.

Some SPCers maintained a concept of the "way to power," at least insofar as it can be inferred from a party pamphlet of 1913, which meant shifting "the political power now in the hands of the economic masters" into the hands of the workers through a legal, peaceful "transformation of capitalist property into collective wealth." This political method, "by the very nature of things," was to be preferred over the "economic method" because it was "the only method compatible with the intellectual development of modern time." For only when such material and intellectual development of workers had occurred could a full transformation to socialism take place. "As soon as the working class learns how to organize an efficient and powerful working class political party, based upon the fundamental tenets of social democracy, just so soon will it discover and travel the way to power."[221] Exactly how this political party was to set about to dismantle capitalist property relations peacefully was never plainly laid out, and the debate over whether it required a revolutionary "dictatorship" functioning temporarily to achieve this transition, through which the ruling class would be disarmed, was just beginning.[222]

The implicit hegemonic position, often quietly sustained by subsequent historians, was that, acting in a "state of exception," and confronting a threat to order of unknown dimensions, the regime behaved reasonably in reining in the strike and arresting its leaders. The question of *sovereignty* trumps all others. In this liberal conception, the argument of sovereignty is unanswerable: the state *had* to protect its exclusive control over legitimate violence. As Mitchell and Naylor note, a surprising element in the response of senior figures within the regime was their calm acceptance of the growth of extraparliamentary squads and vigilantes. Opponents of the strike were interested in using the militia, and on occasion even referred to the formation of private armed organizations of young men, a strategy reminiscent of the Fascist movement in Italy – yet one whose illegality was not critiqued by key figures within the state.[223] Authoritarianism was fused with liberal political economy to create an "exceptional state" of decades-long permanence.

After the strike, monies voted by Parliament to be used for expenses associated with the Great War were channelled, as Mitchell illustrates, into what was essentially a private prosecution of the strike leaders. In a way, this was a more decorous, "Canadian" form of private justice that in the United States was more clearly marked as vigilantism. The federal government was the paymaster for a prosecution launched by leading members of the Citizens' Committee of 1000, under little-used provisions of the Criminal Code that, subject to the consent of the provincial attorney general, allowed for prosecutions by private citizens or organizations.[224] Had the taxpayers' money not been made available, it is doubtful that the citizens, public-spirited as they doubtless were, would have wanted to spend the vast amounts required. Behind the majestic solemnities of courtroom justice we find backstage payoffs, stool-pigeons' reports, and brazen conflicts of interest.

The Politics of Citizenship

The tensions between state sovereignty and grassroots democracy came into focus in debates over citizenship. Although there was, legally, no such thing as "Canadian citizenship," both right and left in Winnipeg argued as though there was. They did so in starkly contrasting languages. The Citizens' Committee of 1000 made an implicit argument about the boundaries of citizenship by never making it apparent who or what its members were. They were a self-selected vanguard of citizens, professedly neutral, but in actuality militantly opposed to the strike. From the standpoint of the right wing, the *citizen* was a person of property and substance – a loyal British subject menaced by foreign doctrines and alien agitators. It was an emphatically Anglo-Canadian, middle-class, conformist approach to the concept of "the citizen." The approach was parallelled in the Law and Order League in Brandon, the Citizens' Committee of Calgary, and many other bodies.[225]

In this framework, the non-British came to be "aliens," people intrinsically in opposition to the "British Constitution." The Citizens saw the events of 1919 as "an assault on the modern British liberal state and the fundamental liberties of free-born Englishmen." They found "acknowledged Bolsheviki" even within the Winnipeg Trades and Labour Council. They vowed to defend "that Constitution which for 200 years has been the wonder of the world and the proudest boast of the Englishman."[226] It was a political program endlessly repeated in the appropriately named Winnipeg *Citizen*, which appeared as the Citizens' Committee organ on 19 May. The liberal citizen of the *Citizen* was constructed as an innocent bystander confronting a labour movement hijacked by militants. It was a plain case of "middle class citizens" fighting "the machinations of a number of confessed Bolshevists."[227] In this political language, to be a striker was to forfeit your symbolic citizenship. Every individual and event placed within this conceptual framework acquired a new meaning.

Within one set of rules, Fred Dixon was a respectable "citizen" – he had, after all, been elected to the Manitoba legislature. Within the *Citizen's* set of rules, his symbolic citizenship was forfeited. As a mere "soapbox orator," he did not make the cut. Roger Bray, within one set of rules, might be regarded as a man of honour who had fought for his country. In the *Citizen's* books, he was merely a *poseur*. He had, the paper claimed, never seen the firing lines, and the question of his citizenship had been settled once and for all on 2 June 1919, when he said he was a Bolshevist.[228] The permission placards might, within one set of rules, be seen as a sensible tool that allowed citizens to get through a strike without robbing innocent parties of milk and bread. Within the *Citizen's* discourse, they were miniature *Communist Manifestos*, alive with Soviet menace. In many ways, the *Citizen* and the Citizens appealed to 19th-century liberal definitions of the individual, defined by his self-possession, manliness, and respectability. Citizenship was not a right that inhered in a person by virtue of being born in, or having become a permanent resident, of Canada. It was a recognition of a propertied individualism.

J.A. Calder, a Saskatchewan Liberal MP, affirmed as much when in June 1919 he introduced legislation to exclude from Canada "persons who believed in or advocated the overthrow of constituted government by force or violence or who advocated the unlawful destruction of property." His bill also removed immigrants in prohibited or undesirables classes from the provision "that any immigrant domiciled in the country for five years could not be deported after a special hearing before an immigration department panel." A.J. Andrews of the Citizens was dismayed that the act did not allow for the deportation of British-born radicals, whom he nicely described as a "dangerous class." Meighen accordingly introduced a new amendment, which passed all three readings in both the House of Commons and Senate in the same day. ("*Saving the World*" was so exercised by this unseemly haste that its authors put in the book's subtitle: *Trial by Jury Destroyed by Stampede Forty-Five Minute Legislation*.) At a stroke, many of the British-born strike leaders were shifted from the de facto security of Canadian citizenship to a de jure redefinition as aliens subject to summary deportation. "This," complains Bumsted good-heartedly, "was a blatant example of inequitable harassment by a government that ought to have known better."[229] A Gramscian would reply: a hegemonic crisis is not a dinner party, and the weapon would long remain in the arsenal of the established political order because it served as an effective technique of disciplining subaltern groups and editing out their most objectionable thinkers. At a time of hegemonic struggle, civil liberties are habitually trumped by the arguments of sovereignty. Perhaps most suggestively, by this measure the federal state itself helped "fuse" the many identities of the left. Socialist British-born Canadians could no longer fancy themselves as being insulated from the possibilities of deportation – all of them could henceforth imagine themselves as passengers on board a future *Komagata Maru*.

The debate between the two sides over citizenship shows up in their contrasting construction of three figures – the citizen, the alien, and the Briton. From the liberal right-wing perspective, the citizen was property-holder, a man whose investments in Winnipeg revealed that he truly had a long-term interest in the community. One could forfeit citizenship by holding the wrong opinions. When it surveyed Winnipeg in June 1919, the *Mail and Empire* of Toronto urged the federal government not to "listen to the Counsels of the solemn owls who undertake to utter clap-trap in the name of the citizens. The citizens want to have Winnipeg purged of the gang who did their best to throttle it and set up a rebel Government. Riel was hanged for resorting to arms to do what they were attempting."[230] Dafoe captured this position on citizenship in his analysis of the municipal elections that followed the strike. Alarmed by the possibility of an alliance between the socialists and the single taxers running for municipal office, he alerted the single taxers to the *OBU Bulletin*'s call for new working-class institutions. What, he wondered pointedly, would Henry George have made of that? The "Radical" candidates were "of a type entirely lacking in the qualifications the electors are looking for." As candidates in the grip of a "rabid class consciousness," they obviously failed the tests of rationality and self-possession required by liberal individualism. They sought to establish "class domination" over "public property and services," which, by implication, were properly under the control and management of those true individuals who laboured without these disabilities.[231] The Pope of Canadian liberalism had declared these leftists deficient in the individual qualities inherent in the true citizen.

The strikers' own *Western Labor News* was amazed at how quickly a radical could be redescribed – those who were once "citizens" quickly became "socialists." One moment he or she might be a peaceful citizen, relaxing at home; the next, "handcuffed, placed under heavy guard in automobiles and [driven] at top speed to the penitentiary at Stony Mountain," and even threatened with summary deportation without the formality of a civil trial. But then a "cog slipped," and now "these desperate Red leaders of a frightfully red revolution – Canadian-wide in scope and engineered from Moscow and backed up by unlimited Bolshevist funds from the United States – these dangerous characters are peacefully resting in their own homes with their wives and children."[232]

Within right-wing discourse the alien was the menacing figure behind the strike. It was the alien who threw stones at the mounted police, the alien who kept speaking of the "Soviet," and the alien whose shadowy intrigues and incomprehensible doctrines were menacing "society." "There are in Winnipeg, unfortunately, a handful of English and Scotch agitators, who are openly and even proudly Red Socialists and Anarchists," warned the *Tribune*. "They are held in contempt by their own fellow-countrymen, are despised and loathed."[233] Added another newspaper: "We simply cannot tolerate a peace that is based on the sacrifice of our rights ... a peace in which the bestial foreigner is permitted openly to boast that he will not permit this or not permit that in a British city, flying a British flag, boasting of British law and cherishing British institutions." Rather than compromise the principles of the state, "It would be better ... that half the population should be wiped off the map, rather than submit to the dictates of Bolsheviks, anarchists and thugs."[234]

In response the left went on the offensive. The genuine "alien" was not really the immigrant. No – the true "alien" was the parasite, the profiteer, and the plutocrat. As Mitchell and Naylor note, the Calgary Labour Conference declared outright: the "alien ... is the master class." Radical socialists, who in the past had indulged in some nativism of their own, now firmly turned their back on that tendency.[235] Not only was the master class alien, but it was also, explicitly or implicitly, promoting the very Kaiserism and Prussianism that the soldiers had been fighting in Europe.

Finally, "the Briton" was also a contested category. Within right-wing discourse, the terms "Briton" and "Bolshevik" were antonyms. In demonstrations, British-constituted authority was championed as the antithesis of the political order represented by the strikers. As Reimer points out, the employers tended to emphasize a "racial" or ethnic definition of Britishness. For the left, though, the Briton was a bearer of "a collection of juridical rights and substantive demands to which the strikers laid claim."[236] When Woodsworth called for the democratic control of industry – meaning the progressive elimination of the private capitalist, a "genuinely scientific reorganization of the nation's industry," and an end to profiteering – he was careful to frame his radical ideas in terms of the British Labour Party. As Reimer argues, by building on wartime discourses of patriotism the *Western Labor News* was able to construct a "historically distinct, working-class definition of citizenship and nationhood," which would work "to counter attempts by Winnipeg employers and various levels of government to discredit the strikers, indeed to deny them citizenship." On 11 June 1919, the *Strike Bulletin* even carried a story of a "Hunnish Atrocity," which turned out to be imprisonment of a striker who had been gassed in the War. "By portraying the Canadian government's actions as arbitrary, autocratic and Prussian," Reimer observes, "and contrasting them with the ideals of British democracy and justice, the *Western Labor News* echoed the discursive battle lines of the war."[237] British-Canadian patriotism was sharply contrasted with the questionable loyalty of the profiteer and the war-monger. The strikers themselves pointedly questioned the credentials of the Citizens Committee. "Who are they? Who is their chairman? Who elected them? Where are their headquarters? How many of them are there? Who gave them power over the City Council and the Parliaments? Who? Why? When? Where? What? It is all a mystery to the citizens as a whole," went one owl-like polemic in the strikers' paper. "Who are they? Why their timidity? Who is their chairman? Who? Who? Who?"[238]

In these left representations of recent history, it was the leftist who was imagined as the prototypical citizen, and it was the police who were violating the boundaries that conventionally separated private and public in a liberal order. The "law" was depicted as a set of pistol-packing "outlaws" terrorizing the domestic realm, riding roughshod over the individual's right to privacy, operating secretly instead of openly, resorting to violence instead of moral suasion, breaking up democratic demonstrations, and (in Dixon's mocking description) "twirling their reeking tubes high in the air in Orthodox Deadwood Dick style."[239]

Science, Enlightenment, and Struggle

For many activists, the campaign for a fuller, more democratic concept of citizenship was linked to the creation of new structures, such as the One Big Union, which conformed to the logic of social evolution. The two issues of a *scientific* reorganization of labour and the right to collective bargaining were intertwined even on the ballot that initially authorized the strike. "This coupling of the two issues was probably a mistake," remarks Bumsted.[240] But such a "mistake" might also indicate the difference separating one framework of thought and activism from another.

One of the most interesting things about the OBU movement, as it gained momentum after the Calgary regional convention and became inextricably wound up with Winnipeg 1919, was the project announced in the resolution that went before the workers, which spoke of "scientifically reorganizing" the labour movement – a goal of some consequence in the period of the first formation, in which "science" and "scientifically" were not words to be casually used. The terms referred activists back to the evolutionary theory and triune formula that had long shaped socialist thought and action. The resolution implied that science could be called upon to support a transition from pure and simple trade unionism à la Gompers and Co. to industrial union-ism. Trade unionists were being asked, in other words, to move from the sim-ple homogeneity of crafts to the complex heterogeneity and functional integration of industry – as any good Spencerian would have spotted at a hundred yards. The OBU might be seen anew, and made much more interest-ing, if its founders' first formationist claims that it represented a scientific breakthrough were taken more seriously.

For someone like Woodsworth, relatively new to Spencerian activism, the argument for an organically unified, functionally differentiated union-ism was similar to the case to be made for the unification of the Protestant churches in one united church. One Big Union, One Big Church, One Big Movement: functional, coherent, and differentiated, all such heterogeneous integrations would be far more capable of responding effectively ("scientifi-cally") to the challenges of modernity. All would be organisms more adapted to the era of corporate capital. A socialism crafted to respond to the matrix-event of a newly consolidated and centralized capitalism and incorporating vast amounts of social-evolutionary theory was predisposed to favour any formula for organization that smacked of organic development. Socialists who had absorbed the combined lessons of Spencer and Marx looked forward to a movement whose overall structure would grow ever larger and more unified, and whose ever more specialized and differentiated parts would be harmoniously and scientifically combined in response to its sur-rounding environment.

The strike, then, although it was, as Masters argued, "not an attempt to seize the government by force," was indeed a revolution in a different first formation sense, and much more than "a struggle over wages and hours and collective bargaining."[241] For both Masters and Bercuson, the strikers were "inadvertent revolutionaries." They did not want to create a revolutionary sit-uation. They were, according to Bercuson, trapped into "appearing to be doing so by their own inexperience and lack of planning." Even if they may not have meant to be revolutionary, the Strike Committee was "arrogating to itself the functions of government."[242] But again, what might have been "ar-rogation" from the perspective of mainstream historians was "evolutionary fulfilment" from the perspective of the first formation. Since social evolution entailed an inexorable, all-encompassing, and organically unified process of scientific enlightenment and political empowerment, there was no "ar-rogation" entailed in workers determining, for instance, how bread and milk were to be distributed: they were, rather, naturally growing into positions of authority that they richly deserved because of the functional indispensability of their labour.

Although general strikes had occurred in various places and industries at least since the Pictou County general coalfields strike of the 1880s,[243] what was new in Winnipeg were the numbers and diversities of trades involved. As 1919 progressed the general strike became not so much one tool in the toolbox of the labour movement, but rather a question, a dialectical, system-challenging but also formation-changing question, about how the left might come to power. Again, this theme went back to social-evolutionary theory. In theory such a strike would bring thousands or even millions of isolated, theoretically homogeneous workers together into a new functionally integrated relationship with each other – moving them, that is, from incoherent homogeneity to coherent heterogeneity, from simple isolation to complex integration. Spencer would not have sympathized, to put it mildly, with the Winnipeg General Strike. But he would have grimly recognized, in many of the arguments brought forward on its behalf and in the subsequent playing out of the One Big Union with which it was intertwined, many echoes of his own evolutionary philosophy.

Winnipeg 1919 was, then, at one and the same time a strike for collective bargaining *and* a revolution. The rebels had both *scientific* and *educational* ambitions. Many radicals saw Winnipeg 1919, in large part, as a pedagogical exercise. For example, when the Defense Committee came to reflect in *"Saving the World"* on the lessons of the strike, they noted that the struggle had shown, among other things, "the nature of the class struggle, the ruthlessness and brutality of imperialist capital, the humbug of 'Christianity,' the real purpose of military and semi-military bodies." Yet, more positively, it had also "started men and women to think and to study, to realize the power they possessed if they could use it unitedly."[244] These were not radicals content merely to elect more socialists to office. For these leftists as a group, given their views of conventional political parties as dysfunctional parasites upon social labour, socialism meant something far larger than the election to office of any particular party. They were trying to effect through the means of the Sympathetic General Strike the revolutionary enlightenment and transformation of their society.

In many respects the radicals succeeded brilliantly in this exercise, demonstrating that a city in which many functions had been taken over by workers did not descend into complete mayhem, and launching unprecedented programs of publication and historical reflection. There was something magnificent about the countless scenes in Winnipeg that springtime – of ordinary people taking hold of their own lives, shouting their convictions to the world, coming together in grassroots institutions, and building their own alternative common-sense understandings of the society around them. In these moments were the molecules of a democratic transformation. The strikers' publication *"Saving the World from Democracy"* was, in essence, a defence of rationality and enlightenment in the face of a regime seemingly capable of neither. The veterans who had sacked the Socialist Party headquarters in January 1919 and burned socialist books in the street provided a classic symbol of the depths of resistance to the "people's enlightenment" that the ruling order could call upon. What the returned soldiers did dramatically – attacking the existence of a library, humiliating an alien – the state did less dramatically and more effectively. It attacked the very existence of socialist libraries by prohibiting books, and it attacked the "International," the multicultural and multinational left, by deporting radical aliens. There was a fascinating cultural continuum between burning a library and cracking down on the distribution of the works of Spencer and Plato. There was a lot of "book-burning," literal or symbolic, going on in 1916–19 – not just in the streets, not just in Winnipeg, and not just by crowds of uninformed returned soldiers. The leftists in Winnipeg were, as leftists had been since the establishment of the Canadian Socialist League of the 1890s, people of the books, pressing their science on society. Operating on stages of vastly different dimensions, both the state and soldiers were enacting counter-enlightenment scripts.

The state authorities suspended many of the normal workings of parliamentary government. They staged show trials, banned political parties and the public use of entire languages, looked the other way while right-wing vigilantes roughed up dissenters. They abused and imprisoned conscientious objectors, used concentration camps as a way of disciplining dissidents, and in general comported themselves in ways that good Canadian liberals generally denounce when they read about them in distant times and faraway places. In Winnipeg 1919 all of these actions were taken in the name of the preservation of liberal order – the peace, order, and good government of a Dominion that the liberals themselves – and notably the lawmakers, the authorities, and many scholars – were determined to uphold.

These liberal activists and intellectuals would always find something disturbingly "unplaceable" and "uncanny" about the strike – and this is a view that very much influences how its memory has been shaped. The strike increasingly became a sort of natural disaster, through which resourceful individuals passed, rather than a moment of collective empowerment. Even the dominant images that came down to us – which most memorably show the strike being *crushed* on Bloody Saturday – are misleading, because they select out of the potentially infinite details about Winnipeg 1919 those few that represent it as violent and irrational. Much about the strike defies individualist forms of narrative construction, because so much of it revolves around educational meetings and collective epiphanies, so little around individual deeds and heroic generals.

In the strike's peculiar status as an "anomaly within liberalism," we have, perhaps, the reason as to why so much ink has been spilled about it, with such huge amounts of venom. It disturbs people. Orthodoxy requires that after the perfect storm of Winnipeg 1919, nothing but wreckage – ill feelings, smashed unions, devastated lives – remains. It can incorporate Winnipeg 1919 only by reiterating how completely the left was obliterated, how completely *over* this moment must be. The reversal must be so total and absolute – "Their defeat was as complete a defeat as ever was"[245] – that any positive memory of the moment is impossible. Yet Winnipeg's legacy was much more ambiguous. Certainly when future prime ministers looked back on Winnipeg, they did not do so in the hope of ever seeing its like again. It put up "red flags" – of revolution and of danger – to anyone who would venture again into the monolithic nationalism and social coercion of the government of 1915–20. A prime minister who overlooked that lesson, as Bennett would in the 1930s, ran the very real risk of staging "Winnipeg: The Next Generation." As the *Red Flag* pointed out in a Gramscian moment, in the wake of Winnipeg, what the triumvirate – the capitalists, the state, and the AFL craft unions – had won in the material sense was more than offset by what they had lost in "moral prestige." At "this stage of development," such a defeat was a victory in disguise.[246]

Yet the resonances of Winnipeg went much beyond that. Winnipeg 1919 was a conscious attempt to imagine what new relations of freedom would look like in the post-capitalist future. This future was one in which the science of socialism was free to complete its humanity-restoring mission and inaugurate the people's enlightenment. Much of Winnipeg 1919 was devoted to *performing* in ways that made this future come alive – projecting into the politics of the present day images of a redeemed tomorrow. If we see the strike as in part a performance of future possibilities, one in which the boundaries between art and life were blurred if not effaced, we can start to make better sense of the many aspects of it that were not directly related to labour relations in industry. There was something more important here than just "playing with words," indulging in rhetorical excesses, or getting carried away with the moment. As Vance reminds us, high diction worked powerfully to achieve a usable past. Reconnaissance suggests that, on the left, high diction worked just as powerfully to create a usable future.

The notorious "sign-crime" for which the strike will always be remembered is a case in point – the permission notices (or placards) announcing that a milk or bread delivery wagon was making its rounds as "Permitted by Authority of Strike Committee." Six little words – each of them easily read exactly for what they meant. But – what did they mean? In what context? The permission placards were explosively controversial not for what they said, but for how they *performed* and what they *foretold*. In a sense, no less than the "conscription of wealth," they condensed an entire sociology.

They were props in a play about social interconnectedness and labour's functional indispensability. They were miniature manifestos about the level of functional integration in society. They made visible the arguments of organicism long embraced by the first formation – and foretold an emergent structure of power in which such relations would be governed in an entirely different way. Working from liberal premises, McNaught and Bercuson note that this event was very much a question of perception versus reality: the placards in themselves changed nothing in terms of power relationships. Yet people *perceived* them as symbols of workers' power.[247] A different way of looking at the placards would be to say that they meant different things in different contexts, rather like a playing card might mean something in one game, and something else in another. For some people they might testify to the achievement of working-class power – since their "objective" performative function was to allow for the delivery of bread and milk at the discretion of the Strike Committee. For others they might represent props in the drama of Soviet Rule on the Red River – a performance that would be continued into the show trials of the following year. What was *performed* was in part a future in which the working class was not only paid a decent wage but also honoured as the foundation of a new civilization – indeed, so powerful that its authority ruled the streets.

Writing in Turin's *L'Ordine Nuovo* on 14 June 1919, Antonio Gramsci was convinced that "in Canada the industrial strikes have taken on the overt character of a bid to instal a soviet regime," while all over the world "the people are intensifying their revolt against the mercantilism and imperialism of capital, which continues to generate antagonisms, conflicts, destruction of life and goods, unsated by the blood and disasters of five years of war."[248] His comment foreshadowed years of debate over Winnipeg within the radical left. Just over two years later, on 7 July 1921, Joe Knight, the obu's main organizer in Ontario, addressed the Third Congress of the Communist International in a debate on the leadership's proposal that Communists should enter major established unions, even those under pro-capitalist leadership, rather than orienting themselves primarily to more revolutionary movements like the iww. Knight suggested that Winnipeg 1919 revealed the correctness of the Comintern's proposed strategy. It resembled the spc's "boring from within" tactic that, according to him, had brought them control of the labour council in Winnipeg, influence over all the city's workers, and an almost successful revolution: "A situation was created in which we were only one step away from taking power. Nothing was done in Winnipeg except by order of the strike committee, which was no less powerful than the state itself. Naturally, Winnipeg is not all of Canada. But had the struggle in Winnipeg gripped all of Canada, it would certainly have ended in revolution."

Winnipeg 1919 in this interpretation prefigured the Comintern leadership's strategy of entering into the trade unions.[249] Subsequent Communist treatments of Winnipeg 1919 would present it very differently. Tim Buck would argue that "the grim truth is that the Winnipeg General Strike exposed the fallacy of the theory that: 'The workers can make themselves invincible by simply folding their arms.' That strike marked the high point of the influence of that false theory in North America, and, simultaneously, the beginning of its decline."[250]

In the high diction of the Canadian left, Winnipeg 1919 became a symbol of heroism. The strikers created an event unlike any seen before in North America (in Canada, only the Congress of Industrial Organizations uprising in the 1930s and the Common Front in Quebec in the 1970s bear a close resemblance). What was revealed in Winnipeg was the enormous power of "the people," conceptualized in 1919 as the working class and its allies, coming together to create a hegemonic challenge to the existing political order. It would be remembered as a moment in which democrats confronted autocrats, seekers after truth faced philistine attorneys and book-burners, a fragile alliance of native-born and foreign-born braved the menaces of wrongful imprisonment and deportation. In a landscape of repression, thousands of men and women had struggled to find a new path to the realm of freedom. They dared to reason and to live in the bright clear air of the people's enlightenment.

Expounding a people's enlightenment: Roger E. Bray, for six years a Methodist lay preacher, addresses one of the many mass meetings at Victoria Park in Winnipeg, 13 June 1919. Provincial Archives of Manitoba.

8

Showtime, 1920

*I*n the aftermath of Winnipeg 1919 came the trials. Some, in the form of deportation hearings inflicted upon the "radical aliens," were held in secret. Others were highly visible. They were show trials, meant to instruct Canadians on political proprieties and to punish those who had dared to step over the lines of liberalism. In them we see both the limitations and the achievements of the first formation of the Canadian left.

The logic of the show trials was transparently fallacious. If the Winnipeg General Strike itself was illegal, its organizers were guilty of a crime. The logical thing to do would have been to arrest and try them all – the 50-odd-member Strike Committee, the leaders of the well-known trade unions whose balloting had led to the supposed crime, and the wider circle of co-conspirators in Winnipeg who had played a public role in aiding and abetting an unlawful act. If the strike as a whole was not illegal, but only aspects of it were, the logical course would have been to bring to trial people accused of violating specific sections of the Criminal Code – for damaging property, for instance. If the real crimes of 1919 were not those of "Winnipeg" but those of a Canada-wide Bolshevik conspiracy, the logical thing to do would have been to bring the self-proclaimed Bolsheviks into the dock. All three strategies would have had at least the saving grace of being consistent with the law itself. Not one of these strategies was adopted.

Show trials are only secondarily about the law. They are primarily demonstrations of the might and majesty of the state and its ability to crush its opponents – detaining some without trial, deporting others, and flaying yet more for "sign-crimes" against the hegemonic order. Show trials often manufacture unproved but vast conspiracies made up of people who may never have met each other but are assumed to share a secret purpose. They are exercises in ideological manipulation.

In this case, the show trials were of a piece with the anti-immigration legislation: they generated preposterous lists following no apparent logic except that of naming the Other of liberal order. R.B. Russell, one of the strike's most powerful leaders, was tried in the fall of 1919 and sentenced on 28 December to two years in Stony Mountain Penitentiary. His trial was followed by the trials of seven others – William Ivens, W.A. Pritchard, R.J. Johns, John Queen, George Armstrong, Roger Bray, and A.A. Heaps – which extended from January to March 1920.[1] These eight men were all charged with various counts of seditious conspiracy and "common nuisance." Fred Dixon and J.S. Woodsworth were charged with seditious libel, and three returned soldier-strikers were also charged with "seditious utterances" (though the charges against two of these three were dropped).

Pritchard of the Socialist Party and *Western Clarion* had merely visited Winnipeg to lend his support. He was as guilty of "causing Winnipeg," if indeed that was a crime, as the saintly canon F.G. Scott, who had graced the strike-divided city with his High Anglican presence. Woodsworth, similarly, had dropped in to lend a helping hand (the transparently comic case against him, based in part upon reading a seditious intent into words from the prophet Isaiah, went nowhere). Dick Johns had been in Montreal in the months leading up to the event. The supposed seditious conspiracy linking such disparate men was never proved, for the simple reason that it had never existed. Yet, as in the case of the more famous Moscow trials of the 1930s, a miscellaneous body of evidence could be drawn together in an attempt to show that such a conspiracy had indeed transpired.

Sedition, seditious libel, and seditious conspiracy, it turned out, were all wonderfully flexible terms. Drawing on British legal authority, Judge Thomas Llewellyn Metcalfe established that sedition:

> embraced all those practices, whether by word, deed or writing, which fall short of high treason, but directly tend to have for their object to excite discontent or dissatisfaction; to excite ill-will between different classes of the King's subjects; to create public disturbances, or lead to civil war, to bring into hatred or contempt the Sovereign or the government, the law or constitution of the realm . . . to incite people to unlawful associations, assemblies, insurrections, breaches of the peace.

As for conspiracy, the judge argued that while "the parties must be shown to be pursuing one common intention," it was not necessary to show they had actually joined together to effect some common purpose or had in fact even met.[2] D.C. Masters, not inclined to brash and critical statements about the established order, nonetheless remarked: "One cannot escape the conviction that the real prisoner in the dock was the O.B.U."[3]

Even so, what was in the dock in Winnipeg was not the OBU in a narrow sense – there were no grounds for arresting someone just because he or she was a member of the OBU, which was not an illegal body – but the ideas that the OBU was thought to represent, most obviously the idea of revolution as it had been taken up and transformed by the first formation. The show trials were *staged*, and the purpose of this showtime was to demonstrate the impossibility of all the hopes and dreams that had flourished so remarkably in Winnipeg in 1919. These were *hegemonic performances*, mounted not just to demoralize and even dispose of a particular set of radical leaders regarded as menaces to the established order, but to foreclose the possibilities of living otherwise that had been recently implanted. They also in effect became acts of *historical interpretation*, which would permanently shape the stories that people would tell about Winnipeg. These carefully calculated, intensively researched, and deliberately executed spectacles would, authorities reasoned, both dampen the fires of revolt and show through the routine functioning of the law that firm order was being restored and nothing had been permanently changed. As Tom Mitchell and James Naylor remark: "The workers' revolt was transformed into a criminal venture. In short, the trials of Russell and the other strike leaders were not about bringing criminals to justice; rather they were ideological events designed to mobilize consent for the established order while constructing strict limitations on the legality of any criticism of the state and demands for fundamental change in relations of production."[4] Neither "panic-stricken" responses to disorder (for the moment of popular mobilization had long passed before the show trials were staged), nor "common-sense" responses to violations of the law, the trials were pre-emptive strikes against an emergent realm of enlightened freedom.

The core indictment under which most of the political prisoners were tried covered events dating back to the Walker Theatre meeting of 22 December 1918. Yet as the cases unfolded the "crime" was tracked back for decades. In essence, authoritarian liberals turned on the leftists associated with Winnipeg the same strategies of violence and exclusion they had earlier used on the *Komagata Maru* in 1914 and would later perfect in the violent repression of the On-to-Ottawa Trek in 1935.[5]

The organization of show trials on such a scale requires an immense amount of time and money. The pivotal behind the scenes role was played by the Committee of 1000 and its energetic leader, A.J. Andrews. In 1919 and 1920 Ottawa expended some $196,000 for the prosecution of the supposed "seditious conspirators." The Department of Justice would pay $150,024.40 to lawyers prosecuting the strike leaders, and $12,332.09 to the McDonald Detective Agency for special police and detective services.[6] Now, when the state confronted the socialists, it could draw upon thick dossiers seemingly full of incriminating evidence. As the SPC's *Red Flag* observed on 6 September 1919, "We have been under surveillance by the secret service, not to speak of enthusiastic amateur sleuths, for five years. Our meetings have been under observation. Our mail, both of the party and of individual members, has been scrutinized. For more than three months at a time every letter was opened." Party headquarters had been searched, members' homes raided, correspondence and account books attacked: yet nothing had been found that would put the party leaders behind bars.[7]

The spectacle in the court continued the theme of book-burning and book-banning so characteristic of Canada from 1915 to 1920: again and again, the Crown attacked, through the figures of the men in the dock, the libraries that stood behind them. They aimed to discredit the dissident interpretations of history and society found therein – to find, in essence, a "seditious conspiracy" going back over a hundred years and encompassing much of the North Atlantic radical world. Drawing upon the texts of the international tradition, the prosecutors sought to make of Winnipeg 1919 an offence against world liberal order. Even *The Communist Manifesto*, notwithstanding its presence in university libraries throughout the transatlantic world, and well on its way to becoming the world's most reprinted secular book, would be hauled out as evidence pertaining to the supposed conspiracy of men on a different continent more than 70 years later.

The show trials were staged as massive spectacles, with socialism as a whole called upon to offer justification for its continued existence. The curious result was that rather than minimizing the significance of Winnipeg 1919 or permanently "sealing" it as a disgraceful defiance of liberal order, the trials confirmed its world-historic status. If one side in this brutal affair was plainly dominant, *both* sides contributed to shaping the discourse of Winnipeg as an episode that related directly to the great international left. If the prosecution wanted to focus relentlessly on its imaginary notion of a vast left-wing conspiracy, the left itself presented the trial as a defence of the people's enlightenment and radical humanism. The hundreds of pages from the trial speeches reveal relatively little about the details of the events that occurred in Winnipeg, but much about the traditions of Milton and Marx, Socrates and Spencer. The leftists responded to the challenge thrown down by the state with an amazing demonstration of their intellectual breadth and prowess. They capped their performances with an unprecedented publication program that brought leading speeches and declarations to a wide public. At long last the Canadian left was not just importing but producing its own books.

Show trials have a way of turning on those who stage them. In the short term those people might think they have the last word – and as they predictably send the political prisoners off to penitentiary, in a sense they do. In the long term show trials are a permanent indictment against those who stage them. Nothing can ever redeem the state that orchestrated the show trials of 1920, against men whose only crime was to imagine, and want to put into practice, a different way of organizing the social world. But at the very least the trials did produce something quite tangible: two speeches that would be commemorated by the activated left. In their contrasting articulations of the politics of resistance, the speeches of defendants Dixon and Pritchard provide an arresting glimpse of the legacy of the first formation.

Bargaining with Hegemony: The Case of Fred Dixon

Fred Dixon (1881–1931) was a local fixture. Born in Reading, England, he immigrated to Canada in 1903 and settled in Winnipeg. Soon he gravitated into the city's famous "Mobius Circle," where freethinkers and advanced liberals read Paine, Tolstoy, Ruskin, and Carlyle. Dixon, the single-tax militant, was also – after his arrest for soapboaxing in 1909 – a leader in the Free Speech Defence League. He helped found the Manitoba Federation for Direct Legislation in 1908 and – after a narrow defeat in 1910, with the spc candidate playing a spoiler's role – was elected to the Manitoba legislature in July 1914, where he joined Dick Rigg of the Social Democratic Party (both would be reelected in 1915). There Dixon succeeded in pushing through a bill favouring direct legislation, though the project subsequently foundered in court, where it was established, in essence, that sovereignty was vested in the Crown, not the voters.[8] Dixon was a 19th-century Georgeite abroad in a 20th-century world – a far cry from the Marxists who, repeatedly, dismissed him as a fakir and tried to defeat him at the polls. He was a stubborn democrat and, like so many single taxers, would not be diverted from his scathing critiques of graft and corruption.

Yet he was no mere apologist of liberal order. In March 1918 Dixon rallied to the banner of the new Dominion Labour Party, where he rubbed shoulders with Ivens and soon shared platforms with Russell. At the Walker Theatre meeting of 22 December, Dixon seconded the motion calling upon the government to liberate political prisoners. He "did not believe that a man who follows the dictates of his conscience is necessarily a criminal, and men who were willing to suffer the tortures of the penitentiary rather than be false to their convictions cannot be bad citizens." He poured scorn on the persecution of the socialists and conscientious objectors. Why not arrest those grafters who had palmed off malfunctioning Ross Rifles, defective shells, and paper boots on the poor soldiers of the Great War – on those responsible for "the whole black record of profiteering and graft," who had given "ten thousand times more aid and comfort to the enemy than all the Socialists and conscientious objectors put together"?[9]

Dixon was not officially a socialist – they ran against him in elections – but in 1920 his new Independent Labour Party would run on a platform that called, among other things, for the transformation of capitalist property into social property and production for use instead of profit, as well as direct legislation, collective bargaining, and other social measures. He topped the polls.

Dixon was the kind of radical who built bridges between left liberals and populists on the one hand and socialists on the other: it made sense for the regime to try to silence him.

Much of his crafty intelligence was on display in the Winnipeg courtroom in January 1920. Dixon had a folksy touch that endeared him to the jury, made up – not at all accidentally – of farmers drawn from outside of Winnipeg itself. "I want you to judge this indictment just the same as you would judge a horse," he advised the jurors. "If you were going to judge a horse it would not make any difference whether the horse were put in a red barn with red curtains around the stall and red lights flashed on; if you wanted to judge the horse you would say bring him out into the open; you do not care whether it was an old broken down barn or not." So it was with the case against him. Look at the charges with your "natural vision," he urged the jurors. Take them out of the context of the trick lighting, the theatrical effects, all the legal artificiality, and "judge these articles as you would judge them if you were behind the barn or haystack, or by the kitchen fire after the chores were done."[10]

Dixon's endearing horse sense went beyond the merely metaphorical. When it came to explaining the crucial events of Black Saturday, when the Mounties had charged the peaceful demonstration, Dixon was able to draw upon his knowledge of horses to help the jurors see the events of that day through his eyes. Some of the men in khaki had been riding "green horses," which had "got the better of the men and carried them away," whereas the "red coats had horses used to the work," which explained why they could form up again and regain control. He went for the jugular of the Crown attorney, whom he painted as a man overly fond of ornate and artificial constructs. Can't we just see things eye to eye, he appealed to the jurors, like two farmers chatting over their shared fence? "One learned man said: 'We don't send men to jail unless they have a guilty mind.' I want you to look me square in the eye. You have watched me for two weeks and heard some of the articles I have written and speeches I have made. Do I look like a criminal with a guilty mind? Is my demeanor that?"[11] What free-born, corn-fed son of Manitoba could resist such an honest, plainspoken man?

It was not all just hayseed and hokum. Dixon was not just a mere populist. He defended the new, all-inclusive demands of the labour movement in language that echoed Bland's *The New Christianity*, published that same year. The demand for co-operative industry, and for production for use and not for profit, emerged from the workers' inevitable rise to maturity. Dixon told the jurors a story. A farmer watches his boy grow, "and he knows that some day the boy will say: 'Father, I must have a voice in the management of this farm and my fair share in the products or start a farm myself.' The farmer may hope the day will never come, but in his heart of hearts he knows the boy will grow to manhood and will rightly demand a voice and a share." It was no different with labour. Just like that Prairie boy, labour was growing into manhood. And now, in the natural course of events, it too was "demanding a voice in the management through collective bargaining in order that it may have a fairer share of the wealth it produces."

Now, wasn't this just the sort of thing that happened on farms? Well, it was the same thing in industry. There too, labour had (so to speak) "all growed up," and what could be more natural than to hear it say, "We'd like a share of the management looking towards co-operation." What could be so seditious about that? Why, if the Crown prosecutor had his way, with his artificial talk and high-flown theories and complicated conspiracies – and wasn't he taking up a lot of your time with his fancy-dancy talk? – the farmer who wrote to his newspaper to complain about the local weed inspector could be charged with publishing "seditious libel," just because he was criticizing a "public official when public feeling was running high."[12]

So, what could be so seditious about Fred, your friendly farmer? Why was the prosecutor trying to "build up" an artificial case against him? Dixon jumped on the phrase "building up," which he turned into a metaphor for the prosecutor's overly complicated and overstated case, which was made up not of solid things but of "painted paper bricks." Why connect Dixon to all the radical literature stacked against the defendants, when he had no time or taste for it? "I do not want to read that kind of literature even at the invitation of the crown counsel," he stated.[13] He had read *The Communist Manifesto*, he admitted, but only with the purpose of debating with the socialists. Why link him to the ultra-radicals, when they were always running against him and the Labour Party? Why blame him for the brash actions of a few strikers? Sure, he had said a few radical things in 1919 – and this was an understatement, given that he had provocatively indicted the government as a form of "Kaiserism in Canada" – but men did say such things in the heat of the moment.

Was Dixon a renegade from the first formation? Not really. Many of his arguments went right back to the movement's underlying evolutionary sociology and philosophy. Like them, he positioned himself in a great movement of enlightenment. Socrates, reviled by his peers, was now in the forefront of the world's philosophers. Bruno, who had supported Galileo's heretical assertion that the Earth moved around the sun, had been executed. Milton, now considered one of the British Empire's "brightest stars," had been thrown in jail and persecuted. Now the advocates of collective bargaining, which was just freedom of speech and association applied to the new conditions of industrial life, were also being persecuted for what they believed – as were those who pursued collective bargaining with the General Sympathetic Strike, who – and here Dixon once more seemingly echoed the rhetoric of *A New Christianity* – were simply following the dictates of evolution itself. To denounce the strike was just like denouncing "the wheat for ripening, the river for flowing into the sea, or the boy for growing into a man." It was akin to trying to dam Niagara in the hope that the river would never reach the sea. "Grass will grow, the river will reach the sea, the boy will become a man," Dixon concluded, "and labor will come into its own."[14] Dixon's militant appeals to a kind of "common-sense empiricism," his dogged reliance on pre-existing concepts of the citizen, meant that it was possible to imagine that he was merely calling for minor reforms – and not, as he repeatedly but quietly said, the replacement of production for profit by co-operative production for use.

Dixon stood at the juncture of social democracy and liberalism. Carrying no "atheistic" or seemingly "revolutionary" baggage, he could appear before the jurors as a man just like them, wrongly accused simply because he had tried to defend the British Constitution and the "natural" rights of labour. Yet he also showed marked courage and candour in attacking those whom he claimed, plausibly enough, were destroying British freedoms. Should Arthur Meighen, the prince of the Canadian Tories, be allowed to conspire against the people and rob them of such liberties as trial by jury? Should such freedoms be destroyed "by those assassins of liberty who misgovern Canada?" Should such age-old principles as the presumption of innocence be cast aside, in an Ottawa-orchestrated campaign against fundamental freedoms? Turning to Canadian history, Dixon invoked the names of Louis-Joseph Papineau, William Lyon Mackenzie, and Joseph Howe – all towering figures in a democratic tradition that the new authoritarians were now misrepresenting. No fewer than four times did Dixon remind the jurors that they held his "personal liberty" in their hands, and by extension the whole tradition of the civil rights of Canadian subjects.[15]

Dixon was a warning to the new authoritarians that, although they could mince liberties and invent conspiracies – in ways reminiscent of their contemporary liberal descendants, with their security certificates and abject complicity in inhumanity against prisoners – there were limits beyond which they could go only with danger to their legitimacy. The authorities could push the "Aliens" around (and to his discredit Dixon also distanced himself from them). But they could not overtly trample on the image of the "free-born Briton." They could not proclaim overtly what they were accomplishing covertly, the suppression of free speech and the abrogation of the Magna Carta, because to do so was too radical a breach in the accepted conventions of political life.

Dixon was also a warning to the emergent new left of the 1920s. A Canadian left that could not include a man like Dixon would be cut off from some of the deepest sources of democratic radical opposition – the resistance to the arbitrary exercise of power in the interests of a propertied elite. A Canadian left that could honestly speak Dixon's democratic language and then radically extend it would retain open channels to the sensibilities of many Canadians;

one that disparaged all such talk as "bourgeois democracy" would pay a steep price in isolation and illegitimacy. In Dixon's speech, in which was revealed much of the mentality of the interwar Independent Labour Party, we see in outline the problem that would persistently haunt the Canadian left of the 1920s: how could leftists withstand the co-optive strategies of the liberals and hang on to the core vision of a new world?

Dixon's speech movingly evoked the possibilities of free discussion and debate in an open society. It quietly refrained from noting the social and economic processes by which freedom had been so grossly eroded over the past five years, as witnessed by his trial itself, and it left unguarded the frontier that separated the radical democracy of socialism from the passive-revolutionary strategies of the authoritarian liberals.

Assaulting Hegemony: The Case of William Pritchard

The case against W.A. Pritchard (1888–1981) was infinitely weaker than the feeble case against Dixon. At least Dixon had shouted some angry truths to power in the heat of Winnipeg 1919. He had likened the government to Kaiserism, and hence, in a general sense, had indeed excited "discontent or dissatisfaction" among His Majesty's subjects. He had been in Winnipeg through the great rebellion, served in the strike leadership, and played a public role in revolutionary meetings.

William Pritchard had been away from Winnipeg for most of May and June 1919. He had visited the city to lend his support to the strike and to the socialists involved in its leadership, but no serious scholar would maintain that Pritchard was responsible in any actual way for Winnipeg 1919. He was, if not an innocent, then at most an interested onlooker. Yet Dixon was found innocent, and through a gross miscarriage of justice Pritchard was declared guilty and sent to Stony Mountain Penitentiary. His address to the jury on 23 and 24 March 1920, which takes up 216 pages in its printed form, is a first formation classic.[16]

Perhaps those outcomes occurred because Dixon could more easily present himself to the jury as just another straightforward, everyday person. Perhaps it was because Pritchard, unlike Dixon, drew more from the Marx than the Spencer side of the ideological continuum. He spoke in a Marxian dialect that some jurors might have found difficult to grasp. He was also systematically framed as a crazed insurrectionist by a prosecution keen to bag at least one major target for their paymasters in the Citizens' Committee and the federal government. The architects of a show trial do not worry too much about justice, and Pritchard in Winnipeg in 1920 stood about as much chance of acquittal as did Bukharin in Moscow in 1938.

Born on 3 April 1888 in Salford, near Manchester, Pritchard came from a coal-mining family. By a nice coincidence, his father James had also worked in the local textile mill associated with the family of Engels. The Salford area was a bastion of the Social Democratic Federation, and the younger Pritchard, despite his immersion in the severely evangelical world of the Plymouth Brethren, may well have absorbed some of the Marxism of that organization. He attended the Manchester School of Technology and the Royal Institute of Technology in Salford before apprenticing as a clerk in the building construction business and acquiring a familiarity with lumber that would later prove useful in his life in British Columbia.

In the early 1900s his father James Pritchard travelled across the sea, and then across the Dominion, to take up work in the coal mines of Vancouver Island. James became a member of the Dominion Executive Committee of the spc in 1908. William arrived in Vancouver in 1911 and within two weeks was admitted as a member of the party. He replaced Kingsley as editor of the *Western Clarion* in August 1914, serving in this capacity until mid-1917. After leaving the *Clarion* he took a job as a shipper in a lumber mill, became intensely committed to industrial unionism as a trade unionist, and gained a position on the Vancouver Trades and Labour Council. His speeches took on an increasingly revolutionary aura. "Pritchard did not see a revolution happening in Canada in the immediate future," Peter Campbell explains, but to the socialist's way of thinking there was an "inevitability" about it. As Pritchard put it, "Before the relentless onslaught of the world's class conscious workers, before the impregnability of proletarian science, the devices of our masters and their apologists must fail."[17]

Pritchard was one of the brightest stars in the meetings at the Empress Theatre in Vancouver, where Socialists gathered frequently through 1919 to debate the revolution swirling all around them. In one memorable address he attacked the government's implicit cultural policy of trying to ban books to forestall the revolution that it itself had precipitated. "The ban was placed on Marx and Morgan and Paul Lafargue, and even on Mark Twain and Plato," Pritchard remarked. "They imagined Plato [to be] 'some whiskered individual strolling around Moscow and spitting fire out between his teeth. (Laughter)." He provided readers of the spc's *Red Flag* with the latest word on the Russian Revolution.[18] He was instrumental in distributing the influential pamphlet *Soviets at Work*. On 20 June Pritchard was arrested on his trip home to Vancouver from Winnipeg. As Pritchard himself explained, his arrest and trial were a blatantly political attempt to "frame" both activist and strike in a particular way – essentially, to relate them both to the entire socialist tradition, whose vast output of confiscated literature was well represented in the dock beside him.

"Pritchard was distinctly a man of parts," writes Masters. He was "a fine athlete, a musician of ability who organized juvenile orchestras and male voice choirs, an omnivorous reader who, at the age of eleven, had read Josephus and

Gibbon. A Marxian socialist, he was a brilliant thinker and his Welsh fire made him a most eloquent speaker."[19] Through Pritchard, readers of the *Western Clarion* had been able to learn of the works of many contemporary writers on socialism. He brought his formidable reputation as a socialist thinker to the Western Labour Conference in Calgary, where he argued that the organization of industrial unions complemented the work of socialists in the political sphere. In the One Big Union that emerged from the conference, Pritchard played a significant intellectual role. Rather like Gramsci, who at the same time was combining a passionate concern for the theory and culture of the socialist movement with the organization of new forms of proletarian activism in factory councils, Pritchard was not so much *breaking* with the traditions of the socialist party as he was bringing them into a potentially new, creative relationship with the struggles of the working class. He was never a syndicalist and, perhaps, never really a standard-issue SPCer. He was, rather, an unprecedented combination of the two, someone capable of breathing dramatically new life into the triune formula, and of transforming it into an active force in the fast-changing labour world.

At his trial Pritchard presented the jurors with an extraordinary two-day exposé of his deepest-held beliefs – and the resulting document is in many ways the opposite of Dixon's presentation. If Dixon comfortably adopted the persona of the country boy, simply trying to explain why a manly labour movement was trying to stand on its own two feet, Pritchard confronted the jurors and Crown attorney with the full majesty and rigour of the Marxian school. Pritchard wanted the jurors to re-experience with him something of the long journey that had led him to the stand in 1920. He wanted them to sense something of the excitement of the new social and intellectual force abroad in the land, to appreciate the vast stock of new knowledge and insight stored in the movement's cherished libraries and developed by its leading thinkers. He wanted to give the jurors a palpable sense of the scope of the people's enlightenment that he had been publicizing in Canada.

He did *try* to sound rural, although perhaps he ended up sounding only like a big-city man awkwardly trying to get down with the rustics. For example, as he explained to the jurors, he wanted to put the contemporary demands of socialism into "good, simple language so that you may understand." So, for example, take the concept of revolution: if a grain of wheat fell upon the ground and, in dying, sprang "forth a hundred fold," was that not a revolution? Repeating, without knowing it, Margaret Haile's old metaphor, he referred to a hen laying eggs: "The period of evolution is there; there is the slow growth; the growth of the chick inside the shell until at a certain point in its growth it is faced with that condition, either it dies in its shell or breaks the shell. And the only thing that is hurt is the shell – revolution. Gentlemen, that is a revolution in the organic world."[20]

Hens were duly succeeded in Pritchard's address by cows, whose rhetorical lot it was to exemplify yet more laws of evolution. "You know what it is to be kept up at night because of trouble with the old cow," Pritchard said, once again striving for a folksy tone. "That cow is about to calve. Well, in doing so, she was demonstrating the Law of Change." This same law was at work "throughout everything in the world – birth – growth – decay." Just as the law worked upon chickens and cows, so too did it work upon "social epochs, upon society. . . . And I want to tell you, gentlemen, when they see the calf alongside of the mother cow, they can write whatever Laws they like; they can refuse to see what is taking place in front of them; they can do what they like, gentlemen, but they cannot put that calf back."[21]

When Dixon placed himself rhetorically in the jurors' imagined rural world, he did so as the friendly neighbour, chatting over the fence. Pritchard was more the visiting instructor in Spencerian sociological theory, conscripting rural examples for an all-embracing explanation of the natural and social world. Dixon had constructed himself as the plainspoken enemy of the prosecution's artificial, complicated, and improbable theories. Pritchard attacked the prosecution frontally, using military metaphors to get his point across: "We are not concerned with breaking down every single point; we just want to make a breach, and we are going to make a breach in the bulwarks of the Crown." Pritchard imagined, accurately enough, that in the future historians would "drive the knife of critical research into the very bowels of the bogey that has been conjured forth out of the imagination of certain legal luminaries of this city." If in Dixon ideas came in the shape of comfortable folksy tales about grown-up sons, in the rhetoric of Pritchard they were weapons, "mental dynamite."[22]

Much of this dynamite went to explode the reputation of Crown attorney Andrews. Given that Andrews's case was preposterous and the evidence for it non-existent, Pritchard's attitude was understandable. He pounced on his opponent's every mistake, zeroed in on moments when the learned counsel displayed his abject historical illiteracy, and went so far as to mock Andrews's pompous habit of pointing with his index finger, which Pritchard thought worthy of a Gilbert and Sullivan operetta. He reached the zenith of his furious contempt for the Crown when he came to discuss *The Communist Manifesto*. "Would you want your children to read that?" the Crown had asked, after reciting some of the *Manifesto*'s juicier passages. In reply Pritchard likened Andrews to one of his aunts, a good soul who in her concern for propriety had hidden the racy Old Testament from him. Andrews was no different. He pillaged quotations he did not understand and made mincemeat of ideas he could not grasp. No doubt, if given the chance, he too would have the jurors lock up their Bibles. It was a fine example of the childish nature of the prosecution and indeed of the Crown attorney pushing it forward.[23]

What could one possibly do with a supposed learned counsel who knew no poetry? He did not even know the name of the poet who wrote "The Mask Of Anarchy," in commemoration of the Peterloo Massacre of 1819: "The one thing that has hurt me possibly more than anything else in this case has been the display of learned ignorance that I find among men of the legal profession," Pritchard said with mock sincerity. "Peterloo will be remembered amongst all liberty-loving people in Britain for all time, and that is where that poem came from – Shelly [Shelley]. Aye!"[24]

Pritchard mercilessly held up to deserved contempt the threadbare logic of a liberal show trial whose very existence was an abuse of justice. Dixon's speech epitomized the potential and the problem of labourism: immensely accessible to its audience, yet ultimately politically nebulous in its leftism, uncertain whether to declare its allegiance to the project of a revolutionary social democracy or to cut and run. Pritchard's speech was its exact opposite. It exemplified the beauty and the limitations of the "impossibilist" style – the limitations lying in the many allusions and arguments that surely flew several miles over the heads of the jurors, and the strengths residing in the sense of authority and justification that it gave to one radical to stand up to the system and say, in a modern vernacular one cannot imagine Pritchard himself ever using: "Can you really believe this bullshit?"

Pritchard's speech was preoccupied not with Winnipeg 1919 – his direct knowledge of the events of the strike was obviously limited because he had played almost no direct role in shaping them – but with the latest trends in socialist thought, and especially with socialism as the applied science of social evolution. In a trial that called upon him to nail his colours to the mast and declare his deepest beliefs, a trial that put "socialism" itself in the dock, Pritchard's overpowering theme was that socialism was a project of rational enlightenment, whose forebears included Bruno and Galileo. As Campbell remarks, Pritchard placed himself "in a long line of searchers after truth, misunderstood and persecuted by the societies of which they were members."[25] He did so almost in the manner of a professor struggling, over two days, to introduce a rather slow class to his entire tradition, with the result that the speech, although one of the great classics of Canadian socialist thought, is also something of a kaleidoscopic document, with its detailed discussion on one aspect of socialist thought followed by a series of observations about something completely different.

But the speech makes great sense within its underlying framework of social-evolutionary thought. Pritchard's very opening words spoke of Bruno, burned at the stake in 1600 because he followed Copernicus in declaring that the Earth revolved around the Sun. Then he invoked Galileo, a master of physics, persecuted for having exploded Aristotle's theory about falling bodies. Would a similar fate befall the socialist scientists of the 20th century, the key figures of the later enlightenment? As it had been in the distant past, so it was in 1920: the enemies of enlightenment could be found among the library-destroying censors, superstitious priests, and book-burning crowds. The Crown counsel had argued that this reverence for the scientific tradition revealed a "paucity of originality." Pritchard retorted, "Everyone of us, you and I, have nothing original about us; that we are, everyone, products of a long line of historical development."[26] Pritchard drew here upon a long-standing first formation argument: whenever individual capitalists claimed to be deriving their profits from their ingenious inventions, they deliberately obscured the generations of humble people, mechanics and artisans, scholars and workers, without whose social labour and intellectual efforts none of their innovations would have seen the light of day. A multi-generational, telescopic perspective revealed just how limited and self-interested such an individualistic "Great Man" approach to the forces of production actually was.[27]

Just how worthy of respect, Pritchard demanded, was a political order whose response to the unwelcome truths of science was to ban books – Tyndale's *Fragments of Science*, Darwin's *Origin of Species*, Marx's *Capital*, Spencer's *First Principles*, even (and this was the book-banning that seemed to arouse Pritchard's greatest ire) Morgan's *Ancient Society*? More than any of the imprisonments and deportations, it was the crime of bibliocide that seemingly most offended Pritchard. "A house that has a library in it, has a soul," he said, referencing Plato – and a house with part of the great international "library" of socialism possessed part of "the greatest library of any school of thought of any day in history."[28] Yet socialists who possessed such books were harassed, often on the most trivial grounds. If, for instance, they possessed Marx's *Capital* in its Charles H. Kerr edition, they were in trouble; but if they had exactly the same text in the London edition, published by George Allen, they were in the clear. Where was the logic in that?

As a man who had lost perhaps $1,300 worth of books through such raiding,[29] Pritchard was plainly speaking from his own experience, but he was also trying to convey the social and scientific enormity of the repressive regime's efforts. It was punishing the ordinary people who sought to educate themselves. "Some working men may spend a little change on beer; some working men may spend a little change on billiards or some other game, and some working men may spend a little change on books, and after ten or twelve years they have a library of books which they enjoy and that they read for themselves," Pritchard explained. And then, "Like a bolt from the blue there comes an Order-in-Council, and an entire library of fifteen years' collecting, is blown to the four winds."[30]

The speech also revealed a remarkably undoctrinaire approach to the Marxist framework.[31] Pritchard argued that Marx should be ranked with Darwin as a thinker – "not through his value theory, ingenious though it may be," but rather because of his general contribution to social-evolutionary thought. In essence, he regarded the triune formula not as a sacred element of the tradition but as a useful heuristic aid. In 1920 Pritchard confronted his accusers not with a solid phalanx of certainties, but with a thoroughly modern grasp of the limitations of all human knowledge. "I tell you gentlemen," he explained, "a man who knows a little at all knows how little he knows. And the more he gets to know the more he knows that he knows very little."[32] Against the bright-eyed ideologues of liberal order, pressing for a conviction, Pritchard expressed an honest humanist sense of complexity, multiplicity, and indeterminacy. He had already grasped what Stephen Kern described as the "specificity-uncertainty dialectic" characteristic of modernity[33] – a trait that was by no means universal among 20th-century Marxists.

In the trial the question of religion was once again revealed as a minefield for socialists. The leading counsel for the Crown reminded the court of Pritchard's reported comments at the Calgary Convention disparaging "the late lamented Mr. Christ" as one of the major obstacles confronting workers. Pritchard, sensing the prejudicial damage that such evidence might wreak, poured scorn on the Crown for bringing it up. Was he really being tried on such medieval grounds? If a man was arrested as an alleged horse thief, was it pertinent to ask him whether he put his stock in Martin Luther or in freethinker Robert Ingersoll, or to convict him because he had not read *Pilgrim's Progress*? What did any of that have to do with stealing horses? "Was their case so weak, so vile in its character, and so crazy in its construction that they had to drag into use something which might possibly prejudice your minds against me?"[34] Could they really stoop that low, to inflame the jurors' minds with talk of religion, which had nothing to do with the charge of seditious conspiracy?

Pritchard's line of defence on this question was nuanced and reasoned. As he remarked, "The Crown have sought from the very commencement to build up in your minds that I, forsooth, am an irreligious man." But, he said, he was prepared to admire John Calvin – at least the Calvin who had authored *Religious Toleration*, and not the Calvin who had burned his theological opponents at the stake. Even Holy Scripture could be a useful resource for socialists, not because it was literally true, but because it might contain valuable historical lessons.[35] Pritchard himself used it to draw a parallel between St. Paul, whose teachings overturned the worldview of the Ephesians, and the socialists, now being persecuted because their views challenged the banal conventionalities of liberal thought.

Yet Pritchard was, like so many in the first formation, caught in an uneasy position. Like Dixon an avid reader of Thomas Paine, Pritchard applied Paine's maxim, "To argue with a man who has renounced reason is like giving medicine to the dead," a telling citation in a speech aimed at a Crown that, he repeatedly charged, was whipping up religious prejudice against him.[36] Against demagogic allegations of "atheistic socialism," with their immense possibility to summon up the irrationalistic furies of the bigoted and superstitious, it was almost impossible for a socialist, especially one trapped in such a vulnerable and dangerous position, to defend himself. It was a liberal courtroom that in its effect resembled a Spanish *auto-da-fé*. Pritchard expressed his admiration for Scripture and his respect for believers, some of whom stood with him in the dock, yet his sophisticated doubts and humane reservations were unlikely to have swayed the true believers from their dire certainties.

Against their rigid beliefs Pritchard raised the standard of socialist humanism – and he did the same thing with respect to the Marxist tradition itself, which has not always been as far removed in spirit from a religious orthodoxy as Marx would surely have wished. To some of those who sought to convert socialism into a set of iron dogmas, Pritchard reminded them that Marx himself had opposed all such "socialistic dogmatism." He quoted Marx as saying:

> We will not then oppose the world like doctrinarians with a new principle: here is truth, kneel down here. . . . We expose new principles to the world out of the principles of the world itself. We don't tell it, "Give up your struggles, they are rubbish, we will show you the true war-cry." We explain to it only the real object for which it struggles, and consciousness is a thing it must acquire even if it objects to it.[37]

Pritchard's celebration of this passage from the Marx of 1843 suggested a profound, undogmatic, and deeply democratic sensibility.

In 1920, then, Pritchard – supposedly on the "far left" of the first formation, and persecuted for his involvement with the revolutionary OBU – articulated a fairly mainstream version of political philosophy on the question of the supposed antithesis of revolution and evolution. In July 1919, after he had been arrested, he spoke at Vancouver's Empress Theatre and argued that revolution was part of evolution because "in order to produce something of importance something else must first be destroyed."[38] The chick must escape from its shell – and the people, now encased, suffocated, and benighted by capitalist socialist relations, must struggle for freedom and democracy. Pritchard acknowledged that the word "democracy" had been horribly twisted in political reality and repeatedly abused in political rhetoric: "For the last half century, this word 'democracy' has fallen from the tongues of all the political administrators like a sweet morsel, democracy has been the magic word of beneficial creation, and autocracy, the word of anathema." Still, he unreservedly considered "democracy" itself a good thing. Notably making almost no mention of the Russian Revolution, he expressed his support for the British Constitution – in the sense, again, that it had both required and justified the revolutions of the 1640s and 1680s, whose democratic promise was being fulfilled by the working-class revolution of the 20th century. Pritchard saw no contradiction between dovetailing this reading of the Constitution and the concept of revolution, which, as a moment of evolution, did not necessarily mean "violence, bloodshed, anarchy, chaos," but merely a great, fundamental change.[39]

Pritchard also spent a good deal of time exploring the ideas of the anti-socialists of the day, who had themselves generated a library of books worth consulting. He did not view the anti-socialists with hostility, but regarded their critiques as part of the process through which socialism as a science would be improved. Ideas could not be killed with clubs or driven into oblivion by machine guns, he argued. Rather, they themselves also obeyed evolutionary laws. "If an idea be healthy, if a theory be correct, drag it out into the open and let us look at it. If it be healthy, sunshine will help it to grow; if it be not healthy sunshine will help to kill it." In its attack upon the libraries, and in its complicity with the book-burning mobs and book-banning bureaucrats, the Canadian state was vainly attempting to curtail the intellectual openness and free discussion through which human beings could more logically grasp their underlying position in the planetary process of evolution.

Here, more than in its acts of cruelty and discrimination against individual socialists, lay the principal fault of the postwar authoritarians, Pritchard urged. They deeply distrusted the free discussion of ideas. They failed to grasp that, in "that most pitiless of contests, the contest of opinion," as fact was put up against fact, the truth would come to light.[40] Behind their long lists of prohibited books and periodicals lurked a deep-seated and long-standing fear – a persistent liberal fear of the capacity of the unwashed majority to judge on questions such as property, social order, and democracy. Like Galileo and Bruno, Socrates and Spencer, the working-class truth-seeker confronted imprisonment, ostracism, even death itself – but, however painful or even fatal such challenges, a life lived in pursuit of truth was better than one cast in superstition and ignorance. Better to understand the laws of capitalist development that, for example, governed the production and exchange of commodities in society, just as Galileo had discovered the four moons of Jupiter, than live in a world of illusion. Pritchard's speech, then, disclosed an often-repeated irony of Canadian intellectual and social history: the most ardent defenders of freedom of speech and thought have traditionally been on the left, and the book-banners and book-burners, although often men and women who declaim their "liberalism" most loudly, are generally found on the right.

The key insight of socialism as the science of social evolution was that to understand realities, people had to mobilize the tools of logic and observation to reconstruct the relations hidden beneath appearances – the organic processes that were increasingly tying the entire planet together in one vast socio-economic system. Pritchard re-enacted for the jurors one of the decisive moments of supersedure of the entire first formation – the instant that a person grasped how the humblest elements of everyday life were related to a vast network of forces and relations. "The wheat that you produce on your land ties you up to every other country in the world. The ships that I load and unload connect me, maybe, with the labors of the Chinese coolies of Shanghai, Hong Kong and other oriental ports," he told the jurors. "Gentlemen, take it home to yourselves. How many farmers on this bald prairie, raising grain, does it take to make a coupon-clipper in the wheat pit of Chicago?" Both the farmers and the coupon-clipper were connected by social relations – ones that would survive them as individuals. "How many toiling slaves in the hills of British Columbia and Montana are necessary to make a copper king?" Such a capitalist, who might claim to be a "self-made man," was only possible because of the labour of countless workers. "How many farmers with mortgages on their farms and collection bills from the machinery companies against them does it take to make a wheat king?"[41]

For the jurors' benefit, Pritchard magnificently developed a vision of a globe united as never before by a transformation in the means of production, distribution, and exchange. If the jurors truly wanted to stop the clock and arrest the revolution, they should focus not upon a few advocates of the One Big Union and the Socialist Party but on the vast new forces that were making this new world. More deadly to the existing order than any political revolutionary was the alteration in the forces and relations of production itself – such as the recent cutting of the Panama Canal, which had the effect of creating a vast competitive labour market, throwing some skilled workers into the ranks of the unemployed and thereby creating a larger global social problem. The 20th-century working class confronted not a national, but a planetary system of capitalism – which promised to supply the world's needs more efficiently than at any earlier time, yet also threatened to devastate all previously existing forms of society and thought. Global modernity was no longer merely "monstrous." Rather than meekly submit to it, or retreat into superstition, nostalgia, or magic, those who were truly modern could choose to understand and master the newly globalized realities.[42]

Pritchard's argument can be distilled down to a contrast between the people's enlightenment and the obscurantism and prejudice of a machine government. It was a contest between the library-builders and the book-banners, the men and women who could appreciate *The Communist Manifesto* as one statement within a library of books, and those who almost comically revealed their medieval minds by putting Marx and Engels's text in the dock alongside the prisoners of Winnipeg. How parochial! It had ridiculously fallen to a province in the "Middle West of the Dominion of Canada" to stamp this classic text of 1848 as "poison" and "seditious," all on the learned advice of the Citizens' Committee. And how superficial! The prosecution's entire case rested upon pillaging the vast library of socialism for juicy quotes that somehow proved that every socialist was a violent conspirator, and not the upholder of a scientific program that explained the phenomena of everyday life. They had collected a "mass of correspondence from people all over the world," but then demonstrated that they lacked the intellectual capacity to understand it. They had "dusted out every cobwebbed corner of every shack of every workingman whom they considered suspect" and "dragged forth a battalion of documents of various kinds," but they had then failed to read these documents with intelligence and in their context.[43]

"Out of that mass of documents, out of that mass of correspondence, my learned friends have gone with the microscope and the surgical knife and they have carved out terms, 'red,' 'bolshevik,' . . . 'socialism,' 'evolution,' 'revolution,' 'proletarian,' 'bourgeoisie,' etc." They wrenched sentences from their context, misconstrued words, disembowelled paragraphs – and foisted this mess upon the seven defendants, as though they themselves had made these arguments. In their prosecutorial zeal, they had misquoted even so famous a text as *The Communist Manifesto*, which they tried to shoehorn into their individualistic and ahistorical perspective. They had made the "most exquisite legal crazy-quilt," a vast blanket of misquotations – "words, sentences, acts, utterances – disconnected from each other."[44] They had not only attacked the freedom of speech and thought necessary for a people's enlightenment, but also in doing so exposed their own fundamental intellectual ineptitude.

Implicit in the prosecution was a deep disregard for and distrust of democracy. "No one can doubt that a democratic structure of society is most calculated to secure the happiness of the greatest number," Pritchard declared. Pritchard was convinced that a genuinely *social* democracy would transform not just the bleak "machine politics" of his day but work a far-reaching cultural revolution. He thought that even the humblest struggles for social reform over the past decade and a half suggested "a dim apprehension of this goal of human effort."[45] He even movingly defended, in the face of the prison term almost certainly looming before him, the possibility that elements of liberalism itself could be saved from the liberals who had turned so violently against their own constitution. In reclaiming the word "revolution" from those for whom it only meant "violence, bloodshed, anarchy, chaos; as though it meant everything that could be combed together from the calendar of crime," he sought to validate the possibility of a "democratic revolution," in the sense not of a modest incremental adjustment of liberal order, but of a great political change that would vest real power in working men and women.

For all that they were obviously far apart on many issues, Dixon and Pritchard were united in their sincere conviction that such a thoroughgoing democratic revolution was both possible and necessary. For both of them, above and beyond the return of Canada to formal democratic governance – an obvious and necessary immediate demand – loomed the great goal of a new *social democracy*, in which the old liberal order would be simultaneously cancelled, preserved, and transformed: cancelled as a mere machine of the privileged; preserved insofar as it enshrined the precious freedoms of speech, assembly, and association upon which enlightenment depended; and transformed so that the limited and partial principle of democracy, now reduced to the mere casting of a ballot every so many years, would instead be enlarged to become the active nucleus of political, economic, and social life. By *social democracy*, they meant a democracy that had been radically *socialized*, whose economy and society were so structured that producers would exercise their capacity to judge with respect to the most important and pressing decisions of their lives.

For them the people's enlightenment was not about a self-selected group of well-educated people descending upon the illiterate and uninformed. It was, rather, a question of helping the subaltern classes to consolidate, respect, and preserve the profound knowledge that those classes had already acquired – to have the confidence in their own hard-earned knowledge and the ability to generalize upon that basis to the rest of society in, as a Gramscian would put it, an expansive struggle for hegemony. As Pritchard insisted, the workers were in a real sense "already well-educated." Although very few had undergone a "university 'degradation,'" that was hardly the point: "Education is not something which proceeds from reputed halls of learning; education is the realization of the problems that stand in front of you and me. That is education. And the school of real education is the school of experience in the material world."[46] Pritchard said he had met coal miners "who could argue on points in philosophy and political economy as well as anybody I ever heard," perhaps even better than the esteemed editor of the *Free Press*. As true believers and ideologues, liberals like J.W. Dafoe could not see the limitations of their outmoded worldview. Once the people had confidence in their ability to understand their daily lives and to grasp the underlying logic of their situations, they would inaugurate the profound revolution upon whose victory the fate of humanity depended.

From the depths of repression in 1920 Pritchard's voice reaches out to our own time with an uncanny directness. The struggle for science, the struggle for revolution, and the struggle for human survival all mutually implied each other: all required a post-liberal concept of freedom, in which subalterns exercised the capacity to judge the most fundamental questions of the social order. Copernicus's text *De Revolutionibus* (On revolution) was (Pritchard delightedly pointed out) not just a text about the "revolution of the planets," but a title that had opposed the "learned ignorance of that day," as upheld by the bright-eyed true believers in orthodoxy. In the short term, such ideologues had prevailed – their persecutions, book-burnings, and book-bannings had silenced many critics. In the long term, they had necessarily failed. The people's enlightenment could be delayed, but it could not be destroyed.[47]

Its spokespersons could nonetheless be imprisoned. Preposterously, the Crown was successful in putting Pritchard away. Simply placing Pritchard on trial with six other defendants created the appearance, if hardly the reality, of a conspiracy. Of all the defendants, Pritchard was most closely affiliated with the deeply controversial Socialist Party of Canada and – unlike Armstrong, Russell, and Johns, his fellow SPCers in the dock – he was indeed an "outside agitator." His involvement in the strike could not be explained on the basis of any pragmatic, down-to-earth economic motives. Pritchard had clearly been drawn to Winnipeg not because he was a member of a trade union involved in the strike, but because he was a socialist intellectual who saw the occasion as an important moment in the creation of an alternative society. It may also well be, as Campbell suggests, that given the earlier shocking conviction of Russell in December, and the nature of the charge, that no effective defence was within Pritchard's grasp.[48]

In the show trial of Pritchard and his six fellow conspirators much care was also taken to find the right jury. In April 1920, shortly after the trials concluded, Andrews evidently told Charles Doherty, the federal justice minister, that it was "questionable if we could secure the conviction of these people by other juries."[49] The jurors confronted a mountain of supposed evidence and were perhaps impressed by the very immensity of this "crazy-quilt" of material and the visual display of seven supposed conspirators. Pritchard was trying to teach them about concepts of radical social democracy and scientific enlightenment in an ominous atmosphere, the gathering dusk of an authoritarian liberal reaction that would predominate for the next two decades.

From Polemic to Reconnaissance

Democracy and enlightenment, the empowerment of a newly conscious working class, the defence of reason against intolerance and superstition, the transformation of unexamined certainties about gender and race into open questions subject to rational analysis, and a call to end wars by transforming the property relations underpinning them: on all these fronts, socialists from 1890 to 1920 had done substantial work. As Trotsky, no friend to the now-divided and discredited European parties of the Second International, remarked in *The Bolsheviki and World Peace*, the cultural achievements of this period would outlast the crisis of its major parties: "There has been nothing like it in history before," he said of the International. "It has educated and assembled the oppressed classes. The proletariat does not now need to begin at the beginning. It enters on the new road not with empty hands. The past epoch has bequeathed to it a rich arsenal of ideas."[50] Trotsky's cultural insight applied in a particular way to Canada in this period, when the official parties of the left were so much less impressive than their European or U.S. counterparts, yet in which, somehow, the "party of the left," although a somewhat inchoate network of visionaries, had made living and reasoning otherwise a real possibility in so many local and personal contexts.

Any realistic summation must concede to such liberal sceptics as O.D. Skelton the truth of much of what they dismissively said about these early socialists – and yet take their critique in directions they would not have anticipated. Canada as a liberal project was by design an inhospitable place for democrats and socialists, and those who challenged its core assumptions necessarily risked ostracism and unemployment if they were securely attached to the Dominion, and detention and deportation if they were not. Across the vast archipelago of societies, nations, and communities in northern North America, brought together but loosely by a state designed to implant and enforce classical liberal conceptions of liberty, equality, and property, socialists were for many years unable to create even the semblance of a strong and united political movement. Instead, what we find are many visionaries and radicals primarily oriented to movements outside Canada, from whence they derived their inspiration. In a colonial pattern that has still not altogether vanished, they were often more like fans of distant celebrities than they were the heroes of their own lives.

From 1890 to 1920, when U.S. socialists looked north, they might have simply seen a place that faintly echoed their own struggles and movements – essentially a Minnesota or an Ohio with a few minor wrinkles. "Canadian socialism" was in many ways "U.S. socialism, northern division." The first party was the U.S.-based Socialist Labor Party. In the first homegrown pan-Canadian organization, the star candidates in its first electoral outing were Gaylord Wilshire and Margaret Haile, both of them figures in the U.S. movement; the keynote speaker at its 1901 convention was John Spargo, who would figure repeatedly in the decade that followed as a hallowed authority. The pivotal theorist in the Socialist Party of Canada was U.S. native E.T. Kingsley, and its B.C. activists were deeply involved in labour and socialist circles encompassing the Pacific Northwest on both sides of the border. In the East a figure like Roscoe Fillmore was radicalized in Maine and was also, throughout this period, deeply immersed in the U.S. movement, as suggested by his wartime polemics in the *International Socialist Review*. That Canadian pressure changed the "Industrial Workers of America" into the "Industrial Workers of the World" tells us not just about that admirable organization's planetary perspective but also about how heavily invested many radical Canadians were in a *North American* movement. Many of the most celebrated labour battles of this era featured such familiar organizations as the United Mine Workers of America and the International Ladies' Garment Workers' Union. When in 1911 Toronto revolutionary leftists in Toronto called their party the "Socialist Party of North America," they were identifying themselves with a continent, not a country. Well into the 1920s, it was not at all clear to Bolsheviks in the second formation whether the revolutionary movement should organize separately in Canada or in the United States. It is entirely probable that in 1914 more Canadian leftists would have recognized Eugene Debs (who had intervened directly in the Dominion's left politics), Bill Haywood, or Mother Jones, than any of their homegrown radicals. By some estimates the U.S.-based *Appeal to Reason* outsold most Canadian left publications – it was considered dangerous enough in the Lakehead to lead authorities to attempt to ban it altogether – and the *International Socialist Review* contained many stories hailing the intrepid feats of its Canadian agents, from Sointula to Sydney.[51] *Wilshire's Magazine* published on either side of the border – mainly, it seems, to avoid U.S. postal restrictions.

When British socialists looked across the ocean, they too might have noticed a profoundly colonial movement that echoed their own – a minor chapter in the life of Greater Britain. "Canadian socialism" was in many ways "British Socialism, North American division." British direct investment in the economy and British immigration made the imperial connection an unmistakable element of life. From the late 19th century, labour and "independent labour" parties popped up in industrial communities, testifying in their perplexing diversity and astonishing numbers to a widespread drive in Canada to build something analogous to the labour parties of Britain. When Brits read debates in the *Western Clarion* and *Cotton's Weekly*, or listened to lectures from Keir Hardie, or attended to different voices echoing H.M. Hyndman, they would have been struck again and again by a sense of familiarity, and when they listened to the voices of Canadian radicals their ears would be filled with the accents of Tyneside and Clydeside, Leicester and East London. In the tale of the *Komagata Maru*, they would read of a potential crisis of the British Empire; and in the saga of Isaac Bainbridge the story of a British immigrant who enraged the rulers of a British Dominion by republishing the words of a British anti-war activist.

Many leftists experienced, as a fact of their own lives, the "North Atlantic Triangle" later so brilliantly explored by J. Bartlet Brebner.[52] They were simultaneously British, American, and Canadian, functioning as part of an "English-speaking world." The developments of one part of this world were quickly reported in others. Keir Hardie, Jim Connolly, John Spargo, William Morris, and Edward Carpenter were all Britons well known in both Canada and the United States (the Webbs, although they visited Canada, never seemingly enjoyed quite the same status, and, contrary to legend, their state-centric "Fabianism" did not catch on as a major Canadian tendency).[53] A U.S. celebrity such as Jack London developed a huge following in Britain, as did, curiously, the Socialist Labor Party in Scotland. Canadians who became socialists were in effect entering a North Atlantic triangle of currents and ideas.

Those who arrived in Canada from outside this triangle were often drawn from the crisis-prone empires of continental Europe. Searching for freedom, they encountered an Empire – and in some instances the virtual second serfdom of the sweatshops, labour camps, and national oppression. Their role and influence within the movement in Canada were structured by the hegemony of the English language – which meant that they were in effect often isolated from broader debates and insulated in their own cultural communities. Often such diaspora socialists were seeking to reinvent in Canada the communities of their homelands – as suggested by Kurikka of the Finns and Krat of the Ukrainians, with their respective schemes for cultural regeneration and their enduring links to Europe. Jewish leftists, although they did not have a homeland in that sense, were often immersed in transnational networks of labour activism and radicalism – as suggested by the Arbeiter Ring, garment unions, anarchist circles, and progressive schools, all of which, in Winnipeg, Toronto, and Montreal, could be regarded as Canadian re-enactments of movements in New York City and London. It is suggestive that, within this formation, the country's leading francophone socialist turned more fervently to Esperanto than to the national question in Quebec – which, it would seem, went largely unexamined on the left in this period. It is also striking how wholeheartedly and rapidly many European immigrants experienced revolutionary events in Europe, embracing as their own the heroes of the movement overseas. "At the mention of the assassinated Dr. Karl Liebknecht," remarked an RCMP spy in a vivid portrait of Jacob Penner, "his eyes sparkled and his whole body seemed to shake with emotion."[54]

The most fundamental sceptical point about the first formation, then, might be that it did not actually exist as much more than a figment of the fond historian's imagination. This might be called the "ontological" critique. While there were plainly many leftists and socialists in Canada, and a diversity of groups, they were each so particular to their own cultural context and separated from each other that calling them all a "left" imputes to them an identity they did not, and could not, have shared. They drew from a socialism found throughout the North Atlantic triangle and instantiated it within very particular localities, without much reference to each other. Had they even heard of each other? Did Nova Scotia miners know of Montreal's Saint-Martin and his struggles – or he of them? Or had non-Ukrainians heard of Krat's utopian vision of a Green Vancouver? Were minds outside the Prairie West set afire by the vision of E.A. Partridge, and were activists outside British Columbia inspired by Helena Gutteridge?

My provisional guess is that, within a Canada in which the left was confined to culturally and socially distinct islands, these and other leading figures, famous in their own milieux, were largely unknown outside them. Insofar as these people figured as part of a general "socialist formation" centred on the theory of social evolution, they did so as disjointed and isolated celebrants of an international belief system that they themselves did little to influence. There was, one might say, little that held them together. The parties were tiny and often culturally specific, their struggles local, and even the Canadian left newspapers largely reprinted, not analyses focused on Canada, but polemics and reports from the North Atlantic world, when they were not preoccupied with unlocking the mysteries of evolution and the secrets of the cosmos.

All true – in part. Yet what our liberal-Skeltonian sceptic and our more theoretically savvy ontological critic are both missing is change over time – that is, the slow drawing together of these diverse fragments and individuals into something that, although linked to the North Atlantic triangle, was also distinctly articulated within it. From 1901, with the csl's launching of a pan-Canadian movement and the coming together of emissaries from that movement with revolutionaries in British Columbia to form the Socialist Party of Canada, *some* effective networks were being formed, and gradually small, homogeneous units did become partially integrated into more complex, larger structures – the federal Social Democratic Party and the more centralized One Big Union standing as two bold experiments. If we follow the first formation in its at times excessive enthusiasm for biological metaphors, one could say that the tiny infant conceived in the 1890s and born in 1901 had, under the pressure of the first major labour revolt of 1907–13, developed into a more integrated and free-standing organism.

By the time of the Great War, and fuelled by a sense of urgency international in derivation but necessarily Canadian in its articulation – conscription was, after all, imposed by a national state, as were a host of other repressive measures – this organism faced its own struggle for existence, which it won largely because the very diversity and grassroots nature that made it somewhat inchoate also made it difficult to detect and destroy. In many respects the Great War, which elsewhere (especially in the United States) brought ruin and devastation to the left, in Canada accelerated the integration and enhanced the effectiveness of the country's radicals. For the first time, and as a necessary element of resistance, leftists of all hues and across the country were called upon to mount a coherent program of resistance against the *Canadian state.*

I rather doubt, then, if many non-Montrealers knew of Saint-Martin or if the coal miners in Nova Scotia knew much about Krat. I am willing to bet that most of them had heard of conscription and of the Winnipeg General Strike – and that a good many took the latter to be an inspirational model of resistance. The sceptics are not wrong to insist upon the localism, distinctiveness, and mutual indifference of many of the individuals and communities who sought to live otherwise – but they err when they miss the extent to which such islands of resistance were changing over time. Under the pressure of events and through the conscious strategies of their activists, they were drawing closer together. And such sceptics are also simplistic in seeing only weakness and passivity in the extent to which the left itself was an archipelago – and they miss the depth, tenacity, and grassroots energy of particular neighbourhoods and regions, which could resist hegemony all the more effectively *because* of their relative distance from the mainstream. North-End Winnipeg, the Lakehead, the garment districts of Toronto and Montreal, the Cape Breton coalfields – these would be great citadels of the left that would withstand many a right-wing siege in the years to come.

A sceptic might also raise a second, perhaps more fundamental, point concerning this formation of the left: whether it really achieved anything that might merit the term "enlightenment" (we might call this the "epistemological critique"). For many critics, the first formationists' heavy investment in Darwin and Spencer damns them as social Darwinists, determinists, positivists, and misinterpreters of science. Theirs is often represented as the "Socialism of the Second International," a misguided attempt to see socialism as a local working out of an all-encompassing theory of evolution, one that left no room for the human capacity to make history. Without focusing on the poststructuralist and postmodern critics of the very concept of enlightenment, we can instead reference Gramsci, who was foremost among the later Marxist critics of the *fin de siècle* generation of theorists and activists. In his polemics against the economist Achille Loria and the criminologist Cesare Lombroso, and later against the major Soviet theorist and leader Nikolai Bukharin, Gramsci took particular aim at the extent to which leftism in general and Marxism in particular had become infected with the crudest forms of scientism. Gramsci thought that one of the most damaging errors of this vulgar "sociology" was its "wholesale and uncritical adoption of a methodology borrowed directly from the natural sciences," typified by Bukharin's attempt to enlist evidence from the natural sciences for evidence of revolutionary occurrences in history. Gramsci went so far as to link this intellectual error – he nicknames it "Lorianism" – with the left's inability to counter the rise of fascism. The misapplication of the principles of natural science to history led to bizarre results and worked to undermine the effectiveness of Marxism – and of the absolute historicism upon which it depends.[55] Gramsci would have found many evidences of "Lorianism" in the *Western Clarion, Cotton's Weekly,* and especially the *International Socialist Re-*

view, and no shortage of reverent treatments of Spencer, Haeckel, and a simplified Darwin.

Others have and will find many other grounds for critique. Scholars of religion have moved well beyond Grant Allen, whose anthropological work is irretrievably dated, and beyond reductionist accounts that treat all faiths as evolutionary mechanisms or irrational delusions. Most contemporary gender scholars would treat with scepticism a belief that one "question" can be built around such an essentialist category as "woman," and rightly wonder whether the first formation's fascination with Darwin did not make them unwitting precursors of the most reactionary forms of biological determinism. In contrast to contemporary critical realist thought, not only did many first formationists assume the actual existence of "races," but some also believed that some "races" were better than others. Others, if not racist in this narrow sense, nonetheless were infatuated with grand narratives tracing the development of humanity from savagery to civilization, with implications supportive of colonialism and racism. Moreover, they often unselfconsciously wrote and acted in ways that naturalized British ideals, and barely noticed the existence of other nations within Canada. Time, in short, has moved on – and many first formation positions now seem very dated, where they are not offensive. Contemporary attempts to plant a Marxist seal of approval on Jack London or extend a socialist-feminist sisterhood card to Charlotte Perkins Gilman must reckon with the racism of the first and the genocidal fantasies of the second.

Finally, critics of a more scientific bent may well see the evolutionary framework espoused by the formation as itself irretrievably dated.[56] Working before the new Darwinian synthesis of the 1930s, and before the new physics of the 1920s and 1930s, even well-informed first formationists like Kautsky and Allen internationally, or Pritchard and McKay in Canada, were popularizers of now superseded scientific paradigms. Their core belief that one could develop a One Big Science extending from the cell to socialism, while it may inspire some utopian visionaries, contrasts with the contemporary conviction among scientists and those who admire their work that "the more causes we understand, the more we realize how many causes there are to discover and how little we actually know about the causes we think we know."[57] What first formationists often reported as scientific certainties, we are now more likely to perceive as hypotheses – since the probabalistic revolution was another scientific advance as yet unconsolidated at the time of the first formation.

I agree with most of these fundamental critiques. Yet, as a historian and a proponent of the critical realist method of reconnaissance, I agree with them as *polemics*, not as principles of historical understanding. Their characteristic mode is one in which past thinkers and activists are brought up in an imagined contemporary courtroom, one in which we ourselves, conveniently enough, are judge and jury, unselfconsciously convinced that we in the 21st century have transcended history. Reconnaissance works neither with exculpation by context nor guilt by retrospective association, but by recovering the underlying patterns of thought and action that help make sense of the past as a time and place radically different from our own. As the application of absolute historicism, it suggests that we are ourselves elements of a historical process, working in our own way within frameworks susceptible to future critique and development. It follows Gramsci in arguing that an awareness of the historical conditions of our own position enhances the ability to contribute to social transformation, and hence rejects the supposition that there is a place outside history from which rigorous politico-ethical judgments can be made. Rather than applying to the first formation metaphysical conceptions of truth and ethics, we are called upon to understand "that every 'truth' believed to be eternal and absolute has practical origins and has represented or represents a provisional value,'" including the interpretations of historical materialism itself.[58]

It is on the basis of reconnaissance that I would make the qualified case that the first formationists did construct, even in their errors, some of the preconditions of a more enlightened politics. They generated theoretical insights and empirical information of lasting significance. More fundamentally, they opened up new realms of analytical and political possibility for the left.

On the class question, which socialists down to the 1960s would regard as the most basic issue of left politics, this formation demonstrated a striking transformation. In essence, many of them underwent – especially in the years of the labour revolt of 1907–13, followed by the more renowned uprisings of 1917–20 – a transformation from aloof experts in political economy and sociology to active participants in popular struggles. First formation thinkers were rediscovering *praxis* – in Michael Löwy's words, the "*mediation* by which class *in itself* becomes the class *for itself*," going beyond any passive waiting for "evolution" to fight for the goals that only actual people in a real situation could attain.[59]

A similar pattern was at work in other spheres. The question of religion was (unevenly) transformed from one monopolized by clerical social gospellers or their rationalist free-thought opponents, and transformed into the revolutionary humanism of the labour churches and the co-operative movement. The so-called woman question was transformed from one dominated by male feminists often preoccupied with grand historical schemas and abstract explanations to one put to practical work, and thereby transformed, by *praxis*-oriented feminists, first in struggles against unemployment and domestic oppression, and then in a semi-autonomous feminist peace movement in the Great War. The race question, which in this period subsumed issues of ethnicity, nation, and colonialism, and one which was indeed often racked with vulgarity and error, was also substantially reworked, so that by 1920 a terrain once unselfconsciously theorized in terms congenial to an Anglo-

Canadian elite included newly confident voices and institutions contesting Anglo hegemony, discrimination on the basis of colour, and even the colonial inheritance itself. Finally, and only at the very end of this period – and belonging more properly to the second formation that succeeded it – intellectuals began to raise, with an unprecedented degree of acuteness, the question of the party, arguing that the various questions of the left could only be integrated and political practice focused with the emergence of a cohesive collectivity capable of interjecting itself into history. They did this with a consistency and energy unanticipated in the smaller pedagogical parties and language-based groups of an earlier day. It would be a mistake to think that any of these issues had been settled by 1920, but it would also be an error to overlook evidence, in sphere after sphere, of a working through of contradictions by activists and intellectuals. From this point of view, a significant problem with polemical denunciations of particular formulations of these questions, in addition to their assumption of some metaphysical place outside history from which one may pass such judgments, is that they often reify positions that were subject to debate and transformation. In a way they fall victim to some of the same patterns of vulgarity, decontextualism, presentism, and partiality that Gramsci himself so effectively criticized.

The first formation simultaneously *limited* and *encouraged* a critical realist appreciation of capitalism and the liberal order. It put evolutionary theory to work in a *multitude of ways* – sometimes quite creatively. In a society still characterized by heresy trials, fundamentalist sects, and, in Quebec, a Catholic Church wielding many of the powers of a state within a state, first formationists demanded and to an extent won a space for the democratic discussion of religious positions. Natural-scientific theories of feminism based on sexual selection and parasitology popular with many in this formation have not weathered well, to put it mildly, but a leading point articulated within them – that women's oppression is rooted in material circumstances and the politics of the family – packed a real punch when it surfaced in feminist journalism in the 1910s, and it would be enormously fruitful to feminists in the 1970s and 1980s (when at least some of the works of this cohort were partially recovered). Although it would be stretching things to say that the first formation achieved anything similar on race, nonetheless even here, in socialist openness to the *Komagata Maru* struggle and to the emergence of the diaspora parties and institutions, we find not just Anglo-centric prejudice but an emergent acceptance, in some quarters even a celebration, of ethnic and cultural difference, and even some questioning of "race" itself as a naturalized category of analysis.

And what of that which sets this formation so firmly apart from those which would succeed it on the left – the cosmic perspective, the extraordinary confidence with which its texts took up the telescopic point of view, moving without hesitation from the cell to socialism? Taken literally, this was of course an invitation to determinism and passivity. Yet, on a metaphorical level, as Gramsci himself so astutely noted, such a "mechanical determinism" could become "a tremendous force of moral resistance, of cohesion and of patient and obstinate perseverance."[60] Yes, the workers bludgeoned into submission might admit, we have been defeated *for now* – but wait until the tide of history rolls over our oppressors! The Great War, labour revolt, and the ensuing Great Depression would unsettle the left's earlier conviction that the age of socialism was inevitably about to dawn – a naturalistic vision, often conveyed through images of flowing rivers and maturing individuals, that was already growing more complicated in such fictional works as London's *The Iron Heel* and Francis Beynon's *Aleta Dey*, and in such theoretical treatises as Antonio Labriola's *Essays on the Materialist Conception of History*. The theme of "socialism deferred" can also be read into some of the interwar writings in Canada on psychology and culture, typified by Colin McKay's more sceptical appraisal of Spencer and Hussein Rahim's *The Psychology of Marxian Socialism* of 1921.[61] The "new age" dawning in the 1920s had a more apocalyptic cast than older notions of evolutionary transition. The point remains, and applies to our own day, that a conviction that there are deep-seated historical patterns and trends can intensify a stoical resistance to the oppressions of the present day.

Moreover, from a 21st-century perspective, this cosmic perspective implicitly (and at times actually) allowed first formationists to begin to think of humanity as a species living within a natural world, in a metabolic relationship calling out for rationality and care. Organicism, such as we find it in Engels and Kropotkin, and in Bland and Partridge, could carry the revolutionary implication that humanity as a species has interests, such as its physical survival, and should collectively struggle to attain them. St. Paul's dictum, "We are members of one another," can be read not only as a warning against the hubris of individualism but also as a call for principled revolutionary solidarity with our fellow human beings.

Much first formation thought, building on Spencer's vast evolutionary notions and merging them with Marx's powerful triune formula, anticipated a contemporary environmental consciousness. If, as Gramsci would argue, this sensibility meant that historical specifics often went maddeningly unexplored, and often entailed a disabling sacrifice of the particular and the local to the general and universal, it also meant a radical bracketing of contemporary values and perspectives. The "view from nowhere" – that is, utopia – that we find in Bellamy and Allen, and in Partridge, Krat, and Bland (and, dare one say it, sometimes Marx and Engels) could work as a springboard for imaginative and realistic critiques of the conventional world. As Löwy remarks: "How can we even conceive of a more substantive rationality without resorting to utopias?" – always on condition that any such utopia "be based on real contradictions and real social movements."[62] What was enduringly valuable about the foundational "sublime" element of this early socialism was its hypothesis that, to be alive at any given historical moment meant being part of a vast network of people extending far into the past and far into the future, to which each individual and collectivity is responsible. In its combination of this sensibility with the triune formula of Marx, the first formation bequeathed some important insights that, under our own present conditions of environmental catastrophe, call out for recovery and development.

Gramsci, polemicizing within his own specific context, sometimes took first formation socialism to be as monological as many of its adherents hoped it would become. Yet this reconnaissance has revealed a social-evolutionary moment that was "heteroglossic," with a multiplicity of dialects and forms of activism co-existing within a conception of socialism as a science of social evolution. For this concept of evolution was immensely suggestive yet almost immeasurably complicated in its implications – as so vividly illustrated by Spencer himself, at war with so many of his socialist progeny. Gramsci's own deeply suggestive vocabulary of "organic crises" and "organic intellectuals," which raised evolutionary discourse to a new level of revolutionary sophistication, was nonetheless not itself uninfluenced by first formation insights. Just as Gramsci learned, more than he was willing to concede, from what Trotsky judiciously hailed as the cultural achievements of this early socialism, so too might its cosmic and ethical insights play into today's massive reconstruction of the project of a feasible left on a global level. It is difficult to imagine a 21st-century left capable of fighting for human survival – for such are the stakes – that has not reckoned with the legacies of Marx and Darwin. In struggling to surpass the first Darwinian-Marxist left that emerged more than a century ago, it must at least understand it.

The formation began with so many refusals – of the sweatshops of the cities and the killing coal mines east and west; of the camps and shantytowns, each with its tale of squalor and despair; of the neighbourhoods choked with effluvia and the rivers dying of sawdust; of the empty platitudes of a soulless church and the petty tyrannies of slavish wedlock; of the city's callous cult of mutual indifference and the countryside's soul-destroying isolation; of the pointless pettiness of local politics, steeped in patronage; and the menacing jingoism of imperial politics and its many fevered acolytes. In each refusal, each moment of resistance, each defiant "no," could be found the possibility of supersedure – the insight that the sweatshop and the slum, the coal mine and the camp, the hypocrisies of pastors and the hidden injuries of patriarchy, the bleak futilities of lives misspent in acquisition and destroyed so casually in war, that all of these were but instances of a deeper logic, instances calling out for a deeper resistance. And so, in picket lines and poems, reading groups and religious revivals, in carefully tended libraries and well-turned soapbox performances, from refusal and supersedure, came a realization that, however tentative and vulnerable, *these refusals could be fused, developed, generalized.* Refusal, supersedure, and system could become moments in the generation of a new political reality, a new historical subject, an answer to the liberal leviathan.

For the first time a new logic, a new ethics, a new politics could be injected into the contradictions of capitalism; and persistently working from a new body of knowledge and insight, grounded in rationality and developed in freedom, a cohort of socialists could pass on a legacy to the following generation. Through books and pamphlets, speeches in socialist halls, manifestos of political parties, in a great movement of resistance and enlightenment a new set of hard-earned axioms and truths, a revolutionary science of the possible, could be transmitted over the generations.

The show trials sought to pronounce the last word on Canadian socialism – and instead they helped Canadian socialism to take the measure of its enemy, this liberal order that disgraced the very name of justice with its authoritarian spectacles. In the dramatic conclusion of his speech, Pritchard turned to a glowing passage from a speech from Anatole France, one of the pillars of French socialism – and used those words, it would seem, to cast his voice out not so much to the jury in 1920 but to those who might still be listening to his voice almost a century later.

> Reason, wisdom, intelligence, forces of the mind and heart, whom I have always devoutly invoked, come to me, aid me, sustain my feeble voice, carry it, if that may be, to all the peoples of the world and diffuse it everywhere where there are men of good-will to hear the beneficent truth. . . . A new order of things is born, the powers of evil die poisoned by their crime. The greedy and the cruel, the devourers of people, are bursting with an indigestion of blood. However, sorely stricken by the sins of their blind or corrupt masters, mutilated, decimated, the proletarians remain erect; they will unite to form one universal proletariat and we shall see fulfilled the great Socialist prophecy, "The union of the workers will be the peace of the world."[63]

Pritchard spoke with the defiance and clarity of a man who realizes the prison doors will soon be swinging shut behind him. So many who read the books and spoke the words of the people's enlightenment would disappear into such jails. So many would be deported, some back to torturing and murdering regimes. There would be many sounds of silence, as the defenders of order worked to end an entire political formation's ways of thinking and acting and living. Yet its insights and memories have not disappeared. They would survive the bleakest and most dispiriting ages of liberal and neo-liberal order to sustain the radical social democracy that has always been its nemesis. It proved impossible to kill the new knowledge, and for that we stand in permanent debt to this version of the left in Canada, which nurtured the critical and realist conviction that it is possible to *reason* – it is even necessary to *live* – otherwise.

Notes

Introduction: Reconnaissance and Resistance

1 *Reasoning Otherwise* is the second volume in a projected series of books on the history of the Canadian left from 1890 to the present. In the first book in this series, *Rebels, Reds, Radicals: Rethinking Canada's Left History* (Toronto: Between the Lines, 2005), I set out some ideas for how the history of the Canadian left might be thought and written about in the 21st century.

2 Thomas L. Haskell, *Objectivity Is Not Neutrality: Explanatory Schemes in History* (Baltimore: John Hopkins University Press, 2000).

3 For an excellent discussion of Gramsci's distinctive approach to history, see Peter Thomas, "Historicism, Absolute," *Historical Materialism* 15 (2007), 249–56.

4 This point is powerfully made in Agnes Heller, *A Theory of History* (London: Routledge and Kegan Paul, 1982).

5 To cite E.P. Thompson, *The Making of the English Working Class* (Harmondsworth, Eng.: Penguin, 1970), 13.

6 Raymond Williams, *Keywords: A Vocabulary of Culture and Society* (London: Fontana, 1976), 286–87; Margaret Cole, cited in Henry Ritter, ed., *Dictionary of Concepts in History* (Westport, Conn.: Greenwood, 1986), 418. For a fuller discussion, see McKay, *Rebels, Reds, Radicals*, ch.2.

7 For an exposition of, and debates surrounding, the liberal order framework, see Jean-François Constant and Michel Ducharme, eds., *Liberalism and Hegemony: Debating the Canadian Liberal Revolution* (Toronto: University of Toronto Press, 2008).

8 Robert Stuart, *Marxism at Work: Ideology, Class and French Socialism during the Third Republic* (Cambridge: Cambridge University Press, 1992), 21, 19.

9 This valuable distinction is explored by Quentin Skinner, "Meaning and Understanding in the History of Ideas," *History and Theory* 8 (1969), 3–53.

10 Analogous, but not identical; it is not evident that structures of socio-historical reason operate with the same high levels of theoretical autonomy and incommensurability as the paradigms and problematics described by many philosophers of science. See Thomas S. Kuhn, *The Copernican Revolution: Planetary Astronomy in the Development of Western Thought* (Cambridge, Mass.: Harvard University Press, 1957); *The Road Since Structure*, ed. James Conant and John Haugeland (Chicago and London: University of Chicago Press, 2000).

11 If we judge the significance of the "left feminist moment" of the 1970s to 1990s, for instance, strictly in terms of the size of the membership of the Feminist Party of Canada, the subscription lists of *Broadside*, or the number of people at an International Women's Day march in Toronto, we would be missing much of the story of left feminism.

1: Socialism: The Revolutionary Science of Social Evolution

1 From R.A.H. Morrow, *Story of the Springhill Disaster: Comprising a Full and Authentic Account of the Great Coal Mining Explosion at Springhill Mines, Nova Scotia, February 21st, 1891, including a History of Springhill and Its Collieries; also, a Description of the Underground Workings, Mechanical Operations and Mysteries of the Mine; Reviews of Other Great Coal Mining Disasters; Coal and Its History; Dangers*

of Mining Operations and Safeguards against Accidents in Mines; Explanation of Coal Mining Terms; Lessons from the Great Calamity, Etc. (Saint John, N.B.: R.A.H. Morrow, 1891), 69.

2 For child labour in Canadian coal mines, see especially Robert McIntosh, *Boys in the Pits: Child Labour in Coal Mines* (Montreal and Kingston: McGill-Queen's University Press, 2000).

3 David Frank, *J.B. McLachlan: A Biography* (Toronto: James Lorimer, 1999), 141–42.

4 "The Social Problem," *Amherst Daily News*, 25, 26, 28 Nov. 1898.

5 *Herald* (Montreal), 15 Dec. 1896.

6 See Gerald Friesen, *Citizens and Nation: An Essay on History, Communication, and Canada* (Toronto: University of Toronto Press, 2000); Ruth Sandwell, *Beyond the City Limits: Rural History in British Columbia* (Vancouver: UBC Press, 1998); and Daniel Samson, *The Spirit of Industry and Improvement: Liberal Government and Rural-Industrial Society, Nova Scotia, 1790–1862* (Montreal and Kingston: McGill-Queen's University Press, 2008).

7 Stephen B. Leacock, *Arcadian Adventures with the Idle Rich* (Toronto: McClelland and Stewart, 1959 [1914]), 1, 2.

8 Stephen Leacock, *The Unsolved Riddle of Social Justice and Other Essays: The Social Criticism of Stephen Leacock*, ed. and intr. Alan Bowker (Toronto: University of Toronto Press, 1973 [1920]), 130, 138.

9 The classic exploration of modernity along Marxist lines is Marshall Berman, *All That Is Solid Melts into Air: The Experience of Modernity* (New York: Simon and Schuster, 1982). For an attempt to apply Berman's insights to Canadian history, see Ian McKay, "Introduction: All That Is Solid Melts into Air," in *The Challenge of Modernity: A Reader on Post-Confederation Canada*, ed. Ian McKay (Toronto: McGraw-Hill Ryerson, 1992), ix–xxvi.

10 For a path-breaking study of the earlier world of urban crafts in Canada, see Robert B. Kristofferson, *Craft Capitalism: Craftworkers and Early Industrialization in Hamilton, Ontario, 1840–1872* (Toronto: University of Toronto Press, 2007).

11 See Ian McKay, *The Craft Transformed: An Essay on the Carpenters of Halifax, 1885–1985* (Halifax: Holdfast Press, 1985), 53–54.

12 On *Appeal to Reason*, see George Allan England, *The Story of the Appeal, 'Unbeaten and Unbeatable': Being the Epic of the Life and Work of the Greatest Political Newspaper in the World* (Fort Scott, Kansas: n.d., n.p. [1915]); and an excellent scholarly account covering socialist U.S. journalism of the day: Elliott Shore, *Talkin' Socialism: J.A. Wayland and the Radical Press* (Lawrence: University of Kansas Press, 1988).

13 Will R. Shier, "The Decadence of Capitalism," *Western Clarion*, 16 Jan. 1909, 2.

14 For an intriguing discussion, see M. Neocleous, "The Political Economy of the Dead: Marx's Vampires," *History of Political Thought* 24, 4 (2003), 668–84.

15 W.L. Mackenzie King, *Industry and Humanity: A Study in the Principles Underlying Industrial Reconstruction* (Toronto: Thomas Allen, and Boston and New York: Houghton Mifflin, 1918), 325–30.

16 J.S. Woodsworth, *My Neighbor* (Toronto: University of Toronto Press, 1972 [1911]), 14–16.

17 Gregory P. Marchildon, *Profits and Politics: Beaverbrook and the Gilded Age of Canadian Finance* (Toronto: University of Toronto Press, 1996), 8–11.

18 Kenneth Norrie and Douglas Owram, *A History of the Canadian Economy* (Toronto: Harcourt Brace Jovanovich Canada, 1991), 296.

19 Craig Heron, *Working in Steel: The Early Years in Canada, 1883–1935* (Toronto: McClelland and Stewart, 1988), 12.

20 See Christopher Armstrong and H.V. Nelles, *Monopoly's Moment: The Organization and Regulation of Canadian Utilities, 1830–1930* (Philadelphia: Temple University Press, 1986).

21 Terry Copp, *The Anatomy of Poverty: The Condition of the Working Class in Montreal, 1897–1929* (Toronto: McClelland and Stewart, 1974), 56. See also Bettina Bradbury, *Working Families: Age, Gender, and Daily Survival in Industrializing Montreal* (Toronto: McClelland and Stewart, 1993).

22 Ian McKay, "Strikes in the Maritimes, 1900–1914," in *Atlantic Canada after Confederation*, ed. P.A. Buckner and David Frank (Fredericton: Acadiensis Press, 1985), 216–59.

23 Sarah Carter, *Lost Harvests: Prairie Indian Reserve Farmers and Government Policy* (Montreal and Kingston: McGill-Queen's University Press, 1990), 149.

24 Gerald Friesen, *The Canadian Prairies: A History* (Toronto: University of Toronto Press, 1987), chs. 8, 13; citations at 165, 301. All the data reported in this and the following paragraph derive from Friesen's classic study.

25 Friesen, *Canadian Prairies*, 317.

26 For an examination of Sifton that doubles as an impassioned manifesto of Prairie liberalism, see John W. Dafoe, *Clifford Sifton in Relation to His Times* (Toronto: Macmillan, 1931); and for a brilliant overview of liberalism, democracy, and populism on the Prairies, see David Laycock, *Populism and Democratic Thought in the Canadian Prairies, 1910 to 1945* (Toronto: University of Toronto Press, 1990).

27 See Robert F. Harney, "Montreal's King of Italian Labour: A Case Study of Padronism," *Labour/Le Travailleur* 4 (1979), 57–84.

28 Heron, *Working in Steel*, 86–87.

29 Canada, Minister of the Interior, *Canada* (n.p. [Ottawa], n.d. [c.1902]).

30 Cited in Nicholas Fillmore, *Maritime Radical: The Life and Times of Roscoe Fillmore* (Toronto: Between the Lines, 1992), 30.

31 See Jeremy Adelman, *Frontier Development: Land, Labour and Capital on the Wheat Lands of Argentina and Canada, 1890–1914* (Oxford: Clarendon Press, 1994). This book marks an advance on more neo-nationalist treatments of the region.

32 Tina Loo, *Making Law, Order and Authority in British Columbia, 1821–1871* (Toronto: University of Toronto Press, 1994). For 20th-century B.C. liberalism, see James Murton, *Creating a Modern Countryside: Liberalism and Land Resettlement in British Columbia* (Vancouver: UBC Press, 2008).

33 *Trades Journal* (Stellarton, N.S.), 18 Oct. 1880.

34 For an outstanding account of unemployment in *fin de siècle* Canada, see Peter Baskerville and Eric W. Sager, *Unwilling Idlers: The Urban Unemployed and Their Families in Late Victorian Canada* (Toronto: University of Toronto Press, 1998). For an interesting work on unemployment as an issue for the left, see David Thompson, "Challenging the Canadian Liberal Order: Unemployed Organizations and First Formation Socialism, 1913–1915," unpublished research paper, Queen's University, Kingston, 2007, a preview of his doctoral thesis, "Work, Not Charity: The Left and Unemployment Activism in the Canadian Liberal Order, 1890–1965."

35 See the website <http://www.casaloma.org/> (10 April 2005). In 1912 Socialists used the mansion to serve a different function: as a backdrop to their campaign against social inequities in Toronto. See Gene Howard Homel, "James Simpson

and the Origins of Canadian Social Democracy," Ph.D. thesis, University of Toronto, 1978, 619.

36 See Edwin Black, *War against the Weak: Eugenics and America's Campaign to Create a Master Race* (New York: Avalon Publishing Group, 2004). Spencer would have had no sympathy for any state project that aimed at removing the supposedly "unfit." He had little sympathy with state projects that aimed at anything. For an excellent discussion of similar patterns of "guilt by retrospective association" in the German case, see Robert J. Richards, "The Moral Grammar of Narratives in History of Biology: The Case of Haeckel and Nazi Biology," in *The Cambridge Companion to the Philosophy of Biology*, ed. David L. Hull and Michael Ruse (Cambridge: Cambridge University Press, 2007), 429–51. For Spencer's thoughts on gender and sexuality, see Cynthia Eagle Russett, *Sexual Science: The Victorian Construction of Womanhood* (Cambridge, Mass. and London: Harvard University Press, 1980).

37 One of the major utopian experiments in Canada in the 1890s was a B.C. community named after Ruskin, and when the Socialist Party of Canada launched a book publishing program after the Great War it somewhat incongruously selected William Morris–style poppies to decorate titles on Marxist economics.

38 Zygmunt Bauman, *Liquid Modernity* (Cambridge: Polity Press, 2000), 3.

39 "Cosmos" etymologically descends from the Greek "kosmos," implying not just the universe's infinite expanse, but also its profound order, its "kosmei."

40 Mark Pittinger, *American Socialists and Evolutionary Thought, 1870–1920* (Madison: University of Wisconsin Press, 1993), 123.

41 Stephen Kern, *A Cultural History of Causality: Science, Murder Novels, and Systems of Thought* (Princeton, N.J. and Oxford: Princeton University Press, 2004), 6, 13.

42 Michael Ruse, *Darwinism and Design: Does Evolution Have a Purpose?* (Cambridge, Mass.: Harvard University Press, 2003), 6; Ruse provides an excellent introduction to contemporary debates over teleology and evolution.

43 For a range of studies of the impact of Darwin, see Gertrude Himmelfarb, *Darwin and the Darwinian Revolution* (Chicago: Elephant Paperbacks, 1996 [1959]); R.J. Wilson, ed., *Darwinism and the American Intellectual: A Book of Readings* (Homewood, Ill.: Dorsey Press, 1967); Peter J. Bowler, *Evolution: The History of an Idea* (Berkeley and Los Angeles: University of California Press, 1983); Bowler, *Theories of Human Evolution: A Century of Debate, 1844–1944* (Baltimore and London: Johns Hopkins University Press, 1986); and Bowler, *The Non-Darwinian Revolution: Reinterpreting a Historical Myth* (Baltimore and London: Johns Hopkins University Press, 1988). Especially helpful collections include David Kohn, ed., *The Darwinian Heritage* (Princeton, N.J.: Princeton University Press, 1988); and Jonathan Hodge and Gregory Radick, eds., *The Cambridge Companion to Darwin* (Cambridge: Cambridge University Press, 2003).

44 To adapt a nice formulation in Pittinger, *American Socialists and Evolutionary Thought*, 37.

45 When it comes to countering firm preconceptions, of the scores of books on Spencer see especially Mark Francis, *Herbert Spencer and the Invention of Modern Life* (Stocksfield, Eng.: Acumen, 2007). Francis demolishes the stereotype of Spencer as the architect of 20th-century totalitarianism and "social Darwinism."

46 Cited in Allen Mills, *Fool for Christ: The Political Thought of J.S. Woodsworth* (Toronto, Buffalo and London: University of Toronto Press, 1991), 19.

47 The pivotal text for this "religious Spencerism" is Henry Drummond, *Natural Law in the Spiritual World* (Philadelphia: Henry Altemus, n.d. [1898]).

48 Herbert Spencer, *Social Statics; Or, The Conditions Essential to Human Happiness Specified, and the First of Them Developed* (London: John Chapman, 1851 [reprinted London: Routledge and Thoemmes Press, 1986]), 293, 65.

49 Herbert Spencer, "The Social Organism," in Spencer, *Collected Writings*, vol. 1 (London: Routledge and Thoemmes Press, 1996), 272; the essay was first published in *Westminster Review*, January 1860.

50 Charlotte Perkins Gilman, *Women and Economics: A Study of the Economic Relation between Men and Women as a Factor in Social Evolution* (Berkeley: University of California Press, 1998 [1898]), 101.

51 For Peter Wright, see *Herald* (Halifax), 1 May 1919. As for heavy theoretical works, members of the Riverdale Local of the Social Democratic Party of Canada (Toronto No. 87), for example, could consult, as the 31st book in the Library, M.H. Fitch, *The Physical Basis of Mind and Morals*, 3rd ed. (Chicago: Charles H. Kerr, 1912), a thorough, one might even say tedious, examination of the applications of Spencerian theory (author's collection). The Ukrainian Social Democrats in Winnipeg translated Edward Bellamy, the Dutch Marxist Anton Pannekoek on "Socialism and Darwinism," and Frederick Engels, *Socialism: Scientific and Utopian*. Anton Pannekoek's thoughtful appraisal of *Marxism and Darwinism* was also available in English (Chicago: Charles H. Kerr and Company, 1912). For an excellent study of Charles H. Kerr, see Allen Ruff, *We Called Each Other Comrade: Charles H. Kerr & Company, Radical Publishers* (Champaign: University of Illinois Press, 1997).

52 *Star* (Montreal), 8 Dec. 1903.

53 *Manitoba Free Press*, 9 Dec. 1903; Beatrice Webb cited in Deborah Epstein Nord, *The Apprenticeship of Beatrice Webb* (Amherst: University of Massachusetts Press, 1985), 42; my thanks to Mariana Valverde for pointing out this reference. For Gompers, see George B. Cotkin, "The Spencerian and Comtian Nexus in Gompers' Labor Philosophy: The Impact of Non-Marxian Evolutionary Thought," *Labor History* 20, 4 (Fall 1979), 510–11.

54 See J. Peter Campbell, "'Stalwarts of the Struggle': Canadian Marxists of the Third Way, 1879–1939," Ph.D. thesis, Queen's University, Kingston, 1991, 30.

55 Nolan Heie, "Ernst Haeckel and the Redemption of Nature," Ph.D. thesis, Queen's University, Kingston, 2008, 5, 13, 19. See also Joseph Dietzgen, *The Positive Outcome of Philosophy* (Chicago: Charles H. Kerr, 1908); author's copy from the library of the Socialist Party of Canada; for an illuminating contemporary commentary, see Larry Gambone, *Cosmic Dialectics: The Libertarian Philosophy of Joseph Dietzgen* (Vancouver: Red Lion Press, 1996).

56 Heie, "Ernst Haeckel and the Redemption of Nature," 4, 13, 19.

57 J.H., "Ernest Haeckel, Scientist – An Appreciation," *Red Flag*, 16 Aug. 1919.

58 Drawing upon the summary in David Stack, *The First Darwinian Left: Socialism and Darwinism 1859–1914* (Cheltenham: New Clarion Press, 2003), 11–12.

59 Bliss Carman, "The Soul of Socialism," *Wilshire's Magazine* 56 (March 1903), 30.

60 Socialist Party of Canada, Lindsay, Ont., Local, *Gems of Socialism* (n.p. [Lindsay], n.d. [1916]).

61 See, for instance, the lengthy debate in *The Grain Growers' Guide* in 1912, typified by W. Hordern, Dundern, "Regarding Socialism," 3 April 1912. Proponents of "socialism" often quoted from one edition of the *Encyclopædia Britannica* (implying that socialism was applied Christianity) and its opponents from another.

62 "The Socialist Passes," *Mail and Empire* (Toronto), 25 Dec. 1918.

63 *Globe* (Saint John), 5 Nov. 1910.

64 O.D. Skelton, *Socialism: A Critical Analysis* (Boston and New York: Houghton

Mifflin Company, 1911), 1, 3. For an important study of Skelton and his partner, Isabel, see Terry Crowley, *Marriage of Minds: Isabel and Oscar Skelton Reinventing Canada* (Toronto: University of Toronto Press, 2003).

65 "Socialism – Socialists," *Western Clarion*, 6 Jan. 1906, 4; *Social Democrat* (Chicago), 16 March 1898.

66 *Citizen and Country* (Toronto), 6 April 1900.

67 Possible exceptions would be a number of the anarchists, a little-studied tendency in Canada. Much of the most innovative new work on them is as yet unpublished: see Travis Tomchuk, " 'There Are Anarchists at Large in Winnipeg': Local Anarchists and Commentaries on Anarchism in the Winnipeg Labour Press, 1900–1919," unpublished paper, Queen's University, Kingston, 2005. Tomchuk's impending doctoral thesis, "Transnational Radicals: Italian Anarchist Networks in Southern Ontario and the Northeastern United States, 1900–1950," will greatly enhance our understanding of these activists. Thus far, despite the enormous hype surrounding them, evidence of actual insurrectionary activities has yet to surface. Direct action – sabotage, armed self-defence against the police, and so on – took place in some of the labour wars of the period, but it did not aim at the revolutionary overthrow of the state.

68 This proposition sounded peculiar to a few Marxists of the time. See, for instance, Louis B. Boudin, *The Theoretical System of Karl Marx in the Light of Recent Criticism* (Chicago: Charles H. Kerr, 1920), based upon articles appearing in the *International Socialist Review* in 1905 and 1906: "Spencerianism, that purest expression of capitalism, and not so very long ago the reigning philosophy, is dead and forgotten" (207).

69 F.C. [Florence Custance], "The Socialist Movement in Canada: The Split in the S.P. of N.A.," *The Worker*, 3 April 1926, 4.

70 Frederick Engels, *Anti-Dühring: Herr Eugen Dühring's Revolution in Science*, in Karl Marx and Frederick Engels, *Collected Works*, vol. 25 (Moscow: Progress Publishers, 1987), 26.

71 Frederick Engels, *Socialism: Utopian and Scientific* (New York: International Publishers, 1968), 16. The passage comes from Engels's introduction to the 1892 English-language edition. *Socialisme utopique et Socialisme scientifique* first appeared in 1880.

72 Stephen Kern, *The Culture of Time and Space, 1880–1918* (Cambridge, Mass.: Harvard University Press, 2003 [1983]), 51.

73 Stack, *First Darwinian Left*, 15.

74 Since one of the key places in Marx's *oeuvre* in which this theme was explored was the unpublished notebooks later published as the *Grundrisse*, first formationists cannot really be held accountable for not realizing the extent to which unilinear narratives were distorting his overall interpretation. See Karl Marx, *Economic Manuscripts of 1857–58*, in Marx and Engels, *Collected Works*, vols. 28, 29 (Moscow: Progress Publishers, 1986, 1987); for an interesting discussion, see Walter L. Adamson, "Marx's Four Histories," in Adamson, *Marx and the Disillusionment of Marxism* (Berkeley, Los Angeles, and London: University of California Press, 1985), 13–39. Down to the end of his life Marx maintained that although there are path-specific patterns of development, one cannot simply take one and assume that it encapsulates a universal pattern that all peoples must follow.

75 Cited in Robert Stuart, *Marxism at Work: Ideology, Class and French Socialism during the Third Republic* (Cambridge: Cambridge University Press, 1992), 60. Although Stuart focuses on France, many of his findings accord with Canadian evidence.

76 Social Democratic Party of Canada, *No Compromise, No Political Trading* (n.p. [Toronto?], n.d. [c.1917]). Interestingly, Marx himself did not place the analysis of value at the heart of some of his own major political and historical writing in the 1870s. It is possible to read Marx's *Civil War in France* (1871) without receiving many clues that its author wanted to explain epochal historical changes with reference to the labour theory of value expounded in *Capital*, vol. 1 (1867). See Karl Marx, *The Civil War in France*, in Marx and Engels, *Collected Works*, vol. 22 (Moscow: Progress Publishers, 1986), 307–59.

77 L.M. Brown, "Socialism: What Some Well Known Men Have Said on the Subject," letter, *Herald* (Halifax), 3 March 1908, 9.

78 See Karl Marx, *Critique of the Gotha Programme* (1875), in Marx and Engels, *Collected Works*, vol. 24 (Moscow: Progress Publishers, 1989), 75–99; the pertinent critique is found on 84–88. See also Bryan D. Palmer, *A Culture in Conflict: Skilled Workers and Industrial Capitalism in Hamilton, Ontario, 1860–1914* (Montreal: McGill-Queen's University Press, 1979), 98–107; Gregory S. Kealey and Bryan D. Palmer, *Dreaming of What Might Be: The Knights of Labor in Ontario, 1880–1900* (Cambridge: Cambridge University Press, 1982), 178–83.

79 "Your Ballot Will Change It," *Western Clarion*, 19 Jan. 1907, 4.

80 Skelton, *Socialism*, 132.

81 Peter Campbell, "In Defence of the Labour Theory of Value: The Socialist Party of Canada and the Evolution of Marxist Thought," *Journal of History and Politics* 10 (1992), 61–86. For Untermann, see Hector N. McDonald, "Untermann 'Economics' (?)," *Western Clarion*, 11 Dec. 1909, 3.

82 Stuart, *Marxism at Work*, 64.

83 Roscoe A. Fillmore, "Keep the Issue Clear," *International Socialist Review* 15, 7 (January 1915), 398, 398–99; "How to Build up the Socialist Movement," *International Socialist Review* 16, 10 (April 1916), 616.

84 Stuart, *Marxism at Work*, 127.

85 Colin McKay would attempt to calculate the overall rates of surplus extraction, but in a later period. See Ian McKay, ed., *For a Working-Class Culture in Canada: A Selection of Colin McKay's Writings on Sociology and Political Economy, 1897–1939*, Part IV (St. John's, Nfld.: Canadian Committee on Labour History, 1996).

86 C.W. Springford, "As to Dawson," *Western Clarion*, letter, 6 Aug. 1910, 3.

87 Brown, "Socialism: What Some Well Known Men Have Said on the Subject," letter, *Herald* (Halifax), 3 March 1908, 9.

88 P.F. Lawson, *Herald* (Halifax), letter, 12 Oct. 1906, 4; see also Lawson, *Herald*, letter, 20 Nov. 1906. See also Charles Allen Seager, "A Proletariat in Wild Rose Country: The Alberta Coal Miners, 1905–1945," Ph.D. thesis, York University, Toronto, 1981, 100, 304; and Seager, "Socialists and Workers: The Western Canadian Coal Miners, 1900–21," *Labour/Le Travail* 16 (Fall 1985), 223–59.

89 Socialist Party of Canada, Lindsay, *Gems of Socialism*; "Must Have Been Drinking," *Western Clarion*, 18 April 1908, 1; "A Refugee," "The Nimble Job Chaser Jots Down a Few Notes," *Western Clarion*, 18 April 1908, 1. For additional Maritime debates over the labour theory of value, see J. Cyrus Doull, "When and Where Does the Process of Production Begin?" *Herald* (Halifax), 15 Aug. 1907; Robert P. Neil, *Herald*, letter, 7 May 1908.

90 "The Modern Magician," editorial, *Western Clarion*, 18 April 1908, 2; "The Next Great Act on History's Stage," *Western Clarion*, 4 Jan. 1908, 1; "The Right Sort of Stuff," *Western Clarion*, 4 Jan. 1908, 2.

91 Mc. [D.G. McKenzie], "Exploitation," *Western Clarion*, 4 Jan. 1908, 2.

92 Fillmore, "How to Build up the Socialist Movement," 614.

93 "The Socialist Party of Canada," *Western Clarion*, 18 April 1908, 4.

94 Wilfred Gribble, "The Two-Headed Man," *Western Clarion*, letter, 15 Aug. 1908, 3.

95 J.Y., "From the Coal City," *Western Clarion*, letter, 4 Jan. 1908, 3.

96 Mc. [McKenzie], "As to the Urry Affair," *Western Clarion*, 12 Dec. 1908, 4.

97 Karl Marx, *General Rules and Administrative Regulations of the International Working Men's Association*, in Marx and Engels, *Collected Works*, vol. 23 (Moscow: Progress Publishers, 1988), 3.

98 Stuart, *Marxism at Work*, 476.

99 Ibid., 78.

100 Shier, "Decadence of Capitalism," 2.

101 As William Irvine, suggesting his strong interest in being in a close dialogue with "Marx," told a mass rally of retail clerks: "Remember you are taking part in the great forward movement of the great proletariat." Cited in Anthony Mardiros, *William Irvine: The Life of a Prairie Radical* (Toronto: James Lorimer, 1979), 67.

102 For solicitation of real estate investors, *Western Clarion*, 16 April 1910; for Cobb, *Western Clarion*, 23 Jan. 1910; advertisements, *Western Clarion*, 6 Jan. 1906.

103 Joseph Adams, *Ten Thousand Miles Through Canada: The Natural Resources, Commercial Industries, Fish and Game, Sports and Pastimes of the Great Dominion* (Toronto: McClelland and Goodchild, n.d. [1912]), 192. For suggestive new work on the left and the middle class in the United States, see Robert D. Johnston, *The Radical Middle Class: Populist Democracy and the Question of Capitalism in Progressive Era Portland, Oregon* (Princeton and Oxford: Princeton University Press, 2003); in Canada, see especially Jennifer Marotta, "A Moral Messenger to the Canadian Middlemost: A Reading of *The Family Herald and Weekly Star*, 1874–1914," Ph.D. thesis, Queen's University, Kingston, 2006.

104 Jack Kavanagh, *The 1913 Vancouver Island Miners Strike* (Vancouver: B.C. Miners' Liberation League, 1914), available at Socialist History Project <http://www.socialisthistory.ca/>.

105 For C. Osborne Ward, see his *The Ancient Lowly: A History of the Ancient People from the Earliest Known Period to the Adoption of Christianity by Constantine* (Chicago: Charles H. Kerr & Co., 1900). For important new work on the struggles of the Lakehead working class, see Michel Beaulieu, "Proletarian Prometheus: Socialism, Ethnicity, and Revolution at the Lakehead, 1900–1935," Ph.D. thesis, Queen's University, Kingston, 2007.

106 Socialist Party of Canada, *Workingmen Get Wise*, leaflet no. 6 (n.p. [Vancouver], n.d. [1912]).

107 *Globe* (Saint John), 5 Nov. 1910; Fillmore, *Maritime Radical*, 24, 88; Homel, "James Simpson and the Origins of Canadian Social Democracy," 504.

108 "Incidental to Evolution" [reprinted from *Machinists Monthly*], *Western Clarion*, 17 April 1909, 2; *Cotton's Weekly*, 8 Dec. 1910; "Pioneer," *Herald* (Halifax), letter, 25 Oct. 1906; *Cotton's Weekly*, 7 Jan.1909; Dave Rees, "Labor's Demands Pictured by Labor Leader," *Herald*, 5 June 1919.

109 William Davenport, *Why Not Enjoy What You Produce* (Vancouver: Socialist Party of Canada, n.d. [1912]).

110 Stuart, *Marxism at Work*, 463.

111 Geoff Eley, *Forging Democracy: The History of the Left in Europe, 1850–2000* (Oxford: Oxford University Press, 2002), 52.

112 See E.P. Thompson, *William Morris: Romantic to Revolutionary* (London: Merlin, 1977 [1955]), 269. For an illuminating table of the writings of Marx and Engels

available to English-speaking readers, see Stuart MacIntyre, *A Proletarian Science: Marxism in Britain 1917–1933* (Cambridge: Cambridge University Press, 1980), 91. Among some important unavailable titles for the cohort of 1890–1922: *On the Jewish Question* (1843); *Economic and Philosophical Manuscripts* (1844); *The German Ideology* (1845–46), *Class Struggles in France* (1850); the *Grundrisse* (1857–58). *Critique of the Gotha Programme* (1875) was available in a 1900 translation, but not widely cited.

113 For this theme among the Guesdistes, see Stuart, *Marxism at Work*, 466. For Marx's own response to the iron law, associated with rivals in the First International, see *Value, Price and Profit* (1865), in Marx and Engels, *Collected Works*, Vol. 20 (Moscow: Progress Publishers, 1985), 103–49.

114 I borrow the term "redressers" from E.P. Thompson, *The Making of the English Working Class* (Harmondsworth, Eng.: Penguin, 1970 [1963], 515.

115 For Gronlund, see especially Stack, *First Darwinian Left*, 47–49.

116 Laurence Gronlund, *The Co-operative Commonwealth: An Exposition of Socialism* (Boston: Lee and Shepard, 1890), 79. Gronlund would also leave behind important studies of the French Revolution, and an investigation of the impact of socialism on personal life and religion: *Our Destiny, The Influence of Socialism on Morals and Religion* (1890). He also served as one of the founding figures of the Socialist Labor Party from 1874 to 1884.

117 Pittinger, *American Socialists and Evolutionary Thought*, 50.

118 Dominque Lecourt, "Marx in the Sieve of Darwin," *Rethinking Marxism* 5,4 (Winter 1992), 6–28.

119 Stack, *First Darwinian Left*, 75. The SPC Library in Winnipeg did contain the fuller text of *Anti-Dühring* in its Charles H. Kerr edition (copy in the author's possession).

120 Frederick Engels, "The Part Played by Labour in Transition from Ape to Man," in Frederick Engels, *Dialectics of Nature* (1873–82) in Marx and Engels, *Collected Works*, vol. 25, 461. Contemporaries would not have had access to this text, which was published only in 1925. Of course, the same radical naturalism pervades Engels's other writings of the 1870s and 1880s.

121 Engels, *Socialism*, 54, 61.

122 Ibid., 51, 68, 69, 72.

123 Pittinger, *American Socialists and Evolutionary Thought*, 72. Significantly, in the 1998 edition of *Women and Economics*, in their zeal to present Gilman to contemporary Americans, the "introducers" seek to minimize Gilman's well-documented attachment to socialist currents and, more seriously, erase her deep attachment to the Spencerian paradigm – even to the extent of editing out notes in the original text that led the reader directly to Spencer. In the 1970s *Herland* came to be hailed as a rediscovered classic of socialist feminism. See Charlotte Perkins Gilman, *Herland*, int. Ann J. Lane (New York: Pantheon Books, 1979). For a vigorously revisionist account, see Mariana Valverde, "When the Mother of the Race Is Free: Race, Reproduction, and Sexuality in First-Wave Feminism," in *Gender Conflicts: New Essays in Women's History*, ed. Franca Iacovetta and Mariana Valverde (Toronto: University of Toronto Press, 1992).

124 Gilman, *Women and Economics*, 75, 65, 43, 120, 121, 223.

125 Ibid., 113.

126 Ibid., 209, 301.

127 Pittinger, *American Socialists and Evolutionary Thought*, 198.

128 Grant Allen, "The Political Pupa," in Allen, *Post-Prandial Philosophy* (London: Chatto & Windus, 1894), 132–33, 135, 136.

129 William Greenslade and Terence Rodgers, "Resituating Grant Allen: Writing, Radicalism and Modernity," in *Grant Allen: Literature and Cultural Politics at the Fin de Siècle*, ed. Greenslade and Rodgers (Aldershot, Eng.: Ashgate, 2005), 8; Grant Allen, *The Hand of God and Other Posthumous Essays, Together with Some Reprinted Papers* (London: Watts & Co., issued for the Rationalist Press, 1909), 113.

130 Chris Nottingham, "Grant Allen and the New Politics," in *Grant Allen*, ed. Greenslade and Rodgers, 107.

131 Grant Allen, *The Evolution of the Idea of God: An Inquiry into the Origins of Religions*, rev. ed. (London: Watts & Co., 1903). See also Greenslade and Rodgers, "Resituating Grant Allen," 2; Paul Lafargue, *Causes of Belief in God* (Vancouver: Whitehead Estate, n.d. [1919]), 10, a translation of "Causes de la croyance en Dieu," *La vie socialiste* 10–11 (1905). Allen's *Idea of God* is today also widely referenced on Internet sites devoted to free thought and atheism. For Allen and the spc's official line on religion, see Peter E. Newell, *The Impossibilists: A Brief Profile of the Socialist Party of Canada* (London: Athena Press, 2008), 95–101.

132 Olive Schreiner, *Woman and Labour* (London: T. Fisher Unwin, 1912), 33, 109. 103–4, 175. For discussions of Schreiner, see Ruth Brandon, *The New Women and the Old Men: Love, Sex and the Woman Question* (New York and London: W.W. Norton, 1990), ch. 2; Cherry Clayton, *Olive Schreiner* (New York: Twayne Publishers, 1997). For an excellent collection of primary sources from Schreiner's time period that provide a context for her work, see Marie Mulvey Roberts and Tamae Mituza, eds., *The Exploited: Women and Work* (London: Routledge and Thoemmes Press, 1995), in the series *Sources of British Feminism*.

133 His name is also sometimes given as Pyotr or Piotr Kropotkin (as it might be translated from the Russian).

134 A. Percy Chew, "Kropotkin and Mutual Aid," *The Voice* [Winnipeg], 26 May, 1910. See Phillips Thompson, "Thoughts and Suggestions on the Social Problem and Things in General (1888–1889)," ed. Deborah L. Coombs and Gregory S. Kealey, *Labour/Le Travail* 35 (Spring 1995), 255–56. Kropotkin returned to the Soviet Union after the 1917 revolution and died there, dissatisfied, as were most anarchists, with the direction of the Bolshevik Revolution.

135 Daniel P. Todes, *Darwin without Malthus* (New York: Oxford University Press, 1989). In all of this, as Todes observes, Kropotkin was in the mainstream of Russian evolutionary thought, which agreed with descent with modification but drew the line at natural selection. His point of view seemed more unusual and radical when it was brought into the British context.

136 Peter Kropotkin, *The Conquest of Bread and Other Writings*, ed. Marshall Shatz (Cambridge: Cambridge University Press, 2002), 4–5, 14.

137 Peter Kropotkin, "Anarchist Communism: Its Basis and Principles," in Kropotkin, *Anarchism: A Collection of Revolutionary Writings*, ed. Roger N. Baldwin (Mineola, N.Y.: Dover Publications, 2002 [1970]), 46.

138 Kropotkin, *Conquest of Bread*, 89, 19.

139 Peter Kropotkin, *Memoirs of a Revolutionist* (Montreal and New York: Black Rose Books, 1989), 464.

140 Peter Kropotkin, *Mutual Aid: A Factor of Evolution* (Montreal and New York: Black Rose Books, 1989), 1, 1–2.

141 Kropotkin, *Mutual Aid*, 53. Characteristically, most of Kropotkin's commentators, including George Woodcock, because they are trapped within dated conceptions of Spencer, have swept Kropotkin's blatant indebtedness to Spencer under the car-

pet. For other assessments of Kropotkin and this tendency, see Paul Avrich, *The Russian Anarchists* (Oakland and Edinburgh: AK Press, 2005 [1967]); Brian Morris, *Kropotkin: The Politics of Community* (Amherst, N.Y.: Humanity Books, 2004).

142 Kropotkin, "Anarchist Communism," 53; Kropotkin, *Mutual Aid*, 293.

143 Kropotkin, *Memoirs of a Revolutionist*, 269.

144 Kropotkin, "Anarchism," *Encyclopædia Britannica* 1905, reprinted in *Anarchism*, ed. Baldwin, 284. See also Kropotkin, *Modern Science and Anarchism*, as cited in Marshall Shatz, "Introduction" to Kropotkin, *Conquest of Bread*, xviii. The aim of anarchism, as Shatz notes in his introduction (xviii), "is to construct a *synthetic philosophy* comprehending in one generalization all the phenomena of nature – and therefore also the life of societies." Emphasis added.

145 Margaret Haile, Review of Jack London, *Call of the Wild*, *Wilshire's Magazine*, September 1903, 90–91; Review of Jack London, *Call of the Wild*, *International Socialist Review* 4, 5 (November 1903), 315.

146 As Don MacGillivray demonstrates, the character of Wolf Larsen – the "Sea Wolf" – was based upon the real-life exploits of Alex MacLean of Cape Breton, who underwent the distinctly modern experience of confronting his own fictional image as a "reality" in his own life. See Don MacGillivray, *Captain Alex MacLean: Jack London's Sea Wolf* (Vancouver: UBC Press, 2008).

147 Jack London, *Martin Eden* (n.p.: Quiet Vision Publishing, 2003 [1913]), 75.

148 Jack London, *War of the Classes, Revolution, The Shrinkage of the Planet* (New York and Berlin: Mondial, 2006 [1905]), 28. In *Social Statics*, 380, Spencer explains: "He on whom his own stupidity, or vice, or idleness, entails loss of life, must, in the generalizations of philosophy, be classified with the victims of weak viscera or malformed limbs. . . . Beings thus imperfect are nature's failures, and are recalled by her laws when found to be such. Along with the rest they are put upon trial. If they are sufficiently complete to live, they *do* live, and it is well they should live. If they are not sufficiently complete to live, they die, and it is best they should die."

149 London borrowed the term from British socialist H.G. Wells, using it in an earlier factual account of his experience of East End London, which described many of its residents as the malformed monsters of the environment in which they lived. Jack London, *The People of the Abyss* (London and Stirling, Va.: Pluto Press, 2001 [1903]).

150 Jack London, *The Iron Heel* (New York and Berlin: Mondial, 2006 [1908]), 15, 14, 15, 47.

151 Ibid., 9, 17, 65.

152 Stack, *First Darwinian Left*, 42. For an acute reading of London's "womanizing," see Jonathan Auerbach, *Male Call: Becoming Jack London* (Durham, N.C. and London: Duke University Press, 1996).

153 Leon Trotsky, "Critique of *The Iron Heel*," in *The Critical Responses to Jack London*, ed. Susan M. Nuernberg (Westport, Conn. and London: Greenwood Press, 1995), 137–38; Alex Kershaw, *Jack London: A Life* (New York: St. Martin's Griffin, 1997), 164. For an excellent guide to the response to London's *Iron Heel*, see Francis Robert Shor, *Utopianism and Radicalism in a Reforming America, 1888–1918* (Westport, Conn. and London: Greenwood Press, 1997), ch. 4.

154 Charlie Murray, a long-time left activist in Nova Scotia, told me this story. It would be interesting to hear of other grassroots groups formed under the inspiration of London's writings.

155 Wilfred Gribble, "Jack London: In Memoriam," Jack London Papers, EH, 1916,

112, Henry E. Huntington Library, San Marino, Cal. I thank Don MacGillivray for this reference. See also Wilfred Gribble, *Rhymes of Revolt* (Vancouver: n.p., n.d. [1911?]). Gribble is briefly noticed in James Doyle, *Progressive Heritage: The Evolution of a Politically Radical Literary Tradition in Canada* (Waterloo, Ont.: Wilfrid Laurier University Press, 2002), 37–38.

156 Exactly how much influence each exerted can be debated. To merit inclusion in this discussion, the given evolutionary writer had to initiate an extended discussion from two or more Canadian activists. More general indications of influence would include the re-publication in Canada of their works; their appearance in socialist libraries; extended references to such works in local commentaries on politics and society; and the adoption of the author's titles in semi-official booklists, as well as those marketing books to left-wing audiences.

157 Engels, *Dialectics of Nature*, 334–35.

158 William Irvine, *The Farmers in Politics* (Toronto: McClelland and Stewart, 1976 [1920]), 79.

159 Jonathan Rée, *Proletarian Philosophers: Problems in Socialist Culture in Britain, 1900–1940* (Oxford: Clarendon Press, 1984), 8–9. The well-born Kropotkin was a partial exception to this rule. He was, interestingly, the only one who had engaged in on the spot research outside Europe – in Western Siberia and Manchuria.

160 See Stack, *First Darwinian Left*, ch. 8.

161 In the hands of a theorist like Emile Vandervelde – the future Belgian president of the Second International, who like many others in Europe had been led to socialism first via Darwin rather than Marx, and aimed to effect a "practical union and unison of Biology and Sociology" – the science of parasitology revealed that "mutual aid" was not just sentimental politics, but the key to saving the human species from degeneration. It was a framework that also allowed socialists to theorize those groups who stood outside capitalist production, and in Vandervelde's hands allowed him to indict bankers, financiers, and prostitutes equally as parasites. See Jean Massart and Emile Vandervelde, *Parasitisme Organique et Parasitisme Social* (Paris: Librairie C. Reinwald, Schleicher Frères Editeurs, 1898). Parasitology was developed in religious circles by the Rev. Henry Drummond, who wielded a considerable influence over contemporaries interested in the social gospel, and who sought to transpose Spencer's concepts of evolution into the realm of theology. See Drummond, *Natural Law in the Spiritual World*.

162 Pittinger, *American Socialists and Evolutionary Thought*, 52.

163 Stack, *First Darwinian Left*, 51. Stack argues that by the 1880s Darwinism and socialism "were so intertwined that it makes no sense to regard one as prior to, or making instrumental use of, the other. The language of Darwinism became, for a time, the language of socialism." (The only amendment one might suggest to this perceptive observation is that Darwinism was often filtered through and charged by the particular grid of Spencerian sociology.) "A biological lexicon provided the structure and boundaries for political and philosophical discourse," argues Stack, "and socialists developed their politics amidst evolutionary precepts and in an organic language." Stack, *First Darwinian Left*, 3.

164 Many, for example, wrestled with the new emphases on heredity of the 1890s and early 1900s. Gaylord Wilshire wrote a preface to R.C. Punnett, *Mendelism* (New York: Wilshire Book Co., 1909), that drew out Mendel's implications for socialism.

165 Cohen would go on as editor of the *Freethinker* and president of the National Secular Society to be a formidable presence among freethinkers until 1951.

166 Chapman Cohen, "Evolution," *The Indicator*, 6 Dec. 1919.

167 Note, for instance, David Rees, "Labor's Demands Pictured by Labor Leader," *Herald* (Halifax), 5 June 1919. See also Ruse, *Darwinism and Design*, 315.

168 Untitled item, *Western Clarion*, 18 April 1908, 1. As many socialists themselves struggled to point out, "survival of the fittest" did not mean "survival of the best." See, for example, Charles Walker, "The Doctrine of the Survival of Fittest," *Herald* (Halifax), letter, 11 July 1908.

169 Arthur M. Lewis, *Evolution: Social and Organic*, 6th ed. (Chicago: Charles H. Kerr, n.d. [1919], 21. As Pittinger remarks, Lewis was linked with such major socialist intellectuals as A.M. Simons, Ernest Untermann, and Robert Rives La Monte, who "raised the socialist discussion of scientific issues to its highest level of sophistication": Pittinger, *American Socialists and Evolutionary Thought*, 11. Fillmore thought so highly of Lewis that he purchased a copy of *Evolution Social and Organic* for his nephew H. Leslie Fillmore, which he presented to him in May 1919 (copy in author's possession). For Tim Buck's response to Lewis, see Tim Buck, *Yours in the Struggle: Reminiscences of Tim Buck* (Toronto: NC Press, 1977), 41.

170 Arthur M. Lewis, *Vital Problems in Social Evolution* (Chicago: Charles H. Kerr, 1917), 3, 192.

171 Jim Connell, "Socialism and the Survival of the Fittest," *Western Clarion*, 8, 15, 22, 29 March, 5, 19, 26 April 1913. Connell was otherwise also known as the popularizer of the popular British left-wing song, "The People's Flag."

172 Richard Dawkins, *The Blind Watchmaker* (London: Longman, 1986).

173 "Socialism – Socialists," *Western Clarion*, 6 Jan. 1906, 4.

174 Enrico Ferri, "Fundamental Character of Socialism," *Western Clarion*, 14 Dec. 1907, 2. Ferri would later become notorious for supporting fascism.

175 J.S. Woodsworth, *Strangers Within Our Gates* (Toronto: University of Toronto Press, 1972 [1909]), 67.

176 Mills, *Fool for Christ*, 69.

177 W.H.S., "Revolutions Are Not Made by Law," *Western Clarion*, Aug. 7, 1909, 1.

178 Connell, "Socialism and the Survival of the Fittest."

179 W.E. Anderson, "Dewberry, Alta.," *Western Clarion*, letter, 16 April 1910, 3; Clifford Butler, "The Nation-Builder. These Be Thy Gods, O Israel. Give Me the Golden Calf," *Western Clarion*, 6 Aug. 1910, 1; *Western Clarion*, 6 Jan. 1906.

180 T. Phillips Thompson, *The Politics of Labor* (Toronto: University of Toronto Press, 1975 [New York and Chicago, 1887], 63, 73; Homel, "James Simpson and the Origins of Canadian Social Democracy," 386.

181 W.U. Cotton, ed., *Cotton's Compendium of Facts*, 3rd ed. (Cowansville, Que.: Cotton's Co-operative Publications, n.d. [1913]), 5.

182 Thompson, *Politics of Labor*, 63–64; *Citizen and Country*, 23 March 1900.

183 *Citizen and Country*, 6 April 1900; *Cotton's Weekly*, 2 Dec. 1909; Ferri, "Fundamental Character of Socialism," 2.

184 Fillmore, "Keep the Issue Clear," 616.

185 "Socialism is not patriotism," advised the *Gems of Socialism*. "Under patriotism the people have nothing to say. Under Socialism the people have all to say." Socialist Party of Canada, Lindsay, *Gems of Socialism*, 8.

186 A detailed critique can be found in Marc Angenot, *Le marxisme dans les grands récits: Essai d'analyse du discours* (Quebec: Les Presses de l'Université Laval, 2005), a close critique of the Guesdistes.

187 Richard Hofstadter, *Social Darwinism in American Thought*, rev. ed. (Boston: The Beacon Press, 1955, 31–32.

188 "Impossibilism" received its first major introduction into Canadian left history

with the important and innovative work of Ross McCormack, though he did not intend "Impossibilism" to be the pejorative term that it would become. According to McCormack, the impossibilists generally shared three fundamental convictions: "first, that capitalism could not be reformed and attempts at amelioration had no place in the class struggle; second, that trade unions could not benefit all workers in the short run or any workers in the long run; and third, that class-conscious political action was the only means by which the proletariat could destroy the wage system and establish the co-operative commonwealth." A. Ross McCormack, *Reformers, Rebels, and Revolutionaries: The Western Canadian Radical Movement 1899–1919* (Toronto: University of Toronto Press, 1991 [1977]), 54. The binary "possibilism/impossibilism" is not innocent – it comes loaded with polemical force. Those who live within the realm of possibility are by implication more "real" than those who are obsessed with the impossible, which carries the unmistakable hint of irrationality. The reductionist reading attributes an unchanging "line" to people who, in fact, were often engaged in fierce debates over their core positions, and proved they would change them if they had to. In McCormack's hands the "impossibilists" are sometimes treated as though they were early versions of the Stalinists. Only recently, in the fine revisionist work of Peter Campbell, has a more respectful note been struck: Peter Campbell, *Canadian Marxists and the Search for a Third Way* (Montreal and Kingston: McGill-Queen's University Press, 1999). For the European roots of the concept, see Claude Willard, *Les guesdistes: Le mouvement socialiste en France (1893–1905)* (Paris: Éditions sociales, 1965), 20–22; and Stuart, *Marxism at Work*, 140–56. Yet, interestingly, some recent works generally sympathetic to the SPC have embraced the term as an apt designation for uncompromising advocates of the single-plank platform. See especially L. Gambone, *The Impossibilists: Selections from the Press of the Socialist Party of Canada and the One Big Union, 1906–1938* (Montreal: Red Lion Press, 1995), and Newell, *Impossibilists*, both valuable additions to the literature. I still find the category somewhat problematic: first because most Marxists believe that capitalism as an entire system is intrinsically unreformable; second, because the term was (to my knowledge) only rarely used in Canada, and not as a self-designation (I know of no group that applied the term to themselves, nor any publication called *The Impossibilist*); and third because both in practice and theory most SPCers, especially after 1911, did not adopt so categorical an approach to trade unionism. When I use "impossibilist" in this text I encase it in quotation marks and use it to denote a scholastic style of Marxist discourse implicitly or explicitly disparaging of all "immediate" or "palliative" struggles that fell short of the "abolition of wage slavery." I do not use it as a pejorative term.

189 See Thompson, *William Morris*, ch.7.

190 *Cotton's Weekly*, 1 April 1909.

2: The Emergence of the First Formation in Canada, 1890–1902

1 Some historians indicate that the Toronto and Montreal groups emerged at the same time. Roughly the same pattern would be followed by many socialist organizations: a group in one locality would organize, be declared the "headquarters," and assume the functions of an executive body.

2 G. Weston Wrigley Sr., "Socialism in Canada," *International Socialist Review* 1, 11 (May 1901), 685–89. For Wrigley Sr., see Ramsay Cook, "Wrigley, George Weston," in *Dictionary of Canadian Biography*, vol. 13, ed. Ramsay Cook (Toronto: University of Toronto Press, 1994), 1111–15.

3 See Paul Buhle, "Socialist Party," in *Encyclopedia of the American Left*, ed. Mari Jo

Buhle, Paul Buhle, and Dan Georgakas (New York: Oxford University Press, 1998), 767–74. The daily papers included the *Jewish Daily Forward*, the largest-circulation Yiddish-language newspaper in the world, and *Appeal to Reason*, for a time the most widely circulated political weekly in the entire country. For the vote statistics, see *International Socialist Review* 17, 8 (February 1917), 507.

4   Robert Stuart, *Marxism at Work: Ideology, Class and French Socialism during the Third Republic* (Cambridge: Cambridge University Press, 1992), 274.

5   For example, the federal socialist vote in 1911 barely exceeded 6,000, with no candidate saving his deposit, at a time when socialists in smaller European countries were amassing vote counts in the hundreds of thousands.

6   These impressionistic statistics are reported in Alexander Trachtenberg, ed., *American Labor Year-Book, 1917–1918* (New York: Department of Labor Research of the Rand School of Social Science, 1918), 291.

7   For a good overview of the 1920s, see Craig Heron, "National Contours: Solidarity and Fragmentation," in *The Workers Revolt in Canada, 1917–1925*, ed. Craig Heron (Toronto: University of Toronto Press, 1998), 275.

8   See Peter Campbell, *Canadian Marxists and the Search for a Third Way* (Montreal & Kingston: McGill-Queen's University Press, 1999).

9   "*Blocco storico*" was also earlier translated as "historic bloc," but, as Adam David Morton observes, this convention may misleadingly place "too much emphasis on the momentous, one-off, or literally 'historic' formation of such a bloc," rather than on its capacity to interpret and reshape historical processes. See Adam David Morton, *Unravelling Gramsci: Hegemony and Passive Revolution in the Global Economy* (London and Ann Arbor, Mich.: Pluto, 2007), 218, n.8, who in turn draws upon Derek Boothman, "Introduction," in Antonio Gramsci, *Further Selections from the Prison Notebooks*, ed. and trans. D. Boothman (London: Lawrence and Wishart, 1995), xi – xii; Wolfgang Fritz Haug, "Rethinking Gramsci's Philosophy of Praxis from One Century to the Next," *Boundary 2* 26, 2 (1999), 111.

10   For the origins of this concept, see Jeffrey L. McNairn, *The Capacity to Judge: Public Opinion and Deliberative Democracy in Upper Canada 1791–1854* (Toronto: University of Toronto Press, 2000).

11   Geoff Eley, *Forging Democracy: The History of the Left in Europe, 1850–2000* (Oxford: Oxford University Press, 2002), 3.

12   See Frederick Engels, "Notes on My Journey through America and Canada," in Marx and Engels, *Collected Works*, vol. 26 (Moscow: Progress Publishers, 1990), 581–82.

13   On this pattern of uneven and combined development – on which the literature is immense – see especially David Harvey, *Justice, Nature and the Geography of Difference* (Oxford: Basil Blackwell, 1996).

14   Gene Howard Homel, "James Simpson and the Origins of Canadian Social Democracy," Ph.D. thesis, University of Toronto, 1978, 68–69. For an examination of Georgeite ideas in Canada's two largest cities, see Gregory Levine, "The Single Tax in Montreal and Toronto, 1880 to 1920: Successes, Failures and the Transformation of an Idea," *The American Journal of Economics and Sociology* 52, 4 (October 1993), 417–32. For illuminating discussions, see Ramsay Cook, *The Regenerators: Social Criticism in Late Victorian English Canada* (Toronto: University of Toronto Press, 1985), and his "Henry George and the Poverty of Canadian Progress," Canadian Historical Association, *Papers*, (1977), 142–57; and Allen Mills, "Single Tax, Socialism, and the Independent Labour Party in Manitoba: The Political Ideas of F.J. Dixon and S.J. Farmer," *Labour/Le Travail* 5 (1980), 33–56.

15 For Goldwin Smith on Henry George, see Arnold Haultain, ed., *Goldwin Smith: His Life and Opinions* (Toronto, n.d.), 184.

16 S.T. Wood, "Social Amelioration: The Contrast Between Doing Good and Doing Right," *The Canadian Magazine* 11, 6 (October 1898): 461–66. See also Carl Berger, "Wood, Samuel T.," in *Dictionary of Canadian Biography*, vol. 14, ed. Cook (Toronto: University of Toronto Press, 1998), 1080–81, who emphasizes Wood's essentially liberal reasons for advocating the single tax.

17 See Martin Robin, *Radical Politics and Canadian Labour* (Kingston: Industrial Relations Centre, Queen's University, 1971 [1968]), 23.

18 Robin, *Radical Politics and Canadian Labour*, 33.

19 David Stack, *The First Darwinian Left: Socialism and Darwinism 1859–1914* (Cheltenham, Eng.: New Clarion Press, 2003), 33.

20 The revolts of the 1870s have yet to be brought together in one study. For some local indications, see Ian McKay "The Crisis of Dependent Development: Class Conflict in the Nova Scotia Coalfields, 1872–1876," *Canadian Journal of Sociology* 13, 1–2 (1988), 9–48.

21 For a fascinating discussion see Stephen Cole, "Commissioning Consent in Canada: The Royal Commission on the Relations of Labour and Capital, 1886–1889," Ph.D. thesis, Queen's University, Kingston, 2007.

22 For George's impact in Canada in general, see Robin, *Radical Politics and Canadian Labour*, 23–33; Russell Hann, "Brainworkers and the Knights of Labor," in *Essays in Canadian Working Class History*, ed. Gregory S. Kealey and Peter Warrian (Toronto: McClelland and Stewart, 1976), 41–42; Ramsay Cook, "Henry George and the Poverty of Canadian Progress," *Papers*, Canadian Historical Association, 1977, 142–57. For interesting contemporary discussions of the single tax in Canada, see Frank W. Williams, "The Labor Question from One Angle," letter to the *Busy East* (Sackville, N.S.), January 1914, 21; "The Single Tax Movement," *Chronicle* (Halifax), 10 Sept. 1890. For an astute assessment of the limitations of Georgeism and the "labour party strategy," via a critique of Engels's unduly optimistic appraisal, see Eric Thomas Chester, *True Mission: Socialists and the Labor Party Question in the U.S.* (London and Sterling, Va.: Pluto Press, 2004), ch. 2.

23 Matthew Beaumont, *Utopia Ltd.: Ideologies of Social Dreaming in England 1870–1900* (Leiden, The Netherlands, and Boston: Brill, 2005), 1–2, 45.

24 Beaumont, *Utopia Ltd.*, 24.

25 See Edward Bellamy, *Looking Backward 2000–1887* (New York: Bantam, 1983 [1888]), 72.

26 Morris, cited in Beaumont, *Utopia Ltd.*, 42.

27 Stephen Leacock, "How Mr. Bellamy Looked Backwards," in Leacock, *The Unsolved Riddle of Social Justice and Other Essays: The Social Criticism of Stephen Leacock*, ed. and int. Alan Bowker (Toronto: University of Toronto Press, 1973 [1920]), 132.

28 Arthur Lipow, *Authoritarian Socialism in America: Edward Bellamy and the Nationalist Movement* (Berkeley: University of California Press, 1982).

29 Laurence Gronlund, *The Co-operative Commonwealth: An Exposition of Socialism* (Boston: Lee and Shepard, 1890), viii. For the Halifax discussion of Bellamy, see *Acadian Recorder* (Halifax), 31 May 1898. For a more hostile Canadian view, see W.A. Douglas, "Bellamy's Blunders: A Review of 'Equality,' " *The Canadian Magazine* 10 (January 1898): 268–70.

30 W.A. Pritchard, "Looking Backward," Foreword to Edward Bellamy, *Looking Back-*

ward 2000–1887 (Vancouver: The Totem Press, 1934), iii. Typical of the "radical planism" taking hold in the 1930s, Pritchard also drew attention to the "accomplishments of Soviet Russia and its Five-year Plan."

31 John David Bell, "The Social and Political Thought of the Labor Advocate," M.A. thesis, Queen's University, Kingston, 1975, 54. For the "Parable of the Water Tank," see Edward Bellamy, *Equality* (New York: D. Appleton and Company, 1897), ch. 23.

32 For a fascinating discussion, see W.R. Fraser, "Canadian Reactions," in Sylvia E. Bowman et al., *Edward Bellamy Abroad: An American Prophet's Influence* (New York: Twayne Publishers, 1962), 137–50, 458–60.

33 "This morning I was up at 8, did not sleep very well last night, wrote all morning on article on Socialism, also read through phamplet [sic] 30 pages by Engles [sic] Socialism Utopia to Science. There is much in it. There is something about Socialism which interests me deeply. There is truth in it – it is full of truth, not much that is strange and obscure." Mackenzie King Diary, 13 Aug. 1897. The Diary at the Library and Archives Canada (LAC) is online at <http://king.collectionscanada.ca>. My thanks to Margaret Bedore for bringing this material to my attention.

34 Cited in Bell, "Social and Political Thought of the Labor Advocate," 12.

35 Craig Heron, "Labourism and the Canadian Working Class," *Labour/Le Travail* 13 (Spring 1984), 53. For the Knights of Labor and working-class politics in the 1880s, see Gregory S. Kealey and Bryan D. Palmer, *Dreaming of What Might Be: The Knights of Labor in Ontario, 1880–1900* (Cambridge: Cambridge University Press, 1982), esp. ch. 6.

36 Robin, *Radical Politics and Canadian Labour*, 27.

37 Ian McKay, " 'By Wisdom, Wile, or War': The Provincial Workmen's Association and the Struggle for Working-Class Independence in Nova Scotia, 1879–97," *Labour/Le Travail* 18 (Fall 1986), 13–62.

38 Pierre Berton, "Introduction" to Phillips Thompson, "Thoughts and Suggestions on the Social Problem and Things in General (1888–1889)," ed. Deborah L. Coombs and Gregory S. Kealey, *Labour/Le Travail* 35 (Spring 1995), 238.

39 The details in this and the following paragraphs are drawn from Hann, "Brainworkers and the Knights of Labor," wherein Hann memorably evokes the world of Phillips Thompson in Toronto from 1883 to 1887.

40 Hann, "Brainworkers and the Knights of Labor," 40.

41 Royal Commission on the Relations of Capital and Labour, *Evidence – Ontario* (Ottawa: Queen's Printer, 1889), Phillips Thompson, 98–103.

42 T. Phillips Thompson, *The Politics of Labor* (Toronto: University of Toronto Press, 1975 [New York and Chicago: 1887], 109. One might say that Thompson was initiating an anti-party theme on the Canadian left that would persist powerfully until the 1940s.

43 Ibid., 21–22.

44 Ibid., 84, 87–88, 89, 112. For a direct quote, see 83. Thompson also published a major critique of Spencer in *Labor Advocate*, 3 April 1891.

45 Thompson, "Thoughts and Suggestions," 244.

46 Ibid., 241, 244, 248–49, 271. For a discussion of Spencer's concept of the "internuncial system," see Lester Frank Ward, *Contemporary Sociology* (Chicago: American Journal of Sociology, 1902), 15–16.

47 These "Nationalists" were partisans of Bellamy's ideal of "The Nation," not Canadian "nationalists" in today's sense of the phrase. For an interesting discussion of

this moment, see Cook, *Regenerators*, ch. 9. Cook probes the connections between theosophy and Bellamyism in Canada.

48 See Bell, "Social and Political Thought of the Labor Advocate," passim. The *Labor Advocate* published 44 issues from 5 Dec. 1890 to 21 Oct. 1891.

49 *Labor Advocate* (Toronto), 13 March 1891.

50 Bell, "Social and Political Thought of the Labor Advocate," 44. *Citizen and Country* would remark in 1899: " 'An eminent financier in New York,' whose name is not given to the public, .is promoting a company to buy Ireland. Why not? One landlord would oppress the people no more than many landlords do. After that, Socialism." *Citizen and Country*, 24 June 1899.

51 The Ottawa newspaper *Capital Siftings* "carried two new columns in the fall of 1894 – 'Socialists' Corner,' a potpourri of classic socialist quotations, and 'Socialist Labor Party,' penned by 'Karl Marx, Junior,' " note Kealey and Palmer, *Dreaming of What Might Be*, 245. This is an early instance of an identification, albeit jocular, with "Marx" as a centre of political identity. It would seem that the first "Marxists" emerged, along with the Socialist Labor Party, in the mid-1890s.

52 *Citizen and Country*, 13 July 1900.

53 Janice Newton seemingly goes so far as to link him with the Fabians, British advocates of gradualism and the permeation of the mainstream parties with socialistic ideas. Her formulation is somewhat ambiguous: "Canadian feminists, radicals, and Fabian socialists, including Phillips Thompson, Helena Gutteridge, Dr Emily Stowe, and Flora MacDonald Denison, were among the supporters of theosophy in Canada." Janice Newton, *The Feminist Challenge to the Canadian Left, 1900–1918* (Montreal and Kingston: McGill-Queen's University Press, 1995), 22. It is not completely clear whether Thompson is here considered as a "radical" or a "Fabian socialist."

54 Berton, "Introduction" to Thompson, "Thoughts and Suggestions," 238–39.

55 Cited in Homel, "James Simpson and the Origins of Canadian Social Democracy," 75.

56 Phillips Thompson, "Capitalism and Corruption," *Citizen and Country*, 15 July 1899; *Citizen and Country*, December 1899.

57 See Homel, "James Simpson and the Origins of Canadian Social Democracy," 75. See also Gene Homel, " 'Fading Beams of the Nineteenth Century': Radicalism and Early Socialism in Canada's 1890s," *Labour/Le Travail* 5 (1980), 7–32, an excellent introduction to Toronto politics of the period.

58 For Colin McKay, see Lewis Jackson and Ian McKay, "Introduction," in *For a Working-Class Culture in Canada: A Selection of Colin McKay's Writings on Sociology and Political Economy, 1897–1939*, ed. Ian McKay (St. John's, Nfld.: Canadian Committee on Labour History, 1996), xi-lii. Incidentally, Colin McKay is not related to the present author.

59 *Herald* (Montreal), 22 March 1902.

60 James Brierley to Mackenzie King, Mackenzie King Papers, vol.1, Reel c-1902, 17 Sept. 1900, LAC.

61 C.M. [Colin McKay], "Experience in Montreal Jail," *Herald*, 17 June 1899.

62 In McKay's home town of Shelburne, Rev. D.V. Warner would a few years later bring out *The Church and Modern Socialism*, in which he admitted the severity of socialist criticism of the church and struggled for a Christian-socialist reconciliation. See D.V. Warner, *The Church and Modern Socialism: An Essay* (Truro, N.S.: News Publishing Co., 1909).

63 *Herald*, 19 Dec. 1896.

64 *Morning Chronicle* (Halifax), 10 Aug. 1901.

65 See Rev. William Thurston Brown, "Extrication or Permeation – Which?" *Wilshire's Magazine*, February 1902, 44.

66 Colin McKay, "Why Workingmen Distrust Churches: The Herald Secures an Expression of Opinion from a Prominent Labor Writer on the Reasons for Indifference," *Herald*, 24 Nov. 1900. The text is also available in McKay, ed., *For a Working-Class Culture in Canada*, 56–59.

67 "Socialist Labor Party of Canada," *The People's Library* 1, 3 (April 1899), 47. The chronology of the growth of SLP branches is not altogether clear; it may well be that Halifax was the site of the first SLP, and hence by one measure the "birthplace" of organized socialism in Canada. The SLP's own phrase was that the Socialist Labor Party of Canada was a "recent offshoot" of the U.S. party.

68 Colin McKay [attributed], "Our Socialists. An Insight into Their Aims and Strength," *Herald*, 30 Nov. 1899.

69 The discussion in this and the following paragraphs draws on McKay, ed., *For a Working-Class Culture in Canada*, "Introduction" and Part I, "If Christ Came to Montreal."

70 Royal Commission on the Relations of Capital and Labour, *Evidence – Quebec* (Ottawa: King's Printer, 1889), testimony of J.M. Fortier.

71 This text can be found in *Citizen and Country* (Toronto), 4 Dec. 1899, and is also printed in McKay, ed., *For a Working-Class Culture in Canada*, 43–47.

72 McKay, ed., *For a Working-Class Culture in Canada*, 59.

73 Most of the biographical details about Spargo in this section are drawn from Marku Ruotsila's fascinating and thorough *John Spargo and American Socialism* (New York: Palgrave Macmillan, 2006), which takes Spargo from his socialist youth to his reactionary old age. On socialist ideas in the United States, see Daniel Bell, *Marxian Socialism in the United States* (Ithaca, N.Y. and London: Cornell University Press, 1996 [1952]); Anthony V. Esposito, *The Ideology of the Socialist Party of America, 1901–1917* (New York and London: Garland Publishing, 1997). For a large collection of documents, see Albert Fried, ed., *Socialism in America: From the Shakers to the Third International, A Documentary History* (New York: Columbia University Press, 1992). For Britain, see Stanley Pierson, *Marxism and the Origins of British Socialism: The Struggle for a New Consciousness* (Ithaca, N.Y. and London: Cornell University Press, 1973).

74 Ruotsila, *John Spargo*, 11.

75 Ibid., 13, 17.

76 E.P. Thompson, *William Morris: Romantic to Revolutionary* (London: Merlin, 1977 [1955]), 341, 342.

77 Ruotsila, *John Spargo*, 23–24.

78 Ibid., 37.

79 See Keith Walden, *Becoming Modern in Toronto: The Industrial Exhibition and the Shaping of a Late Victorian Culture* (Toronto: University of Toronto Press, 1997).

80 For an excellent description of this promotional side of socialism, see Elliott Shore, *Talkin' Socialism: J.A. Wayland and the Radical Press* (Lawrence: University of Kansas Press, 1988). As Shore says of Wayland, the entrepreneur behind the *Appeal to Reason* and *Coming Nation*, two wildly popular left magazines in the United States: "Throughout his life [Wayland] remained largely what he already was: a real-estate speculator and a sharp businessman who used his talents to advance the cause of American socialism" (28).

81 Colin McKay, "The 1901 Socialist Convention," letter, *The New Commonwealth*, 5 June 1937.

82 A.H. Ross, "Recalls 1901 Ontario Socialist Convention," letter, *The New Commonwealth*, 29 May 1937.

83 Spargo was here echoing a position, often cited by Canadian socialists, that was first made famous by Thomas Carlyle (who debated the "Negro Question" with John Stuart Mill). John Spargo, *Where We Stand: A Lecture by John Spargo. Originally Delivered under the Title: 'Our Position; Economic, Ethical and Political'* (New York: Comrade Publishing Company, 1902), 13–14.

84 Spargo, *Where We Stand*, 17–18.

85 Ibid., 4.

86 Ibid., 6.

87 Ibid., 19–20.

88 Ibid., 5.

89 Karl Marx, *Economic and Philosophic Manuscripts of 1844*, in Marx and Engels, *Collected Works*, vol. 3 (Moscow: Progress Publishing, 1975), 304: "Natural science will in time incorporate into itself the science of man, just as the science of man will incorporate into itself natural science: there will be *one* science."

90 Spargo, *Where We Stand*, 7. Spargo was citing Engels's 1888 introduction to the English edition of *The Communist Manifesto*. See Marx and Engels, *Collected Works*, vol. 26, 517.

91 In his later polemic with Goldwin Smith, Spargo would comment – with a typical Hyndmanesque disparagement of the working class – that workers were often distracted by cheap amusements: "A sensational novel, produced in a week, may have, and often does have, greater exchange value than a work by a great thinker like Herbert Spencer, owing to the greater demand." See John Spargo, *Capitalist and Laborer: An Open Letter to Professor Goldwin Smith, D.C.L. in Reply to His Capital and Labor; and Modern Socialism: A Lecture Delivered at the New York School of Philanthropy* (Chicago: Charles H. Kerr & Company, 1907), 58–59.

92 Spargo, *Where We Stand*, 6–7.

93 Ibid.

94 Here was a "mild and palatable Christian Socialism," writes Robin, adding for good measure: "far removed from the harsh, ranting doctrinaire-Marxism of the DeLeonites." Robin, *Radical Politics and Canadian Labour*, 34.

95 Spargo, *Where We Stand*, 20.

96 Ibid., 22–23.

97 Just over a month before, George Wrigley Sr. had sought to distance the Canadian Socialist League from militant utterances from the Socialist Labor Party which, Wrigley intimated, had caused some members of the Woman's Christian Temperance Union to infer that socialists were anarchists (and therefore sought to bar the CSL from using their rooms). "No Anarchists They: Socialist League Deplores Assassination of McKinley," *Globe* (Toronto), 20 Sept. 1901.

98 Unlike the earlier speech, "The Struggle Between Anarchism and Socialism," *The Comrade*, November 1901, is not clearly identified as the written version of the Toronto speech. I am inferring the connection between the two. The connection is not as certain as in the earlier case, but the contemporary Toronto newspaper coverage suggests the plausibility of doing so.

99 A.H. Ross, "Recalls 1901 Ontario Socialist Convention"; *World* (Toronto), 30 Nov. 1901.

100 Marx, *Contribution to Critique of Hegel's Philosophy of Law, Introduction* (1844), in Marx and Engels, *Collected Works*, vol. 3, 182.

101 As Homel has revealed, Smith's relationship with the Toronto working class and socialist movement was complex. The prominent Toronto leftists all seemingly felt obliged to have Smith as an interlocutor for their emerging socialism. They all felt a need to remain in close contact with a self-confessed old-fashioned liberal of the 19th century. For his part, Smith took a warm interest in the labour movement, donated books to the Labour Temple, and retained a favourable impression of Toronto's leading leftist, James Simpson – although not so favourable that he could overlook his unpardonable adherence to the highly inflammatory Socialist Party of Canada. Homel, "James Simpson and the Origins of Canadian Social Democracy," 159.

102 C. McK., "Socialism Round the Corner," *Herald*, 6 Nov. 1907, reprinted in McKay, ed., *For a Working-Class Culture in Canada*, 47–50.

103 The same hints at senility could be found in a local production by socialist firebrand Wilfred Gribble, who also attacked Smith's aged inability to absorb the new socialist ideas. See Wilfred Gribble to Goldwin Smith, Goldwin Smith Papers, 121 January 1906, cited in Homel, "James Simpson and the Origins of Canadian Social Democracy," 295.

104 Spargo, *Capitalist and Laborer*, 45, 49.

105 Cited in Hann, "Brainworkers and the Knights of Labor," 48.

106 Spargo, *Where We Stand*, 17.

107 Ibid., 21.

108 Untitled item, *Western Clarion*, 18 April 1908, 1.

109 Evidence for such a division of opinion within the CSL is adduced by Homel, drawing from correspondence internal to the League written by J.A. Martin. Homel, "James Simpson and the Origins of Canadian Social Democracy," 159.

110 The letter was signed on behalf of "Ontario Socialists" by James Simpson, Chairman, and G. Weston Wrigley, secretary. See University of Vermont, Burlington, Vermont, John Spargo Papers, Spargo Collection, Box 1, File 1–35, Addresses, speeches, essays and other writings: Appreciation Plaque, Ontario Socialist League, January 1902, James Simpson and G. Weston Wrigley to John Spargo, January 1902.

111 Cited in Eley, *Forging Democracy*, 115.

3: The Class Question

1 Claude Larivière, *Albert Saint-Martin, Militant d'Avant-Garde (1865–1947)* (Laval: Les Éditions coopératives Albert Saint-Martin, 1979).

2 Larivière, *Albert Saint-Martin*, 53, 74, 89–90, 90–91 (direct quotations here and throughout the chapter are my translation).

3 Gene Howard Homel, "James Simpson and the Origins of Canadian Social Democracy," Ph.D. thesis, University of Toronto, 1978, 416, 480, n.28.

4 My thanks for this information to Peter Graham, whose forthcoming biography of Charlie O'Brien is keenly awaited.

5 Edmund Fulcher, "Brandon, Man.," *Western Clarion*, 7 Aug.1909, 3.

6 Rayner, "Jottings From Vancouver Meeting," *Western Clarion*, 16 April 1910, 3.

7 Philip S. Foner, *The Industrial Workers of the World 1905–1917*, vol. 4 (New York: International Publishers, 1965), 207. For a more detailed account, see Mark Leier, *Where the Fraser River Flows: The Industrial Workers of the World in British Columbia* (Vancouver: New Star Books, 1990), 57–89. Free speech battles also erupted in Saint John and Moncton in the Maritimes. Foner's account of the free

speech fight was strongly contested by Jack Scott in *Plunderbund and Proletariat: A History of the IWW in B.C.* (Vancouver: New Star Books, 1975), essentially on the grounds that Foner overstated the extent of the freedom conceded; Leier provides a sensible mediation of the debate in *Where the Fraser River Flows*, 87–88, n.46.

8 Jeffrey L. McNairn, *The Capacity to Judge: Public Opinion and Deliberative Democracy in Upper Canada 1791–1854* (Toronto: University of Toronto Press, 2000).

9 For an exhaustive, and at times exhausting, institutional account of the intricacies of building labour parties and the semi-fictional "Canadian Labour Party" in Canada, see Martin Robin, *Radical Politics and Canadian Labour* (Kingston: Industrial Relations Centre at Queen's University, 1971 [1968]); for a rewarding interpretation of the Ontario pattern, see James Naylor, *The New Democracy: Challenging the Social Order in Industrial Ontario, 1914–1925* (Toronto: University of Toronto Press, 1991), chs. 3, 4.

10 This theme can be drawn out most plainly in Fillmore's polemical articles in the *International Socialist Review*, which (although the writer takes care to identify himself as a member of the SPC) are written entirely from the subject position of "We, the American Socialists." See Roscoe Fillmore, "Keep the Issue Clear," *International Socialist Review* 15,7 (January 1915), 398–403, and "How to Build up the Socialist Movement," *International Socialist Review* 16,10 (April 1916), 614–18.

11 For a stimulating analysis underlining the sharp differences between the Canadian parties and the SPD, see Moses Baritz, Review of Robert Michels, *Political Parties: A Sociological Study of the Oligarchical Tendencies of Modern Democracy* (1915), in *Western Clarion*, April 1917. Baritz undoubtedly, in this SPC-related organ, overlooked aspects of authoritarianism in the Canadian experience, but he was not wrong to notice that as bureaucracies, the Canadian parties could not hold a candle to their European counterparts. In other countries, such as those studied by Robert Michels, one could make the case that within Second International organizations, the initial educational objectives of socialist bodies had been displaced by the interests of party machines, succumbing to an iron law of oligarchy. Yet, as Baritz remarked, the patterns that Michel underlined did not seem to apply in Canada, where socialist parties retained their educational focus and generated small bureaucracies by European standards.

12 A. Ross McCormack, *Reformers, Rebels, and Revolutionaries: The Western Canadian Radical Movement 1899–1919* (Toronto: University of Toronto Press, 1991 [1977]), 18.

13 Western exceptionalism has been a major theme in literature on the Canadian left. Ross Johnson, author of a substantial and immensely useful thesis on the topic, argues that British Columbia was the "home front" for the socialist party. See Ross A. Johnson, "No Compromise – No Political Trading: The Marxian Socialist Tradition in British Columbia," Ph.D. thesis, University of British Columbia, Vancouver, 1975. For David Bercuson, looking more specifically at coal miners, the argument for Western exceptionalism takes on an almost eugenic hue. He vividly contrasts the "in-bred" coal-mining communities of Nova Scotia, breeding generation after generation in stagnant pools of paternalism, with the presumably more wholesome and less incestuous atmosphere of British Columbia, where workers confronted an "industrial frontier" with ruthless employers, far more dangerous coal mines, and a heterogeneous population. Bercuson, "Labour Radicalism and the Western Industrial Frontier, 1897–1919," *Canadian Historical Review* 58 (1977), 154–75. Bercuson's use of statistics in this widely read article is question-

begging, in part because of their selectivity and more essentially on the grounds of their reliability, because some figures conflate different measures for coal tonnage in British Columbia and Nova Scotia.

14 Johnson, "No Compromise – No Political Trading," 49.

15 Ibid., 213–14.

16 Homel, "James Simpson and the Origins of Canadian Social Democracy," 253.

17 Larivière, *Albert Saint-Martin*, 59. Saint-Martin won 504 votes out of 3,924 cast – 13 per cent – with percentages topping 25 per cent in nine of the 77 polls, and 34 per cent in one poll. The Socialist Party in British Columbia in 1903 won 4,787 votes out of 59,688 cast – about 8 per cent. Johnson, "No Compromise – No Political Trading," 184. Hawthornthwaite in British Columbia received 486 votes in 1903, and 455 in 1907. See Peter E. Newell, *The Impossibilists: A Brief Profile of the Socialist Party of Canada* (London: Athena Press, 2008), 34, 80.

18 O.D. Skelton, *Socialism: A Critical Analysis* (Boston and New York: Houghton Mifflin Company, 1911), 309.

19 At roughly the same time Socialists in Finland were routinely winning over 300,000 votes from a population of 3.3 million. On the eve of the Great War the Social Democratic Party in Germany had 1,085,905 members and commanded a vote of about 4,250,000. For a fascinating table, see Donald Sassoon, *One Hundred Years of Socialism: The West European Left in the Twentieth Century* (London: Fontana, 1997), 10; there are reflections on the Canadian pattern in *Cotton's Weekly*, 21 Aug. 1913. According to G.R.F. Troop, who wrote what was perhaps the first postgraduate thesis on the topic of Canadian socialism, "The official party membership varied widely. At the time of the formation of the Social Democratic Party it was estimated that the new organization had about 2,000 dues-paying members, while the old Socialist Party of Canada retained 1,300. At the close of 1914 the Social Democratic Party consisted of 230 locals divided as follows: Ont. 82; B.C. 46; Alta. 45; Sask. 20; Man. 28; Que. 8; N.S. 1. The membership is given as 5,380. That of the S.P. of C. was probably rather less." See G.R.F. Troop, "Socialism in Canada," M.A. thesis, McGill University, Montreal, 1921, 58.

20 Often overlooked in such counts are the revolutionary and radical unions. The American Labor Union, Western Federation of Miners, and Industrial Workers of the World were major forces in the West at times before the Great War. With almost 8,000 strikers in 1912, the IWW might well have had more members than the two socialist parties combined. Socialist-led industrial unions included the United Mine Workers, roughly 11,000-strong in Nova Scotia's District 26 and slightly more numerous in the West's District 18. A major ingredient of the years 1911–14 was the emergence and consolidation of effective trade unionism in the garment trades, often under socialist leadership.

21 That party, the Provincial Progressive Party, was a stillborn attempt to bring socialists and labourites together. For a discussion of Debs's role, see Robin, *Radical Politics and Canadian Labour*, 59.

22 For a path-breaking account of mining communities in British Columbia that emphasizes the British connection, see John Douglas Belshaw, *Colonization and Community: The Vancouver Island Coalfield and the Making of the British Columbian Working Class* (Montreal and Kingston: McGill-Queen's University Press, 2002); see also Jeremy Mouat, *Roaring Days: Rossland's Mines and the History of British Columbia* (Vancouver: UBC Press, 1995); John R. Hinde, *When Coal Was King: Ladysmith and the Coal-Mining Industry on Vancouver Island* (Vancouver and Toronto: UBC Press, 2003).

23 McCormack, *Reformers, Rebels, and Revolutionaries*, 67.

24 This distillation recalls the points made by Robert Stuart and noted in chapter 1, p.49–50. See Stuart, *Marxism at Work: Ideology, Class and French Socialism during the Third Republic* (Cambridge: Cambridge University Press, 1992).

25 Robin, *Radical Politics and Canadian Labour*, 3.

26 See especially Barry Ferguson, *Remaking Liberalism: The Intellectual Legacy of Adam Shortt, O.D. Skelton, W.C. Clark, and W.A. Macintosh, 1890–1925* (Montreal and Kingston: McGill-Queen's University Press, 1993).

27 Robin, *Radical Politics and Canadian Labour*, 9.

28 Paul Buhle, "Socialist Labor Party," in *Encyclopedia of the American Left*, 2nd ed., ed. Mari Jo Buhle, Paul Buhle, and Dan Georgakas (New York and Oxford: Oxford University Press, 1998), 760. The Halifax organizer was A.M. Muirhead, who subsequently tried to "warn off" interlopers from the Canadian Socialist League from "his" territory. Muirhead evidently wrote to the csl: "I learn that you have written our friend, John Thomas Bulmer, looking toward the formation of a branch of the Social Democratic party in this city. This being so, I beg to advise that the socialist movement here, as elsewhere, is in the hands of the Socialist Labor party. Any branch of the debauchery started here will be taken in hand and smashed. On behalf of the revolution. A.M. Muirhead, organizer section Halifax N.S., S.L.P. of Canada." *Citizen and Country* (Toronto), 6 April 1900.

29 Mark Pittinger, *American Socialists and Evolutionary Thought, 1870–1920* (Madison: University of Wisconsin Press, 1993), 102, 101. One of De Leon's great contributions to the movement was his translation, not subsequently held to be flawless, of August Bebel's *Woman under Socialism*, which throughout North America came to be ranked with Engels's *The Origin of the Family, Private Property and the State* as an authoritative socialist treatise on the position of women.

30 Frank Girard and Ben Perry, *The Socialist Labor Party 1876–1991: A Short History* (Philadelphia: Livra Books, 1993), 21. For a biography of Daniel De Leon, see L. Glen Seretan, *Daniel De Leon: The Odyssey of an American Marxist* (Cambridge, Mass.: Harvard University Press, 1979). Readers interested in exploring De Leon at greater depth might wish to consult the on-line library of his works currently under preparation: <http://www.marxists.org/archive/deleon/pdf/index.htm>. For titles that interestingly suggest how his legacy was interpreted by slpers, see Arnold Petersen, *Daniel De Leon: Disciplinarian* (New York: New York Labor News Company, 1943); and *Daniel De Leon: From Reform to Revolution 1886–1936* (New York: New York Labor News Company, 1937).

31 Buhle, "Socialist Labor Party," 763.

32 For example, Colin McKay in this period was working hard to build international unions affiliated with the afl in Montreal and wrote for the *American Federationist*, the afl paper. See Colin McKay, "The French Canadian as a Trade Unionist," in *For a Working-Class Culture in Canada: À Selection of Colin McKay's Writings on Sociology and Political Economy, 1897–1939*, ed. Ian Mckay (St. John's, Nfld.: Canadian Committee on Labour History, 1996), 68–70. For an indispensable guide to this period of the afl in Canada, see Robert Babcock, *Gompers in Canada: A Study of American Continentalism before the First World War* (Toronto: University of Toronto Press, 1974).

33 Girard and Perry, *Socialist Labor Party*, 23. With his term "The Kangaroos" De Leon was referring to the arbitrary and irregular Kangaroo Courts commonly found in the Western United States.

34 *Citizen and Country*, 6 April 1900.

35 *Herald* (Montreal), 30 Nov. 1899; *Citizen and Country*, 15 June 1900, 6 April 1900.

36 *Citizen and Country*, 13 Jan.1900; see also *The People's Library* 1, 3 (April 1899), 47.

37 *Citizen and Country*, 13 Jan. 1900.

38 See *The Social Democrat* (Chicago), 6, 13 Jan. 1898.

39 McCormack, *Reformers, Rebels, and Revolutionaries*, 20.

40 *Citizen and Country*, 9 Dec. 1899.

41 Johnson, "No Compromise – No Political Trading," 99. As we shall explore in chapter 6, anti-Asian activism was also found earlier in the province's Knights of Labor.

42 Debs's gibe about "mixed pickles" was directed at the program of the Provincial Progressive Party in British Columbia, which seemed in 1902 about to become a dominant force on the provincial left, before it was scuttled by more revolutionary socialists. This platform, wrote one supporter, "is one which should commend itself to all reasonable men. The convention recognized that it was dealing with conditions, not theories, and therefore eliminated the millennium dawn features which so frequently handicap a good movement." Debs, not conventionally presented in the Canadian literature as an "impossibilist," derided the PPP as "a middle class movement, which proposes to take a short cut to power and distribute official favours. In this party is to be found anarchists, single taxers, direct legislationists, cast off capitalist politicians and many honest but misguided men who know little or nothing about socialism." It was in this context that he described its platform as a "jar of mixed pickles." See Robin, *Radical Politics and Canadian Labour*, 58–60.

43 For a useful source book on the revisionist debate, see H. Tudor and J.M. Tudor, eds., *Marxism and Social Democracy: The Revisionist Debate 1896–1898* (Cambridge: Cambridge University Press, 1988). The assumption that the "revisionist debate" played a decisive influence on the Canadian left before the 1940s has yet to be comprehensively explored. I am a sceptic.

44 Canadian Socialist League, *Program and Declaration of the Canadian Socialist League* (Montreal: Canadian Socialist League, 1899), unpaginated.

45 "Canadian Socialism," *Citizen and Country*, 23 Feb. 1900.

46 G. Weston Wrigley, "Socialism in Canada," *Citizen and Country*, 4 May 1899.

47 *Globe* (Toronto), 20 Sept. 1901.

48 Johnson, "No Compromise – No Political Trading," 93–94.

49 Pittinger, *American Socialists and Evolutionary Thought*, 248. As Pittinger remarks, although *Wilshire's* never tired of promoting the Darwin-Spencer-Marx triad, Wilshire himself had an imperfect grasp of evolutionary theory and tended to centre his analysis on the "Problem of the Trusts." "Wilshire," Pittinger emphasizes, "always saw Spencerian cosmic evolution as the larger framework within which Marxist socialism must develop" (131).

50 Gaylord Wilshire, "A Parliamentary Candidate," *Wilshire's Magazine*, May 1902, 76.

51 Gaylord Wilshire, "My Campaign in West Elgin," *Wilshire's Magazine*, July 1902, 21; and Wilshire, "My Canadian Manifesto," *Wilshire's Magazine*, June 1902, 65–66.

52 Wilshire, "My Campaign in West Elgin," 21.

53 Linda Kealey, *Enlisting Women for the Cause: Women, Labour, and the Left in Canada, 1890–1920* (Toronto: University of Toronto Press, 1998), 98.

54 Johnson, "No Compromise – No Political Trading," 119, 68.

55 "Canadian Socialism," *Citizen and Country*, 23 Feb. 1900.

56 Johnson, "No Compromise – No Political Trading," 100. Johnson also provides details about the various publications. *Citizen and Country* moved west in 1902. R. Parmeter Pettipiece, proprietor of the *Lardeau Eagle*, assumed control of *Citizen and Country* and the Social Progress Company through 1901 and 1902, and the publication, now named the *Canadian Socialist*, became the official organ of the B.C. Socialist Party, formed in 1901. In the spring of 1903 the *Nanaimo Clarion*, a paper run by the Revolutionary Socialist Party of Canada, merged with the *Bulletin* of the striking United Brotherhood of Railway Employees workers; and the first issue of the new paper, named the *Western Clarion*, saw the light of day, as a tri-weekly with a circulation of 6,000, on 7 May 1903. See Johnson, "No Compromise – No Political Trading," 175. With a few interruptions, it would publish until 1925. Although not owned by the party, it was represented on its Executive Committee. For important new work on Pettipiece as a socialist journalist, see David Thompson, "The 'Indignity of Speaking for Others': The Early Brainwork of R. Parm Pettipiece and the *Lardeau Eagle*," unpublished paper, University of Victoria.

57 *Citizen and Country*, 4 May, 17 Aug. 1900. For example, one Lou Garofsky of Toronto won special commendation from Wrigley for his work as a traveller for *Citizen and Country*: "The men approached, for the most part, have never heard of the paper, but Lou fetches them. In one mail this week he sent us 34 cards from a garment workers' convention in Detroit. The subscriptions were 13 from New York, two each from Pennsylvania, Massachusetts and Illinois, and one each from Missouri, Kansas, Indiana, Ohio, Quebec and Ontario. *Citizen and Country*, 2 Dec. 1899. Another item also provides a glimpse of another such traveling agent for socialism: "R.F. Langford, an active social reform worker in Ottawa, is now travelling as a commission agent in Manitoba, and he will probably go as far west as Vancouver, B.C. Our comrades in the west who meet him will find in him an agreeable comrade."*Citizen and Country*, 2 Dec. 1899.

58 "An Endless Chain. For Citizen and Country," *Citizen and Country*, 11 March 1899.

59 *Citizen and Country*, 9 March 1900.

60 Those books were Anna Sewell's *Black Beauty*, Rev. Charles Kingsley's *The Water Babies*, T.S. Arthur's *Ten Nights in a Bar Room*, George Meredith's *Diana of the Crossways*, and I. Marvel's *Dream Life*. "Every boy and girl should read these books. Each one is a gem . . ." *Citizen and Country*, 11 Nov. 1899.

61 *Citizen and Country*, 15 July 1899; *Citizen and Country*, 11 Nov. 1899.

62 *Citizen and Country*, 17 Aug. 1900, 2 Dec. 1900. Perhaps because it was generally considered a tough book to read, *Capital* was dropped from the list on 2 Dec. 1900.

63 Homel, "James Simpson and the Origins of Canadian Social Democracy," 156, 160.

64 Burns in the *Social-Democratic Herald* (Chicago), 16 June 1900, cited in Johnson, "No Compromise – No Political Trading," 104.

65 Johnson, "No Compromise – No Political Trading," 128.

66 Ibid., 129–130.

67 Ibid., 184.

68 Ibid., 187. Johnson's unpublished thesis remains an indispensable source for discussions of early British Columbia socialism.

69 McCormack, *Reformers, Rebels, and Revolutionaries*, 28.

70 Johnson, "No Compromise – No Political Trading," 208.

71 See Gerald Tulchinsky, *Taking Root: The Origins of the Canadian Jewish Community* (Toronto: Lester Publishing, 1992), 317, n.18.

72 Cited in Homel, "James Simpson and the Origins of Canadian Social Democracy," 156.

73 Craig Heron, "Labourism and the Canadian Working Class," *Labour/Le Travail* 13 (Spring 1984), 73.

74 Cited in Eric Leroux, *Gustave Francq: Figure marquante du sydicalisme et précurseur de la FTQ* (Montréal: vlb éditeur, 2001), 109.

75 See William M. Dick, *Labor and Socialism in America: The Gompers Era* (Port Washington, N.Y.: Kennikat Press, 1972).

76 Leroux, *Gustave Francq*, 113–15.

77 Robin, *Radical Politics and Canadian Labour*, 90, 91.

78 Socialist Party of Canada, *Socialism and Unionism* (Vancouver, n.d. [1910],) 5, 12–13.

79 Ibid., 13, 11.

80 *Western Clarion*, 6 July 1911, cited in Robin, *Radical Politics and Canadian Labour*, 95.

81 Robin, *Radical Politics and Canadian Labour*, 101. Aided by the concentration of the coal miners' votes and the ongoing wrenching disturbances in the coalfields, the B.C. Socialists consistently punched above their weight in terms of their votes and seats. In 1912, now divided into two parties, they were able to win 25 per cent of the vote in the ridings they contested, and became the opposition – although, revealingly, they were unable to capitalize on this position to become the real opposition in the eyes of the public. See Johnson, "No Compromise – No Political Trading," 262.

82 Johnson, "No Compromise – No Political Trading," 206. The 1906 convention was held in Fernie.

83 Mark Leier, "Workers and Intellectuals: The Theory of the New Class and Early Canadian Socialism," *Journal of History and Politics* 10 (1992), 98. This article also appeared in *Making Western Canada: Essays on European Colonization and Settlement*, ed. Catherine Cavanaugh and Jeremy Mouat (Toronto: Garamond, 1996), 133–153. Compared to countries with more developed and sophisticated left historiographies, of the sort that would be considered "old hat" in most of Europe, we have a very partial grasp of the social basis of the left, though Leier's analysis of Vancouver has suggestively brought forward fascinating ideas about the urban base of the spc's "upper echelon." For important work on "middle-class socialism" in Europe, see Carl Levy, ed., *Socialism and the Intelligentsia 1880–1914* (London and New York: Routledge & Kegan Paul, 1987).

84 Rayner, "Jottings from Vancouver Meeting," *Western Clarion*, 16 April 1910, 3.

85 Leier, "Workers and Intellectuals," 97.

86 Jacques Rancière, *The Nights of Labor: The Workers Dream in Nineteenth Century France* (Philadelphia: Temple University Press, 1989).

87 George Ross Kirkpatrick, *The Socialist and the Sword* (Vancouver: Socialist Party of Canada, n.d. [1912?]).

88 Alf Budden, *The Slave of the Farm: Being Letters from Alf. Budden to a Fellow Farm Slave and Comrade in Revolt* (Vancouver: Socialist Party of Canada, Dominion Executive Committee, 1914), 58.

89 Will. R. Shier, "Spreading the Gospel," letter to the *Western Clarion*, 15 Aug. 1908, 3.

90 *Cotton's Weekly*, 5 Aug. 1909.

91 *Western Clarion*, 6 Aug. 1910.

92 Wilfred Gribble, "Tale of a Tour. Ninth Installment," *Cotton's Weekly*, 5 Aug. 1909.

93 Homel, "James Simpson and the Origins of Canadian Social Democracy," 455.

94 Wilfred Gribble, "Toronto Local," *Western Clarion*, 18 April 1908, 3.

95 *Cotton's Weekly*, 1 April 1909; Robert Hunter, "The Red Special," *Western Clarion*, 15 Aug. 1908, 2.

96 W.G. Gribble, "Correspondence," *Western Clarion*, 20 April 1907, 4.

97 *Cotton's Weekly*, 1 April 1909.

98 "One Side, Facts for Ontario Socialists," *Western Clarion*, 23 Jan. 1910, 3.

99 "Not People," *Western Clarion*, 24 Dec. 1910, 1.

100 "One Month's Slaughter," *Western Clarion*, 20 April 1907, 1.

101 Aileen Kraditor, *The Radical Persuasion, 1890–1917: Aspects of the Intellectual History and the Historiography of Three American Radical Organizations* (Baton Rouge: Louisiana State University Press, 1981).

102 "The Modern Magician," editorial, *Western Clarion*, 18 April 1908, 2.

103 E.T.K. [E.T. Kingsley], "Notes by the Way," *Western Clarion*, 15 Aug. 1908, 1.

104 Wilfred Gribble, "A Call to Arms from an Ontario Comrade," *Western Clarion*, 16 Jan. 1909, 1; C.W. Springford, "As to Dawson," letter to *Western Clarion*, 6 Aug. 1910, 3.

105 Western Clarion, 6 Jan. 1906, 2; H. Norman, "Justice in Vancouver," *Western Clarion*, 7 Aug. 1909, 1.

106 "The Machine," editorial, *Western Clarion*, 22 Jan. 1910, 2.

107 *Western Clarion*, 15 Aug. 1908, 3.

108 *Cotton's Weekly*, 2 Dec. 1909; McKenzie cited in McCormack, *Reformers, Rebels, and Revolutionaries*, 56.

109 Stuart, *Marxism at Work*, 106.

110 *What's the Matter with Canada?* (n.p [Vancouver], n.d. [1908]), Ottawa: Canadian Institute for Historical Microreproductions, CIHM/ICMH series no. 83256, 1997 [election pamphlet for F.H. Sherman, Socialist candidate in Calgary]; Socialist Party of Canada, Lindsay, Ont., Local, *Gems of Socialism* (n.p. [Lindsay], n.d. [1916]), 17, 4.

111 McCormack, *Reformers, Rebels, and Revolutionaries*, 31.

112 David Frank, *J.B. McLachlan: A Biography* (Toronto: James Lorimer, 1999), 109.

113 I thank Robin Bates for sharpening this point in his critique of an earlier draft of this chapter.

114 Gribble, "Correspondence."

115 Johnson, "No Compromise – No Political Trading," 229.

116 "Nationalization of Land," *Cotton's Weekly*, 7 Jan. 1909.

117 Johnson, "No Compromise – No Political Trading," 226.

118 W.R.S., "Chips from a Blockhead," *Cotton's Weekly*, 2 Dec. 1909; Nicholas Fillmore, *Maritime Radical: The Life and Times of Roscoe Fillmore* (Toronto: Between the Lines, 1992), 62.

119 "The Modern Sisyphus," editorial, *Western Clarion*, 16 April 1910, 2.

120 "A Comrade of Toronto Defends the Socialists," *Western Clarion*, 20 April 1907, 1, 4.

121 Charles Allen Seager, "A Proletariat in Wild Rose Country: The Alberta Coal Miners, 1905–1945," Ph.D. thesis, York University, Toronto, 1981, 232–34; character appreciation from *Western Clarion*, 22 April 1911, cited at 266, 266, n.75. For O'Brien's speeches, see F. Blake, comp., *The Proletarian in Politics: The Socialist Position as Defined by C.M. O'Brien, M.L.A., in the Alberta Legislature* (n.p. [Vancouver]: Socialist Party of Canada, n.d. [1910]). Among other articles,

O'Brien wrote a "History of Socialism and Its Growth in Canada" for the *District Ledger* in 1912.

122 Blake, *Proletarian in Politics*, 6, 3–9.

123 McCormack, *Reformers, Rebels, and Revolutionaries*, 64. See Daniel De Leon, *A Socialist in Congress: His Conduct and Responsibilities* (New York: New York Labor News Company, 1963 [1912]) for a detailed account of how De Leon differed from the legislative tactics of the famous U.S. "sewer socialist" Victor Berger. For the French parallel, see Stuart, *Marxism at Work*, esp. 270. As Stuart notes, the Guesdists were the first to denounce the sin of "parliamentarianism," and even though they elected a good many deputies, they construed their role as one of broadcasters for the wider cause. Jules Guesde, an obscure editor, might reach an audience of thousands with his editorials, but as a parliamentary orator he could reach millions.

124 Fillmore, "Keep the Issue Clear," 402.

125 Fillmore, "How to Build up the Socialist Movement," 617.

126 This famous spc slogan was borrowed from Wilhelm Liebknecht, *No Compromise, No Political Trading*, trans. A.M. Simons and Marcus Hitch (Chicago: Charles H. Kerr, Unity Library, No.102, 1900).

127 W.H. Stebbins, "No Compromise," letter to *The Voice* (Winnipeg), reprinted in *Western Clarion*, 18 April 1908, 3.

128 In his book *Maritime Radical*, Nicholas Fillmore details, celebrates, and analyzes his grandfather's career; I draw the biographical details in the following paragraphs from this study.

129 Fillmore, *Maritime Radical*, 3.

130 Ibid., 21.

131 Ibid., 24.

132 Burbank's left-wing secularism, possibly implicit between the lines in the practical texts consulted by Fillmore, became clearer in his defiant *Why I Am an Infidel* (Girard, Kan.: Haldeman-Julius Co., 1926).

133 Fillmore, *Maritime Radical*, 45, 46.

134 Ibid., 53. See, for more details, the superb pioneering article by David Frank and Nolan Reilly, "The Emergence of the Socialist Movement in the Maritimes, 1899–1916," *Labour/Le Travailleur* 4 (Fall 1979), 85–113.

135 Frank, *J.B. McLachlan*, 126.

136 According to *Cotton's Weekly*, 24 Oct. 1912, Cumberland boasted 350 subscribers; Cape Breton South, 346.

137 Fillmore, *Maritime Radical*, 78.

138 Roscoe Fillmore, "Slave Delusions: Workers Care for All Interests But Their Own," *Western Clarion*, 24 Dec. 1910, 1.

139 "The Lone Fighter," *Cotton's Weekly*, 5 Aug. 1909.

140 Fillmore, "Keep the Issue Clear," 398.

141 Robin, *Radical Politics and Canadian Labour*, 101–2.

142 As Leier notes, Parker Williams moved from the spc to the sdpc in 1916 before abandoning both parties to run as an "independent socialist." In 1916, he campaigned for Liberal candidates in Vancouver. Williams won his seat in 1916 but resigned in 1917 when the Liberals appointed him to the Workmen's Compensation Board. Mark Leier, *Rebel Life: The Life and Times of Robert Gosden, Revolutionary, Mystic, Labour Spy* (Vancouver: New Star Books, 1999), 43–45.

143 Arthur J. Wilkinson and J.L. Pratt, "Social Democratic Party: Statement of Reasons for Leaving the Socialist Party of Canada," *The Voice*, 30 April 1909.

144 The details in this paragraph are drawn principally from Robin, *Radical Politics and Canadian Labour*, 110–12.

145 J.W. Ahlqvist, "The Socialist Movement in Canada before the War," *The Worker*, 27 Feb. 1926, 4.

146 I acknowledge here my general indebtedness to Tadeusz Adam Kawecki, "Canadian Socialism and the Origin of the Communist Party, 1900–1922," M.A. thesis, McMaster University, Hamilton, 1981. To my knowledge, this party – soon to become the single largest left party in the Dominion – has never been the subject of a Ph.D thesis, published monograph, or even substantial article. Many general patterns have to be pieced together, somewhat precariously, from unpublished theses and incidental references. Consequently, much of this initial reconnaissance will require revision as more research is done. For interesting new material on the local politics of the SDPC in the Lakehead, see Michel Beaulieu, "Proletarian Prometheus: Socialism, Ethnicity, and Revolution at the Lakehead, 1900–1935," Ph.D. thesis, Queen's University, Kingston, 2007.

147 *Cotton's Weekly*, 19 March 1914. The estimates did not include the 64 Finnish locals, which had grown to 362 in March 1914. See also Kawecki, "Canadian Socialism and the Origin of the Communist Party." Kawecki draws on details from the *Industrial Banner*, a major labour paper.

148 Ahlqvist, "Socialist Movement," 4.

149 Kawecki, "Canadian Socialism and the Origin of the Communist Party," 96.

150 David Thompson, "Challenging the Canadian Liberal Order: Unemployed Organizations and First Formation Socialism, 1913–1915," unpublished research paper, Queen's University, Kingston, 2007. Thompson explores a previously hidden history of SDPC activism among the unemployed in various locations. The information in this paragraph comes from his study.

151 *Western Clarion*, 17 Dec. 1910, cited in Kawecki, "Canadian Socialism and the Origin of the Communist Party," 88.

152 F.C. [Florence Custance], "The Socialist Movement in Canada. The Split in the S.P. of N.A.," *The Worker*, 3 April 1926, 4. The strategy of "industrializing" members would become a major phenomenon in the 1960s in France and the United States. See Kristin Ross, *May '68 and Its Afterlives* (Chicago and London: University of Chicago Press, 2002); Max Elbaum, *Revolution in the Air: Sixties Radicals Turn to Lenin, Mao and Che* (London and New York: Verso, 2002).

153 *Cotton's Weekly*, 4 June 1914, cited in Kawecki, "Canadian Socialism and the Origin of the Communist Party," 97.

154 Quotations from: Kawecki, "Canadian Socialism and the Origin of the Communist Party," 97; *Cotton's Weekly*, 7 Aug. 1913; *The Voice*, 25 June 1915, cited in Kawecki, "Canadian Socialism and the Origin of the Communist Party," 99.

155 The slogan was actually used on the SDPC's membership cards. See Social Democratic Party of Canada, *No Compromise, No Political Trading* (n.p. [Toronto?], n.d. [c.1917]); membership card in the Kenny Collection, Thomas Fisher Rare Book Library, University of Toronto.

156 That the two parties resembled each other on the ideological level is suggested by McCormack, *Reformers, Rebels, and Revolutionaries*, 74–75. Little evidence for the SDPC as an advocate of "revisionism" à la Bernstein or of Fabian-style gradualism has surfaced. In my view, a map that reduces the SPC to "impossibilism" and the SDPC to "possibilism" is seriously misdrawn. All three of the parties that emerged from the 1911 split were committed to the triune formula. None resembled the parliamentary "social democrats" that some historians were yearning to find in

the pre-war past of the Canadian left. For a different interpretation, see Newell, *Impossibilists*, 105–8.

157 In this case we are fortunate to have the book-length study by Larivière, *Albert Saint-Martin*, which in 1979 opened up a new vista into the infrequently studied early history of the socialist idea in Quebec. The following few paragraphs on Saint-Martin are largely derived from this study, supplemented by my own researches in the *Western Clarion* and *Cotton's Weekly*.

158 See especially Fernande Roy, *Progrès, Harmonie, Liberté: Le libéralisme des milieux d'affaires francophones de Montréal au tournant du siècle* (Montreal: Boréal, 1988). An older pattern of interpretation, which marks Larivière's fine study of Saint-Martin, suggested an almost "totalitarian Catholicism," whereas more recent books have brought out the power, at both the local and national levels, of a liberal order.

159 Saint-Martin even travelled to Europe in spring 1905 to attend an Esperanto Congress at Boulogne-sur-Mer in France. In 1906 he established an Esperanto publication, *La Lumo*, and in 1907 organized a Montreal Esperanto Cooperative, which operated two food outlets and experimented in communal living. Esperanto was, perhaps, Saint-Martin's way of imagining how living otherwise might actually work. Saint-Martin would also be involved with a "socialist commune," Le Kanado, at Lac des Ecorces. For the leading Marxist critique of Esperanto as a form of linguistic utopianism, see Peter Ives, *Gramsci's Politics of Language: Engaging the Bakhtin Circle and the Frankfurt School* (Toronto: University of Toronto Press, 2004), 16–52. For an impressive history of Esperanto, with many insights into its connections with socialism, see Peter G. Forster, *The Esperanto Movement* (The Hague, Paris, and New York: Mouton Publishers, 1982).

160 For an imaginative study of "popular liberalism" in Montreal, see Patrice Dutil, *Devil's Advocate: Godfroy Langlois and the Politics of Liberal Progressivism in Laurier's Quebec* (Montreal and Toronto: Robert Davies Publishing, 1994). With respect to labour and the left, see the foundational work of Eric Leroux, *Gustave Francq: Figure marquante du syndicalisme et précurseur de la FTQ* (Montréal: VLB éditeur, 2001), 103–5.

161 Larivière, *Albert Saint-Martin*, 29.

162 Ibid., 30.

163 Ibid., 32.

164 Ibid., 45.

165 Gouin had unseated Premier Parent through Byzantine manoeuvres within the Liberal Party, orchestrated in part by the *rouges* and proponents of a more secular educational system.

166 Larivière, *Albert Saint-Martin*, 48.

167 Ibid., 55.

168 Ibid., 55–56.

169 See Irving Abella and David Millar, eds., *The Canadian Worker in the Twentieth Century* (Toronto: Oxford University Press, 1978), 75.

170 Robin, *Radical Politics and Canadian Labour*, 95.

171 SPC notables such as E.T. Kingsley and Jack Kavanagh supported the Miners Liberation League, even though doing so could hardly be squared with the SPC's single-plank platform. The SPC leadership may well have felt constrained to do so by the solidarity of rank and file members of the Socialist Party, trade unions, and the IWW (whose ideas were influential within the League). See Leier, *Rebel Life*, 31; Leier, *Where the Fraser River Flows*, 62.

172   George Hardy, *Those Stormy Years: Memories of the Fight for Freedom on Five Continents* (London: Lawrence & Wishart, 1956), 53–54.

173   For a study of the remarkably parallel case of the Guesdists, see Stuart, *Marxism at Work*, 198–99.

174   Hardy, *Those Stormy Years*, 54.

175   For the minutes of the iww's founding convention, see <http://www.iww.org/culture/library/founding/part12.shtml> (accessed 15 May 2005). After a proposal to call the union the "Industrial Workers of America," John Riordan, a Canadian delegate, pointed out the ambivalent feelings that such a title might arouse among Canadians. See also Leier, *Where The Fraser River Flows*, 36; and Beaulieu, "Proletarian Prometheus."

176   Joyce L. Kornbluh, "Industrial Workers of the World," in *Encyclopedia of the American Left*, ed. Buhle, Buhle, and Georgakas, 356–57.

177   See Larry Peterson, "The One Big Union in International Perspective: Revolutionary Industrial Unionism, 1900–1925," *Labour/Le Travailleur* 7 (Spring 1981), 41–66.

178   Salvatore Salerno, *Red November, Black November: Culture and Community in the Industrial Workers of the World* (Albany: State University of New York Press, 1989), 37.

179   Hardy, *Those Stormy Years*, 54–55.

180   Leier, *Rebel Life*, 31. Leier queries the accuracy of Hardy's account, which he suggests may have been significantly reshaped by intervening political loyalties.

181   Leier, *Where the Fraser River Flows*, 117.

182   Ibid., 92.

183   Foner, *Industrial Workers of the World*, 229.

184   David Schulze, "The Industrial Workers of the World and the Unemployed in Edmonton and Calgary in the Depression of 1913–1915," *Labour/Le Travail* 25 (Spring 1990), 53, 62–63, 68.

185   Foner, *Industrial Workers of the World*, 156; Leier, *Where the Fraser River Flows*, 66.

186   Salerno, *Red November, Black November*, 7.

187   Cited in ibid., 7.

188   See Foner, *Industrial Workers of the World*, 151. For other descriptions, see Franklin Rosemont, *Joe Hill: The IWW and the Making of a Revolutionary Working Class Culture* (Chicago: Charles H. Kerr, 2002). In a discussion of Paul Jordan-Smith's *Cables of Cobweb* (1923), Rosemont notes that Jordan-Smith was inspired by the ideas of an autodidact named Parker H. Seccombe, who was head of the "Spencer-Whitman Center" and editor of its magazine, *Tomorrow* (495–96). There would seem to be much suggestive evidence here of a deeper and more long-lasting penetration of Spencerian evolutionary ideas than an earlier literature had noticed. I thank David Thompson for this reference.

189   Foner, *Industrial Workers of the World*, 151; Robert L. Tyler, *Rebels of the Woods: The I.W.W. in the Pacific Northwest* (Eugene: University of Oregon Press, 1967), 26–27.

190   For more on the Wobblies' distinctive cultural forms, see Salerno, *Red November, Black November*, 151. For a wonderful study of one case, see Larry Peterson, "The Intellectual World of the iww: An American Worker's Library in the First Half of the Twentieth Century," *History Workshop Journal* 22,1 (1986), 153–72.

191   Cited in Melvyn Dubofsky, *We Shall Be All: A History of the IWW*, 2nd ed. (New York: Quadrangle, 1974 [1969]), 153. Dubofsky very valuably underlines the Wobblies' debt to Darwin.

192 Cited in Salerno, *Red November, Black November*, 75, 77.

193 For discussion and illustration, see Buhle, Buhle, and Georgakas, *Encyclopedia of the American Left*, 217–18.

194 For a predictably dyspeptic account of the Wheel's impact upon the theorists of the postwar One Big Union, see David J. Bercuson, *Fools and Wise Men: The Rise and Fall of the One Big Union* (Toronto: McGraw-Hill Ryerson, 1978), 124: "In a scientific age this carefully divided wheel, with its spokes representing different groups and subgroups of industry and with a general administration at the hub, appealed to those who styled themselves scientifically minded. . . . The secessionists felt called upon to play around with such diagrams."

195 Roseline Usiskin, "Towards a Theoretical Reformulation of the Relationship Between Political Ideology, Social Class, and Ethnicity: A Case Study of the Winnipeg Jewish Radical Community, 1905–1920," M.A. thesis (Sociology), University of Manitoba, Winnipeg, 1978; "The Winnipeg Jewish Radical Community: Its Early Formation 1905–1918," in *Jewish Life and Times: A Collection of Essays* (Winnipeg: Jewish Historical Society of Western Canada, 1983): 155–68. For pioneering work in the history of anarchists in Canada, see Travis Tomchuk, " 'There Are Anarchists at Large in Winnipeg': Local Anarchists and Commentaries on Anarchism in the Winnipeg Labour Press, 1900–1919," unpublished paper, Queen's University, Kingston, 2005. On Emma Goldman in Canada, see Theresa Moritz and Albert Moritz, *The World's Most Dangerous Woman: A New Biography of Emma Goldman* (Toronto: Subway, 2004).

196 *Cotton's Weekly*, 1 April 1909.

197 Any re-evaluation of Simpson's role must acknowledge Homel's detailed, almost magisterial, thesis, upon which most of the following paragraphs rely: Homel, "James Simpson and the Origins of Canadian Social Democracy." This fascinating work, which takes Simpson's story up to 1914, deftly explores a wide range of archival sources. It mounts a strong defence for Simpson as one of the founding figures of "Canadian Social Democracy" and provides a compellingly detailed study of a central socialist figure and invaluable insights into the organization of socialism in Toronto, then as now a pivotal city for the Canadian left.

198 See Tim Buck, *Yours in the Struggle: Reminiscences of Tim Buck* (Toronto: NC Press, 1977), 42. In characterizing Simpson as someone who "wanted to get elected," Buck was overlooking Simpson's many years as an SPC and SDPC militant. Thanks to Homel, "James Simpson and the Origins of Canadian Social Democracy," we can now situate Simpson more fully in the context of the first formation.

199 Homel, "James Simpson and the Origins of Canadian Social Democracy," 375.

200 Ibid., 191–92, 193.

201 Ibid., 195.

202 Ibid., 212.

203 Ibid., 217.

204 Ibid., 245, 253–54, 255, 336.

205 Ibid., 475, 624.

206 Ibid., 696, 159.

207 Ibid., 195, 218. Homel's Simpson was attracted to "Socialism's idealism," to a "Canadian socialism substantially derived from religious and ethical beliefs," and to the British Labour Party. Homel's own abstract of the thesis does not even mention the SPC, incontestably the party which Simpson himself selected, from a range of choices, from 1903 to 1910. And yet, with a good historian's passion for

detail and complexity, Homel has actually produced an invaluable account that shows, contrary to his own wishes, that Simpson was essentially on the same page as Kingsley and the spc in most respects.

208   Ibid., 221, 242, 423.

209   Ibid., 529.

210   Ibid., 702.

211   Skelton, *Socialism*, 161, 159.

212   Ian MacPherson, *Each for All: A History of the Co-operative Movement in English Canada, 1900–1945* (Toronto: Macmillan, 1979), 8, 46.

213   Ibid., 27, 28, 34.

214   For reflections on this phenomenon in the succeeding period, see John Varty, "Growing Bread: Technoscience, Environment and Modern Wheat at the Dominion Grain Research Laboratory, Canada, 1912–1960," Ph.D. thesis, Queen's University, Kingston, 2005.

215   MacPherson, *Each for All*, 46.

216   Ibid., 36.

217   MacPherson, *Each for All*, 36, 43–48.

218   See William Kirby Rolph, *Henry Wise Wood of Alberta* (Toronto: University of Toronto Press, 1950), 63.

219   Anthony Mardiros, *William Irvine: The Life of a Prairie Radical* (Toronto: James Lorimer, 1979), 99. The disciple in question is Irvine.

220   Friesen, *The Canadian Prairies: A History* (Toronto: University of Toronto Press, 1987), 319.

221   This judgment might well be revised by future work on socialism and the agrarian question in Canada. For outstanding contemporary analyses of the agrarian question, see A.M. Simons, *The American Farmer* (Chicago: Charles H. Kerr, 1902); V.I. Lenin, *Capitalism and Agriculture in the United States* (New York: International Publishers, 1934), drawn from the Russian original of vol. 22 of his *Collected Works*. For important new work on the social and cultural history of the Western agrarian revolt, see Bradford James Rennie, *The Rise of Agrarian Democracy: The United Farmers and Farm Women of Alberta, 1909–1921* (Toronto: University of Toronto Press, 2000); Lyle Dick, *Farmers 'Making Good': The Development of the Abernethy District, Saskatchewan 1880–1920* (Ottawa: Environment Canada, 1989); Jeffery Taylor, *Fashioning Farmers: Ideology, Agricultural Knowledge and the Manitoba Farm Movement, 1890–1925* (Regina: Canadian Plains Research Center, University of Regina, 1994). Among much interesting U.S. work, see Jim Bissett, *Agrarian Socialism in America: Marx, Jefferson and Jesus in the Oklahoma Countryside 1904–1920* (Norman: University of Oklahoma Press, 1999), with its highly useful bibliography; Lawrence Goodwyn, "The Cooperative Commonwealth and Other Abstractions: In Search of a Democratic Premise," *Marxist Perspectives* 3 (1980), 8–42; and James Green, *Grass-Roots Socialism: Radical Movements in the Southwest, 1895–1943* (Baton Rouge: Louisiana State University Press, 1978). For interesting Canadian comments, see Newell, *Impossibilists*, 45–47.

222   "Canadian Socialist League," *Citizen and Country*, 13 Jan. 1900.

223   Cited in Eley, *Forging Democracy*, 93. Once again, it seems that Kautsky and Co. were much more orthodox than Marx himself, who immersed himself in Russian sources from 1871 to 1883 and seems to have concluded that it would be a huge error to ignore "the democratic potential of peasant communal organization" and "the Russian peasantry's primacy as a revolutionary force" in the socialist struggle.

See Teodor Shanin, *Late Marx and the Russian Road: Marx and 'the Peripheries of Capitalism'* (New York: Monthly Review Press, 1983).

224 Reginald Whitaker, "Introduction" to William Irvine, *The Farmers in Politics* (Toronto: McClelland and Stewart, 1976 [1920]), xxxiv.

225 *What's the Matter with Canada?* 5–6.

226 Budden, *Slave of the Farm*, 5–6, 44–45.

227 Socialist Party of Canada, *Wage-Earner and Farmer* (n.p. [Vancouver], n.d. [1912?]).

228 Rolph, *Henry Wise Wood of Alberta*, 62–63.

229 Mardiros, *William Irvine*, 86–87.

230 C.M. Christianssen, "Small Farmers and the Socialist Movement," *Red Flag*, 24 May 1919.

231 Socialist Party of Canada, *The Working Class and Master Class* (Vancouver: Socialist Party of Canada, 1912 [1910]), unpaginated.

232 W.E. Hardenburg, *What Is Socialism? A Short Study of Its Aims and Claims* (Vancouver: Dominion Executive Committee, Socialist Party of Canada, n.d.), 28.

233 Will R. Shier, "The Decadence of Capitalism," *Western Clarion*, 16 Jan. 1909, 2.

234 Karl Marx and Frederick Engels, *The Communist Manifesto* (London and New York: Pluto Press, 2000), 48; Marx and Engels, "Manifesto of the Communist Party," in *Collected Works*, vol. 6 (Moscow: Progress Publishers, 1976), 494.

235 John Rivers, "Among the Heathen," *Western Clarion*, 15 Aug. 1908, 3; W.J. Curry, "The Asiatic Invasion: Its Cause and Outcome," *Western Clarion*, 12 Dec. 1908, 4 (continuation of earlier story); Socialist Party of Canada, Lindsay, Ont., *Gems of Socialism*, 13. In one address to his Canadian admirers, Keir Hardie noted that there were "hoboes" at both ends of the social scale – both the decadent idler and the lazy vagabond were slated for disappearance under socialism. Keir Hardie, "When Labor Rules the World," *Western Clarion*, 6 Jan. 1906, 1.

236 For an early version of what promises to be a major work that will change our vision of the Canadian left and the unemployed, see Thompson, "Challenging the Canadian Liberal Order." For unemployed activism in the United States, see especially Franklin Folsom, *Impatient Armies of the Poor: The Story of Collective Action of the Unemployed 1808–1942* (Niwot: University Press of Colorado, 1991).

4: The Religion Question

1 Charles M. Sheldon, *In His Steps* (Grand Rapids, Mich.: Zondervan Publishing House, 1967 [1896]), 2, 6–7, 8, 9, 12, 15, 39, 41.

2 See, for instance, http://www.carmical.net/articles/wwjd.html; and http://www.worldnetdaily.com/news/article.asp?ARTICLE_ID=41363; http://www.luc.edu/publications/loyolamag/summer2001/jesus.htm; http://www.biblebb.com/files/MAC/mac-lkl2.htm; http://www.rapidnet.com/~jbeard.wwjd.htm (all accessed 25 May 2005). I suspect that a thorough search of just some of the 9,110,000 sites Google then linked to "WWJD" would generate many more products. Sometimes "WWJD" has a socially progressive edge, as in the contemporary ecological slogan: "What Would Jesus Drive?"

3 Sheldon, *In His Steps*, 230.

4 Ibid., 232,

5 *Citizen and Country*, 25 March 1899.

6 See Rosemary R. Gagan, *A Sensitive Independence: Canadian Methodist Women Missionaries in Canada and the Orient, 1881–1925* (Montreal and Kingston: McGill-Queen's University Press, 2003); Ruth Compton Brouwer, *New Women for*

God: Canadian Presbyterian Women and India Missions, 1876–1914 (Toronto: University of Toronto Press, 1990).

7 In Russia, Dostoevsky's *The Brothers Karamazov* contained these remarks: "Socialism is not merely the labor question, … it is above all things the atheistic question, the question of the form taken by atheism today, the question of the tower of Babel built without God, not to mount to Heaven from earth but to set up Heaven on earth." Fyodor Dostoevsky, *The Brothers Karamazov* (New York: Modern Library, 1949), 26, as cited in John Sanbonmatsu, *The Postmodern Prince: Critical Theory, Left Strategy, and the Making of a New Political Subject* (New York: Monthly Review Press, 2004), 11.

8 For central studies in this debate, see David B. Marshall, *Secularizing the Faith: Canadian Protestant Clergy and the Crisis of Belief, 1850–1940* (Toronto: University of Toronto Press, 1992); and Nancy Christie and Michael Gauvreau, *A Full-Orbed Christianity: The Protestant Churches and Social Welfare in Canada, 1900–1940* (Montreal and Kingston: McGill-Queen's University Press, 2003).

9 For discussions of this struggle, see Jennie MacLean, "Parrots, Picnics and Psychic Phenomena: The Feminism, Nationalism and Social Reform of Eva Circé-Côté in *Le Monde Ouvrier*'s Montreal, 1900–1914," M.A. thesis, Queen's University, 2000; Andrée Lévesque, "La Citoyenneté selon Éva Circé-Côté," in *Résistance et transgression* (Montréal, éditions du Remue-ménage, 1994). For accounts of the Ultramontanes, see Roberto Perrin, *Rome in Canada: The Vatican and Canadian Affairs in the Late Victorian Age* (Toronto: University of Toronto Press, 1990), a balanced and judicious study; for contemporary left polemics, see especially Daniel De Leon, *The Vatican in Politics: Ultramontanism* (New York: New York Labor News, 1928).

10 Claude Larivière, *Albert Saint-Martin, Militant d'Avant-Garde (1865–1947)* (Laval: Les Éditions coopératives Albert Saint-Martin, 1979), 7.

11 Finding Aid, Marshall J. Gauvin Collection, University of Manitoba, Elizabeth Dafoe Library. See <http://www.umanitoba.ca/librairies/units/archives/ead/html/gauvin.shtml#a2> (10 Aug. 2004).

12 Richard Allen, *The Social Passion: Religion and Social Reform in Canada 1914–28* (Toronto: University of Toronto Press, 1973), 4.

13 See Ian McKay, "Strikes in the Maritimes, 1900–1914" in *Atlantic Canada after Confederation*, ed. P.A. Buckner and David Frank (Fredericton: Acadiensis Press, 1985), 216–59.

14 Cited in Ramsay Cook, *The Regenerators: Social Criticism in Late Victorian English Canada* (Toronto: University of Toronto Press 1985), 182.

15 Kidd, *Social Evolution*, 2nd ed. (New York: Macmillan and Co., 1894), 353.

16 See Henry Drummond, *Natural Law in the Spiritual World* (Philadelphia: Henry Altemus, n.d. [c.1898]).

17 John Webster Grant, *A Profusion of Spires: Religion in Nineteenth-Century Ontario* (Toronto: University of Toronto Press, 1988), 65.

18 Peter Campbell notes the examples of Irish Catholics Jack Kavanagh and Jack Leheney. See Peter Campbell, *Canadian Marxists and the Search for a Third Way* (Montreal and Kingston: McGill-Queen's University Press, 1999), 10. Certainly a few prominent people of the early 20th century – Joe Wallace of Halifax, who would go on to become one of Canada's best-known "Red poets," was one – both became socialists and remained in close touch with their Catholicism.

19 See O.D. Skelton, *Socialism: A Critical Analysis* (Boston and New York: Houghton Mifflin Company, 1911), 309; George Hardy, *Those Stormy Years: Memories of the*

Fight for Freedom on Five Continents (London: Lawrence & Wishart, 1956), 38; and "The Relations between Capital and Labour," *Sun* (Saint John), 22 Jan. 1906, 7.

20 "Product of the alcohol-steeped brains . . ." cited in Grant, *Profusion of Spires*, 200; "Pope Leo xiii and the Working Class," *Western Clarion*, 7 Aug. 1909, 2.

21 Colin McKay, "The French Canadian as a Trade Unionist," in *For a Working-Class Culture in Canada: A Selection of Colin McKay's Writings on Sociology and Political Economy, 1897–1939*, Part IV, ed. Ian McKay (St. John's, Nfld.: Canadian Committee on Labour History, 1996), 68–70.

22 Allen Mills, *Fool for Christ: The Political Thought of J.S. Woodsworth* (Toronto, Buffalo and London: University of Toronto Press, 1991), 45.

23 One major heresy trial took place in the Presbyterian Church in 1893, when Rev. John Campbell was charged for a lecture he delivered to the Queen's theological alumni and student body on "The Perfect Book and the Perfect Father." It seemingly called into question the infallibility of the Bible, queried the depiction of God's character in the Old Testament, and discounted the image of a God sitting in judgment upon sinners. He was found guilty by the Presbytery of Montreal, a judgment overturned on appeal. David B. Marshall, *Secularizing the Faith: Canadian Protestant Clergy and the Crisis of Belief, 1850–1940* (Toronto: University of Toronto Press, 1992), 79–80. Both William Irvine and Salem Bland encountered the reality or spectre of heresy charges in their careers.

24 Michael Gauvreau, *The Evangelical Century: College and Creed in English Canada from the Great Revival to the Great Depression* (Montreal and Kingston: McGill-Queen's University Press, 1991), 127, 4.

25 For an outstanding study of the most public attempt to create a new form of Christianity accessible to working-class people, see Lynne Marks, *Revivals and Roller Rinks: Religion, Leisure, and Identity in Late-Nineteenth-Century Small-Town Ontario* (Toronto: University of Toronto Press, 1996).

26 Cook, *Regenerators*, 187, 189.

27 Allen, *Social Passion*, 17.

28 Drummond, *Natural Law in the Spiritual World*, xii – xiii, 10.

29 *Citizen and Country*, 1 April 1899; George D. Herron, *Between Caesar and Jesus* (New York: Thomas Y. Crowell & Co., 1899), 45–46.

30 For interesting work on this central issue, see Brian Trainor, "The Language of Temperance in Nineteenth-Century Ontario," M.A. thesis, Queen's University, Kingston, 1993; Craig Heron, *Booze: A Distilled History* (Toronto: Between the Lines, 2003).

31 Herron, *Between Caesar and Jesus*, 49.

32 Edward M. Penton, "The Ideas of William Cotton: A Marxist View of Canadian Society, 1908–1914," M.A. thesis, University of Ottawa, 1978, 134. Penton guesses that Marx received slightly more attention in *Cotton's*.

33 *Citizen and Country*, 4 May 1899, 13 Jan. 1900.

34 A partial list of prominents would include Rev. E.S. Rowe, Professor A.J. Hunter, and James Simpson; in Halifax, Rev. Professor Carruthers, Rev. J.L. Donaldson, and Rev. R.R. Osgood Morse; in Saint John, W.F. Hatheway; in Fredericton, H.H. Stuart; in St. Thomas, R.N. Price; in Woodstock, T.A. Forman; in British Columbia, Annie Chapman and James Cameron. The Toronto left featured season after season of Christian socialist speakers from 1898 to 1904. Among frequently mentioned titles were a number by Rev. F.D. Maurice: *Tracts on Christian Socialism*, *Tracts by Christian Socialists*, *God and Mammon: A Sermon to Young Men*, and *Social Morality*.

35 Tim Buck, *Yours in the Struggle: Reminiscences of Tim Buck* (Toronto: NC Press, 1977), 26–27.

36 *Globe* (Toronto), 25 Feb. 1901; *Sun* (Saint John), 8 Oct. 1909.

37 *Citizen and Country*, 21 Oct. 1899.

38 J. Cyrus Doull, letter to the *Herald* (Halifax), 26 Nov. 1906; *Herald*, 3 March 1908; *Sun* (Saint John), 20 Dec. 1909.

39 *Herald*, 11 Feb. 1920; "Old Collier," letter to the *Herald*, 31 Oct. 1906; *Citizen and Country*, 25 March 1899.

40 Morse in *Herald*, 3 March 1906; E.W. Wilcox, "Who Are the Socialists?" *Amherst Daily News*, 24 Nov. 1908; L.M. Brown, "Socialism: What Some Well Known Men Have Said on the Subject," letter to the *Herald*, 3 March 1908, 9; Socialist Party of Canada, Lindsay, Ont., Local, *Gems of Socialism* (n.p. [Lindsay], n.d. (1916).

41 *Citizen and Country*, 2 Feb. 1900, 23 March 1900.

42 Gauvreau, *Evangelical Century*, 195, 198; *Herald*, 4 Feb. 1907.

43 "Canadian Socialist League," *Citizen and Country*, 6 April 1900.

44 *Morning Chronicle* (Halifax), 10 Aug. 1901.

45 Colin McKay, "Why Workingmen Distrust Churches," in *For a Working-Class Culture in Canada*, ed. McKay, 56–59.

46 "The Response to McKay's Challenge," in *For a Working-Class Culture in Canada*, ed. McKay, 60–62; McKay, "What Workingmen Expect of the Church: A Rebuttal by Colin McKay," in *For a Working-Class Culture in Canada*, ed. McKay, 62–67.

47 Walter A. Ratcliffe, *Jesus and Socialism: An Address Delivered in Union Hall, Brantford, Ont.* (n.p., n.d.), see esp. 4, 3, 19, 17; *Citizen and Country*, 24 June 1899, 2 Feb. 1900.

48 *Herald*, 19 Oct. 1920, 6; Wm. Parker, "Fort William, Ont.," letter to *Western Clarion*, 6 Aug. 1910; Gene Howard Homel, "James Simpson and the Origins of Canadian Social Democracy," Ph.D. thesis, University of Toronto, 1978, 32.

49 Richard Allen, "Introduction" to Salem Bland, *The New Christianity* (Toronto: University of Toronto Press, 1973 [1919]), xii, xiv. For a much fuller discussion of Bland, and an outstanding comprehensive biography that also sheds a rare light on the culture and society of *fin de siècle* Canada, see Richard Allen, *The View from the Murney Tower: Salem Bland, the Late-Victorian Controversies, and the Search for a New Christianity*, vol. I (Toronto: University of Toronto Press, 2008).

50 In contrast, much U.S. evangelicalism brought to present-day Canadians is of a "pre-millennialist" cast: only the future second Coming of Christ will redeem a depraved humanity.

51 Bland, *New Christianity*, 25, 26, 22.

52 Allen, "Introduction," viii.

53 Bland, *New Christianity*, 17, 27.

54 Ibid., 22, 27.

55 Ibid., 23.

56 Cited in ibid., 32.

57 Ibid., 9, 18.

58 Ibid., 16.

59 Ibid., 52.

60 Ibid., 16, 55.

61 Ibid., 51–52.

62 Ibid., 54.

63 Ibid., 28.

64 It was true that the triune formula was not *fully* explicit: at least in *The New Chris-*

tianity, there is no sustained attempt to speak of the labour theory of value, and class struggle is apprehended only as it is transcended in a higher functional harmony.

65 V.I. Lenin, cited in David McLellan, *Marxism and Religion* (London: Macmillan, 1987), 4. As McLellan notes, Lenin's views on religion underwent a significant modification after his study of Hegel during the First World War. For a Marxist analysis that draws heavily from Grant Allen's work, see Paul Lafargue, *The Origins and Evolution of the Idea of the Soul*, trans. Charles H. Kerr (Chicago: Charles H. Kerr, 1922); for a less anthropological approach, see Karl Kautsky, *Foundations of Christianity: A Study in Christian Origins* (New York and London: Monthly Review Press, 1972 [1925]).

66 See Salvatore Salerno, *Red November, Black November: Culture and Community in the Industrial Workers of the World* (Albany: State University of New York Press, 1989), 149, for a nice cartoon from the *Industrial Worker*, 11 June 1910. Sometimes this slight was delivered in a rather good-natured way, as in this report from a meeting of the fledgling SPC local in Windsor, Ont.: "The meeting was continued until 11 p.m., a good many taking part in the discussion, even to a [the] fossil remains of [the] Middle Ages, a sky-pilot." Lorne Wilkie, "Windsor's Baptism of Fire," *Western Clarion*, 7 Aug. 1909, 4.

67 As Varpu Lindström-Best remarks, "At first glance the Finns in Canada seem to be a very religious and homogeneous group; as late as 1931, 88.3 per cent declared that they were Lutheran. At the same time, many held bitter, anti-religious sentiments. Furthermore, a mere 3 per cent of the Finns who claimed to be Lutheran in the census report had actually bothered to join the church in Canada." Anticlericalism, she observes, had deep roots in Finland, where the Finnish Lutheran Church enjoyed a measure of recognition from the state. Varpu Lindström-Best, *Defiant Sisters: A Social History of Finnish Immigrant Women in Canada* (Toronto: Multicultural History Society of Ontario, 1988), 115. Ukrainian immigrants were divided between Eastern-rite Catholics and the Orthodox. Many left-wing Ukrainians seem to have identified with secularly-minded rebels against the Russian Empire more closely than with these faith communities. Among the Jews, often emigrants also from the Russian Empire, were such figures as Moses Baritz and Sophie Mushkat, both aggressively anti-religious in their socialism. Janice Newton makes the interesting suggestion that the SPC provided an attractive option for secular Jews, who were unlikely to see a left defined in terms of Christian socialism as one they could call their own. Janice Newton, *The Feminist Challenge to the Canadian Left, 1900–1918* (Montreal and Kingston: McGill-Queen's University Press, 1995), 25. Peter Campbell adds the idea that both Jews and Gentiles could find in social science a way of transcending their religious and national particularities. Campbell, *Canadian Marxists and the Search for a Third Way*, 19.

68 John Lyons, "An Explanation," letter to *Western Clarion*, 24 Dec. 1910, 3.

69 *Citizen and Country*, 9 Dec. 1899, 4 Nov. 1899, 2 Dec. 1899.

70 Cited in Homel, "James Simpson and the Origins of Canadian Social Democracy," 156–57.

71 *Herald*, 26 July 1906.

72 Cited in Michael Boudreau, "The Emergence of the Social Gospel in Nova Scotia: The Presbyterian, Methodist and Baptist Churches and the Working Class 1880–1914," M.A. thesis, Queen's University, Kingston, 1991, 63–64.

73 See Janice Newton, "The Alchemy of Politicization: Socialist Women and the Early Canadian Left," in *Gender Conflicts: New Essays in Women's History*, ed. Franca

Iacovetta and Mariana Valverde (Toronto: University of Toronto Press, 1992), 129. As Homel relates, when SPCers were brought up on free speech charges in Toronto, one Russian Jew refused to kiss the Bible. The Judge, saying "I don't want to make martyrs of you," allowed those arrested to leave the court without sentence. Homel, "James Simpson and the Origins of Canadian Social Democracy," 419.

74 Ruth Frager, *Sweatshop Strife: Class, Ethnicity, and Gender in the Jewish Labour Movement of Toronto 1900–1939* (Toronto: University of Toronto Press, 1992). For Krat, see Nadia Kazymyra, "The Defiant Pavlo Krat and the Early Socialist Movement in Canada," *Canadian Ethnic Studies* 10, 2 (1978), 38–54.

75 Lindström-Best, *Defiant Sisters*, esp. ch.4.

76 Ross A. Johnson, "No Compromise – No Political Trading: The Marxian Socialist Tradition in British Columbia," Ph.D. thesis, University of British Columbia, Vancouver, 1975, 68, 116, 159–160, the last citing *Western Socialist*, 27 Sept. 1902; see also *Citizen and Country*, 12 Aug. 1899.

77 Homel, "James Simpson and the Origins of Canadian Social Democracy," 278; Campbell, *Canadian Marxists*, *passim*; David Frank, *J.B. McLachlan: A Biography* (Toronto: James Lorimer, 1999), 85–86.

78 Colin McKay, "Christianity and the Social Crisis," *Eastern Labor News*, 1 Feb. 1913; and Colin McKay in *For a Working-Class Culture in Canada*, ed. McKay, 343. See also Donovan E. Smucker, *The Origins of Walter Rauschenbusch's Social Ethics* (Montreal and Kingston: McGill-Queen's University Press, 1994); Paul M. Minus, *Walter Rauschenbusch: American Reformer* (London: Macmillan, 1988); and Christopher H. Evans, *The Kingdom Is Always but Coming: A Life of Walter Rauschenbusch* (Grand Rapids, Mich.: William B. Eerdmans, 2004).

79 *Western Clarion*, 18 April 1908; *Cotton's Weekly*, 2 Dec. 1909.

80 Cook, *Regenerators*, describes Ingersoll's impact. Significantly, Ingersoll is indirectly debated in one of the earliest discussions of "socialism" in Nova Scotia in the *Trades Journal* of the PWA. At least two of the leading socialist secularists of the early 20th century noted the influence of Ingersoll's writings on their outlook. For Ingersoll's reception by the socialist Finns of Toronto, see William Eklund, *Builders of Canada: History of the Finnish Organization of Canada 1911–1971* (Toronto: Finnish Organization of Canada, 1987), 118. For a diverting history of free thought in the United States during this period, see Susan Jacoby, *Freethinkers: A History of American Secularism* (New York: Henry Holt, 2004), 186–267. For a fascinating study of the Freemasons' milieu, see Patrice Dutil, *Devil's Advocate: Godfroy Langlois and the Politics of Liberal Progressivism in Laurier's Quebec* (Montreal and Toronto: Robert Davies Publishing, 1994); for Richardson, see Barbara Roberts, *A Reconstructed World: A Feminist Biography of Gertrude Richardson* (Montreal and Kingston: McGill-Queen's University Press, 1996).

81 Grant, *Profusion of Spires*, 132.

82 J.H. Burroughs, *Religion Thy Name Is Superstition* (Vancouver: Socialist Party of Canada, n.d. [1912]), unpaginated.

83 John Spargo, *Capitalist and Laborer: An Open Letter to Professor Goldwin Smith, D.C.L. in Reply to His Capital and Labor; and Modern Socialism: A Lecture Delivered at the New York School of Philanthropy* (Chicago: Charles H. Kerr & Company, 1907), 20; Eugene V. Debs, "Jesus, the Supreme Leader" (March 1914), at <http://www.marxists.org/history/usa/parties/spusa/1914/0300-debs-jesussupreme> (27 May 2005).

84 "In These Days of Peace," editorial, *Western Clarion*, 4 Jan. 1908, 2; "Merry Christmas," editorial, *Western Clarion*, 24 Dec. 1910, 2.

85 Burroughs, *Religion Thy Name Is Superstition*; Wilfred Gribble, "Tale of a Tour: Ninth Installment," *Cotton's Weekly*, 5 Aug. 1909.

86 J. Reay, "Garrulous Sky Pilot Promptly Called Down," *Western Clarion*, 14 Dec. 1907, 1.

87 P.F. Lawson, "All It Produces Is Labor's Right," letter to the *Herald*, 13 Aug. 1907; W.G. Gribble, "Correspondence," *Western Clarion*, 20 April 1907, 4; Mc. [D.G. McKenzie], "Stick to Your Last," *Western Clarion*, 18 April 1908, 2.

88 J.G. Shearer, "The Growing Interest of the Churches in the Labor Movement," *Western Clarion*, 15 Aug. 1908, 2.

89 Burroughs, *Religion Thy Name Is Superstition*; "The Modern Jupiter," *Western Clarion*, editorial, 19 Oct. 1912.

90 W.J. Curry, "The Educational Forces of Society," *Western Clarion*, 15 Dec. 1906, 3; Alfred J. Gordon, "A Reply: To Mr. Crews, of Guelph, Ont.," *Cotton's Weekly*, 5 Aug. 1909. The point can be found in Karl Marx, "The Communism of the *Rheinischer Beobachter*," in Karl Marx and Frederick Engels, *On Religion* (Moscow: Progress Publishers, 1975), 73–77.

91 "Cause and Effect," *Cotton's Weekly*, 5 Aug. 1909; Curry, "Educational Forces of Society."

92 Paul Lafargue, *Causes of Belief in God* (Vancouver: SPC, Whitehead Library no. 6, n.d. [1920?]); Socialist Party of Canada, Lindsay, *Gems of Socialism*; *Western Clarion*, 24 Dec. 1910.

93 *Cotton's Weekly*, 8 Dec. 1910; J.H., "Ernst Haeckel, Scientist – An Appreciation," *Red Flag*, 16 Aug. 1919, front page.

94 Percy Rosoman, "Socialists vs. So-Called Socialists," *Western Clarion*, 24 Dec. 1910, 4; Ed Fulcher, "About It, and About," letter to *Western Clarion*, 11 Dec. 1910, 3.

95 H. Siegfried, "Revelstoke Socialists," *Western Clarion*, 7 April 1906, 4; *Cotton's Weekly*, 2 Dec. 1909; Robin Adair, "The Coming of the Storm," *Western Clarion*, 19 Jan. 1907, 3.

96 Rosoman, "Socialists vs. So-Called Socialists."

97 Roscoe A. Fillmore, "Is Socialism Against Religion?" *Cotton's Weekly*, 2 Dec. 1909.

98 Roscoe Fillmore, "Oleaginous If Not Original," *Western Clarion*, 16 April 1910, 1.

99 Roscoe A. Fillmore, "Keep the Issue Clear," *International Socialist Review* 15, 7 (January 1915), 399.

100 "Probus," letter to the *Herald*, 4 Feb. 1908. The voters did not seem to be scared off by the case made by Probus, given that in 1910 Landry won more votes in Springhill on the Labor Party platform than did the other two mainstream parties combined.

101 *Cotton's Weekly*, 3 June 1909, 7 Jan. 1909. When historians Christie and Gauvreau write that "most progressive ministers eschewed the political manifestations of socialism because they undermined the solidarity of the community by pitting class against class and because they struck at individual conversion, the very foundation of evangelism," they capture the conventional liberal position. Christie and Gauvreau, *Full-Orbed Christianity*, 16–17. Yet the socialist rejoinder would be that, in this and other cases, it was not the "political manifestations of socialism" that had "undermined the solidarity of the community," but the denial of the workers' basic social and political rights by capitalists like Cowans. Socialists theorized, but they did not invent, the social divisions, class violence, and systemic cruelty of modern Canadian capitalism.

102 Fillmore, *Maritime Radical*, 74. For Stuart's efforts, see H.H. Stuart, "Socialism

and Religion," talk at Springhill, *Eastern Labor News*, 17 June 1911; "Is Socialism Wrong in This?" *Eastern Labor News*, 24 June 1911.

103 Cited in Fillmore, *Maritime Radical*, 84.

104 Cited in Eklund, *Builders of Canada*, 118.

105 Arthur M. Lewis, *Evolution Social and Organic*, 6th ed. (Chicago: Charles H. Kerr and Company, n.d. [1910]), 133.

106 Arthur M. Lewis, *The Struggle between Science and Superstition* (Chicago: Charles H. Kerr, 1915), 186–87.

107 *Globe* (Toronto), 22 Sept. 1910.

108 Moses Baritz, "Christianity and Socialism," *Globe*, 31 Sept. 1910.

109 "Socialism and Christianity," editorial, *Globe*, 31 Sept. 1910.

110 *Globe*, 22 Sept. 1910. To a contemporary ear this commentary has a slightly anti-Semitic overtone – seemingly playing off Baritz's obviously Jewish name and underlining his newness to the community.

111 William James, "Socialism Truest Christianity," *Globe*, 23 Sept. 1910.

112 *Globe*, 22 Sept. 1910.

113 *Globe*, 23 Sept., 24 Sept. 1910.

114 *Globe*, 26 Sept. 1910. See also Peter E. Newell, *The Impossibilists: A Brief Profile of the Socialist Party of Canada* (London: Athena Press, 2008), 95–101.

115 Curry, "Educational Forces of Society."

116 Finding Aid, Marshall Gauvin Collection, University of Manitoba, Elizabeth Dafoe Library, Special Collections. To complicate matters, in his early years Gauvin often went under the anglicized version of his name, "Govang."

117 See, for an on-line critique of Gauvin <http://www.frontline-apologetics.com/gauvin_review.htm> (25 May 2005).

118 See Marshall J. Gauvin [Govang], "Historical Reflections and the Labor Movement," *Eastern Labor News*, 3, 24 April, 1, 8 May 1909.

119 *Eastern Labor News*, 22 June 1912.

120 *Eastern Labor News*, 8, 15 May 1909.

121 Gauvin evidently dusted off this rapturous paean to rationalism and delivered it once again shortly after the First World War. We cannot be 100 per cent positive that the manuscript of the talk in the Gauvin Papers at the University of Manitoba is exactly the same talk he gave years before; very likely he edited some points. Yet enough details in the published text line up with the description in the contemporary newspapers to suggest that it is at the very least an edited and revised version of the talk he gave in Moncton before the war.

122 Marshall J. Gauvin, "An Appeal for Truth in Religious Teaching," unpublished manuscript, Gauvin Collection, University of Manitoba, 11.

123 Ibid., 4–5.

124 Marshall J. Gauvin, *The Illustrated Story of Evolution* (New York: Peter Eckler Publishing Co., 1921), 16, 119.

125 *Herald*, 27 Feb. 1908; Pritchard cited in Harry Gutkin and Mildred Gutkin, *Profiles in Dissent: The Shaping of Radical Thought in the Canadian West* (Edmonton: NeWest Press, 1997), 131; the John McKay case in *Herald*, 17 Sept. 1909, 2; John Taylor, *Ottawa: An Illustrated History* (Toronto: James Lorimer, 1986), 136.

126 Karl Marx, "Contribution to the Critique of Hegel's Philosophy of Law. Introduction," (1844) in Karl Marx and Frederick Engels, *Collected Works*, vol. 3 (Moscow: Progress Publishers, 1975), 175.

127 Karl Marx, "The Communism of the *Rheinischer Beobachter*," (1847) in Karl Marx and Frederick Engels, *Collected Works*, vol. 6 (Moscow: Progress Publishers, 1976),

231; Marx and Engels, "Manifesto of the Communist Party," (1848) in Marx and Engels, *Collected Works*, vol. 6, 508; Karl Marx, *Capital: A Critique of Political Economy*, vol. 1, trans. Ben Fowkes (New York: Random House, 1977), 173; see also Marx and Engels, *Collected Works*, vol. 35 (Moscow: Progress Publishing, 1996), 90.

128 See Grant Allen, *The Evolution of the Idea of God: An Inquiry into the Origins of Religions* (London: Watts and Co., issued for the Rationalist Press Association, 1903); *The Hand of God and Other Posthumous Essays, Together with Some Reprinted Papers* (London: Watts and Co., issued for the Rationalist Press, 1909); Lafargue, *Origin and Evolution of the Idea of the Soul*; Kautsky, *Foundations of Christianity*.

129 David McLellan, *Marxism and Religion* (London: Macmillan, 1987), 1, 72.

130 Michael J. Buckley, S.J., *Denying and Disclosing God: The Ambiguous Progress of Modern Atheism* (New Haven and London: Yale University Press, 2004), 102.

131 McLellan, *Marxism and Religion*, 3.

132 See Karl Marx, "Economic and Philosophical Manuscripts of 1844" (1844) in Marx and Engels, *Collected Works*, vol. 3, 306.

133 McLellan suggestively remarks that Marx's evolutionary account of the history of religious belief does not substantially differ from that of Spencer. McLellan, *Marxism and Religion*, 21.

134 For an illuminating collection of contemporary documents, see Andrew Pyle, *Agnosticism: Contemporary Responses to Spencer and Huxley* (Bristol: Thoemmes Press, 1995).

135 Herbert Spencer, *First Principles* (London: Williams and Norgate, 1867), in Herbert Spencer, *Collected Writings*, vol. 5 (London: Routledge/Thoemmes Press, 1996), 20, 24.

136 John Spargo, *The Common Sense of Socialism: A Series of Letters Addressed to Jonathan Edwards, of Pittsburg* (Chicago: Charles H. Kerr & Company, 1911), 37, 157.

137 John Spargo, *The Spiritual Significance of Modern Socialism* (New York: B.W. Huebsch, 1911), 17.

138 Spargo, *Spiritual Significance*, 82, 83–84.

139 J.Y., "From the Coal City," letter to *Western Clarion*, 4 Jan.1908, 3.

140 *Herald*, 7 Dec. 1908, 4; Morrison Davidson, "Socialism and Sex," *Western Clarion*, 14 Dec. 1907, 4.

141 *Cotton's Weekly*, 5 Jan. 1911.

142 Linda Kealey, *Enlisting Women for the Cause: Women, Labour, and the Left in Canada, 1890–1920* (Toronto: University of Toronto Press, 1998), 135.

143 Roscoe A. Fillmore, "Is Socialism Against Religion?" *Cotton's Weekly*, 2 Dec. 1909.

144 On Spinoza, see Jonathan I. Israel, *Radical Enlightenment: Philosophy and the Making of Modernity 1650–1750* (Oxford: Oxford University Press, 2001).

145 Frederick Engels, *Landmarks of Scientific Socialism*, ed. and trans. Austin Lewis (Chicago: Charles H. Kerr and Company, 1907) – copy in my possession stamped "Socialist Party of Canada, Winnipeg Local No. 1"; Michael Hendrick Fitch, *The Physical Basis of Mind and Morals* (Chicago: Charles H. Kerr, 1912) – copy in my possession stamped "The Property of Riverdale Local, No. 87, S.D.P. of C"; Sinclair is cited in James Doyle, *Progressive Heritage: The Evolution of a Politically Radical Literary Tradition in Canada* (Waterloo, Ont.: Wilfrid Laurier University Press, 2002), 45.

146 For a critical evaluation, see Mary Midgley, *Evolution as a Religion: Strange Hopes and Stranger Fears* (London and New York: Methuen, 1985). For a provocative

outline of the science/ religion debate, see Peter J. Bowler, *Monkey Trials and Gorilla Statements: Evolution and Christianity from Darwin to Intelligent Design* (Cambridge, Mass. and London: Harvard University Press, 2007). See also Robert T. Pennock, "Biology and Religion," in *The Cambridge Companion to the Philosophy of Biology*, ed. David L. Hull and Michael Ruse (Cambridge: Cambridge University Press, 2007), 410–28.

147 Margaret Haile, "The International Race for the World's Market," *Wilshire's Magazine*, October 1903, 65.

148 Gaylord Wilshire, *Socialism: A Religion* (New York: Wilshire Book Company, n.d. [1906]).

149 For some sources on this artistic colony, see Jan Allen, ed., *Bon Echo: Dreams and Visions* (Kingston: Agnes Etherington Art Centre, 1993); Mary Savigny, *Bon Echo: The Denison Years* (Toronto: Natural Heritage Books, 1997); Robert Stacey and Stan McMullin, *Massanoga: The Art of Bon Echo* (Toronto: Penumbra Press, 1998); Michelle Lacombe, "Songs of the Open Road: Bon Echo, Urban Utopians, and the Cult of Nature,"*Journal of Canadian Studies*, Summer 1998. On Bucke, see S.E.D Shortt, *Victorian Lunacy: Richard M. Bucke and the Practice of Late Nineteenth-Century Psychiatry* (Cambridge: Cambridge University Press, 1986); and Michael Robertson, *Worshipping Walt: The Whitman Disciples* (Princeton and Oxford: Princeton University Press, 2008), ch. 3. For Whitman's deep attachment to Peter Doyle and other working-class men, see Richard Bucke, ed., *Calamus: A Series of Letters Written during the Years 1868–1880 by Walt Whitman to a Young Friend (Peter Doyle)* (Boston: Laurens Mayard, 1897; reprinted, Kessinger Publishing Legacy Reprints, n.d.).

150 J.B. McLachlan, "Labor in Nova Scotia Has Won Triumphs," *Herald*, 31 Dec. 1920, 9.

151 See Tim Hilton, *John Ruskin* (New Haven, Conn. and London: Yale University Press, 2002); Elliott Shore, *Talkin' Socialism: J.A. Wayland and the Radical Press* (Lawrence: University Press of Kansas, 1988), 36–39. For interpretations of Ruskin, see Tim Hilton, *John Ruskin* (New Haven, Conn. and London: Yale University Press, 2002); Wolfgang Kemp, *The Desire of My Eyes: The Life and Work of John Ruskin*, trans. Jan ven Heurck (New York: Farrar, Straus and Giroux, 1990); Judith Stoddart, *Ruskin's Culture Wars: Fors Clavigera and the Crisis of Victorian Liberalism* (Charlottesville and London: University Press of Virginia, 1998). For a particularly discerning Marxist commentary on Ruskin, see Michael Löwy and Robert Sayre, *Romanticism against the Tide of Modernity*, trans. Catherine Porter (Durham, N.C. and London: Duke University Press, 2001), 127–46. As they point out, "ignorant of the structural imperatives that govern modernity, Ruskin seems to put all his hopes in individual awareness and action" (145), yet nonetheless he was often a foundational influence upon both labourists and socialists in the early 20th century.

152 Fillmore, "How to Build up the Socialist Movement," *International Socialist Review*, 16, 10 (April 1916), 615, 617.

153 For an excellent discussion, see Cook, *Regenerators*. Janice Newton, *Feminist Challenge*, argues that theosophy had a particular appeal for women because of "its belief in a woman-centred divinity" (22). Yet theosophists themselves would probably have contested this description of a doctrine they persistently described as a *philosophical* approach to religion, rather than a free-standing religion in its own right.

154 For an on-line link to Blavatsky and her teachings, see <http://www.theosociety.org/pasadena/key/key-1.htm> (10 March 2005).

155   W.H.G. Armytage, *Heavens Below: Utopian Experiments in England, 1560–1960* (London: Routledge and Kegan Paul 1961), 374; I was drawn to this quotation by Diana Chown, "Introduction," in Alice A. Chown, *The Stairway*, ed. by Diana Chown (Toronto: University of Toronto Press, 1988), xxxii. For a more recent account, with descriptions of settlements that Canadians found inspiring, see Gillian Darley, *Villages of Vision: A Study of Strange Utopias*, rev. ed. (Nottingham: Five Leaves Publications, 2007). For U.S. experiments in utopian intentional communities, see Robert S. Fogarty, *All Things New: American Communes and Utopian Movements, 1860–1914* (Chicago and London: University of Chicago Press, 1990); Francis Robert Shor, *Utopianism and Radicalism in a Reforming America, 1888–1918* (Westport, Conn. and London: Greenwood Press, 1997).

156   See Eklund, *Builders of Canada*, 102.

157   Kevin Wilson, *Practical Dreamers: Communitarianism and Co-operatives on Malcolm Island* (Victoria: British Columbia Institute for Co-operative Studies, 2005), 25.

158   Kealey, *Enlisting Women for the Cause*, 108.

159   John David Bell, "The Social and Political Thought of the Labor Advocate," M.A. thesis, Queen's University, Kingston, 1975, 104–5.

160   "A Jap Speaks Out," *Cotton's Weekly*, 20 Aug. 1909. In Vancouver in 1911, the remarkable Sikh socialist Hussain Rahim also dedicated his energies to the formation of a Hindu Temperance Association. Peter Campbell, "East Meets Left: South Asian Militants and the Socialist Party of Canada in British Columbia, 1904–1914," *International Journal of Canadian Studies* 20 (Fall 1999), 46.

161   Irvine cited in Anthony Mardiros, *William Irvine: The Life of a Prairie Radical* (Toronto: James Lorimer, 1979), 22, 30–31.

162   J.B. McLachlan, "Where Would Robert Burns Stand Today in Labor Problems?" *Herald*, 24 Jan. 1908; W.F. Hatheway, *Canadian Nationality, The Cry of Labor and Other Essays* (Toronto: William Briggs, 1906), 212; McNamara cited in *The Voice* (Winnipeg), 1 May 1914. I thank David Thompson for this reference.

163   Chown, *Stairway*, 13.

164   Francis Marion Beynon, *Aleta Dey* (London: Virago Press, 1988 [1919]), 44, 55, 81, 147, 190–91.

165   Grant, *Profusion of Spires*, 59.

166   Robert Blatchford, *God and My Neighbor* (London: Clarion Press, 1903), 22–23.

167   *Globe* (Saint John), 5 Nov. 1910.

168   *Cotton's Weekly*, 5 Aug. 1909.

169   *Citizen and Country*, 7 Dec. 1900; Socialist Party of Canada, Lindsay, *Gems of Socialism*.

170   J. Stitt Wilson, "A Morning Meditation," *Cotton's Weekly*, 2 Dec. 1909.

171   "What the Socialists Ask," *Cotton's Weekly*, 6 Jan. 1910.

172   Louis Aubrey Wood, *A History of Farmers' Movements in Canada: The Origins and Development of Agrarian Protest 1872–1924* (Toronto: University of Toronto Press, 1975).

173   "Partridge of Sintaluta" [E.A. Partridge], *A War on Poverty: The One War That Can End War* (Winnipeg: Wallingford Press, n.d. [1926]); citations in the following pages are from v-vi, 59, 112, 204, 9–10, 89, 107, 114, 15, 163–65, 159.

174   Those who would scoff at the detailed blueprint for Partridge's "Realm of Freedom" might consider Bauman's argument with respect to most utopian projections, which are designed to show that what seems to be solid and predictable in the present moment can be redescribed as a set of conflicting

projects for the future: "Utopias weaken the defensive walls of habit, thus preparing their destruction by a dramatic thrust of condensed dissent, or their gradual erosion by the vitriolic solution of utopian ideas." They are not intrinsically "flights from reality," but rather different ways of exploring its present-day contradictions. Zygmunt Bauman, *Socialism: The Active Utopia* (London: George Allen and Unwin, 1976), 16.

175 Spencer, *First Principles*, 123; Partridge, *War on Poverty*, 204.

176 Partridge, *War on Poverty*, 165.

177 Ibid., 208.

178 Martin Buber, *Paths in Utopia*, trans. R.F.C. Hull (Boston: Beacon Press, 1966 [1949]), 9, 13.

5: The Woman Question

1 *Citizen and Country*, 16 May 1902.

2 Sadly, it would appear that Ontario's claim to have the first woman candidate in the entire British Empire is undermined by Catherine Spence, who ran as a candidate in Southern Australia in 1897. Women won the right to vote in New Zealand in 1893, but it was not until 1919 that women candidates there contested seats in a general election. My thanks to Chris McCreary for his help in researching this point.

3 Gene Howard Homel, "James Simpson and the Origins of Canadian Social Democracy," Ph.D. thesis, University of Toronto, 1978, 124.

4 Cited in Catherine L. Cleverdon, *The Woman Suffrage Movement in Canada* (Toronto: University of Toronto Press, 1974 [1950]), 161; see J.W. Longley, *Love* (Toronto: Copp, Clark, 1898).

5 At the same time the much more predictable diatribes of the *Western Clarion* about gender – which echoed equally sexist positions developed in England by Belfort Bax – have gained far more attention. See Karen Hunt, *Equivocal Feminists: The Social Democratic Federation and the Woman Question 1884–1911* (Cambridge: Cambridge University Press, 1996), 27.

6 A most interesting essay on Margaret Haile is as yet unpublished: see Ingrid Ericson, "'When Will We Awake from This Fatalism?' An Essay on First-Wave Socialism, Maternal Feminism, and the Case of Margaret Haile," cognate essay, Queen's University, Kingston, 2007.

Few other historical accounts spend much time on Haile, who not only complicates the master narratives of liberalism, but also disrupts some of the narratives of feminist historiography, according to which both "maternal feminism" – a category embracing an extraordinary diversity of contradictory positions – and sexist men silenced the socialist feminists. In many respects Haile's historiographical fate epitomizes the irony of how this socialist-feminist moment has been treated in the secondary literature: in the (justified) polemical struggle to highlight the limitations of socialist organizations on the women's movement, subsequent historians have inadvertently obscured and even silenced the feminists who created a powerful discourse within the broader socialist formation.

Cleverdon, in her magisterial *Woman Suffrage Movement in Canada*, does not notice Haile at all. In her briskly revisionist *Liberation Deferred? The Ideas of the English-Canadian Suffragists, 1877–1918* (Toronto: University of Toronto Press, 1974 [1950]), Carole Lee Bacchi notes the presence of one group, the "Old Guard" in her terminology, associated with Toronto's Dr. Augusta Stowe-Gullen, Montreal's Agnes Chesley, Winnipeg's Francis Marion Beynon, and Vancouver's Helena Gutteridge, which continued to raise "feminist" issues such as marriage, the motherhood role, and educational and occupational opportunities. On the other hand were the "social reform suffragists," who were "intent on preserving the traditional allocation of sex roles." The feminists, she argues, "invariably" drew their support from "the self-supporting women," whereas the social reform advocates included "many more working women who decided that the most pressing problems were social not sexual, and a large number of housewives for whom the problem of sexual discrimination was more remote." She passes over Haile's candidacy in silence (36).

Although Janice Newton does notice Haile's candidacy, she essentially agrees with Mary Jo Buhle, who regards Haile as a woman who "clung to the notion of the home as a traditional source of woman's power" and to "domesticity as a special feminine preserve," and highlights her connection to the Woman's Christian Temperance Union. Haile emerges as a person who "often used the differences between men and women, rather than equality-based arguments, to argue for radical social change." Janice Newton, *The Feminist Challenge to the Canadian Left, 1900–1918* (Montreal and Kingston: McGill-Queen's University Press, 1995), 17–18; Mary Jo Buhle, *Women and American Socialism* (Urbana, Chicago, and London: University of Illinois Press, 1981), 117.

In her pioneering work on this period, Linda Kealey notes that Haile emphasized in her campaign that the enfranchisement of women was but "a step towards the ultimate goal of socialism," and that her candidacy drew the support of Augusta Stowe-Gullen. She also underlines the significance of May Darwin, another CSL militant, who had urged women to join the socialist movement because women and children were "the greatest sufferers from the competitive system." The presence of other middle-class women reformers as supporters of Haile's candidacy suggested "the common ground sometimes shared by feminists and socialists." Linda Kealey, *Enlisting Women for the Cause: Women, Labour, and the Left in Canada, 1890–1920* (Toronto: University of Toronto Press, 1998), 97.

7 Margaret Haile, "Some of the Theories of Party Organization: Before the Form of an Instrument Is Decided There Must Be a Clear Conception of the Use to Be Made of It," *Social Democratic Herald* (Chicago), 22 June 1901; see <http://www.marxisthistory.org>.

8 *Social Democratic Herald*, 2 Dec. 1897. I would like to thank Ingrid Erikson for sharing her research notes on Margaret Haile with me.

9 Haile, "Some of the Theories of Party Organization." The quotations in the following paragraphs come from this same source.

10 Ibid.

11 For commentary, see *Citizen and Country*, 16 May 1902.

12 Cited in Mary Jo Buhle, *Women and American Socialism, 1870–1920* (Urbana: University of Illinois Press, 1983), 94; *Justice* (Providence, R.I.), 19 May 1894.

13 See Margaret Haile, "The Leaves of Life Are Dropping One by One," *Wilshire's Magazine*, 60 (July 1903), 30–32; "Capital Unions vs. Labor Unions," *Wilshire's Magazine*, September 1903, 71–75; "Peace on Earth," *Wilshire's Magazine*, 1 Dec. 1903, 30; "The International Race for the World's Market," *Wilshire's Magazine*, October 1903, 66–67; "A Guess on the Merger Decision," *Wilshire's Magazine*, June 1903, 19.

14 Newton, *Feminist Challenge to the Canadian Left*, 24. The book examines "the three largest English-speaking socialist organizations in the years preceding World War I," which in Newton's view were the CSL, SPC, and SDPC. A significant drawback of much of the literature on the feminists and socialists of *fin de siècle*

Canada is its pervasive assumption that points about the U.S. Socialist Party can be imported holus-bolus into the very different context of Canada, which lacked any one strong socialist party in this period. For leading U.S. titles exploring organized socialism and feminism, see Sally M. Miller, ed., *Flawed Liberation: Socialism and Feminism* (Westport, Conn.: Greenwood Press, 1981); Buhle, *Women and American Socialism*. For an outstanding collection on the history of the European socialist feminists, see Marilyn J. Boxer and Jean H. Quataert, eds., *Socialist Women: European Socialist Feminism in the Nineteenth and Early Twentieth Centuries* (New York: Elsevier, 1978).

15 Newton, *Feminist Challenge to the Canadian Left*, 10, 6, 12, 42, 11.

16 Kealey, *Enlisting Women for the Cause*, 13, 14, 92, 223.

17 Ibid., 119; Newton, *Feminist Challenge to the Canadian Left*, 15, 25, 63, 139.

18 Newton, *Feminist Challenge to the Canadian Left*, 68.

19 Kealey, *Enlisting Women for the Cause*, 111–12.

20 Newton, *Feminist Challenge to the Canadian Left*, 24, 126.

21 Kealey, *Enlisting Women for the Cause*, 8.

22 Newton, *Feminist Challenge to the Canadian Left*, 11. Kealey, *Enlisting Women for the Cause*, presents the most complete and detailed portrait of women on the Canadian left for this period. She provides fascinating portraits of women activists in the movement, and persistently underlines the concrete difficulties confronting women. Her account is substantially different in tone from that of Newton, *Feminist Challenge to the Canadian Left*, marking a step towards a more post-polemical appreciation of the structures shaping the various movements of the left. Nevertheless, both books leave the impression that socialist feminism was essentially stifled by its enemies on the left.

23 See Anne Lopes and Gary Roth, *Men's Feminism: August Bebel and the German Socialist Movement* (Amherst, N.Y.: Humanity Books, 2000). Hunt, *Equivocal Feminists*, 41–42, notes this assumption in the case of Belfort Bax. As Bacchi notes of the founding of the Canadian Woman Suffrage Association, men played an important role; the association had 46 male and 49 female members in 1883, and an executive of 7 men and 12 women. Included among the suffrage militants was Phillips Thompson. See Bacchi, *Liberation Deferred?* 28.

24 This interpretation challenges the notion that the "traditional male left" had always relegated women's issues to the periphery. Recent European historiography has revealed the extraordinary extent to which the woman question was foundational to socialist politics in many countries. In Germany, Geoff Eley notes, Bebel's *Woman under Socialism* was regarded as "German socialism's founding text," whose "maximum program" for women's rights (legal equality and the suffrage, but also dress reform and emancipated sexuality) was influential for many generations. Geoff Eley, *Forging Democracy: The History of the Left in Europe, 1850–2000* (Oxford: Oxford University Press, 2002), 99–100. Of course, such theoretical centrality rarely translated into actual political power for women in the major socialist parties.

25 See Charles Allen Seager, "A Proletariat in Wild Rose Country: The Alberta Coal Miners, 1905–1945," Ph.D. thesis, York University, Toronto, 1981, 296–97, 324; see also James H. Gray, *Red Lights on the Prairies* (Toronto: Macmillan of Canada, 1971), 177–81.

26 See Enrico Ferri, *Socialism and Modern Science*, trans. Robert Rives La Monte, 3rd. ed. (Chicago: Charles H. Kerr and Company, 1912), 20–22. For a good discussion, see Mark Pittinger, *American Socialists and Evolutionary Thought, 1870–1920*

(Madison: University of Wisconsin Press, 1993), 188–89. Women's waged employment was pronounced, by Italian sociologist Guglielmo Ferrero, "deleterious to society, throwing men out of work, endangering women's health, and lessening their grace." See Cynthia Eagle Russett, *Sexual Science: The Victorian Construction of Womanhood* (Cambridge, Mass. and London, England: Harvard University Press, 1989), 144. For a fascinating introduction to this theme in Canada, see Wendy Mitchinson, *The Nature of Their Bodies: Women and Their Doctors in Victorian Canada* (Toronto: University of Toronto Press, 1991).

27 See Herbert Spencer, *Social Statics; Or, The Conditions Essential to Human Happiness Specified, and the First of Them Developed* (London: John Chapman, 1851 [reprinted London: Routledge and Thoemmes Press, 1986]), 173; John Stuart Mill, *The Subjection of Women*, new ed. (London: Longmans, Green, 1906).

28 Charlotte Perkins Gilman cited in Russett, *Sexual Science*, 151.

29 Kealey, *Enlisting Women for the Cause*, 124. Canadians who did not read the publication directly were often exposed to reprints from it (and its successor *Progressive Woman*) in their local socialist press. See *Cotton's Weekly*, 12 Aug. 1909, 11 March 1909; and *Western Clarion*, 16 Jan. 1909.

30 Lopes and Roth, *Men's Feminism*, 30.

31 Ibid., 33. Bebel became, for example, increasingly more radical on the question of abortion as he worked, according to Lopes and Roth, for "almost half his life" on the various editions, expanding the book to "some three times its original length."

32 Cited in Lopes and Roth, *Men's Feminism*, 38.

33 Lopes and Roth, *Men's Feminism*, 31, 66.

34 Cited in Lopes and Roth, *Men's Feminism*, 71.

35 Varda Burstyn, "Economy, Sexuality, Politics: Engels and the Sexual Division of Labour," *Socialist Studies/ Etudes Socialistes*, 1983, 19–39. As Newton notes, Toronto spc women organized a "Socialist Women's Study Club" in September 1908, which met until the following summer. In order "to understand the position of women in capitalist society and their status in previous stages of development, the group began with Engels's *Origin of the Family, Private Property and the State*, later reading other socialist works. Newton, *Feminist Challenge to the Canadian Left*, 133. Engels's book was also translated into Finnish and published in the Finnish socialist publication *Toivo* in Toronto between 1902 and 1904. Kealey, *Enlisting Women for the Cause*, 133; Varpu Lindström-Best, *Defiant Sisters: A Social History of Finnish Immigrant Women in Canada* (Toronto: Multicultural History Society of Ontario, 1988), 145.

36 See Frederick Engels, *The Origin of the Family, Private Property and the State: In the Light of the Researches by Lewis H. Morgan* (1884), in Karl Marx and Frederick Engels, *Collected Works*, vol. 26 (Moscow: Progress Publishing, 1990), 129–276. Quotations to the *Origin* are to the more readily available 1942 edition, which was the same translation as the one read in the early 20th century: Frederick Engels, *The Origin of the Family, Private Property and the State, in the Light of the Researches of Lewis H. Morgan*, vol. 22, Marxist Library, Works of Marxism-Leninism (New York: International Publishers, 1942 [1884]).

37 Morgan's "rediscovery of the original mother-right *gens* as the stage preliminary to the father-right *gens* of the civilized peoples has the same significance for the history of primitive society as Darwin's theory of evolution has for biology and Marx's theory of surplus value for political economy." Engels, *Origin of the Family, Private Property and the State*, Preface to the Fourth Edition, 16.

38 Engels, *Origin of the Family, Private Property and the State*, 50. Engels was

influenced here by some of the more speculative currents of 19th-century anthropology. For an illuminating discussion of Bachofen et al., see Cynthia Eller, *The Myth of Matriarchal Prehistory: Why an Invented Past Won't Give Women a Future* (Boston: Beacon Press, 2000), 30–35.

39 Juliet Mitchell, *Women's Estate* (New York: Random House, 1971), 80.

40 As Geoff Eley puts it, "The more consistent the socialism, one might even say, the more easily feminist demands were postponed to the socialist future, because a sternly materialist standpoint insisted that none of these questions could be tackled while capitalism perdured." Eley, *Forging Democracy*, 23.

41 For example, looking at an article by George Paton on "Women in Society" in *Western Clarion* in 1912, Newton underlines the conservative nostalgia of Paton's vision: "*The Western Clarion* reiterated that it was capitalism that destroyed the home. The growing trend of women to enter the paid labour force was cited as one means by which it did so: 'Capitalism has torn woman from the home, thrust her into the economic field in competition with the opposite sex, grinds her life into profits and ultimately forces her to sell her body in order to live. Capitalism today is fast destroying the home, the palace, that we are told woman should exclusively occupy as her position in society.' She must 'fight side by side with her proletarian male partner, under the Socialist banner in the modern world for the *restoration of that which she lost* in primitive times, 'liberty and equality'; also for the establishment of the home where peace, happiness and plenty will be the rule" (emphasis added). This argument is essentially nostalgic: "capitalism forced women out of the home; socialism would restore them." But this is a misleading interpretation. The emphasis on the "restoration of that which she lost in primitive times" means not a return to women's confinement to the domestic sphere, but the restoration (in modernized socialist form) of women's ancient equality and power. It meant undoing the (hypothetical and ancient) "world-historic defeat of the female sex." Paton was glossing Engels, not describing an actually remembered past reality. Newton, *Feminist Challenge to the Canadian Left*, 63.

42 Engels, *Origin of the Family, Private Property and the State*, 31, 62–63.

43 See Lise Vogel, *Woman Questions: Essays for a Materialist Feminism* (New York: Routledge, 1995), ch. 5, "Engels's *Origin*: A Defective Formulation," 76. The entire discussion is a path-breaking critique of Engels's work.

44 Engels, *Origin of the Family, Private Property and the State*, 72–73. That the most convincing models for such a "free monogamy" are to be found in the contemporary gay community – a sexual minority ridiculed by Engels – suggests that the Founding Father's economic determinist analysis could not grasp, by a long shot, all that went into the subordination of women by heterosexual men.

45 The concept of the matriarchy has not fared at all well in recent social-science or feminist writing. See Eller, *Myth of Matriarchal Prehistory*. Colin McKay, for one, who never lost his enthusiasm for the "Marx-Morgan synthesis," proclaimed that "Man came to the headship of the family only after bloody battles" in a 1931 article published posthumously in 1940. "Patriarchy – father rule – appeared when property became important enough as a means of power for the males to challenge the rule of the females." Colin McKay, "How Private Property Began," *Advertiser* (Kentville, N.S.), 8 Feb. 1940, 16, adaptation of "The Evolution of Property," *Canadian Unionist*, March 1931, 239–41.

46 See Socialist Party of Canada, *The Evolution of Human Society* (Vancouver: Socialist Party of Canada, 1912); Gerald Desmond, *The Struggle for Existence* (Vancouver: SPC, n.d. [1911]). Revealingly, even in his founding address to the Canadian

Socialist League, Spargo very selectively used Engels's *The Origin* without – remarkably enough – "getting" the point about women themselves having endured a "world-historic" defeat. See John Spargo, *Where We Stand: A Lecture by John Spargo. Originally Delivered under the Title: 'Our Position; Economic, Ethical and Political'* (New York: Comrade Publishing Company, 1902), 6–7.

47 Hunt, *Equivocal Feminists*, 27. For a suggestive and helpful discussion, see Janet Hannam and Karen Hunt, *Socialist Women: Britain, 1880s to 1920s* (London and New York: Routledge, 2002), especially ch. 3, "Constructing the Woman Question," 57–78.

48 Hunt, *Equivocal Feminists*, 25.

49 Olive M. Johnson, *Woman and the Socialist Movement* (New York: New York Labor News, 1908), 3, 37, 34, 36. The book was published under the auspices of the "Socialist Women of Greater New York."

50 John Spargo, *Socialism and Motherhood* (New York: B.W. Hubesch, 1914), *passim*.

51 Galton cited in Angus McLaren, *Our Own Master Race: Eugenics in Canada, 1885–1945* (Toronto: McClelland and Stewart, 1990), 15; Karl Pearson, *National Life from the Standpoint of Science* (London: Adam and Charles Black, 1905), 106. Eugenic arguments suffuse Margaret Sanger's campaign for birth control: see Margaret Sanger, *Woman and New Race* (New York: Truth Publishing, 1920). For an interesting discussion, see Lucy Bland, *Banishing the Beast: Sexuality and the Early Feminists* (New York: New Press, 1995), Part 3, "The Politics of Fertility Control and Sex." With the exception of some borderline cases such as Woodsworth in the Great War period, it appears that Canadian leftists rarely followed this eugenics path. In Canada Woodsworth, then director of the Bureau of Social Research, brought out a series of five articles in 1916 that touched on the problem of "mental defectives." Like many of his contemporaries, Woodsworth worried that such "defectives" were reproducing themselves with abandon, confronting Canada with the prospect of "race suicide." As Allen Mills suggests, these articles represented a shift in Woodsworth's thought away from his earlier social Protestantism to a more secular, "scientific" approach. Allen Mills, *Fool for Christ: The Political Thought of J.S. Woodsworth* (Toronto, Buffalo and London: University of Toronto Press, 1991), 55–56. As McLaren reveals, Tommy Douglas wrote his M.A. thesis on "Christian sociology" with this approach. In this thesis, Douglas argued for the restriction of marriage to those holding certificates of health, segregation of the unfit on state farms where the sexes would be separated, limitation of some subnormal families by doctors' discreet provision of birth-control information, and finally "sterilization of the defective." McLaren, *Our Own Master Race*, 8.

52 Ian McKay, ed., *For a Working-Class Culture in Canada: A Selection of Colin McKay's Writings on Sociology and Political Economy, 1897–1939*, Part IV (St. John's, Nfld.: Canadian Committee on Labour History, 1996), 41.

53 Alice A. Chown, *The Stairway*, ed. and with an Introduction by Diana Chown (Toronto: University of Toronto Press, 1988), 5. Of course, this is put in the mouth of a semi-fictional character, but the character's life so closely parallels Chown's own that it is difficult not to conclude that she was writing autobiographically.

54 Ruth Frager, *Sweatshop Strife: Class, Ethnicity, and Gender in the Jewish Labour Movement of Toronto 1900–1939* (Toronto: University of Toronto Press, 1992), 127.

55 Cited in Frager, *Sweatshop Strife*, 139.

56 Ibid.

57 Diana Chown, "Introduction" to Chown, *Stairway*, xxxix, xl.

58 Diana Chown, "Introduction" to Chown, *Stairway*, xxxii, ix; Chown, *Stairway*, 89.

59 Chown, *Stairway*, 61, 79.

60 Even his fan Ernest Crosby, who acclaimed him as a "poet and prophet," wrote of his poems celebrating Greek love, "He has manfully grappled with the problem and he deserves our thanks for his courage and frankness, but I do not believe that much is to be expected from close friendships of a romantic nature between persons of the same sex." Ernest Crosby, *Edward Carpenter: Poet and Prophet* (London: Arthur C. Fifield, 1905), 46. For important work on Edward Carpenter, see Tony Brown, ed., *Edward Carpenter and Late Victorian Radicalism* (London: Frank Cass, 1990); Chushichi Tsuzuki, *Edward Carpenter 1844–1929: Prophet of Human Fellowship* (Cambridge: Cambridge University Press, 1980); and, of particular interest with regard to Carpenter's religious viewpoint, Antony Copley, *A Spiritual Bloomsbury: Hinduism and Homosexuality in the Lives and Writing of Edward Carpenter, E.M. Forster, and Christopher Isherwood* (Lantham, Md.: Lexington Books, 2006); Sheila Rowbotham, "Edward Carpenter: Prophet of the New Life," in Sheila Rowbotham and Jeffrey Weeks, *Socialism and the New Life: The Personal and Sexual Politics of Edward Carpenter and Havelock Ellis* (London: Pluto Press, 1977); and, for an important collection of his writings on sex, see Noel Greig, ed., *Edward Carpenter: Selected Writings*, vol. 1, *Sex* (London: GMP Publishers, 1984).

61 Chown, *Stairway*, 51.

62 Ibid., 273.

63 Ibid., 270.

64 For example, in elections in January 1899, it ran Marie Westland for School Trustee in Ward 6 in London, Ont. See Socialist Labor Party, *The People Library* 1, 3 (New York, 1899), 47. Here one finds it difficult fully to agree with Wayne Roberts, who argues that the SPC was the first in Canada to grant women full membership rights. See Wayne Roberts, " 'Rocking the Cradle for the World': The New Woman and Maternal Feminism, Toronto 1877–1914," in *A Not Unreasonable Claim: Women and Reform in Canada 1880s–1920s*, ed. Linda Kealey (Toronto: Women's Press, 1979), 43.

65 *Cotton's Weekly*, 2 Dec. 1909; M. Wisdom, "Women's Rights," *Cotton's Weekly*, 1 April 1909.

66 SDPC cited in Roberts, " 'Rocking the Cradle for the World,' " 44; Colin McKay in McKay, ed., *For a Working-Class Culture in Canada*, 42.

67 As in the case of James Simpson: see Homel, "James Simpson and the Origins of Canadian Social Democracy," 624.

68 Anthony Mardiros, *William Irvine: The Life of a Prairie Radical* (Toronto: James Lorimer, 1979), 24; McKay, ed., *For a Working-Class Culture in Canada*, 192.

69 Eley, for example, underlines the extent to which the European left tended to fudge on the central issue of the suffrage, both marginalizing women when it chose the electoral route because "voteless female workers didn't matter" and deriding as a "bourgeois" diversion struggles for women's political rights. Eley, *Forging Democracy*, 103.

70 For an illuminating account of Beynon, see Ramsay Cook, "Francis Marion Beynon and the Crisis of Christian Reformism," in *The West and the Nation: Essays in Honour of W.L. Morton*, ed. Carl Berger and Ramsay Cook (Toronto: McClelland and Stewart, 1976), 187–208.

71 Francis Marion Beynon, "The Country Home," *Grain Growers' Guide*, 12 June 1912, 9.

72 Francis Marion Beynon, "The Woman's Page of Yesterday, Today and Tomorrow," *Grain Growers' Guide*, 25 Dec. 1912, 10.

73 Francis Marion Beynon, "'We Don't Believe in Women,'" *Grain Growers' Guide*, 18 Nov. 1912, 10.

74 "A Northwest Woman," "A Tight-Wad's Wife," letter to *Grain Growers' Guide*, 18 Nov. 1912; see also "A North-West Woman," "A North-West Woman in Self-Defence," *Grain Growers' Guide*, 15 Jan. 1913, 10.

75 "A True Friend of Unhappy Wives," "A Man Who Is a Disgrace to the Name," letter, *Grain Growers' Guide*, 18 Nov. 1912.

76 "A SUFFERER," "Wives Unpaid Servants," *Grain Growers' Guide*, 27 Nov. 1912, 10. For more commentary on the issue, see Rose Turrell, of Dauphin, Man., "Answers Paul Emphatically," letter to *Grain Growers' Guide*, 18 Dec. 1912; "Contented," "Not a Tight Wad's Wife," *Grain Growers' Guide*, 25 Dec. 1912.

77 "Mother of Three," "A Woman's Hopeless Position," *Grain Growers' Guide*, 8 Jan. 1913, 10.

78 "A North-West Woman," "A North-West Woman in Self-Defence," *Grain Growers' Guide*, 15 Jan. 1913, 10.

79 "Mothers of the Race," editorial, *Grain Growers' Guide*, 2 April 1913.

80 "A Prairie Wife," *Grain Growers' Guide*, 16 Oct. 1912 [reprinting Ottawa *Citizen*].

81 Francis Marion Beynon, "The Country Homemakers," *Grain Growers' Guide*, 26 June 1912, 13.

82 Francis Marion Beynon, "Is There Injustice to Women in This?" *Grain Growers' Guide*, 7 May 1913.

83 Francis Marion Beynon, "'We Don't Believe in Women,'" *Grain Growers' Guide*, 18 Nov. 1912.

84 Francis Marion Beynon, "The New Man," *Grain Growers' Guide*, 14 Aug. 1912, 9.

85 Francis Marion Beynon, "'We Don't Believe in Women,'" *Grain Growers' Guide*, 18 Nov. 1912, 10; "For Debaters on Woman Suffrage," *Grain Growers' Guide*, 24 Dec. 1913; and "The Woman's Movement," *Grain Growers' Guide*, 10 July 1912, 9.

86 Francis Marion Beynon, "The Woman's Movement," *Grain Growers' Guide*, 10 July 1912, 9, 17 July 1912, 9.

87 Francis Marion Beynon, "The Woman's Movement," *Grain Growers' Guide*, 17 July 1912, 9. On the other hand, she viewed with some misgivings the entry of men into occupations, such as domestic science, traditionally associated with women. Citing Schreiner, she noted the discrepancy between women's seeming indifference as "one of the old traditions of our race comes toppling about our ears" and men's outrage that had greeted women when they dared to breach the walls of male-dominated professions. Francis Marion Beynon, "Men Invading Woman's Sphere," *Grain Growers' Guide*, 20 Aug. 1913.

88 Francis Marion Beynon, "The Country Home," *Grain Growers' Guide*, 12 June 1912; *Grain Growers' Guide*, 25 Dec. 1912.

89 Francis Marion Beynon, "'We Don't Believe in Women,'" *Grain Growers' Guide*, 18 Nov. 1912, 10; Francis Marion Beynon, "The Poor Wives of the Well-to-Do," *Grain Growers' Guide*, 9 Oct. 1912; "A Northwest Woman," "A Tight-Wad's Wife," letter to *Grain Growers' Guide*, 18 Nov. 1912 (response of Beynon); "A True Friend of Unhappy Wives," "A Man Who Is a Disgrace to the Name," letter, *Grain Growers' Guide*, 18 Nov. 1912.

90 Francis Marion Beynon, "The Poor Wives of the Well-to-Do," *Grain Growers' Guide*, 9 Oct. 1912.

91 Ibid.

92 Francis Marion Beynon, "Effective Household Economy," *Grain Growers' Guide*, 12 June 1912; Francis Marion Beynon, "Hundreds Want Booklet," *Grain Growers' Guide*, 18 Sept. 1912. As she explained some months later, "Housekeeping has been discovered to be a science and the proper sanitary care of our homes and children, the intelligent up-bringing of the growing generation, the woman's right to take up land and to have a voice in the affairs of the nation have crept into the woman's page and crowded the beauty notes nearly out of existence." Francis Marion Beynon, "The Woman's Page of Yesterday, Today and Tomorrow," *Grain Growers' Guide*, 25 Dec. 1912, 10.

93 Mrs. Lawrence Doran, Ponoka, Alta., "Women Lagging Behind," *Grain Growers' Guide*, 11 Dec. 1912 (comment of Beynon).

94 Francis Marion Beynon, "Harking Back to those Women's Clubs," *Grain Growers' Guide*, 24 July 1912.

95 "Just Seventeen," "The Man's Side of the Problem," *Grain Growers' Guide*, 11 Dec. 1912, 10; "Mothers of the Race," editorial, *Grain Growers' Guide*, 2 April 1913.

96 Francis Marion Beynon, "Woman and War," *Grain Growers' Guide*, 31 July 1912, 9.

97 J.M.C., Rocanville, Sask., "Favors Militarism," letter to *Grain Growers' Guide*, 7 Aug. 1912, 11.

98 It would be interesting to explore the possibility that Beynon was influenced in her narrative by the actual death of Gertrude Richardson's father, thought by his family to have been indirectly caused by mob violence at the time of the Boer War.

99 Olive Schreiner, *Woman and Labour* (London: T. Fisher Unwin, 1912), 158: "The fact is, that modern fiction being merely a description of human life in any of its phases, and being the only art that can be exercised without special training or special appliances, and produced in the moments stolen from the multifarious, brain-destroying occupations which fill the average woman's life, they have been driven to find this outlet for their powers as the only one presenting itself. How far otherwise might have been the directions in which their genius would naturally have expressed itself can be known only partially even to the women themselves."

100 Francis Marion Beynon, *Aleta Dey* (London: Virago Press, 1988 [1919]), 48, 13.

101 Beynon, *Aleta Dey*, 248. Beynon was perhaps making a deft reference to the anti-authoritarian traditions of the Freemasons. See Albert Pike, *Morals and Dogma of the Ancient and Accepted Scottish Rite of Freemasonry, prepared for the Supreme Council of the Thirty Third Degree for the Southern Jurisdiction of the United States* (Charleston, 1871), where this phrase immediately follows on from the observation: "The foulness of the slaves is a direct result of the atrocious baseness of the despot."

102 Beynon, *Aleta Dey*, 92.

103 Ibid., 161.

104 Yet when *Aleta Dey* was revived in the 1980s, its advocates presented it as a *critique* of socialism. Editor Anne Hicks remarks that "the political socialism represented by the fictional American lawyer, Ned Grant, was slick and over-confident" (xiv – xv). She misidentifies one of the novel's key characters.

105 Beynon, *Aleta Dey*, 192.

106 Ibid., 172.

107 Barbara Roberts, '*Why Do Women Do Nothing to End the War?*' *Canadian Feminist-Pacifists and the Great War* (Ottawa: Canadian Research Institute for the Advancement of Women, CRIAW Papers, 1985), 13, citing the *Grain Grower's Guide*, 10 Jan. 1917.

108 Beynon, *Aleta Dey*, 217.

109 At least one of the more *outré* charges of sedition to arise from the massive revolt in Winnipeg 1919 stemmed from the direct quotation of this biblical authority.

110 H.G. Wells, *Socialism and the Family* (London: A.C. Fifield, 1906), 58: "Motherhood . . . is regarded by the Socialists as a benefit to society, a public duty done." For Wells it was a "monstrous absurdity" that women should have to earn their living in waged employment while also "bearing and rearing children in their spare time" (59).

111 Grant Allen, *The Woman Who Did* (Boston: Roberts Bros., 1895). Wells, *Socialism and the Family* (especially 48), targeted Allen as a romantic apostle of free love. For an earlier statement linking socialism to the defence of marriage as an institution, see Karl Heinzen, *The Rights of Women and the Sexual Relations*, trans. Emma Heller Schumm (Chicago: Charles H. Kerr, 1891). For *fin de siècle* sex radicals, see Joanne E. Passet, *Sex Radicals and the Quest for Women's Equality* (Urbana and Chicago: University of Illinois Press, 2003); Hal D. Sears, *The Sex Radicals: Free Love in High Victorian America* (Lawrence: The Regents Press of Kansas, 1977); Taylor Stoehr, ed., *Free Love in America: A Documentary History* (New York: AMS Press, 1979).

112 O.D. Skelton, *Socialism: A Critical Analysis* (Boston and New York: Houghton Mifflin Company, 1911), 216 (emphasis added).

113 John Spargo, *The Spiritual Significance of Modern Socialism* (New York: B.W. Huebsch, 1911), 64; N.M.T., "Socialism Would Destroy The Home," *Western Clarion*, 7 Aug. 1909, 1.

114 Socialist Party of Canada, Lindsay, Ont., Local, *Gems of Socialism* (n.p. [Lindsay], n.d. [1916]); Newton, *Feminist Challenge to the Canadian Left*, citing the *Clarion*, 114, 115.

115 The racial and gender politics of the panic have been nicely dissected by Mariana Valverde, " 'When the Mother of the Race Is Free': Race, Reproduction, and Sexuality in First-Wave Feminism," in *Gender Conflicts: New Essays in Women's History*, ed. Franca Iacovetta and Mariana Valverde (Toronto: University of Toronto Press, 1992), 3–25. For an excellent study of *fin de siècle* feminists' appropriation of evolutionary theory and the ways in which they constructed men as the "primitive Other" against which feminists were forces of civilization, see Bland, *Banishing the Beast*.

116 August Bebel, *Woman under Socialism*, trans. Daniel De Leon (New York: New York Labor News Company, 1917), 146; Engels, *Origin of the Family, Private Property and the State*, 66. Grant Allen thought much the same way: because of the absurd rules regarding sex and marriage, men were unrealistically compelled to choose between an unhealthy and unnatural celibate lifestyle or the brothel.

117 Charlotte Perkins Gilman, *Women and Economics: A Study of the Economic Relation between Men and Women as a Factor in Social Evolution* (Berkeley: University of California Press, 1998 [1898]), 5.

118 Charlotte Perkins Gilman, *Moving the Mountain* (New York: Charlton Co., 1911), 254.

119 Schreiner, *Woman and Labour*, 82–83n, 240.

120 Bland, *Banishing the Beast*, xiii. Newton notes the motif of men as "beasts or reptiles" in the commentary of Mary Cotton Wisdom, which she implicitly endorses. See Newton, *Feminist Challenge to the Canadian Left*, 130. See also Morrison Davidson, "Socialism And Sex," *Western Clarion*, 14 Dec. 1907, 4. The British radical drew a parallel between prostitutes and blacklegs who worked below the standard rate of wages.

121 Arthur Bullard, "The Only Possibilism," *Western Clarion*, 16 April 1910, 3.

122 Amy Campbell Johnston, "White Slavery," *British Columbia (B.C.) Federationist*, 12 Dec. 1913.

123 *B.C. Federationist*, 6 March 1914. This was an echo of a position developed by Frances Swiney, for whom see Sheila Jeffreys, *The Spinster and Her Enemies* (London: Pandora, 1985). Swiney was read extensively in British Columbia in this period.

124 Newton, *Feminist Challenge to the Canadian Left*, 128.

125 Estelle Baker, *The Rose Door* (Chicago: Charles H. Kerr, 1911), 192.

126 For an invaluable collection on the left and gay sexuality from Marx's day to the late 20th century, see Gert Hekma, Harry Oosterhuis, and James Steakley, eds., *Gay Men and the Sexual History of the Political Left* (New York and London: Haworth Press, 1995).

127 J. Donald Wilson, "'Never Believe What You Have Never Doubted": Matti Kurikka's Dream for a New World Utopia," in *Finnish Diaspora*, vol. 1, ed. Michael G. Karm (Toronto: 1981), 143–44.

128 Edward Bellamy, *Looking Backward 2000–1887* (New York: Bantam, 1983 [1888]), 149.

129 Bebel, *Woman under Socialism*, 164–65. For a fascinating later development in Germany, building in part upon Bebel's work, and upon the sexology of Magnus Hirschfield, see Lillian Faderman and Brigitte Eriksson, trans. and eds., *Lesbian-Feminism in Turn-of-the-Century Germany: Stories and Autobiographies* (Weatherby Lake, Mo.: Naiad Press, 1980).

130 Eleanor Marx and Edward Aveling, *The Woman Question* (1886), reprinted in Marie Muvley Roberts and Tamae Mizuta, eds., *The Reformers: Socialist Feminism* (London: Routledge/ Thoemmes Press, 1995), 18.

131 See William Greenslade and Terence Rodgers, eds., *Grant Allen: Literature and Cultural Politics at the Fin de Siècle* (Aldershot, Hants.: Ashgate, 2005), 11; and Grant Allen, *The Story of the Plants, with Illustrations* (London: George Newnes, 1895), 90–91, as cited in Greenslade and Rodgers, eds., *Grant Allen*, 20, n.60.

132 Gilman, *Women and Economics*, 31, 142–43; Gilman, *Moving the Mountain*, 111.

133 Schreiner, *Woman and Labour*, 85–87. It was perhaps fortunate for Schreiner's peace of mind that she did not know more about the personal life of Alexander the Great.

134 Ibid., 243, 241–42, 75–76n, 107–108.

135 In Curry's Schreineresque synopsis of the history of Rome, "degenerate rulers" had failed to meet the challenge of the "virile barbarian invaders." In the 20th century, the stereotypically bloated and unmanly capitalist class, "decadent through luxury and idleness," might not fully understand the revolution portended by the coming of workers and commodities from Asia. See W.J. Curry, "The Asiatic Invasion: Its Cause and Outcome," *Western Clarion*, 12 Dec. 1908, 4.

136 Cited in Russell Hann, "Brainworkers and the Knights of Labor," in *Essays in Canadian Working Class History*, ed. Gregory S. Kealey and Peter Warrian (Toronto: McClelland and Stewart, 1976), 55.

137 Spargo, *Where We Stand*, 9–10; C.W. Springford, "As to Dawson," letter to *Western Clarion*, 6 Aug. 1910, 3.

138 Colin McKay, "The Mate from Maine," in *Windjammers and Bluenose Sailors: Stories of the Sea by Colin McKay*, comp. Lewis Jackson and Ian McKay (Lockeport, N.S.: Roseway Publishing, 1993), 119–130.

139 "Trusteeship Candidates," *Western Clarion*, 6 Jan. 1906, 4.

140 "Socialism – Socialists," *Western Clarion*, 6 Jan. 1906, 4; "Manitoba Provincial Executive," *Western Clarion*, 17 April 1909, 3; Wilfrid Gribble, "Revolution!" *Cotton's Weekly*, 14 Dec. 1907, 1; Curry, "Asiatic Invasion," 4; "The Break of Dawn," *Cotton's Weekly*, 5 Aug. 1909.

141 Alf Budden, *The Slave of the Farm: Being Letters from Alf. Budden to a Fellow Farm Slave and Comrade in Revolt* (Vancouver: Socialist Party of Canada, Dominion Executive Committee, 1914), 28; *Western Clarion*, 6 Jan. 1906, 2.

142 See Martin Henry Blatt, *Free Love and Anarchism: The Biography of Ezra Heywood* (Urbana and Chicago: University of Illinois Press, 1989); and Sheila Rowbotham, *A New World for Women: Stella Browne – Socialist Feminist* (London: Pluto Press, 1977). In this period Emma Goldman was one of the most renowned apostles of enlightened sexuality; see Candace Falk, *Love, Anarchy and Emma Goldman* (New York: Holt Rinehart, 1984).

143 See Kevin Wilson, *Practical Dreamers: Communitarianism and Co-operatives on Malcolm Island* (Victoria: British Columbia Institute for Co-operative Studies, 2005), 32; Wilson, " 'Never Believe What You Have Never Doubted,' " 142, 143.

144 See Angus McLaren, "Sex Radicalism in the Canadian Pacific Northwest, 1890–1920," *Journal of the History of Sexuality* 2, 4 (1992), 527–46. For Forster Kerr (and her publisher) "Lucifer" – probably meaning not the rebellious archangel who was held to be the same as Satan, but the planet Venus appearing before sunrise as the morning star – was the symbol of the early stage of a sexual enlightenment.

145 Dora Forster, *Sex Radicalism as Seen by an Emancipated Woman of the New Time* (Chicago: M. Harman, 1905), 28, 26, 20, 8, 26–27, 46–47, 51 (the last coming from R.B. Kerr, "Darwin, Weismann and Harman," printed as an addendum to the pamphlet). Forster would subsequently develop a Gilmanite critique of women's economic dependence in *Cotton's Weekly* in 1909, as noted by Kealey, *Enlisting Women for the Cause*, 107.

146 Cited in Kealey, *Enlisting Women for the Cause*, 103.

147 Lindström-Best, *Defiant Sisters*, 149, 71, 72–74, 75.

148 Theresa Moritz and Albert Moritz, *The World's Most Dangerous Woman: A New Biography of Emma Goldman* (Vancouver: Subway Books, 2001), 17.

149 C. Gasquoine Hartley, *Woman's Wild Oats: Essays on the Refixing of Moral Standards* (London: T. Werner Laurie, 1919), 69, 209, 229.

150 See "Debating Sexuality in Halifax, 1920: Mrs. Donald Shaw and Others," in *The Challenge of Modernity: A Reader on Post-Confederation Canada*, ed. Ian McKay (Toronto: McGraw-Hill Ryerson, 1992), 336, 339; see also *Herald* (Halifax), 5 April 1920.

151 The *Western Clarion* also opened its advertising columns to "The People's Bookstore," which offered customers a wide range of books on "Science and Marriage." *Western Clarion*, 23 Jan. 1910, 4.

152 Bebel, *Woman under Socialism*, 343–44.

153 "Partridge of Sintaluta" [E.A. Partridge], *A War on Poverty: The One War That Can End War* (Winnipeg: Wallingford Press, n.d. [1926], 148–49.

154 Grant Allen, "The New Hedonism," *Fortnightly Review* 61, 55 (March 1894), 377–92.

155 An indication of how this change affected the woman question might be gleaned from the declining place of "objectivizing" physical descriptions of women in socialist literature. In the 1890s Charles H. Kerr could still publish Karl Heinzen's *Rights of Women*, with such passages as: "I have had opportunity to make

manifold observations among both sexes of the most diverse nations. The most beautiful women – in order to speak of these – I have found in America and England, at least in so far as concerns color and contour of face" (145). It was "undeniable," according to Heinzen, "that woman is inferior to man in the vigor and logic of her thought as well as of her will" (135).

156 This and a number of the following examples come from Kealey, *Enlisting Women for the Cause.*

157 Roberts, " 'Rocking the Cradle for the World,' " 43, 44.

158 Linda Kealey, *Enlisting Women for the Cause,* 127.

159 Roberts, " 'Rocking the Cradle for the World,' " 43.

160 Kealey, *Enlisting Women for the Cause,* 135.

161 Roberts, " 'Rocking the Cradle for the World,' " 44.

162 Newton, *Feminist Challenge to the Canadian Left,* 37.

163 The story of the women of the Finnish-Canadian left has been brilliantly told by Lindström-Best, *Defiant Sisters.*

164 Lindström-Best, *Defiant Sisters,* 140–47.

165 Frager, *Sweatshop Strife,* 101.

166 Mercedes Steedman, *Angels of the Workplace: Women and the Construction of Gender Relations in the Canadian Clothing Industry, 1890–1940* (Toronto: Oxford University Press, 1997), 81, 83.

167 Frager, *Sweatshop Strife,* 120–30.

168 Her story has been interestingly recorded by Irene Howard, *The Struggle for Social Justice in British Columbia: Helena Gutteridge, the Unknown Reformer* (Vancouver: UBC Press, 1992), and this description relies heavily on that biography and on the back files of the *B.C. Federationist.*

169 See Howard, *Struggle for Social Justice in British Columbia.* Howard notes that Gutteridge had a photograph of one of the Pankhursts hung on a wall of her home even into her old age (62).

170 Howard, *Struggle for Social Justice in British Columbia,* 75.

171 [Helena Gutteridge], "How I Became a Socialist" [review of Helen Keller], *B.C. Federationist,* 14 Nov. 1913.

172 M.G., "The New Idea," *B.C. Federationist,* 12 Dec. 1913.

173 Howard, *Struggle for Social Justice in British Columbia,* 76

174 B.M. Burns, "Women and Socialism," *B.C. Federationist,* 31 Oct. 1913.

175 Ibid.

176 Anonymous [Helena Gutteridge], "Commonsense and Vice," *B.C. Federationist,* 31 Oct. 1913.

177 H.G. [Helena Gutteridge], "Woman's Work," *B.C. Federationist,* 16 Jan. 1914.

178 Amy Campbell Johnston, "Woman's Independence," *B.C. Federationist,* 16 Jan. 1914.

179 Ida Douglas Fearn, "Food for Thought," *B.C. Federationist,* 23 Jan. 1914; Mrs. Ernest Lloyd, "Progress," *B.C. Federationist,* 23 Jan. 1914. For M. Spillman, the connections between disenfranchisement and degeneration were obvious. More educated women had more intelligent, brighter, and quicker children. This inheritance of acquired characteristics could be observed in the United States, where freer and better-educated women produced "more virile, more go-ahead" men. M. Spillman, "Why Women Should Vote," *B.C Federationist,* 30 Jan. 1914.

180 H.G. [Helena Gutteridge], "Mothers, Children and Deserted Wives," *B.C. Federationist,* 30 Oct. 1914.

181 Howard, *Struggle for Social Justice in British Columbia,* 68.

182 *B.C. Federationist*, 7 Nov. 1913.

183 H.G. [Helena Gutteridge], "Miners' Wives Keen Suffragists," *B.C. Federationist*, 14 Nov. 1913.

184 J.D.F., "Slums," *B.C. Federationist*, 20 Feb. 1914.

185 H.G. [Helena Gutteridge], "Mothers, Children and Deserted Wives," *B.C. Federationist*, 30 Oct. 1914.

186 *B.C. Federationist*, 27 Nov. 1914.

187 This description builds on a useful definition developed by Frager, who restricts the term "feminism" to the "explicit conviction that women have been (and still are) fundamentally subordinated to men, combined with an explicit commitment to oppose this subordination." Frager, *Sweatshop Strife*, 5.

188 Kealey, *Enlisting Women for the Cause*, 8. Drawing what to my eye looks like far too sharp a line between the "scientific socialism" of the SPC and the supposed reformism of the SDPC, Kealey argues that the scientism of the first, especially its reliance on biology, worked against the socialist feminists, because it allowed the orthodox Marxists to argue that sex differences were beyond the remit of historical materialism (256).

189 Kealey, *Enlisting Women for the Cause*, 118.

6: The Race Question

1 *Province* (Vancouver), 21 July 1914.

2 In addition to contemporary newspaper sources, details about the vessel are drawn from Hugh Johnston, *The Voyage of the Komagata Maru: The Sikh Challenge to Canada's Colour Bar* (Delhi: Oxford University Press, 1979); Robie L. Reid, "The Inside Story of the 'Komagata Maru,'" *British Columbia Historical Quarterly* 5, 1 (1941), 1–23; Rajini Srikanth, "The *Komagata Maru*: Memory and Mobilization among the South Asian Diaspora in North America," in *Re/collecting Early Asian America*, ed. Josephine Lee, Imogene L. Lim, and Yoko Matsukawa (Philadelphia: Temple University Press, 2002), 78–91; W. Peter Ward, *White Canada Forever: Popular Attitudes and Public Policy Toward Orientals in British Columbia*, 3rd ed. (Montreal and Kingston: McGill-Queen's University Press, 2002); Eric W. Morse, "Some Aspects of the Komagata Maru Affair, 1914," Canadian Historical Association, *Historical Papers* (1936), 100–8; and Eric Wilton Morse, "Immigration and Status of British East Indians in Canada: A Problem in Imperial Relations," unpublished M.A. thesis, Queen's University, Kingston, 1936, 72–75. Morse's thesis, although rather roughly presented (and often overlooked in writings on the incident), is an unusual document in that it received a close reading from many of the principal actors, including Robert Borden and Mackenzie King, and is partly based on difficult to obtain confidential files; Reid's article is in essence a defence of the local Immigration officials, of whom he was one, and a rebuttal to Morse's charge that they mishandled the situation. For the story of the *Komagata Maru*, see also the film *Continuous Journey*, produced and directed by Ali Kazimi (Canada, 2004).

3 *Times* (Victoria), 23 May 1914.

4 Franca Iacovetta, Michael Quinlan, and Ian Radforth, "Immigration and Labour: Australia and Canada Compared," *Labour/Le Travail* 38 (Fall 1996), 96.

5 *B.C. Federationist*, 10 April 1914.

6 *Sun* (Vancouver), 22 June 1914.

7 *Sun*, 23 June 1914; *B.C. Federationist*, 26 June 1914; *News Advertiser* (Vancouver), 24 June 1914. On the same night in New Westminster, labour men endorsed a mass anti-Hindu meeting, which one alderman broadened to include a demand

for the removal of all the "Asiatics" who were supposedly capturing many local industries and driving out the local merchants. *Sun*, 25 June 1914.

8 *Sun*, 23 June 1914.

9 *B.C. Federationist*, 5 June 1914.

10 *Province*, 22 June 1914.

11 In addition there was a 1908 agreement by the Canadian Pacific Steamship Co. not to sell tickets to East Indians who could not be admitted into Canada.

12 Reid, "Inside Story of the Komagata Maru," 10.

13 Morse, "Immigration and Status of British East Indians in Canada," 90; Morse, "Some Aspects of the Komagata Maru Affair," 103.

14 Srikanth, "*Komagata Maru*," 85.

15 For an excellent analysis, see Uday Singh Mehta, *Liberalism and Empire: A Study in Nineteenth-Century British Liberal Thought* (Chicago and London: University of Chicago Press, 1999).

16 For general context, see C.A. Bayly, *Indian Society and the Making of the British Empire* (Cambridge: Cambridge University Press, 1988); Judith M. Brown, *Modern India: The Origins of an Asian Democracy*, 2nd. ed. (Oxford: Oxford University Press, 1994); for the emergence of radicalism, see Arun Coomer Bose, *Indian Revolutionaries Abroad, 1905–1922* (Patna: Bharati Bhawan, 1971); James Campbell Ker, *Political Trouble in India, 1907–1917* (Delhi: Oriental Publishers, 1973) – a documentary collection of confidential intelligence reports that contains fascinating Canadian materials.

17 Sohan Singh Josh, *Tragedy of Komagata Maru* (New Delhi: People's Publishing House, 1975), 10.

18 See Carl Berger, *The Sense of Power: Studies in the Ideas of Canadian Imperialism 1867–1914* (Toronto: University of Toronto Press, 1970). For more recent reflections on Canada's identity within the Empire, see Phillip Buckner and R. Douglas Francis, eds., *Canada and the British World: Culture, Migration, and Identity* (Vancouver: UBC Press, 2006).

19 *Sun*, 23 May 1914.

20 Ward, *White Canada Forever*, 84, 90.

21 *Province*, 11 June 1914, 4 June 1914.

22 D.M.C. Farr, ed., *Life and Letters of Sir Wilfrid Laurier*, vol. 2 (Toronto: McClelland and Stewart, 1965), 352.

23 On 9 June 1914 the owners cabled Captain Yamamoto to leave the next day, unless the $15,000 still owing for the charter and other items were paid. *Province*, 10 June 1914.

24 Andrew Parnaby and Gregory S. Kealey, "The Origins of Political Policing in Canada: Class, Law, and the Burden of Empire," *Osgoode Hall Law Journal* 41, 2/3 (Fall/Summer 2003), 211–39.

25 Srikanth, "*Komagata Maru*," 86

26 *Sun*, 23 May 1914.

27 Srikanth, "*Komagata Maru*," 84. As Srikanth suggests, the telegram from the governor of Hong Kong was apparently overlooked, an error that the Canadians came to regret during the two months that the ship was anchored in Vancouver Harbour. This would certainly fit within an overall pattern of disarray and confusion within the ruling regime on the question.

28 *Province*, 23 July 1914, 4 June 1914, 15 July 1914; *B.C. Federationist*, 15 May 1914; Bourassa quoted in Morse, "Immigration and Status of British East Asians in Canada," 41.

29 *Province*, 24 June 1914; Morse, "Immigration and Status of British East Asians in Canada," 26.

30 "Race," though it appears throughout this chapter, is a highly problematic term, used in perplexingly incongruous and contradictory ways by contemporaries. Although it would be wearisome to place it in quotation marks or italics throughout to indicate my analytical distance from this contemporary usage, readers should be aware that it is never being used as though it neutrally described an underlying biological pattern or represented a reputable scientific theory.

31 Patricia E. Roy, *The Oriental Question: Consolidating a White Man's Province, 1914–41* (Vancouver: UBC Press, 2003).

32 Kipling cited in Ninette Kelley and Michael Trebilcock, *The Making of the Mosaic: A History of Canadian Immigration Policy* (Toronto: University of Toronto Press, 1998), 123. See also Sean Mills, "The Empire Within: Montreal, the Sixties, and the Forging of a Radical Imagination," Ph.D. thesis, Queen's University, Kingston, 2007, ch. 3.

33 For factual background on South Asian immigration, see in addition to the sources on the *Komagata Maru*, Paramjit S. Judge, *Punjabis in Canada: A Study of Formation of an Ethnic Community* (Delhi: Chankya Publications, 1994).

34 "It seems to me . . ." in Ward, *White Canada Forever*, 84; Srikanth, "*Komagata Maru*," 83.

35 See Colin Kidd, *The Forging of Races: Race and Scripture in the Protestant Atlantic World, 1600–2000* (Cambridge: Cambridge University Press, 2006), 10. According to Kidd, "Subcontinentals from India were classed as 'Hindu' in three [U.S.] censuses between 1920 and 1940, in the following three counts as White, and from 1980 as 'Asian' " (10). The category "Hindu" is thus a prime example of the fluidity and scientific emptiness of racial categories. Morse, "Immigration and Status of British East Indians in Canada," 4, n5, argues that the term "Hindu" had a peculiar convenience in Canada, to refer to "a native of Hindustan." Yet, revealingly, those of British origin born in India, although "natives of Hindustan" in one sense, were not, legally or culturally, "Hindus."

36 Woodsworth, *Strangers Within Our Gates* (Toronto: University of Toronto Press, 1972 [1909]), 154. Writing in 1936, and from a perspective by no means hostile to the officials bent on excluding the South Asians, Morse skilfully skewered the climatic argument. Sikhs, he recalled, were famous throughout the British Empire for their exploits on behalf of its rulers – they had been among its hardiest soldiers, campaigning in such places as Afghanistan, Tibet, and (later) the trenches of Flanders. By the mid-1930s, many such Sikhs had survived 25 B.C. winters without seeming to be much the worse for it. Morse, "Immigration and Status of British East Indians in Canada," 5. Governor General Lord Grey conceded the point. After studying comments from a Vancouver doctor familiar with the adaptation of an earlier immigration of Sikhs to local conditions, he wrote that it would be "impossible in future to urge climatic considerations as a reason for discouraging on humanitarian grounds, the emigration of Sikhs to British Columbia.' " Morse, "Immigration and Status of British East Indians in Canada," 28. Of course the "climate argument" – that non-Whites could not easily adapt to northern climates – was on its face inherently illogical. Non-White Aboriginal peoples had lived in the Arctic for hundreds of years.

37 Robert J.C. Young, *Colonial Desire: Hybridity in Theory, Culture and Race* (London and New York: Routledge, 1995), 94.

38 *Province*, 6 July 1914.

39 See Zygmunt Bauman, *Liquid Modernity* (London: Polity Press, 2000). Bauman uses "liquid modernity" as a term to describe a phase of modernity in which nothing keeps its shape, and social relationships and institutions are changing at such a pace that the very experience of being a human being has profoundly changed. He uses it, in short, to describe the 21st-century world. By using the term here, I am suggesting that Canadians in 1914 already perceived a threatening "liquefaction" of their societies, to which they responded by imagining ever more solid, essentialized, and anti-modern identities.

40 Morse, "Immigration and Status of British East Indians in Canada," 20–21, citing S.N.B. Singh, "Canada's New Immigrant," in *Canadian Magazine* 28 (1907), 387; *London Times*, 19 March 1908; J.B. Williams, "Canada's New Immigrant," in *Canadian Magazine* 28 (1907), 384.

41 *Sun*, 14 May 1914, 23 May 1914, 23 May 1914; *Province*, 21 July 1914.

42 Pollogue Pogue, "The Canned Hindus," *Sun*, 18 June 1914; *Province*, 25 June 1914, 18 July 1914.

43 Pollough Pogue, "From India's Coral Strand," *Sun*, 19 June 1914; *Colonist* cited in Ward, *White Canada Forever*, 83–84.

44 Cited in Kelley and Trebilcock, *Making of the Mosaic*, 147.

45 See Jennifer Marotta, "A Moral Messenger to the Canadian Middlemost: A Reading of *The Family Herald and Weekly Star*, 1874–1914," Ph.D. thesis, Queen's University, Kingston, 2006.

46 Michael Banton, "Historical and Contemporary Modes of Racialization, "in *Racialization: Studies in Theory and Practice*, ed. Karim Murji and John Solomos (Oxford: Oxford University Press, 2005), 52–53.

47 Constance Backhouse, *Colour-Coded: A Legal History of Racism in Canada, 1900–1950* (Toronto: Osgoode Society for Canadian Legal History and University of Toronto Press, 1999), 5.

48 André Siegfried, *The Race Question in Canada* (Toronto: McClelland and Stewart, 1966 [1907]), Lionel Groulx, *L'Appel de la race* (Montreal: Éditions Fides, 1980 [1922]).

49 Edmond Demolins, *Anglo-Saxon Superiority: To What It Is Due* (New York: R.F. Fenno, 1899), 132; Tony Bennett, Lawrence Grossberg, and Meaghan Morris, eds., *New Keywords: A Revised Vocabulary of Culture and Society* (Oxford: Blackwell, 2005), 294; David Roediger, *The Wages of Whiteness: Race and the Making of the American Working Class* (London and New York: Verso, 1991), 133.

50 Roediger, *Wages of Whiteness*, 25.

51 Edmund Bradwin, *The Bunkhouse Man: A Study of Work and Pay in the Camps of Canada 1903–1914* (Toronto: University of Toronto Press, 1972 [1928]), 92; Irene Howard, *The Struggle for Social Justice in British Columbia: Helena Gutteridge, the Unknown Reformer* (Vancouver: UBC Press, 1992), 94.

52 Craig Heron, *Working in Steel: The Early Years in Canada, 1883–1935* (Toronto: McClelland and Stewart, 1988), 77. For a more theoretical statement of this insight, see E. San Juan, who argues that race emerges out of the raw materials furnished by class relations and the ups and downs of colonial/ capitalist expansion and imperial hegemony. Race functions to regulate the price of wage labour within and outside the territory of the metropolitan power, and also lends to relations of domination and subordination an air of naturalness and fatality. See E. San Juan, *Racial Formations/ Critical Transformations* (Atlantic Highlands, N.J.: Humanities Press, 1992); *Beyond Postcolonial Theory* (New York: St. Martin's Press, 1998); *Racism and Cultural Studies* (Durham, N.C.: Duke University Press, 2002).

53 Banton, "Historical and Contemporary Modes of Racialization," 52–58.

54 Bob Carter, *Realism and Racism: Concepts of Race in Sociological Research* (London and New York: Routledge, 2000), 2–3. See also Elizar Barkan, *The Retreat of Scientific Racism: Changing Concepts of Race in Britain and the United States Between the World Wars* (Cambridge: Cambridge University Press, 1991). Science, especially since the discoveries of the Human Genome Project, has discredited this race concept. Today it is conventionally accepted that classifying human populations into races was an exercise that mistakenly extrapolated from superficial, literally skin-deep differences, to reach untenable conclusions about them.

55 Mariana Valverde, *The Age of Light, Soap and Water: Moral Reform in English Canada, 1885–1925* (Toronto: McClelland and Stewart, 1991), 109–10; James W. St. G. Walker, *"Race," Rights and the Law in the Supreme Court of Canada: Historical Case Studies* (Waterloo, Ont.: Osgoode Society for Canadian Legal History and Wilfrid Laurier University Press, 1997), 13; Nancy Leys Stepan, "Race, Gender, Science and Citizenship," in *Cultures of Empire: Colonizers in Britain and the Empire in the Nineteenth and Twentieth Centuries*, ed. Catherine Hall (New York: Routledge, 2000), 71; Backhouse, *Colour-Coded*.

56 W.G. Smith, *A Study in Canadian Immigration* (Toronto: Ryerson Press, 1920), 60.

57 Backhouse, *Colour-Coded*, 3, 4.

58 Karl Kautsky, *Are the Jews a Race?* (London: Jonathan Cape, 1926), 64–65; a translation of *Rasse und Judentum*, first published in 1914.

59 David Roediger, *Towards the Abolition of Whiteness* (London and New York: Verso, 1994), 2; Backhouse, *Colour-Coded*, 15.

60 For useful overviews, see James Miller, *Skyscrapers Hide the Heavens: A History of Indian-White Relations in Canada* (Toronto: University of Toronto Press, 1989); Olive Patricia Dickason, *Canada's First Nations: A History of Founding Peoples from Earliest Times* (Toronto: McClelland and Stewart, 1992); Sarah Carter, *Aboriginal People and Colonizers of Western Canada to 1900* (Toronto: University of Toronto Press, 1999). For a path-breaking study of anthropology and Native Canada, see Noel Dyck and James Waldram, eds., *Anthropology, Public Policy and Native Peoples in Canada* (Montreal and Kingston: McGill-Queen's University Press, 1993). On "the Indian" as a category of evolutionary thought, see Roy Harvey Pearce, *Savagism and Civilization: A Study of the Indian and the American Mind*, rev. ed. (Berkeley: University of California Press, 1988); for an innovative overview incorporating contemporary critical theories of race and racialization, see Augie Fleras and Jean Leonard Elliott, *Unequal Relations: An Introduction to Race, Ethnic, and Aboriginal Dynamics in Canada*, 5th ed. (Toronto: Pearson Prentice Hall, 2007).

61 See Eric L. Goldstein, *The Price of Whiteness: Jews, Race, and American Identity* (Princeton and Oxford: Princeton University Press, 2006). For a path-breaking study of evolutionary theory as interpreted by Jewish intellectuals in Montreal, see Gordon Dueck, "The Salamander and the Chameleon: Religion, Race and Evolutionism in the Anglo-Jewish Press, Montreal, 1897–1914," Ph.D. thesis, Queen's University, Kingston, 1999.

62 Edward Said, *Orientalism* (New York: Pantheon, 1978).

63 *Sun*, 22 June 1914.

64 *Province*, 6 July 1914.

65 Pollough Pogue, "From India's Coral Strand," *Sun*, 19 June 1914; Baxter in *Sun*, 23 June 1914.; Reid in *Province*, 6 July 1914.

66 For a classic study of the theme, see Roy Harvey Pearce, *Savagism and Civilization:*

A *Study of the Indian and the American Mind* (Berkeley: University of California Press, 1988).

67 Morse, "Immigration and Status of British East Indians in Canada," 96; *Debates of the House of Commons*, 1914, 1239–44.

68 *Sun*, 22 June 1914.

69 Parnaby and Kealey, "Origins of Political Policing in Canada," 225.

70 Ibid., 231. Parnaby and Kealey also draw particular attention to *Swadesh Sewak* (Servant of the country), a Gurmukhi-language publication in Vancouver.

71 *Sun*, 22 June 1914.

72 Justice Morrison declared that the Immigration Act did not apply to an alien tourist such as Rahim who entered Canada before the passage of the revised Immigration Act. He was hence not affected by an order-in-council passed since the coming into force of the Act. See *In re Rahim*, 16 *B.C. Reports*, 1911, 471.

73 Hopkinson cited in Parnaby and Kealey, "Origins of Political Policing in Canada," 233; Peter Campbell, "East Meets Left: South Asian Militants and the Socialist Party of Canada in British Columbia, 1904–1914," *International Journal of Canadian Studies* 20 (Fall 1999), 38.

74 *Industrial Banner* (Toronto), reprinted in *B.C. Federationist*, 12 June 1914; *B.C. Federationist*, 29 May 1914; Hawthornthwaite in Campbell, "East Meets Left," 39.

75 *Province*, 6 July 1914.

76 For the labour council, see Gene Howard Homel, "James Simpson and the Origins of Canadian Social Democracy," Ph.D. thesis, University of Toronto, 1978, 579–81; Bruce in *Mail and Empire* (Toronto), 27, 28 Jan. 1912.

77 James H. McVety, "Suggests Violence in Case Asiatics Are Landed," *B.C. Federationist*, 5 June 1914; *B.C. Federationist*, 26 June 1914.

78 *Daily News-Advertiser* (Vancouver), 18 July, 19 July 1914.

79 *B.C. Federationist*, 24 July 1914.

80 Campbell, "East Meets West," 43.

81 *Province*, 30 June 1914. In the reportage, Bird is said to have relied upon the definitions accessible to him in an encyclopedia.

82 Cited in Campbell, "East Meets West," 46.

83 Ibid., 47.

84 Ibid., 48. Those reported by Hopkinson's informants to be involved included such prominent South Asians as Bhag Sing, Balwant Sing, and Gharib Singh. Campbell suggests that Hopkinson's information about Rahim and the others forming a local must be treated cautiously.

85 Campbell suggests that Rahim apparently attended his last Dominion Executive Committee meeting on 23 Oct. 1914. On 21 November the Committee acquired new headquarters, and Rahim, after his arrest, did not return to his position.

86 Campbell, "East Meets Left," 51–52, 38, 41–42; *Sun*, 22 June 1914. Ever since the brutal handling of priest Bhawgan Singh in November 1913 – although a writ of habeas corpus had been granted by Mr. Justice Morrison in his case, Malcolm Reid ignored the telegram and deported him anyway – much of the Sikh community especially had been outraged by a sense that their religion was under siege. Protest meetings erupted in Victoria and Vancouver, and, as Morse remarks, "It [the Bhawgan Singh case] did great harm in helping to spread sedition among the East Indians on the Pacific Coast." Morse, "Immigration and Status of British East Indians in Canada," 75–76.

87 Campbell, "East Meets Left," 36; "Local Vancouver No. 1, S.P. of C.," *Western Clarion*, 4 Jan. 1908, 3.

88 Parnaby and Kealey, "Origins of Political Policing in Canada," 229.

89 *Sun*, 23 May 1914; *Province*, 17 June 1914.

90 *Province*, 20 June 1914, 23 July 1914, 6 July 1914, 21 July 1914.

91 Morse, "Some Aspects of the Komagata Maru Affair," 108.

92 For the Montreal paper, see *Province*, 21 July 1914; for Skelton, Farr, ed., *Life and Letters of Sir Wilfrid Laurier*, vol. 2, 52n.

93 *Province*, 23 July 1914. The newspaper thought these weapons would emit powerful, incapacitating odours.

94 Morse, "Immigration and Status of British East Indians in Canada," 90.

95 Ibid., 90.

96 *Province*, 23 July 1914, 22 July 1914.

97 Srikanth, *"Komagata Maru,"* 79–80.

98 As Campbell suggests, "In the Punjab, in organizations like Kirti Kisan, the educational emphasis of the Socialist Party of Canada lived on." Campbell, "East Meets Left," 56.

99 *Province*, 20 July 1914.

100 Srikanth, *"Komagata Maru,"* 78.

101 David Goutor, *Guarding the Gates: The Canadian Labour Movement and Immigration, 1872–1934* (Vancouver and Toronto: UBC Press, 2007), 23.

102 Kelley and Trebilcock, *Making of the Mosaic*, 111–12.

103 Ibid., 114.

104 Donald Avery, *"Dangerous Foreigners": European Immigrant Workers and Labour Radicalism in Canada, 1896–1932* (Toronto: McClelland and Stewart, 1979), 37.

105 Kelley and Trebilcock, *Making of the Mosaic*, 155. It was never proclaimed, perhaps because Laurier was worried about diplomatic problems with the United States or by the prospect of a backlash among Afro-Canadian voters in Nova Scotia and Southwestern Ontario.

106 For an interesting discussion, see Fleras and Elliot, *Unequal Relations*, 29.

107 Kelley and Trebilcock, *Making of the Mosaic*, 140–41; Goutor, *Guarding the Gates*, 210.

108 Avery, *"Dangerous Foreigners,"* 34.

109 F. Hyatt, "The Struggle for Life," letter to *Western Clarion*, 17 April 1909, 3.

110 Bradwin, *Bunkhouse Man*, 198.

111 Cited in Kelley and Trebilcock, *Making of the Mosaic*, 132.

112 Smith, *Study in Canadian Immigration*, 146.

113 Karl Polanyi, *The Great Transformation: The Political and Economic Origins of Our Time* (Boston: Beacon Press, 1971 [1944]), 76.

114 To reference E.J. Hobsbawn, "The Machine Breakers," in *Labouring Men: Studies in the History of Labour* (London: Weidenfeld and Nicolson, 1964), 7.

115 Bradwin, *Bunkhouse Man*, 234–35.

116 Woodsworth, *Strangers Within Our Gates*; J.S. Woodsworth, *My Neighbor: A Study of City Conditions* (Toronto: University of Toronto Press, 1972 [1911]). The two Woodsworth books are exhibits A and B in many a seminar dramatization of the shortcomings of a past generation, annually dissected (in whole or in part) by legions of students hunting for signs of anti-immigrant intolerance, nativism, and racism. Sometimes, misleadingly, they are interpreted as the writings of the socialist left: see, among many others, Kelley and Trebilcock, *Making of the Mosaic*, 134.

117 Kenneth McNaught, *A Prophet in Politics: A Biography of J.S. Woodsworth* (Toronto: University of Toronto Press, 1959), 4–5.

118 Ibid., 39.

119 Grace MacInnis, *J.S. Woodsworth: A Man to Remember* (Toronto: Macmillan, 1953), 83.

120 For a very different appraisal, see McNaught, *Prophet in Politics*, 8, 25, 46. McNaught essentially sees *Strangers Within Our Gates* as "basically a statement of facts" (46). The title may have been derived from *Deuteronomy* 16: 14 – "And thou shalt rejoice in thy feast, thou, and thy son, and thy daughter, and thy manservant, and thy maidservant, and the Levite, the stranger, and the fatherless, and the widow, that *are* within thy gates" – or from *Exodus* 20:10 – "But the seventh day *is* the sabbath of the LORD thy God: *in it* thou shalt not do any work, thou, nor thy son, nor thy daughter, thy manservant, nor thy maidservant, nor thy cattle, nor thy stranger that is within thy gates." Perhaps these passages establish that the immigrants will be assessed according to religious standards, without clearly implying whether they are to be invited to the great Canadian feast, or morally regulated according to the rules of Sabbath observance.

121 Woodsworth, *Strangers Within Our Gates*, 12.

122 Ibid., 32.

123 Ibid., 128–29.

124 Contemporary reviewers were well aware that Woodsworth was no socialist in 1909. A review of *Strangers* in *The Voice* (Winnipeg), 30 April 1909, suggested that the writer, although respecting Woodsworth, by no means regarded him as a "socialist."

125 Drummond's argument was that individual Catholics, who relied upon clerical "external sources" for their spirituality, were the human equivalents of such semi-parasites as the hermit crab. In Woodsworth's view, weaning Catholics away from their bad, unprogressive habits of dependency meant they would evolve their own reformation, based on public schools, easy access to the Bible, and so on. Woodsworth, *Strangers Within Our Gates*, 256.

126 Woodsworth, *My Neighbor*, 10.

127 Woodsworth, *My Neighbor*, 14, 28; Ian McKay, ed., *For a Working-Class Culture in Canada: A Selection of Colin McKay's Writings on Sociology and Political Economy, 1897–1939*, Part IV (St. John's, Nfld.: Canadian Committee on Labour History, 1996), 45.

128 Woodsworth, *My Neighbor*, 55–56. John Graham Brooks was a contemporary social critic.

129 Perhaps it could be more readily aligned with the newer strains of liberalism, often associated with Queen's University and epitomized by Skelton and Adam Shortt, analyzed so well by Barry Ferguson. See Barry Ferguson, *Remaking Liberalism: The Intellectual Legacy of Adam Shortt, O.D. Skelton, W.C. Clark, and W.A. Macintosh, 1890–1925* (Montreal and Kingston: McGill-Queen's University Press, 1993).

130 Woodsworth, *Strangers Within Our Gates*, 29

131 Ibid., 154, 122, 109, 231.

132 Ibid., 16, 17, 32, 90, 154, 154, 158, 253.

133 Ibid., 46, 71.

134 Ibid., 154.

135 Adele Perry, *On the Edge of Empire: Gender, Race, and the Making of British Columbia 1849–1871* (Toronto: University of Toronto Press, 2001).

136 Heron, *Working in Steel*, 77.

137 Ibid., 79.

138 Ian McKay, "Industry, Work and Community in the Cumberland Coalfields, 1848–1927," vol. 1, Ph.D. thesis, Dalhousie University, Halifax, 1983, 384–97.

139 Goutor, *Guarding the Gates*, 40, 76–77.

140 Ibid., 54, 56, 56–57.

141 Ibid., 55.

142 See Michael Boudreau, "Crime and Punishment in the City of Order: Halifax, 1917–1935," Ph.D. thesis, Queen's University, Kingston, 1996, ch. 6.

143 Cited in Goutor, *Guarding the Gates*, 41.

144 Ibid., 41, 109, 56, 38–39, 6. See also Karen Dubinsky and Adam Givertz, "It Was Only a Matter of Passion: Masculinity and Sexual Danger," in *Gendered Pasts: Historical Essays in Feminity and Masculinity*, ed. Kathryn McPherson, Cecilia Morgan, and Nancy Forestell (Toronto: Oxford University Press,), 65–79.

145 Goutor, *Guarding the Gates*, 99.

146 John A. Cooper, "Canadian Democracy and Socialism," *The Canadian Magazine* 3, 4 (August 1894), 332–36; Janice Newton, "The Alchemy of Politicization: Socialist Women and the Early Canadian Left," in *Gender Conflicts: New Essays in Women's History*, ed. Franca Iacovetta and Mariana Valverde (Toronto: University of Toronto Press, 1992), 118, citing *Cotton's Weekly*, 20 May 1909; *Herald* (Halifax), 2 Sept. 1919, 6.

147 Charles Allen Seager, "A Proletariat in Wild Rose Country: The Alberta Coal Miners, 1905–1945," Ph.D. thesis, York University, 1981, 99–100, 272, 274–75, 277.

148 Cited in Avery, *"Dangerous Foreigners,"* 71.

149 McKay, "Industry, Work and Community in the Cumberland Coalfields," vol. 1, 322; Heron, *Working in Steel*, 85.

150 Gillian Creese, "Exclusion or Solidarity? Vancouver Workers Confront the 'Oriental Problem,' " *B.C. Studies* 80 (Winter 1988–1989), 36–37.

151 *Citizen and Country*, 6 April 1900.

152 *Sun* (Saint John), 20 Jan. 1909, 8.

153 Colin McKay, "The French Canadian as a Trade Unionist," in *For a Working-Class Culture in Canada*, ed. McKay, 68–71.

154 "The Socialist Party of Canada," *Western Clarion*, 4 Jan. 1908, 3.

155 Socialist Party of Canada, *The Working Class and Master Class* (Vancouver: Socialist Party of Canada, 1912 [1910]); Homel, "James Simpson and the Origins of Canadian Social Democracy," 96.

156 For Phillips Thompson and the CSL, see Phillips Thompson, "Anglo-Saxon Jingoism," *Citizen and Country*, 9 Dec. 1899; for Butler, see Deborah Stiles, " 'The Dragon of Imperialism': Martin Butler, Butler's Journal, the Canadian Democrat, and Anti-Imperialism, 1899–1902," *Canadian Historical Review* 85, 3 (September 2004), 481–505.

157 "People Who Live in Nests," *Western Clarion*, 16 Sept. 1905; "No Slaves under Old Glory," *Western Clarion*, 19 Oct. 1905; "Digging the Panama Ditch," 12 Aug. 1905. I am indebted to Andrew Cooke for these references.

158 "Partridge of Sintaluta" [E.A. Partridge], *A War on Poverty: The One War That Can End War* (Winnipeg: Wallingford Press, n.d. [1926]), 195; William Irvine, *Cooperative Government* (Ottawa: Mutual Press, 1929), 139.

159 *Sun*, 29 Oct. 1904, 10 Jan. 1910.

160 Karl Marx and Frederick Engels, *The Communist Manifesto* (London and New York: Verso, 1998), 58; "Manifesto of the Communist Party" (1848), in *Collected Works*, vol. 6 (Moscow: Progress Publishers, 1976), 502. For the Internationale in 40 languages, see <http://www.hymn.ru/internationale/index-en.html> (Feb. 24 2008).

161 See Karl Marx to Sigfrid Meyer and August Vogt, 9 April 1870, in Marx and

Engels, *Collected Works*, vol. 43 (Moscow: Progress Publishers, 1988), 471–76. One reading of this letter on racial divisions in England suggests that race was not merely an illusion, but a hegemonic relationship, with a reality not reducible to class exploitation or understandable apart from it.

162 See Lawrence Krader, ed., *The Ethnological Notebooks of Karl Marx* (Assen: Van Gorcum, 1972).

163 Defense Committee, *W.A. Pritchard's Address to the Jury in The Crown vs. Armstrong, Heaps, Bray, Ivens, Johns, Pritchard, and Queen* (Winnipeg: Wallingford Press, 1920), 137; and see McKay, ed., *For a Working-Class Culture in Canada*, 185–88.

164 McKay, ed., *For a Working-Class Culture in Canada*, 188; Mark Pittinger, *American Socialists and Evolutionary Thought, 1870–1920* (Madison: University of Wisconsin Press, 1993), 171.

165 Socialist Party of Canada, *Socialism and Unionism* (Vancouver, n.d. [1911]), 11. The *Manifesto of the Socialist Party of Canada* (Vancouver, 1910), perhaps the party's most widely circulated document, was essentially a succinct history of humanity, "from Savagery to Civilization." See the World Socialist Movement website: <http://www.worldsocialism.org/canada/manifesto.1910.htm>.

166 Sydney Olivier, *White Capital and Coloured Labour*, Socialist Library, no. 4 (London: Independent Labour Party, 1910).

167 Kautsky, *Are the Jews a Race?* 66, 75. For support for this controversial appraisal of Kautsky as an interesting theorist of the Jewish question, see Jack Jacobs, "Karl Kautsky: Between Baden and Luxemburg," in *Essential Papers on Jews and the Left*, ed. Ezra Mendelsohn (New York and London: New York University Press, 1997), 483–528. Jacobs points out that Kautsky never discusses Marx's own writings on "The Jewish Question," which he possibly thought gave the impression of anti-Semitism.

168 See Pittinger, *American Socialists*, ch. 9, pungently entitled, "Outsiders of Evolution: Immigrants, Blacks, and Women."

169 Alf Budden, *The Slave of the Farm: Being Letters from Alf. Budden to a Fellow Farm Slave and Comrade in Revolt* (Vancouver: Socialist Party of Canada, Dominion Executive Committee, 1914), 13; E.T.K. [E.T. Kingsley], "Notes by the Way," *Western Clarion*, 15 Aug. 1908, 1.

170 See, for example, W.J. Curry, "The Asiatic Invasion: Its Cause and Outcome," *Western Clarion*, 12 Dec. 1908.

171 For the blunt racism of prominent figures in U.S. socialism, such as Victor Berger, see David Shannon, *The Socialist Party of America: A History* (New York: Macmillan, 1955). As Berger declared in the *Social Democratic Herald*: "There can be no doubt that the negroes and mulattoes constitute a lower race – that the Caucasian and indeed even the Mongolian have the start on them in civilization by many thousand years – so that negroes will find it difficult ever to overtake them" (50). The party itself generally argued that in abolition of wage slavery lay the "sole salvation" of Afro-Americans (51). I am not aware of any Canadian equivalents.

172 Goutor, *Guarding the Gates*, 43; Philip Girard, " 'His Whole Life Was One of Continual Warfare': John Thomas Bulmer, Lawyer, Librarian and Social Reformer," *Dalhousie Law Journal* 13, 1 (May 1990), 376–405; Phillips Thompson, "Thoughts and Suggestions on the Social Problem and Things in General (1888–1889)," ed. Deborah L. Coombs and Gregory S. Kealey, with introduction by Pierre Berton, *Labour/Le Travail* 35 (Spring 1995), 245–46; Norman Penner, ed., *Winnipeg 1919: The Strikers' Own History of the Winnipeg General Strike* (Toronto: James Lewis & Samuel, 1973), 70.

173   J.T. Mortimer to Sifton, 22 June 1899, quoted in D.J. Hall, *Clifford Sifton*, vol.1, *The Young Napoleon, 1861–1900* (Vancouver: UBC Press, 1981), 268; Ross A. Johnson, "No Compromise – No Political Trading: The Marxian Socialist Tradition in British Columbia," Ph.D. thesis, University of British Columbia, Vancouver, 1975, 99, 274, citing the *Western Clarion*, 26 March 1910. Howard notes that, in a report to the Royal Commission on Labour, J.H. McVety had urged separate schools for Oriental children because they were "a bad moral influence" on White children. See Howard, *Struggle for Social Justice in British Columbia*, 94.

174   Howard, *Struggle for Social Justice in British Columbia*, 113.

175   Mark Leier, *Red Flags and Red Tape: The Making of a Labour Bureaucracy* (Toronto: University of Toronto Press, 1995), 169–70. J.B. McLachlan, letter to the *Herald*, 30 Jan. 1908, 2; C.M. [Colin McKay], "The Conqueror Comes," *Herald* (Montreal), 20 Sept. 1900; *Citizen and Country*, 11 May 1900.

176   Curry, "Asiatic Invasion," 4. For an interesting discussion of Spencer on this issue, see Daniel Becquemont and Laurent Mucchielli, *Le cas Spencer: Religion, science et politique* (Paris: Presses Universitaires de France, 1998), 166–168.

177   Jim Connell, "Socialism and the Survival of the Fittest," *Western Clarion*, 8, 15, 22, 29 March, 5, 19, 26 April 1913.

178   Cited in Linda Kealey, *Enlisting Women for the Cause: Women, Labour, and the Left in Canada, 1890–1920* (Toronto: University of Toronto Press, 1998), 9.

179   "Heterodox Economics" [H. Ashplant], "The Chinese Problem," *Citizen and Country*, 11 March 1899; Thompson (*Labor Advocate*, 22 May 1891) cited in Goutor, *Guarding the Gates*, 66.

180   Socialist Party of Canada, Lindsay, Ont., Local, *Gems of Socialism* (n.p. [Lindsay], n.d. [1916]), unpaginated; George Ross Kirkpatrick, *The Socialist and the Sword* (Vancouver: Socialist Party of Canada, n.d. [1912?]); Socialist Party of Canada, *The Working Class and Master Class* (Vancouver: Socialist Party of Canada, 1912 [1910]).

181   *Western Clarion*, 12 Sept. 1908, 24 May 1913, as cited in Creese, "Exclusion or Solidarity?" 37; Socialist Party of Canada, Lindsay, *Gems of Socialism*.

182   *Cotton's Weekly*, 5 Jan. 1911.

183   Cited in Avery, *"Dangerous Foreigners,"* 53.

184   Ibid., 55.

185   Seager, "Proletariat in Wild Rose Country," 97.

186   Kautsky, *Are the Jews a Race?* 87–88.

187   The beginnings of a more general theorization of diaspora socialism can be discerned in Paul Buhle, *Marxism in the United States: Remapping the History of the American Left* (London and New York: Verso, 1987), and in an important U.S. collection on immigrant radicals, Paul Buhle and Dan Georgakas, eds., *The Immigrant Left in the United States* (Albany: State University of New York Press, 1996).

188   Cited in Avery, *"Dangerous Foreigners,"* 64.

189   Bradwin, *Bunkhouse Man*, 108.

190   Avery, *"Dangerous Foreigners,"* 61, citing *Robochyi narod*, 22 Jan. 1914.

191   Gerald Tulchinsky, *Taking Root: The Origins of the Canadian Jewish Community* (Toronto: Lester Publishing, 1992), 259. For Jewish-Canadian leftism in this period, see especially Simon Belkin, *Le Mouvement Ouvrier Juif au Canada 1904–1920*, trans. Pierre Anctil (Montreal: Septentrion, 1999), which first appeared in Yiddish in 1956. For more general context on Jewish culture in Montreal, see Pierre Anctil, ed., *Through the Eyes of the Eagle: The Early Montreal Yiddish Press 1907–1916* (Montreal: Véhicule Press, 2001), which includes

interesting labour and socialist materials. For the international context, see Ezra Mendelsohn, ed., *Essential Papers on Jews and the Left* (New York and London: New York University Press, 1997); Adam M. Weisberger, *The Jewish Ethic and the Spirit of Socialism* (New York: Peter Lang, 1997), which, in a study of Germany, focuses on a messianism traceable back to Judaism as an often subtle element of a Jewish affinity for socialism.

192 Kealey, *Enlisting Women for the Cause*, 129.

193 W.G. Gribble, "Correspondence," *Western Clarion*, 20 April 1907, 4.

194 See R. Usiskin, "Towards a Theoretical Reformulation of the Relationship between Political Ideology, Social Class, and Ethnicity: A Case Study of the Winnipeg Jewish Radical Community, 1905–1920," M.A. thesis (Sociology), University of Manitoba, Winnipeg, 1978.

195 R. Usiskin, "The Winnipeg Jewish Radical Community: Its Early Formation 1905–1918," in *Jewish Life and Times: A Collection of Essays* (Winnipeg: Jewish Historical Society of Western Canada, 1983), 168.

196 Ruth Frager, *Sweatshop Strife: Class, Ethnicity, and Gender in the Jewish Labour Movement of Toronto 1900–1939* (Toronto: University of Toronto Press, 1992); for one example, see *Morning Chronicle* (Halifax), 10 Aug. 1901.

197 MacInnis, *J.S. Woodsworth*, 92–93; for Baritz, see "One Side, Facts for Ontario Socialists," *Western Clarion*, 23 Jan. 1910, 3. For an excellent overview, see Tulchinsky, *Taking Root*.

198 Avery, *"Dangerous Foreigners,"* 59–60.

199 Many of the organizational intricacies of the Ukrainian socialist movement in Canada can be unearthed from Peter Krawchuk's informative 1979 study, based on the movement's leading newspapers: *Chervonyi prapor* (Red flag, 1907–8), *Nova hromada* (New community, 1911–12), *Robochyi narod* (1909–18), and *Robitnyche slovo* (1916–18). See Peter Krawchuk, *The Ukrainian Socialist Movement in Canada (1907–1918)* (Toronto: Progress Books, 1979). The distilled history here omits some important organizations and figures discussed in the work of Krawchuk and others. Added to the left historian's familiar hazard of changing organizational names are the complexities introduced by the Ukrainian-Canadian left's international ties: for example, although it is in general correct that the "Ukrainian Social Democrats" attained leadership in 1911, some of those loyal to the SPC before and after the break of 1911 also went under the name "Social Democrats" because this was the term most commonly used in Ukraine itself. For additional context, see Jaroslav Petryshyn and L. Dzubak, *Peasants in the Promised Land: Canada and the Ukrainians, 1891–1914* (Toronto: James Lorimer and Company, 1985), esp. 154–69.

200 Krawchuk, *Ukrainian Socialist Movement*, 11.

201 Cited in Krawchuk, *Ukrainian Socialist Movement*, 12–13.

202 Krawchuk, *Ukrainian Socialist Movement*, 63, 91.

203 Even given the irrationalities of racial description, this labelling required a radical suspension of disbelief: a pocket of Norway actually lies to the east of Finland.

204 Smith, *Study in Canadian Immigration*; Bradwin, *Bunkhouse Man*, 102.

205 Varpu Lindström-Best, *Defiant Sisters: A Social History of Finnish Immigrant Women in Canada* (Toronto: Multicultural History Society of Ontario, 1988), 154.

206 Report of interview with J.W. Ahlqvist in William Eklund, *Builders of Canada: The History of the Finnish Organization of Canada 1911–1971* (Toronto, 1987), 118–19, 120.

207 Eklund, *Builders of Canada*, 147.

208 Homel, "James Simpson and the Origins of Canadian Social Democracy," 159.

209 Interview in Eklund, *Builders of Canada*, 121.

210 MacInnis, *J.S. Woodsworth*, 108–9.

211 Ibid., 110, 111.

212 Peter Campbell, " 'Not as a White Man, Not as a Sojourner': James A. Teit and the Fight for Native Rights in British Columbia, 1884–1922," *left history* 2, 2 (Fall 1994), 39, 46. For a different interpretation, see Wendy Wickwire, " 'We Shall Drink from the Stream and So Shall You': James A. Teit and Native Resistance in British Columbia, 1908–22," *Canadian Historical Review* 79, 2 (1998), 199–236.

213 For the context of these struggles, see Cole Harris, *Making Native Space: Colonialism, Resistance, and Reserves in British Columbia* (Vancouver and Toronto: UBC Press, 2002); and Paul Tennant, *Aboriginal Peoples and Politics: The Indian Land Question in British Columbia, 1849–1989* (Vancouver: UBC Press, 1990).

214 Campbell, " 'Not as a White Man, Not as a Sojourner,' " 57, 50. Partly in response to the outcry he helped to orchestrate, Ottawa backed down on 17 Jan. 1918.

215 *Red Flag*, 9 Aug. 1919. For a strong postwar SPC critique of the "White Man's Burden" with respect to the First Nations, see *Red Flag*, 26 April 1919. For Native peoples within liberal order, see for the early history of the North American context Robert A. Williams Jr., *The American Indian in Western Legal Thought: The Discourses of Conquest* (New York and Oxford: Oxford University Press, 1990); and for Canada, Sidney L. Harring, *White Man's Law: Native People in Nineteenth-Century Canadian Jurisprudence* (Toronto: University of Toronto Press, 1998). No study of the Canadian left and First Nations from 1890 to 1920 has (to my knowledge) been attempted, but for a fascinating biography that suggests ways in which the two topics could be linked, see Donald B. Smith, *Honoré Jaxon: Prairie Visionary* (Regina: Coteau Books, 2007), a study of Louis Riel's secretary, labour party supporter, and anarchist activist.

216 J. Donald Wilson, "Matti Kurikka and A.B. Makela: Socialist Thought among Finns in Canada, 1900–1932," *Canadian Ethnic Studies* 10,2 (1978), 18.

217 See several illuminating articles by Wilson, from which the facts and quotations about Kurikka and Makela in these paragraphs are principally derived: J. Donald Wilson, "Matti Kurikka: Finnish-Canadian Intellectual," *BC Studies* 20 (Winter 1973–74), 50–65; " 'Never Believe What You Have Never Doubted': Matti Kurikka's Dream for a New World Utopia," in *Finnish Diaspora*, vol. 1, *Canada, South America, Africa, Australia, and Sweden*, ed. Michael G. Karnia (Toronto, 1981), 131–53. See also Wilson, "Matti Kurikka and A.B. Makela," 9–21.

218 Wilson, " 'Never Believe What You Have Never Doubted,' " 135–36.

219 Ibid., 133, 136, 137.

220 Kevin Wilson, *Practical Dreamers: Communitarianism and Co-operatives on Malcolm Island* (Victoria: British Columbia Institute for Co-operative Studies, 2005), 25.

221 Wilson, " 'Never Believe What You Have Never Doubted,' " 139

222 Ibid., 148; Wilson, "Matti Kurikka and A.B. Mäkelä," 13.

223 Wilson, "Matti Kurikka and A.B. Mäkelä," 13,14.

224 Ibid., 18.

225 Nadia Kazymyra, "The Defiant Pavlo Krat and the Early Socialist Movement in Canada," *Canadian Ethnic Studies* 10, 2 (1978), 38–54. These paragraphs on Krat are entirely indebted to Kazymyra's study.

226 See Paul Crath [Pavlo Krat], *Koly ziishlo sontse: opovidannia z 2000 roku* (Toronto: Z drukarni Robitnychocho slova, 1918); available on microfiche, Canadian

Institute for Historical Microreproductions, CIHM/ICMH Microfiche series, no.81062, 1996.

227 Walter Smyrniw, "The First Utopia in Ukrainian Belles Lettres: Pavlo Krat's Koly Ziishlo Sontse," *Canadian Slavonic Papers* 38, 3/4 (September-December 1996), 405–19.

228 Lindström-Best, *Defiant Sisters*, 150, 151. For more work on Kannasto, see Samira Saramo, "Women Made of Iron: Sanna Kannasto and Finnish Socialist Women in Early-Twentieth-Century Lakehead," unpublished paper, York University, Toronto, 2007; and, for her wider context, " 'A Socialist Movement Which Does Not Attract the Women Cannot Live': The Strength of Finnish Socialist Women in Port Arthur, 1903–1933," in *Essays in Northwestern Working Class History*, ed. Michel S. Beaulieu (Thunder Bay, Ont.: Lakehead University Centre for Northern Studies, 2008).

229 Mushkat's career has been brought imaginatively to light by Linda Kealey, upon whom this account primarily relies. See Linda Kealey, "Sophie," *New Maritimes*, November 1987, 12–13; also, Janice Newton, *The Feminist Challenge to the Canadian Left, 1900–1918* (Montreal and Kingston: McGill-Queen's University Press, 1995). A more recent contribution is that of Jack Switzer, "Sophie Mushkat McClusky: Alberta's Strident Socialist," *Alberta History* 54, 3 (Summer 2006), 21–24.

230 Nicholas Fillmore, *Maritime Radical: The Life and Times of Roscoe Fillmore* (Toronto: Between the Lines, 1992), 48. Fillmore thought so highly of his sexist witticism that he committed another version of it to print in the *Western Clarion* in 1909: "They are well posted and the lady Comrades can talk plain straight Socialism without ever once mentioning ice cream, bob-bons, directoire gowns or peach-basket hats. Take note of this, lady Comrades of the S.P.C." Roscoe A. Fillmore, "Moncton, N.B.," letter to the *Western Clarion*, 7 Aug. 1909.

231 Kealey, "Sophie," 13.

7: War, Revolution, and General Strike

1 Leon Trotsky, "The Bolsheviki and World Peace," *Mail and Empire* (Toronto), 8, 12, 14, 18, 19, 21, 23, 24, 25, 26, 28 Jan. 1918. For the complete text, see Leon Trotsky, *The Bolsheviki and World Peace* (New York: Boni and Liveright, 1918).

2 For descriptions of Trotsky's life in New York, see Pierre Broué, *Trotsky* (Paris: Fayard, 1988), 162–68.

3 *Mail and Empire*, 14 Jan. 1918.

4 Library and Archives Canada (LAC), MG 28, IV, Trotskyist Collection, interview with Maurice Spector. Spector was interviewed on CBC's "Horizon," 2 Feb. 1964.

5 *Varsity* (Toronto), 3 Jan. 1918.

6 Chief Press Censor's Files, Microfilm Reel T-94, LAC; Ernest J. Chambers, Chief Press Censor for Canada, to Sir Robert Falconer, President, University of Toronto, 6 Jan. 1918; Ernest J. Chambers to "The Editor," *Varsity*, 6 Jan. 1918; Ernest J. Chambers to H.J. Hamilton, Manager, University of Toronto Press, 6 Jan. 1918.

7 *Mail and Empire*, 28 Jan. 1918. See also V.I. Lenin, *The Soviets at Work*, 5th ed. (New York: Rand School of Social Science, 1919).

8 *Mail and Empire*, 8 Jan. 1918.

9 "Bolsheviki as Hierarchy," *Mail and Empire*, 18 Feb. 1918.

10 For a study of the culture of recruiting and the salience of local networks of patrons and clients, see Paul Maroney, " 'The Great Adventure': The Context and Ideology of Recruiting in Ontario, 1914–17," *Canadian Historical Review* 77,1 (January 1996), 62–98.

11 See Ian McKay, "The 1910s: The Stillborn Triumph of Progressive Reform," in *The*

Atlantic Provinces in Confederation, ed. E.R. Forbes and D.A. Muise (Toronto and Fredericton, University of Toronto Press and Acadiensis Press, 1993), 192–229.

12 Cited in William English Walling, ed., *The Socialists and the War: A Documentary Statement of the Position of the Socialists of All Countries; With Special Reference to Their Peace Policy* (New York: Henry Holt, 1915), 171–72.

13 Ian Angus, *Canadian Bolsheviks: The Early Years of the Communist Party of Canada* (Montreal: Vanguard Publications, 1981), 11, documents the controversial opinions of J.H. Burroughs, then editor of the *Western Clarion*: "An editorial by Burroughs in the October 24, 1914 issue declared support for the allies against 'German culture,' and expressed the hope that Germany would soon be crushed."

14 Craig Heron and Myer Siemiatycki, "The Great War, the State, and Working-Class Canada," in *The Workers' Revolt in Canada, 1917–1925*, ed. Craig Heron (Toronto: University of Toronto Press, 1998), 12–13.

15 Jonathan Vance, *Death So Noble: Memory, Meaning, and the First World War* (Vancouver: UBC Press, 1997).

16 McKay, "1910s"; see also Ian Milligan, "Sedition in Wartime Ontario: The Trials and Imprisonment of Isaac Bainbridge, 1917–1918," *Ontario History* 100, 2 (Autumn 2008), 32–59.

17 Geoff Ewen, "Quebec: Class and Identity," in *Workers' Revolt in Canada*, ed. Heron, 122.

18 For interesting new work on this notorious shooting, see Mark Leier, "Plots, Shots, and Liberal Thoughts: Conspiracy Theory and the Death of Ginger Goodwin," *Labour/Le Travail* 39 (Spring 1997), 215–24.

19 Party News, *Western Clarion*, 15 Jan. 1920.

20 Borden cited in Craig Heron, "Introduction," in *Workers' Revolt in Canada*, ed. Heron, 5; *Catholic Register*, 6 March 1919, 1 May 1919, as cited in Theresa Catherine Baxter, "Selected Aspects of Canadian Public Opinion on the Russian Revolution and on Its Impact in Canada, 1917, 1919," M.A. thesis, University of Western Ontario, London, 1972, 75.

21 *Globe* (Toronto), 21 Dec. 1918, 6, cited in Baxter, "Selected Aspects of Canadian Public Opinion," 35; *Herald* (Halifax), 2 Dec. 1920, 3, 28 Nov. 1919; "Bolshevism on Wheels, "*Mail and Empire*, 20 Dec. 1918.

22 Wright in *Herald*, 1 May 1919; review of E.J. Dillon, *Eclipse of Russia*, *Mail and Empire*, 8 Oct. 1918; "Curb Socialism after the War," *Mail and Empire*, 4 Sept. 1918.

23 "Fewer Jews among Bolsheviki," *Mail and Empire*, 11 Feb. 1918; *B.C. Federationist*, 24 Jan. 1919 – a piece reprinted in the paper and by no means reflective of its own editorial position; "Jews and Socialism," *Mail and Empire*, editorial, 21 Nov. 1917. John Spargo wrote an entire book to combat the impression that Bolshevism was Jewish; see Spargo, *The Jew and American Ideals* (New York and London: Harper & Brother Publishers, 1921).

24 "Russia Queered Allies in Finland," *Mail and Empire*, 11 Sept. 1918; "Ukrainians and the Other Russians," *Mail and Empire*, 5 Feb. 1918.

25 "Trotzky," *Mail and Empire*, 14 Jan. 1918.

26 Stephen Leacock, "The Bolshevik Spectre Frightens an Uneasy Conscience," *Herald*, 18 Dec. 1918 (reprinting Montreal *Star*).

27 With obviously much more limited resources, the left struggled valiantly to rebut such propaganda. See, for example, "Frozen Brains of Manufacturers' Association: A Comment on the Frozen Breath of Bolshevism," *Red Flag*, 24 May 1919. Against the image of the Russian wolf, whose "Frozen Breath of Bolshevism" turned productive industries into desolate ruins, *Red Flag* retorted with a cutting satire on

the "Frozen Brains of the Manufacturers' Association" (which everyone suspected was behind the campaign). "The whole civilized world stands today tottering upon the brink of a social revolution. The kept press of the ruling class, with its prostitute scribblers, are working overtime vilifying the Russian workers because they have overthrown their parasitic masters and taken the management of their own affairs into their own hands." The left also tried to expose the "Behind the Scenes" intrigues that accounted for the film *Bolshevism on Trial*: "Motion Picture Play Exposed," *Red Flag*, 3 May 1919.

28 Note Ross A. Johnson, "No Compromise – No Political Trading: The Marxian Socialist Tradition in British Columbia," Ph.D. thesis, University of British Columbia, Vancouver, 1975, 336–37; *Canadian Annual Review*, 1918, 308; *Western Clarion*, 15 Oct. 1918.

29 "Bolshevikism Soon Ran Its Course," *Mail and Empire*, 16 Sept. 1918; *Saturday Night*, 28 June 1919, 1; Aitken in "Curb Socialism After the War," *Mail and Empire*, 4 Sept. 1918.

30 Baxter, "Selected Aspects of Canadian Public Opinion," 83.

31 Cited in "Truth Will Out," editorial, *Western Clarion*, 16 July 1920; Leacock, "Bolshevik Spectre Frightens an Uneasy Conscience."

32 Antonio Gramsci, *Selections from the Prison Notebooks*, ed. and trans. Quintin Hoare and Geoffrey Nowell-Smith (London: Lawrence and Wishart, 1971), 210.

33 For an excellent overview, see Gregory S. Kealey, "Spymasters, Spies, and Their Subjects: The RCMP and Canadian State Repression, 1914–1939," in *Whose National Security? Canadian State Surveillance and the Creation of Enemies*, ed. Gary Kinsman, Dieter Buse, and Mercedes Steedman (Toronto: Between the Lines, 2000), 18–33.

34 Cited in McKay, "1910s," 205.

35 R. Craig Brown and Ramsay Cook, *Canada, 1896–1921: A Nation Transformed* (Toronto: McClelland and Stewart, 1974), ch. 12, 249; McKay, "1910s."

36 Vance, *Death So Noble*, 34.

37 Paul Fussell, *The Great War and Modern Memory* (Oxford: Oxford University Press, 2000), 248.

38 Vance, *Death So Noble*, 265.

39 See James McArthur Conner and the Social Democratic Party of Canada, *Why Send Canadian Nickel to Kill Canadian Soldiers?* (n.p. [Toronto], n.d. [1916] (election broadsheet).

40 Socialist Party of Canada, Local No. 3, *"All I Possess"* (n.p. [Winnipeg], n.d. [November, 1918]).

41 Ibid.

42 See Karl Liebknecht, *Militarism* (Toronto: William Briggs, 1917). A copy of this book in the author's collection is stamped "No. 87," and "Socialist Party of Canada, 204 Bannatyne Ave., Winnipeg, Manitoba." Liebknecht argued in terms of social-evolutionary theory that "Militarism is one of the most important and energetic manifestations of the life of most social orders, because it exhibits in the strongest, most concentrated, exclusive manner the national, cultural, and class instinct of self-preservation, that most powerful of all instincts" (2).

43 Grace MacInnis, *J.S. Woodsworth: A Man to Remember* (Toronto: Macmillan, 1953); Ian Milligan, "The Trials and Imprisonment of Isaac Bainbridge, 1917–1918," unpublished research paper, Queen's University, Kingston, 2006, 35. This detail comes from the recollections of Bainbridge's son, who recalls that the family even took care to hide its copies of the *Encyclopædia Britannica*.

44 "Report re Bolshevism in Winnipeg District," Winnipeg, Man., 4 March 1919, Re: Jacob Penner, in RCMP Files, File 117–89–57 Supp. H, Solicitor-General's Reading Room, Ottawa.

45 *B.C. Federationist*, 31 Jan. 1919; see also "Stop Press News," *Red Flag*, 8 March 1919.

46 Norman Penner, ed., *Winnipeg 1919: The Strikers' Own History of the Winnipeg General Strike* (Toronto: James Lewis & Samuel, 1973), 157. This is a reissue of Winnipeg Defense Committee, *"Saving the World from Democracy." The Winnipeg General Sympathetic Strike May-June 1919. Trial by Jury Destroyed by Stampede Forty-Five Minute Legislation. Workers Arrested and Rushed to Penitentiary to Smash Strike. Leading Lawyers, Members of Employers' Committee of 1000. Engaged By Federal Government to Prosecute Workers. Strike-Arrests-Trials-Penitentiary* (Winnipeg: n.d. [1920]). In this text I generally cite the 1970s reissue of *The Strikers' Own History*, as Penner, ed., *Winnipeg 1919*, which is more likely to be accessible to the average reader.

47 For the fuller picture, see Jeffrey A. Keshen, *Propaganda and Censorship during Canada's Great War* (Edmonton: University of Alberta Press, 1996).

48 *Red Flag*, 11 Jan. 1919, 8 March 1919, 27 Sept. 1919.

49 *B.C. Federationist*, 7 Feb. 1919.

50 The anti-war path to the left can be traced back at least to the Boer War. Phillips Thompson had polemicized brilliantly against "Anglo-Saxon Jingoism" in 1899. The South African War confounded all Spencerian hopes that "militant" societies had been rendered passé by social evolution. See Phillips Thompson, "Anglo-Saxon Jingoism," *Citizen and Country*, 9 Dec. 1899. So clearly was *Citizen and Country* identified with the anti-war position that its canvassers complained that they could barely do any active work. At the same time, the newspaper's anti-war position won it a hearing even in Prince Edward Island and on Nova Scotia's South Shore, areas not normally reached by socialist teachings. *Citizen and Country*, 9 March 1900; see also 2 Feb. 1900, 2, 9 March 1900. In the following years the SPC hammered the anti-war message home wherever it could. On the Toronto School Board James Simpson crusaded against cadet training and even against flying flags on the anniversary dates of significant battles. Vancouver SPCers sought places on their school board by promising to teach children that "the war-like spirit is fomented and kept alive simply to serve the selfish ends of a privileged few; that war can never be justified except when waged in defence of the life and liberties of a people." Gene Howard Homel, "James Simpson and the Origins of Canadian Social Democracy," Ph.D. thesis, University of Toronto, 1978, 447; *Western Clarion*, 6 Jan. 1906. Benjamin Wilson, a U.S. socialist visiting Halifax in 1908, succinctly defined socialism as "a peace society." *Herald*, 7 Dec. 1908. George Ross Kirkpatrick of the Socialist Party in the United States, in an SPC reprint, *The Socialist and the Sword*, put the anti-war message with all the SPC's customary delicacy: "A sword is a three-foot razor with which the working class obligingly and stupidly cuts its own throat in war. . . . Patriotism is perfect and glorious in proportion as the starved slave is willing to fight for a fat master." George Ross Kirkpatrick, *The Socialist and the Sword* (Vancouver: Socialist Party of Canada, n.d. [1912?]). For a useful general discussion, see Richard J. Evans, *Comrades and Sisters: Feminism, Socialism and Pacifism in Europe 1870–1945* (New York: St. Martin's Press, 1987).

51 Roscoe Fillmore, "How to Build up the Socialist Movement," *International Socialist Review* 16,10 (April 1916), 616.

52 J.S. Woodsworth, *Re-Construction from the Viewpoint of Labor* (Winnipeg: Hecla Press, n.d. [1920]).

53 Craig Heron, "National Contours: Solidarity and Fragmentation," in *Workers' Revolt in Canada*, ed. Heron, 269.

54 Cited in David J. Bercuson, *Fools and Wise Men: The Rise and Fall of the One Big Union* (Toronto: McGraw-Hill Ryerson, 1978), 85.

55 Ibid., 125.

56 Cited in Martin Robin, "Registration, Conscription, and Independent Labour Politics, 1916–1917," in *Conscription 1917*, ed. Ramsay Cook, R. Craig Brown, and Carl Berger (Toronto: University of Toronto Press n.d. [1969]), 62.

57 *Canadian Annual Review*, 1917, 298.

58 "'Wade in Blood up to the Knees': Advice Contained in the Pamphlet Issued in City by Bolsheviki," *Mail and Empire*, 27 Nov. 1918.

59 See *Peace and the Workers* (n.p. [Toronto], n.d. [1918]), now available on the Socialist History Project website <www.socialisthistory.ca> (accessed 25 April 2005). Ian Angus, the ranking authority on this period in Toronto, considers it probable that this leaflet came from the Socialist Party of North America.

60 Cited in Heron and Siemiatycki, "Great War, the State, and Working-Class Canada," 21.

61 Nolan Reilly, "The Emergence of Class Consciousness in Industrial Nova Scotia: A Study of Amherst, 1891–1925," Ph.D. thesis, Dalhousie University, Halifax, 1983, 256. For an article drawn from this thesis, see Nolan Reilly, "The General Strike in Amherst, Nova Scotia, 1919," *Acadiensis* 9 (Spring 1980), 56–77.

62 See Ian McKay and Suzanne Morton, "The Maritimes: Expanding the Circle of Resistance," in *Workers' Revolt in Canada*, ed Heron, 43–86.

63 *Eastern Federationist*, 29 March 1919.

64 Kenneth McNaught, *A Prophet in Politics: A Biography of J.S. Woodsworth* (Toronto: University of Toronto Press, 1959), 92; Allen Mills, *Fool for Christ: The Political Thought of J.S. Woodsworth* (Toronto, Buffalo and London: University of Toronto Press, 1991), 81; Maurice Spector, "A Criticism of the Bourgeois Element in Mr. Woodsworth," *The Worker*, 17 July 1926. Mills does note that Woodsworth does not fit easily into the "gradualist" mould in which McNaught had placed him.

65 Cited in MacInnis, *J.S. Woodsworth*, 104–5.

66 Cited in ibid., 115–17.

67 Ibid., 119–20.

68 Ibid., 99.

69 Cited in McNaught, *Prophet in Politics*, 96.

70 It is difficult to square this candid declaration by Woodsworth with both Mills's and McNaught's strenuous efforts, revealingly parallelled by a host of Communists, to make the post-1917 Woodsworth a consistent and thorough anti-Marxist.

71 J.S. Woodsworth, "What Does Radical Labour Want?" *Maclean's Magazine* 35, 7 (1 April 1922), 12, 32.

72 Will R. Bird, *And We Go On: A Story of the War by a Private in the Canadian Black Watch; a Story without Filth or Favor* (Toronto: Hunter-Rose, 1930).

73 Colin McKay, in *For a Working-Class Culture in Canada: A Selection of Colin McKay's Writings on Sociology and Political Economy, 1897–1939*, ed. Ian McKay (St. John's, Nfld.: Canadian Committee on Labour History, 1996), xliv.

74 *Herald*, 30 May 1919, 6.

75 Heron and Siemiatycki, "Great War, the State, and Working-Class Canada," 24.

76 See Barbara Roberts, *A Reconstructed World: A Feminist Biography of Gertrude Richardson* (Montreal and Kingston: McGill-Queen's University Press, 1996), 48, 103. This brilliant book has guided the discussion of Richardson throughout these pages.

77 C.K. Ogden and Mary Sargant Florence, *Militarism versus Feminism: An Enquiry and a Policy Demonstrating that Militarism Involves the Subjection of Women* (London: George Allen and Unwin, 1915), 106–7.

78 Roberts, *Reconstructed World*, 122.

79 Barbara Roberts, 'Why Do Women Do Nothing to End the War?' *Canadian Feminist-Pacifists and the Great War* (Ottawa: Canadian Research Institute for the Advancement of Women, CRIAW Papers, 1985), 23.

80 Cited in Roberts, *Reconstructed World*, 150.

81 Cited in ibid., 1.

82 See Thomas P. Socknat, *Witness Against War: Pacifism in Canada, 1900–1945* (Toronto: University of Toronto Press, 1987), 56. The wider North American context of the Women's Peace Party can be explored in such works as Marie Louise Degen, *The History of the Woman's Peace Party* (New York: Garland Publishers, 1972 [1939]); Linda Kay Schott, "Women Against War: Pacifism, Feminism, and Social Justice in the United States, 1915–1941," Ph.D. thesis, Stanford University, 1985; Barbara Steinson, *American Women's Activism in World War I* (New York: Garland Publishers, 1982). Not until the 1970s, with the Feminist Party of Canada, do we find so emphatic an attempt to organize an autonomous political party by and for women.

83 Roberts, *Reconstructed World*, 111.

84 Cited in Roberts, 'Why Do Women Do Nothing to End the War?' 25.

85 Cited in Roberts, *Reconstructed World*, 186.

86 The element of truth within the tale was that the Bolshevik Revolution, as the path-breaking research of Wendy Z. Goldman suggests, did envisage far-reaching changes for family policy and social life. See Wendy Z. Goldman, *Women, the State and Revolution: Soviet Family Policy and Social Life, 1917–1936* (New York: Columbia University Press, 1993). For a fascinating recent study, drawing upon many grassroots sources, see Gregory Carleton, *Sexual Revolution in Bolshevik Russia* (Pittsburgh: University of Pittsburgh Press, 2005).

87 *Mail and Empire*, 26 Oct. 1918. As for other gender-bending characters, I have found no Canadian comment on male homosexuality under the Bolsheviks. Still, one wonders if word of the Bolsheviks' rather backhanded relaxation of anti-sodomy laws – by repealing the pre-existing criminal code, they had repealed them as well – had not reached the ears of the Halifax *Herald* editor, whose denunciations of the "mad orgy of revolutionary perverts" in Russia have, shall we say, a certain edge to them. *Herald*, 18 Sept. 1918.

88 Roberts, *Reconstructed World*, 200–1. For the argument that feminist struggles against militarism raised the image of the "disorderly woman" more clearly than that of the "moral mother," see Kathleen Ann Kennedy, " 'We Mourn for Liberty in America': Socialist Women, Anti-Militarism, and State Repression, 1914–1922," Ph.D. thesis, University of California, Irvine, 1992, 221.

89 This discussion of the prosecution, not to say persecution, of Bainbridge draws heavily on the work of Ian Milligan, "The Trials and Imprisonment of Isaac Bainbridge, 1917–1918," unpublished paper, Queen's University, Kingston, 2006, and " 'Seemingly Onerous Restrictions': Sedition in Ontario, 1914–1919," M.A. research paper, York University, Toronto, 2007.

90 See C.H. Cahan, *Socialist Propaganda in Canada: Its Purposes, Results, and Remedies* (Montreal, 1918), 7–8. The absence of an extensive literature on the SDPC makes it difficult to assess Bainbridge's work within it.

91 For Bainbridge's letter, see LAC, RG 6, Series E, Vol. 604, File 279–7, Reel T-91, Secretary of State Files; Milligan, "Isaac Bainbridge," 91–92. For a fascinating discussion that helps situate this transnational moment of the Canadian left, see Benjamin Isitt, "Mutiny from Victoria to Vladivostok, December 1918," *Canadian Historical Review* 87, 2 (June 2006), 223–65.

92 See *The Awakener*, May 1920 (n.p. [Toronto]); for its background, see Marcus Graham, ed., *Man! An Anthology of Anarchist Ideas, Essays, Poetry and Commentaries* (London: Cienfuegos Press, 1974), xii. Green remembered contacting "a good many comrades" in Toronto, where "we formed a forum where lectures were held." I thank Travis Tomchuk for these references.

93 *Herald*, 18 Dec. 1918. A general study of the many and intricate networks binding radicals from similar cultural backgrounds together has yet to be written, but the existing evidence suggests vibrant transnational communities of struggle seeking to import the Bolshevik example into North America.

94 *Mail and Empire*, 6 July 1918, 18 Dec. 1918.

95 *Mail and Empire*, 26 Sept. 1918.

96 *Mail and Empire*, 29 July 1918.

97 *Mail and Empire*, 21 Oct. 1918.

98 *Herald*, 15 Nov. 1918.

99 *The Voice* (Winnipeg), 18 Dec. 1914.

100 Irwin St. John Tucker, *The Price We Pay* (Toronto: Social Democratic Party of Canada, n.d. [1917]). "I. Bainbridge," literature agent of the party, used this pamphlet to promote other pieces of socialist literature: *The History of Canadian Wealth* (Gustavus Myers), *Socialism for the Farmer* (Ameringer), *The Genesis and Evolution of Slavery* (Kingsley), and *Common Sense and Socialism* (Spargo).

101 *Canadian Forward*, 28 Oct. 1916.

102 See Angus, *Canadian Bolsheviks*, 32.

103 Isaac Bainbridge, "Canada – The Melting Pot," *Canadian Forward*, 28 Oct. 1916. Ian Milligan steered me towards this fascinating article.

104 Bill Waiser, *Park Prisoners: The Untold Story of Western Canada's National Parks, 1915–1946* (Saskatoon and Calgary: Fifth House, 1995), 4–5.

105 Ibid., 8, 10.

106 John Herd Thompson, *Ethnic Minorities during Two World Wars* (Ottawa: Canadian Historical Association, Booklet No. 19, 1991).

107 Waiser, *Park Prisoners*, 11, 15, 16, 20, 46.

108 Johnson, "No Compromise – No Political Trading," 354, n.49; see also *Canadian Annual Review*, 1918, 308; *Western Clarion*, 15 Oct. 1918. By 1920 many SPC writers were more critical. Still, some offered to guide Lenin and Trotsky so that they might avoid mistakes in the future. "Other types of critics are those who are not given to hysteria, who look on things coolly and dispassionately, and who, having thoroughly digested the works of Marx, Engels, and all the recognized authorities on scientific socialism, can show Lenin and Trotsky, or any other of the executive heads of the Bolsheviki just where they made their initial mistakes, and how they continue to make an ever increasing number from day to day." See Frank Cassidy, "Russia and Us," editorial, *Western Clarion*, 1 Sept. 1920.

109 "Proletarian Dictatorship," *B.C. Federationist*, 24 Jan. 1919 [reprinting the *Butte Bulletin*].

110   *Canadian Forward*, 24 June 1918.

111   *The Voice*, 16 Nov. 1917; *Western Labor News*, 7 Jan. 1919; and *Labor Star* (Vancouver), 6 Feb. 1919, 20 March 1919, all cited in Baxter, "Selected Aspects of Canadian Public Opinion," 112, 113, 115. *The Voice* was superceded, argue Mitchell and Naylor, because it failed to reflect "the new militancy of the local labour movement." Tom Mitchell and James Naylor, "The Prairies: In the Eye of the Storm," in *Workers' Revolt in Canada*, ed. Heron, 187.

112   *The Soviet*, 18 April 1919; see Socialist History Project website <www.socialisthistory.ca/Docs/docs.htm> (accessed 25 April 2005).

113   Angus, *Canadian Bolsheviks*, 36–37.

114   Ewen, "Quebec," 129.

115   James Naylor, "Southern Ontario: Striking at the Ballot Box," in *Workers' Revolt in Canada*, ed. Heron, 161.

116   Ibid., 144, 158, 161, 169.

117   *Red Flag*, 21 June 1919; Socialist Party of Canada, Winnipeg Local No. 3, "An Answer and a Challenge," *Western Clarion*, 16 Sept. 1920.

118   See, for example, a speech by J. Harrington in Vancouver, as reported in *B.C. Federationist*, 7 Feb. 1919.

119   *B.C. Federationist*, 17 Jan. 1919; Woodsworth in *B.C. Federationist*, 17 Jan. 1919.

120   Pritchard in *Red Flag*, 15 Feb. 1919; for Social Democratic Party of Manitoba, see *Canadian Forward*, 10 April 1918; "Want Ban Lifted on Socialist Press," *Mail and Empire*, 17 Dec. 1918.

121   "J. Simpson Praises the Bolsheviks," *Mail and Empire*, 19 Feb. 1918.

122   Bessie Beatty, "Russian Bolshevism, Tyranny or Freedom," *B.C. Federationist*, 7 Feb. 1919, reprinted from *The Public*; Louis Fraina, "A Problem in Tactics," *Red Flag*, 28 Dec. 1918; "The Bolsheviki at the Forum," *B.C. Federationist*, 24 Jan. 1919. See also Paul Buhle, *A Dreamer's Paradise Lost: Lewis C. Fraina/Lewis Corey (1892–1953) and the Decline of Radicalism in the United States* (Atlantic Highlands, N.J.: Humanities Press, 1995).

123   Peter Campbell, *Canadian Marxists and the Search for a Third Way* (Montreal and Kingston: McGill-Queen's University Press, 1999), 83.

124   Borrowing some phrases and images from Chad Reimer, "War, Nationhood and Working-Class Entitlement: The Counterhegemonic Challenge of the 1919 Winnipeg General Strike," *Prairie Forum* 18, 2 (Fall 1993), 219.

125   Cited in Penner, ed., *Winnipeg 1919*, 79.

126   Reimer, "War, Nationhood and Working-Class Entitlement," 224–25.

127   D.C. Masters's *The Winnipeg General Strike*, first published in 1950 and reissued in 1973 (Toronto: University of Toronto Press), was followed by David Jay Bercuson, *Confrontation at Winnipeg: Labour, Industrial Relations, and the General Strike* (Montreal and Kingston: McGill-Queen's University Press, 1990), first published in 1974; Kenneth McNaught and David Bercuson, *The Winnipeg Strike: 1919* (Toronto: Longman Canada, 1974), and J.M. Bumsted, *The Winnipeg General Strike of 1919: An Illustrated History* (n.p.: Watson Dwyer Publishing Limited, 1994). Among these general interpreters of Winnipeg, Bercuson stands out as an authoritative guide to the city's past history of industrial relations and to the strike's role within the "prairie fire" of Western regional revolt and also as the major proponent of the "Children's Crusade" critique.

128   Robson cited in Bumsted, *Winnipeg General Strike*, 64; *Winnipeg Telegram*, 28 June 1919, cited in Penner, ed., *Winnipeg 1919*, 218.

129   McNaught and Bercuson, *Winnipeg Strike*, 25, emphasis added. Yet what does it

mean to be "literally held in subjugation"? The workers were not compelled by law or coerced by force to be members of the international unions. Elsewhere Bercuson argued that Western workers, living on an industrial frontier where their hopes for a better life were disappointed by such realities of capitalism as uncaring employers and unsafe coal mines, accordingly became radicals – whereas their Eastern counterparts generally did not. In the in-bred, closed, stagnant Nova Scotia coal-mining towns, Bercuson argues, there was not much stimulus for radicalism. David Bercuson, "Labour Radicalism and the Western Industrial Frontier, 1897–1919," *Canadian Historical Review* 58 (1977), 154–75.

130 See Mitchell and Naylor, "Prairies," 182–230.

131 Bumsted, *Winnipeg General Strike*, 22.

132 McNaught and Bercuson, *Winnipeg Strike*, 101.

133 Norman Penner, "Introduction" to *Winnipeg 1919*, ed. Penner, ix–xxiii.

134 Alf Budden, *The Slave of the Farm: Being Letters from Alf. Budden to a Fellow Farm Slave and Comrade in Revolt* (Vancouver: Socialist Party of Canada, Dominion Executive Committee, 1914), might be considered a contender, although it is not in essence a very Canada-focused book. Gustavus Myers, *History of Canadian Wealth* (Chicago: Charles H. Kerr, 1914; reprinted as *A History of Canadian Wealth*, Toronto: James Lewis & Samuel, 1972), might also be considered a contender, but it is the work of a U.S. muckraker who, as Stanley Ryerson points out in his "Introduction" (xvi-xvii), was heavy with facts and light on theory. One might also reference the *Manifesto of the Socialist Party of Canada* (Vancouver, 1910; 5th ed., 1920), which is thought to have sold over 39,000 copies internationally; again, it is not particularly focused on Canada. See Peter E. Newell, *The Impossibilists: A Brief Profile of the Socialist Party of Canada* (London: Athena Press, 2008), 93.

135 Bercuson, *Confrontation at Winnipeg*, 102.

136 McNaught and Bercuson, *Winnipeg Strike*, 111, drawing on Masters, *Winnipeg General Strike*, 130; Bercuson, *Confrontation at Winnipeg*, 179.

137 This new reconnaissance builds on the inspiring work of an emerging third generation of Winnipeg strike scholars, including Tom Mitchell, James Naylor, and Chad Reimer.

138 Bercuson, *Confrontation at Winnipeg*, 4.

139 McNaught and Bercuson, *Winnipeg Strike*, 49.

140 Jacob Penner, "Recollections of the Early Socialist Movement in Winnipeg," *Marxist Quarterly* 2 (Summer 1962), 23–30.

141 Bumsted, *Winnipeg General Strike*.

142 Roseline Usiskin, "Towards a Theoretical Reformulation of the Relationship Between Political Ideology, Social Class, and Ethnicity: A Case Study of the Winnipeg Jewish Radical Community, 1905–1920," M.A. thesis (Sociology), University of Manitoba, Winnipeg, 1978, *passim*.

143 Ernest Chisick, "The Origins and Development of the Marxist Socialist Movement in Winnipeg, 1900–1915," M.A. thesis, University of Manitoba, Winnipeg, 1972, 13.

144 See Alan F.J. Artibise, *Winnipeg: A Social History of Urban Growth 1874–1914* (Montreal and London: McGill-Queen's University Press, 1975), 132.

145 Don Avery, "The Radical Alien and the Winnipeg General Strike of 1919," in *The West and the Nation: Essays in Honour of W.L. Morton*, ed. Carl Berger and Ramsay Cook (Toronto: McClelland and Stewart, 1976), 211. For an interesting collective biography of North-Enders, see Harry Gutkin with Mildred Gutkin, The *Worst of Times, the Best of Times: Growing up in Winnipeg's North End* (Markham, Ont.: Fitzhenry and Whiteside, 1987).

146 For this suggestion, see Roland Penner, *A Glowing Dream: A Memoir* (Winnipeg: J. Gordon Shillingford Publishing, 2007), 23–24.

147 Reimer, "War, Nationhood and Working-Class Entitlement," 227.

148 Bercuson, *Confrontation at Winnipeg*, 82.

149 See Brian McKillop, "Citizen and Socialist: The Ethos of Political Winnipeg, 1919–1935," M.A. thesis, University of Manitoba, Winnipeg, 1970, 38. See also A.B. McKillop, "The Socialist as Citizen: John Queen and the Mayoralty of Winnipeg, 1935," *Manitoba Historical Society Transactions*, Series 3, No.30 (1973–74).

150 Jack London, *The Dream of Debs: A Story of Industrial Revolt* (Chicago: Charles H. Kerr & Company, n.d. [1909]), 7, 32. A copy of this pamphlet was in the Vancouver library of the Independent Labour Party.

151 Mitchell and Naylor, "Prairies," 180.

152 Bercuson, *Confrontation at Winnipeg*, 77.

153 Penner, ed., *Winnipeg 1919*, 146, 69.

154 Ibid., 100.

155 Bercuson, *Confrontation at Winnipeg*, 178.

156 In their exciting new work on the workers' revolt in the Prairies, Mitchell and Naylor ask an important question. If you set the "bar of radicalism" as high as possible, and ask if workers would put their jobs and wage standards at risk by gestures of solidarity with the acts of their comrades in Winnipeg, "whose goals were unclear and whose outcome was far from uncertain," the answer, "astonishingly . . . is yes in several cases." Mitchell and Naylor, "Prairies," 196.

157 This rethinking of the strike as an attempt to form a historical bloc is one of the most promising new interpretive thrusts, developed in important work by Reimer, "War, Nationhood and Working-Class Entitlement," 221.

158 Bumsted, *Winnipeg General Strike*, 38.

159 A. Ross McCormack, "Radical Politics in Winnipeg: 1899–1915," Historical and Scientific Society of Manitoba, *Papers*, Series III (29), 1972–73, 86; on Ivens, Harry Gutkin and Mildred Gutkin, *Profiles in Dissent: The Shaping of Radical Thought in the Canadian West* (Edmonton: NeWest Press, 1997), 61, 80. The "tremendous egotist" comment comes from Fred Tipping.

160 See Richard Allen, *The Social Passion: Religion and Social Reform in Canada 1914–28* (Toronto: University of Toronto Press, 1973), 117.

161 Joanne Carlson Brown, "The Form without the Power? Wesleyan Influences and the Winnipeg Labour Church," Canadian Society of Church History, Annual Conference, *Historical Papers 1994*, 72–73.

162 Penner, ed., *Winnipeg 1919*, 74.

163 Brown, "Form without the Power," 71.

164 *Red Flag*, 21 June 1919.

165 Allen, *Social Passion*, 163.

166 Masters, *Winnipeg General Strike*, 50.

167 Allen, *Social Passion*, 116.

168 Brown, "Form without the Power," 65. Brown rebuts the common arguments that the Labor Church was a church "in form only – one that lacked any power at all," and that it lacked a genuine theology, by drawing attention to the Methodist forms and extraordinary range of activities associated with the congregation.

169 Ibid., 72.

170 Gutkin and Gutkin, *Profiles in Dissent*, 86; Masters, *Winnipeg General Strike*, 49–50.

171 Penner, ed., *Winnipeg 1919*, 147–48, 157, 91, 137.

172 Gutkin and Gutkin, *Profiles in Dissent*, 223–24.

173 Ibid., 230.

174 Linda Kealey, *Enlisting Women for the Cause: Women, Labour and the Left in Canada, 1890–1920* (Toronto: University of Toronto Press, 1998), 224.

175 Mary Horodyski, "Women and the Winnipeg General Strike of 1919," *Manitoba History* 11 (Spring 1986), 28, 34. Eric Angel also explores this incident in his unpublished thesis on Winnipeg: "Workers, Picketing and the Winnipeg General Strike of 1919," M.A. thesis, Queen's University, Kingston, 1995, 75.

176 See Mitchell and Naylor, "Prairies," 185; Horodyski, "Women and the Winnipeg General Strike of 1919," 30.

177 Horodyski, "Women and the Winnipeg General Strike of 1919," 34.

178 Mitchell and Naylor, "Prairies," 82, makes this point well.

179 Ruth Frager, *Sweatshop Strife: Class, Ethnicity, and Gender in the Jewish Labour Movement of Toronto 1900–1939* (Toronto: University of Toronto Press, 1992), 6.

180 Gutkin and Gutkin, *Profiles in Dissent*, 250.

181 Avery, "Radical Alien and the Winnipeg General Strike," 215, 221.

182 Ibid., 220–221, citing *Manitoba Free Press*, 22 May 1919.

183 On deportation, see Barbara Roberts, *Whence They Came: Deportation from Canada, 1900–1935* (Ottawa: University of Ottawa Press, 1988); for a general study of deportation in the U.S. context, see Daniel Kanstroom, *Deportation Nation: Outsiders in American History* (Cambridge, Mass. and London: Harvard University Press, 2007).

184 Heron and Siemiatycki, "Great War, the State, and Working-Class Canada," 23–24.

185 Masters, *Winnipeg General Strike*, 36. More work on this point should address the complication of some immigrants' tendency to anglicize their names.

186 Penner, ed., *Winnipeg 1919*, 70, 83, 77–78.

187 Bercuson, *Confrontation at Winnipeg*, 127, who on the same page also asserts that "charges that the strike was alien-lead [sic] were completely false." It might be safer in the light of new evidence to say that they were "exaggerated."

188 Citation from RCMP Files, Solicitor-General's Reading Room, Ottawa, Jacob Penner, File 117–89–57, Supp.H., "Report re Bolshevism in Winnipeg District," Winnipeg, Man., 4 March 1919; see also Reports for 7 March, 19 July, 19 Aug. 1919; 9 Nov. 1921. I thank Stefan Epp for guiding me to this information.

189 Penner, ed., *Winnipeg 1919*, 115.

190 See Avery, "Radical Alien and the Winnipeg General Strike," 218–19.

191 Mitchell and Naylor, "Prairies," 183.

192 Penner, ed., *Winnipeg 1919*, 52–53; Reimer, "War, Nationhood and Working-Class Entitlement," 232.

193 Mitchell and Naylor, "Prairies," 184.

194 This second option aligns with the interpretation put forward by Penner, *Glowing Dream*, 24.

195 Avery, "Radical Alien and the Winnipeg General Strike," 225.

196 Reimer, "War, Nationhood and Working-Class Entitlement," 232.

197 Penner, ed., *Winnipeg 1919*, 78. Interestingly, in making this point, the *Bulletin* noted the Nova Scotia case of mine bosses seeking strikebreakers in Eastern Europe.

198 Penner, ed., *Winnipeg 1919*, 78.

199 Ibid., 29.

200 Reimer, "War, Nationhood and Working-Class Entitlement," 232.

201 Mitchell and Naylor, "Prairies," 184.

202 Penner, ed., *Winnipeg 1919*, 227.

203   Avery, "Radical Alien and the Winnipeg General Strike," 217.

204   Penner, ed., *Winnipeg 1919*, 19; Bumsted, *Winnipeg General Strike*, 65.

205   Penner, ed., *Winnipeg 1919*, 159, 219.

206   Angel, "Workers, Picketing and the Winnipeg General Strike," 31, n.28.

207   Avery, "Radical Alien and the Winnipeg General Strike," 224.

208   Ibid., 222.

209   "the barriers to color ..." cited in Mitchell and Naylor, "Prairies," 184; Penner, *Glowing Dream*, 24.

210   Mitchell and Naylor, "Prairies," 187.

211   Central titles include Defense Committee, *"Saving the World from Democracy"*; Defense Committee, *W.A. Pritchard's Address to the Jury in the Crown vs. Armstrong, Heaps, Bray, Ivens, Johns, Pritchard, and Queen* (Winnipeg: Wallingford Press, 1920); and Defence Committee for the Dominion Labor Party, *Dixon's Address to the Jury. An Argument for Liberty of Opinion* (Winnipeg: Israelite Press, 1920).

212   Mitchell and Naylor, "Prairies," 176–77.

213   Penner, ed., *Winnipeg 1919*, 114.

214   Cited in Reimer, "War, Nationhood and Working-Class Entitlement," 228–29.

215   Penner, ed., *Winnipeg 1919*, 45.

216   Ibid., 150.

217   Penner, ed., *Winnipeg 1919*, 7, 12.

218   Ibid., 156.

219   *Western Labor News*, cited in Mitchell and Naylor, "Prairies," 215.

220   Defense Committee, *W.A. Pritchard's Address to the Jury*, 72.

221   J.B. Osborne, *The Way to Power* (Vancouver: Dominion Executive of the Socialist Party of Canada, n.d. [1913]), 15–16.

222   The idea was certainly present in Lenin's *The Soviets at Work*, read extensively at this time. See Nikolai [V.I.] Lenin, *The Soviets at Work: The International Position of the Russian Soviet Republic and the Fundamental Problems of the Socialist Revolution* (New York: Rand School of Social Science, 1919). Those who have dined out for years on tales of spc craziness should pause before the Winnipeg evidence. Undoubtedly the party's "impossibilist" style was often not its strong suit. Yet it is striking that it was the spc that seemingly spoke most directly to many workers in 1919 – certainly those who reprinted passage after passage of its analyses in their historical account of the strike. Interestingly, however fiercely many pre-war spcers had derided the usefulness of immediate demands, their postwar successors rarely desisted from making them – as suggested by their calls for the end of dictatorial government by order-in-council.

223   Mitchell and Naylor, "Prairies," 208.

224   Tom Mitchell, " 'Legal Gentlemen Appointed by the Federal Government': The Canadian State, the Citizens' Committee of 1000, and Winnipeg's Seditious Conspiracy Trials of 1919–1920," *Labour/Le Travail* 53 (Spring 2004), 13.

225   Mitchell and Naylor, "Prairies," 202.

226   Mitchell, " 'Legal Gentlemen Appointed by the Federal Government,' " 17–18.

227   Cited in Penner, ed., *Winnipeg 1919*, 55.

228   Ibid., 55, 57.

229   Bumsted, *Winnipeg General Strike*, 48.

230   Penner, ed., *Winnipeg 1919*, 177.

231   Dafoe, "The Calibre of the Radical Candidates," editorial, *Manitoba Free Press*, 24 Nov. 1919, as discussed in McKillop, "Citizen and Socialist."

232 Penner, ed., *Winnipeg 1919*, 181–82.

233 Ibid., 73.

234 *Winnipeg Evening Telegram*, 12 June 1919, as cited in McKillop, "Citizen and Socialist," 46.

235 Mitchell and Naylor, "Prairies," 184.

236 Reimer, "War, Nationhood and Working-Class Entitlement," 231.

237 Ibid., 220, 231; Penner, ed., *Winnipeg 1919*, 211, 139.

238 Mitchell and Naylor, "Prairies," 211; Penner, ed., *Winnipeg 1919*, 112.

239 Penner, ed., *Winnipeg 1919*, 184.

240 Bumsted, *Winnipeg General Strike*, 38.

241 Masters, *Winnipeg General Strike*, xv.

242 Bercuson, *Confrontation at Winnipeg*, 179; McNaught and Bercuson, *Winnipeg Strike*, 111.

243 Although Pictou County was most likely the largest single strike in the 19th century in the sense of worker days lost, this general strike has yet to find an historian.

244 Penner, ed., *Winnipeg 1919*, 216.

245 Bercuson, *Confrontation at Winnipeg*, 205.

246 "The S.P.C. and Organized Labor," editorial, *Red Flag*, 30 Aug. 1919.

247 McNaught and Bercuson, *Winnipeg Strike*, 54.

248 Antonio Gramsci, "The Revolutionary Tide," *Selections from Political Writings (1910–1920)*, ed. Quintin Hoare, trans. John Mathews (New York: International Publishers, 1977), 61.

249 "Joe Knight Speech to the Comintern, 1921," trans. and presented by John Riddell <http://www.socialisthistory.ca/Docs/Leninist/Knight_21.htm> (accessed June 2008). I thank John Riddell for drawing this speech to my attention.

250 Tim Buck, *Canada and the Russian Revolution* (Toronto: Progress Books, 1967), 66–67. As he wrote in an earlier book: "Working-class pride in the solidarity of the workers of Winnipeg could not blind Canadian Marxists to the fact that the ideas represented by its leaders were wrong." Tim Buck, *30 Years, 1922–1952: The Story of the Communist Movement in Canada* (Toronto: Progress Books, 1952), 19.

8: Showtime, 1920

1 See Tom Mitchell, "Repressive Measures: The Committee of 1000's Campaign against Radicalism after the Winnipeg General Strike," *left history*, 3 & 4 (Fall 1995–Spring 1996), 133–67.

2 Cited in J.M. Bumsted, *The Winnipeg General Strike of 1919: An Illustrated History* (n.p.: Watson Dwyer Publishing Limited, 1994), 67.

3 D.C. Masters, *The Winnipeg General Strike* (Toronto: University of Toronto Press, 1973 [1950]), 133.

4 Tom Mitchell and James Naylor, "The Prairies: In the Eye of the Storm," in *The Workers' Revolt in Canada, 1917–1925*, ed. Craig Heron (Toronto: University of Toronto Press, 1998), 213.

5 Sadly, some mainstream historians have regarded such obvious miscarriages of justice with indifference. As W.L. Morton remarked, "It is to be noted ... that the strike had been a real challenge to public order; it had caused deep fears; the victors were comparatively lenient and the sentences in the circumstances relatively mild." Cited in Bumsted, *Winnipeg General Strike*, 73. "He jests at scars, that never felt a wound." Even Masters seems to lend some credibility to the proceedings: "In a way the O.B.U. was a conspiracy to secure control of the country.... Many radicals have talked about the dictatorship of the proletariat in much the same way that many professed Christians talk about the coming of the

Kingdom of Heaven on earth." See Masters, *Winnipeg General Strike*, 133. Yet the OBU was not an illegal organization, and there is nothing in the Criminal Code to forbid discussion of the "dictatorship of the proletariat." David Bercuson gives the show trials virtually no attention in *Confrontation at Winnipeg: Labour, Industrial Relations, and the General Strike* (Montreal and Kingston: McGill-Queen's University Press, 1990), or in his book co-authored with Ken McNaught, *The Winnipeg Strike: 1919* (Toronto: Longman Canada, 1974). Interestingly, Skelton, writing at the time, thought that only if one could show that "the men in question believed in extreme communist organization of society" *and* "had been trying this spring to put it in force by conspiracy and revolution" could the policy of arrests be justified. He was sceptical on both counts. O.D. Skelton, "The Western Strikes," *Queen's Quarterly*, 27 (July 1919–April 1920).

6 Mitchell, "Repressive Measures," 133–67; Tom Mitchell, "'Legal Gentlemen Appointed by the Federal Government': The Canadian State, the Citizens' Committee of 1000, and Winnipeg's Seditious Conspiracy Trials of 1919–1920," *Labour/Le Travail* 53 (Spring 2004), 11.

7 *Red Flag*, 6 Sept. 1919.

8 See Harry Gutkin and Mildred Gutkin, *Profiles in Dissent: The Shaping of Radical Thought in the Canadian West* (Edmonton: NeWest Press, 1997), 24.

9 Norman Penner, ed., *Winnipeg 1919: The Strikers' Own History of the Winnipeg General Strike* (Toronto: James Lewis & Samuel, 1973), 14.

10 Defence Committee for the Dominion Labor Party, *Dixon's Address to the Jury. An Argument for Liberty of Opinion* (Winnipeg: Israelite Press, 1920) [hereafter *Dixon Speech*], 13.

11 *Dixon Speech*, 87, 94.

12 Ibid., 68, 73.

13 Ibid., 13, 8.

14 Ibid., 67, 68.

15 Ibid., 5, 3, 6, 98, 9.

16 For the text, see Defense Committee, *W.A. Pritchard's Address to the Jury in the Crown vs. Armstrong, Heaps, Bray, Ivens, Johns, Pritchard, and Queen (R.B. Russell was tried previously) Indicted for Seditious Conspiracy and Common Nuisance, Fall Assizes, Winnipeg, Manitoba, Canada, 1919–1920* (Winnipeg: Wallingford Press, n.d. [1920]), hereafter cited as *Pritchard Speech*. Others have discussed this speech as well: see Peter Campbell, *Canadian Marxists and the Search for a Third Way* (Montreal and Kingston: McGill-Queen's University Press, 1999), 92–93; and Bryan Palmer, "System Failure: The Breakdown of the Post-War Settlement and the Politics of Labour in Our Time," *Labour/Le Travail* 55 (Spring 2005), 334–35.

17 Cited in Campbell, *Canadian Marxists and the Search for a Third Way*, 87. The brief description of Pritchard's life here relies heavily on Campbell's excellent sketch in this book.

18 *B.C. Federationist*, 3 Jan. 1910; "Pritchard-Makovski Debate," *Red Flag*, 15 Feb. 1919; W.A. Pritchard, "Russia under the Soviets," *Red Flag*, 26 April 1919, 3 May 1919, 10 May 1919, 17 May 1919, 24 May 1919, 31 May 1919.

19 Masters, *Winnipeg General Strike*, 8.

20 *Pritchard Speech*, 120, 73.

21 Ibid., 73–74.

22 Ibid., 15, 3, 13.

23 Ibid., 13–14, 48–49.

24 Ibid., 81.

25 Campbell, *Canadian Marxists and the Search for a Third Way*, 93.

26 *Pritchard Speech*, 8–9.

27 For a similar critique, based on the work of Paul Lafargue, see Colin McKay, "Property and Progress," in *For a Working-Class Culture in Canada: A Selection of Colin McKay's Writings on Sociology and Political Economy, 1897–1939*, ed. Ian McKay (St. John's, Nfld.: Canadian Committee on Labour History, 1996), 170–76.

28 *Pritchard Speech*, 10.

29 Campbell, *Canadian Marxists and the Search for a Third Way*, 251, n.76.

30 *Pritchard Speech*, 182.

31 For a very different impression of Pritchard's supposed "theoretical absolutism," see Gutkin and Gutkin, *Profiles in Dissent*, 94.

32 *Pritchard Speech*, 44, 32.

33 Stephen Kern, *A Cultural History of Causality: Science, Murder Novels, and Systems of Thought* (Princeton, N.J. and Oxford: Princeton University Press, 2004), 13.

34 *Pritchard Speech*, 54.

35 Ibid., 17.

36 Ibid., 13.

37 Ibid., 42. Pritchard was quoting from Marx's letter to Arnold Ruge, September 1843, first published in *Deutsch-Französische Jahrbücher*, 1844. See Karl Marx and Frederick Engels, *Collected Works*, vol. 3 (Moscow: Progress Books, 1975), 144, for a slightly different translation.

38 See Campbell, *Canadian Marxists and the Search for a Third Way*, 92.

39 *Pritchard Speech*, 127, 72, 74.

40 Ibid., 13.

41 Ibid., 66.

42 Ibid., 83.

43 Ibid., 5–6.

44 Ibid., 5–6, 34.

45 Ibid., 129.

46 Ibid., 118. Dixon reaches for the same idea in his speech: he refers to his writing on the defeat of the strike in 1919: "The workers have simply gone to school once more. They have experienced another demonstration that in union there is strength. That the way to greater victory is through greater unity. Their conviction that it must be each for all and all for each has been deepened. The bond of union between all workers has been strengthened by common sacrifice for a common end. While impressing the need for collective bargaining and better wages upon the community mind, the workers have themselves been taking a university course in politics and economics." *Dixon Speech*, 70.

47 *Pritchard Speech*, 213.

48 Campbell, *Canadian Marxists and the Search for a Third Way*, 93.

49 Mitchell, " 'Legal Gentlemen Appointed by the Federal Government' Trials,' " 41.

50 Trotsky, "The Bolsheviki and World Peace," *Mail and Empire*, 12 Jan. 1918.

51 For the Lakehead and *Appeal to Reason*, see Michel Beaulieu, "A Proletarian Prometheus," ch. 2; for Canadian notices in *The International Socialist Review*, see "News and Views," October 1913, 246, for news from Sointula. A more thorough analysis of Canadian reports in U.S. left publications would be useful to fill in gaps in the record of the movement. *Appeal to Reason*, said to have 14,000 subscribers in Canada, was banned (according to Dorothy Steeves) in May 1906. See Dorothy G. Steeves, *The Compassionate Rebel: Ernest E. Winch and His Times* (Vancouver: Boag Foundation, 1960), 18.

52 John Bartlet Brebner, *North Atlantic Triangle: The Interplay of Canada, the United States, and Great Britain* (Toronto: McClelland and Stewart, 1966 [New Haven: Yale University Press and Toronto: Ryerson Press, 1945]).

53 Such New Brunswick "Fabians" as W.F. Hatheway actually drew more from New England transcendentalism and Bellamyism – and not very much, it seems, from the Webbs or their circle. See W. Frank Hatheway, *Canadian Nationality, the Cry of Labour, and Other Essays* (Toronto: William Briggs, 1906).

54 "Report re Bolshevism in the Winnipeg District," 7 March 1919.

55 Antonio Gramsci, *Prison Notebooks,* ed. Joseph A. Buttigieg, trans. Joseph A. Buttigieg and Antonio Callari, vol. 1 (New York: Columbia University Press, 1992), especially 43–64 and section 25. See also Lucio Colletti, "Marxism as a Sociology," in *From Rousseau to Lenin: Studies in Ideology and Society* (London: NLB, 1969), 3–44.

56 For an interesting brief for the defence of the Marxist philosophy of science, see Helena Sheehan, *Marxism and the Philosophy of Science: A Critical History* (Atlantic Highlands, N.J.: Humanities Press International, 1985); for a critique of Marxism's scientific credentials, see Gavin Kitching, *Marxism and Science: Analysis of an Obsession* (University Park: Pennsylvania State University Press, 1994).

57 Stephen Kern, *Cultural History of Causality,* 13.

58 Antonio Gramsci, *Selections from the Prison Notebooks,* ed. and trans. Quintin Hoare and Geoffrey Nowell-Smith (London: Lawrence and Wishart, 1971), 406.

59 Michael Löwy, *The Theory of Revolution in the Young Marx* (Leiden and Boston: Brill, 2003), 173–74.

60 Gramsci, *Selections from the Prison Notebooks,* 336.

61 Hussein Rahim, *The Psychology of Marxian Socialism,* Book One, *The Human Nervous System and the Principles of Nerve Energy* (Vancouver: The Author, 1921). Rahim's continuing links with the SPC are suggested by W.A. Pritchard's Foreword.

62 Michael Löwy, "From Marx to Ecosocialism," *Capitalism, Nature, Socialism: A Journal of Socialist Ecology* 13, 1 (March 2002), 121–33.

63 *Pritchard Speech,* 283. Pritchard's speech cites France's speech virtually verbatim. France's speech was reported in the French socialist newspaper *L'Humanité* and reprinted in *The Nation* (New York), 6 Sept. 1919. It is highly probable that *The Nation* was the source upon which Pritchard drew.

Index

Aallotar temperance society 330
Aboriginal peoples 5, 362, 391–92, 393, 406, 412; assimilation of 220, 225; conscription of 407; land rights of 407; marginalization of 24; "primitive communism" and 391, 406–7; restrictions on religious beliefs of 364; subordination of 359, 390
accumulation vs. sovereignty 378
l'Action Catholique 221
Adair, Robin 248
Adams, Joseph: *Ten Thousand Miles Through Canada* 5
Addams, Jane 443
Afghanistan 355, 358
African immigrants, marginalization of 361
Afro-Americans 396, 407; *see also* Blacks
agnosticism, Spencerian 218
agrarian protest 201
agrarian question 145, 198–208; *see also* farmers
agrarian socialists 200
agricultural technology 204–5
agriculture: immigrant workers and 374; migratory labour and 384
Ahlqvist, J.W. 177–78, 250; 404–5
Aika 324, 404, 409
Aitken, Max (Lord Beaverbrook) 22, 350
Aitkins, Sir James 425–26
Albert (N.B.) 165, 170–71
Alberta 25; coal miners in 156; labour struggles in 129; postwar labour parties in 128; Trades and Labor Congress 165
Alberta and Great Waterways Railway Company 167
Alberta Farmers' Co-operative Elevator Company 201
alcohol abuse 341
Alger, Horatio 91
"alien," construction of 485, 487, 488; foreign 332, 387–88, 420, 422, 441, 451–53, 475–80, 497
alienation: religious 241; urban 18; veterans' 441
alien registration and internment 452–54
Allen, Grant 55, 66, 68, 69, 97, 225, 246, 247, 254, 258, 259, 328, 523, 526, 585n116; *The British Barbarians* 59; *The Evolution of the Idea of God* 59; marriage and 59; religion and 59; Spencer and 58; *The Woman Who Did* 59, 315, 324
Allen, Richard 221, 225, 233, 471
All I Possess (Winnipeg SPC) 428
Almazoff, Moses 480

Amalgamated Clothing Workers of America (ACWA) 331
Amalgamated Society of Engineers 462
amalgamations 96
American Federationist 389
American Federation of Labor (AFL) 36, 96–97, 136, 137, 184; secession from 433
American Labor Union 553n20
anarchism 61–63, 80, 93, 106, 111–12, 192, 276, 324, 423, 446, 464, 471, 536n67, 541n144; anti-British 364; as unbridled individualism 112; Jewish 192; socialist 62; synthetic philosophy of 63; vs. Marxism 152; vs. socialism 112
anarchist communism 61, 447
anarchy, economic 57
Anderson, W.E. 73
Andrews, A.J. 486, 499, 508–9, 517
Anglican Church, *see* Church of England
Anglo-Saxon superiority 359, 395
Angus, Ian 606n59
Angus, R.B. 353
annexationism, democracy vs. 90
Anning, Amelia 297
anti-Bolshevism 423, 425–26
anti-capitalism 392, 438, 449
anti-Catholicism 221
anticlericalism 237, 241, 243
anti-conscription activism 449
Anti-Conscription League 444
anti-feminism 29
Antigonish (Nova Scotia), Bishop of 327
anti-immigrant violence 476
anti-immigration 387, 497
anti-imperialism 95, 368
anti-militarism 34, 389, 438, 443, 449, 454
anti-modernism 29
anti-monopoly 134
anti-poverty activism 338, 341
anti-racism 369, 398
anti-religious sentiment 237
anti-secularization 219–20
anti-Semitism 331, 392, 401
anti-socialism 513
anti-unemployment activism 341, 452
anti-unionism 71, 163
anti-war activism 421–22, 430, 436–39, 440, 443–46
Appeal to Reason 20, 130, 147, 519, 544n3, 549n80

638

Reasoning Otherwise

Marquis Book Printing Inc.

Québec, Canada

2008

    This book has been printed on 100% post consumer waste paper, certified Eco-logo and processed chlorine free.